Strawberries in Winter

To Mitch
Cohen
with
warm regards
– hope he finds
it interesting
Thomas 22 Sept 2009

Thomas Nowotny

STRAWBERRIES IN WINTER

On Global Trends and Global Governance

PETER LANG
Frankfurt am Main · Berlin · Bern · Bruxelles · New York · Oxford · Wien

Bibliographic Information published by Die Deutsche Bibliothek
Die Deutsche Bibliothek lists this publication in the Deutsche Nationalbibliografie; detailed bibliographic data is available in the internet at <http://dnb.ddb.de>.

Printed with financial support of Bundesministerium für Bildung, Wissenschaft und Kultur in Wien.

ISBN 3-631-51527-8
US-ISBN 0-8204-6507-0

Printed in Germany 1 2 4 5 6 7

www.peterlang.de

Table of Contents

Why I Wrote This Book

I entered school in my hometown Vienna, Austria two years before the end of World War II. It was at that time that I and my elder sister learned from the greengrocer at the corner that the Nazis were murdering Jews ("making soap out of their bones and lampshades out of their skin," the greengrocer said). We suspect that he listened to Allied radio transmissions – something that, if discovered, meant certain death at the hands of the Nazis. In early 1945, bombs launched from British planes hit some houses in the block we were living in. I remember how that made our air raid shelter tremble. Yet that was far less unsettling than seeing a corpse for the first time in my life. I found the body in a park shortly before Allied forces entered Vienna. I now believe that the corpse had simply been deposited there because it had been impossible to transport it to the cemetery and to arrange for a proper interment.

The two following years were terrible. Sometimes I was so hungry that I ate potato peels taken from the dustbin. The winter of 1946/1947 was exceptionally cold. We just had enough fuel to heat the smallest room in our apartment; and even that was only every other day or so. But in this, our family was still lucky. Many Viennese froze to death.

Austria had become a desperately poor country and it remained largely rural. A quarter of the work force was still employed in agriculture. Hans Morgenthau, who visited Vienna as a State Department expert, wrote a highly negative report on the economic prospects of my home country. He saw none.

We were fortunate to live in the sector of the city occupied by American troops. But the Soviet headquarters (the "Kommandatura") were only half a mile away. We knew that people entered the building to never be seen again. In 1951 the Communists attempted a putsch against the elected government. It failed, but only narrowly.

Today Austria is amongst the wealthiest countries of the world. It ranks number eight in per capita income. Its over-fed, coddled citizens feel fully entitled to this elevated position. Two generations ago, politics were marked by civil war and dictatorship. Today democracy is functioning smoothly and, this too, is seen as the natural state of affairs. It is greeted less with appreciation than with boredom.

The increase in Austria`s wealth has been exceptionally rapid. So was the return to, and the consolidation of, democracy. Yet, in a way, Austria just reflects what happened all over the world. On a global scale too, the developments of the last fifty years have been spectacular. In the short span of just one quarter of a century, global wealth has tripled. Within half a century, the size of the world population has doubled. Average life expectancy has risen by nearly 20 years. More than half of the states on our planet are now ruled democratically. In the "West", at least, no major power has been involved in a war against another major power.

Just as Austrians accept their good fortune as a matter of fact and do not doubt their having merited it, the world also accepts this astounding transformation as if it were the most natural thing to have happened – as if events and developments could not have run in any other direction. The world has left behind, it seems, memories of large scale disasters; of whole continents being ravaged by famine; of all of its surface being contested between mutually hostile imperial powers; of the vast majority of humans slumbering in numb illiteracy and ignorance. Is forgetting this past justified? Is humanity really that safely afloat on a broad stream that carries it forward into an ever brighter future? Are catastrophes such as world wars and world economic crises nothing but relatively minor and merely temporary disturbances in this vast stream?

Sticking to mere figures and looking at the broad trends only, we could come to share such cool optimism. For what are the 20 million killed in the Second World War when compared to the three billion humans that have been added to the world population in the last fifty years? How minor is the loss of wealth caused by the World Economic Crisis if this loss is set against the unprecedented growth of world wealth that has occurred since? Indeed – this vast, broad stream of improvement in human condition seems to move onwards, irrespective of what we do or fail to do. It seems to move along irrespective of the success or failure of governance in nations, and of success or failure of governance in global affairs.

That conclusion does not sit well. Fortunately, we shy away from callously accepting as negligible the death of a few million in a famine here or in a war there. Such Olympic equanimity also runs counter to the extra caution that seems to be genetically programmed in humans. Better be prudent about the future. Better ward against risks it might harbour. Better to err on the side of pessimism than to be irresponsibly optimistic.

But there is one even more cogent reason to dispense with such equanimity. The past cannot instruct us on the future. The changes we described – the increase in wealth and in the size of the global population – are not merely quantitative. They have changed the nature of the global system. The past, therefore, cannot provide us with lessons for the future. In the past, lack of governance, or failed governance, might not have affected the vast, broad trends in the world very much. From now on it will, and it will do so to an ever greater extent.

Yet we are not up to the task. We are far from being able to truly direct these large developments politically. We even fail to come to grips with the task intellectually. Our concepts and our discourse are still those of a bygone era. This bygone era was defined – or was thought to be defined – by whether power over the globe was held by just one state; or shared between two states; or between several states. And this still holds centre stage in the present political discourse: whether the world is "unipolar" or "multipolar"; and how the various "poles" live out their alleged hostility to one another; whether, and to what extent, Americans are "anti – European"; and whether, and to what extent, Europeans are "anti – American"; and whether both of them might not be confronted by powers of an ominous "axis of evil" that is hostile to all that is "Western", regardless of whether it comes from the United States or from Europe.

Such discourse does not help us to understand and deal with the deeper and more challenging problems of our planet. It does not help us to deal, for instance, with the question of what can be done to narrow the ever widening gap between the very poor and the very wealthy countries. It does not instruct us as to how to prevent genetic engineering from running far ahead of our capacity to remedy some of its highly dangerous consequences. It does not enlighten us in the decision on whether and how to react to global warming.

Those are the new challenges. But we have not even become better at dealing with the old, traditional ones: what to do about aggression, envy, internal disorder, breakdown of states, competitive armament, large scale organised crime, terrorism, decay of democratic virtue, a willful military, etc. With the states of the world having become more interconnected, these traditional challenges have also acquired a new and more threatening dimension.

I retain in vivid memory the horrors experienced in my childhood. I lived through them in a country that, before, had thought of itself as being a haven of civility and a beacon of modernity. The personal experience of breakdown and disaster, and the experience of my country in the twentieth century has taught me that such a sense of calm security might be illusionary. It has alerted me to the danger that such cock-sure self-confidence and thoughtless indolence might be as misplaced today as it had been misplaced ninety years ago, before Central European arrogance was shattered in World War I. The future is not assured by some invisible hand that shields us from serious and more permanent mishaps, and that would make continue the flow of that broad beneficial stream that carried us forward over the last fifty years. The future will be defined by our success or failure to shape it through effective governance.

So this is a book about these tasks that we face, and about the tools we have acquired to accomplish them. It is also about why we see some things as being relevant and others not. It discusses the ideas we have on how to best organise the common, political action and, accordingly, it deals with political theories.

We will start out by sketching developments in the global economy; in world population and in the ensuing demographic shifts; in urbanisation; in the production and consumption of food, of raw materials and of energy. We will assess how all of this impacts upon the world ecosystem. On all of this we have ample data. The conclusions we may draw thus seem rather straightforward – even if they run counter to accepted wisdom on occasion.

Matters become more difficult when we enter fields where relations between the physical, the social and the political within and among states become more diffuse: crime and other social disfunctionalities; recurring economic crises; war; civil war; terrorism and poverty. While we know at least some things about what causes poverty and inequality within states, and while we know a few things about what to do about that, less is known about the true causes of the inequality as it exists between states and about remedies that could narrow this gap.

We study how the three dominant regions of the world – the US, Europe and Japan – have fared in this global system; how they relate to one another; and whether they will be joined – or challenged – by the emergence of China as the fourth coagulation point of global power.

All this will lead us to the question that is most difficult to answer. This is the question of how this complex web of an ever-closer interdependence is being held together; whether markets do it all by themselves and, if not, who then exercises control over the markets and especially over the financial markets. We ask whether the stability and predictability of the system is being assured by the United States acting as a reliable "hegemon"; or whether that is done either by international organisations, or by global "civil society" acting through thousands of "International Non-Governmental Organisations".

We conclude with an outlook on the future of the nation state and of democracy; with descriptions of some obvious changes in the way global relations and global governance is structured; and, finally, with speculations on further developments that are likely or possible over the next fifty years.

Altogether this is a vast undertaking and I am very aware of the dangers I incur in leaving the sheltered waters of some academic niche and venturing out without my flanks always being covered with the armour of all the latest literature on this or that specific issue. But I hope to make up for that through my having also known the real thing, through my having been intimately connected both to national and international politics and by my having learned what they can, and what they cannot achieve.

I am grateful to Peter Lang Publishing for taking the risk of entering these unsheltered waters with me; and to the Austrian Ministry for Education, Science and Culture for having supported this venture. I am grateful to my wife for having read the manuscript over and over again in its many evolving versions. I could not have completed the book without my graduate students Daniela Mussnig and Vedran Dzihic helping me in putting together and tidying up the draft.

I hope that their efforts and mine have not been in vain. It will not have been in vain if I succeed in moving readers to viewing the world from a different perspective, and into realising that they are not merely passive spectators. It is up to all of us whether the twenty-first century will bring a repeat of the disaster wrought in the twentieth century, or whether we will have become better able to care for ourselves and our planet.

I retired from diplomatic service some years ago. In a few years I will also retire from teaching. As I watch my grandchildren play cops and robbers, I wonder what their life will turn out to be. Will it be as favoured as my life has been by the experience of half a century of peace and human progress? Or will their lives be as fraught with disaster as were the lives of the generation to which my own parents belonged? Having withdrawn from the realms directly connected to politics, I have fewer and fewer tools to make a difference. But I can still write, and this is why I wrote this book.

The Global System, Global Trends and Why We Know at Least a Few Things About Them

We are not given to ponder every detail of our daily, routine life. We do not take special note of things we are accustomed to. It cannot be otherwise. Were we to stop and reflect on what we are familiar with already, we would become immobilised by the enormity of the task. But it is exactly for that reason that we frequently fail to take note of things that creep into our daily life so slowly that we do not reflect on all the implications of some new additions in our basket of the routine and trivial.

When we go to the supermarket in January to buy lettuce and strawberries, we know by routine that we will find them on the shelves. We would be surprised were we to find instead a sign: "sorry – no lettuce, come again in spring when the first fresh deliveries will have arrived from local green-houses". Such a break with the expected would make us reflect on the fact that, in winter, lettuce and strawberries do not come from local suppliers, but from quite some distance. They have been hauled to the North either by plane or by trucks travelling thousands of miles. One of the reasons we have failed to pay any attention is the low price of strawberries and lettuce, even in winter. They do not cost much more than the local variety we may purchase in late spring and summer. But shouldn't we be surprised by this fact?

And while taking the strawberries and the lettuce to the check-out counter, we still may wonder about things other than their low price. They are available not just because of cheap long distance transport in refrigerator trucks, or in the cargo holds of airplanes. Finding cheap lettuce and strawberries on the shelves of supermarkets in winter also is contingent on a lot of other preconditions. For example, everybody in the long supply chain has to be paid. Everyone in the supply chain must be sure that the payment will arrive reliably. The wholesaler that purchases the goods from the growers must be certain that they conform to the prevailing "phytosanitatry" rules – the food and drug laws that protect the consumer who finally will buy the fruits and vegetables. Roads suitable for heavy and fast travelling refrigerator trucks must have been built and maintained, as well as functioning airports to accommodate big transport planes, and air controllers and air control systems to guide the planes to their destination. Somebody must set the schedule for the heavy, fast-travelling trucks and for the giant airplanes, and so on. We could think of many, many other preconditions that have to be met for strawberries and lettuce to be cheap to buy even in winter. But while we try to mentally draw up a list, the lady at the check-out will wonder about our pensive look and why we have not started to unload on her counter the items we took from the shelves.

While we carry the bags to the parking lot, we start to ponder another related question. Who sees to it that all of these preconditions are actually being met? Who arranges and co-ordinates the process? Who, in the end, is in charge? Obviously a host of persons and institutions are involved. Many of them will be governmental. And that is why each nation has a government. Governments are there to devise and enforce rules and to co-ordinate private actors where the market fails to do so. But then we realise that the long and complex supply chain for the lettuce and the strawberries does not stop where the power of governments stops – namely at national borders. The trucks or airplanes might be owned by a foreign company. Drivers and pilots might be citizens of different countries. The products themselves could have been grown on farms in foreign states. Banks in still another state might have done the financing of the trade. Industries in yet another foreign nation might have supplied the pesticides that had been sprayed on the lettuce and on the strawberries. The national government itself has no control and power over these foreigners. Yet these foreigners do observe rules, as otherwise co-operation with them would be difficult or even impossible. Their sticking to rules and their co-operation must have become routine too; routine to the extent that you, the consumer of the lettuce and the strawberries, do not even notice it and reflect upon it. Still it is worth thinking about: who is in charge of such very complex systems? Who prevents the failure and breakdown of such a routine, daily co-operation? Who governs? How can we be certain that such complex systems will continue to function? Will they always continue to function?

One can do without strawberries and lettuce in winter. But modern societies cannot do without electricity. Its being there to use is also something we accept matter-of-factly. If we turn the switch we expect lights to go on. We would be surprised if it remained dark because the generators in power stations have ceased to turn. Yet they could very well cease to turn if power stations ran out of fuel. Much of this fuel comes from foreign countries. In Japan and Europe the majority of fossil fuels are imported, and a sizeable and growing percentage of fossil fuels are also being imported by the United States. What would happen if this supply from foreign countries were to stop for one reason or another – and this for a lengthier period of time? Computers would stop. Food would rot. Travel would cease. In short, life as we know it and as we have been accustomed to would come to an end. And that could happen in a very literal sense. Many would die. But when switching on the light, we hardly think of such contingencies.

I am a European born before the Second World War. My childhood memories are of bombs and of the night sky being lit by burning refineries; of soldiers breaking down doors with guns under their arms. Having lived these experiences, I still marvel at something persons younger than me, or persons living in America accept as the quasi natural state of affairs. I realise and appreciate that for more than half a century our lives have not been disturbed by a major war. Wars did occur. But such wars as those over Korea, Vietnam, Iraq, or Afghanistan were quite minor in historic comparison. Yet earlier on, and ever since the 18th century, many of the wars have been world-wide. Those who lived in the 18th century experienced nearly as many years of war as years of peace. At that time war, and even world wide war, was, so to say, "normal". Now it is not. We expect peace to be the normal state of affairs. Is this but a pleasant illusion? Were the last fifty years only the exception to a general rule and would wars continue to belong to human affairs like thunder to lightning?

One other childhood memory is haunting too. Once my father disappeared to return one day later pale, exhausted and trembling. He drew me into a corner and asked me quietly whether I really had made disparaging remarks about the Führer to colleagues in primary school. I had. And someone had learned about it. In the end, also the local office of the GESTAPO. My father was held for a day-long questioning and was released under threats to keep closer watch over his family. Today, in the wealthy countries, few carry the burden of such memories. In fact, we expect to live in democracies. We do not fear or expect secret police to knock at the door at four o'clock in the morning. We accept democracy like we accept the absence of major wars: as something thoroughly normal. Doing so, we fail to observe the many pre-conditions for peace and for democracy. How are these pre-conditions met? Will they always and reliably be met?

In order to make peace and democracy possible, many have to co-operate. Much of this co-operation has to be international. Universities offer courses on “international relations”. Banks have “international” departments. At airports, one queues up for “international” flights. We accept this term “international” and do not question what it implies. Yet it implies a bold generalisation about the world system. There would be no substance to this world system as such. What we observe out there – beyond our borders – would just be the result of actions “inter nations”[1]. Nations, and nothing else, would form the building blocks of the global system. If we want to know something about this sphere beyond the national frontiers, it would suffice for us to register and analyse how different nations act towards each other.

1 In a similar vein, the economy is often pictured as just the result of preferences of individual actors.

States still do much, and even most, of the co-ordination and control that is needed to maintain the present, complex global system. They may have ceded some of their prior tasks to other organisations. Nonetheless, we cannot explain the big, centennial developments by just looking at what states do or at what they have done. To prove the point, let us do a mental experiment and view things from a different perspective. Let us assume that every fifty years or so extraterrestrials from a superior civilisation[2] would scan the earth with their equally superior scientific instruments and log what they find. What observations on the earthlings would these extraterrestrials have noted down over the last two hundred years?

Their log would contain little of what is contained in course books and readers on international relations. These superior beings in another solar system might, per chance, have observed a nuclear explosion or two; or the turbulences of world wars. But they would not have read the transcripts of the debates in the General Assembly of the United Nations and they would have failed to take note of the latest diplomatic manoeuvre in the Middle East. Altogether, the curious extraterrestrials would thus have ignored much of what is seen as essential in "international relations". They would, however, have observed an astounding and major transformation of this distant planet. They would not have failed to note that the planet's population had doubled within the short span of just 50 years. They would take note of the sudden disappearance of smoke stacks, of the advance in agriculture, of the explosive growth of mega-cities and of cities in general, of a vast cloud of radio wave-emittances suddenly shrouding the earth, of the transformation of the planet's surface by highways, and of the many big and fast ships that ply the seas.

The extraterrestrials would compare this latest entry in their log with the one made two hundred years before. They would conclude that changes had indeed accelerated on this distant blue planet. Give them another couple of thousand years, they would say, and these earthlings might very well catch up with us and merit a personal visit. After all, they have emerged in their present form, naked and semi-starved just a mere 80,000 years ago.

---

2 I invite the reader to a galactic perspective: 10 billion stars in our galaxy; one percent of them has planets = 100.000 million. One percent of these can support life = 1million. 10 percent of these can support more complex and advanced forms of life =100.000. On one third of them, life is further advanced than on our own little blue planet = 33.000. To traverse the galaxy at a (physically feasible) speed – one third the speed of light – would take just 10 million years. In that – cosmologically short – period, the most superior species of the galaxy should have been able to colonise all inhabitable planets. So – where are they?

We will therefore discard, for a time, the traditional notion of "international relations" and share this intra-galactic perspective. Like extraterrestrials, we will look at the wider picture. We ignore the particulars. We no longer concern ourselves with the details of transactions "inter nations". Instead, we will try to conceive of the world as one single big system. We assume as truly relevant just the changes in this wider picture.

In this supremely detached view, even World War II would not make that much of a difference. Europe would have been removed from the pinnacle of power and from the top of the international pecking order even without this big war. Most of the poor countries would have remained poor irrespective of the accidental turns in their history. The British and French Empires would have crumbled under any imaginable international constellation. Any economic system not conforming to, or being compatible with, the principles of markets would have perished just as Communism did. All these things could have happened a bit earlier; or a bit later. But it is highly plausible that they would have happened anyhow.

This is not to imply that politics, political institutions and political governance are irrelevant. Quite on the contrary. They are a part of this vast process of global transformation. But they and the economy co-evolve together. They are mutually contingent. Economic evolution cannot occur in the absence of effective governance; and in the absence of wealth and economic growth, governance can do very little to improve the human lot.[3] We shall deal with that issue of governance at some lengths later on in the last chapters of this book: Who, which institutions are in charge? Are they up to the task? Have they adapted and will they continue to adapt? Or will their failure to do so undermine the global system that, due to its complexity, direly needs effective governance?

But before we can address these questions, we first have to establish how exactly the world system has evolved and in which direction it is likely to evolve in the future. That is not an easy task. In the absence of any communication with the wise extraterrestrials, we have to rely on our own wits and observations. We certainly will also seek counsel from those scientists that specialise in investigating such questions. What do they see as the important trends? What changes in the very nature of the world do they believe to be the salient ones? Unfortunately, even prominent political scientists fail to provide us with consistent answers as they disagree amongst each other on the nature of these changes. What is considered as central by one is being considered trivial by another.

3 In order to be effective, such governance has, for example, to be democratic (that is susceptible to change and adaptation according to the wishes of those who are affected by it).

There is little agreement between authors on what would be the strategic variable of change. Some believe that the strategic variable is the changes in the relative military weight of states and regions. Some believe it to be changes in the relative economic weight. Others still perceive of culture and identity or ideas as defining the nature and dynamics of the world system.

If political scientists disagree with each other on the nature of the truly salient trends that transform the global system, such disagreement becomes even more marked if, next to political scientists, we ask the wider group of social scientists on how they view the issue. Economists have their vision and interpretation of the world; historians another one; anthropologists yet a third; sociologists a fourth; and so on.

Constructivism

Such open disagreement on even the most basic questions seems to sustain those who discard the notion that some objective reality could be depicted in a "scientific" manner. All we may know is how people speak about what they want to have accepted as "real". All we have is their "discourse". This discourse is a "social construct". It reflects the interests and predilections of those powerful and prestigious enough to make their own discourse prevail over other, alternate "discourses".

In a state established and held together by sheer physical coercion, for example, those at the top are those (males) that can wield this power of physical coercion. In such a country, the discourse on the nature of the political and global system will be shaped by the interests of the rulers to maintain and legitimise their power of coercion. They will define the state as the institution with a monopoly of physical coercion (Max Weber). They will define international relations as the mirror image of the relative capacity of each of these states to inflict physical damage on another state.

This is the so called "realist" school of international relations.[4] It prevailed even in recent times, when the "West" was mobilising for the Cold War. Later, in the sixties, the international discourse was influenced and determined, to no small extent, by the visions, wishes and interests of those numerous states that had just escaped from under the yoke of colonialism. Now, at the beginning of the 21st century, when financial markets are dominant, the prevailing discourse on world affairs tends to be shaped by the perspective and interests of those that own or manage financial capital.

4 Personified, for example, by H. Morgenthau and his "Politics Among Nations"

It is claimed that a discourse would constitute the only "reality" accessible to us. Any attempt to go beyond this discourse and try to discover the "true" reality it hides would be in vain. Any such attempt would create but another, alternate discourse. In its turn, this discourse, too, would be shaped by the position and interests of those powerful enough to have it accepted. All we can do is to "deconstruct" each discourse and to excavate, so to say, the hidden agenda imbedded in it.[5] If we "deconstruct", for example, the above mentioned discourse of the so called "realists", it would become evident that this discourse transports and legitimises the agenda of an aggressive and phallocratic warrior class.

To a large extent, and to the point of being trivial, such claims are just a confirmation of the obvious. Of course, each discourse is a social construct. The very language we use in communicating (and thinking) is a social construct. If born in China, one will grow up learning Chinese, and not German or Spanish. Accepting Chinese words, one accepts with them the meanings that have been assigned to them in a social process. It is equally obvious that truth is what is accepted as truth. And in the choice between what is accepted as true and what is not accepted as true, this choice certainly reflects the position of those who have the power, prestige or social function to imprint their seal of approval upon a certain supposition.

The issue is not whether a discourse is a social construct. It certainly is. The issue is why we accept certain discourses and why we reject others. This cannot just be explained by the power and interests of various groups as they are imbedded in each distinct discourse. We rejected the notion of the earth being flat and the centre of the universe not because the religions that earlier on had the power to impose such an old fashioned, geo-centric notion have waned. We reject the flat-earth and geo-centric view because it is impractical. It is not functional. It does not explain phenomena as well as the modern notion of the earth being a sphere and of the universe being an expanding, four dimensional space filled with energy and visible and invisible matter.

Certainly, in the realm of global studies too, what we accept as "real" is also a social construct. But, as in other fields of science, in the field of international studies, such constructs have to be tested for their usefulness in explaining things. We expand knowledge by discarding less functional explanations

5 Part of the attraction of "deconstruction" to its practitioners must be the sense of omnipotence it conveys. They have power to see behind the veil, to unmask others, to free themselves of claims by others on what is real and what is not real. This claim accommodates a childish yearning for omnipotence that, frequently, is also found among intellectuals.

for more functional ones; just as a species less suited to a certain ecological niche is being replaced by one better adapted to survive in it (an evolutionary theory of knowledge).

It is not just the powerful and mighty that make one discourse prevail over another discourse. Today this is mainly the function of scientists. In the course of modernisation, social functions have become differentiated. In this process, scientists have been assigned the task to test the usefulness of new propositions and explanations. There is no one in sight who could compete with scientists in this function. This also holds true in the realm of political science and of international studies. If we want to know whether the world population grows, or if we wish to establish the causes of recent violent conflicts, we do not turn to soothsayers. Neither will we turn to those at the top of the social/political/ economic pecking order – to elected politicians or to the managers of large banks. We will call for a scientific response to our questions and we expect these responses to come from scientists.

Chaos Theory

But in posing such questions to political scientists, do we not request something that is clearly impossible? We ask political scientists to explain developments that take place in very complex systems. To live up to that expectation and in order to offer true explanations, political scientists must do more than just tell a story of what has happened. That would just be "history". Political scientists have to be more ambitious. They aspire to discover and show the final causes of political developments. To succeed, they would have to class some events or developments into category one and others into category two. Success in their endeavour would presuppose knowledge on which variable is present in class one and not present in class two. It would also require knowledge on how exactly this one variable interacts with the countless other ones present in each of these two societies. Clearly this is a difficult task and impossible in many instances.

The difficulties reside in the complexity of social and political systems. In a simple system with just two or three variables[6], there is usually just one possible outcome or "solution". In such a simple system one might safely predict, by a simple equation, that "when A times B then = C". However, systems even a bit more complex have already several "solutions"[7]. Highly complex systems

6 that relate to one another in a "linear" fashion

7 As economists, with their predilection for expressing things via mathematics, discovered quite some time ago.

with highly complex equations have an impossibly large number of solutions. Predictions, thus, are no longer possible. These systems are "chaotic".[8] We cannot say what will happen when. This applies, of course, also to the very complex global system.

If we cannot make such firm predictions in the inherently chaotic global system, does this also imply that we are unable even to discern regularities or some of the major lines of development or trends in this system? We may attempt an answer to this question by drawing a parallel to another chaotic system – namely, the weather system. We still are not able to precisely predict weather over the long term – even though the variables coming into play in meteorology are fewer than those that shape the global system. We cannot predict, for example, how the weather will be on 1 January 2006. We still can predict though, with some certainty, that in January the temperature will be lower than in August of the same year. We can by now also predict with a certain confidence that, due to the trend of global warming, the first week of October 2040 will be somewhat warmer than this first week of October 2003.

The term "chaos" conveys an impression of utter confusion – of the absence of any discernible patterns and trends. But this is NOT what chaos theory implies. In fact, the many feasible "solutions" of complex, multi-variable, non-linear equations aggregate around distinct patterns ("fractals"). The notion of a pattern does not imply that each figure is identical to the other one. Quite on the contrary – each of the specimens will be distinct; just as no lime leaf is exactly like another limeleaf. Nonetheless, when we see a lime leaf we immediately recognise it as such; just as a psychiatrist will recognise depressions as such without any depressed person behaving in exactly the same manner as another depressed person. A political scientist will immediately recognise an authoritarian system, and again, each one of these authoritarian systems as being distinct from the others. Social scientists thus have learned to recognise the patterns, the "fractals", formed by chaotic systems. Such fractals can be arranged around a path, a trend. Even in chaotic systems one may thus:

1) discern patterns and
2) discern trends

8 The novel Jurassic Park by Crichton is built around the unpredictability of complex and, therefore, chaotic systems. It warns against ignoring it. The scientist/entrepreneur in charge of establishing a theme park for dinosaurs is very careful. He believes he has thought about all eventualities. But as the system of the park is so complex, he cannot predict all of these possible consequences; and he is therefore unable to ward against them and control them.

> We have come to discern patterns and trends in the chaotic meteorological system. In the same way we may also discern patterns and trends in the global system.

Both chaos theory and the notion of "discourse" discourage us to follow, in social science, the usual path of scientific inquiry used in “hard” science. Traditionally, social sciences have made some a priori assumptions on what they perceived to be the true nature of humans or of nations. They then made some assumptions on how – given this unchangeable nature of humans or of nations – these would react to this or that change in their environment. And only at the latest stage of their inquiry did they attempt to match these theoretical considerations with reality. Through this match they sought corroboration of exactly what they had assumed from the beginning – namely the existence of some form of immutable law that governs humans and societies.

But given the many variables that influence human, social or political behaviour, political science has not been very successful when using such methods. The aim of emulating "hard" science, and the hope of finding some iron laws akin to the eternal laws of physical motion, have been in vain.

Political science (just as economics) is thus well advised to follow the example of meteorology – to abandon all a priori assumptions on how the weather should behave and just start gathering data on what patterns we may actually observe. This has also been the path followed by another science that deals with very complex systems – namely biology – that deals with the complexity of living things. At the beginning of modern biology there was a systematic effort to observe regularities and trends and to classify them according to discernable patterns.

But even when using this very same methodology as biologists, the task of the political scientist still remains difficult. Unlike the biologist, he has to deal with humans that are aware of their situation. Even if their behaviour is triggered by some outward circumstances, they, in turn, react to these circumstances and thus change them. They do so with a special intent and purpose. This purposeful action might be an individual one. Or it might be a purposeful collective action, that is, a political action. We therefore cannot describe the global system while neglecting the fact that it is also shaped by purposeful, political human action. We have to include the political in our overview of the global system.

If we now look at the dominating patterns and at the vast and truly long-term trends, which are the most potent ones? It is difficult NOT to assume that it is the increase in the wealth. It is difficult NOT to assume that this increase has driven most other major global trends.[9] So let us look at this trend first.

Levels of World Economic Performance, 1500-1992

	1500	1820	1992
World Population (million)	425	1068	5441
GDP Per Capita (1990 $)	565	651	5145
World GDP (billion 1990 $)	240	695	27995
World exports (billion 1990 $)	n.a.	7	3786

Source: http://www.j-bradford-delong.net

World economic expansion did not just start with the invention of the steam engine in the 18th century. It began earlier. In the time between 1500 and 1820, the world economy expanded enough to permit the world's population to more than double while still increasing its per capita GDP by a fifth[10]. As shown in the graph below, the development became truly unprecedented and dramatic from 1820 on. The rise in the world's wealth has been explosive.

The picture below is that of a "J"-shaped curve. The development is cumulative. The acceleration (the economic growth rate) seems to be constant at least; and wealth thus accumulates in a "geometric" fashion.

9 This notion of a techno-economic evolution being the basis for most of the economic, social, political and cultural developments is – of course – a Marxist notion. Surprisingly, this Marxist notion is nonetheless shared by utterly conservative institutions. These are (like the IMF and the Wall Street Journal = "Wall Street Journal Marxism") also convinced of technology and of the economy being the prime movers of society. And all who thought – and preached – otherwise have been proven wrong again and again as, for instance, all of the "anti modernists" who – starting from the German Romantics – thought it possibly both wiser and, lastly, inevitable that humankind would try to reclaim its earlier phase of pre-modern innocence.

10 "Progress" did not start with the invention of the steam engine and automatic spinning in the late 18th century. It is generally agreed by now that it had already started in the Middle Ages; and that it had, at its base, a political / social revolution that established the (relative) security of private property; and that permitted long distance commerce. In the 12th century already, bankers in Genoa provided credits to good clients at a real interest rate of 2 percent (something modern bankers can do only in very rare instances).

Estimated Global GDP per capita 0-2000

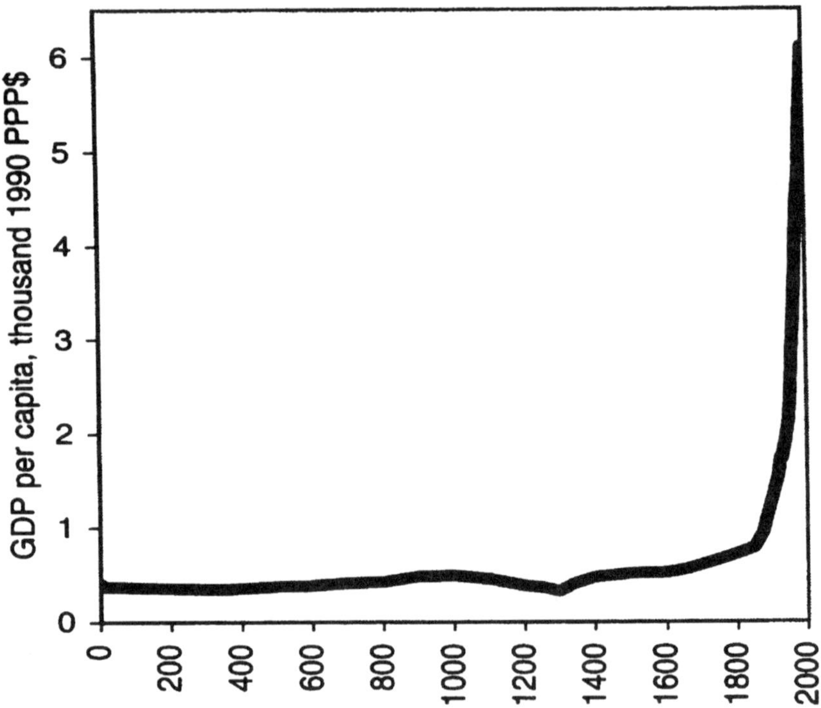

Source: DeLong 2000a

This "J" is the sum of developments in a number of quite different countries, each of them at a different stage of economic development and each of them having evolved at a different pace. If we dis-aggregate this average and look first just at those countries that have become wealthy already, we find that the latest arrivals – the "newly rich" so to say – have grown at a faster pace. This is visually expressed in the graph below. It shows the economic development of the present members of the "club of the rich countries". The first curve – the one that is flattest – portrays economic growth in the first country to industrialise – namely Great Britain. Great Britain was succeeded by France, then by Germany, then by the US, then by Japan, and so on. Each of the successors was faster in the accumulation of wealth than its predecessor.

Income per head in selected, presently wealthy economies 1800-2000
(in 000's, 1985 US Dollars)

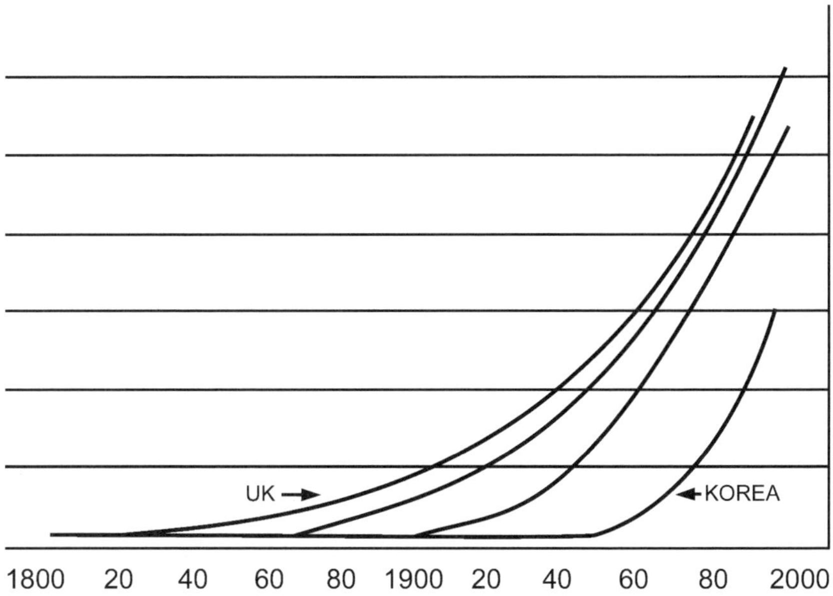

Source: Maddison 1995

Basically, economic development is a process of learning. And the process of learning can itself be learned. Each late-comer can therefore do better than those that came before him. The steepest and last curve is the one for Korea. The rise in wealth that Britain achieved in the 150 years between 1800 and 1950 was accomplished by Korea in a period of just 50 years, between 1950 and 2000.

Of course, the "J"-shaped curve on the development of the whole world economy does not reflect the economic record of single countries or regions. Some of them might do better than the average. Others might do worse. Countries might fall back in their relative economic rank. One prominent example is Argentina. At the end of World War I it ranked among the world's wealthiest. By now it has come close in poverty to its traditionally poorer neighbour – Brazil.

A more recent example is provided by New Zealand. In 1965 its per capita income was still 25 percent above the (OECD) average of all wealthy countries.

Thirty years later it was 38 percent below this average. While other economies grew, the economy of New Zealand remained stagnant.[11]

Countries might even fall back in absolute wealth. They might become poorer than they had been before. The movement upwards or forwards might be interrupted by recessions and financial crises. It might even be interrupted more seriously by longer periods of stagnation. Twenty years ago the world (and nearly all experts) was convinced that the further economic rise of Japan was inevitable. It would become "the super state" (Herman Kahn) – or "number one". This has not happened. The bubble in the Japanese real-estate and stock markets burst and the implosion was followed by a period of stagnation and even decline.[12]

May we, nonetheless, feel certain about the overall picture and the long term perspective? May we still assume that, for the world taken as such and on the average, economic growth will continue? May we still be confident that, fifty years from now, this average will be substantially higher than it is at present?

Some claim we may not do so as ours will be an "age of discontinuity". In this age, all long-term trends will be broken. The explosive rise in the world's population, the disappearing costs for transport and communication, and the revolution in information technology will bring a rupture with the past. We would have entered a world totally different from what it was decades ago. We therefore should refrain from projecting the past into the future.

Yet, since the onset of the industrial age, each new generation has been convinced they were standing at such a breaking point in history. Each generation was deeply impressed by the recent advances in technology. It is even likely that previous generations had better reasons for holding on to such beliefs. The inventions that were made in the fifty years between 1860 and 1910, for example, certainly had a more profound social and economic impact than the inventions made in the last fifty years. These last fifty years have seen major breakthroughs in the field of electronics and computing (transistor and memory-chip) and in microbiology. These technological changes did indeed impact upon the socio-economic

11 It is difficult to ascertain how much of this stagnation is due to factors that could not be affected by policy choices (or not easily so), like the reliance on agricultural production and exports (with their worsening terms of trade), and how much is due to bad policy choices. It seems likely that bad policy did have some place in this discouraging non-development. Many blame the ultra-liberal policies of the centre-left (!) government for that.

12 This failure of Japan also contains a warning to other wealthy and hitherto successful nations. Especially to the US. As we will point out, there are troubling parallels between pre-collapse Japan and present USA. The Japanese crisis might be the harbinger of a fate that even could befall the world economy as such. After all, we still do not possess suitable tools to avert such an eventuality. The World Economic Crisis of the thirties could very well be repeated at the dawn of the 21st century.

order and they will continue to do so in the coming decades. But this impact was not as monumental as the impact of inventions made in the last decades of the 19th and in the first decades of the 20th centuries such as, for example, the:

- telegraph
- telephone
- light bulb
- electric generator
- electric motor
- artificial fertiliser
- discovery of the nature of contagious diseases
- basic sanitation and running water for the masses
- internal combustion engine
- motor car
- aeroplane
- radio
- cinema, and so on

The technologies that entered upon the scene after 1950 are significant in many ways and their application will deeply affect individual and collective life. But in their capacity to advance well-being and economic growth, the impact of these new technologies is less revolutionary than we proclaim it to be. At their best, the technical/scientific/economic innovations of the last decades will just permit a continuation[13] of the past trends in economic evolution. In that sense, ours is not an "age of discontinuity". We are thus justified to assume that past trends will continue.

But this might not be true if we look not just at the long-term but at the very, very distant future. In the very, very long term, one hundred or two hundred and fifty years from now, the trend might indeed be broken. It might be that by then the very nature of human society might be transformed in ways that cannot be predicted. Presently, the economy and its constraints structure both the lives of individuals and the policies of nations. But this could change. Economic gain has been the dominant motive in societies in the relatively short period of the last three or four hundred years only. Yet, if seen against the background of millenia, this has been only a short-lived exception. We therefore cannot exclude the pos-

13 Which does not preclude – as we shall see – that on a world-wide scale economic development does indeed accelerate (due mainly to a "catching up" of those who had been left behind until now).

sibility that this exception might draw to an end; and that in the very distant future, societies will again be guided by other than purely economic motives.[14]

This leads to another general observation. We have assumed the world economy will grow at an ever faster pace. But what about those countries which are already very wealthy? Will they also grow at an ever more rapid pace? Or will their development become slower? Economic theory would predict that it would. Their development would follow the shape of an "S". Several points on this curve should be of special political significance.

The "S" curve, reflecting many biological and social processes and – inter alia – economic growth

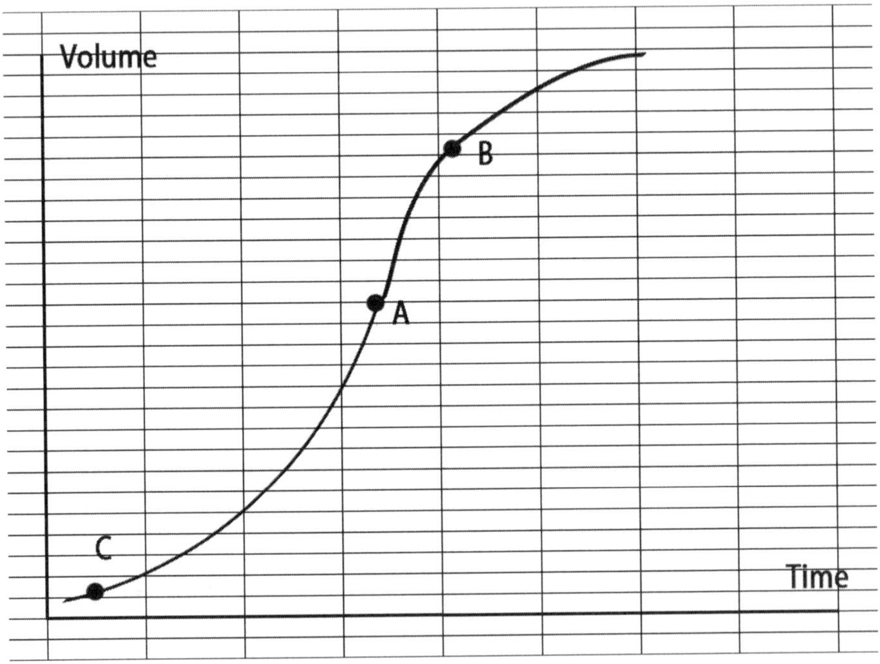

14 Some maintain that this has already occurred with the arrival of a "post-materialist" age. Empirical evidence and our own life experiences do, however, not sustain that proposition. Over the last decades, humans have certainly not turned less "materialistic".

Point A marks the end of the process of "catching up". Point B signals the fact that the country has joined the rank of the other highly developed nations, and now will have to compete with the best.

Instructed by economic theory, we assume that at both of these turning points, growth will become slower. But actually we know very little about this deceleration. Do all countries slow in a similar way once they have reached a certain level of wealth? If this were so, those at the top would still stay at the top; and those a bit behind would always stay a bit behind. But experience shows that this is not always the case. Late-comers were able to overtake earlier champions – just as the US overtook Great Britain.

Point C on the lower part of the "S"-curve signals the onset of faster growth. Obviously, economic growth had also occurred before, though it was slower (like the growth of the West European economy in the time between 1500 and 1820). Several questions arise. Is this prior, slow growth a pre-condition for the subsequent faster one? And, more importantly, are all countries of the world on such an "S"-curve? Would all of them eventually reach this point "C" and then start to develop more rapidly?

We shall deal with both sets of questions at quite some length at later stages. We shall look more closely at the dynamics of these countries that are wealthy already and that dominate the world economy. We will also address the question of if and how poor countries might exit from "non-development".

At this point, though, we should emphasise that since 1820 the world economy has grown rapidly, and that it has done so at an ever faster pace. We assume that this development is connected to – and has largely driven – other developments that have profoundly changed our world over these two hundred years.

The World Economy – Long Term Trends

Over the last two hundred years, the growth of the world economy has accelerated. As the graph below demonstrates, this acceleration became more pronounced after World War II. Between 1945 and 1970, that is, in a mere quarter of a century, world real income tripled.

World GDP 1900-1997
In 1990 US $ billion

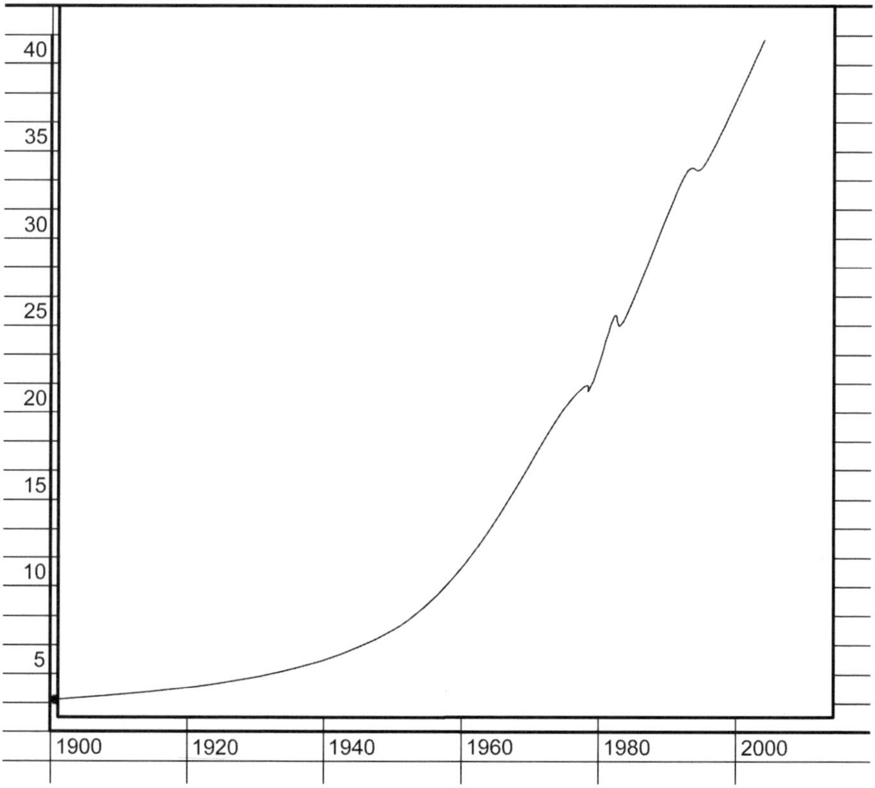

Source: Maddison 1995

During the last decades, this growth of the world GDP has been at an annual average rate of 3%. This is above the long term historic trend. Could this imply that world economic growth will continue at this faster pace?

GDP per capita
in 1990 USD – in a 56 country sample

	1820	1870	1900	1913	1950	1973	1992
12 Western European Countries							
Austria	1 295	1 875	2 901	3 488	3 731	11 308	17 160
Belgium	1 291	2 640	3 652	4 130	5 346	11 905	17 165
Denmark	1 225	1 927	2 902	3 764	6 683	13 416	18 293
Finland	759	1 107	1 620	2 050	4 131	10 768	14 646
France	1 218	1 858	2 849	3 452	5 221	12 940	17 959
Germany	1 112	1 913	3 134	3 833	4 281	13 152	19 351
Italy	1 092	1 467	1 746	2 507	3 425	10 409	16 229
Netherlands	1 561	2 640	3 533	3 950	5 850	12 763	16 898
Norway	1 004	1 303	1 762	2 275	4 969	10 229	17 543
Sweden	1 198	1 664	2 561	3 096	6 738	13 494	16 927
Switzerland	-	2 172	3 531	4 207	8 939	17 953	21 036
UK	1 756	3 263	4 593	5 032	6 847	11 992	15 738
Arith. Average	1 228	1 986	2 899	3 482	5 513	11 694	17 412
4 Western Offshoots							
Australia	1 528	3 801	4 299	5 505	7 218	12 485	16 237
Canada	893	1 620	2 758	4 213	7 047	13 644	18 159
New Zealand	-	3 115	4 320	5 178	8 495	12 575	13 947
USA	1 287	2 457	4 096	5 307	9 573	16 607	21 558
Arith. Average	1 236	2 748	3 868	5 051	8 083	13 828	17 475
5 South European Countries							
Greece	-	-	-	1 621	1 951	7 779	10 314
Ireland	954	1 773	2 495	2 733	3 518	7 023	11 711
Portugal	-	1 085	1 408	1 354	2 132	7 568	11 130
Spain	1 063	1 376	2 040	2 255	2 397	8 739	12 498
Turkey	-	-	-	979	1 299	2 739	4 422
Arith. Average	-	1 194*	1 676*	1 788	2 259	6 770	10 015
7 East European Countries							
Bulgaria	-	-	-	1 498	1 651	5 284	4 054
Czechoslovakia	849	1 164	1 729	2 096	3 501	7 036	6 845
Hungary	-	1 269	1 682	2 098	2 480	5 596	5 638
Poland	-	-	-	-	2 447	5 334	4 726
Romania	-	-	-	-	1 182	3 477	2 565
USSR	751	1 023	1 218	1 488	2 834	6 058	4 671
Yugoslavia	-	-	-	1 029	1 546	4 237	3 887
Arith. Average	-	876*	1 174*	1 527*	2 235	5 289	4 627

	1820	1870	1900	1913	1950	1973	1992
7 Latin American Countries							
Argentina	-	1 311	2 756	3 797	4 987	7 970	7 616
Brazil	670	740	704	839	1 673	3 913	4 637
Chile	-	-	1 949	2 653	3 827	5 028	7 238
Colombia	-	-	973	1 236	2 089	3 539	5 025
Mexico	760	710	1 157	1 467	2 085	4 189	5 112
Peru	-	-	817	1 037	2 263	3 953	2 854
Venezuela	-	-	821	1 104	7 424	10 717	9 163
Arith. Average	-	783*	1 311	1 733	3 478	5 017	5 949
11 Asian Countries							
Bangladesh	531	-	581	617	551	478	720
Burma	-	-	647*	635	393	589	748
China	523	523	652	688	614	1 186	3 098
India	531	558	625	663	597	853	1 348
Indonesia	614	657	745	917	874	1 538	2 749
Japan	704	741	1 135	1 334	1 873	11 017	19 425
Pakistan	531	-	687	729	650	981	1 642
Philippines	-	-	1 033	1 418	1 293	1 956	2 213
South Korea	-	-	850	948	876	2 840	10 010
Taiwan	-	-	759	794	922	3 669	11 590
Thailand	-	717	812	846	848	1 750	4 694
Arith. Average	609*	638*	775	872	863	2 442	5 294
10 African Countries							
Côte d'Ivoire	-	-	-	-	859	1 727	1 134
Egypt	-	-	509	508	517	947	1 927
Ethiopia	-	-	-	-	277	412	300
Ghana	-	-	462	648	1 193	1 260	1 007
Kenya	-	-	-	-	609	947	1 055
Morocco	-	-	-	-	1 611	1 651	2 327
Nigeria	-	-	-	-	547	1 120	1 152
South Africa	-	-	-	1 451	2 251	3 844	3 451
Tanzania	-	-	-	-	427	655	601
Zaire	-	-	-	-	636	757	353
Arith. Average	-	-	-	-	893	1 332	1 331

Source: Maddison 1995

We have assumed that a major contribution to fast growth has come from some still poor but big countries and/or vast regions entering a phase of early and thus rapid economic expansion. We assumed that such latecomers evolve at a faster pace than those already past this early stage of development ("catching up effect").

Let us therefore look at how certain regions and countries have evolved over the last 200 years in order to find out whether this is a valid assumption.

Two hundred years ago, the United States and Western European countries formed the group of the wealthiest. At that time already, this group was also fairly coherent. Measured in per capita GDP, the difference between the then wealthiest (UK) and the poorest[1] (Italy and Germany) did not exceed 30%. A hundred years later, this distance had widened to a dramatic one to three ratio with a per capita GDP of 4.593 in the UK and 1.746 in Italy. Since then, the gap has narrowed. Today, we are basically back where we were in 1820 with a difference in wealth of about 30%.

Eastern European countries have always been poorer. In 1820, their per capita wealth was about 40 percent below that of Western Europe. They then lost ground and the gap in wealth grew wider. It widened even dramatically in the last years under Communism and in the early Post-Communist era. Now their per capita GDP is no more than 25% of the "Western" one.

In the countries of the outer periphery, among those most remote from the centres of early modernisation, the relative decline was even more pronounced. In India, for instance, per capita wealth was half that of Western Europe in 1820. Now it is less than 10%.

Figures on per capita GDP are very relevant, of course. For each country they signal its stage of economic development. But besides that, the absolute size of each country's GDP is relevant too as it points to the sheer weight[2] a country has in the world economy.

---

1 We except Finland, at that time part of – very poor – Russia.

2 This is, of course, just the quantitative aspect. The economic "weight" – or power – of a country is also determined by the type of goods it produces; with an advantage going to those countries that produce high value added goods and, in doing so, use cutting edge technology.

The ten leading economies in 1820 and 1992

	GDP (million 1990 $)	GDP as Per Cent of World Total %	Population (000s)	Population as Share of World Total %
		1820		
1. China	199 212	28.7	381 000	35.5
2. India	110 982	16.0	209 000	19.6
3. France	37 397	5.4	30 698	2.9
4. UK	36 164	5.2	21 240	2.0
5. Russia	33 779	4.9	45 005	4.2
6. Japan	21 831	3.1	31 000	2.9
7. Austria	13 460	1.9	14 268	1.3
8. Spain	12 975	1.9	12 203	1.1
9. USA	12 432	1.8	9 656	0.9
10. Prussia	11 864	1.7	11 214	1.1
Top Ten Total	490 096	70.5	765 284	71.7
World	694 772	100.0	1 067 894	100.0
		1992		
1. USA	5 675 617	20.3	255 610	4.7
2. China	3 615 603	12.9	1 167 000	20.9
3. Japan	2 417 603	8.6	124 336	2.3
4. Germany	1 359 696	4.9	80 576	1.5
5. India	1 188 096	4.2	881 2001	6.2
6. France	1 030 356	3.7	57 372	1.1
7. Italy	939 685	3.4	57 900	1.1
8. UK	927 772	3.3	57 848	1.1
9. Russia	801 837	2.9	149 400	2.7
10. Brazil	756 014	2.7	156 012	2.9
Top Ten Total	18 712 219	66.8	2 987 254	54.9
World	28 000 037	100.0	5 440 983	100.0

Source: As these estimates refer to countries within the boundaries of the years specified, they are taken from Tables H2 and H3 for France, Germany, India, Russia and the UK. Otherwise from Appendices A and C. "Austria" refers to the Austrian half of the Austro-Hungarian Empire. The Polish and Finnish provinces are not included in the 1820 figure for Russia.

Source: Maddison 1995

In 1820, China had the biggest economy by far. It produced 29 percent of the world's wealth[3]. India came second. The contribution of the United States was a mere 1,8 percent.

By 1992 these relations had changed. The mismatch between the size of populations and their share in the world's wealth had become stark indeed. With 4,7 percent of the world's population, the United States produced 20,3 percent of the world's wealth. China, on the other hand, (which in 1992 already had replaced Japan (!!) as the world's second most weighty economy)[4] produced

3 But this already was less than would have corresponded to its 35% share in the then world population.

4 If one does not count the European Union as a single unit. For if one does, the Union would by now be the world's biggest economy. These figures compare GDPs in purchasing power parities.

12,9 % of the world's wealth, while its share in the world's population stood at 20,9%.

Let us now take a look at the dynamics of this process – its course over the last two hundred years. The table below indicates when, and how far, various countries fell back in relation to the economic growth of the United States. We have to realise, of course, that this growth of the United States has been very rapid (as we have seen, the US had increased their share in the world's wealth from 1,8 percent in 1820 to 20,3% in 1992). So most of the other countries and regions have indeed fallen back if compared to the very dynamic US. Europe was no exception and over the first half of the 20th century its economic growth was lower than growth in the US.

Falling behind and catching up: rates of divergence from or convergence towards the per capita GDP level of the USA, 1820-1992
(annual average compound rate of growth)

	1820-1913	1913-50	1950-92		1820-1913	1913-50	1950-92
Austria	-0.46	-1.40	1.71	Argentina	n.a	-0.85	-0.93
Belgium	-0.27	-0.89	0.85	Brazil	-1.27	0.27	0.50
Denmark	-0.32	-0.04	0.47	Chile	n.a.	-0.60	-0.42
Finland	-0.45	0.30	1.09	Colombia	n.a.	-0.18	0.16
France	-0.40	-0.48	1.01	Mexico	-0.81	-0.64	0.20
Germany	-0.19	-1.29	1.67	Peru	n.a.	0.52	-1.37
Italy	-0.63	-0.75	1.79	Venezuela	n.a.	3.62	-1.42
Netherlands	-0.52	-0.53	0.59				
Norway	-0.64	0.52	1.08	Bangladesh	-1.35	-1.88	-1.29
Sweden	-0.50	0.51	0.26	Burma	n.a.	-2.85	-0.40
Switzerland	n.a.	0.44	0.10	China	-1.22	-1.88	1.94
UK	-0.29	-0.76	0.05	India	-1.28	-1.86	0,00
				Indonesia	-1.09	-1.71	0.80
Australia	-0.15	-0.86	0.00	Japan	-0.83	-0.67	3.70
Canada	0.14	-0.20	0.32	Pakistan	-1.18	-1.89	0.27
New Zealand	n.a.	-0.26	-0.75	Philippines	n.a.	-1.83	-0.65
				South Korea	n.a.	-1.79	3.85
Greece	n.a.	-1.08	2.05	Taiwan	n.a.	-1.18	4.18
Ireland	-0.39	-0.81	0.93	Thailand	n.a.	-1.57	2.16
Portugal	n.a.	-0.37	2.02				
Spain	-0.71	-1.42	2.02	Côte d'Ivoire	n.a.	n.a.	-1.26
Turkey	n.a.	-0.83	0.99	Egypt	n.a.	-1.53	1.33
				Ethiopia	n.a.	n.a.	-1.73
Bulgaria	n.a.	-1.32	0.21	Ghana	n.a.	0.05	-2.31
Czechoslovakia	-0.55	-0.21	-0.34	Kenya	n.a.	n.a.	-0.62
Hungary	n.a.	-1.14	0.02	Morocco	n.a.	n.a.	-1.05
Poland	n.a.	n.a.	-0.37	Nigeria	n.a.	n.a.	-0.16
Romania	n.a.	n.a.	-0.09	South Africa	n.a.	-0.41	-0.81
USSR	-0.78	0.15	-0.74	Tanzania	n.a.	n.a.	-1.11
Yugoslavia	n.a.	-0.49	0.26	Zaire	n.a.	n.a.	-3.27

Source: Derived from Table 1-3.

But then, in the period between 1950 and 1992, Western Europe was, on the contrary, more dynamic than the US, although it came from further behind and was just "catching up". Overall, and through all these 200 years, South (Latin) America was less dynamic than North America; and, unlike Western Europe, it was less dynamic also in the period immediately after World War II.

In the rest of the world, the dynamics of the economy were very uneven. In Africa, the average annual growth rates lagged behind those of the US by more than one percent. In stark contrast, some East Asian countries, notably Japan, South Korea and Taiwan (Chinese Taipeh) grew fully four percent faster than the US in the time after 1950[5].

Economic growth is accompanied by an accumulation of real capital (that is capital actually invested in a work-place)[6]. The more capital available to each worker, the more productive this worker.

The table below shows that the wealthy countries of Western Europe[7] and Japan now roughly equal the United States in the amount of capital at the disposal of each worker.

Gross non-residential capital stock per person employed, 1950-92

	1950	1973	1992	1950	1973	1992
	(in 1990 international dollars)			(USA = 100)		
France	18 120	48 815	103 162	31	57	92
Germany	18 312	58 210	101 855	32	68	91
Netherlands	29 564	65 787	87 962	51	77	78
UK	12 444	35 399	64 892	22	42	58
Japan	7 752	34 777	113 376	13	41	101
USA	57 600	85 178	112 261	100	100	100

Source: Maddison (1995a)

5 Growth in China set in rather late in the early eighties, and while growth is very fast now, the average for the period 1950-1992 is low because of this late onset of rapid development.

6 There is some discussion on whether this accumulation of capital actually **triggers** or precedes economic growth. Karl Marx thought so. He believed that a "primitive accumulation", e.g. through slave trade, would precede the "capitalist" accumulation. In any case – it is clear that growth cannot continue for any lengthy stretch of time without such an accumulation.

7 As in many other fields, the UK is again an exception. There, the amount of capital available to each worker was still half of the amount available to a US worker – perhaps a consequence of the massive export of British (portfolio) capital.

In 1950, French workers could use just a third of the amount of capital that had been invested for each work place in the US; in Japan just one seventh. This drawing even in the period of just forty years was contingent on high investment rates. In Europe and Japan they were substantially above those of the US. One of the consequences of this accumulation of capital is a high productivity for each hour worked. In France it is even higher than in the US[8].

Labour productivity level (GDP per hour worked) in advanced capitalist countries, 1870-1992 (US level = 100)

	1870	*1913*	*1929*	*1938*	*1950*	*1973*	*1992*
Austria	62	57	44	39	32	65	83
Belgium	94	70	64	61	48	70	98
Denmark	67	66	68	61	46	68	75
Finland	37	35	34	36	32	57	70
France	60	56	55	62	45	76	102
Germany	70	68	58	56	35	71	95
Italy	46	41	38	44	34	66	85
Netherlands	103	78	84	72	51	81	99
Norway	48	43	45	50	43	60	88
Sweden	54	50	44	49	56	77	79
Switzerland	77	63	72	68	69	78	87
UK	115	86	74	69	62	68	82
Arith.Average	69	59	57	56	46	70	87
Australia	147	103	86	83	69	72	78
Canada	71	82	69	61	77	81	87
USA	100	100	100	100	100	100	100
Japan	20	20	24	25	16	48	69

8 This is not the case if one measures productivity as per person in the employed and unemployed work force. If so measured, France would still lose out against the US due to its higher unemployment and due to the fact that weekly work-time has been reduced while during the last three decades it had been raised (!!) in the US.

Labour productivity level (GDP per hour worked) in medium and low income countries, 1950-1992 (US level = 100)

	1950	1973	1992		1950	1973	1992
Greece	20	46	59	Argentina	49	47	41
Ireland	30	43	71	Brazil	19	24	23
Portugal	20	42	48	Chile	37	38	37
Spain	21	46	69	Colombia	22	25	27
Arith. Average	23	44	62	Mexiko	24	33	29
CZH	29	34	62	Peru	23	27	15
Hungary	21	28	25	Venezuela	71	82	58
Poland	19	24	21	Arith. Average	35	39	33
USSR	24	28	19	Bangladesh	6	3	4
Arith. Average	23	29	23	China	7	6	10
				India	5	4	5
				Indonesia	8	8	12
				Pakistan	6	6	9
				Philippines	11	11	10
				South Korea	10	14	29
				Taiwan	9	18	38
				Thailand	6	7	15
				Arith. Average	8	9	15

Source: Maddison 1995

Note that in the meantime, and in relation to the US, productivity per work hour even declined in many of the poorer countries (the East Asian "tiger-countries" again being the glaring exception).

The table below on the growth phases in the various regions of the world permits us to draw some more general conclusions:

Phases of growth by major region, 1820-1992
(annual average compound growth rate)

Phases of Growth by Major Region, 1820-1992
(annual average compound growth rate)

	1820-70	1870-1913	1913-50	1950-73	1973-92	1820-1992
			GDP			
Western Europe	1.7	2.1	1.4	4.7	2.2	2.2
Western Offshoots	4.3	3.9	2.8	4.0	2.4	3.6
Southern Europe	1.0	1.5	1.3	6.3	3.1	2.1
Eastern Europe	1.6	2.4	1.6	4.7	-0.4	2.0
Latin America	1.5	3.3	3.4	5.3	2.8	3.0
Asia*	0.2	1.1	1.0	6.0	5.1	1.9
Africa	0.4	1.1	3.0	4.4	2.8	1.9
World	1.0	2.1	1.9	4.9	3.0	2.2
			Population			
Western Europe	0.7	0.7	0.5	0.8	0.3	0.6
Western Offshoots	2.8	2.1	1.2	1.5	1.0	1.9
Southern Europe	0.3	0.4	0.9	1.4	1.4	0.8
Eastern Europe	0.9	1.3	0.4	1.2	0.7	0.9
Latin America	1.3	1.8	1.9	2.7	2.3	1.8
Asia*	0.1	0.6	0.9	2.1	1.9	0.9
Africa	0.3	0.7	1.9	2.4	2.9	1.3
World	0.3	0.8	0.9	1.9	1.8	1.0
			GDP per Capita			
Western Europe	1.0	1.3	0.9	3.9	1.8	1.5
Western Offshoots	1.4	1.8	1.6	2.4	1.4	1.7
Southern Europe	0.6	1.1	0.4	4.9	1.7	1.4
Eastern Europe	0.7	1.0	1.2	3.5	-1.1	1.1
Latin America	0.2	1.5	1.5	2.5	0.5	1.1
Asia*	0.1	0.6	0.1	3.8	3.2	1.0
Africa	0.1	0.4	1.0	2.0	-0.1	0.6
World	0.6	1.3	0.9	2.9	1.2	1.2

Source: Maddison 1995

Economic growth spread out from an historic centre and the leader – the United Kingdom – was soon joined by other Western European countries, by North America[9] and, later, by Japan.

Led by economic theory, we assumed that in the already wealthy countries economic development would become slower. But actual figures show that, up until now, this slow-down has not set in. In the period between 1820 and 1992, the overall GDP of Western Europe increased at roughly the same constant speed. Compared to the 19th century, growth in European per capita GDP even seems to have been a bit more rapid in the 20th century. These figures, therefore, do not sustain the theoretical notion of economic growth slowing down with increasing wealth. At least up until now, the predictions of economic theory have not been sustained by actual data.

9 ..and Australia.

As mentioned, most of the time the US GDP grew faster than the GDP of Europe. If we subtract, however, the effects of population growth and just look at the development of the per capita GDP, the dynamics of Europe (average annual growth = 1,5%) do not differ very much from the dynamics of the US (average annual growth = 1,7%). Western Europe slid back in the first half of the 20th century, but caught up in the time between 1950 and 1973. Since then, (and except for the late nineties) the development of European per capita GDP has been moving more or less parallel with the US (more on that in the chapter on the "Triad").

If we except a few countries, wealth has also grown in regions other than North America, Europe and Japan. But it did so only if calculated in absolute terms. In relative terms, and in relation to those that were already wealthy, many countries that had been poor 200 years ago fell behind even further with the gap to the wealthy increasing markedly.

The spread of economic dynamics has therefore been very uneven. We tend to assume that, nonetheless, and eventually, more countries would join the "growth league". This optimistic assumption seems justified only if we take the very long term view. Until now, and over the past 200 years, however, the track record has not been that encouraging. Many poor countries have failed to enter a phase of dynamic, self-sustaining growth. Or – like Latin America – they have been unable to sustain it.[10]

Nonetheless, those countries that did join the growth league recently (like China) or are about to join it (like India) are very populous ones. Their economy is likely to expand vigorously. If one excepts Japan, the rest of Eastern and South Eastern Asia will also remain on the path of rapid expansion with the crisis of 1997 having proven to be but a brief interruption of a continuing steep rise. The World Bank expects fast growth to continue in East Asia and the Pacific and to extend also into South Asia. Growth should also remain vigorous in some of the formerly Communist countries, which will continue their "catching up".

10 This sombre conclusion is in stark contrast to the optimism prevailing in the poorer states in the sixties, when many of them had gained or re-gained full independence and when they expected rising wealth to accompany their newly found freedom.

Forecast real GDP growth per capita 1998-2008

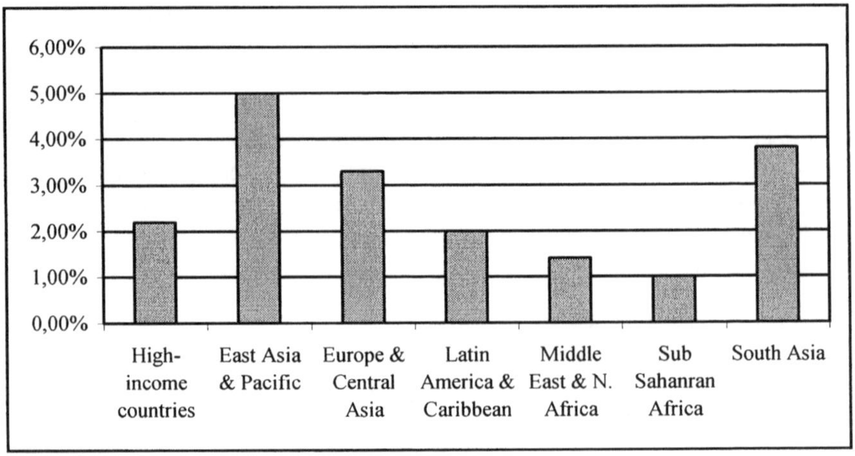

Source: World Bank 1999

The addition of this mass of rapidly expanding wealth will allow for the continuation – and probably even an acceleration – of world economic growth. As we have noted before, and as it also becomes evident from the above table, in the past, the rates of growth of the world economy have indeed tended to rise, being higher now than they were at the onset of the industrial age[11].

Data thus confirm an assumption of world economic development still following the shape of a "J curve", with wealth increasing exponentially and with the speed of growth still rising.

This very broad picture prompts two equally broad comments:

The species of humans has existed for 4 million years; and in their present form as homo sapiens for 80.000 years. Over this long period, the outward conditions of its existence had changed but very slowly. Over the last two hundred years, and particularly over the last fifty years, these changes in the outward conditions have, however, become dramatic. This revolutionary transformation in the conditions of human existence could, of course, not have been accompanied by an equally rapid change in our genetic make-up and programmes. But it has not

11 (even if one ignores as exceptional the "golden age" of the time between 1950 and 1973 when the world per capita wealth rose by an impressive average of 4,9 percent each year).

been accompanied either by any dramatic changes in our cultures[12]; nor by any profound changes in our political institutions. This should cause concern.

The second observation is on the divergence between economic theory and actual developments. One main tenet of economic theory is on the declining marginal utility of the inputs of additional labour and of additional capital. As countries grow wealthy, capital would accumulate. But as more and more of it becomes available, its "marginal utility" would decline. One added unit of capital would therefore produce fewer and fewer results. Capital would thus migrate to places still at an earlier stage of development where returns promised to be much higher. This would stimulate growth in these still poorer places. Growth in rich countries would slow; and it would increase in the poorer countries.

But this is not what we actually observe. If compared to prior phases of their economic evolution, economic growth has not slowed in the wealthy countries. It might even have accelerated. On the other hand, many of the poor countries have not profited from growth and from the inflow of capital. We therefore have to question and perhaps even to jettison the theory on a "declining marginal utility" of capital. The opposite of its claims might actually be true. The more capital available, the more productive a society or polity. The effects might be cumulative. Greater wealth would produce conditions for further rapid increase in wealth. On the other side, absolute and relative poverty might increase the risks of remaining poor.

12 Significantly, these revolutionary changes are hardly reflected in how we view and interpret the global system. We still use notions like "realism" or "liberalism" that were developed in much earlier phases of our history. Many "realists", for example, still make reference to the Greek historian Thucydides, fully convinced that his teachings are still valid in a world which , however, has become totally transformed.

Technology and the Changing Structure of the Economy

The expansion of the world economy implies repeated shifts in the economic tasks assigned to each nation. This runs counter to the teachings of the early British economist David Ricardo. He thought that their tasks would be assigned to specific nations, as it were, by laws of nature. The competitive advantages of specific nations would thus be immutable and this would make for an immutable division of labour. Britain, for instance, would be destined to forever produce cloth, and Portugal to produce wine now and forever in the future.

Evidently – this has not been the case. Britain has not retained its competitive advantage in textiles[1]. The competitive advantage in the production of textiles has shifted "downwards" to countries in the earliest phase of industrialisation. The most advanced countries, on the other hand, enter into new, high value added productions, supplanting those that had migrated to the poorer countries ("flying geese pattern" with every new "goose", that is, with every new production and technology taking the lead in the wedge of flying geese).

This wheel of change now turns faster. Products that were considered "cutting edge" a mere twenty years ago, products that were scarce and thus could produce high ("rent") income, these products now have to compete over their price. They have become mere "commodities". Margins of return in their production have become narrow. Witness the example of memory chips. Once they were considered the very embodiment of modernity. By now they mainly are produced in countries which have not yet attained full economic maturity – like South Korea and Taiwan (with Malaysia and other South East Asians in hot pursuit).

Within the course of one "product cycle", various tasks have thus been assigned to countries according to their position on the ladder of economic development[2]. The rich countries introduce, use and profit from the latest technology. The poorest countries, on the other hand, produce with the most traditional tech-

---

1 Remarkably, and as we will show later, the advantage in agricultural production seems to shift away from the poor and towards the wealthy countries. Note for instance the agricultural export of wealthy Denmark and the wealthy Netherlands, the leading position of France and Italy in the production and the export of wine, and the US exports of cereals and soya.

2 In a later chapter we will look into the question as to whether this promotes or impedes the poorer nations from narrowing the gap in wealth that separates them from the rich nations of the world.

nology. How does that affect economic growth? A few countries that used to be poor have developed very rapidly. But, as we have seen, and contrary to the predictions of economic theory, economic growth in the already rich countries has not slowed down. And indeed, as we have seen, growth usually slackens after a period of "catching up" draws to its end. Yet, contrary to theory, and as we have mentioned growth remained more or less constant after that point.

% Share of memory-chip market

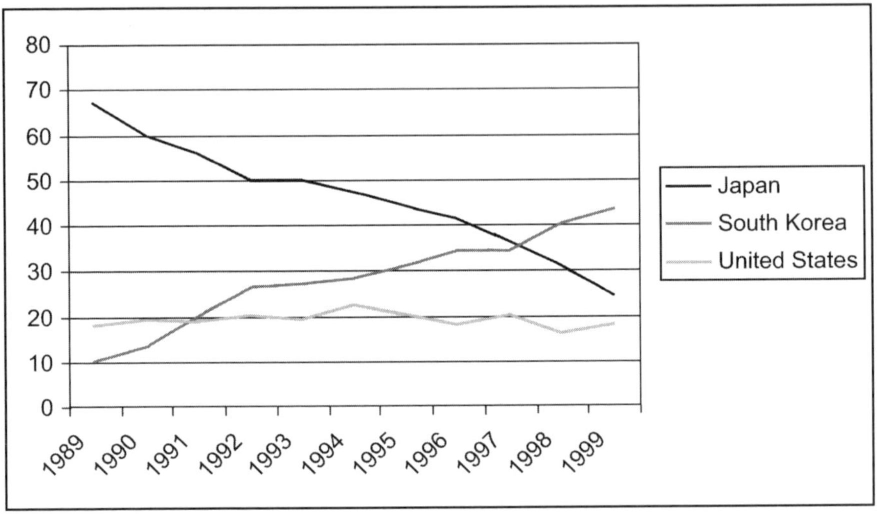

Source: Cahners In-Stat Group

We thus need to revise the theories on economic development. Obviously other things than the addition of new capital have a more profound impact. The other, and much more crucial, factor is the capacity of ceaseless innovation. Wealthy nations remain economically dynamic because they retain the capacity to innovate; because they are able to position themselves again and again at the leading edges of new "product cycles". The constant flow of innovation has, up until now, compensated for any "declining marginal utility of capital".

How to explain economic growth

Originally, economists assumed development to be driven by just two "factors of production": labour and capital. In the course of growth, capital would increasingly substitute for labour. As the supply of labour was seen as being sufficient at all times[3], capital thus was seen as the one crucial, strategic factor needed for growth. One would just have to add capital and everything else would follow.[4]

This notion still seems basically sound to quite a number of powerful institutions. Development banks, for example, still act as if their lending of capital would provide the most essential and only truly relevant input to growth. This view is shared by many others that own or administer capital. They too are convinced that capital and the immediate interests of capital should reign supreme. All that would be needed for a sound economic policy would be a due regard for this, their crucial role and, thus, respect for "shareholder value".

That such views are still widely held – and still inform policy – is surprising. We should have known better for quite some time. More ample data and more refined statistical methods have permitted us to disaggregate those factors that, at first, were assumed to be the only ones to promote or to impact up on economic growth. Using these methods, statisticians discovered that the traditional explanations of economic growth were rather shaky. Addition of labour and addition of capital make just a minor contribution. Some even maintain that the addition of these two inputs would explain ten percent of the variance in economic performance at best. Other inputs would make up for the remaining ninety percent.

The fact that things other than labour and capital are central in promoting growth becomes evident from another attempt to portray the working of a national economy. One may picture an economy as one giant grid of inputs and outputs, with the various productive units using the outputs of other units as their own input (input-output analysis, Leontief). If one uses this instrument for economic planning – as was done in the Soviet Union – one has to assume as constant in each productive unit (in each square on the checker-board) the relationship between input and output. But, on each square of the checker-board, the relation between input and output is, of course, defined by the

3 Not least because of the large rural/agricultural labour force that could be shifted into industrial production.

4 When discussing the dilemma of poor countries and the attempts to assist them through development aid, we shall return to probe further into how this simplistic notion has misled policy.

methods and conditions of production. In a dynamic economy these methods and conditions are bound to change. Soviet central planning could not adapt to these necessary changes. It could not predict them and could not provide for them. This was one of the causes of its ultimate failure. Evidently, the input output analysis that tries to portray and guide an economy, cannot explain the most important input into the growth of an economy.

But what is this big unknown that promotes economic growth much more efficiently than the mere addition of capital and labour and that is alleged to explain ninety percent of the variance in growth? Obviously, it cannot be just one single factor. Originally, one had been tempted to obscure this obvious fact by naming the big unknown "technological change". But that implies a not very useful extension to the meaning of the term "technological change". One could extend this meaning to include not just the effects of applied scientific discovery; but also to include the effects of innovation in the way things are produced; in the way enterprises are managed and financed; in the way stocks are being held to a minimum; in the way personnel resources are optimised; etc. Yet even when so extended, the term "technological change" would still not catch many of those things that decide economic success or failure.

Other factors thus enter next to the factor of a broadly defined "technological change". One of these additional factors has been called "human capital". The term designates public and private investment in schooling and other investments that improve the qualification of the workforce. Yet another element was presented as relevant more recently. It is called "social capital"[5]. The word was meant to stand for the capacity for co-operation and concertation. This capacity is different in different societies. When looking at the record of economic success and failure, it becomes plausible that this capacity to co-operate and concert is indeed decisive in achieving success in both the political and the economic realm.

Finally, one should not neglect the contribution of institutions. Raising wealth necessitates an ever more pronounced division of labour. It must be sustained by both formal and informal rules, and by institutions capable of enforcing them.

Taken together, all these factors determine the capacity of a society to innovate the process of production. Yet, there can be no question, that among

---

5 The neat attribution of growth to various and distinct factors remains a somewhat dubious exercise. New capital, for instance, will automatically bring new technology, and new training for workers. The general societal and political set-up surrounding economic success is probably not given the credit and attention it would deserve; etc.

the various factors to promote innovation, technology in its narrow sense of applied science remains important.

New technology may impact on production by being used by either the very same firm or country the discovery originated from. Or new technology might enter by being used by a firm or country other than the one in which it was first discovered. This second path of technological change is the more common one.

But what exactly is the impact of such technological innovation? And what may we assume about its impact in the medium- and long-term future? In the first chapter of the book, we have maintained, rather cavalierly, that the impact of more recent technological changes and innovations would not differ very dramatically from the impact that earlier technological changes had on economic growth in previous periods. We even assumed that the boost given by technological innovation might be weaker today than it had been in the time between 1875 and 1940.

Yet, it is not that easy to precisely measure the contribution new technology (in its narrow sense) makes to economic performance. Certainly, much research is done and much technology is developed in the wealthy countries; and very little of that occurs in the poor countries. Yet the linkage between growth and the amount of research is not as clear as we tend to assume. Wealthy countries are not simply and mainly wealthy because they finance and produce path-breaking technological innovations. And poor countries are not simply poor because they fail to do so.

Some OECD countries that grew very fast in the 1990's had invested rather little in research and development. Such had been the case, for example, with Denmark or Ireland. On the other hand, Japan had invested a lot yet could hardly register any growth at all.

Also, it is just a handful of OECD countries that have a positive "technology balance of payments". Very few countries receive more in patent fees than they have to pay out in patent fees. Yet among those with a negative balance of technology payments are very important countries like Germany, and rather fast growing ones like Finland.

As it seems, economic growth in a specific country is not boosted very much by an increase in the volume of research and development done there. A very comprehensive study done by OECD (Bassanini et al. 2001) concludes that the

Expenditure on R&D in the OECD countries 1980s and 1990s, total expenditure on R&D as percentage of GDP

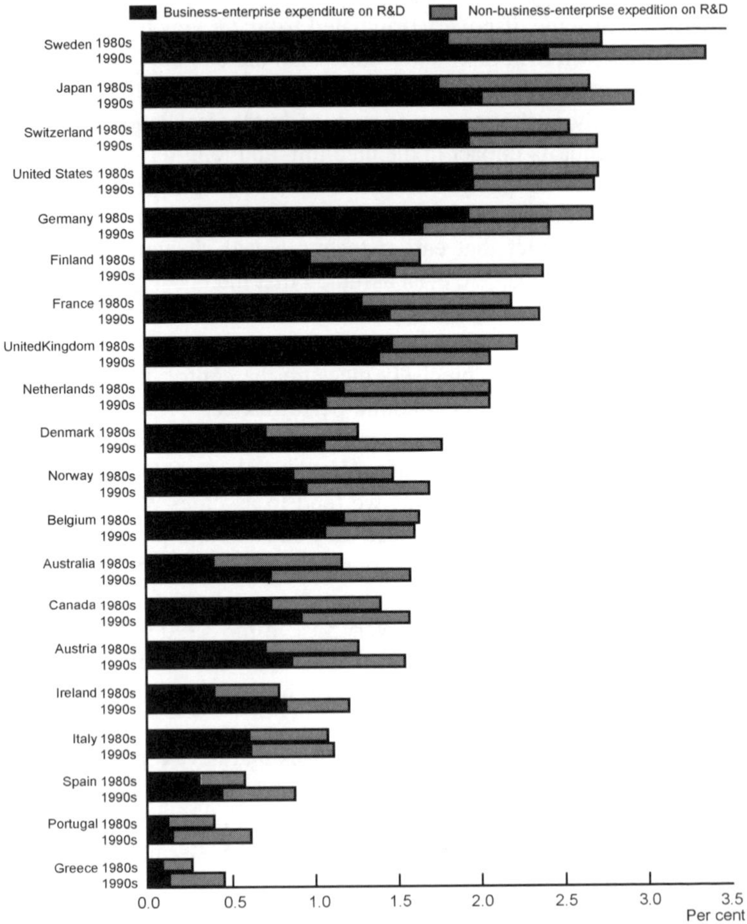

Source: OECD

impact of R+D expenditures is real but relatively small.[6] Certainly, much more relevant is the ability to integrate new technology into production regardless of

6 Thus contradicting an earlier OECD study that found no correlation whatsoever between economic growth on one hand and R+D expenditures on the other.

whether this technology was developed at home or abroad. The UK technological leadership in the fifties (among other things, the jet airplane and radar were developed there) did not impede the subsequent relative but drastic economic decline of Britain. On the other hand, countries did very well that mainly used imported technology. As it seems, the key to the success of an enterprise or of a country is mastery of the skills involved in linking solutions to particular needs. This does not imply that the solutions that are being used had been developed from scratch and by their own efforts.

The application of technologies invented somewhere else can spread very fast. Witness the use of the internet invented by the US military. It was just in the 80s that the broader public started to access it. Yet, if measured in percentages of the population that accesses the internet today, the US is no longer the leader. It has been surpassed by Norway and Singapore.

Poorer countries are not just disadvantaged in the creation of new technology. More important is that they are disadvantaged, too, in the application of technology that has been invented somewhere else. This is true specifically for information technology (the mastery of which is crucial today for integration into the world economy). Only a miniscule part of the population of poor countries has access to the internet.

The IT divide
Personal Computers per 1.000 people, 2000

	Economies	*GNI $ billions 2000*	*Population millions 2000*	*GNI per capita $ 2000*
Less than 5.0	30	684	1,729	400
5.0-19.9	32	1,583	2,021	780
20.0-49.9	24	1,660	684	2,430
50.0-199.9	38	3,704	507	7,300
200.0 or more	29	23,430	834	28,090
No data	54	254	282	900

Source: World Bank Atlas 2002

Yet, there are exceptions. Even the poorer countries may profit solidly from the latest technologies. India did. Its soft-ware industry has managed to compete on a global scale.[7]

7 Note: speaking English helps.

Software exports from India

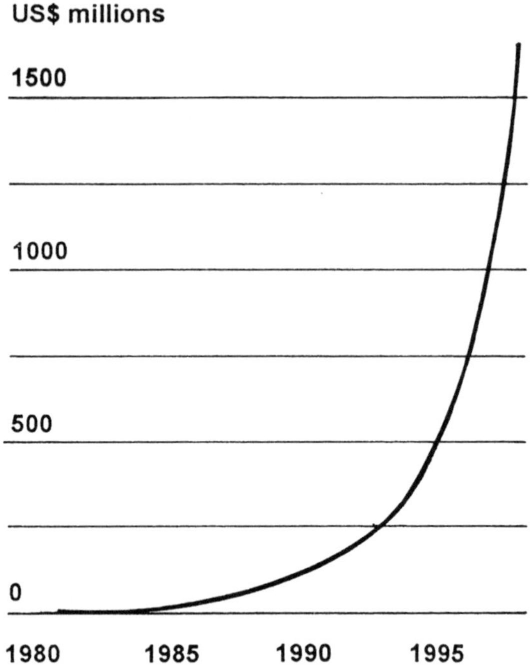

Source: Economist

In the past, even advanced technology had been some sort of "public good" which could be acquired by anyone willing and able to use it; either for a fee (patents), or for free. The question is whether this will hold true for the future also, and whether new technologies will thus continue to spread rapidly. It might be that new hurdles will impede such rapid spread. There is a distinct tendency:

a) for research to move from the academic or the otherwise free realm into the corporate realm;

b) within corporations to no longer sell the findings of their researchers, but to keep it for themselves for "strategic" reasons: Microsoft is not likely to sell to Netscape crucial parts of a new software.

Holdings of biotechnological patents has shifted sharply towards the private sector

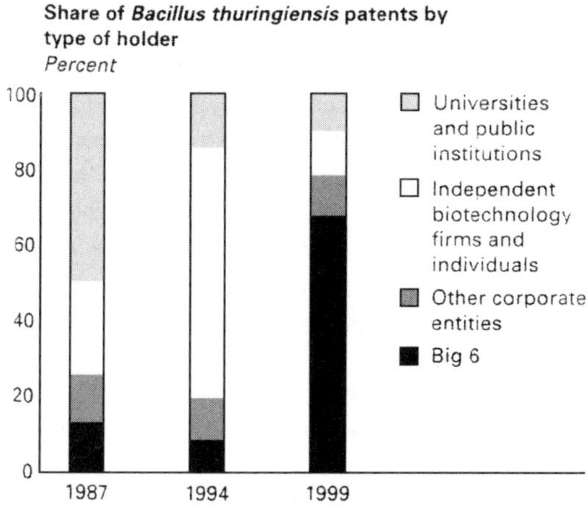

Source: de Janvry and others 2000

Up until now, these tendencies to restrict the spread of new technology have not yet translated into a true change of the large overall trend. This trend has, on the contrary, run in the other direction. The time has become shorter for firms and countries to hold on to an exclusive monopoly for a new technology. At the turn of the century it still took 30 years for a competitor to appear on the horizon; at the end of the 20th century it takes just three and a half years.

Interval between the introduction of innovation and the entry of competitors

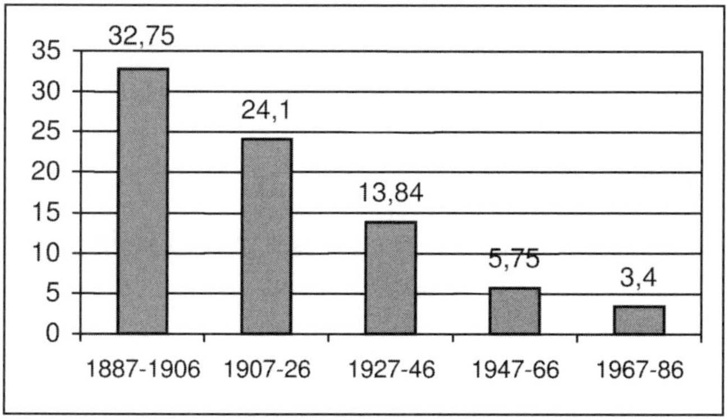

Source: Baumol 2002

Will all wealthy countries (newcomers and the established rich) continue to expand their economy at the quasi normal historic pace? Or will this pace become slower – at least in the long-term future? Several arguments other than the declining marginal utility of capital are used to sustain the second alternative of growth becoming slower eventually. One of the causes could be the increase in the size of the tertiary sector of their economy, which produces "services" instead of food and raw materials (the "primary" sector), or industrial goods (the "secondary" sector). In the "primary" and "secondary" sectors it has been possible to replace human labour by machines to a large extent. The table below demonstrates that with the production of coal. In the US, this production more than doubled over the last 50 years. Nonetheless, the number of miners was cut in half. That implies that productivity per worker grew by more than 400 percent.

Mining of coal in the US 1950 –2000
(production in million tons –left scale; number of miners – in thousand –right scale)

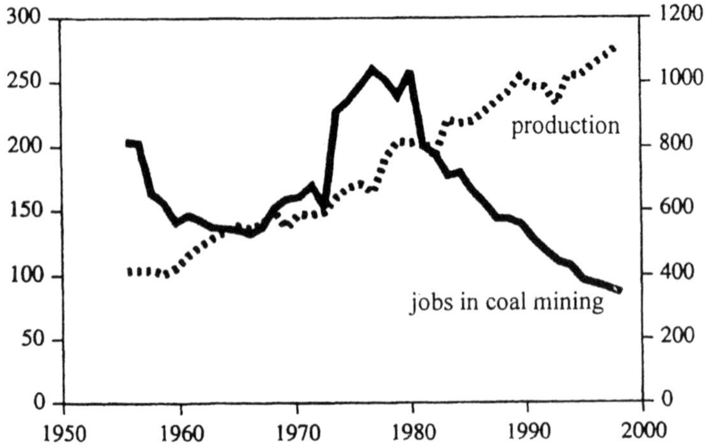

Source: US Department of Labour

In the same period the number of persons employed in the US in the tertiary sector has grown fourfold.

Number of persons employed in US primary and secondary production vs. persons employed in the service sector, 1950 –1999
(in million)

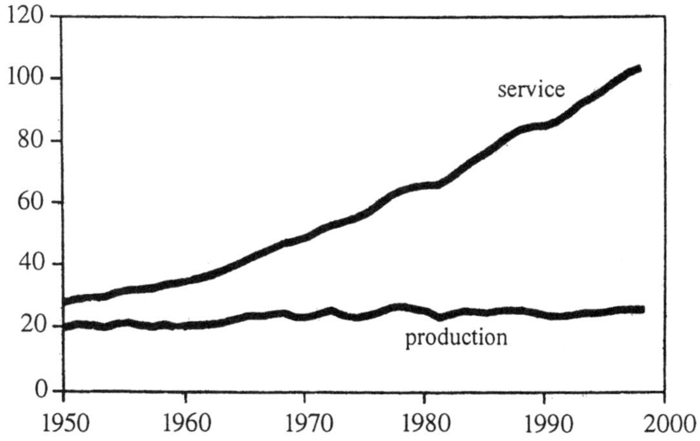

Source: US Dep. of Labour

This growth of the service sector reflects, in part, a rising demand due to rising wealth (such as demand for eating out; or demand for new forms of entertainment; or demand created by more students attending university and thus needing educators; or for care for the infirm elderly, the numbers of which are rising due to longer life-expectancy; etc.). But the growth of employment in the service sector also reflects the very slow rise of productivity in this sector. Many of those services which had already been available at a lower stage of economic development cannot be rationalised the same way as industrial or agricultural production has been rationalised. In the long run, this is bound to slow growth in the very rich countries where the volume of production in the tertiary sector has come to dwarf that in the industrial and agricultural sectors.

Three kinds of arguments are, however, brought forth against this pessimistic conclusion.

1) The proponents of the "new economy" maintain that the electronic revolution now also permits the rationalisation of the production of services. Yet there is little evidence for that actually occurring (see chapter on the "New Economy"). Even if we suppose that it has profited from all electronic wizardry presently

available, up to now the rise in productivity in the tertiary sector has remained modest in comparison to the rise of productivity in the industrial sector.

2) According to one other argument, the growth of the service sector is a mere statistical phenomenon with no counterpart in the real economy. The rising volume of the service sector only reflects increasingly common "outsourcing". Once, cleaning crews used to be employed directly by factories. The workers so employed were "industrial workers". Now, cleaning services are "outsourced". Specialised cleaning firms are contracted to keep factories in order. The persons employed by these cleaning firms are no longer "industrial workers". They are now "service" workers, though they do the same kind of job and though their activity is connected to industrial production. The same holds true for many researchers, accountants, lawyers, truckers etc. Once these were employed directly by factories. They were thus counted as "industrial workers". Now they sell their services (either directly or via an employer) to these factories; and thus have become "service workers". Nonetheless, their input remains intimately connected to industrial production. Their services are essential for industry being able to increase productivity.

3) The third argument points to the changing nature of services and to the fact that some of them are "high value added" activities. A good number of these can be exported and imported the way industrial products are exported and imported.

It is true that many – and even most – of the services are still being produced and consumed locally. They therefore do not enter international trade. The services of an Indian hairdresser or an Indian house-cleaner can only be produced and consumed in India. They cannot be sold abroad. These activities therefore do not affect the international economic standing of India. The same holds true for the similar services rendered in wealthy countries. If a Danish firm sells complex technical products abroad that are much in demand, there also will be much demand for the Danish currency as foreigners try to buy these high-tech products. The Danes selling them will become wealthy and will also be able to pay good salaries to Danish hairdressers and house-cleaners. As a consequence, these will earn much more than their Indian counterparts, though they do the same job as their Indian counterparts and though they also produce for the local market only. As this example demonstrates, the relative wealth of a country is determined not in its "sheltered sector" but in that "open" sector of production that is subject to international competition.

However, not all service activities are in this sector of the economy that is sheltered from foreign competition. A sizeable – and growing – part is now also in the "exposed" sector. The production done in this "exposed" tertiary sector, thus, may augment the economic clout of a country in the same way it is being augmented by the export of high value-added industrial products. The products of this "exposed" part of the service sector are very complex. Creating them calls for much know-how and specialisation. Selling them abroad entails high profits. Examples abound: financial services offered world-wide by the City of London; Hollywood movies; international consulting and engineering; etc. All such services have potent and expanding global markets. Exporting these services can contribute at least as much to the relative economic standing of a country as does the export of industrial products.[8]

The service sector of high income countries is thus bifurcated into a part with high productivity; and into a part with low productivity (accompanied more often than not by low wages).[9] Both of these sub sectors have expanded quickly. If we now wish to know how this affects the prospects for future economic growth, and how this affects the distribution of income, we will have to gauge the relative weight of each of these two sub–sectors; and subsequently guess how this, their relative weight, will evolve.

Matters are further complicated by this distinction being very crude and neglecting an important part of the work force. For what weight and significance are we to accord to those that cannot easily be classified as belonging to either the one or to the other of these two groups. What about judges, university professors, law makers, urbanists, civil servants etc.? Their functions are essential. If effective in their work, they will provide a competitive advantage to their country. If ineffective, they might burden it with a serious competitive disadvantage.

A look at the service sector of the economy has thus raised some important questions. Let us retain a few tentative answers:

1) It is likely that, in the very long run, in the very mature economies the growing weight of the service sector will somewhat depress growth.

2) Large parts of the service sector no longer operate in the "sheltered" sector of the economy. These services are now sold world wide. The share that such service-products have in international commerce is increasing. Many of these services are very complex. They are thus the equivalent to what "cutting edge technology" is in industrial production.

---

8 One prominent example is tourism. Many poorer countries were successful in developing tourism. Yet the main tourist destinations remain in the very wealthy countries. Five states that are all very wealthy top the list of countries visited most frequently. In sixth place comes China, with just one third of the number of visitors going each year to number one, which is France.

9 Robert Reich divides them not into two, but three distinct sectors: a) routine production service (e.g. transport); b) in person service (e.g. hairdresser); c) symbolic analytic service (e.g. public relations, investment banking).

Being competitive and achieving rapid growth is contingent upon a number of factors, not all of them narrowly economic ones. The quality of public institutions, for instance, is an essential pre-condition of growth.

The continued fast dispersion of technological innovation is one of the reasons why the world economy continues to grow rapidly and why economic latecomers may enter a phase of "catching up". But, on the other hand, there also has to be a continuous stream of original, first innovations of products and processes. This stream of original inventions and first applications must not dry up. For the stream to continue to flow, entrepreneurs and firms must be able to profit from such innovations and first applications. They also must be able to profit handsomely, so as to compensate for the risks which, by necessity, accompany each such step into the not yet proven; into the unknown. Firms taking such risky steps thus must be able to use to their advantage their standing at the cutting edge of a new product cycle. (They must be permitted to reap a rent income.[10])

Continuous innovation thus depends on a precarious balance. On one hand, the original inventors and pioneers must be able to maintain a privileged, quasi-monopolistic position at least for some time. That is, they must be able to control and occasionally to block the dispersion of an invention that makes their production more profitable. On the other hand, continuous world economic growth depends on the rapid dispersion of such innovations. Up until now, it has been possible to maintain this balance – at least in a rough way and with many (especially the poorer) falling by the wayside.

Yet another and perhaps even more precarious balance is also a precondition for the continued growth, not just of single countries, but also of the world economy as such. We have talked about innovation as if it implies nothing other than using, to general acclaim, the discoveries made by some tinker in his garage-shop. That's the pussy cat image of innovation. But, in reality, it appears more frightening. Frequently, it will look like some dangerous, invincible animal stomping the land. It will impact like "gales of destruction", wreaking havoc on what we have become accustomed to and on what we have come to depend on.

Innovation and the accompanying rise in productivity has been particularly rapid in the realm of agriculture. In my own country, Austria, a quarter of the workforce of 4,5 million were still employed in agriculture at the end of World War II. A generation later, one million jobs in agriculture had been wiped out. Many villages and whole valleys were deserted. The bastions of rural existence and culture disappeared. Farms that had been family homesteads since the Middle Ages fell into disrepair. Young men who stuck to their farms had difficulties in finding spouses.

---

10 Guaranteed to them in many cases through patent laws.

Other parts of the workforce have lived similar, unsettling, traumatic experiences. Where I have my summer home in the Alps, salt had been mined since Roman times. The whole culture of the little town is deeply shaped by this tradition. Salt miners held a high social rank. On festive occasions they wore black velvet uniforms – not too dissimilar to the black velvet uniforms worn at the royal English court. The salt miners maintained well endowed cultural and civic organisations. Their houses were spacious, the town wealthy. Five years ago, though, the salt mine, in production for 2000 years, was closed for good. Unemployment in the small town is high now. And even if new jobs could be created quickly, a way of life has been destroyed.

The "gales of innovation" do not just destroy the status, wealth, and the tradition of workers. They also destroy capital that has been invested. Railroad tracks decay next to the more heavily used roads – just as a hundred and fifty years ago canals decayed next to the then more profitable railroads. The wealth of those that had invested in canals or railroads is being blown away by these gales of change.

Yet all this destruction is a necessary companion of innovation. New things and processes have to take the place of old things and processes. They have to drive out and destroy those old products and processes. One may resent and fight this process – just as the Luddites did when they opposed the replacement of the old hand looms by steam or water driven power looms. But the Luddites have come to stand for the futility of such battles. Had they succeeded, they would have done so at a very high price to the public. Their stopping innovation would have halted economic development. We would still be stuck with the poverty of early 19th century Britain.

So this is one side of innovation and economic growth: never ending change; a never ending disruption of the routine; a blatant disrespect for tradition and continuity; a state of permanent insecurity. Yet it is obvious that humans cannot exist and function when nothing is predictable and when even their physical survival could be called into question.[11] A more complex economy is in even more dire need of predictability and continuity. It has been pointed out, for example, that secure property rights are the indispensable base of any economic development. Nobody is willing to invest if he or she must fear that he or she will not be able to reap the rewards of this investment, because the property one has invested in, has been seized by someone else – without the original owner having any chance of re-establishing his rights through the intervention of the police or

11 This is why the US economist Dan Rodrik believes a high level of public social security to be a pre-requisite for opening up to the many uncertainties of international trade: the greater this openness – the higher the level of social protection.

through the intervention of courts. Few will work if uncertain as to whether they will be paid. Few will part with savings if they have to doubt that the bank they deposit them in will be able and willing to return them on request. Trusted, firm, reliable institutions must be in place in order to provide this essential predictability, stability and security. In their absence economies would collapse.

So for economic growth to happen and to continue, societies, individuals and firms must be able to count on many things not changing. But for economic growth to happen, societies, voters and enterprises must also be willing to contemplate and suffer the deep perturbations of a ceaseless revolution in the external circumstances. They must be willing to expose themselves to the hard blows of the never-ending "gales of creative destruction". They must be able to accommodate both of these contradictory principles. Not all societies can.

Lastly, there is a contradiction in the whole theory on economic growth. It is equally difficult to resolve. At the cost of somewhat simplifying the issue, we might term this the contradiction between the "endogenous" and the "exogenous" explanations of economic growth. The "endogenous" explanation assumes that – once started by some impetus – growth will feed upon itself. Growth could be explained by the dynamics unleashed in the process of economic growth.

The "exogenous" explanation of economic growth, on the other hand, implies that the dynamics of growth cannot be explained from factors that arise within this process, but by factors that act from the outside.

This difference has far reaching implications. In this book we will therefore touch upon them rather frequently. Were we to adhere to the "endogenous" explanation, we would have to assume, for example, that those at the top of the economic pecking order will stay there forever. The first one will always remain the first one. And the last one will always remain the last one.

Looking for evidence to confirm this thesis, we find it to be contradictory. On the one hand economic growth does indeed seem to be a cumulative process. Obviously, there is a strong tendency for those on top to stay on top – or at least to stay among the first ones. And there also is an obvious tendency for the losers to remain losers – at least for quite some while. But as Robert Reich remarked, at least in the past, most of the leading nations have been able to maintain their top position for three generations at best[12]. In the ranks below, the relative positions have also changed frequently. Who would have thought that Ireland would advance to a spot ahead of its former master the UK? Or that Korea – dirt poor 30 years ago – would be accepted as an OECD member into the club of the wealthy.

---

12 Witness for example the loss of the British leadership position in the early 20th century.

Yet the "exogenous" theory, too, is not fully sustained by actual historical data. The inflow of capital had thus been pictured as one of the possible external triggers of economic development. Yet, in many cases, this has not been so. Sometimes – as for example with the oil-exporting Arab countries – the inflow even had the clear negative effect of stunting economic diversification and growth. Similarly, liberalising external trade has been beneficial in some instances; and detrimental in others.

Economics parades as the most evolved of all social sciences. Made confident by the use of refined mathematic methods, it is not given to self-doubt and thus has no qualms about freely offering its good advice to politics. Yet economists cannot provide answers to some of the most pressing, the most important questions put to them: Why do some nations develop? And why do others fail to do so? Will the rich always remain the rich; and the poor always the poor? What is the most relevant, the single most "strategic" ingredient behind economic success?

Perhaps economists would do well to heed the good advice of old Socrates: the most important knowledge is being very well aware of all the things one does not know.

World Population Growth and its Implications
(with a short sub chapter on female empowerment)

The Anglo-Austrian historian Eric Hobsbawm has described the 20th century as having been “short and disastrous”. But this view would not be shared by those intelligent beings on that distant other planet in another solar system who scan our earth with their sophisticated scientific instruments. These distant observers would conclude that, for the earthlings, this twentieth century must have been the most successful period in their 4 million year history. They multiplied by four. After all, growth in its numbers is the main criterion for measuring the success of a species.

World population 1750-2020
(in billion)

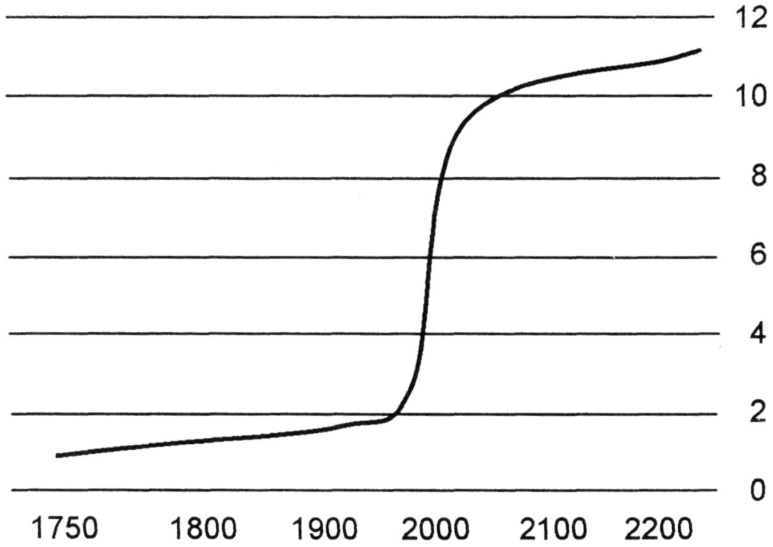

Source: UNDP

Seen from that far, the growth of the earth’s population must seem exponential, with the number of persons living on earth increasing at an ever faster pace. At first sight, thus, this development also seems to have the form of a “J”; and thus seems to be similar to the exponential increase in global wealth. But looking closer, we discern an important change that occurred in the mid-sixties. The growth rates that had increased until then, started to become smaller. What we see is not a "J" curve but an "S" curve, with the point of inflexion already having been reached in the mid-sixties.

From now on, population growth will become slower. This reversal is reflected in the sequence and results of predictions about the future size of the world population: the more recent this prediction, the smaller the size of the population predicted. What is behind, first, this rapid rise in the world population and, then, the sudden slowdown of this growth?

What happens is that the death rate falls dramatically due to health improvements like clean drinking water, basic sanitation, vaccination. These improvements become accessible even in very poor countries. Prior to that, not only was the death rate high; but so was the fertility rate (= number of births per woman) so as to compensate for this high death rate. Yet the fertility rate remains elevated even after the death rate has started to decline. It then takes some time for the fertility rate to also become lower. The graph below shows the development of those two rates in the first modernising country, namely in the United Kingdom. There, the decline in the birth rate lagged behind the decline in the death rate by a century and a half!

Birth rate and death rate in the UK 1700-1988

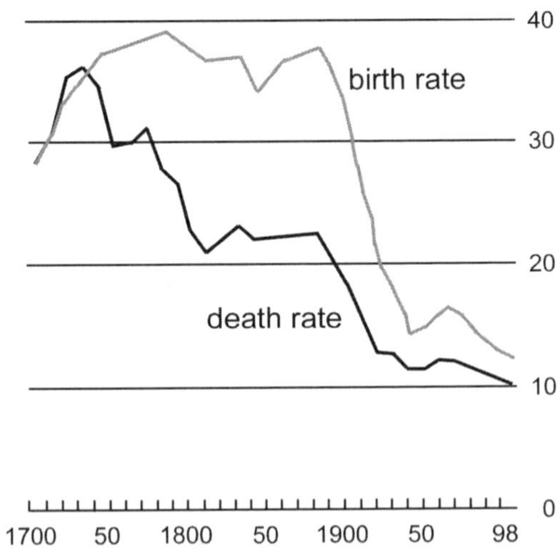

Source: The Economist

Countries now in the early stages of economic development do follow this pattern. Death rates decline before fertility rates. The pattern is different, though, in as much as both the decline of death rates and the decline of fertility rates are now much more abrupt; and even more abrupt for the death rate. Hence a population explosion in poor countries. Populations in these countries now grow faster than the fast growing population of 19th century Britain.

Cultural Adaptation

Just as the information stored in genes is essential for the survival of an animal, the "information" stored in the mores, values and cultures[1] *of a society is also essential for the survival of this society. And this information is adapted to circumstances just as the genetic information is adapted to a certain ecological "niche" inhabited by a certain species. If the circumstances change, the culture also changes so as to adjust to a new situation and so as to enable the society to survive under these changed, new circumstances. But this cultural adaptation is a slow process. It follows the change of circumstances only with a certain time lag. Primitive circumstances with high chances of premature death demand high fertility rates so as to keep the population constant. Then circumstances change. The risk of premature death becomes smaller. Values, mores adapt. But this is a slow process. According to still prevalent cultural codes, high store is still being put in having a large number of children*[2]*. Ultimately the fertility rate also decreases. Yet this movement is less precipitous than the decline of the death rate.*

But even long entrenched, culturally defined human behaviour can change quite rapidly: In Europe, the two latecomers to modernisation – Spain and Italy – provide an example. Notwithstanding their "family oriented" cultures, fertility rates have shrunk dramatically within just a few decades and now are the lowest in Europe.

Perhaps fertility rates could decrease as quickly and dramatically in other parts of the world too; and perhaps there are other reasons for that not happening. Fertility rates might remain high for a simple reason – namely because birth con-

1 Called "memes" – the cultural equivalents of genes – by Richard Dawkins.

2 And especially sons: The first small-talk question you will receive in many North African countries is: "How many sons do you have?" (My negative answer caused interlocutors to pity me).

trol is not available[3]. In merely material terms, this should not be a major obstacle to lowering the fertility rate. Birth control is not expensive.

Fertility rates in European countries[4] (1995-1999)

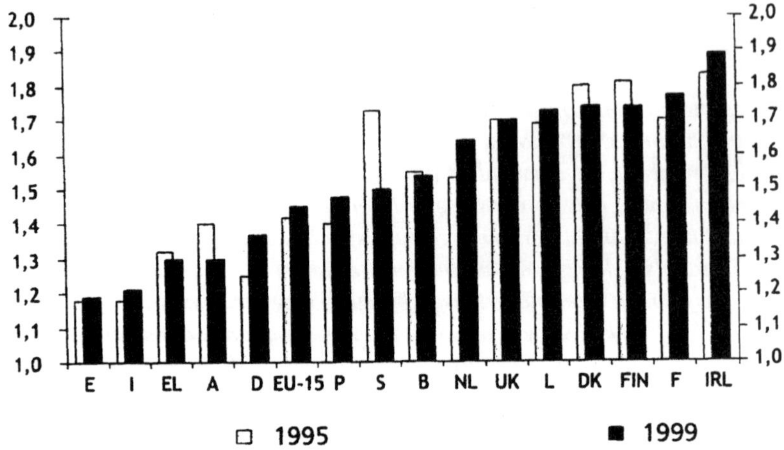

Source: Eurostat

---

3 More primitive and less efficient forms of birth control have existed since time immemorial – as, for example, the vinegar drenched sponge used by Roman ladies. Other more cruel forms were common. Infanticide was widely practised not only in China, but also in Europe up to the 18th century. Or children were simply abandoned, most of them to certain death. Bosweth (1988) estimates this to have been the fate of one in four children born in 18th century European cities (hence the many "foundling hospitals").

4 In no European country, save Albania, is the fertility rate at the replacement level of >2: necessary to keep population at least constant. The differences that exist among European countries provide food for thought and reflection. In the wealthy Scandinavian countries, fertility rates have risen over the last five years. In wealthy Austria they have declined even though Austria – together with France – is the country most generous in providing financial incentives to families that raise children.

Unmet need for family planning among married women for select countries

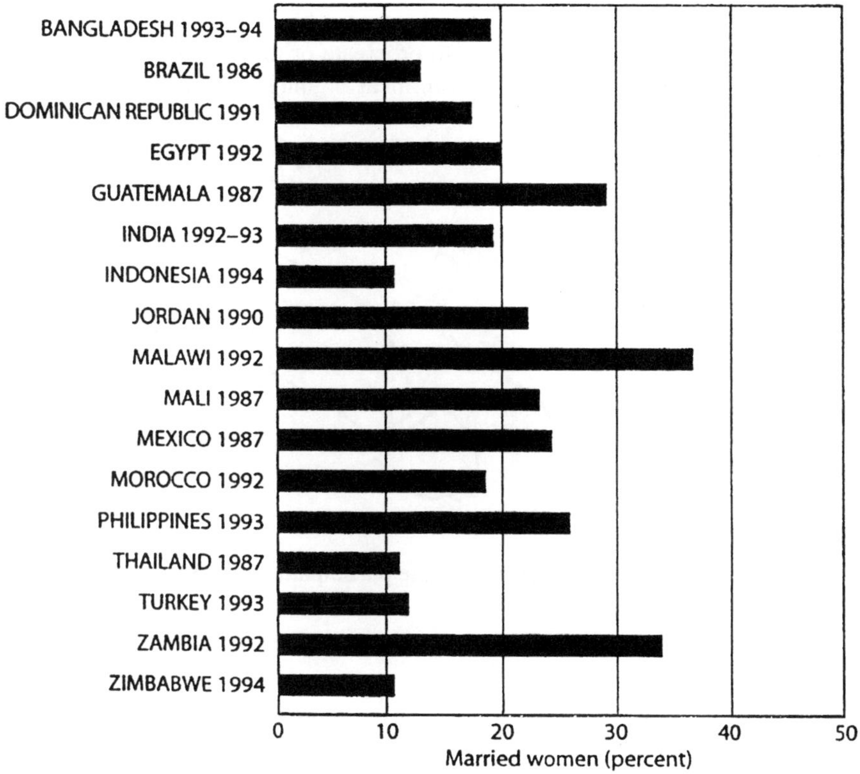

Source: Scientific American, January 2000

Sub Chapter: the Global Gender Revolution

Yielding to the pleasures of sex (in its heterosexual version) has been coupled with procreation until now. This is no longer the case in countries where women have access to effective and reliable birth control. There, procreation and sex have become de-coupled. The effect on gender relations has already been, and will continue to be, momentous.

It is no longer the male who decides on procreation; but – thanks to birth control – the female. Yet according to socio-biology, the decision on procreation, on the survival of one's genes, is the most central one there is. He or she who decides on procreation wields ultimate power. Before birth control became effective and widely available, this decision rested with the male. He therefore could impose his version of a division of labour – and an inferior status – on the female. But now the decision on whether the genes of a couple will survive in a following generation, now this decision to procreate or to not procreate has shifted to the female. Therefore, female empowerment is going to advance.

The evolution of authority

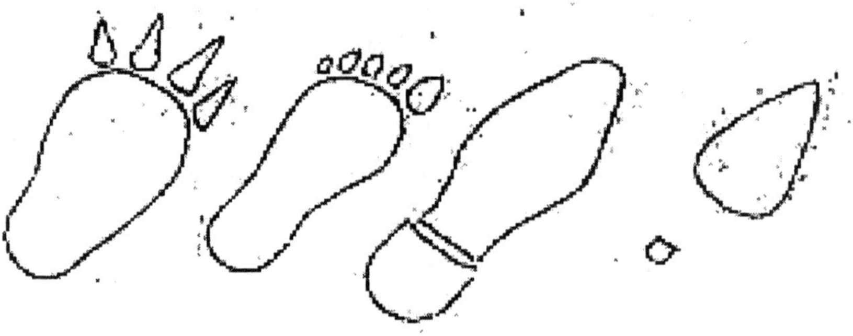

This finds expression in a rising female participation in the labour force.[5]

Female labour force as a percentage of female population; USA, EU-15, and Japan

	1970	*1974*	*1988*	*1991*	*1994*	*1997*	*1999*
US	30.2	33.1	43.8	44.2	45.3	46.1	46.6
EU-15	26.7	28.5	35.2	36.9	36.9	37.9	38.5
Japan	38.6	35.7	39.7	42.0	42.2	42.9	42.6

Source: Eurostat

5 In some countries, which are in the earlier phase of modernisation, the reverse might be true and female participation rates might actually decline. Such countries are still at the very first stages of modernisation. Tiny increases in wealth permit the realisation of a traditional role model. Thanks to the slight improvement in material circumstances, the female who was "out there" to assure the mere survival of the family can now remain at home and thus conform to the vision of comfort, propriety and homeliness of her male master.

In all three members of the triad – US, EU and Japan – female participation in the labour force has increased dramatically over the last 30 years.[6] The participation of males in the labour force, on the other hand, has remained more or less constant in the US, increased somewhat in Japan but has decreased substantially in Europe, falling by more than 13%.[7]

Male labour force as a percentage of male population from 15-64 years of age

	1970	*1974*	*1988*	*1991*	*1994*	*1997*	*1999*
US	85.4	85.4	85.0	85.2	85.5	85.4	84.8
EU-15	90.6	87.5	79.9	80.3	78.5	78.2	77.5
Japan	88.7	90.5	86.8	88.8	90.5	92.1	92.4

Source: Eurostat

The social, political and economic advance of females is reflected in other figures as well as those on labour force participation. In the wealthier countries, they are now even with males in access to education. In some of those countries, the traditional numeric predominance of male over female university students has reversed. Educators believe that female students find it easier to submit to the rigor and discipline of tertiary education.

Formal education has, by now, become the main precondition for reaching the higher ranks in professional life. There is thus reason to believe that the female scaling of the bastions of university education presages their ultimate massive influx into these higher ranks (which up to now have frequently not been that accessible to females).

Changes in the mode of production further promote this process of female empowerment. The information society puts a premium on networking and cooperation, and makes rigid hierarchies dysfunctional. Networking has been connected with females; and the need for strict hierarchical structures with males. Furthermore, today's production calls for nimbleness and not for sheer physical strength. This shift again favours females over males. Finally, the likelihood of wars is receding and with it the need – and excuse – for male aggressiveness.

6 Remarkably, it is higher in Japan than it is in Europe.

7 There are reasons to believe that the labour force participation of females will always remain a bit below the male participation rates, as females will continue to be hampered by the onerous task of child bearing and child rearing. Notwithstanding a greater willingness of males to share these tasks, they will remain incumbent upon females to a large extent.

Surprisingly, females also seem better equipped to deal with the harshness of unexpected change and with the burden of risk and uncertainty. In Europe, the daughters of first generation immigrants generally do much better in adapting to the mores and requirements of the country their parents had chosen to live in. Sons have greater difficulties. Similarly, females were better able to deal with the strains of the transition from a Communist, centrally planned economic system to a market economy. Male life expectancy declined in Russia by more than five years. Female life expectancy by just one year. This ability to cope will certainly be a premium in a world system which, by necessity, will be marked by momentous and frequently unexpected change.

But will that shift in gender relations in its turn, also have a deep impact on the world system? Will it change its nature? The answer is open. If the past is a guide we should assume that – at least at first – not very much will change. Some of the great historic rulers were women: Catherine the Great of Russia, Christine of Sweden, Elisabeth I of England, Maria Therese of Austria. In their use of power, including military power, they were not less ruthless than their male counterparts. One might contend that these were women who lived in, and had to adjust to, a male dominated society. Things would be different if women were to become dominant in society. That might or might not be the case. We simply do not know.

*

With that, back to the demographic prospect of the world by 2050. It is assumed that, by then, fertility rates world wide will have converged to a point of somewhat above 2 births per female. This is the reproduction level. If fertility falls below this rate (and it is much below this rate in nearly all European countries), the population shrinks. The graph below is based upon the assumption that, ultimately, fertility rates in the now wealthy countries will remain a bit below the re-production level; and that they will remain a bit above this level in the less developed countries.

Total fertility rates: Estimates 1950-1995 and medium variant projections 1995-2050

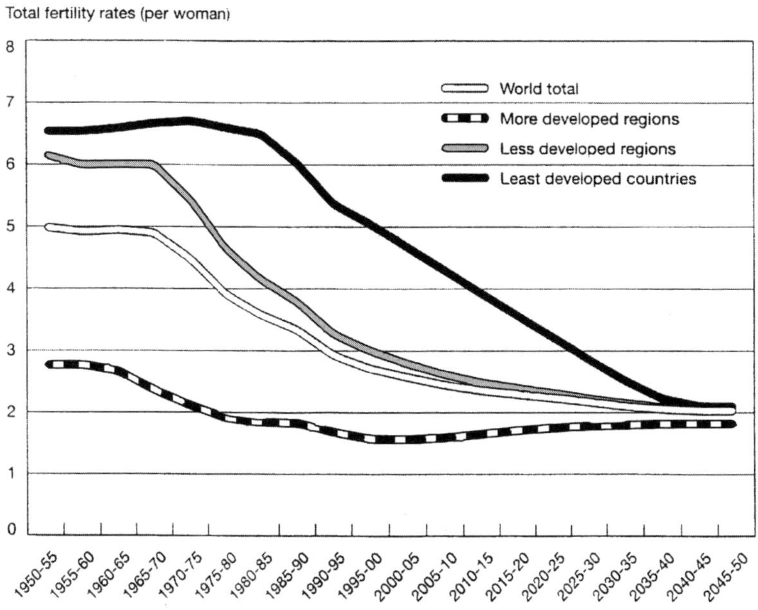

Source: United Nations Population Division, 1999

In the next decade, though, the differences in the fertility rates will persist and these differences will cause further shifts in the relative demographic weight of states and regions. Until 2050, the increase of population will be nearly exclusively in the poorer countries, whereas from 2030 on, the population of the wealthy countries will even decline a bit.

World population 1950-2050 industrial and developing countries
(in billions)

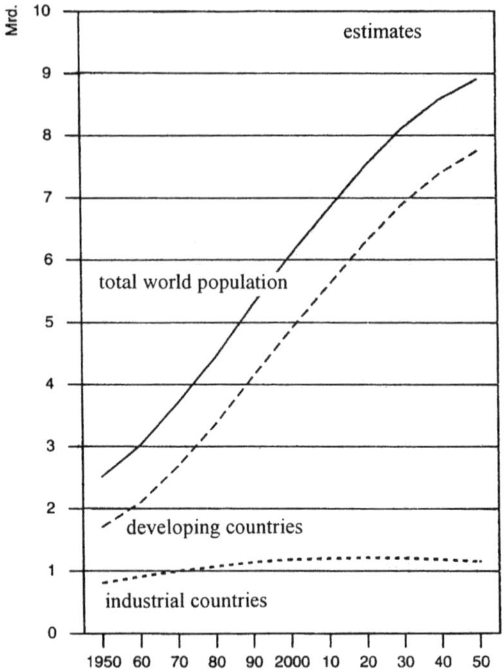

Source: UN, World Population Fund 1998

If we look at the future demographic weight of continents, we can see that, in 2050, the share of Asia in the world population will be about as large as it is today with fully sixty percent. The share of the Americas will remain constant too; that of Japan and Europe will shrink. The share of Africa will rise markedly.

World population, 1999 and 2050, by continents

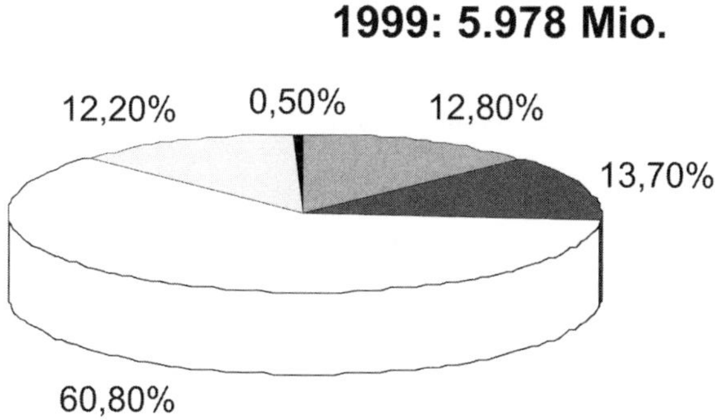

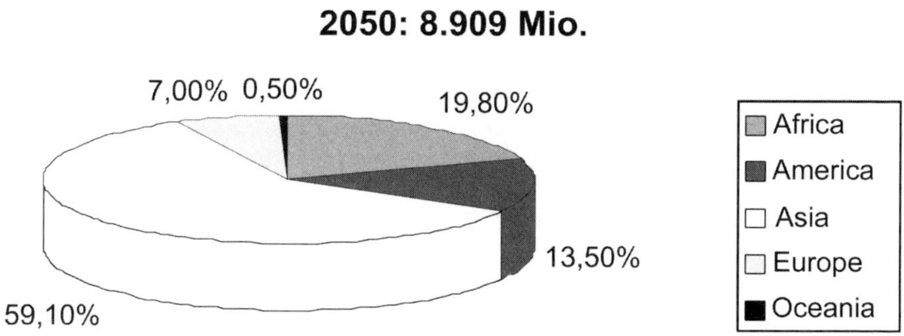

Source: UN Population Fund

Among the less wealthy countries of the world, developments will be uneven, too. Those countries already fairly advanced on the path of economic development will register just a modest progression in the size of their population; whereas in these mere fifty years, the population of some very poor countries will increase by about 150%.

Rate of Increase of Population 1999-2050	
Taiwan	+ 11%
Thailand	+ 21%
Ethiopia	+ 177%
Nigeria	+ 124%
Pakistan	+ 127%

By 2050, India will have become more populous than China. No single European country will be among the 20 most populous ones. From the "Triad" countries, the US will remain near the top in the ranking of the most populous countries (but it will rank far below the two Asian giants China and India; and a bit after Pakistan). Japan will have dropped back to rank no. 17 – just after Russia which will occupy rank 16 – also after having experienced a strong decline in the number of citizens.

Ultimate world population size under different assumptions
(in billions)

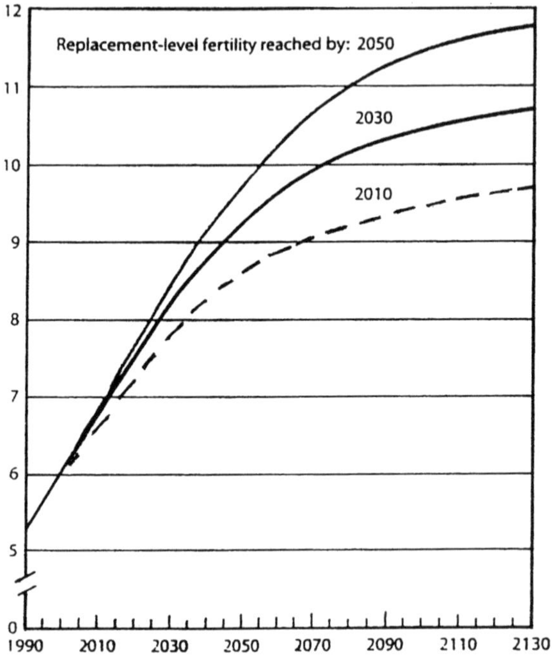

Source: UN Population Fund

Let's take the even wider perspective and look beyond 2050. The world population will continue to grow even thereafter (while fertility rates will be low, there will be more women in reproductive age). But this further growth of the world population will be relatively slow. It is assumed to cease altogether a century later with between 9 and 12 billion people inhabiting the globe.

The growth and decline of human populations had once been determined and constrained by physical factors that could not be changed by human will (the amount of food available, the incidence of disease, etc). Those physical factors are no longer that relevant. On occasion, though, they might become relevant again. A warning in that direction is provided by the decline of life expectancy in some African countries like Botswana and Uganda. The decline is not due to the wider use of birth control. It is the consequence of AIDS.

Changes in life-expectancy in three African countries

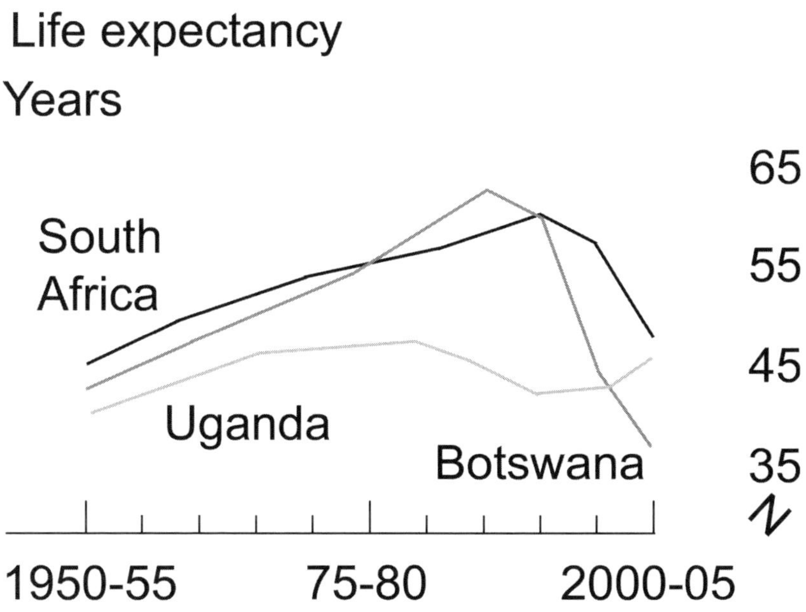

Source: UN Population Fund

AIDS is a scourge which made its appearance just thirty years ago. It is not clear whether it will continue to have its demographic impact only in African countries; or whether it could also have such an impact in other regions of the world. (In some countries, like Russia, HIV infection has risen markedly in recent years.)

AIDS might be followed by similar unexpected, unpleasant surprises. Bacteria adapt to antibiotics. New strains develop that may become resistant even to the most potent combination of antibiotics. In fact, this is what has already happened with an especially aggressive form of tuberculosis. In the race between new drugs and such new strains[8], the enemy might win out more frequently in the future. Just as AIDS does now, such new and incurable diseases would certainly also impact on demographic developments.

Nonetheless, at present, and at least in the wealthy countries, the main constraint on population size is not the external one of disease, hunger or war. In the wealthy countries, demographic developments are determined by the presence or the absence of the wish to reproduce. These preferences can change. Such changes could oblige us to discard all of the above projections on the future size of the world population.

Attitudes towards child bearing already changed once in the wealthy countries; and already once this affected the demography of these countries. One of the previous graphs in this chapter was on the fertility rates and it also shows how this rate developed in the wealthy countries in the time between the end of World War II and 1960. In that period, fertility declined less rapidly than we would have expected by just projecting the trends of the past. This – relatively minor – aberration is called the "baby boom". It had a profound impact on all aspects of economic, political and cultural life in Europe and the United States. The generation that created this "baby boom" had suffered through the uncertainties and tragedies of economic depression and war. It sought attachment, warmth, security. It thus resurrected and implemented the ideal of the nuclear, multi-child family. We cannot exclude that such sentiments might come to prevail once again. In fact, they might be about to do so.

In some of the wealthiest, "trend setter" countries of North America and Scandinavia, fertility rates have begun to rise again. Could it be that, in these countries, citizens have become fed up with gross consumerism? Could it be that, in these countries, we witness a renaissance of the family[9] and the associated values? Could that signal a turning away from the sphere of paid work and consumption and a yearning for bonding and attachment that is being produced by the family? Could it be that the number of children and not the size of home or car will become the dominant status symbol?

Predictions are risky – especially those concerning the future.

Notwithstanding such uncertainties, what we have found still provides a solid enough base to permit us to pose some questions and attempt some tentative an-

8 Science fiction has frequently toyed with the vision of some genetic experiments running sour by creating new forms of bacteria or other life that could destroy humankind or its ecological base. This is a vision that cannot be cast aside as completely eccentric and irrelevant.

9 Although of families of a new type.

swers as to the future demographics of the world and on how they connect to the global system:

1) the "population bomb" is not about to explode.

2) the long term outlook is quite positive. Wealth rises in the form of a "J" curve. That is true at least for the mid term future and at least as long as major countries that are still poor will enter a phase of catching up and of rapid, self-sustaining growth. The world population, however, is growing in the form of an "S" curve. We can superimpose this curve on the "J" curve of economic growth and we show these two curves in the graph below.[10]

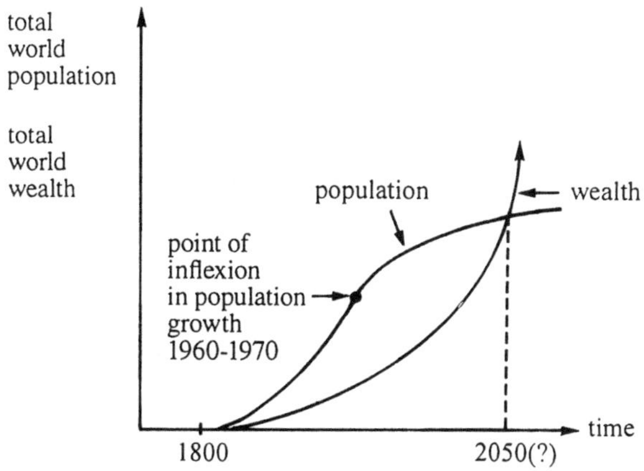

As this graph makes evident, the past decades were difficult for the poorer part of the world and the coming decades will not be different in that respect. In these poorer parts of the world, population growth was still rather fast compared to the wealth increase, which was not yet at full speed. Eventually though, this is going to change; and at some point the "J" curve of rising wealth will cut across the "S" curve of a growing world population.

The relationship between rising wealth and slower population growth

The exact relationship is not that clear[11]. We do not know what causes what. Does rising wealth cause a slower growth in the size of the population? Or, in-

10 The graph does not aspire to be statistically correct and it lacks, for instance, precise scales. Its purpose is to express the dynamics of two processes.

11 Recent evidence would suggest that high fertility is as much a symptom of poverty as a cause (IBRD 2002).

versely, does a slower population growth prompt a rise in wealth? It might be that the linkage, if it exists, is not the same at all times and in all places. Some countries with a rapidly expanding population might still grow economically (as India has done recently), while other countries with a slow population growth might remain poor (as, for example, Argentina). But whatever such deviations in individual countries may be, over the long run and on the average, the relationship between rising wealth and fewer offspring has been rather tight.

One thing is obvious though: fewer children imply that a smaller percentage of the 0-60 year old population is dependent and not part of the work force. A slowdown of population growth thus reduces this burden of the not – yet – employed under 15 years of age.

3) At the outset of the industrial revolution two hundred years ago, the per capita income in what today are the wealthiest and the poorest countries did not differ that much. According to Maddison, in 1820 the per capita GDP of India was behind the UK per capita GDP by not more than 50%[12]. The demographic weight of the presently wealthy countries has already been reduced drastically. It will continue to shrink. The demographic weight of the presently poor countries has grown very much.

We have to assume that, in the long term future, per capita income in the presently poor countries[13] will eventually return to its "normal" level. That implies that the situation will be restored to what existed at the outset of the industrial age. The differences in the per capita GDP of the presently poor and the presently rich countries will have disappeared. If this were to happen, economic weight would be added to the demographic weight of the poorer countries (especially the two most populous ones, India and China). Inevitably, the present world dominance of the "Triad" (US, Japan, Europe) will come under effective challenge already in the mid-term future (2040-2060).

---

12 According to Maddison whom we have quoted in the preceding chapter. Others (Bairoch) even maintain that in 1800 the per capita income of India, China and Britain would have been roughly even.

13 Or at least in most of them.

The Ageing of Societies

Rapidly growing populations are young on the average. In some still poorer countries, the percentage of the population that is under 15 years of age may thus exceed 50%. As birth rates decline, this segment of the population will shrink. The population will become older on the average. In addition, rising wealth not only corresponds to falling birth rates. It also corresponds to a rising life expectancy. Within just one single generation, life expectancy rose by no less than ten years in East Asia and by seven years in the average of all OECD countries.

Trends in life expectancy, 1970-1998 (years of life)

Region	*1970*	*1982*	*1993*	*1997*	*1998*
East Asia and Pacific	59	66	68	69	69
Europe and Central Asia	n.a.	68	69	69	69
Latin America and Caribbean	61	65	68	70	70
Middle East and North Africa	53	60	65	67	68
South Asia	49	55	60	62	62
Sub-Saharan Africa	44	48	50	51	50
Developing Countries	55	61	64	65	65
OECD	71	75	77	78	78

Source: World Bank

Those over 60 years of age will form a growing part of the population. Well before the start of the new century, the two groups, namely those over 60 and those under 15, were of equal strength in Europe. By now, the first group clearly outnumbers the second group.

With some time lag, the still poorer countries will follow. If these countries are taken as a group, the size of the population under 15 and the size of the population over 60 will become even by 2050; that is merely fifty years after the same thing happened in Europe.

For the moment though, the rich countries and the poor countries still face different problems. While rich countries will have to build old age homes, the poor ones will have to build schools. In poor countries, families centre around children. In rich countries they centre around the elderly. Already now, families in the wealthy countries spend more of their free time on caring for their elders than they spend on caring for their young.

Development of the age structure in wealthy and in poorer countries; 1950-2050, in %

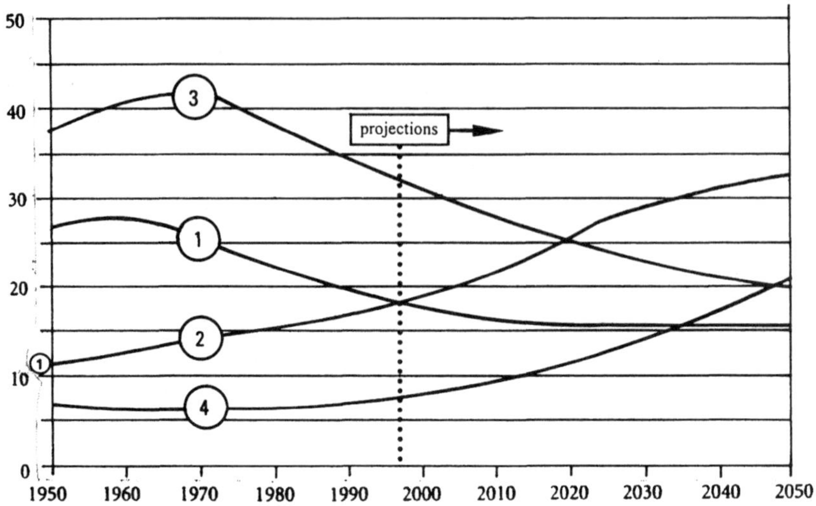

1 = wealthy countries, share of the population under 15 years
2 = wealthy countries, share of the population over 60
3 = poorer countries, share of the population under 15
4 = poorer countries, share of the population over 60

Source: UNDP

In the wealthy countries this demographic trend will result in a marked rise in the number of those who have retired from the work force. The trend will be particularly strong in Japan and in Europe, where this development will have peaked in 2030.

Youth dependency (0-14 as percentage of 15-64) and old-age dependency ratios (65+ as percentage of 15-64), estimates 1950-95 and projections 1995-2050 (medium variant)

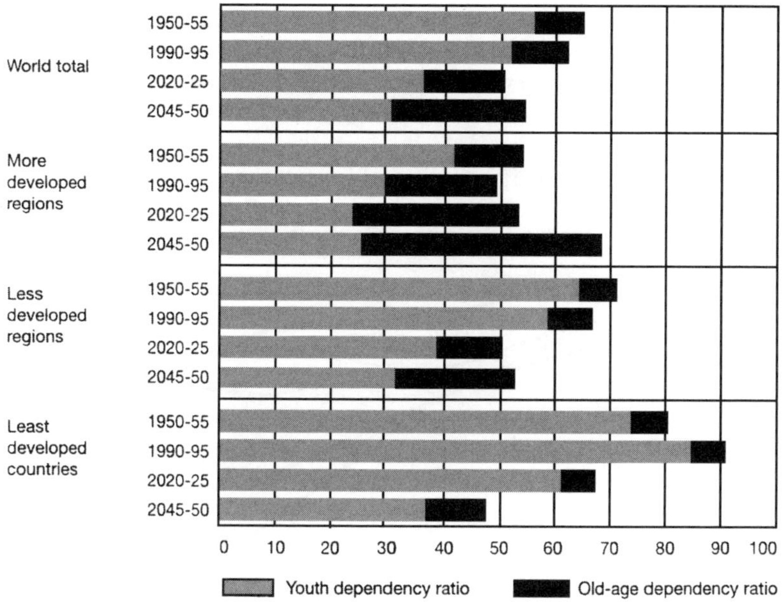

Source: United Nations Population Division, 1999

Demographic trends in the EU according to age-classes

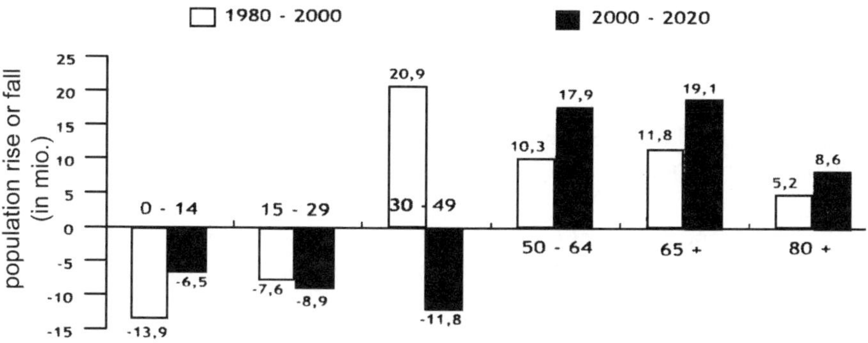

Source: Eurostat

The problem is being accentuated by the fact that, at the same time, the age of retirement is getting lower (instead of rising to compensate for the demographic trends and for the longer life expectancy). When, after World War II, the old age pension insurance was extended to blue collar workers in Austria, the average life expectancy of a manual labourer was lower than the mandatory age of retirement (then and now, still 65). In the meantime, the actual average age of retirement has dropped to 58 years, while the Austrian average life expectancy inches closer to 80 (81 years for females, 75 years for males) .

Percentage of people aged 55-64 still working full-time

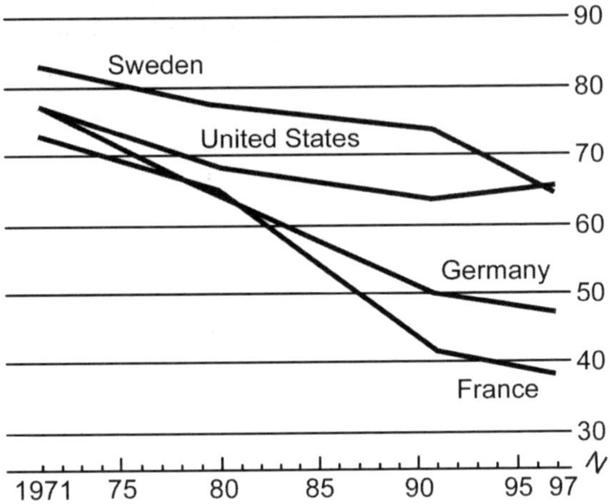

Source: Eurostat, OECD

The above graph shows the US to be an odd exception, with the actual age of retirement rising – something against the trend in most other OECD countries. The number of years spent in the labour force before retirement decreased in the other OECD countries, in line with rising wealth and productivity. This was not the case in the United States. For a few years, Americans have started to again work longer in their life. They have also started to work more hours per week.

This is one of several instances that prompt the question as to the nature of the US "exceptionality". Is this "working longer again" a US exception because the US is exceptional (Calvinist culture, pressure of competitive consumption)? Or does the US march in a direction others will also choose sooner or later? The second explanation carries some weight at this moment as in the

EU there now is consensus on the need to master the looming pension crisis mainly by raising the actual age of retirement.[1]

Old age used to bring drastic reductions in income. This is no longer the case. Retirement income has been raised in relation to the income of persons still active in the work force. Life-plans and life-styles of the retired are now based on the expectation that their income will not be much lower than what they had gained when they still were employed.[2]

Pensioners standard of living as percentage of the general population's 1998

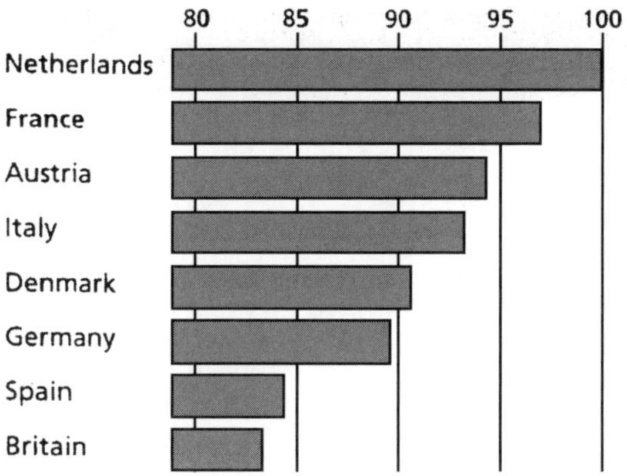

Source: OECD

---

1 To balance the system with all other parameters remaining unchanged , the actual age of retirement would, for example, have to be raised by fully 10 years in Austria. That leads to the question of whether jobs could actually be found for all those that thus would be obliged to remain in the work force.

2 Originally, the old age pension was conceived of as an insurance in the case that one would survive into old age but – due to this old age – would no longer be able to participate in the labour force. This is reflected in the terms used to designate such schemes: Social Security, Pensions-Versicherung, Securité Sociale. All these terms denote their original purpose as having indeed been one of insurance. But as wealth increased and life expectancy rose, such schemes have changed their character. By now they are entitlements to work-free rent income. The profile of the retirees has also changed. It no longer corresponds to some fragile, grey-haired person sitting listless in the afternoon sun. Today, retirement correlates with the image of golf club wielding or tennis-ball-smashing well-tanned persons; or to agile grandparents driving their mobile homes back and forth over the US continental divide as they venture from one state to another.

The above statistics on money income still do not provide the full picture and still underestimate the privileged position of the retired in the wealthy countries. The young, those at the start of their professional life, have to pay back student loans (increasingly common also in Europe). They have to establishe a family and/or buy and furnish a house or flat. In all but a few of the OECD countries (e.g. Australia or Belgium) the poverty rate among those over 65 is therefore lower than the average poverty rate.

Poverty rates for individuals by age and gender (poverty line defined as 50 percent of the median equivalent disposable household income)

Country	All adults and children			Adults aged 18-64			Adults aged 65 and over		
	Total	Male	Female	Total	Male	Female	Total	Male	Female
Australia 1994	12.3	–	–	9.8	9.4	10.4	15.1	14.7	15.4
Belgium 1992	5.4	5.3	5.4	4.4	4.2	4.8	8.2	8.5	7.9
Canada 1994	11.2	10.6	11.7	10.6	9.4	11.8	2.1	2.3	2.3
Denmark 1992	5.3	5.2	5.3	5.5	5.2	5.5	4.6	4.1	4.9
Finland 1995	4.0	4.1	3.9	4.1	4.1	4.1	1.0	0.6	1.3
France 1989	14.0	14.2	13.9	14.1	14.1	14.1	13.4	13.9	13.1
Germany[2] 1994	12.2	10.5	12.6	11.6	10.5	12.6	8.3	8.7	7.6
Israel 1992	15.3	–	–	12.1	11.7	12.5	13.5	12.7	13.6
Italy 1995	16.0	16.3	15.7	16.1	15.9	16.5	6.8	7.4	6.4
Luxembourg 1994	4.9	4.8	5.0	4.0	3.5	4.7	2.1	2.5	2.0
Netherlands 1991	6.5	6.4	6.6	6.0	5.5	6.6	3.5	4.0	3.1
Norway 1995	4.4	4.4	4.4	5.1	4.8	5.3	1.1	1.3	0.9
Poland 1995	15.7	16.4	15.0	13.8	15.1	13.5	8.9	8.8	9.0
Russian Federation 1995	21.1	–	–	20.8	21.3	20.7	13.5	9.9	15.2
Spain 1990	10.6	–	–	9.9	9.9	10.2	6.7	6.5	6.9
Sweden 1992	5.4	5.0	5.1	6.7	6.7	6.6	1.9	1.1	2.5
Taiwan, China 1995	6.9	6.7	7.2	5.2	5.0	5.6	17.2	16.2	18.4
United Kingdom 1995	13.3	13.3	13.2	10.9	10.6	11.4	6.9	5.9	7.6
United States 1995	19.9	18.5	21.2	16.4	14.8	18.5	16.6	12.8	19.2

Source: OECD

Between the old and the young, financial and other burdens have thus been re-distributed. They have been lifted from the old and have been added to the load that the younger generation is bearing. Inevitably this will breed resentment not only against the elder, but also against the political systems that force the younger ones to finance the leisure pursuits of their elders.

Such financing can either be done by a levy on the wages of those still working ("pay as you go system"); or by the returns on the capital invested in a fund ("funded systems"). The pension insurance can be either public or private[3]. We cannot enter the discussion on the advantages and draw-backs of the systems. Suffice to say that, even in funded systems, the income of the retired population will have to be paid from the income of those still in the working force. It also will have to be guaranteed by the state in one form or another.

The ageing of populations will increase the demand for health services. Their price and volume will rise for other reasons too. However, it is clear that becoming older implies more fragile health and thus a more intense use of remedies. In the OECD countries, the rise in the costs of health care that may be attributed to the ageing population is as massive as the rise in expenditure for old age pensions. By 2050, both will consume 6.7% more of the GDP than they did in the year 2000. This implies that, for those two kinds of added expenditures only, taxes would have to be raised by roughly 15%. That is not a pleasant prospect, especially for those who are convinced of the moral and practical advantages of keeping taxes at a minimum.

Age related spending
Projected increase from 2000 to 2050 in percentage points of GDP

	Old age pensions	Health care	Other*
OECD average	3.4	3.3	-0.7

*child/family benefits and "early retirement" programmes

Source: Leibfritz 2002

What then will be the other implications of this shift in demographic weight towards older persons?

1) The population of the poor countries will be young and the population of the wealthier countries much older. We may assume that this will also affect the

3 For reasons not readily evident, the World Bank has exerted massive pressure to transform the European public pay as you go pension systems into funded ones.

whole climate of global relations. Young are more risk prone[4], entrepreneurial, and aggressive. Older people are more prudent, cautious and less enterprising. This might heighten tensions between rich and poor countries.

2) Caring for a rapidly growing old, non-working population will impose heavy burdens upon citizens and governments of wealthy countries. This might come at the cost of lower investment in the future and of disengagements in the international realm.

3) A rising part of the population in wealthy countries will own capital (either through pension funds or directly). The supporters of "shareholder value" will thus have a numerous and politically powerful constituency, even if and where the protection and promotion of this shareholder value is detrimental to the real economy (as it often is) .

4) Whereas some decades in the late 20th century were coloured by a youth culture, that is, the culture of the young not engaged in the workforce, the future might be coloured by a "grey" culture of retired idlers. They also might set the tone politically. As did the youth culture, this "grey" culture would also oppose and weaken the work ethic. Unlike the youth culture, a grey culture would, however, shun experimentation, be basically hostile to things and persons not familiar, and be diffident about the wider world. Clearly such inclinations are more difficult to reconcile with globalisation than those that come naturally to a younger population.

---

4 One aspect of ageing and of ageing societies is an increase in aversion to war. If, in a poor country, a family has four sons, and one of them dies on the battlefield, then this is considered tragic and the fallen will be honoured and remembered as a hero. If, in a rich country, a family has a son, and if he is the only child and killed in war, then this is more than a tragedy, this is the end, this is a price not worth paying for any cause.

Migration and the Dilemmas of "Multi-Culturalism"

If all wealthy countries are taken together, their population will shrink. Within that group, developments will diverge. The US will be the only major wealthy nation to register a substantial growth of population in the time between 2000 and 2050. If one excepts Ireland[1], all European countries will have fewer inhabitants by 2050.

Population, % change, 2000-2050

Source: UN Population Fund

Since the seventies, the area of what is now the European Union has been an area of net immigration.[2] Since the mid eighties, this inflow has become more

---

1 and Albania (not included in the above graph)

2 Migration (or better: mobility of labour) within the EU is not impeded by any obstacles and, according to "freedom of movement" (and with a very few exceptions), every EU citizen can work in any EU country he or she pleases. But surprisingly,

marked. Yet, even if immigration were held at the level it has reached in the eighties, the population of the EU would still decline from the year 2020 onwards. To keep the population constant after that point, immigration into the EU would have to rise further.

Factors driving the growth or decline of the EU(15) population

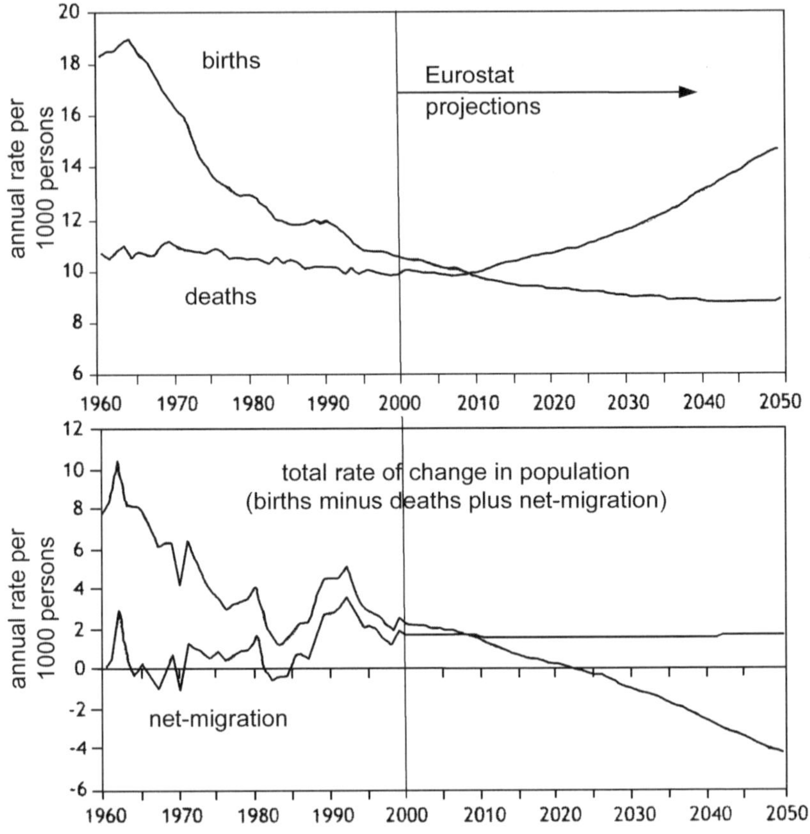

Source: Eurostat – Bevölkerungsstatistik, Daten 1960-1999

---

not that much use is made of this freedom. Most immigrants into EU countries come from outside the EU, and only a fraction from other EU members.

Very likely this is what is going to happen and we may expect that immigration into the EU will rise indeed, just as immigration into the US was increasing in the late 20th century. We may expect that in this field, too, Europe would eventually come to emulate the US.

Immigrants granted legal residence in the United States
(actual numbers 1960-1995; and projection to 2025)

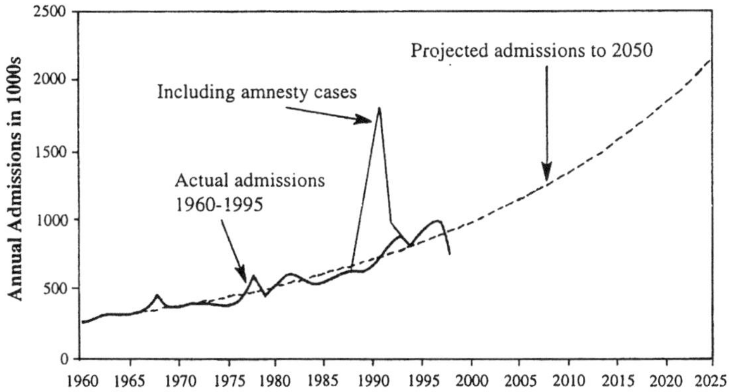

The estimates for 1995 through 1998 include 500,000 applicants already living in the US whom the INS expected to approve but whose cases it had not finished processing. The projected admissions for 1998–2025 assume that annual admissions continue to rise by 3.2 percent a year, as they did between 1965 and 1998, and assume no new amnesties.

Source: 1998 Statistical Yearbook of the Immigration and Naturalization Service

The flow of migration is determined by "push" and "pull" factors.

Poverty, hopelessness, insecurity, war and unemployment are push factors. They push migrants outwards from their previous residences. In order to be effective, this push has to be quite massive. People are attached to their roots. Emigrating means cutting them. This implies losses in tangible and intangible investment (investment, for instance, in houses; investment in the web of personal relationships one has built; or investment in language skills one will no longer be able to use). So powerful motives are needed for writing off all of these investments with the decision to migrate to another country.

Pull factors, on the contrary, are those that make a country attractive as a haven for immigrants. A thriving economy of the new host country is such a pull factor. Yet the most powerful pull factor is simply the immigration policy of the recipient country. We assume that official policy will tend to promote immigration so as to increase the pool of labour in periods when the economy is doing well. When, however, the economy becomes depressed, immigration policy would tend to become restrictive, so as to avoid a growth of the pool of unemployed.

The importance of the "Pull Factor"
Legal immigration into the US 1820-1990

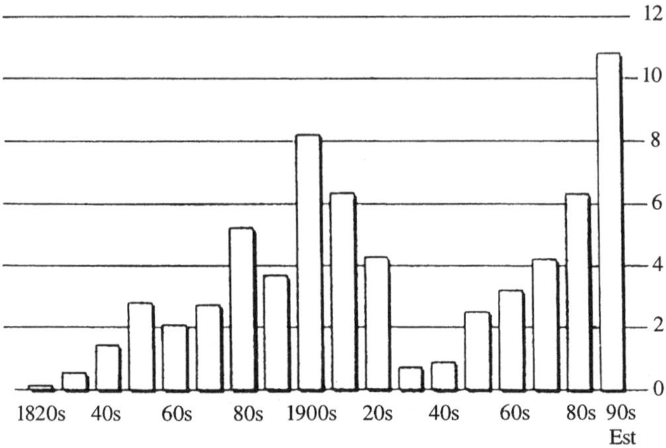

Source: US Immigration and Naturalisation Service

The table above makes obvious that the push and pull of economics can be tempered or even be overruled by official policy. Immigration into the US soared in the nineties when the US performed very well. But, on the other hand, immigration into the US declined in the time between 1900 and 1930, when the US economy was also expanding rapidly. This decline in immigration can therefore not have been due to a lesser lure by a less dynamic US economy. It was due to a change in US immigration policy which became more restrictive at the beginning of the 20th century.

We may conclude that wealthy and economically dynamic countries with a stagnant or declining population do not automatically suck in ever wider flows of immigrants. They will tend to. But, over the medium term, politics will remain the gatekeeper. One cannot exclude, for instance, that even with demand for labour being very high in the EU, and with the employers clamouring for more foreign workers being admitted, immigration policy of the EU would remain restrictive. At least over the medium term of two or three decades, the rising European xenophobia[3] could prompt European politicians to close the doors to new immigrants even if the demographic and economic situation would not warrant such course of action. Recently, anti-immigrant emotions have indeed started to impact quite markedly on the European political agenda. They had certainly influenced the results of recent elections in France, Denmark, the Netherlands and Austria. The trend has even been felt in the UK which prides itself on its liberal tradition.

Anti-immigrant sentiments on the rise in the UK
(answer to the question "What would you say are the important issues facing Britain today?")

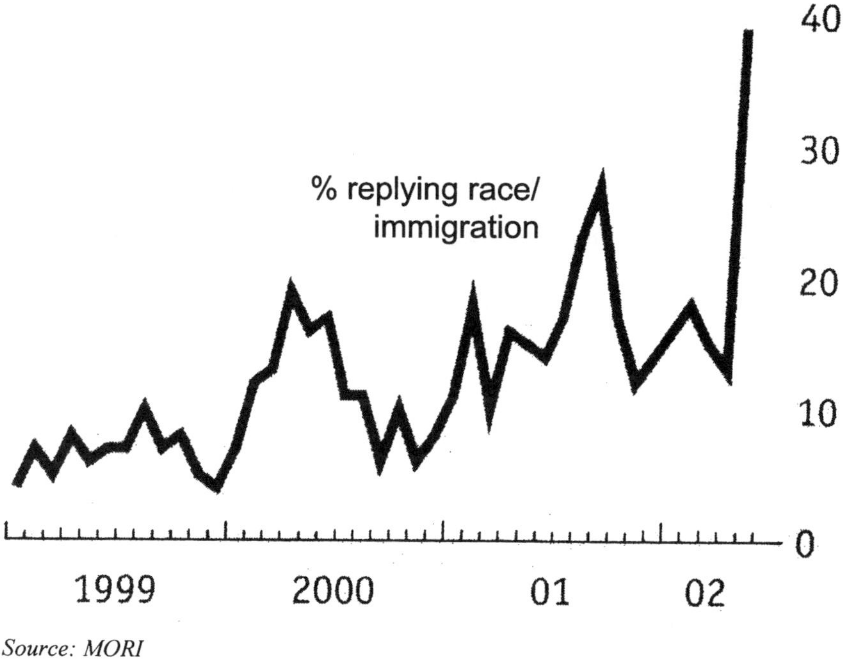

Source: MORI

Official policy has – of course – little impact on the level of illegal immigration. Yet this flow of illegal immigrants can be substantial – especially in border regions where a wealthy country adjoins a poorer one (California and Texas in

3 Just as at the beginning of the 20th century, the anti–immigrant sentiment in the US forced politicians into tightening immigration policy, notwithstanding the favourable economic situation.

the US, Spain, Italy, Austria and Germany in the EU). Even authoritarian-totalitarian regimes like the Communist ones found it hard to hermetically seal their frontiers. Liberal democracies are even less able to do so.

Difficult to stop, illegal immigration does cause severe problems to both the migrants and the recipient countries. In the recipient countries, unregistered, undocumented workers ("sans papiers" in France) may undermine the social systems and the established contractual framework between employees and employers. Migrants themselves have to survive without being able to rely on this safety net of social legislation. Furthermore, many of them have entered with the help of organised crime; with the help of gangs that specialise in smuggling migrants across borders. The prices these gangs demand for those services are high and cause many of their clients to remain in some form of indentured labour. Finally, like drug trafficking, this is an ample source of income for organised crime.

The number of illegal and legal immigrants is augmented by the number of asylum seekers. In theory, a state could do very little to affect their numbers, as all states are under a treaty obligation (Geneva Refugee Convention) to take in asylum seekers. But with the numbers of asylum seekers growing, recipient countries attempt to interpret as narrowly as possible this obligation. Also, the burden imposed on recipient countries has been distributed very unevenly. The number of asylum seekers per 1000 of the resident population varies markedly even between EU countries.[4]

4 Hence the long-standing attempts to even the burden within the EU and to unify the rules and procedures that apply to asylum seekers.

Asylum applications and net migration in 2001
(per 1000 of resident population)

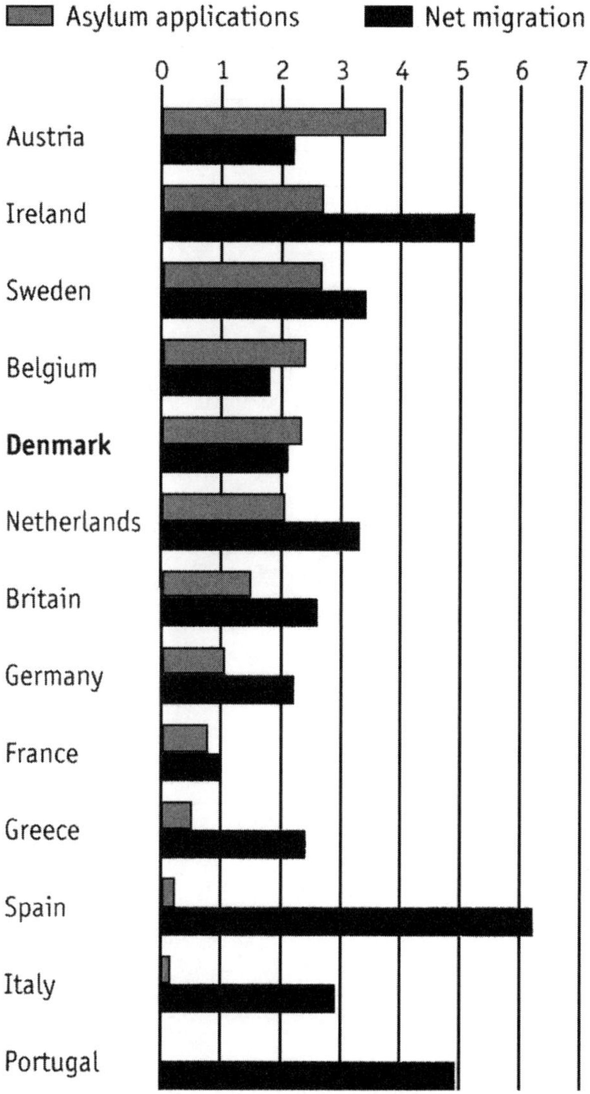

Source: Eurostat; OECD; UNHCR

Foreign population as % of total population

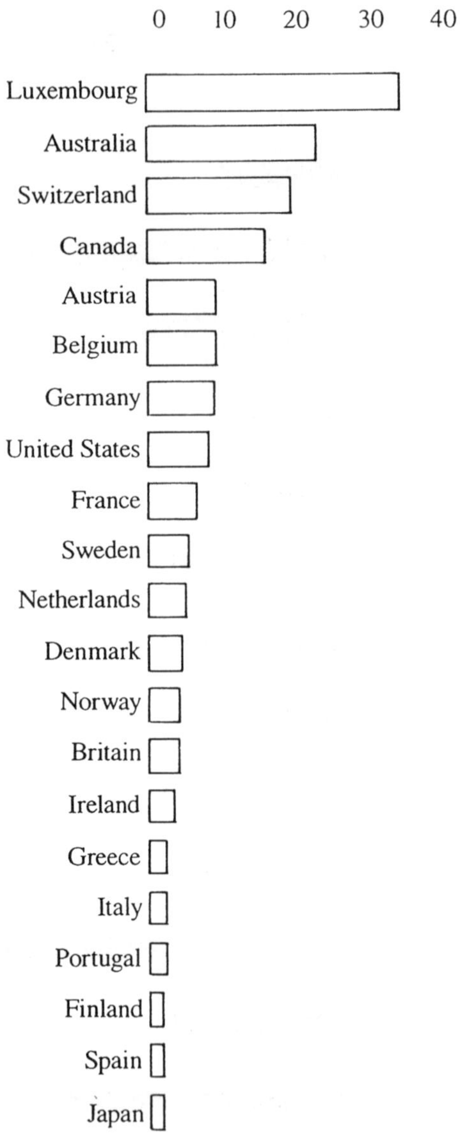

Source: OECD

As we have seen, politics may have a decisive role in curtailing legal immigration; in stemming the flow of illegal immigrants; and in restricting the inflow of asylum seekers. In the future too, political decisions will therefore have an impact on the numbers of those who enter into the wealthy countries in order to live and settle there. But, if we again take the very, very long perspective, we should assume that these flows will become wider on the average. Politics can interrupt this tendency for a decade or two, but not for an indeterminate period. Already now, in the wealthy countries, the percentage of the foreign population[5] is quite high.

Japan is an odd, but significant exception to this rule. All other wealthy countries have a "Western tradition" and culture. Japan shares in this tradition in parts only, as it has largely maintained its very specific culture and institutions. It also has retained, as it seems, its insistence on "purity", and finds it difficult to accommodate and integrate foreigners. Even those ethnic Koreans that have lived there for three generations have not been integrated. This will negatively affect the long term dynamics and thus the long term future of Japan.

In the time between 1990 and 2000, the lion's share in the growth of the EU population already came from immigration.

5 "Foreign" means residents with a nationality other than the one of the host country. The size of this "foreign population" is thus also dependent upon the ease or difficulty in accessing the citizenship of the host country. In Austria and Switzerland, for example, the hurdles to acquiring citizenship are high, and the "foreign population", thus, is sizeable.

Growth in the EU population; in %; divided into the two components of growth

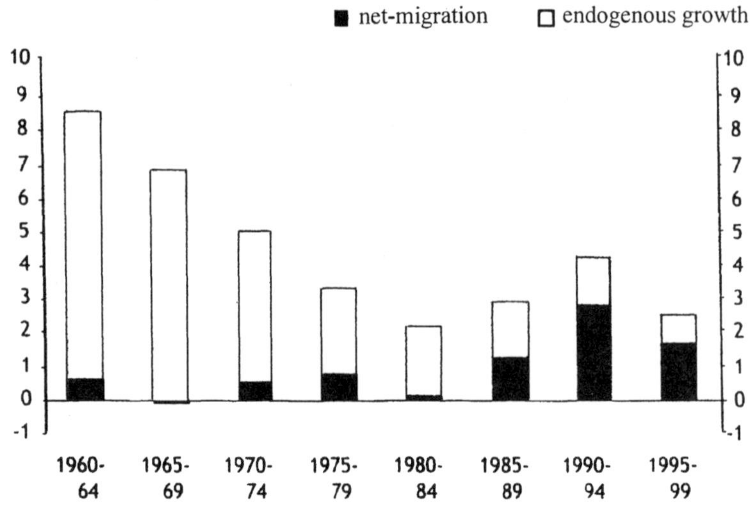

Source: Eurostat – Population Statistics

Immigrants to the EU used to come mainly from regions close to Europe; largely from Northern Africa and Western Asia. But increasingly, they will also come from regions farther away in which case the pressure of a rapidly growing population is especially acute. That has already happened in the US. Immigrants into the US first came mainly from Europe, later from Mexico and the Caribbean. Now Asians also constitute a massive share of new US immigrants. Inevitably and ultimately, this will result in a smoothing of the edges that divide cultures and ethnicities. The wealthy countries of immigration will become less homogenous ethnically and culturally.[6]

Losing inhabitants through migration impacts upon the countries of origin. The exodus of qualified labour ("brain-drain") might have some negative conse-

6 Though one has to caution against the notion that, in a state of pristine innocence, states (or their predecessors) would have been ethnically, culturally, racially homogenous. I always enjoyed telling the French that their "ancêtres les Gallois" had actually been Bavarians, and that, later on, they had become Romans/Italians; to transmute – as the name "France" signals – into a Teutonic tribe. Similarly, I enjoyed mentioning to Brits their Celtic (=Austrian), Phoenician, Roman, Danish, Teutonic and French ancestry.

quences. The substantial investments in education seem to get lost as, instead of the country of origin, the country of immigration will henceforth profit from them. But then, quite a few of the emigrants might return again with new skills and the readiness to apply them in their original home countries. *"A survey by the Public Policy Institute of California has found that half of the foreign-born (particularly Chinese and Indian) highly skilled immigrants in Silicon Valley (that were contacted in this survey)... have set up subsidiaries, joint ventures, subcontracting operations or other businesses in their countries of origin."* (Financial Times, 10 June 2002)[7] And remittances from emigrants do certainly form an important source of income for many poor countries (as e.g. Albania, Egypt or the Philippines).

Immigration raises the wealth of the recipient countries: more workers equals more work done, equals bigger GDP. Obviously too, for the immigrants themselves, the move into the new country implies economic gains. Were it otherwise, they would remain in their native countries. But the voters that ultimately decide on immigration laws and immigration policies would pose a different question: does immigration raise the per capita wealth of the population already there?

Studies have attempted to provide an answer to this question. They differ somewhat in their findings. But they seem to converge around the conclusion that the effect on the wealth of resident population is positive but relatively minor.

Yet the focus of such studies is too narrow. The dynamics of the US, its capacity to turn around and innovate, its impressive vitality and creativity, cannot be explained while neglecting the massive contribution of immigrants. This is confirmed by the foreign names of many of the US Nobel prize winners; and by the fact that the majority of science students at US universities is now of Asian origin. In my own home country, Austria, the German-language refugees that entered after World War II ("Volksdeutsche") have made a decisive contribution to the dynamics of the after-war period. Many of the mid-sized and technologically leading Austrian enterprises were founded by these refugee-immigrants.

Wealthy countries with a stagnant population therefore make special efforts to attract and select those immigrants that do offer such skills. In fact, they have started to compete against each other in their search for such assets. Software specialists from India are one such group that is wooed by immigrant countries. Being successful in attracting them might provide the immigrant country with a strong competitive edge in the development of software.

7 Overseas, Chinese have contributed as much as 70% of China's Foreign Direct Investment. Overseas Indians still provide 10% of India's incoming FDI.

US H1-B visas issued to indian workers (thousands)

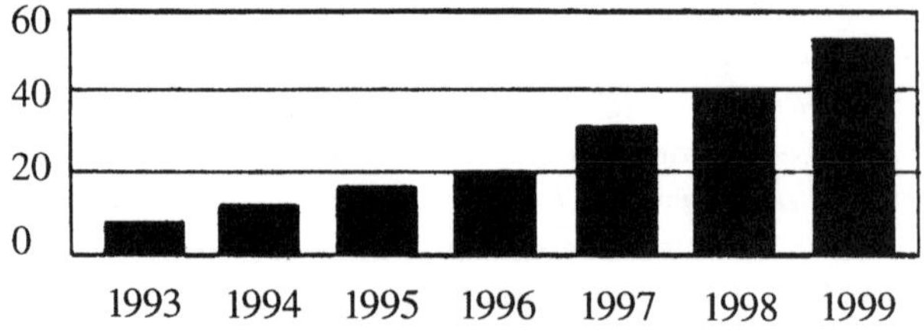

Source: India's National Association of Software and Service Companies, U.S. State Department Investor's Business Daily, July6, 2000, p. A10

But there is a downside to this. In the recipient countries, different groups of the population are affected differently by the arrival of immigrants. Most of these immigrants enter into low paying jobs[8]. They thus increase the supply of semi-skilled or unskilled labour. Due to technological changes, the wages in this segment of the labour market were in decline already. Now they are depressed even further. It is no accident that anti-immigrant feelings are strongest in this insecure blue-collar population, threatened by a loss of status and wealth.

A risk of a different nature derives from cultural diversity induced by the growing size and diversity of an immigrant community. Such diversity has more than merely positive aspects and consequences. Cultural diversity might escalate into multi-culturalism and this multi-culturalism, again, might escalate to the extent of weakening those common values and institutions that sustain a polity and that provide it with the basis for effective collective action.

With this argument we enter treacherous ground. Anti-immigration policy has always played on this argument, and it has always been used to justify xenophobia. In the big, traditional haven countries like the US, Australia or France, historic experience has not supported such fears. On the contrary, it has proven them unjustified. In each of these countries, first generation immigrants tended to cling to their old culture. But the following generations did integrate into the new home country. Sometimes they did so very rapidly. This held true even for immigrants from countries with cultures very different from the host country's: It holds true, for instance, for Asians immigrating into the United States.[9]

---

8 Even if they have a higher qualification in their country of origin.

9 Half of the second generation ethnic Asian immigrants into the US marry American spouses.

The big question is whether this will hold true for the future as well. May we expect that future immigrants will again integrate into the society and culture of their new home countries? The question is pertinent since at least some factors at work now could make future integration more difficult than it has been in the past.

a) Ease of communication: immigrants now may stay in daily contact with their country of origin. Visible proof is given by the forests of satellite dish antennas sprouting in immigrants' quarters. The evening news immigrants listen to will frequently be from the country of origin.

b) Double citizenship (once very rare) is becoming more common and accepted.

c) Intermarriage: in some of today's big immigrant communities, it is the rule and not the exception for marriages to be arranged with brides or bridegrooms from the country of origin, who then join their spouse in the country of immigration. Children thus grow up in households where the language of the host country is not spoken. This puts them at a serious disadvantage in the subsequent school career, and this again threatens them with subsequent economic and social marginality.

d) Shrinking public space and disappearance of institutions that integrate: the conscript armies are being replaced by professional armies. Sports are being followed on television instead of being experienced at stadiums. Team sports are in decline, local shops and pubs are closing. Schools become more segregated along lines of class and income. There are fewer opportunities for immigrant newcomers to mingle with the indigenous locals.

e) Formal education is becoming ever more important in opening the gates to integration and professional advance. This venue of advancement will not be easily accessible to many of the first and second generation immigrants; whereas historic patterns of advancement (petty shops, semi-skilled labour) will tend to disappear.

f) The now common agreements on the international transfer of acquired pension entitlements facilitate the return into the country of origin after the age of retirement has been reached. Life plans are shaped by this – frequently unfulfilled – promise of a "homecoming". This lowers the intention to adjust to the new home country.

It is not easy for wealthy states to deal with this issue of growing diversity. On the one hand, they will have to fight against intolerance and the repression of cultural diversity. On the other hand they have to prevent their states from fracturing into disconnected islands of separate cultures and identities which, between them, share little of what is common.

In his novel "Sybil", the 19th century British prime minister Disraeli worried about a future with *"two nations between whom there is no intercourse, who are ignorant of each others' habits, thoughts and feelings as if they were.... inhabitants of different planets... who are ordered by different manners and are not governed by the same law."* This was written at the end of the 19th century. By and large, the 20th century has not confirmed such fears. Within the wealthy nations, at least, differences have not grown, but have evened out.

Yet it seems that the tide has turned. As we shall see, differences in wealth and income widen again. Another threatening and deep divide is the one opening between an estranged "underclass" and the rest of society. The third divide that may come to split wealthy countries is the one between co-existing, but widely differing, ethnic-cultural groups which – as Disraeli feared – do indeed have little in common and do not wish it to be otherwise. There is a distinct danger that these three deep and probably widening cleavages might add up (with certain immigrant communities sliding into the underclass and into poverty).

Up until now, groups of immigrants had always eventually integrated into the societies of their new home countries with this process being a bit faster in the US and a bit slower in Europe. As mentioned, it is not clear whether this will also be the case in the future. It is certain though, that migration movements from the poor to the wealthy regions of the world will increase and become rather massive[10]. Nonetheless, and if counted in percentage points of the resident population, this migration would still be inferior to the one that occurred in the time between 1850 and 1910. It will be inferior, certainly, to what free markets for labour would demand and accommodate. Globalisation has brought the "free mobility" for goods and services. It has done the same for capital. It has not done the same for labour. Even in the present wave of globalisation, the geographic mobility of labour will remain circumscribed and partial only. Mobility of labour will remain more constricted than it had been at an earlier instance of globalisation in the era between 1850 and 1910.

Migration is, so to say, a natural thing. It is a quasi natural safety valve to ease pressures that arise from natural causes or from divergence in the level of economic development. Efforts to curtail this freedom are still of a rather recent origin. Till the end of the 19th century and during the first big wave of globalisation, only a few European countries had issued passports. Visas were unknown. There were, thus, few legal obstacles to limit migration. Nonethe-

10 With the possible exception of Eastern Asia.

less, this liberal regime still did not open the sluices for a vast, wholesale exchange of populations, as migration was limited by physical factors. The prices for long distance geographic displacement were still very high compared to average annual income. In Europe, such displacement was thus reserved either for the very wealthy or for those Europeans who would scratch together their life's savings to pay for the crossing of the Atlantic. For nearly all other inhabitants of the globe such journeys were clearly beyond financial reach. When the price of long distance travel started to drop, however, at the end of the 19th century, the potential for the permanent displacement of great numbers of humans grew accordingly. And states started to regulate and curtail migration.

This has created a dichotomy in the global economic/political system. Capital may move freely. Labour may not do so. Prices for capital and labour are each set by the marginal opportunity costs, by the reward they may get at their best possible employ. As workers from poor countries may not migrate freely to wealthy countries, these opportunity costs of wages will be low as they will correspond to the best possible employment in their own, poor country with its low productivity of labour. Capital, on the other hand, may migrate.

As we have seen, economic growth and the growth of productivity does not slow down in wealthy countries. In these countries, the productivity of capital therefore also remains high. Interest rates that are high world-wide correspond to this high productivity of capital. This will facilitate capital gaining shares in the world income; and labour losing shares in the world income.

If the free movement of capital was restricted, and if labour was able to migrate freely between nations, it would be otherwise. The share of labour would rise and the share of capital would decline.

Is it thus the greed of capital which has caused barriers to go up that restricts free migration? Not really. The political and social systems are clearly not equipped to deal with population exchanges that would indeed be massive were they not controlled by politics. Such freedom would be detrimental not just to capital, but – more directly – to the workers in wealthy countries. Their wages would come under severe pressure.

But even if it does not reach the full potential it would have were it not restricted by politics, migration between nations will remain substantial. It will be fuelled by the demographic pressure of a rapidly growing population in poor countries, and of a stagnating or even declining population in most of the wealthy countries. It will be fuelled, too, by the gap in absolute wealth between these two groups of countries becoming wider in the foreseeable future.

This will impact on political systems and upon global governance. We have assumed as likely that immigrant groups will integrate into their new home countries less rapidly and less readily than they have done in the past. In relation to their former and their present home state, they will remain in an in-between position for quite some time. They are no longer full citizens of their country of origin; and – at least in an emotional and sociological sense – not full citizens yet in their new home country. They will participate in both realms (and this will be facilitated by ever more common dual citizenship). Indeed, such "diasporas" of emigrants/immigrants already have quite some impact politically. Witness, for example, the Armenian diaspora in France, the Greek, or Cuban diaspora in the US; the Baltic diaspora in Canada; or the world-wide Tamil diaspora that affects policies towards Sri Lanka.

But this political clout of a diaspora is just one facet of a more common phenomenon: the weakening of ties that bind humans to a state; and to one state only.

Urbanisation – Modernisation

The increase (within two generations) of the world population from two to six billion brought more than a merely quantitative change. It also brought qualitative change as it altered the nature of human society and affected the political systems both on a global and on a national level. One such obvious change is urbanisation. The vision of a world population of presently 6 billion tends to conjure up images of teeming villages. These images are misleading. Half of the world population is now urban.

Percentage of the urban population according to regions 1950-2015

	1950	1975	1995	2015
Africa	14,4	25,2	34,9	46,4
Asia	15,3	22,2	33,0	45,6
Latin America	41,4	61,2	73,4	79,9
Industr countries	54,9	69,9	74,9	80,0
World	29,7	37,8	45,3	54,4

Source: UNO, World Urbanisation Prospects: the 1996 revision, New York 1998

Urban living implies living closer together. It was thought that this would cause problems. Humans are "territorial animals". They were assumed to need, and fight for, undivided, physical territory[1]. Squeezing too many humans into too tight a space would run counter to this prime instinct and would cause discomfort and non-suppressible aggression. But evidently this prediction has not come true. Humans seem to like cities. Otherwise they would not choose to live in them. They seem to prefer the comforts of togetherness to the satisfaction of lording over a vast piece of empty land.[2]

1 The instinct evidently lies at the root of the general preference for individual houses, surrounded by (mostly useless) green space.

2 This is not to imply that mega-cities would not pose special problems that are difficult and costly to remedy. Such difficulties arise in the realm of transportation, pollution or waste-removal.

In the 19th century, urbanisation progressed rapidly in what was then called the "Civilised World". In the 20th century it was mainly the cities in the poorer countries that registered a prominent increase in population.

Development of the urban and of the rural population in wealthy and in poor countries
(in billion)

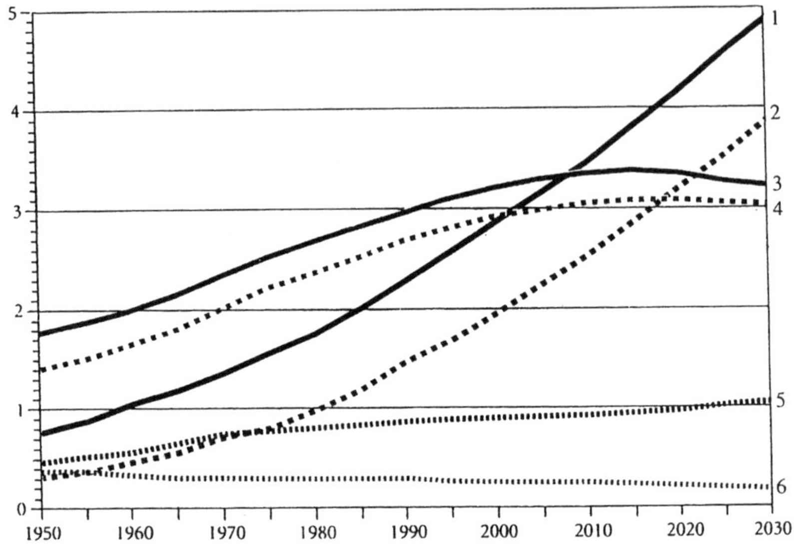

1 = urban population world – wide
2 = urban population in poor countries
3 = rural population world – wide
4 = rural population in poor countries
5 = urban population in wealthy countries
6 = rural population in wealthy countries

Source: UN Population Division 2000

At present, the urban population is growing at a moderate pace in the wealthy countries of the world; while their rural population is declining at a moderate pace. In the poorer countries, the rural population will still grow a bit till 2010; but already fifty years ago, the urban population in the poorer countries started to expand very rapidly. Somewhere around 2015, in these countries, too, the urban population will therefore surpass the rural population in its numbers.

Whilst cities in the poorer states are growing rapidly, the pace of this growth is not too different from the pace of urbanisation in the Europe or in the US of the last century, when industrialisation in these countries entered into the age of mass production and cities developed around the railroad hubs. But as these urban centres in the poorer countries are already very big at present; and bigger than the cities of Europe and the US were in the late 19th century, the population increase in absolute numbers will also be more sizeable; and in their mass these mega cities now dwarf the big urban agglomerations of 19th century Europe and North America. By 2000, not a single European city ranked among the megacities with more than 10 million inhabitants. Nearly all of these are located in what once had been called the "Third World".

Megacities of the world

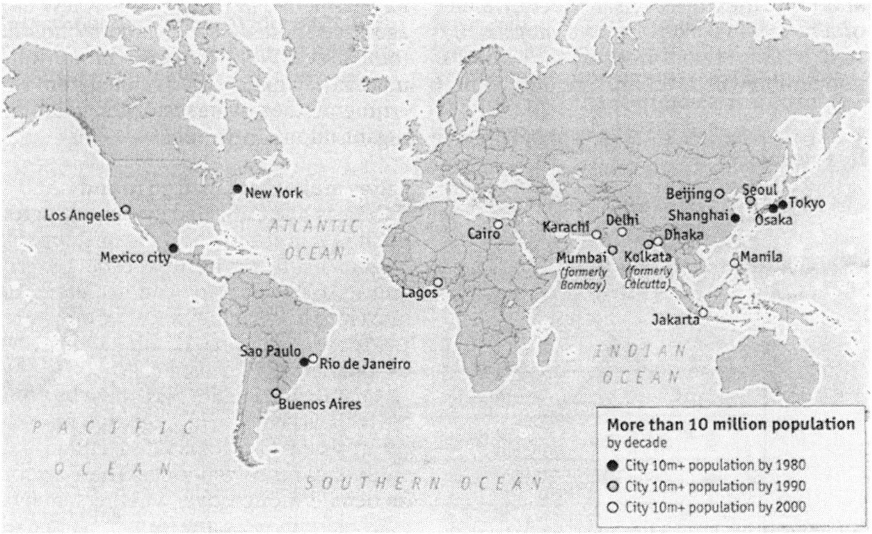

Source: UN-HABITAT

Ranking the world's cities according to the number of their inhabitants, one discovers that fascinating shifts have taken place over the centuries. Not a single truly "European city" can be found among those ten cities that had the most inhabitants a thousand years ago. We have returned to this state of affairs. But even those changes that have occurred just over the last hundred years are startling: comparing the list of 1800 with the list from 2000, we find that just two cities (Edo = Tokyo, and Peking) appear on both of them.

Population of the world's then biggest cities 1000, 1800, 1900 and 2000
(cities = urban agglomerations; in million)

1000	*1800*	*1900*	*2000*
Cordoba 0.45	Beijing 1.10	London 6.5	Tokyo 28.0
Kaifeng 0.40	London 0.86	New York 4.2	Mexico City 18.1
Constantinople 0.30	Canton 0.80	Paris 3.3	Bombay 18.0
Angkor 0.20	Edo 0.69	Berlin 2.7	São Paolo 17.7
Kyoto 0.18	Constantinople 0.57	Chicago 1.7	New York 16.6
Cairo 0.14	Paris 0.55	Vienna 1.7	Shanghai 14.2
Baghdad 0.13	Naples 0.43	Tokyo 1.5	Lagos 13.5
Nishapore 0.13	Hangchow 0.39	St. Petersburg 1.4	Los Angeles 13.1
Hasa 0.11	Osaka 0.38	Manchester 1.4	Seoul 12.9
Anhilveda 0.10	Kyoto 0.38	Philadelphia 1.4	Beijing 12.4

Edo = old name of Tokyo

Source: 1000-1900: Tertius Chandler, Four Thousand Years of Urban Growth: A Historical Census (Lewiston. NY: Edwin Mellen Press, 1987); 2000 from UN World Urbanisation Projects, The 1996 Revision (New York 1998)

But contrary to wide-spread belief, even in the poorer countries mega cities will not be the ones to grow fastest. Most of the increase in urban population will be in smaller cities with populations of less than 500.000 inhabitants.

Population growth in cities of various sizes
(5-year increases in %)

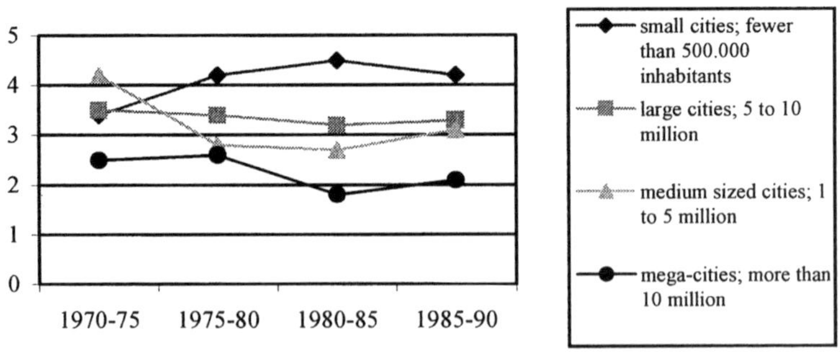

Source: Habitat 2002

In fact, already now, most of the world's urban population lives in cities with less than 500.000 inhabitants.

World urban population according to the size of their cities
(in percentages of the whole world urban population)

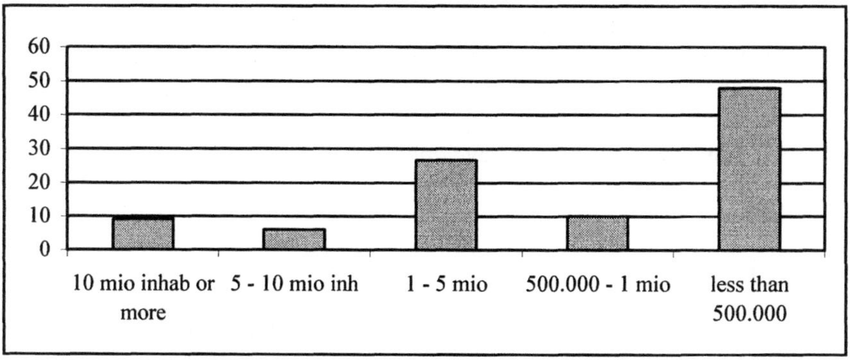

Source: Habitat 2002

Environmental health, welfare, and living conditions

	City product category			
Indicator	**Low**	**Lower-middle**	**Upper-middle**	**High**
Household connections (percent)	48,0	78,8	92,9	99,9
water	45,6	68,7	84,3	99,9
sewerage	45,6	93,6	95,0	100,0
electricity	72,3	93,6	95,0	100,0
Water consumption	88	181	232	247
liters per person per day in all settlements				
Wastewater treated percent treated	29,4	58,7	68,2	97,4
Solid waste disposal (percent) sanitary landfill or incinersted	30,7	41,4	37,5	77,7
other (open dump, recycled, burned)	85,9	58,9	62,2	22,3
Under-five mortality per 1,000	104,2	39,7	25,8	6,2
Households below the locally defined powerty line (percent)	31,7	23,2	16,0	6,9
Sample size (cities)	49	36	25	20

Source: UN-habitat Global Urban Indicators Database 1998

Per capita of inhabitant, very big cities are more expensive to run than smaller cities. But even on big cities, some basic urban services can be provided at relatively low costs. "Graduating" in the ranking from "poor" to "low middle income" (that is from a per capita GDP of less than 750 US$ to a per capita GDP of between 751 to 2.499 US$) implies that instead of just half, a full 80% of a city's population might be provided with access to safe water.

Nonetheless, the quality of urban life is closely related to a country's income. The "city development index" (put together by UN Habitat) closely relates to the UNDP-"Human Development Index" which, as we shall see, is again closely related to average national income.[3]

City development versus human development

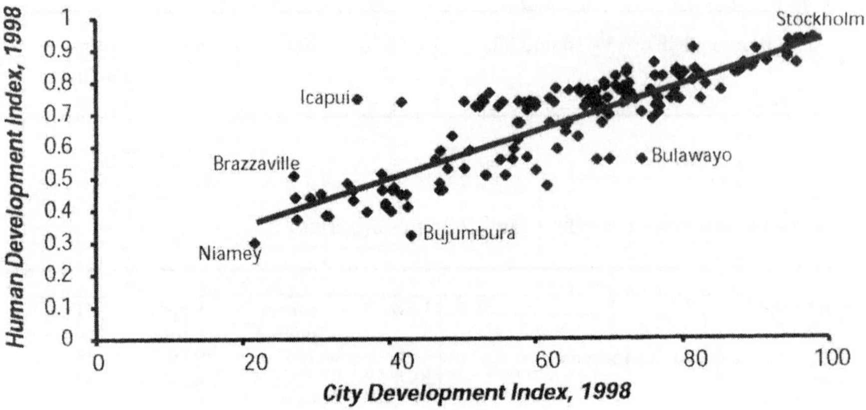

The change from a preponderantly rural to a preponderantly urban society has a profound impact upon individuals, families, nations. It also impacts heavily upon the global systems. Farmers, and especially subsistence farmers, do not participate very much in an economy based upon a division and a specialisation of tasks. Their existence is dependent upon, and is given shape and meaning by, reliance on and intercourse within a narrow group. In urban surroundings, on the contrary, they will come to depend upon many more, and frequently faraway, persons and institutions. They will become connected to the national and the global polity and economy.

3 The correlation between quality of urban life and average wealth is, of course, not so tight as to not account for some deviations. In some cities, quality of urban life is worse than one would expect on the basis of average income; and in some – like Seoul or Hanoi – it is better.

Some believe that this change from a rural environment to an urban one is a change for the worse. And indeed, many have always been uneasy about cities. They have portrayed cities as cesspools, as havens of vice, as parasites on the sound rural body of the "Volk". This anti-urban instinct is part of the political folklore the world over. But evidence does not support such "reactionary" pessimism. On the contrary, those living in cities are healthier, wealthier, more productive, better educated, more open and communicative.[4] In short, they lead better lives, on the average, than those still living in rural surroundings.

Of course, the "on the average" implies just that. In fact, within the big cities, living conditions can vary dramatically. Infant mortality – a clear sign of stark deprivation – is four times higher among the poor than among the wealthy inhabitants of the same cities in India, Turkey, and Egypt.

High inequality in infant mortality in urban areas

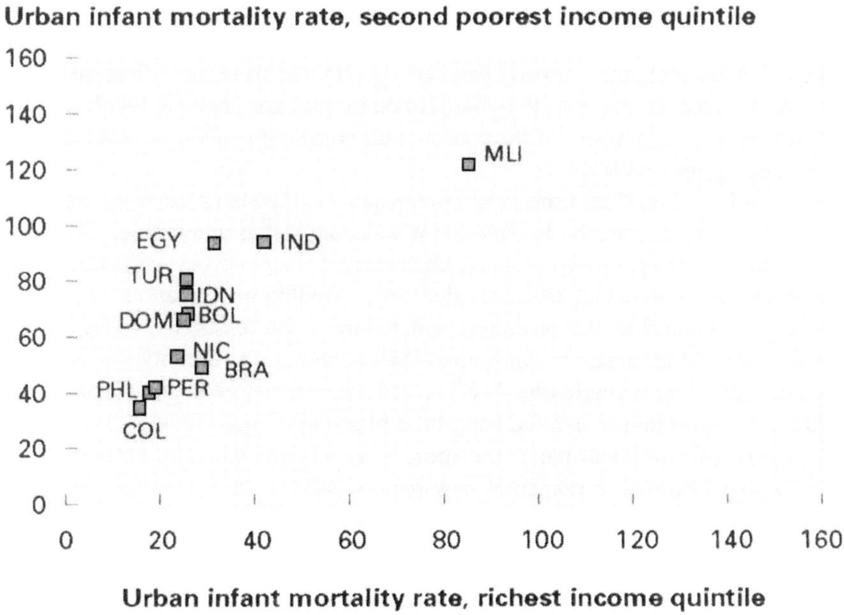

Source: World Development Report 2003

---

4 This is a judgement on the **average** of urban dwellers. This average should not obscure the dismal living conditions in some of the urban slums with living and social conditions even worse than those of the rural proletariat.

Notwithstanding such abject poverty as it prevails in urban slums, those are still misguided who glorify and romanticise village life. Evidently, they have never lived it in these self-enclosed quarters themselves. They have not experienced its stultifying, petty oppression, its claustrophobia, its sheer hopelessness and lack of perspective. Urbanisation offers an escape. It is part of the process of modernisation; and the essential ingredient of this modernisation is the gradual loosening of humans from the bondages of rigid ties and unilateral dependency.

Modernisation and Countertrends

"Modernisation" is an ill – defined notion. It could denote, and was perhaps sometimes intended to denote, a process that would lead nations all over the world to ultimately resemble the most modern nation – which was conveniently assumed to be the United States. According to the now prevailing definition, however, "modernisation" is meant to denote a process in which personal bonds and human identities become diversified. Citizens emancipate from the exclusive identification with one – mostly smaller – group and from identification with just one social role. In the end, they participate in, and are identified with, a number of different groups, some of them even with conflicting aims; some of them with overlapping membership.

Once in pre-modern times and circumstances, the status, identity, and role of an individual was strictly defined and it was considered immutable. The place in the village pecking order remained unchanged for succeeding generations of the same family. The rituals that provided order, rhythm and meaning remained the same over centuries: the weddings and funerals, the feasts, the religious observances; etc. Modernisation cut humans loose from such certainty. Several identities substitute for a single one. Social roles might be adopted and discarded. Suddenly one is no longer just the son of the blacksmith, but a student of mechanics, a member of a political party, the spouse of someone who has been selected by one's own free will, a reader of newspapers, etc. To deal with the ensuing tensions between such differing roles and identities, the principles of rationality and tolerance have to be internalised. Society is transformed in this process. Science takes the place of belief. Interest replaces vision. The relative replaces the absolute.

Norbert Elias defined this process as the essence of "civilisation"[5]. To him, the process seemed both benign and inevitable as it provides humans with the wherewithal for expanding experience and for free rational choice. Nonetheless, at all times, this process prompted more opposition than support. For, in the long run, the process of modernisation might very well be experienced as something liberating. But in the meantime, the process is also deeply unsettling as most humans do not relish freedom as much as they cherish routine and security.

Escaping the pettiness of villages enhances the scope of choice and freedom. But this gain implies, at the same time, a loss of certainty. This is a painful and disorienting experience. People are cut loose and have to redefine their lives and social roles. When losing the certainty of old bonds and beliefs, humans are therefore tempted to look for "Ersatz-Villages" that could regain for them what has been lost. Narrow nationalism is one of these remedies. Nationalism substitutes for the lost, close community of the village which is replaced by an "imagined" community, by the fictional community of the nation. The fictionality or artificiality of this construct creates problems. Nationalism encourages citizens to all feel part of one big family. Actually though, one member of this family knows very little about the other members, and – were he or she to know them – he or she would perhaps not be enchanted by this acquaintance. Personal interests will also diverge widely in this fictive family or fictive village. Special efforts are therefore necessary in order to maintain the fiction of closeness and communality so as to hold this fictive village or family together. History is being interpreted in a way so as to create and sustain the notion that historic fate has welded the inhabitants of a state into a true community that always has been and always will be united to face the "*slings and arrows of outrageous fate*". Frequently this coherence is sought by a proven expedient. It is done by finding and picturing the outsider, the alien.

By necessity, each group that wishes to establish itself more permanently must draw a line between insiders and outsiders. These efforts are, however, especially noxious if undertaken with the intent of creating and defining a nation. In this case, more often than not, the outsider becomes the enemy. In fact, most modern nations have defined themselves against the "enemy alien". The French have defined themselves against the English; the Germans against the French; the Americans against the British; the Italians against the Pope and against the Austrians; etc.

---

5 And the theologian Teilhard de Chardin saw in it even the realisation of a divine plan of human liberation and redemption with individuals gaining ever more freedom in their moral choices.

The option for the Ersatz-Village of nationalism, the option of tempering the shock of modernisation by seeking shelter in the fictive community of a nation thus comes at a price. It is the price of hostility towards outsiders and the price of intolerance towards those insiders that do not conform to the picture book image of national identity.

Political mass parties as they have emerged in the last half of the 19th century have provided another sort of “Ersatz-Village”. The theory of “modernisation” would make us believe that we are now about to exit from this phase of politics. Nationalism and mass parties have just tempered but not thwarted the trend to “modernisation”. In the end, citizens have become truly “modernised”. They would have learned to feel comfortable with multiple identities and ever changing roles. They no longer need the crutches of support provided by either nationalism or by mass parties.

Or this, at least, had been the standard interpretation provided by social science until quite recently. But does it still hold? Will modernisation indeed prevail? Or should we expect new counter movements against rationality and modernisation as they find expression in

- identity politics,
- a surge of fundamental religion,
- a matter-of-fact acceptance of irrationality (New Wave in California),
- the xenophobia of populist parties, etc

We shall return to these urgent questions at several instances. But we should retain that, notwithstanding modernisation, the need for identity and security is primeval. This need and yearning might be scoffed at by persons of high rank who feel secure in their elevated place in society. Their wealth and social status cushions them against the vagaries of continuous change and disruption that are inherent in any modern economy. They thus are amply supplied with what is in short supply with persons in a lower station of life and in poorer conditions.

Clearly, the need for security and belonging has to be met in any social order that aspires to permanence and peace. Walls of ancient cities have stood as symbols for this kind of continuity and security. Today’s cities should not be mistaken for mere shelters either. They will also have to provide a sense of security and continuity. They have to provide a “home”[6].

What about the future of cities and about the future geographic pattern of human settlement? In the more advanced countries, mega-cities have ceased to

6 The fact that more than 10% of the US population lives in trailer parks might therefore bode ill for the future of the US.

grow. In those countries, the population first moved to suburbs (suburbanisation), and later on into smaller cities and towns that lie close to one another and form vast regions of high population-density (as for example in the German Ruhrvalley or the US Boston-Washington corridor). Peripheral spaces continue to thin out. Sooner or later, this pattern is likely to come to prevail in all parts of the world.

But does the world hold enough resources to accommodate a population that will at least double before ceasing to grow any further; that will be wealthier; and which will live in cities that are expensive to maintain? At first sight, doubts on that seem well founded, especially if one were to assume that all of the future generations, in all countries of the world, would consume as much raw materials as do the citizens of the presently wealthy countries. Seven times as much minerals would be consumed if each citizen of the world used as much of them as a citizen of the US.

How much more raw materials would be necessary if each citizen of the world used as much of them as a citizen of the US

Raw materials	Increase in present production that would be necessary
minerals	7 times the present output
metals	2 times
wood-products	5 times
synthetics	11 times
total	6 times

Source: Grecia Matos, USGS Reston, 1998

It thus seemed reasonable to doubt whether the output of raw materials could keep up with the expected increase in the world's population and wealth. Sooner or later the planet would run out of some essential raw materials. And indeed, this was a prediction that was made in the early 70's by the Club of Rome. But even before disappearing altogether from the world markets, as had been predicted by the Club of Rome, rising demand for raw materials would meet a declining supply. Necessarily, thus, the predictions of the Club of Rome imply a stark rise in the price of raw materials. Necessarily, such a rise should also have happened in the past, as, in the past demand for raw material had already risen rapidly. But this is not what we observe.

According to the price index of the British "Economist", real prices of industrial raw materials have declined by 80% over the last 150 years. The trend has not been broken in the recent past. It even has become more pronounced.

Economist's industrial price index 1840-2000 (real prices of items like rubber, aluminium, timber, cotton, etc.)

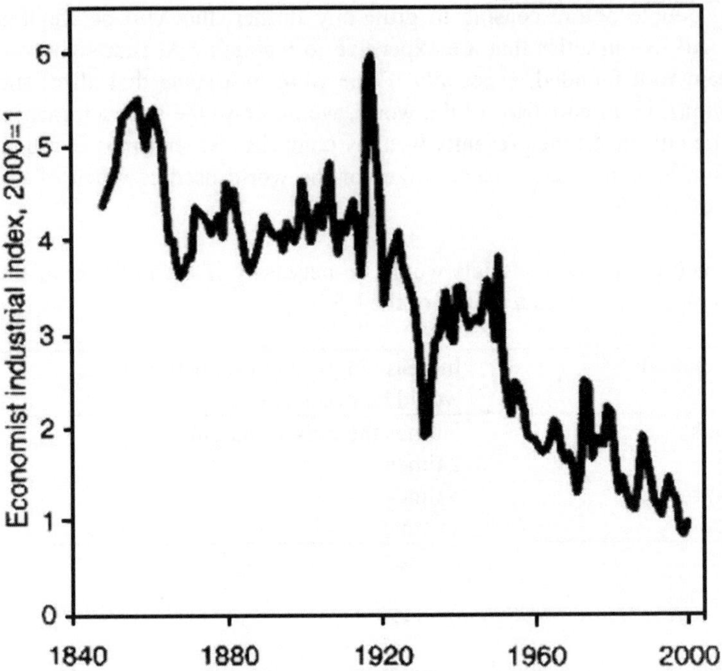

Source: Economist

That holds true also for the most basic of all raw materials – namely for staple food. Though the world population has grown at an accelerated pace since 1820, food has not become more expensive.

Starting from the beginning of the 19th century, that is, starting with the full onset of the industrial revolution, in the United Kingdom the real price of wheat has fallen steadily. It did so even in a period in the mid 19th century when the British population grew rapidly. Today the UK real price of wheat is an insignificant fraction of what it was 200 years ago. On the – very big – scale we use in the graph below, it does not even register properly.

Wheat price in Great Britain, 1316-1999
(1999 British Pound per ton, real prices adjusted by the US deflator)

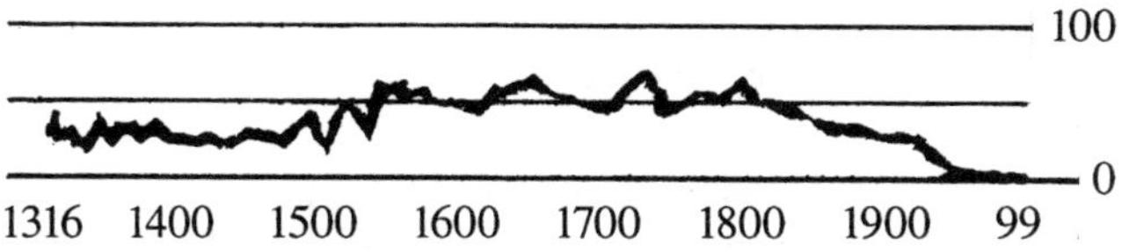

Source: Mitchell B., British Historical Statistics, UK Ministry of Agriculture, 1999

Three hundred years ago one thought that agriculture would be the key to, and the only true source of, wealth ("physiocrats"). Today such claim would strike us as being scurrilous. Regions in wealthy countries that rely on agriculture exclusively (as do, for instance, many of the US Plains States), suffer impoverishment and an exodus of their population. The back-sliding of formerly wealthy Argentina in the first half of the 20th century, and the decline of New Zealand in the second half, are examples of the declining fortunes of the exporters of agricultural raw materials.

In the above graph another thing catches our attention and calls for comment. The line leading up to 1800 is very jagged. Till then, real prices of wheat were subject to violent swings (reflecting alternating scarcity and abundance on the British isles). Since 1800, the line has been basically smooth. The wheat market became integrated world wide and thus was no longer affected by the swings in production of just one single country (brought about, for instance, by local draught). World trade in cereals has created a better balance between demand and supply. Local famines have thus disappeared – at least in most of the countries and certainly in all wealthier ones.

> Real prices of raw materials and of agricultural commodities are in long-term decline. In the very short term though, these prices may be subject to sudden and drastic swings. While these swings do not affect the long term trend, they are particularly severe on countries that still have to rely on the export of just one, or just a few of such raw materials.
>
> International commodity price agreements and funds are intended to control and stabilise the international market price of certain widely used raw materials and commodities, like wheat, tin, copper, oil, cocoa, etc. However, meeting this goal is difficult. At their best, such arrangements may smoothen out minor and short term perturbations. But, in doing so, they have to keep an eye on the long term downward trend of commodity prices. At the risk of oth-

erwise resulting in failure, all such arrangements have to accommodate these long term trends. They cannot fight them. This also holds true for the CAP (Common Agricultural Policy) of the European Union. The EU and European farmers also have to accept and adjust to the obviously inevitable downward trend in the price of agricultural products.

These are, at least, the lessons of the past. But is it truly legitimate to rely upon them and to project into the future the trends of the last hundred years? Or might we not have passed a turning point? Could it be, for example, that we have already reached the limits of further expansion in agricultural production? Could it be that the world population will be thus worse fed in the future?

This is not simply a question of calories; but a question also of diet. It might perhaps be possible, it is argued, to maintain the present level of per capita caloric intake.[1] But it clearly would not be possible to maintain the present diet with its high meat consumption. It would be even less possible to extend the consumption patterns of Western countries (with their proclivity for expensive meat) to the rapidly growing population of the rest of the world. As they escape poverty, people desire to eat more meat. The animals slaughtered to provide it are avid consumers of cereals. But they are not very efficient in transforming their feed into meat. Three to five pounds of cereal chicken feed translate into just one pound of chicken[2] meat. Demand for cereals would thus not simply rise in parallel with the growing world population. It would rise much faster as the world wide demand for meat would increase and, with it, the demand for cereals to feed all those animals that humans would like to slaughter and eat. At present, 38% of grain crop is being fed to animals. This percentage rate is bound to go up.

And indeed, the world production of cereals has grown continuously since 1950. In fact, production has increased fourfold in a period of just 50 years. Production per capita, that is, world production divided by the world's population, has also grown.[3]

---

1 It just takes 700 square meters to grow a sufficient vegetarian diet for one person – and that without any artificial chemical inputs (State of the World Population 2001).

2 Still, chickens are more efficient converters of feed into meat than other animals (as for instance cattle or pigs) .

3 Nonetheless, a troubling message seems hidden in the following, right hand graph on the per capita world food production. For the last twenty years it has tended to stagnate. Evidently, this cannot be due to lagging demand which we assume rises together with rising incomes and with the wish to consume more meat. Does this more recent development in the last 20 years bode ill for the long-term future? Does it signal a reversal of a long-term trend? Such a reversal is not likely. The reasons for the 20-year stagnation in the per capita consumption of cereals are short-term ones only. It was caused, for example, by the decline of agricultural production in the Commu-

World cereal production
(in mio tons)

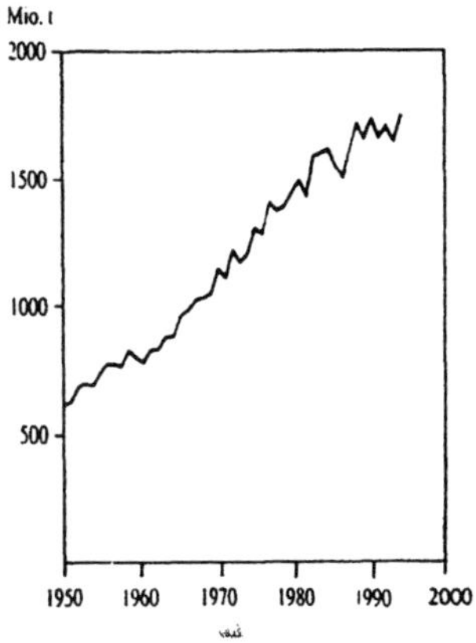

Per capita world cereal production
(in kg)

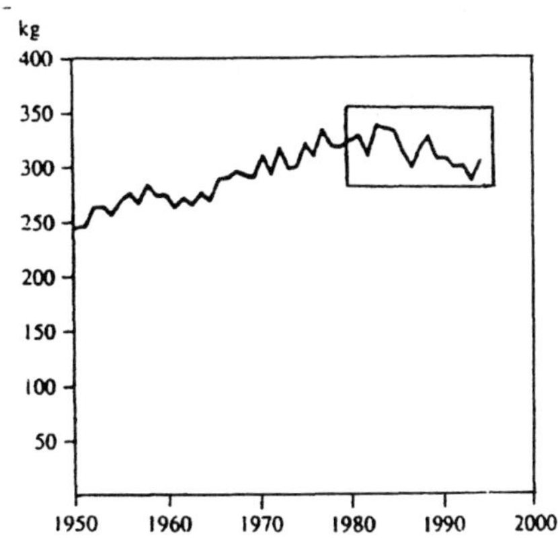

Source: International Food Policy Research Institute

World cereal production per hectare

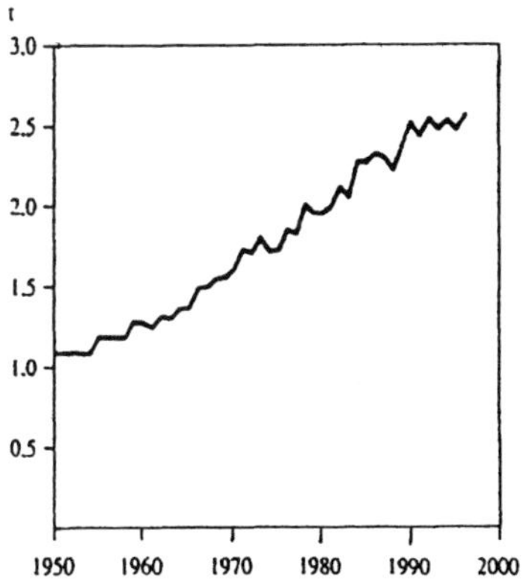

World agriculturally used surface and fertiliser use per capita

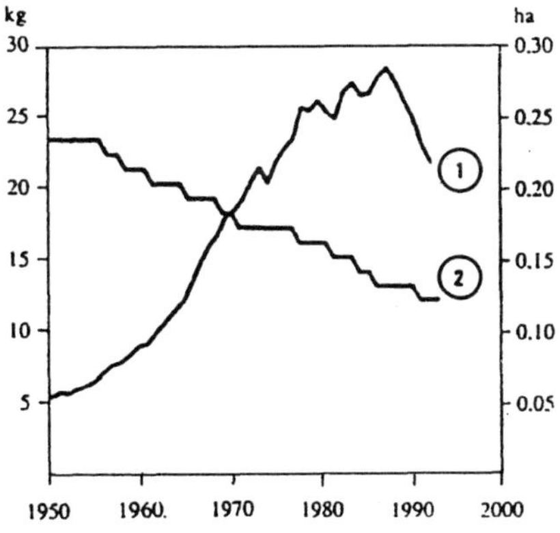

1 = fertiliser consumption
2 = agricultural surface

Source: International Food Policy Research Institute

---

nist and the post-Communist countries; and by changes in EU-agricultural policies that put a premium on letting fields lay fallow.

The increase in world cereal production came about through a dramatic increase in per hectare yields. And it came about in spite of the fact that the agricultural surface available per capita of the world population shrunk; and it came about in spite of the reduced application of fertilisers.

There still seems to be ample space for a further rise in the per hectare output. In Sub–Sahara Africa it is at a mere fifth of that in the United States (while among the wealthy countries, hectare yields seem to converge).

Cereal yields
(tonnes per hectare)

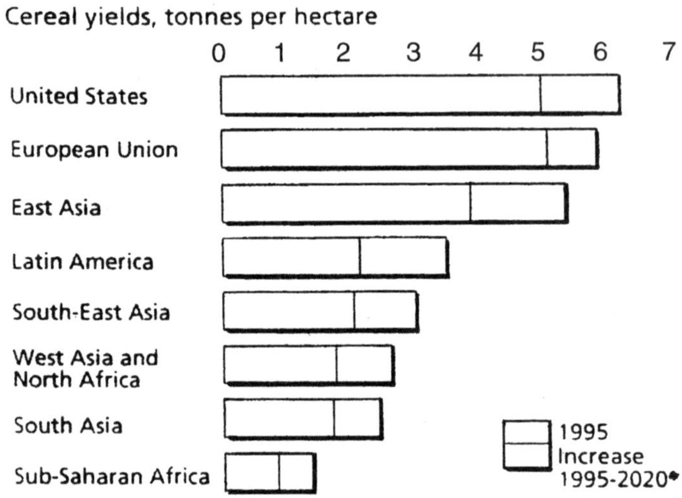

Source: International Food Policy Research Institute

Over and above that, there is still much land that is suitable for agriculture but that is not being used for that purpose. The biggest such resources are located in Latin America and Sub-Saharan Africa. On the other hand, no such reserves exist in South Asia. There, on the contrary, much land is being used in an unsustainable way. Some of it has even been lost for agricultural production by over-use, unsuitable practice or through urbanisation. Even so, world-wide, the reserves of land that could be used for agriculture are still bigger by far than the land lost or endangered by unsustainable exploitation.

Availability of crop land
(million hectares)

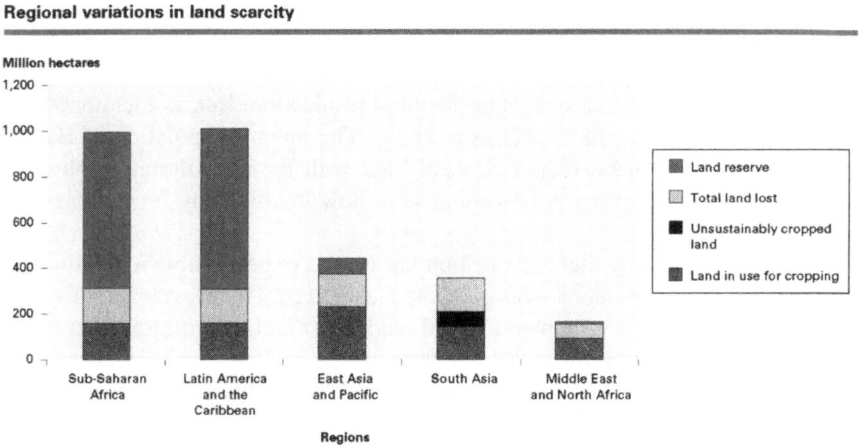

Source: IBSRAM (International Board for Social Research and Management) 2001

Optimism over these ample reserves of agricultural land needs to be tempered though. First, such reserves do not exist for some of the poorer parts of the world (especially South Asia). Second, in both Latin America and Sub-Saharan Africa, the full use of such reserves might not be feasible due to environmental constraints (such as the need to preserve at least a part of the forest cover).[4] Finally, the high percentage of land having become overused or unusable in the Middle East or South Asia points to the dangers of desertification or of other dire results of unsustainable exploitation. Many of these consequences are impossible to reverse later on. That implies the permanent loss of ecological and agricultural assets.

But – again as seen on a global level and in terms of world-wide averages – the world-wide agricultural surface would not have to be expanded in order to accommodate the growing food demand of a growing world population. Basically these needs could be covered by simply increasing hectare yields.

4 In my home country – Austria – ecological problems are not caused by rising demand and rising prices for agricultural products; but by their decline. They have, inter alia, caused alpine pastures to be abandoned; and hedges and orchards to be uprooted and ploughed under.

Overall, and on the world-wide average, lack of agricultural surface therefore should not become a major bottleneck on the course of a further rise in agricultural production. According to a study done by the International Institute of Applied Systems Analysis (IIASA), such a bottleneck could, however, come to exist in some few, very poor and at the same time very populous countries – as, for instance, Bangladesh. There, scarcity of suitable land could indeed become the strategic limit to an expansion of agricultural production. But, as mentioned, this does not hold true for the world as a whole. The hungry population of Bangladesh and of other places could be easily fed with the agricultural surpluses of other countries (the question remaining as to how it would pay for the import of the needed foodstuff).

This is not to imply that malnutrition has ceased to be a problem. It still is one for the 800 million persons who go hungry each day. The persistence of hunger in a world of plenty is a human, a moral, and also a political disaster that cannot be excused or explained away. Nonetheless, we do have to appreciate that malnutrition has receded over the last decade not only in relative but also in absolute terms.

Number and percentage of malnourished people 1990-92 and 1996-98

	East Asia	*Latin America and the Caribbean*	*Near East/ North Africa*	*South Asia*	*Sub-Saharan Africa*	*Developing World*
Number of malnourished (millions)						
1990-92	283	59	25	299	162	828
1996-98	181	55	36	294	186	792
Percent malnourished						
1990-92	17	13	8	27	35	21
1996-98	12	11	10	23	34	18

Source: FAO The State of Food Insecurity in the World, Rome 2000

The persistence of hunger among more than 10 percent of the world's population cannot be ascribed to unavoidable fate. As we have seen, it is not due to the fact that global agricultural production has already reached the physical limits to any further expansion. The persistence of hunger is an outrage exactly because it is avoidable. It could be made to disappear by the proper political, institutional and economic remedies.

According to traditional economics and the theory of "comparative advantage", poorer countries were destined to be and remain the "natural" exporters of agricultural products; and industrial countries are destined to remain their main importers. But the comparative advantage in agricultural production has now shifted. Agricultural production has become very capital intensive.[5] Also, modern agriculture has come to rely on a complex network of suppliers and buyers which is difficult to establish in poor countries.

Therefore, not the poor but the wealthy countries have become the main exporters of basic agricultural products. This trend will continue. The pattern assumed as being "natural" by early economists will be reversed. Poor countries will concentrate increasingly on the production of (at first simple) industrial products. While the wealthier countries, with very extensive agriculture and vast (corporate) farms, will become the main suppliers of (staple) foodstuff.

Buyers and sellers, imports and exports 1995-2020
(in mio tonnes)

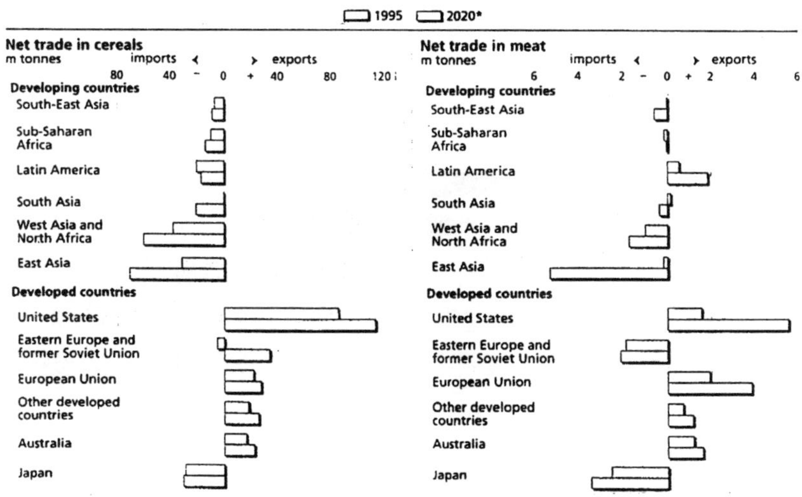

Source: International Food Policy Research Institute

Politics have always impacted upon agricultural production. We therefore have to assume that this will remain to be the case with agricultural production being determined not just by economic, but also by political constraints. Even

5 In Austria, for example, more in terms of machinery is invested in a single work place in agriculture than is invested in one workplace in industry (about 100.000 euro).

wealthy countries, with their agricultural surpluses and with their well-to-do consumers who spend but a small fraction of their income on food, cannot desist from political intervention in the agricultural markets. They subsidise agricultural production either via higher prices consumers have to pay; or directly from the state budget.

There are some purely tactical-political reasons for that. Agricultural lobbies are powerful everywhere (see the example of the US sugar cane growers). But there are more solid reasons, too, for this kind of intervention: having sufficient food reserves for times of crisis; avoidance of drastic changes in prices otherwise unavoidable in view of the inelasticity of supply and demand; maintaining the landscape; etc.) .

Farmer's subsidies as % of gross farm revenue

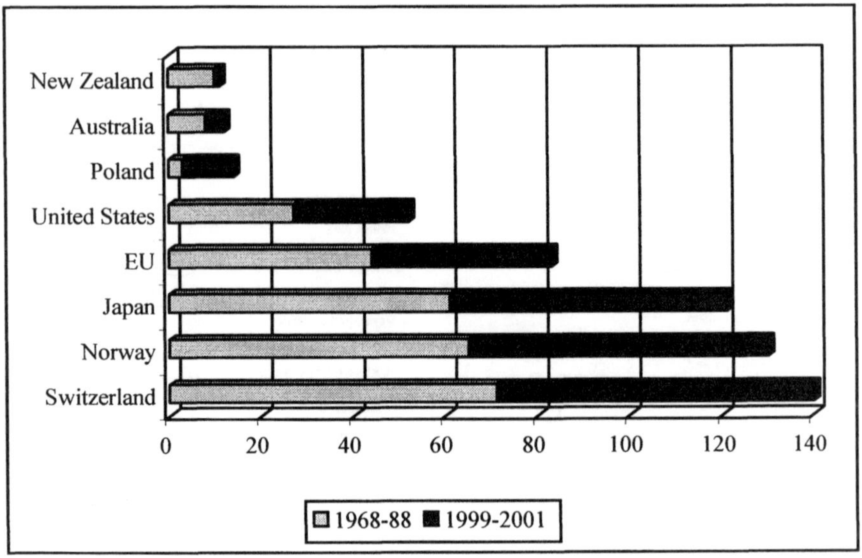

Source: OECD

As agricultural products are traded internationally, such political interventions do have an international aspect. Frequently, trade in agricultural products is shrouded in controversy and political conflict. This will remain so in the future and will thus continue to impact on global governance.

Agricultural production is not just affected by such politics; or just by the width of the surface available for growing food. It is also affected, and increasingly so, by irrigation – by the amount of water available for agricultural purposes.

World-wide water use

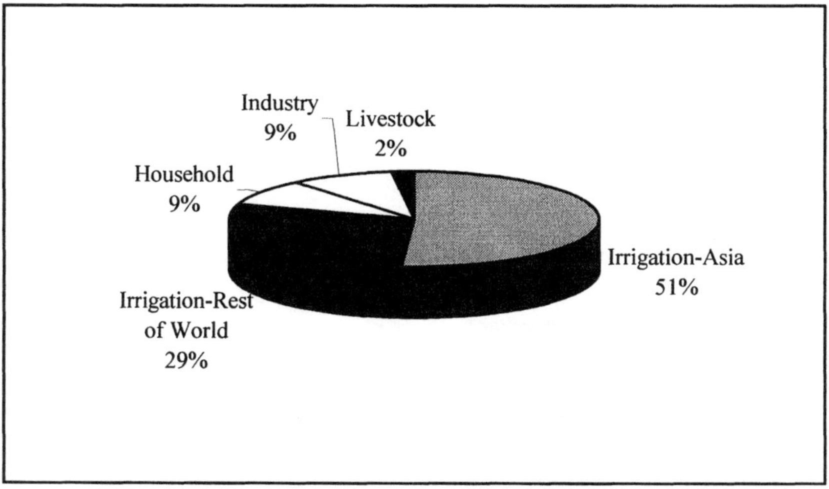

Source: Global Water Partnership

Agriculture is the major user of water. The area irrigated world-wide for agricultural purposes increased from 90 million to 250 million hectares between 1950 and 1993.

The growing use of water in agriculture has lead to some serious problems in some regions and countries: aquifiers have been depleted ("mining of water"); due to repeated flooding, salt has been washed up from below and the top soil has become encrusted with salt and is thus useless for agriculture; or groundwater has become polluted by nitric fertilisers. The problems are exacerbated by the fact that much of the irrigated surface is in the poor countries, with limited funds available to compensate for, and correct, the negative consequences of widely used irrigation. Unfortunately, poor countries are also disproportionally those where the problems of aridity are most troubling, and where, at the same time, few alternatives are available to agriculture as a source of income. Poor countries thus might not be able either to finance the progress to sounder irrigation technologies; nor to develop sufficient jobs in the industrial sector of the economy.

Global irrigated agricultural surface 1950-1993
(in mio hectares)

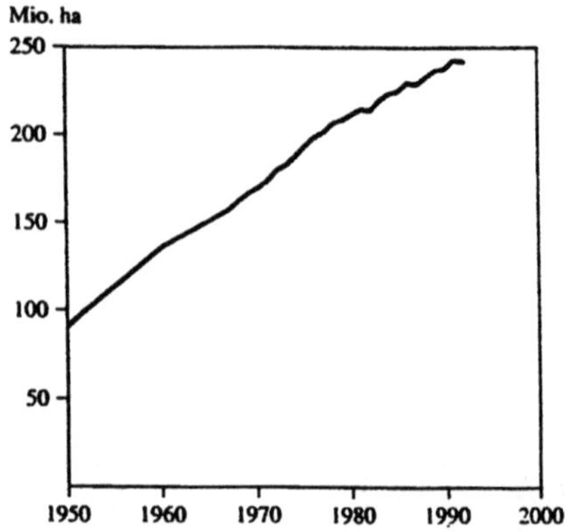

Source: US Department of Agriculture

Inevitably, such conflicting claims over scarce and/or under-priced resources like water do become political. If such conflicting claims arise over the same water resource but in different countries, they become issues in international relations and, frequently, sources of international contestation. Examples are the differences between Syria, Turkey and Iraq over the use of water from the Euphrates-Tigris twin rivers; or the conflicting claims of the Central Asian republics on the Oxos river.

> Water, water everywhere and not a drop to drink:
>
> Only 2,5% of the water on earth is sweet water; only 0,007 % is potentially usable by humans. This still would make for (renewable) sweet water reserves of 1.800 cubic metres per capita. Just one third of that volume would be consumed if every citizen of the world used as much water as his or her counterpart in a very wealthy country.
>
> That might lead to the optimistic conclusion that there is enough sweet water on earth for everyone. But such optimism is unfounded as these global figures hide serious problems which exist on a regional or local level. Fresh water is abundant in some parts of the world, most of which tend – at the same time – to be the wealthy ones in the temperate zones of the earth. And water is scarce in other, mainly poorer parts.

But shouldn't there be an evident solution to this problem? All one would have to do, we could surmise, is to divert water from the moist areas into the more arid ones. Unfortunately, that cannot be done on the large scale required. The vast financial resources and the technical means for such a large transfer are not – yet(?) – available. Neither do we have the political and other institutions that could manage such gigantic multinational projects. In fact, institutional and political hurdles frequently even prevent such transfer schemes from becoming operative within one single country.

Securing the water supply for a growing and increasingly wealthy population will thus become a serious issue. As it cannot be tackled on a global scale, it has to be dealt with on a more limited geographic scale and with the economic and political resources at hand. A realistic pricing of irrigation water is one of the tools which is already available. Many consumers, and especially the agricultural ones, do not pay the real (replacement) costs[6] of the water they use. These costs are "externalised" and paid for by the public. This can happen through tax money being used for the construction of reservoirs, dams, canals, and pipelines. Or the public might be forced to pay by shouldering the high cost of water scarcity that falls upon the society as such.

Raising the price of water to the level of replacement costs would limit its use to where it is most needed and productive. Modern technology too can, by now, reduce the amount of water used for irrigation. Modern water saving technology (drip irrigation) could reduce the wasteful irrigation by flooding. It also would be less damaging environmentally than traditional methods of irrigation. There is still ample room for a broader application of this technology.

But even with such economic and technological innovations, some places on earth (especially Northern and Eastern Africa, the Middle East and Central Asia, the Western Plain States of the US, and Northern China) would still face water shortages in the not too distant future. Desalination seems to offer a way around this problem. Due to an evolution of technology, the price for desalinated water has fallen. But costs still are too high to permit desalinated water being used in agriculture. It is still too high by half even for use in urban consumption.[7] A crucial component of the price of desalinated water is the price of energy (which is being used amply even in the more modern and less energy intensive process of

6 The replacement costs are particularly high with the depletion of the so-called paleontological acquifiers (in for example Saudi-Arabia or Western China). These are, to a large extent, non-renewable resources. Water there is being "mined" at an alarming rate. In Northern China the water table under the wheat producing areas is falling at a rate of five feet per year.

7 This is for the world average. In certain places, with difficult access to other sources of sweet water, desalination has by now become competitive.

desalination by osmosis). Were the real price of energy to fall further, desalination might add substantially to the water supply. But, as we shall argue, such a decline in the real price of energy is not likely to come about.

The growing scarcity of water is therefore bound to raise its price. This will create and /or accentuate distributional problems. The rich and the rich countries will have few difficulties in paying these higher prices and, thus, to maintain and increase their consumption of water. The poor and the poorer countries will be constrained to limit their consumption. And – as we have seen – it is mainly in the poor countries that the problems of water stress and water scarcity will become most acute. In some of the poor countries, water scarcity will thus become a hurdle on the path of economic development. As we have seen, water scarcity will also feed tensions between some water scarce countries and their neighbours. Nonetheless and overall, scarcity and the rising price of water will not become an insurmountable barrier on the way to overall future economic development.

As households consume only 9 percent of all water used, the insufficient supply of water is not the main obstacle in meeting the needs of households. The problem is one of financing, building and maintaining the distribution networks. Providing potable, clean water to all is a prime task, not least because it is the most efficient tool to combat early death. Success in this task would prevent half a billion persons from becoming seriously ill each year.[8] Unfortunately, not much progress seems to have been made on this front in recent years.

Population with access to an improved water source

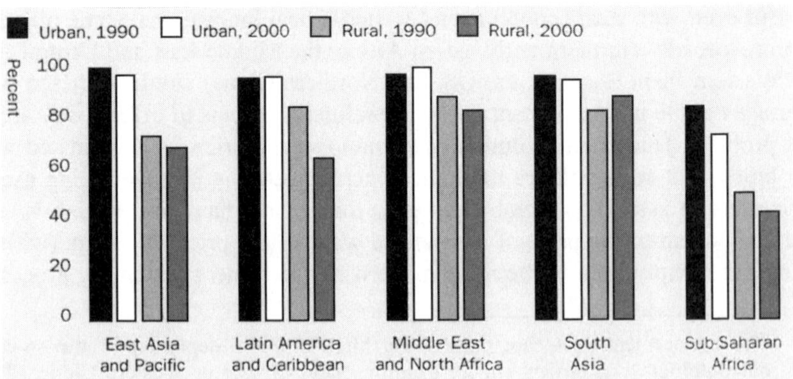

Source: WHO and Wolrd Bank staff estimates

8 World Bank 1992

What general conclusions can be drawn then on the future supply of raw materials, food, and water, and on how this supply will impact upon the global system?

Contrary to predictions, scarcity of raw materials does not present a hurdle to future growth of global wealth. Scarcity of raw materials will not impede the elimination of poverty. Nor will prosperity become threatened by a long-term rise in the prices of raw materials. On the contrary, some problems may arise from the obviously inevitable long-term decline of these prices.[9]

Looking at global figures and on world averages, we have found little to sustain the Malthusian notion of a growing world population running out of food. Ample supplies of arable land are untapped yet. But even if one were not to use them, the possible increase in hectare yields on existing arable surfaces would be sufficient to feed a growing world population and to feed it sufficiently well.

These global figures do, however, hide grievous regional or national problems. The possibility of extending hectare yields (or agricultural surface) are limited in many of those countries that register a high population growth, and that, until now, have not managed to create sufficient non-agriculture jobs. One of the consequences is a rise in (mostly subsistence) farming in marginal lands, which may damage these lands to the extent that these surfaces become not just useless but even major environmental problems.

Climate change and water scarcity accentuate these problems. Water scarcity will restrain the further expansion of irrigated agriculture. Some of the poorest countries, which rely upon irrigation, will be affected most negatively. The change in the world's climate due to global warming will heighten such difficulties. Climate change will also deepen the problems of water scarcity in already arid states. Some of them, as the US Plains States or South European Mediterranean countries, are wealthy. Most are not. Agricultural yields will thus rise in the temperate zones; and drought problems will increase in some of the subtropical and tropical regions. Desertification will, for example, progress in the Sahel-Zone of Sub-Saharan Africa.

Due to these developments and due to progress in agricultural productivity even in poor countries, millions will lose their traditional economic base in agriculture. Large scale migrations have solved similar problems in the past. But if "globalisation" has made it easier for goods, services and capital to cross national borders, it has not done the same for labour and migrants. On the contrary, the barriers have become higher. The bridges between the realms of wealth and the

9 It is in the interest of both consumers and producers that this be a smooth process with wild swings in prices being evened out to the extent possible. But – as experience has shown – this is a feat difficult to achieve.

realms of poverty have become more fragile; and hopes of ever crossing them more distant.

Poor tropical and subtropical countries might retain the edge in a few fields of agricultural production like cocoa, rare fruits and vegetables, spices, cut flowers, etc. But basic foodstuffs like wheat, corn, soy, beef, milk powder will increasingly come from the already wealthy countries which will be able to add the advantage of more efficient agricultural production to the existing advantage in high value-added industrial production and in high value services.

Notwithstanding a growing per capita food production, the problem of hunger (euphemistically termed: "under-nourishment") does persist at an intolerably vast scale of nearly 800 million. As mentioned, hunger exists not because not enough food is available world-wide. Hunger among those 800 million is due to this food not being distributed justly and efficiently on both the national and on the international levels. Starvation is the result not of absolute scarcity, but of poverty and bad governance.

Just as in the realm of food, in the realm of water, too, absolute scarcity is not the real issue. Overall, there is enough water to even meet the demand of all poor persons were they to consume the same amount as persons living in the rich parts of the world. The problem is that the water is not in the places that need it most urgently. And where it will become technologically feasible to make it available[10], it will become available at steeply rising costs only.

Some of the solutions to tackle water stress and water scarcity need to involve more than one country. They thus call for intra-regional co-operation. This might result in a joint definition of common interest and in co-operation between adjoining nations. But this might also have the opposite effect of fanning conflict. Many have predicted that this latter consequence would be the more likely one. But this dire prediction has not been born out until now. Conflicting claims over water have not – yet – figured as the prime cause of violent conflict.

10 In some places of the world – e.g. in South Africa – the scarcity of water will be technological indeed. This implies that no more water would become available even if its price were increased. In most other water problem countries, economic solutions are feasible with more water becoming available at a higher price.

Oil and Other Sources of Primary Energy

The rise in the world's wealth, in the world's per capita production, calls for older technology being replaced again and again by newer technology. But this growth also depends upon another input: on the use of energy. Technological and economic progress would not have been possible had it not been supported by a growing use of energy.

World supply of energy 1750-2000
(in Exajoule = 10^{18} Joule)

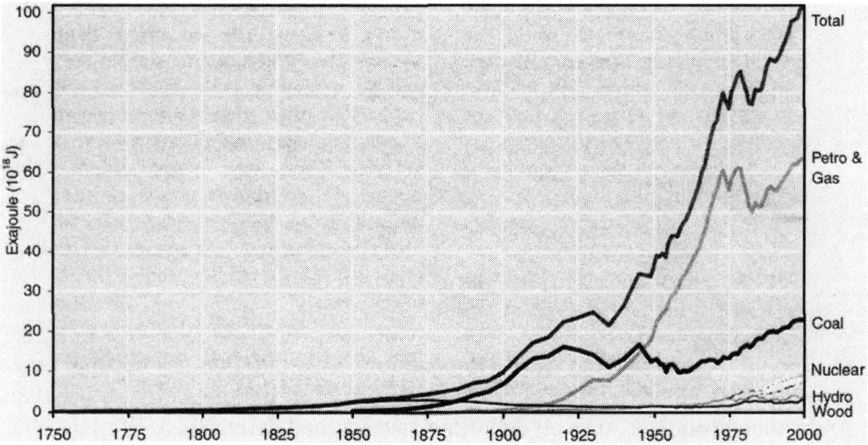

Source: Energy Information Administration 2000

Originally, and when emerging from the African savannahs, homo sapiens had at its disposal nothing but his own muscle power. The muscle power of draught animals was added in the late Neolithic age. Then, later still, came the power of water mills, of windmills and the power of sails to drive ships. In the production of heat, wood was replaced or supplemented, first by charcoal and peat, and then, since the Middle Ages, by coal. The steam engine came in the late 18th century, followed by the steam turbine and, shortly thereafter, by the electric motor and by the internal combustion engine. Oil started to supplement coal at the end of the 19th century and natural gas made a powerful entry later on and now is the source of primary energy – the use of which is expanding most rapidly.

If measured against what it costs to maintain one human being (one "human power" muscle engine) the price of energy has dropped continuously. The real price of energy thus has followed a trend that can be pictured by a reversed "J" curve; and the amount of energy at the disposal of, and used by – on the average – each human being has risen. Up until quite recently, the use of energy has therefore grown more rapidly than wealth itself.

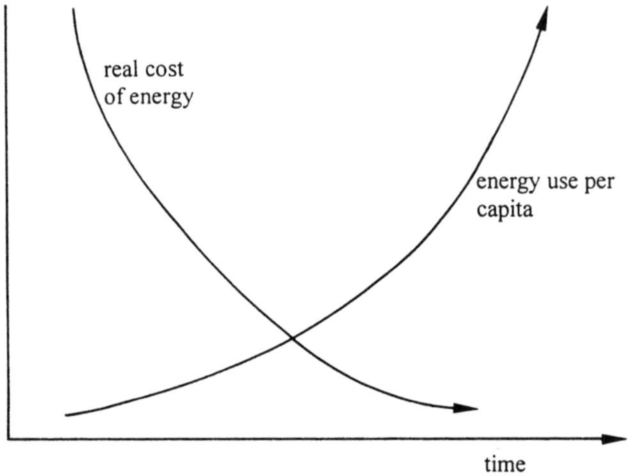

Should we expect both trends to continue? This question has become urgent since the first oil price shock of 1973. A new bout of fighting between Israel and Arabs then prompted Arab oil exporting states to halt deliveries to Western countries. This action in turn permitted the cartel of major oil exporting countries (Organisation of Petrol Exporting Countries = OPEC) to drastically raise the price of crude oil. In the wealthy oil consuming countries, this resulted in an unprecedented combination of inflation and economic stagnation. Poorer oil consuming countries went heavily into external debt. Other "oil shocks" followed with renewed hikes in the price of crude oil.

These crises demonstrated that primary energy (muscle, wind, solar, fossil fuels, hydro-power etc.) is not simply a raw material like any other. It is the very basis for all production. The availability and price of primary energy determines the price and availability of many other basic goods and materials. As we have seen, if the price of energy were low enough, it would be economically feasible to convert, by desalination, sea water into water for irrigation, and thus make deserts bloom. Were the real price of energy low enough, most of the metals we use could be simply extracted from sea water; or from very low quality ore. Vegetables could be grown economically in green houses north of the polar circle, etc. In short: the amount and price of energy available to humans determines to a large extent the scope, nature and limits of production.

As the real price of energy became lower over the centuries, many other goods and materials became more plentiful and cheaper too. But the succeeding oil crises now raise doubts as to whether this historic downward trend in the price of energy is to continue.

Different carriers of primary energy are fungible over the very long term only. It is only in the very long term that one can substitute, say, solar power for oil and natural gas. In the short and medium run, oil driven power stations cannot be simply converted to burn bio mass; and automobiles cannot be converted to using hydrogen instead of gasoline for fuel.

That makes the demand for each form of primary energy rather inelastic over the short to medium term. This holds true, in particular, for oil. If the exporters of oil succeed in forcing up the price of their product, consumers cannot simply switch to using other sources of energy. They have no choice but to pay the higher prices for oil.

World energy consumption 1990 and 1997
(in mio tons of oil)

Source of energy	*1990*		*1997*	
	Total in mio. tons of oil entities	Percentage share	Total in mio. tons of oil entities	Percentage share
Coal	501	55	2122	22
Oil	18	2	2940	30
Gas	9	1	2173	23
Nuclear energy	0	0	579	6
Renewable energy*	383	42	1833	19
Total	911	100	9647	100

*bio-?, water, wind, geo-thermic, and solar energy

Source: IEA

Oil is the most important source of primary energy at present. As such it also sets the prices of other carriers of primary energy. If oil gets more expensive, those who sell other forms of primary energy will hike their prices too. Due to the low (short-term) elasticity of demand, these changes in price can be abrupt and steep.

It is just in the 20th century that oil has gained this dominant role. In 1900, coal still covered 55% of the energy need; and renewable energy (mostly biomass) another 42%; while oil contributed no more than 2%. A hundred years later, oil covered, with 30%, the biggest share of needs. The share of renewable energy had shrunk to 19%; and that of coal to 22%. The contribution of nuclear energy is a far from negligible 6%.

So let us look at the trends in the price and availability of oil. The price of oil has gone up since the seventies. It now fluctuates between 20 and 30 US$ per barrel (which is, in fact, the present OPEC target range). Yet this rise is still rather moderate. The real price (that is the price discounting inflation) is just a bit above what it had been before the first oil crisis.

Oil price per barrel
(in real and nominal terms)

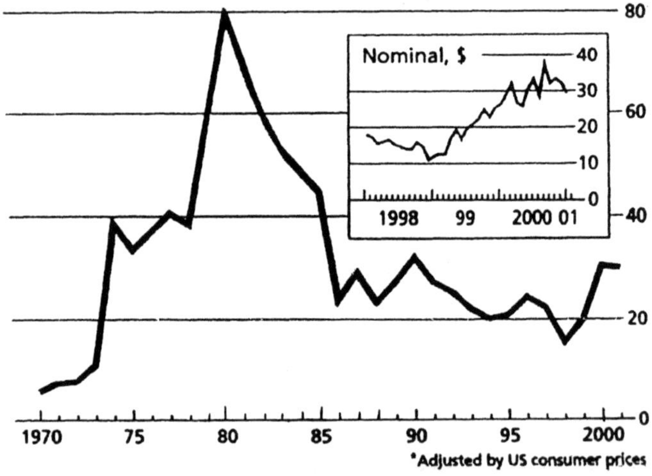

Source Financial Datastream

Since 1950, oil consumption has evolved differently in different regions of the world. Everywhere, it dropped markedly in reaction to the sudden surge of the oil price in the seventies. Since then it has remained more or less constant in Europe, with a tendency to a slight rise since 1985. In the US, this tendency of rising consumption was much stronger. In Asia, however, oil consumption has doubled and Asia now ranks before Europe and behind the US as the second biggest consumer.

Consumption of oil
(in million tons)

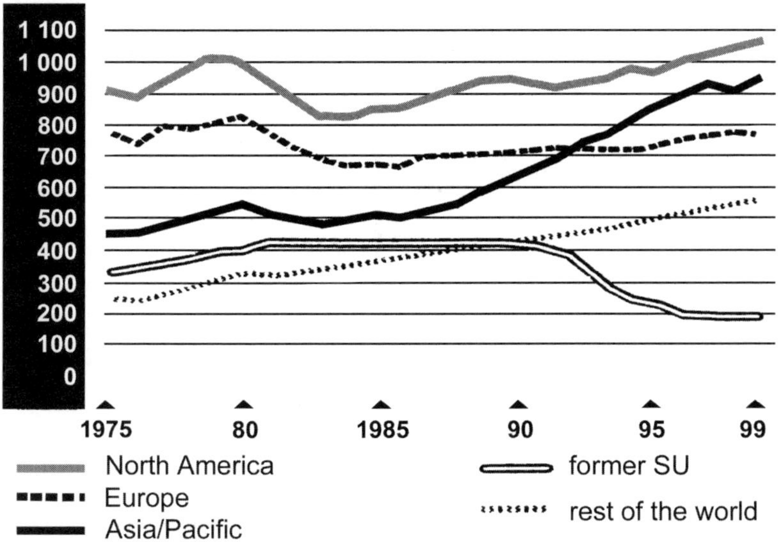

Source: IEA

As we have to assume that the demand of Asia will continue to grow in line with its rapidly expanding population and economy, world consumption of oil will thus continue to expand.

Inevitably, this prompts the question as to the limits of that development. At that pace of consumption, would the world not soon run out of oil? Wouldn't the reserves become exhausted?

The table below, drafted by the US Department of Energy, provides a tentative answer – albeit on a very grand historic scale. Within this century the rise in consumption will outpace the pace of the discovery of new oil reserves.[1] At the midst of this century, at the latest, shrinking supply would force world oil consumption to decline.

---

1 With some claiming that this has happened already.

World oil production and known resources
(estimates; in billion barrels)

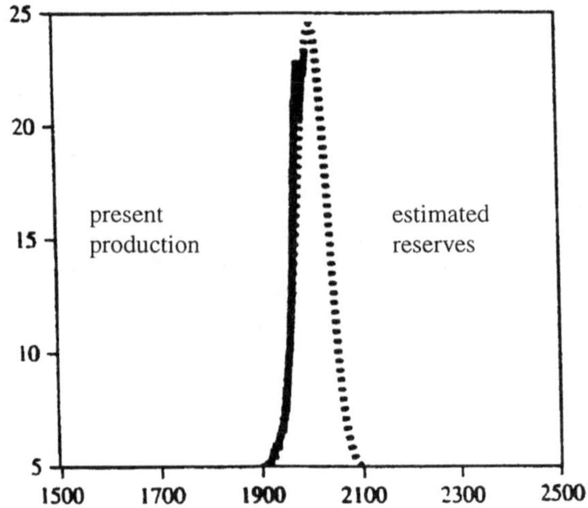

Source: US DOE

At first sight, such predictions do have a certain plausibility. We automatically assume that, eventually, all oil wells will become exhausted. But it is not that easy to arrive at some more precise predictions. Technology, politics and economics can make for widely divergent prospects. What may be considered a "reserve" does not just depend on geological data and upon the technology available for extracting oil. To no small extent what can be considered a reserve also depends on economic factors and especially upon the going market price for crude oil. Take, for example, the question as to the actual size of the oil deposits on the Alaska "North Slope". With a price of oil of more than 24 US$ per barrel, those reserves would amount to 7 billion barrels; with a price of less than 12 US$, they would hardly exist at all. If the price of crude oil is high, it pays to use the expensive technologies needed to extract oil even under the severe conditions in these high latitudes. If the price of crude oil is low, exploitation of these deposits is no longer economically feasible. The reserves cease to exist. The "known" in "known reserves" therefore depends not just on the scope of exploration, or on the prevailing technologies in extraction, but also on the market price of crude oil.

There is quite some oil not only under the Alaskan "North Slope", but also around Greenland and in other forbidding places. Whether these deposits can be considered "reserves" will depend on the price of crude oil and upon the evolution of the techniques of searching for and drilling for oil and on the techniques used to transport it. Assuming present technological trends to continue (with the fuller exploitation of existing fields, and with exploring and drilling becoming cheaper); and also assuming constant or slightly rising real prices for oil, experts conclude that the volume of "reserves" so determined is quite large still. Just 20% of all reserves that exist or had existed have been pumped up until now. Yet, however the situation might evolve, and even if significant new productions open in other regions of the world, it is certain that most reserves are and will be in the Middle East. The reserves of the Middle East (and North Africa) are sufficient to permit it to produce at its 1998 level for another 83 years. In the US, on the other hand, oil reserves would be depleted in 10 years if the present level of production is maintained. The EU-15 is in an even worse position. Its reserves would be depleted in just 6 years.

Years of remaining oil production at 1998 rate
(reserves of crude oil measured as a multiple of production in 1998)

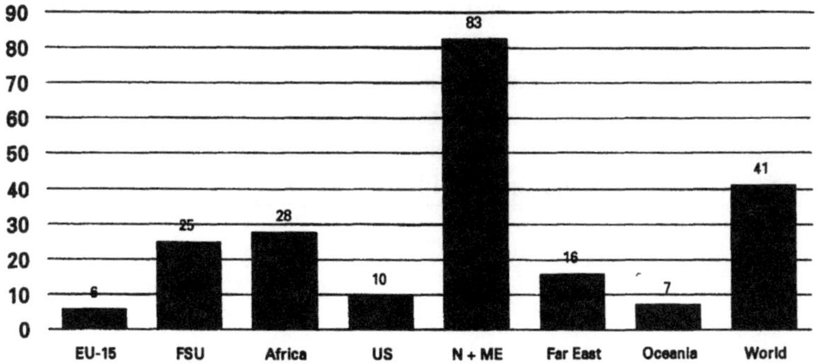

FSU: former Soviet Union; N+ME: Near and Middle East.

Source: Eurostat

Unfortunately, the main producers of oil in the Middle East and North Africa are rather unstable states: Algeria and Libya, Eastern Saudi Arabia, Southern and Northern Iraq, Kuwait, and Southern Iran. In maintaining its oil consumption, the world will therefore become even more dependent on a region that is politically, socially and economically volatile.[2]

Could it be that there is some connection between easy income from oil exports on the one hand, and, on the other hand, the political instability and the difficulties in economic development and modernisation that countries of this region encounter?

In the world, those countries whose wealth stands on firm foundations have never been dependent on just one commodity – the sale of which brings a high "rent income". On the contrary, some of the wealthiest countries – like Switzerland, Denmark, or Japan – are devoid of any natural resources that would be easy to exploit and to export.

High rent income from the easy exploitation of natural resources discourages both political/social modernisation and economic development. The exploitation of oil and natural gas creates substantial revenues. Some of them are paid out as wages or they reach the broad public in other ways (for instance by generous state subsidies for housing or for medical treatment). In resource-rich countries, this pushes up the wages and makes these wages uncompetitive with those of other countries[3]. Any other production than that of the one exported raw material will thus shrink and imports will cover all needs of the local consumers. No technical or commercial skills are developed.

Income from the exploitation and export of one single raw material is also easy to control. Inevitably, this control will be political. A few hundred soldiers suffice to secure an oil-field and thus to secure both wealth and power to the one who can command these soldiers[4].

---

2 The US "National Intelligence Council 2000" assesses the medium term prospects of the region as follows: "...little positive change...prospects for increased demographic pressures, social unrest, religious and ideological extremism, and terrorism directed both at the regimes and their Western supporters."

3 This is the so called **"Dutch Disease"** – a term coined in view of the fate of the Netherlands when its huge natural gas fields started to produce. Norway has gone to great lengths to avoid similar dangers and has thus put much of the oil income into reserves.

4 Worse still than oil are diamonds. To extract oil you need a minimum of stability; diamonds can be extracted even under chaotic conditions.

In a rain-fed agriculture[5], wealth is produced all over the territory by small farmers. In an industrial society it is produced in thousands of independent enterprises. It is difficult to control these thousands of economic producers of wealth. The ruler cannot simply replace, or control by his soldiers, thousands of managers, inventors, workers. In such countries economic decision making and economic power is thus decentralised. This decentralisation is a precondition for a functioning market economy. But economic decentralisation and economic independence of citizens is a precondition, too, of democracy. Both democracy and a market economy are difficult to evolve where power and economic decision making are centralised, as they are in countries where the pumping of oil is the near exclusive source of wealth. Dependence on the export of oil might be one of the main reasons for democratisation lagging in the Arab world.

Freedom and oil

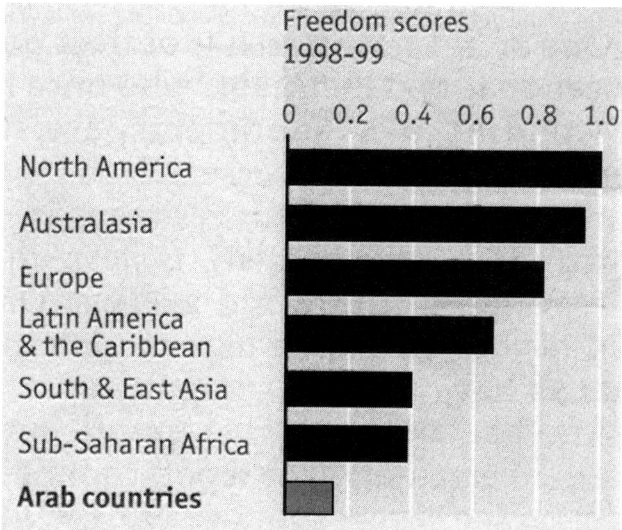

Source: Arab Development Report

5 In "**Oriental Despotism**" **Wittfogel** claimed that, for that reason, despotic rule could not evolve in the countries with moderate climate and a rain-fed agriculture; but could in the orient where the vast **irrigation** system permitted and/or needed centralised control.

For oil producing countries the key challenge is to use the oil income so as to develop other sources of income, instead of passively having these other sources of income wither in the warm wind of comfortable rent-income. The challenge is to use oil income to integrate into the world economic system instead of having it purchase an exit from the world economic system. Indonesia, for example, has succeeded in seizing the chances offered by the first alternative. Nigeria has opted for the second and worse one.[6]

To conclude this outlook on the future of oil: sooner or later oil output will peek. Forecasts as to when this will happen vary widely and they have changed repeatedly. Most would assume this to happen in 20 years at the earliest; and in 50 years at the latest. But even before that, oil will become more expensive. In addition, reliance on oil will be risky in view of the non-stable nature of the region which will produce most of it in the future.

So we should expect growing use of other sources of energy. With the supply of oil from wells declining, and with the price of oil rising, growing use will be made of the oil that can be extracted from oil shale and tar sands. There is nearly as much oil stored in them as is stored in oil wells. Would these sources become exhausted too, natural gas will be there to meet the increased demand for fossil energy. At the present rate of consumption the known reserves of gas would last for nearly a century.

6 Also, coming to rely on the income from oil as the main source of government revenue makes the government lose interest in building and expanding an **alternate tax base** (and makes it ill prepared for the moment when the oil wells will have run dry).

Price of natural gas and production years left
(at the average of 1975-99 consumption)

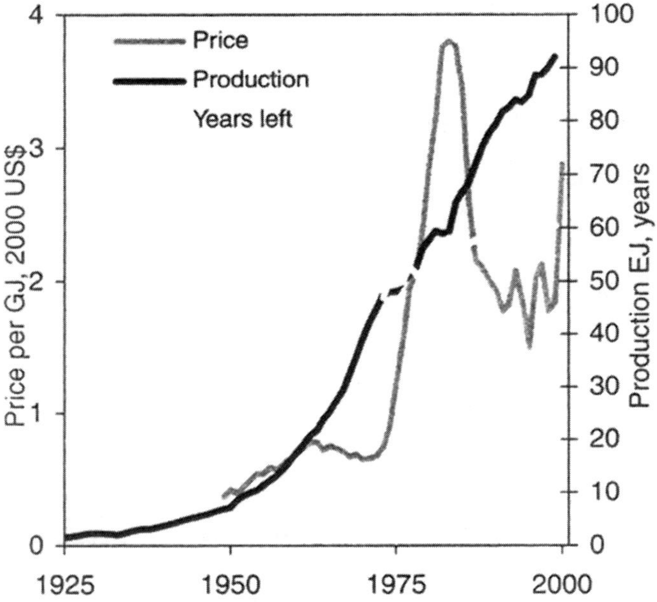

Source: EIA 1999

Other, non-fossil sources of primary energy will develop in the meantime. They already do so. Wind power has in fact become commercially competitive. Electricity produced in coal or gas fired plants costs about 6 US cents per KWh. Costs for wind generated electricity had fallen to this level before the turn of the millennium. If technological development is to continue at the pace of recent years, photo–voltaic energy might follow the pattern set by wind energy.

Price per KWh for energy generated from wind, solar-electric or solar-thermal sources

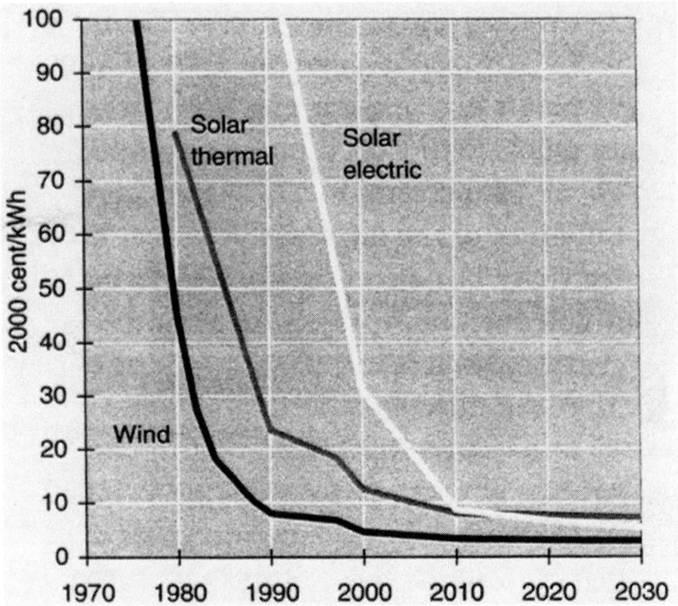

Source: US Department of Energy

Share of global energy production by different sources

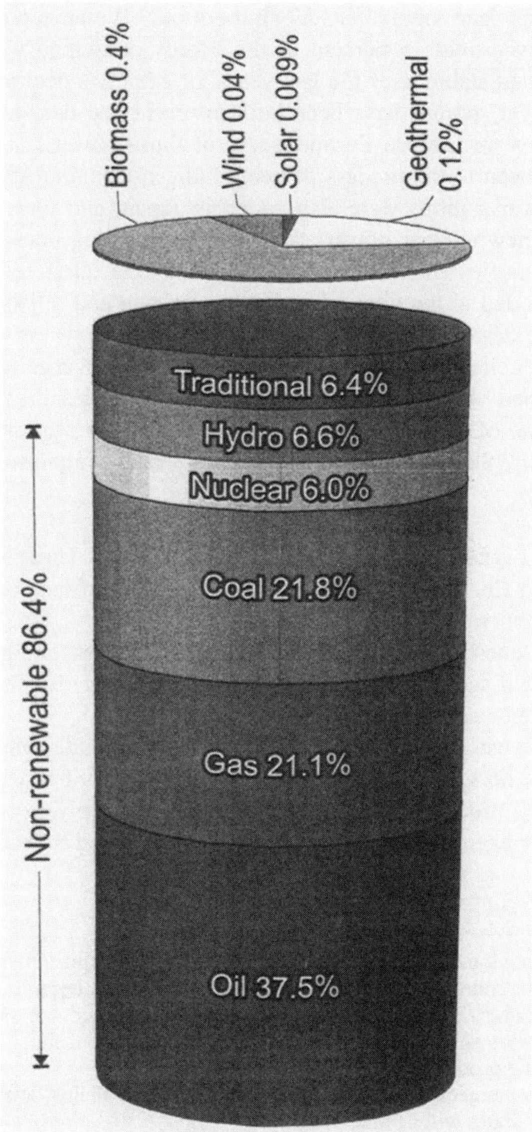

Source: US Dept of Energy/EIA 2000

At present, both of these new carriers of primary energy still cover a minuscule fraction of our energy needs. But this market share is expanding rapidly.[7]

What about nuclear energy? DOWN but not out? We have noted that nuclear stations presently provide 6 percent of the energy consumed world-wide. That share has remained stable over the last years, or even has declined a bit, as few new nuclear power stations have been built in recent decades, and hardly any in the rich countries. In Eastern Europe, some of those power stations were completed that had been in the process of being built in Communist/Soviet times. A few nuclear power stations were also added in Japan; and recently Finland has decided to add new nuclear power stations to the existing ones. In some of the less wealthy countries (like North Korea or Iran) the quest for nuclear power seems less grounded in the hope of accessing a cheap and reliable source of energy; than in the desire to access weapons-grade Plutonium[8] (as it is produced in the reactors of nuclear power stations). Nonetheless, the surge in nuclear power plants capacity had basically come to an end in the seventies already.

Will that state of affairs continue or could there be a renaissance of nuclear power generation? Several powerful factors are arranged against such an eventuality:

a) Concerns over safety. Accidents like the one on US Three Mile Island or in Soviet/Ukrainian Chernobyl, could make vast stretches of land unusable and uninhabitable for generations to come[9].

b) Essential questions connected to the use of nuclear energy have still not been resolved. No solution has been found, in particular, for the safe and final deposit of spent nuclear fuel.

c) The high costs of this form of energy. Cost estimates vary. But it seems certain that they lie substantially above the present cost of producing electricity in gas, coal or oil fired plants[10]. The costs have risen steeply, not least because of the ever more stringent security precautions now stipulated by public authorities.

---

7 As is made obvious by the obtrusive sight of wind-farms spread over the landscape.

8 Though most countries are part of the Nuclear Non-Proliferation Treaty; and thus have subjected their reactors to scrutiny by the International Atomic Energy Agency. Scrutiny by this agency should prevent Plutonium in spent fuel – rods being channelled into the production of nuclear weapons.

9 There is the connected question as to how to insure against such accidents. Ultimately, only states will be able to do so.

10 This is so even if one is to exclude from these costs the costs connected with the ultimate disposal of spent fuel and the – high – costs of decommissioning nuclear plants.

d) Transporting electricity is fairly expensive. A premium is thus put upon moving productions close to consumers. In doing so, one may also use for home and office heating the – otherwise wasted – energy of the cooling systems ("co – generation"). It is for this reason that there is a move from big to smaller and de-centralised power plants [11]. Big remote nuclear plants are thus at a disadvantage.

There are some countervailing arguments that support electricity being generated in nuclear power stations:

a) security of supply of fuel;
b) they do not emit "greenhouse gases" (see next chapter);
c) much lower costs in terms of human lives lost. Chernobyl, the worst accident that has happened till now will have cost a maximum of a hundred lives (even if one is to include in this number the number of people still to die over the next five decades as victims of the higher radiation caused in the area by the accident). Compared to that, 5.160 coal miners were killed in one country (China) and in one year (2001) alone. To the numbers so killed have to be added the numbers of those who die as a consequence of the high emissions from these coal fired plants[12];
d) a new generation of inherently safer reactors ("pebble-reactors").

Holding these arguments against each other, it does not seem likely that nuclear power will gain an advantage soon.

At present, per capita energy consumption differs widely between the world's regions. Compared to the Europeans, North Americans consume twice as much per head. Europeans on their turn consume three times as much per head as East Asians.

These differences will even out – at least eventually and somewhat. They already have done so in the past. The major share of the increase in the world's energy consumption between 1980 and 2000 was already caused by the rise of consumption in now less developed countries, as they moved closer to the per capita consumption in Europe and North America. If all industrial countries are taken together, per capita energy consumption will remain constant in that group. It will remain constant even though their per capita wealth will continue to rise.

---

11 Technological developments have facilitated this shift; as well as the use of natural gas for fuel.

12 Among them radioactive radiation from soot – which is at a higher level overall than the radiation seeping out of nuclear plants.

Energy consumption per head 1995
(gigajoules)

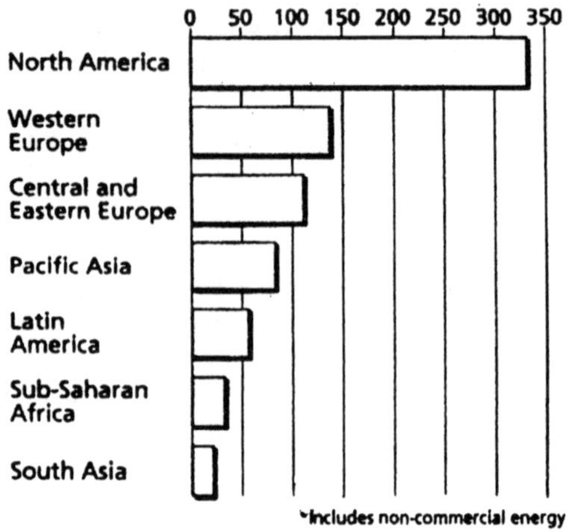

Source: World Energy Assessment

Global primary energy consumption
(quadrillion BTU)

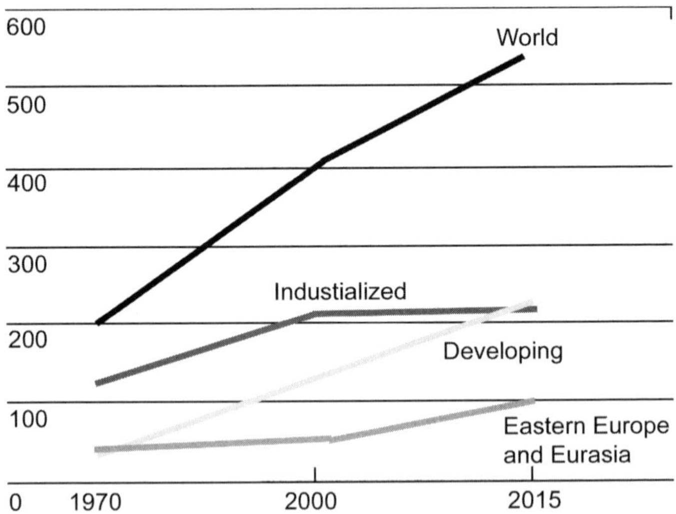

Source: International Energy Outlook 1998; US Dept of Energy

Such a development brings the reversal of a prior long-term trend. Until the first oil crisis in 1973, as we had mentioned at the outset, each additional percentage point of GDP had been produced with a more than one percent added input of energy. The "energy-intensity" of production had risen as it had since time immemorial. Since the early seventies, however, one added percentage point of GDP is produced with an added input of energy that is smaller than one percent. In the wealthy countries "energy-intensity" of production is declining.

Energy intensity varies within the group of rich countries. Some rich countries use still exorbitantly much energy for each unit of the GDP, some much less. Energy intensity is lowest in Japan. There it has remained constant over the last decade. The very high energy intensity of the US is declining; and so is the energy intensity in Europe (although less rapidly than in the US).

Energy intensity
(Gross inland consumption per unit of GDP in 1990 prices; kg of OE per 1000 Euro)

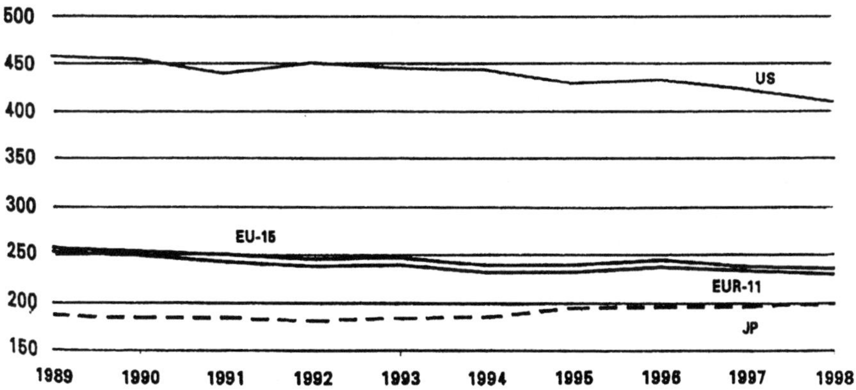

Source: Energy, yearly statistics, 1998, Eurostat

SUMMING up we should retain:

The era will come to an end when oil was dominant in the supply of energy. But this will be a slow and drawn-out process. Oil will continue as the main source of primary energy at least for several decades still. After that, it will be supplemented by natural gas as the main carrier of energy. This will bring us rather close to the end of this century. Alternate, non-fossil sources of primary energy will develop rapidly but nonetheless will still cover a relatively minor share of the energy demand – given the minuscule contribution they provide today and given the technical and economic uncertainties surrounding them. The future of nuclear power is uncertain too. One may predict a renaissance of nuclear energy; or, on the other hand, its final demise.

The price of crude oil will probably rise in real terms as consumption rises and as the volume of known reserves no longer expands. This will also boost the prices of other forms of energy. This hike in the price of energy will accelerate transition to other forms of primary energy.

As the price hike of primary energy will be gradual and relatively moderate, it will not impose a limiting factor on world economic growth. The energy consumption of the now wealthy countries will either remain stable or expand but little. The consumption of the poorer countries, on the contrary, will grow markedly.

Much more serious than the problem of gradually rising real prices for energy is the problem of short-term bottlenecks and/or short-term sudden and violent changes in this price. This volatility is difficult to remedy as it is caused by low elasticity in both supply and demand.

The problem of the price volatility is enhanced, furthermore, by the inherent instability of the Middle East which will become more dominant than it already is in the supply of oil. This instability may once more lead to either shortages or over-supply of crude oil and thus, once more, to drastic if only short-term swings in the price of energy. Also, the function as holder of the main oil reserves will continue to make the Middle East a strategically important region – something that might lead outsiders to directly intervene in that region though such interventions might prove counterproductive as they might heighten insecurity instead of promoting stability.

Atmospheric Emissions and the Management of the Global Commons

The world population is likely to double, expanding by another 6 billion people. The world's consumption will grow even faster, as overall wealth will increase. Insufficient supply of energy and insufficient supply of food and raw materials are not likely to become serious bottlenecks in this process. But might it be that nature would? Might the world's ecological system fails to support such growth? Could it become impaired to the point of collapse?

And indeed, as a consequence of human exploitation, ecosystems may collapse. There are historic precedents. Such collapses occurred on two islands when humans destroyed some key elements of their ecosystems. In medieval Iceland overgrazing lead to severe soil erosion and thus to a decline in agricultural production, to starvation and to a shrinkage in population. A similar tragedy occurred on the Easter Islands. Such precedents do provide a warning. What happened on those small islands could perhaps happen to the world as such, which – in a sense – is also but a tiny, isolated island suspended in the vast ocean of the solar space.

Up until quite recently, humans were not aware of such dangers. Humankind still acted according to the bible's injunction to "subdue and master nature". Only in the last decades has it dawned that this might be a recipe for disaster; and that one would have to learn how to live with and in nature. It has become evident that humans would have to adapt their ways if they do not wish to endanger their own survival.

But has this lesson been truly learned? And will it be heeded? Let us look at how we have fared until now. And let us first look at how we have treated the air we breath. Basically, we have treated it as a depository for gaseous emissions. Some of these emissions impair health directly. Others, like the Fluorocarbons, destroy the ozone layer of the upper atmosphere and thus destroy a shield that largely filters out dangerous ultra-violet radiation. Still other emissions build up in the atmosphere and prevent the Earth from radiating heat into space – like the glass of a greenhouse that keeps the heat of this greenhouse from radiating outside ("greenhouse effect"; greenhouse gases).

Carbon-dioxide is the major component of these green-house gases. It is emitted mainly through the burning of fossil fuels. As carbon dioxide continues to build up in the atmosphere, the surface of the earth will become warmer. Examinations of the ice core of ancient glaciers prove the connection between higher temperatures and the carbon dioxide content of the atmosphere.

Global warming – historical temperature variations and CO_2 concentration

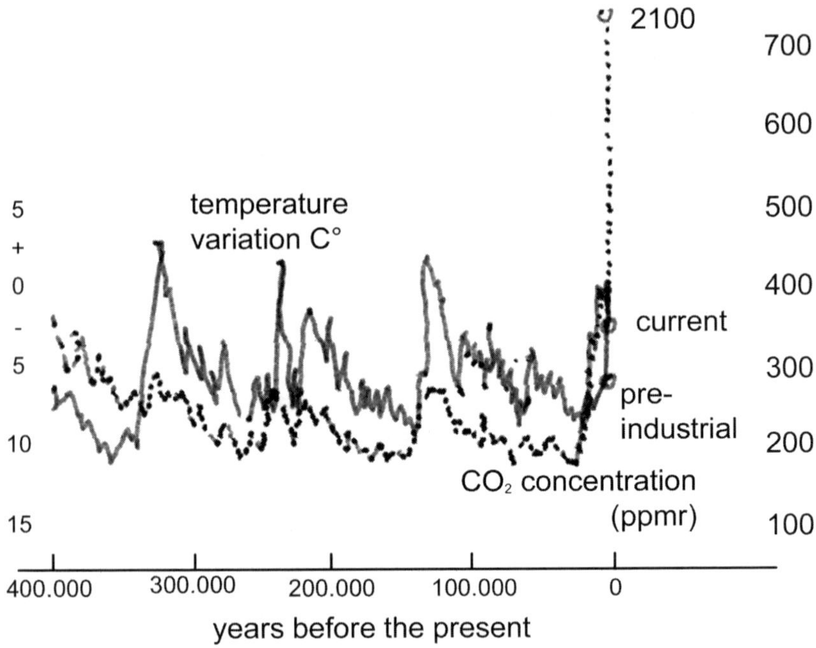

Source: CDIAL, Oakridge National Laboratory

This connection holds true also for the more recent past. Since the midst of the nineteenth century, with the massive increase in the burning of coal, the emissions of carbon dioxide into the atmosphere have risen[1] and the surface temperature on earth has increased by roughly a centigrade and a half.

---

1 This is the conclusion of an international council of scientists who advise the UN on that issue. But some – a minority – still doubt this connection between man made emission of carbon dioxide and the rise in the temperature of the earth surface. They claim that this rise is still within what can be seen as quite common variations as they also have occurred in the past, without power stations exhaling CO_2 into the atmosphere. Climate is a very complex system.

Average temperature on the earth's surface 1866-1998
(in centigrades)

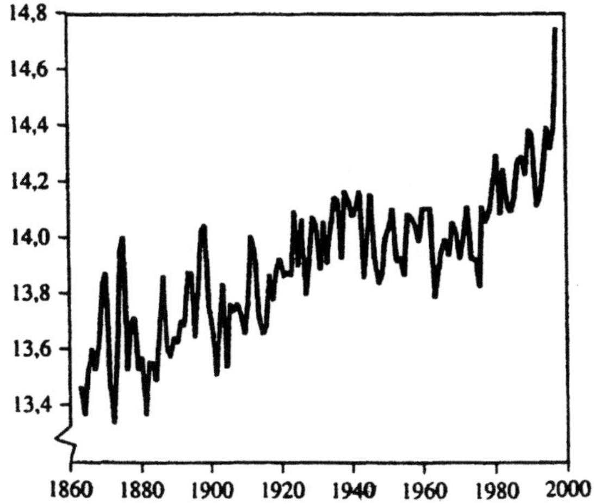

Source: Goddard Institute

So over both the very, very long term of millennia, and for the more recent past of the last 150 years, we may establish this close connection between the CO_2 content of the atmosphere on one hand and the surface temperature on the other hand. But it is true that much is still unknown about the exact causal chain. Vast "CO_2 sinks" exist in the form of bio-mass, in the form of limestone rocks and – especially – in the form of the vast oceans. In these sinks, CO_2 is stored and thus withheld from the atmosphere. It is not clear at what rate is is released from these "sinks". Notwithstanding all these uncertainties, the majority of scientists has come to conclude that the connection between the rise in the atmosphere's CO_2 content and the rise in the temperature is indeed a causal one; and that the rise in the CO_2 content of the atmosphere is indeed the consequence of human activity.

Many uncertainties also exist as concerns the consequences of global warming. Some of these consequences might even be beneficial. Agriculture, for example, might be extended further into northern regions[2]. But most of the conse-

2 But even that is not certain for Europe. One of the consequences of global warming might be that the Gulf Stream ceases to flow. Were this to happen, citizens of London and Frankfurt would become woefully aware that they live in the same latitude

quences will be negative. And, on average, they would hurt those countries most heavily that are ill off already. Countries that are arid (and most of them are poor at the same time) would become more arid still and might convert to full deserts. One of the most damaging consequences could be the rise in the sea level[3], with the water stored in the polar caps melting into the sea as the temperature rises. If this were to happen, some low lying islands – like the Maldives – could disappear completely. The same fate could befall the densely populated delta regions of some of the great rivers (like the Nile, the Ganges or the Mississippi).

So while much is unknown still in this complex web of interrelationships between temperature and CO_2 emissions, it does seem prudent not to wait for full clarity before taking action. It seems prudent to lower the emission of greenhouse gases.

The precautionary principle

Many of humankind's actions will deeply affect the environment. Some of these effects will reach deep into the future. Some of them will be irreversible. Many of them will be hard to predict. Ten thousand years hence, what will, for example, be the state and the effect of nuclear waste stored deep underground in salt domes? How will the reduction of the forest cover affect this or that species? What negative health effects from breathing dust-free air only; or from the wide use of antibiotics?

It seems inscribed in human genes to use extra caution when risks and dangers are unknown. Travelling in cars is risky, but these risks are known and evident. The use of cars has thus become routine and people do not shy from it even in view of the relatively high risks involved. The long term effects of a higher exposure to radiation[4], on the other hand, are not that evident and known. Humans thus are much more prudent in exposing themselves to this unknown risk. Thus the deep scepticism towards nuclear energy; and thus the

as the Ainus of Labrador. The Gulf stream acts as a kind of giant warm-water heating system that permits orchards and vineyards to bloom in Europe in latitudes in which, in North America and Asia, pines hardly survive.

3 Some claim that the opposite might happen with the sea level actually dropping. More precipitation would fall around the North – and the South Pole. Notwithstanding global warming, both regions would still be cold enough to convert that precipitation into ice. Yet the long term history does not seem to support this notion. Cold temperatures have indeed coincided with low sea levels. During the last ice age, for example, the sea levels were low enough to permit settlers to cross on dry land what is today the Bering strait and start settling in North America. Similarly, settlers migrated into the UK via dry land that today is buried under the Channel.

4 Either from nuclear fission or from heightened ultra – violet radiation)

alarm over the widening of the "ozone hole" that permits more ultraviolet radiation to reach the earth's surface.

This "precautionary principle" in view of unknown risks also informs global governance. It has even become expressly enshrined in international law; as, for instance, in the Rio Declaration (on sustainable development): "*Where there are threats of serious or irreversible damage, lack of full scientific certainty shall not be used as a reason for postponing cost-effective measures to prevent environmental degradation.*"

The US leads the world in CO_2 emissions – both in absolute numbers and on a per capita basis. Other industrialised countries with a near equal level of per capita wealth, have only half of the CO_2 per capita output. The US, thus, has ample scope for reducing its CO_2 emissions.

Ranking of countries by the volume of their CO2 emissions from the burning of fossil fuels and from the production of cement

(1995)

Rank	*Country*	*Total emissions (in 1,000 t)*	*Per capita emissions (in t)*
1	USA	5,468,564	20.5
2	PRChina	3,192,484	2.7
3	CIS	1,818,011	12.2
4	Japan	1,126,753	9.0
5	India	908,734	1.0
6	Germany	835,099	10.2
7	Great Britain	542,140	4.3
8	Ukraine	438,211	4.5
9	Canada	435,749	14.8
10	Italy	409,938	7.2
11	South Korea	373,592	8.3
12	Mexico	357,834	3.9
13	France	340,085	5.9
14	Poland	338,044	8.8
15	South Africa	305,805	7.4
16	Indonesia	296,132	1.5
17	Australia	289,808	16.2
	World	22,714,561	3.9

Source: WRI, 1998

The US is closely followed by China. This is not only because China is populous, but also because it still relies to a large extent on the burning of coal for home-heating, for industrial use, and for the generation of electricity. Compared to the burning of other fossil fuels, the burning of coal causes disproportionally large emissions of greenhouse gases.

In view of the likely and very damaging consequences of global warming, the political pressure grew to reduce the emission of "greenhouse gases". That has led to the 1997 "Kyoto Protocol". For the wealthy countries, it has set legally binding targets for lowering these emissions. The treaty would initiate one of the most comprehensive – and costly – projects of international co-operation in environmental policy. Because, or in spite, of that, the project remains controversial. Many fear that it will fail to deliver on its intended purpose.

Global emission of CO_2, 1950-2050
in 1000 tons

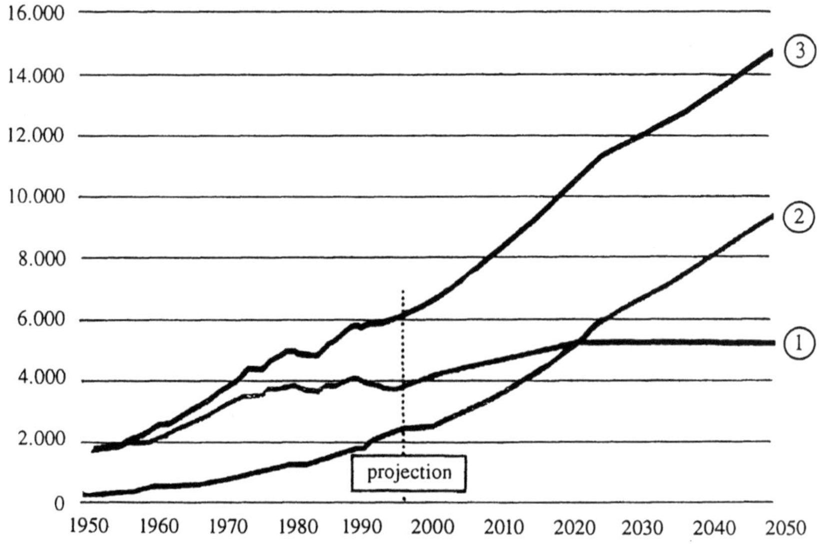

1 = industrial countries
2 = developing countries
3 = global

Source: World Watch Institute

One of its weaknesses is the failure to also tie in the poorer countries. Constricted by the protocol, the wealthy (Annex I) countries might indeed manage to stop the rise in their greenhouse gas emission by 2020. But even when the rich (Annex I) countries reduce their greenhouse gas emissions, those from the poorer countries will continue to grow and will continue to grow even in the more distant future. They will do so at a rapid pace. Fifteen years from now, developing countries will release more CO2 into the atmosphere than the now wealthy countries.

So even if the rich countries all comply with the Kyoto protocol, the world wide emissions of greenhouse gases will continue to rise. All that this compliance would do is to postpone the effects of global warming by a mere six years. That is, the same high temperatures would be reached but just six years later. Yet this small gain would come at a very high price. It would cost several times more than what is being disbursed by the wealthy countries for development assistance to poorer countries[5]. Necessarily, this raises the question as to whether this is money well spent and as to whether these high sums should not be better used for other purposes.

Notwithstanding all its imperfections, the Kyoto Protocol does provide evidence of the resolve, of at least many countries, to enter into far-reaching and expensive commitments for the sake of protecting the global environment.

While it is difficult and costly to ward against global warming, emissions other than CO_2 are easier to control and to reduce. This has been the case – notably – for emissions of sulphur dioxide. The decline was partly caused by the declining role of coal as the primary source of energy. But that reduction in SO_2 emissions was also caused by conscious political action; as is shown by the example of the Netherlands pictured in the graph below.

5 The "sceptical environmentalist" Bjorn Lomborg estimates these costs to amount to a staggering annual 900 billion US dollars for all OECD countries by 2050. I do not know all of the details underlying this estimate; and believe it to be too high mainly by the acceptance of too high a discount rate for future benefits. But even while rejecting such numbers as inflated, we should not doubt the substantial costs of compliance with the Kyoto Protocol. Whether realisation of this fact justifies US president George W Bush pronouncing the Kyoto Protocol "dead" is another question altogether.

SO_2 emissions (in 1,000 t) – linking policy to emission reductions in the Netherlands

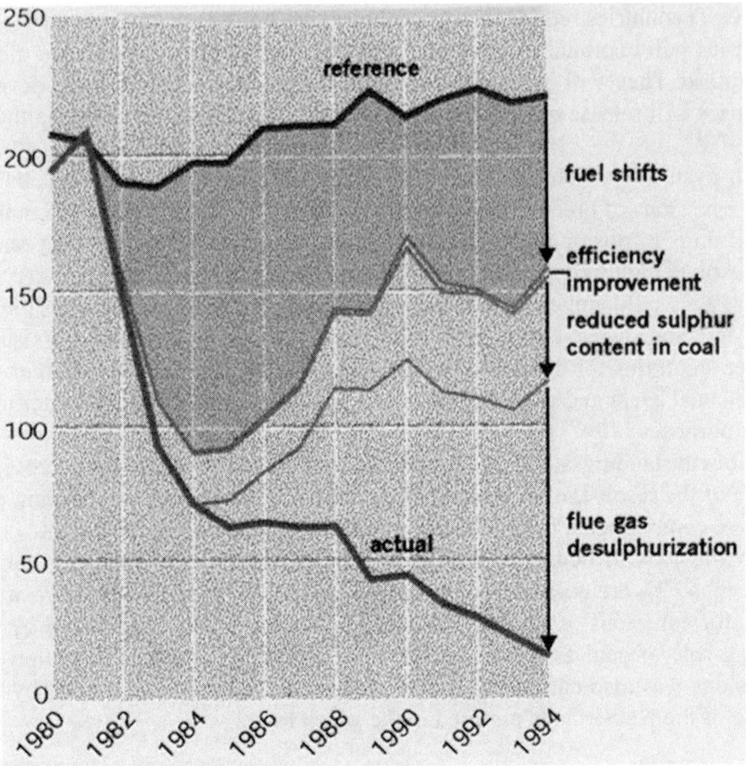

Source: UNEP 2002

The community of nations has been even more successful in reducing the emission of CFC gases. These are the prime culprits behind the opening of the "ozone hole". CFC gases break down the ozone molecules in the upper atmosphere. As mentioned, these molecules shield the earth from much of the ultraviolet radiation emanating from the sun. Higher exposure to this radiation causes health problems – mainly through more frequent skin-cancer. Growing wealth coincided with rapidly rising use and emission of CFC gases. But, this trend of rising CFC emissions was broken within less than a decade. This clearly is the effect of global political action ("Montreal Protocol").

Annual production in CFC gases peaked in the eighties and has dropped to near zero by now.[6] As a consequence, CFC concentration in the upper atmosphere has started to drop too.

The annual global production of CFC gases

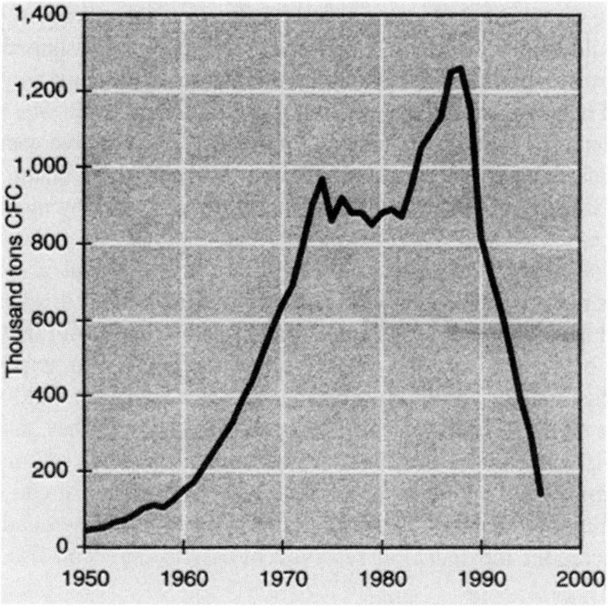

Source: Blackmore 1996

"Commons" were patches of land that were not owned by any individual farmer but by the community of farmers, as such, and that were used and exploited by each member of that community. The so-called "global commons" belong to humankind as such. We already have dealt with one: the air we breath. But there are others that can be exploited, used and abused by individual human beings, corporations or states:

Water
The fish in the ocean
Wetlands and other valuable biotopes

6 Poorer countries receive financial assistance from wealthier ones so as to phase out their CFC production.

Bio-diversity = the diversity of flora and fauna
Unique landscapes

The danger is that we repeat in these "global commons" that what happened in the British commons. These patches of common pasture were over-used at the price of their rapid decline in productivity. Each farmer could realise a nice profit from sending one additional cow or sheep to feed on the commons. On the other hand, he would gain very little in return for investing in the sustained use of these commons (by ploughing or fertilising them). The improvements in yield thus secured would accrue to all villagers and not to him alone. Little was thus invested in the maintenance of the commons and much was done to overuse and damage them. The subsequent and inevitable decline in the fertility of the commons is termed the "tragedy of commons". It is one of the reasons why most of the commons have ceased to exist.

Such situations, where private gain (either of an individual, a corporation, or a state) does not add up to a public good, are rather frequent in social, economic and political life. They are particularly frequent in international life. One example is provided by the exploitation of the fish of the oceans. In some parts of the oceans, stocks have become reduced severely, with the result that, notwithstanding the ultra modern equipment of fishing vessels, the catch has shrunk. In some traditional fishing areas (North Sea, Great Banks), the stock of some species of fish has become so low that it has become doubtful whether it can recover even after all fishing has ceased. This has been the case on the Newfoundland banks – once considered the inexhaustible reservoir of easy to catch cod-fish.

Newfoundland cod-catch (tons) 1850-2000

Source: World Bank 2002

The rise of aquaculture partly compensates for the decline of fishing on the open seas.

Annual catches of the EU 15 fishing vessels
(in 1000 tons)

	1988	1993	1997
all over the world	7.404	6.592	6.750
in the North Atlantic	174	83	37
aquaculture production	910	912	1.187

Source: Eurostat

And, in a way, what we see here is a repeat of the development that – much earlier – had led humans to turn from hunters-gatherers into farmers. This implies – of course – a break up of the commons and the establishment of property rights on the high sea. In various forms this development will also touch other commons – like, for example, the commons of rare fauna. Animals that (due to the destruction of their habitat) can no longer be preserved in the wild will be preserved in game parks and zoos (either owned privately or by communes and states). The wild roaming animals that used to be common property of mankind will have become the property of either communes or of corporations.

But even so, much "global governance" – much conscious and joint effort by the international community-will still be necessary to preserve those commons where problems cannot be solved by simply turning them over to private ownership.

Many cultures share the myth of primeval innocence; of a paradise since lost through human guilt and intervention. Many yield to the temptation to also view environmental issues from this perspective. But first there is the question as to whether paradise has ever existed and as to whether, instead of being pleasant, life in these primeval conditions had not been rather nasty. Second, and even if paradise had existed, it would have been equipped for a few million humans only. It could not have provided the homestead for the present 6 billion citizens of the world. Third, we have long since ceased to live in something that could be called "pure nature".

Some of the unique landscapes Europeans cherish and protect are not natural at all but the result of human intervention. Forests once covered what today is the Hungarian Puszta, the barren Adriatic islands and the northern European Heaths. The forests Austrians are so fond of, are mostly planted. Hardly any primeval forest exists in Austria.

The issue, thus, is not one of returning to primeval innocence, but to shape our environment in a way that is acceptable, and perhaps, on occasions, even pleasing. A growing world population and poverty complicates this task. Rising wealth eases it. The worst environmental problems now are not in the wealthy but in the poor countries. Growing wealth creates a vast number of these problems; but it also helps to solve them.

Indeed, in many cases we may discern a positive correlation between rising wealth and improvements in the environment. This runs counter to a general perception which correlates growing wealth with growing environmental problems. But that perception reflects just the experience in the more distant past. For, in the first phase of industrialisation and modernisation, such sombre assessment had indeed been justified. In the first phase of industrialisation, environmental problems did increase more rapidly than the wealth created in the process.

The connection between GDP per capita and SO_2 pollution in 47 cities and 31 countries
(income in 1985 ppp US Dollars)

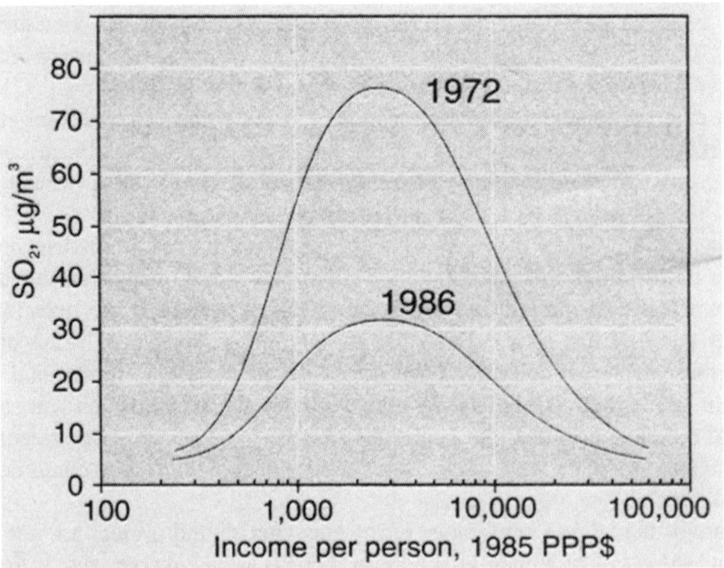

Source: World Bank 1992

Yet from a certain point on, the relationship became reversed. From that point on, rising wealth correlated with diminishing environmental problems. This process is pictured in what has been called the "environmental Kuznets curve" (in reference to the economist who correlated growing overall wealth first with rising, and then with declining, inequality). The graph below provides an example of such an "environmental Kuznets curve" by pointing to the correlation between wealth and the level of SO_2 emissions.

Similar relationships exist for other emissions; for the dropping oxygen content of rivers (caused by waste over-load); for safe or unsafe waste disposal; etc. These findings should not surprise us. Upon reflection, it seems quite natural that humans should try to use their wealth to eliminate threats to their safe – and pleasant – existence.

But even that argument is still based on the notion of a trade-off between faster economic growth on one hand and more efficient environmental protection on the other. Probably, this notion has to be revised too. Perhaps it even has to be inverted. It might be that, instead of a trade-off, we are faced with positive feedbacks; with better environmental protection making for greater overall economic efficiency. The United Nations Industrial Development Organisation – UNIDO – has composed an index on "Competitive Industrial Performance – CIP". The graph below shows a positive correlation to exist between industrial competitiveness and environmental protection measured by the amount of CO_2 emitted[7] for each unit of GDP.

7 It is, of course, a bit problematic to use just this single indicator for measuring the quality of environmental policies.

Regression of competitive industrial performance index values on carbon dioxide emissions
(log model – 1998)

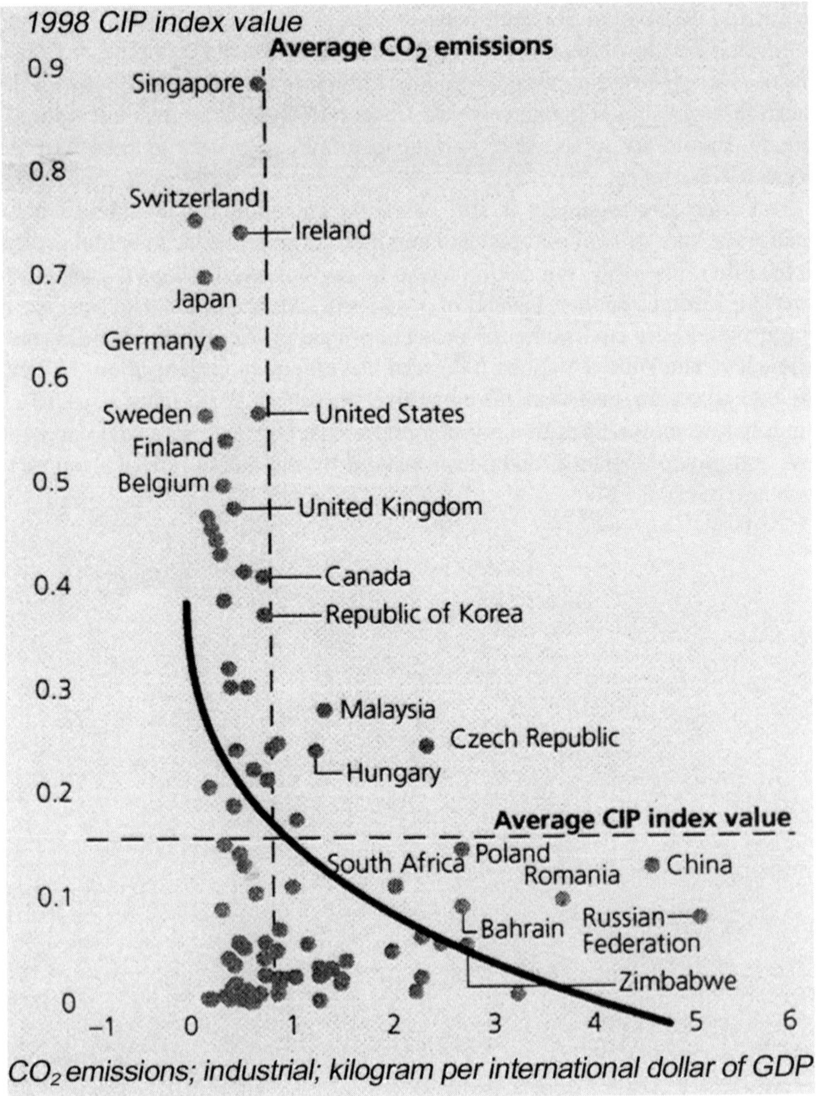

Source: UNIDO, 2002

We should be cautious, though, in generalising from those examples and coming to believe that all – or even the more pressing – environmental problems could be solved and would be solved eventually, provided the worlds' wealth will continue to rise.

Some damage cannot be repaired because such damage has become irreversible. Once a species has become extinct, it is extinct now and forever. Once heavy metals have poisoned vast patches of soil, there is no remedy short of the wholesale removal of that soil to another place where it will continue to stay as it is – namely poisoned. Once a marsh has been drained and paved over, it cannot be brought back into existence, etc.

Second, many of the success stories on environmental degradation that has been followed by environmental improvement refer to remedial action that can be done, and that has been done, in one, single country only. Values and interests converge more easily in just one country than within a wider group of several countries or even on a world-wide scale. Also, single countries do have the governmental and other institutions needed for effective collective action. The regional and or global institutions that deal with environmental problems (such as the United Nations Environmental Programme – UNEP) are much weaker and less efficient in comparison. "Problems of collective action" thus are more difficult to resolve on an international level. They are easier to solve on the national level. Nonetheless, many, and increasingly more, environmental problems would call for effective and strong remedial action on a regional, or even on a global level.

In view of these difficulties, one has to appreciate that it is exactly in the field of environmental protection that progress in global co-operation and global governance has been most rapid. The example of the Montreal Protocol (on the phasing out of CFC production) demonstrates that such global co-operation and problem solving can advance very rapidly and that it may advance even against the opposition of very concrete and firm economic interests. The "Kyoto Protocol" demonstrates that – generally – the interest in, and engagement for, such global solutions is higher, the wealthier the country. We therefore should expect that, in the long run, the "environmental Kuznets curve" will also hold true for fields where the elimination of environmental problems needs the co-operation not just within countries, but also between countries. But progress in that direction is far from automatic and assured. The willingness and capacity to co-operate does not extend to all countries and all issues that have to be addressed.

We should, however, note a phenomenon which we shall investigate more closely later on. It is exactly in this field of environmental policies that states have ceased to be the sole players. Analysing the decision-making in this realm, we have to acknowledge the important function not just of states; but the function also of transnational civil society, of the scientific community, of transnational corporations; and of international organisations of various sorts. The rather dense global co-operation in these fields cannot be explained while ignoring the contributions made by these many new international actors.

Damage to the Social Environment

Massive global trends transform the global system and alter the conditions of personal life. Population growth, the expansion of the world economy, urbanisation, the increase in the consumption of energy and raw materials may seriously impair the world's ecosystem. Whether the outcome will actually be a negative one, that, however, will not be determined by some blindly acting force that would drive humanity along a pre-determined path. The final outcome will depend upon conscious choices and upon purposeful joint action – upon political action on a communal, national and global scale. The question is whether humankind is actually capable of acting in such a way so as to deal with and correct for the negative consequences of a growing world population and of growing wealth.

According to pessimistic environmentalists, humankind is not equipped to act in such a purposeful and foresighted manner. Inevitably, thus, the growth of population and the rise in material wealth is bound to destroy the ecological base of human existence. Pessimistic environmentalists are right in having reason for concern. Nonetheless, their fear of a wholesale destruction has not been justified up until now. Humans have managed to preserve and repair the ecological base of their existence. Yet another kind of fear is perhaps better founded. The fear, namely, that progress in wealth has become self destructive not by destroying the ecological base of humankind, but by destroying its social base; by destroying group cohesion; the sense of mutuality and commonality; the sense of propriety, of virtue and of civic mindedness. This damage to the social environment is worse in its consequences than the damage inflicted by growing wealth upon the global ecological system.

Dealing with that claim prompts some very basic questions as to what constitutes human nature; as to what constitutes a social group; and as to what constitutes a state. We cannot deal with all of these questions. But we may, at least, mention some of them that have a more direct bearing on our investigation of the global system.

States and political institutions are here to solve the problem of collective action. The tasks and choices involved have already been captured by Rousseau in his well-known fable of the stag hunt. In a "state of nature", before any form of political authority became established, a group of males gather for a stag hunt. They join forces because each one alone would not be capable of cornering and killing the quick footed and potentially dangerous animal. The positive pay-off for their joining forces could be big. Each one of the hunters could gain a solid chunk of high protein stag meat. But the hunting party is not favoured by luck. Erring through the forest it finds no stag. Finally, one after the other deserts the hunting party. Doing so, each of the deserters makes a simple calculation. On the way home, each can be pretty certain to catch a little rabbit. This is a feat which each of them can accomplish all by himself. Of course, the quantity of meat on one small rabbit is less by far than the quantity of meat each could cut from a stag that they would have killed together. Pondering on whether to desert or not to desert the stag hunting party, each one assumes that all other members of the party think about the same thing. Each assumes that the others also assume that others might desert, and each of the deserters then has ample time to kill a rabbit, whilst those that stick to the group waste their time in pursuing a hunt that has become hopeless because there are simply no longer enough males to find, corner and kill the prey. The hunting party dissolves. In the long run, each of them is worse off for that. But they will have learned from that experience. For quite some time, at least, they will refrain from going hunting together again. The price they pay for that is that all of them will be less well fed. They would have been better off if all of them would have persisted in their joint effort, and tried yet another hunt after the failure of the first one.

Now let us look at the mechanism and implications of this mini-drama[1].

For an optimal outcome the hunting party will have to stay together. But for that to happen each of its members must trust the others not to desert. If he does not, distrust becomes a self-fulfilling prophecy. Furthermore, the members must actually be capable – physically and mentally – to work together in a common endeavour. They must communicate with one another in order to achieve the necessary coordination in completion of their common task[2].

As it is not difficult to surmise, the hunting party does indeed stand for the state and for other communal efforts. The dissolution of the hunting party stands for that failure of trust and cohesion that can undermine states and other communal enterprises. Do modern states and modern communal institutions face this danger of losing the necessary base of trust and willing co-operation? Are these dangers greater the further advanced a society is in the accumulation of material wealth?

---

1 A now better known and more modern version of this fable is generally known as the prisoner's dilemma – short "PD". It is more cumbersome to render and less plausible than J. J. Rousseau's parable of the stag hunt.

2 A bit naively, Rousseau thought that this could be achieved by the members of the hunting party signing a "contract social" – a kind of mini-constitution of their common nascent state.

The discussion of this issue has a long history and it cuts across ideological divides. There are the old reactionaries (like Joseph de Maistre) who saw modernity as destructive. Conservative romantics like Ferdinand Toennies juxtapose the rational and coldly efficient "Gesellschaft" to the warmth of the more natural "Gemeinschaft". Some progressive leftists are "communitarians" and believe that the most serious damage inflicted by capitalism has been its rupturing of communal ties.[3] Market liberals as well as many Leftists would contest all of that. For them the communal is non existent.[4] Individuals would and should do nothing more than "maximise" their personal benefit ("utility"). To pursue this goal, they would not need the crutches of a "community".

The American political scientist Robert Putnam has tried to provide an empirical base to this debate ("Making Democracy Work" and "Bowling Alone"). In doing so, he has re-vitalised the concept of "social capital". As Putnam uses it, the term stands for the stock of trust a society has in its common institutions; and the willingness, tradition and routine a society has in actually using these institutions. Robert Putnam tries to demonstrate that this "social capital" is an essential pre-requisite for a functioning economy and polity. Comparing the inferior performance of Southern Italy to the good economic and political performance of Northern Italy, he traces the cause of this difference to the lack of proper "social capital" in the Southern part of the Italian peninsula. In "Bowling Alone", Robert Putnam provides arguments and evidence for the claim that with the progress in material wealth, "social capital" is likely to become depleted – just as the stock of non-renewable sources of energy would become depleted by economic growth. Human material progress would thus in the end destroy the very foundation it is based upon.

Some developments sustain such pessimism:

- Clearly, the family as the most basic type of community is in decline;
- Mental illness and other forms of social disfunctionality become more common;

---

3 As for instance Richard Owen and other early British Socialists; or the modern left-leaning sociologists Anthony Giddens and Amitai Etzioni. Inasmuch as he has a concrete political vision and programme (and, contrary to evidence, I do believe that he has), the British Prime Minister Tony Blair has also to be counted among the left **"communitarians"**; claiming as he does, that a society would not just be defined by the rights its members hold (or by the entitlements they have been assigned); but equally so by the obligations its members are ready to assume.

4 According to the UK ex-Prime Minister Margaret Thatcher: "there is no such thing as 'society' ".

- An "underclass" has become permanently established in wealthy countries and grows even in times of prosperity;

- Core institutions and values essential for the survival of small local communities are being eroded. These communities degrade into mere dormitories for commuters without any collective substance or soul;

- Voluntary organisations atrophy;

- All human activities are being commercialised. Thus they no longer promote human bonding[5];

- Public space is being reduced;

- Various groups of societies segregate according to intelligence as education follows intelligence; status follows education; and marriage follows status[6];

- Geographic segregation according to status and income is becoming more acute;

- The pseudo-connectedness provided by television hides but deepens the actual isolation of individuals;

- In the most advanced of the "modernisers", the United States, citizens seem no longer able to agree on acceptable behaviour, on standard norms, and are less subject to informal social sanctions. Courts are therefore called to resolve even the most trivial conflicts.

This last example of the courts intruding into the most trivial aspects of life merits close scrutiny as it highlights some essential issues and developments. It highlights – as some previous examples have done – the scope of the US exceptionality. The proclivity of US citizens to rush to court is something still specific to Americans; as is the proclivity of these courts to rule in such trivial matters and to do so with quasi-legislative power. But at this point, that is not our major concern.

5 O. Wilde: a cynic is a person who knows the price of everything and the value of nothing.

6 This is a complex argument: intelligence used to be distributed in society at random, with the son or daughter of a simple worker having as much chance of being intelligent as the children of a baron. The education system was not open to all at that time. Now it is. Hopefully (that is far from certain) it will select the brightest. Educational status (and no longer traditional social rank) is now decisive for the choice of a partner. Intelligent female marries intelligent male; and as intelligence is genetically determined for at least 50%, their offspring will also tend to be more intelligent and will again marry intelligence.

Source: New York Herald Tribune

The aspect more pertinent to our overall argument is that this growing role of courts is but one other example of a general trend: informal social rules and constraints are being replaced by formal ones; informal institutions are being replaced by formal institutions. Generally, the formal institutions are believed to be superior in efficiency and effectiveness to their informal cousins. But this is not necessarily so. US courts have, for example, started to interfere in the teacher-pupil relationship. This has helped neither teachers, nor pupils, nor the educational system. Scarce money is now withdrawn to pay for lawyers, courts and indemnities. In addition, the lien between teacher and pupil is handicapped by having to bear the burden of court definitions and prescriptions. This brings out the other troubling and more general aspect of this development in the US. A classroom is based on a give and take between teachers and pupils. It functions because society and parents trust it to function; because they trust teachers to make an effort and to be fair; and because they trust pupils to accept their role and to profit from it. Once this basic trust evaporates (inter alia in courtroom tangles), the base of the institution "school" starts to crumble with it. Teachers will cease to teach. Pupils will cease to learn. Parents and citizens in general will cease to pay. As many other common institutions, schools, too, rest on a base of basic trust. They cannot function in its absence.

Humans are social beings; they are defined by and in their social relations. They would not even be able to speak (and thus think) without having been surrounded by community since infancy. We could not function without being imbedded in a web of reciprocal ties. Human existence is emptied out if this is no longer the case and if humans become isolated. Unfortunately, all of the ills just mentioned above seem to indicate that this emptying out of humans and this withdrawal from communality is well advanced already.

"There is a place that takes you back to that time of innocence. A place where the biggest decision is whether to play kick-the-can or king-on-the-hill. A place of caramel apples and cotton candy, secret forts and hopscotch on the streets. That place is Celebration – a new American town of block parties and Fourth of July Parades; of spaghetti dinners and school bake sales, lollipops and fireflies in a jar".

This is the header of an advertising text trying to lure inhabitants to the newly created, wholly artificial city "Celebration" owned by Disney and situated near its entertainment complex in Orlando, Florida. This key part of the sales pitch is notable for what it does not say; and for the sentiments and longings it appeals to.

It does not refer to the material aspects of the new habitation: size and number of rooms, insulation, cost for heating and air conditioning, availability of a garage, costs of financing, etc. It does not even refer to some other key issues of city living: like crime, schools, public transportation, recreational and shopping facilities, etc.

It blatantly appeals to a sense of lost innocence; the sense that much of the communal has disappeared in modern America; and might be recuperated under the sheltering wings of the Disney Corporation. Obviously, this is the main selling point: Celebration is a place where you will no longer be isolated; but again be inserted into a thriving and supportive community.

So if this is the sales pitch of the marketing strategists of "Celebration" and Disney, they must be quite certain that the sentiment they appeal to is widely shared by Americans. Is such a sentiment a mere fantasy; a romantic and unrealistic yearning for a return to childhood? Or shouldn't we credit those who hold it with some sense of realism and capacity for objective judgement?

For an answer, use the rule of the thumb: public opinion is more often right than wrong.

Pessimists usually attract wider audiences than optimists and we therefore tend to ignore positive messages. In this specific case, we might thus overlook altogether different symptoms that all point in the opposite direction of humans becoming more and not less interconnected and communal:

- Modern societies are less cruel. The death penalty has been abolished in most wealthy countries. Animal fights for public amusement have been banned.
- The more modern the society, the less corrupt (in general). This implies that the informal communal sanctions against corruption have become more potent.
- While the traditional family is in decline, people still cherish family life. Finding a partner and founding a family still ranks as a top priority among young people. The high rate of divorce might just express disappointed high hopes. Also, there are "new" forms of family life like: unmarried couples living together, or homosexual permanent bondings. These developments do not support the notion that humans have rejected close attachment to a "significant other" and now prefer to live as loners.
- New forms of commonality substitute for older ones. The INTERNET has created virtual communities. Professional associations thrive. Few things have grown faster than professional magazines.
- In offices and in office culture there is strong emphasis on the communal. The new office architecture with its open spaces provides visual proof.
- Democracy is becoming the dominant form of government world-wide. Yet a democratic polity can only exist on the basis of shared values, reciprocity and commonality.

These examples could prove that the need and the capacity for connectedness and commonality has not decreased as a consequence of modernisation. They show that we now have wider and more conscious choices about whom to connect to. Other indicators, too, would sustain the optimistic claim that the accumulation of material wealth does not automatically destroy the urge and capacity for social bonding. Neither would it obstruct participation in the "civic society". This participation is higher in the wealthier EU-countries, like Denmark and the Netherlands, than in poorer EU-countries like Portugal and Spain. Participation in organisations of civil society is rising together with wealth also in the "threshold countries" of Eastern Asia and Latin America.

Growing participation in civil society organisations 1981-97

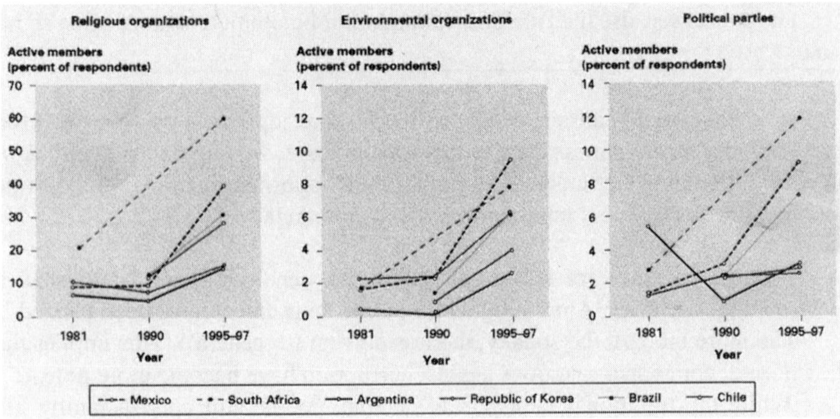

Source: World Value Survey

But it is problematic anyhow, to juxtapose the individual and material on one side to the immaterial and communal on the other. This differentiation is highly artificial. Because what seems to be individual and material at first sight, is actually and au fond social. Who would really wish for the bigger car were it not a sign of social rank; and thus of communal esteem that one hopes to gain. Who would drive a Mercedes if it were not for others looking at it and – rightly – interpreting it as a claim to social rank and approval?

This example points to a type of inherent scarcity that no amount of economic progress will be able to overcome:

Many goods we yearn for are so called positional goods[7]. Such goods cannot be reproduced at will. They are sought exactly because they are scarce and, by their being scarce, they signal social rank. If such goods became abundant they would not signal high rank anymore and thus would be worthless for exactly that reason[8]. Who would relish driving a Mercedes if everyone could afford to buy that heavy car? Who would pay a fortune for the carbon in diamonds, were they not rare and thus available only to the rich who flaunt them as visible signs of their success (just as military wear their badges as signs of rank)?

7 A. Hirsch: "Social limits to growth".

8 Example from J. Schumpeter: the silk stockings of Queen Elizabeth. When they were so very scarce, they signalled royal rank. Nowadays nylons of greater smoothness and transparency are worn even by cleaning ladies.

That is why there will always be competition between individuals and nations, regardless of how wealthy they have become. Greater wealth might even increase the virulence of this competition, as ever newer and ever more costly symbols have to be created to signal high social standing[9]. The economist Lord Keynes predicted in the 1930s that his grandchildren would no longer care very much for material possessions. Two generations later, in the sixties, it looked, for a time, as if this prediction would become true. One thought we had entered the era of "post-materialism". Youngsters exchanged their suits and costumes for sweatshirt and jeans and frolicked in the mud of Woodstock.

Oh where is Woodstock now? Where are the flower-children? Time has bypassed them. Against their hope and vision, the race of competitive consumption has not slackened. It has accelerated and has become even more merciless. Hippies and Dylan Thomases no longer provide role models for the young. DINKs (double income, no kids) do. Nobody, except a few ivory tower sociologists, still talks about "post-materialism". The rest read life-style magazines and shopping guides.

The competition for inherently limited status symbols keeps the economic engine humming. But other arguments might also be offered to explain the continuing urge to increase material wealth:

- One has not found a substitute for labour as the organising principle of private and social life. Those substitutes that have been tried are worse in their effect upon society. The society would become militarised if people were to yearn for valour and bravery instead of working at the hilt so as to finance ostentatious consumption.
- We should appreciate the fact that today the majority of citizens are "materialistic" and acquisitive. Being so, at least they do not ape the vices of former idle ruling classes. If they were to come to act like the former ruling classes, their future and the future of their nations would be bleak.
- The never ending revolution of economic change is needed so as to prevent a petrifaction and a re-feudalisation of society. Stagnant feudalism is – so to say – the "natural social order". If not held in constant motion and turmoil

9 Why, among the very rich nations of this planet, the obsession with "competitiveness"? Whom would they want to be competitive against as a group? Are they competing against the Martians? And why, between them, this obsession with having found the right formula, the need to impose the model on others and claiming its universal significance? Is it truly because we wish for still higher material wealth; or is it not because we want to demonstrate that we are more valorous, tougher, more intelligent; with better right to be offered respect and acknowledgment?

by the ceaselessly humming economy, societies would lapse into this natural order. Continuous economic change prevents such petrifaction.

- Neo-Marxists claim that the process of accumulation of capital is incessant by its very nature. This accumulation is the essential characteristic and it needs labour to produce the necessary "Mehrwert".

- Financial capital has over – wrought expectations and unrealistically high claims to profit. It therefore has to seek ever new productions if such high gains still are (or seem) possible.

Paid work will therefore continue to structure our personal life as well as the whole society. No feasible alternatives are in sight. Yet not all of the consequences of that unidirectional quest are positive. One of the negative consequences is unemployment. We tend to work more than necessary. We thus deprive others of the chances to also participate in the work force.

Economists provide many explanations for the persistence of unemployment; and for the fact that, over the last decades, it has grown in the rich countries instead of declining[10]. But whatever these explanations, underlying all of them is the assumption that working at least 40 hours a week is and should be the norm. Yet this assumption should be questioned. Why do we automatically reject the alternative of people opting for leisure instead of income and preferring to exchange some added leisure for some added income?

One person works full time, 40 hours a week and earns 1000 US dollars a week. The other person does not work, is unemployed and therefore is without wage-income. The two could make a deal that would imply no added cost to the employer. They could share leisure and income. Each of them would earn 500 US dollars; and each of them would work for just 20 hours a week.

Though this solution is so obvious, it is rarely taken even in countries with high unemployment. Not only is there massive opposition from the employers; workers too are ambivalent about such options. Frequently, they also oppose it. Few governments have thus dared to venture into this terrain[11].

The opposition of employers is explained easily. They prefer a high level of unemployment. This makes for docile workers and moderate trade unions. The scepticism of workers is more difficult to explain. One would expect that the preference for leisure grows together with rising wealth, and that people would

10 It started to recede a bit recently; in the US, since the mid eighties; in Europe since the mid nineties.

11 The solution was tried by the socialist government of France; but was partly rescinded later on by the following conservative French government.

like to "purchase" more leisure time with their added income; just as they generally prefer to purchase more ample homes and finer food. But they don't.

People remain addicted to competitive consumption. They do not desire the freedom of leisure time more than the added income that permits them to spend more on their shopping. "Virtue" is being attached to buying as much as possible; and no virtue is being attached to frugality or to taking more time out for leisurely pursuits.

James Madison remarked in one of his "Federalist Papers" that no polity can do without "virtue". *"To suppose that any form of government will secure liberty and happiness without any VIRTUE in the people, is a chimerical idea."*

True! But different societies and different polities are based upon different forms of "virtue". "Virtues" are usually defined as those internalised rules that are very much functional for the preservation of the existing socio-economic order; and beneficial, in particular, to those that dominate in this order.

In a society dominated by males, the woman was considered virtuous who blindly obeyed her husband and who meekly tolerated his abuse. In feudal/warrior societies, virtue was defined as the readiness for senseless sacrifice and for resolve against all odds in physical combat. Catholicism marked as virtuous those who devoted themselves to duties at the cost of even embracing the repellent (like licking the wounds of lepers). Early capitalism found virtuous those who were diligent, sober, punctual, parsimonious. Males, warrior princes, bishops and early capitalists very much profited from such definitions of "virtue".

If, in late capitalism, the virtues of early capitalism are in decline, what does that tell us about the new rulers and their interests? Virtue is attached to long working hours and high spending; to mobility and shiftlessness instead of permanence; to ruthlessness instead of accommodating friendliness; to information instead of knowledge and wisdom.

Yet limits seem to exist as to the extent the notion of "virtue" may be redefined in the interest of the rulers and dominators. T. Friedman cites the British social scientist Edward Carr with the following quotation: "*.. forming connections is one of the most defining characteristics of human beings.. asking us to break such connections, to re-invent ourselves, think in short term and stay flexible sets us all adrift...we do not bond with other; we "team". We do not have friend;, we have contacts. We are not members of enduring, nurturing communities; we are nodes in ever shifting, coldly utilitarian networks."*

The word "nurturing communities" used by Carr is significant. As mentioned, humans are social beings. They only become true persons in the relation to and by insertion into a community of other humans. Ignoring that truth and cutting these bonds, opens the vista into a future without precedent. It is a future fraught with dangers. Until now, the process of civilisation has involved moving persons closer to one another; enlarging their interface; enriching their intercourse. The jury is out on whether this process has now truly become reversed. There are many symptoms to make us surmise that this is what really is happening; and fewer symptoms certainly to indicate that a new communality substitutes for the old one.

But let us turn from such abstract considerations to some more mundane statistics. Many of them provide fodder to the pessimists which see material progress as self-destructive. As mentioned, material progress has put at siege the most basic of all communities, namely the traditional family. Increasingly, marriage is tentative and no longer for life. In Sweden, nearly half of all marriages end in divorce.

Marriages and divorces per 1000 people. EU-15

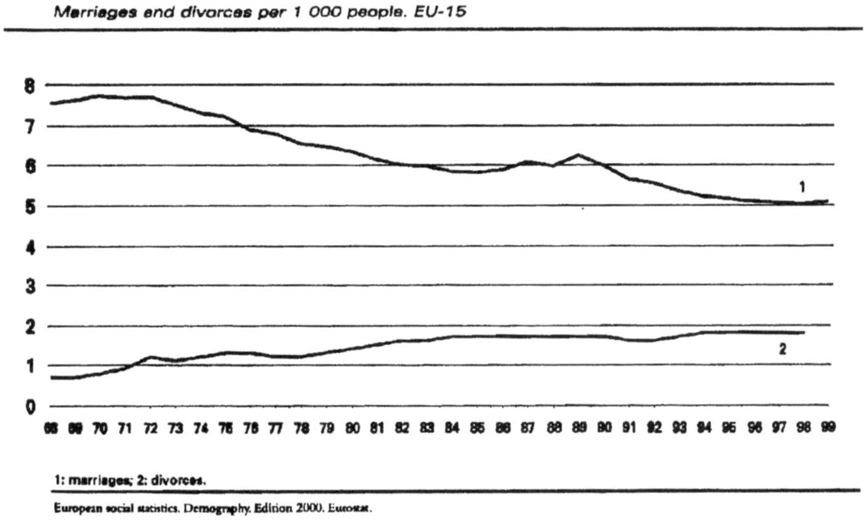

Source: Eurostat 2000

That might be for the good, with each side then being free to seek someone better suited as a new partner. But, however that may be, personal happiness or unhappiness of the couple is not the main reason for concern over the decay of the traditional family. The fate of children is. In addition to those left with single parents after a divorce, the numbers of those have risen dramatically who are born out of wedlock. In Sweden, this is now the majority.

Percentage of children born out of wedlock
European countries, 1993-1999

European countries	*1993*	*1999*
Austria	26.3	30.5
Denmark	46.8	44.9
France	34.9	40.7
Germany	14.8	22.1
Greece	2.8	4.0
Ireland	19.9	30.9
Italy	7.4	.
Netherlands	13.1	22.8
Norway	44.4	.
Poland	8.2	11.7
Sweden	50.4	55.3
Spain	10.8	

Source: Eurostat

The reason for concern is, therefore, not respect for traditional morals; but worry about the effects of single parenthood upon all of these children. If there is a consensus in social science, then it is upon the fact that children in single parent families are disadvantaged seriously in nearly all respects. They do worse at school and later in professional life, are more liable to become unemployed and criminal, more liable to become or stay poor, to use drugs, etc[12].

Not only does the number of single parent households grow. So does the number of those who live all by themselves. In some cases, that might correspond to their preferences. In many cases it will not be so, but will be enforced by the death of a partner, by bad luck in finding a spouse, or because of separation enforced by work.

12 Just to be clear about that: these effects exist even if one controls for the effects of income (usually lower in single parent families). Given equal income the child of the single parent family is at higher risk still than the child of a two parent family with comparable income.

Single person US households as a percentage of total households 1890-1990

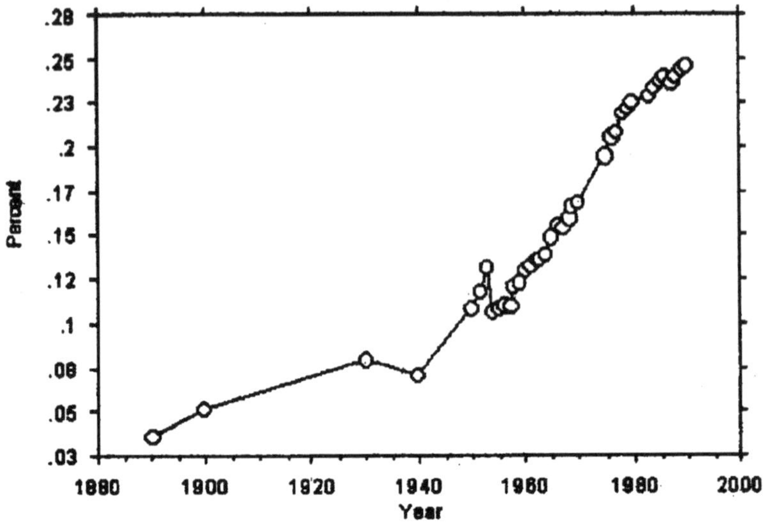

Source: US Bureau of Census

Recorded crimes per 1000 population

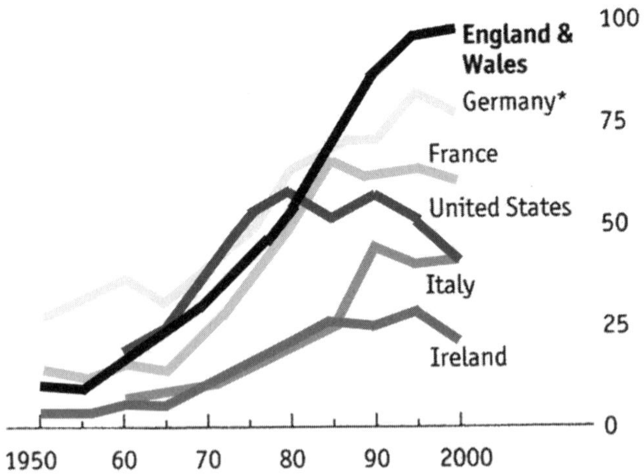

Source: UN population prospects

Material wealth stimulates destructive tendencies. Early on one had assumed it to be the other way round. Crime, for example, was seen as a consequence of poverty. But, as it seems, it is not poverty but growing wealth that correlates with crime. Both in the US and in Europe, crime rates have risen together with wealth in the years since World War II.[13]

Suicidal, self-destructive tendencies also seem to increase with increasing wealth. Obviously, suicide rates are also culturally defined – that is, they differ according to the different cultures of different countries. But there also is a strong correlation to the wealth of that country. Generally: the higher the wealth, the greater the number of suicides.

Suicide in the EU
mortality per 100.000
Male Female

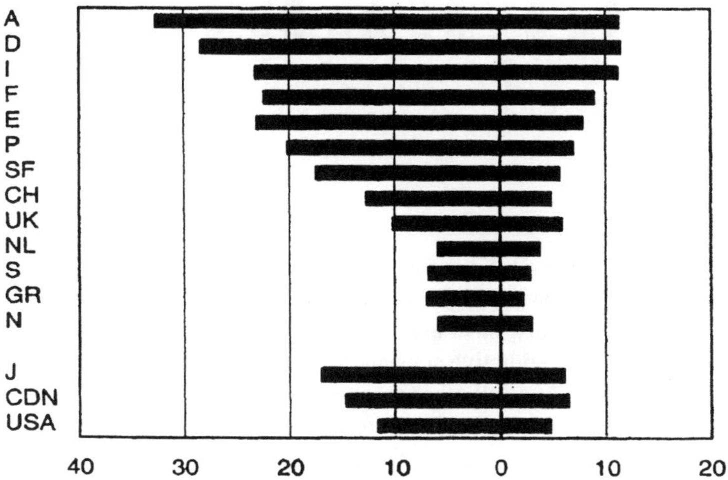

Source: Eurostat

One also may kill oneself through bad habits. In poor countries, premature death comes as a consequence of poverty mostly. As a consequence of hunger, as the consequence of a poor diet, as the consequence of having to drink unsafe water. In rich countries premature death is frequently the consequence of persons using that superior wealth to finance dangerous habits like smoking and drinking.

13 Over the last decade they have levelled somewhat or even declined. But they remain still very high compared to what they were in 1950.

WHO estimates of years of life lost caused by 10 major risk factors

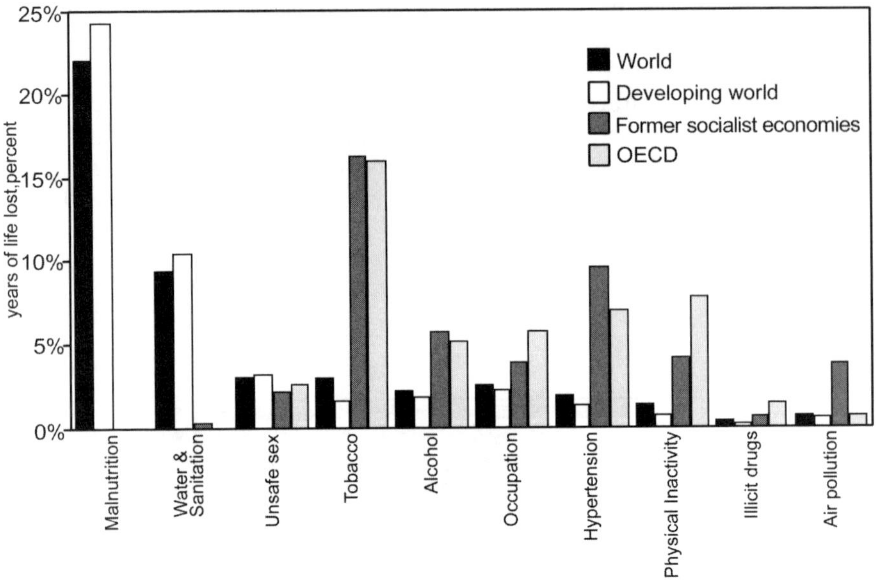

Source: WHO 1996

And finally one can kill oneself – or at least one's own personality via drugs:

Drugs offer a glaring example of some negative consequences of growing wealth. Addictive drugs have always been with us. But different regions of the world used different addictive substances. With globalisation, however, everyone now can use the drugs of all other regions.

In other ways, too, the rising consumption of drugs has been facilitated by modernisation and globalisation. Drugs have become cheaper and more widely available. Evidently, rising demand defies all attempts to control and limit supply. Notwithstanding the long standing "drug war" of the US, more of them entered illegally. The same holds true for Europe. The consequence was a steep drop in the street price.

% decrease in the UK street price of drugs
November 1990 to December 2001

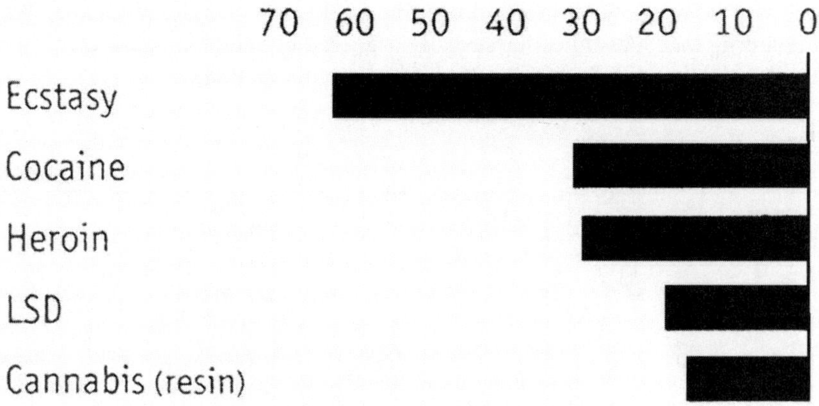

Source: UK National Criminal Intelligence Service

The rising consumption of hard drugs is both a reflection and a cause of a deep seated alienation and marginalisation of parts of the society.

The consequences of the habit for the consumer are very negative: HIV, early death, petty and not so petty crime, pauperisation, marginalisation. For the societies the costs are high too. The highest costs arise from the fact that a substantial part of the economy is being criminalised. As a consequence, organised crime expands and becomes wealthy and powerful enough to corrupt the economic and political system. The ill consequences extend into the international realm. Legitimate governments are destabilised and subverted by this vast network of organised crime. Drug barons build their own mini-states complete with their own private armies (including, as of late, submarines).

The problem will not go away. It will remain with us and it will even grow. Eventually, drug consumption will have to be decriminalised. But decriminalisation will then, in its turn, accentuate other problems arising from the use of drugs. Arduous efforts are still being made by people to arrive at "feeling good". They work hard, for instance, so as to gain approval from their boss. They make efforts to be kind to the spouse in order to be liked by her, etc. All those onerous efforts can be short circuited by drugs. Just pop the pill and you will experience the same "feel good"-effect without any exertion. On the road to this unhappy state of affairs, the border between the legitimate and the illegal (or socially undesirable) use of drugs will become rather fluid. Already now, the anti-depressant drug Prozac is being widely used in the US not to cure real depression but just to make one's day brighter. Drugs will also become more targeted in their effects. There will be drugs for this and drugs for that kind of mood and feeling. What about a drug that substitutes for sexually triggered bonding? It could come to replace the pleasant, but frequently very complicated, real thing.

Dilbert

Source: New York Herald Tribune

In preceding chapters, we have dealt at length with what could impede the growth in the world's population and the growth in its wealth. We have addressed developments that would endanger even the preservation of existing wealth and the maintenance of the existing numbers of persons on our planet. We found that such obstacles and dangers do indeed exist; but that nearly all of them can be lifted by purposeful, joint and timely human action; and by humans adapting their behaviour, their values and institutions to new circumstances.

The problem is that these changes now have become more massive and thus call for more resolute adaptation and/or counter-action. The key variable, the strategic variable, is thus the capacity in human societies to agree on the nature of a challenge, to agree on the nature of the response; and to mount such response in an efficient manner. To do that, they must be able to maintain what the stag hunters in Rousseau's fable have failed to maintain: trust in one another, communication and co-operation with one another.

Countless authors have warned against societies losing that capacity on the road to ever greater wealth. These authors come from different traditions. They have different political preferences. Many may simply mourn the losses that are inevitable with all passage of time. Some of them might be the traditional opponents of modernisation. Yet, as the chorus is so broad, it is difficult to dismiss all that pleading as nostalgic or otherwise irrelevant. Indeed, we have to fear that, basically, these authors are right in seeing trust and the capacity to co-operate as the single most important resource (or raw material so to say). The world might find substitutes for oil, for phosphates. It might learn to use less water; and to catch fewer fish from the oceans. But as all important human efforts are collective, the world as we know it would crumble if the most strategic of all resources became scarce, and humans un-learned how to bond, how to trust, how to co-operate.

Poverty and Income Inequality Within States

The notion is widespread that economic growth just benefits those who are wealthy already. The poor will remain as poor as they always have been: Yet, though widely accepted, this notion is not confirmed by data. World-wide, the poorest fifth of the population does share in rising wealth. The wealthier a country, the lower, in general, the incidence of poverty.[1]

Average annual per capita consumption of the poorest fifth of population
In 1993 US $ (PPP) log scale

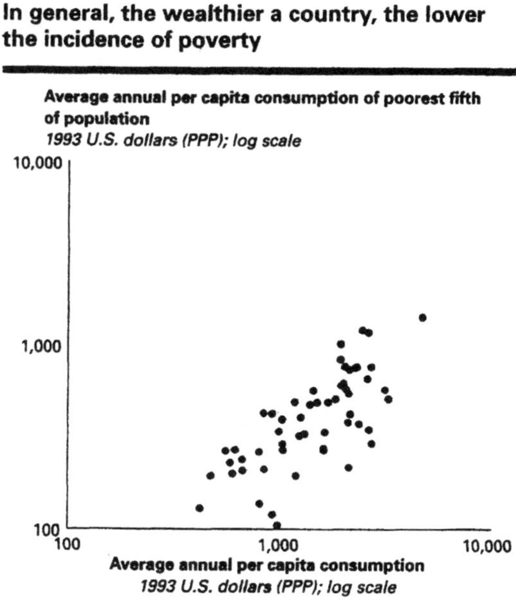

Source: IBRD

1 If poverty is measured by surveys on consumption, the effect of overall rising wealth on poverty is more marked still. A 10% rise in overall wealth would produce a 26% reduction of absolute poverty (Adams jr. 2003).

Measuring poverty

Two methods are used to measure poverty. One may gauge poverty either in absolute terms; or in relative terms. In absolute terms, poverty is gauged against a fixed parameter. In the following examples we use the parameter of the World Bank "of people having to live on less than one US dollar a day". This method is especially useful in low income countries where the problem of poverty is mostly one of simple subsistence, of having enough to survive.

The other method gauges poverty in relative terms (usually: the percentage of the population living from an income that is less than either 50% or 60% of the median income) . In wealthier countries, poverty does not translate into a problem of subsistence, as one can physically survive on very little. In wealthier countries, poverty implies social exclusion; the burden of not being able to share and to connect to the life other people accept as standard. Therefore, in wealthier countries, it is more meaningful to apply the yardstick of relative poverty.

So let us look at absolute poverty first.

Absolute poverty in the world's regions, 1987-1998

	Population covered by at least one survey	*People living on less than $1 a day*				
Region		1987	1990	1993	1996	1998
East Asia and Pacific	90,8	417,5	452,4	431,9	26,1	278,3
excluding China	71,1	114,1	92,0	83,5	55,1	65,1
Europe and Cental Asia	81,7	1,1	7,1	18,3	23,8	24,0
Latin America and the Caribbean	88,0	63,7	73,8	70,8	76,0	78,2
Middle East and North Africa	52,5	9,3	5,7	5,0	5,0	5,5
South Asia	97,9	474,4	495,1	505,1	531,7	522,0
Sub-Saharan Africa	72,9	217,2	242,3	273,3	289,0	290,9
Total	88,1	1183,2	1276,4	1304,3	1190,6	1198,9
Excluding China	84,2	879,8	915,9	955,9	980,5	985,7
	Share of population living on less than $1 a day					
Region	1987	1990	1993	1996	1998	
East Asia and Pacific	26,6	27,6	25,2	14,9	15,3	
excluding China	23,9	18,5	15,9	10,0	11,3	
Europe and Cental Asia	0,2	1,6	4,0	5,1	5,1	
Latin America and the Caribbean	15,3	16,8	15,3	15,6	15,6	
Middle East and North Africa	4,3	2,4	1,9	1,8	1,9	
South Asia	44,9	44,0	42,4	42,3	40,0	
Sub-Saharan Africa	46,6	47,7	49,7	48,5	46,3	
Total	28,3	29,0	28,1	24,5	24,0	
Excluding China	28,5	28,1	27,7	27,0	26,2	

Source: IBRD

Between 1987 and 1998, the number of persons subsisting on less than one US dollar a day has roughly remained stable. But as the world population has grown, the share of this population living on less than one dollar a day has dropped from 28,3% to 24,0 %.

As of 1999, the World Bank had made poverty reduction its main goal. Together with the IMF and the countries concerned, it drafted the Poverty Reduction Strategy Papers that should guide the relevant policies of the country receiving assistance, of the donor countries, and of the International Financial Institutions (IFIs) and of International Organisations (IOs).

Poverty reduction is also one of the "Millennium Goals", set by the worlds' heads of state and government in September of 2000. Poverty – that is the percentage of the population living on less than one US dollar a day – should be halved by 2015. Other millennium goals to be met by 2015 are:

- reduce the infant mortality rate by two thirds
- achieve a 100% enrolment in primary education
- achieve – already by 2005 – gender equality in the enrolment in primary education
- provide access to birth control to all women in reproductive age
- reduce maternal mortality by three quarters

East Asia is well on its way to meeting this target of cutting absolute poverty by 50%. In fact, it will overshoot this target. Other regions are just a little bit above the trajectory to the target (as, for instance, Latin America and the Middle East); or they are below it by a relatively small margin (as e.g. Africa). In Central Eastern Europe and Central Asia, however, absolute poverty has increased dramatically (though from a very low level).

We have maintained that the growth of the world economy would also benefit the poor, and we have shown that, on the average, it does. But that is, of course, a generalisation. We thus have to add a few qualifications:

- Not all countries participate in the rise of overall wealth (we shall deal with that issue later).
- It is not in all countries with rising wealth that the poor can share in this increase of wealth.
- And even where they can, the share that they can cut from the growing cake is very uneven.

So let us analyse how evenly wealth is distributed in the countries of the world; and let us ask whether this distribution changes in the course of economic development; whether it becomes either more equal or less equal.

Reduction of poverty by half till 2015
Percentage of the population having to live from less than 1 US $ a day

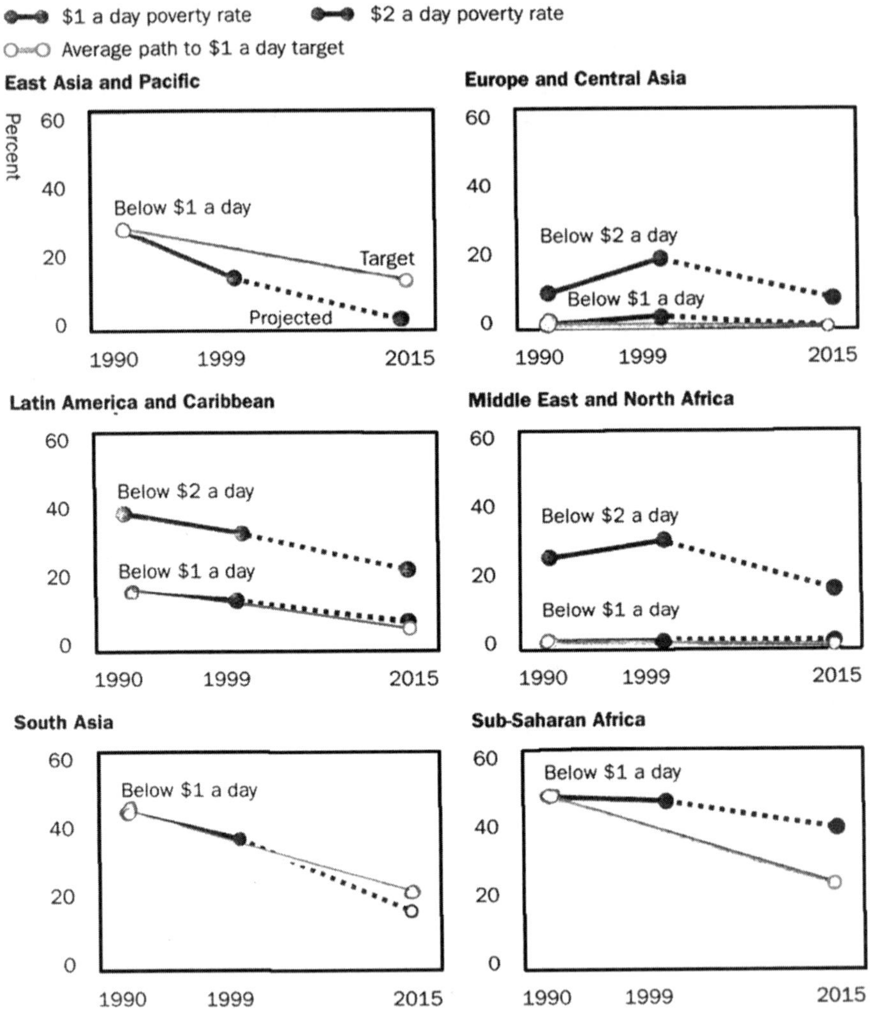

Source: World Bank

The table below provides an answer for the member countries of the European Union. Were it just for this table, we would conclude that greater equality goes hand in hand with a high level of wealth. In the European Union, at least, the correlation is clear: the wealthier the EU member, the more equal the distribution of the income; it being least equal in poor Portugal and Greece; and most equal in wealthy Denmark[2].

Gini[3] coefficient versus average disposable income 1996
EU 15 member countries
Average disposable income

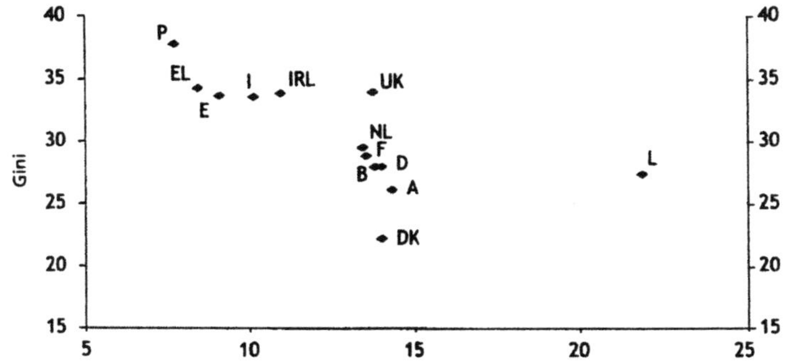

Source: Eurostat

But, on the other hand, this should not make us assume that income inequality is greatest in the poorest countries. This is not so.

On the average, rich countries have a more equal distribution of income. The distribution is less equal in the very poor countries. The distribution is, however, very much less equal in the intermediate countries ("threshold countries", or "emerging markets", or "medium income countries"). If we put the Gini-coefficient (or another yardstick for measuring inequality) on the vertical axis and the time since the onset of economic development on the horizontal axis we arrive at a graphic picture on how inequality developed over the time since economic growth began. It first rises when economic development sets in. Later, it

2 The US, with a high level of wealth and stark inequality of income, is an exception (as they are in many other fields). The other Non – European member of the league of the wealthy – Japan – is, on the other hand, very egalitarian and egalitarian, too, in income distribution. The US Gini coefficient stands at 40, the one of Japan at 25.

3 The Gini coefficient is the most commonly used measure of inequality. The higher the coefficient, the less equal the distribution of income.

declines as countries move up into the league of the truly wealthy.[4] This bell-shaped curve is named the Kuznets curve after the economist who first pointed to this pattern.[5]

Level of wealth and inequality in the distribution of income

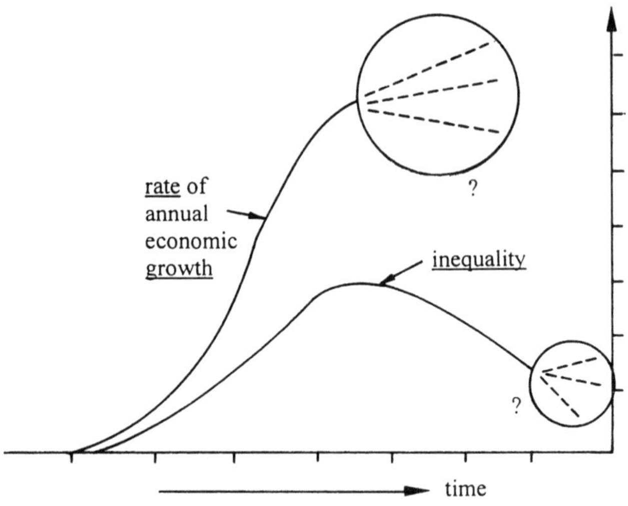

In the above graph the right hand side of the Kuznets curve becomes fuzzy; and we have added a question mark. This is because future developments are uncertain. We are not certain as to how inequality will evolve in these rich countries. Will the income distribution continue to become more equal as overall wealth rises even further? Or will it again become more unequal?

Why does this question matter? The issue of equality is relevant because people care. Equality ranks higher on their agenda than absolute wealth. There is

4 This is in contradiction to the Marxist prediction of growing polarisation. Karl Marx stipulated an ever rising inequality.

5 While it is true that inequality changes in the course of economic development, it is also true that patterns of income distribution vary widely between countries and world regions. These differences seem to remain constant over time. Thus, even if and when having become wealthy, Latin America would still have a very uneven distribution of income.

only a weak correlation between economic growth and the "happiness index"[6] . But this happiness index correlates closely with income distribution. More unequal societies are less happy.

This subjective feeling has its counterparts in social and political reality. The more unequal a society, the less liberal as a rule, the higher the crime rate and the worse other symptoms of social disfunctionality. High inequality also makes for less flexibility and, thus, greater difficulties in adapting to new circumstances. This is because it becomes hard to arrive at consensus and joint action when between citizens differences in income and in life chances are substantial.

There also is a connection to economic performance. Individuals who are wealthy and privileged by high income try to justify and legitimise their elevated position by claiming that their wealth and high income would ultimately benefit all; and that their wealth would, in fact, be a necessary precondition for the material betterment of also the middle and low income classes. Economic history does not sustain such claims.

All East Asian countries, for example, that have achieved rapid economic growth, were, at the same time, very egalitarian. In a similar vein, those European countries that have managed best to escape from the economic doldrums of the nineties were also those European countries with the most equal distribution of income: Sweden, Finland, Denmark, and the Netherlands.

The distribution of income is thus something greatly relevant. Greater equality is an important social goal in itself. But it also is a useful tool for achieving other goals. So how have the rich countries fared in this respect more recently? Has the income distribution become more equal, or less equal? The table below, compiled by the European Commission[7], provides a certain base for an answer as it concentrates on the development of income inequality in the more immediate past between 1975 and 1995.

The insight provided by this table is at odds with the Kuznets theorem of growing wealth always correlating with growing equality. It shows that, in the more recent past, in already wealthy countries, the increase in inequality was even more marked than the increase of inequality in the whole world taken together (which nonetheless was rather strong too).

---

6 "Happiness" is certainly difficult to define and to measure. A whole sub-section of empirical sociology is exclusively devoted to researching this single issue. The above text is based on the findings of A. Oswald and R. Frankel, which ranked national averages in responses to the question: "are you feeling satisfied with your life?"

7 In the extremely interesting and fascinating "Scenarios Europe 2010".

World-wide tendencies in income distribution 1975-1995
(% of countries weighted according to their population)

Countries	*Inequality*			
	increases	*remains constant*	*decreases*	*no visible trend*
Industrial states	71.8	1.2	27	0.0
Eastern Europe	98.1	0.0	0.0	1.9
Former Soviet Union	100.0	0.0	0.0	0.0
Latin America	83.8	0.0	11.4	4.8
South Asia and Middle East	1.4	70.2	14.4	14.0
East Asia	79.4	4.4	16.1	0.1
Africa	31.6	11.9	7.7	48.8
World	56.6	22.1	15.6	5.7

Source: EC, Scenarios Europe 2010

But this does not hold true for all countries. Some of them deviate widely from this trend. In some very few economically successful countries of Europe, inequality has even decreased instead of becoming stronger. In Finland, the Gini-coefficient dropped from 30 to 26 between 1980 and 1990. On the other hand, the increase of income inequality was most pronounced in those wealthy countries that adhere to the gospel of neo-conservative dogma. In the time between 1980 and 1990, the Gini-coefficient increased from:

35 to 40 in New Zealand
27 to 32 in the United Kingdom
32,5 to 35,5 in the US[8]

Neo-conservatives have always maintained that wealth would "trickle down" or that the "rising tide would lift all the ships". This has not happened where neo-conservatives rule. There, wealth has “trickled up”.

The ex-Communist countries, the so-called transition countries, saw a dramatic increase in income inequality. This development was most pronounced in those ex-Communist countries which had been least successful in transforming their economy. The Gini-coefficient rose in

Poland	from	24	to	28
Romania	from	23	to	29
Russia	from	24	to	48
Kyrgyz Rep	from	23	to	55

Source: OECD

8 To rise to a staggering 40 in 1999.

We thus can say that, from now on and on the average, in the advanced countries, further economic growth tends to go hand in hand with a renewed rise in income inequality.

What has caused this reversal of the prior and seemingly secular trend towards greater equality? The main cause seems to have been the development of the labour market. As the era of mass production draws to a close, there now is less demand for unskilled and semiskilled labour and also more supply of this type of labour. Less demand and more supply implies lower wages.

Employment in industry 19 OECD countries 1970-1994
(skilled and non- skilled labour in the industrial sector)

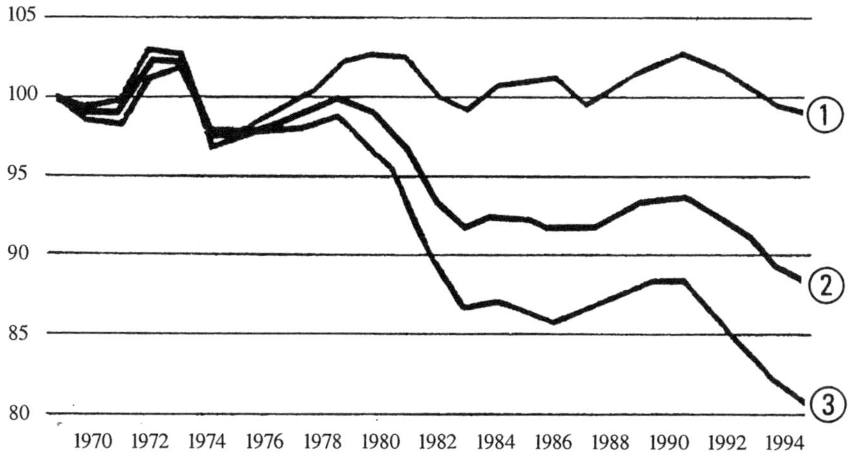

1 = skilled labour
2 = unskilled labour
3 = industry – total

Source: OECD

The liberalisation of world trade has re-enforced this tendency. Labour intensive products are imported from poorer, low-wage countries. These imports substitute for local labour intensive production in wealthy countries. Demand for semi-skilled and unskilled workers decreases in the wealthy countries and the wages drop in this section of the labour market. The demand for skilled workers and employees continues to grow, however. In the US, male high school graduates (that is those with nothing but the compulsory education) therefore saw their real wages reduced by more than 10% between 1979 and 1999; whereas college graduates saw them increase by about 15%.

Real median earning of male workers by educational attainment (1979 = 100)

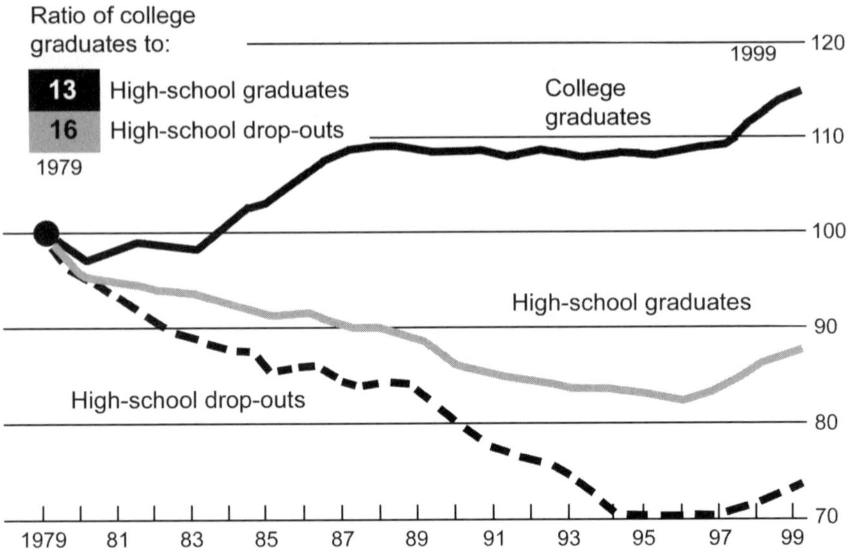

Source : US Department of Labour

Unemployment also affected income distribution, with a large pool of unemployed blue collar workers discouraging wage claims of those with less education. Up until quite recently college graduates, on the other hand, did not have to fear unemployment. They thus were in a better position to claim pay hikes.

Unemployment and level of education
(US – development between March and December 2002)

	Job change since March 2002 In 1,000	*Percentage of labour force 25 and older*
Less than a high school degree	-267	9.7%
High school graduation, no college	-956	30.5%
Some college but no degree	-507	28.0%
College graduate	+369	31.8%

Source: US Department of Labour

The waning strength of labour unions also contributes to the stagnation or low growth of wages in the industrial sector. Union membership fell in the United States and in most[9] Western European countries.

Union membership and employment in the US

Source: US Department of Labour)

A US study – summed up in the table below – tries to evaluate the weight all of these factors – and some other ones – had in widening the cleavage between the remuneration of skilled and of unskilled labour.

The stock of those with better education is growing rapidly. According to this study, this is one potent trend that partly compensates for the rise in inequality and that reduces the wage gap by roughly 40%, as it moderates the wage claims of educated, skilled workers. Among the factors which, on the other hand, make for a wider gap, the most important one is "technological change" (which puts the unskilled at a disadvantage). Trade also makes a notable contribution to inequality. The other "usual suspects", the other explanations, for greater wage inequality carry far less weight. Immigration or the "outsourcing" of tasks, for instance, has but a small effect. Note the relative importance, though, of a minimum wage.

9 It is noteworthy, though, that union "density" fell least where unions are strongest; that is in the Scandinavian countries. It is also worth noting that – contrary to neo-conservative dogma – unemployment was also low in these highly unionised Scandinavian countries (Sweden, Denmark, Finland).

Contrary to the combined wisdom of economists, minimum wages can make a difference. Their lowering increases inequality.

Getting less equal

A. Equalising forces	
Increase in stock of skilled relative to unskilled labour	-40
B. Unequalising forces	
Trade	7
Lower Transport and communication coasts	3
Liberalisation	3
Outsourcing	1
Immigration	2
Falling minimum wage	5
Deunionisation	3
Skill-based technological change	29
Other unexplained	29
TOTAL	**97**
C. Net effect	18

Source: William R. Cline, Institute for International Economics

Underclass, overclass and social mobility

The onset of sustained economic growth shattered the rigidity of traditional societies. It increased geographic mobility as people moved to towns. It increased professional mobility as people changed jobs. And it increased social mobility as people moved into more productive and, thus, better paid employment.

The movement became especially acute with the onset of full scale mass-production in the late 19th and early 20th centuries, with the migration of formerly low paid rural workers to the assembly lines of vast factories. There was a shared vision of that trend persisting. Even if one did not manage to reach a higher station in life oneself, one felt certain that at least one's children would.

Inequality was decreasing in that period. And that inequality which remained was made bearable by this hope of social advancement. Both have changed. Inequality is on the rise again. And the hope is less well founded that one might graduate, eventually, into a higher social class and into a better station in life. Channels of social advancement that were open before now tend to close. There is now less mobility between social classes. The daughters and sons of the wealthy will again become wealthy. Their risk of sliding back again on the social scale is now less than it had been in generations before. The rich stay rich even over several generations.

On the other hand, there is a fair chance for the sons and daughters of the poor to remain poor; at least if the parents were part of the lowest and the most hopeless stratum called the "underclass".

Changes in the mode of production are the main cause for this decline of social mobility. Both the very wealthy "over-class"; and the very poor "underclass" are thus caught in a self-reproducing circle of incentives and disincentives. In the bygone industrial age, skills once acquired could be used for a long time. Those that did not yet possess them could acquire them without too many difficulties. Because of these previously acquired skills, they could draw even with those better paid.

We have transited from the age of mass-industrial production to a knowledge based production. Skills needed are continuously up-scaled and redefined. Those who can do so are at an advantage. Evidently, those already well adapted to the knowledge based production are also better equipped to learn this continuous learning and adaptation. Those that are behind them in social rank will always stay behind. The distance to them will remain the same at best. Probably it will widen. Those worse off may, of course, also have to suffer through continuous training and learning. That will make them advance economically. But those ahead of them already will advance even more rapidly.

Those on the lowest end of the social scale are also caught in a circle of self-reinforcing influences. This circle turns into a downward spiral. Becoming unemployed, for example, they lose those professional skills they had, while frequently lacking opportunity, incentives or aptitude to acquire the more complex new skills instead. They adapt to their negative surroundings and sombre perspectives by moving into the sub-culture of dependency and social isolation; which they bequeath to their offspring, just as those on the opposite end of the social ladder bequeath to their children their own well rewarded patterns of behaviour.

Governments can affect the final distribution of wealth and income. They can do that through taxation; through transfers (like payments for welfare); and they finally can do that through the services they provide, which – intended or not – frequently do not benefit all parts of the population in the same manner.

Let us look at the effect, first, that various government services have on the distribution of income.

One would assume that services provided by the government are of greater benefit to the poor than they are to the rich. But this is not always the case. Even in the wealthy countries, some services actually privilege the wealthy. Free university education, for instance, has this effect. Many European states provide university education for free. They thus heavily subsidise each of their university students with money paid by taxpayers. Yet the vast majority of university students still comes from families with above average income. Once they have graduated they will benefit from their education by, again, drawing higher than average incomes. Free university education thus transfers wealth to those that are wealthy already; or that are likely to have above average incomes.

This somewhat perverse effect of the provision of public services is even more pronounced in developing countries. In poor countries, the rural population is frequently disenfranchised politically, with effective political power being vested only with the urban part of the population and especially with the wealthier part of this urban population. This is reflected in the pattern of state spending. It favours the wealthy part of the urban population. But there are also purely physical reasons for this "negative re-distribution" through government services.[10] Only so much money is available, and it can only be spent in certain places. A telephone system, for instance, will start to be built in the capital and will first benefit the wealthier inhabitants of the capital. The same tends to hold true for running water and some of the more than basic medical services.

Share of the wealthiest and the poorest fifth of the population in the state expenditure for health

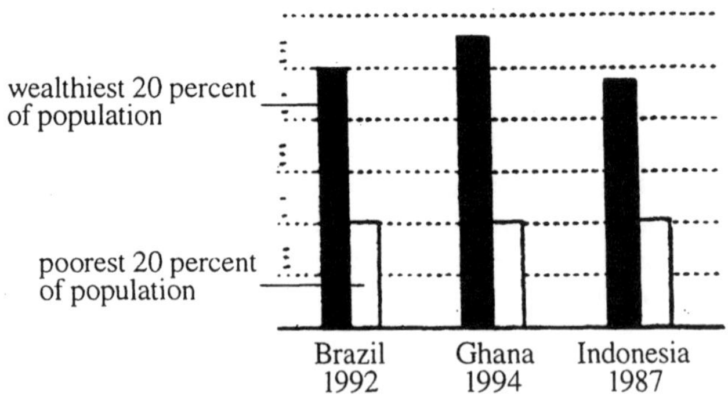

Source UNDP

10 One other and simple reason for the tendency of governments to concentrate efforts on the capital: their power does not extend much beyond.

Of course, many, and even most, of the government services still benefit the poor more than the rich. But, as we have seen, there are limits as to how much can be transferred to the poor by government services. There are limits also as to how much wealth can be "re-distributed" via taxes – by imposing higher taxes upon the rich than upon the poor. In a globalising economy, capital has become very footloose. If taxed too highly in one country, capital simply migrates to another country where it is being treated more leniently[11]. Having to fear an exodus of capital, governments feel constrained to lower taxes on it. Labour does not have this kind of international mobility. Governments thus feel less constrained in taxing labour. As a consequence, taxes on labour have risen while taxes on capital have not (or only moderately so) .

Taxes on capital and labour in the EU

Source: European Commission

11 This, at least, is what governments assume. As we will show in one of the next chapters, this assumption is not necessarily a sound one, supported by actual evidence. In Switzerland, corporate and personal income tax vary widely among the different "cantons".

The great US tax rate turn-around; median families versus millionaires

	Median families' effective tax rate	*Millionaires' families effective tax rate*
1948	5.3%	76.9%
1960	12.4%	85.5%
1970	16.6%	68.8%
1980	23.7%	31.7%
1989	24.4%	26.7%

Source: Phillips 2002

One may understand why governments feel constrained to lower taxes on corporations so as to prevent their moving elsewhere. It is more difficult to understand why they also feel constrained to lower the taxes just on high income. The United States have done so with the effect that the poor and millionaires have become subject to roughly the same income tax rate. But, in other wealthy countries too, marginal tax rates on high incomes have been lowered.

So re-distribution via taxes has become less effective. As it seems, it is not that easy for states to affect income distribution via taxation or via the services it provides. They may, however, affect income distribution through transfers. Generally, wealthier states are better equipped to do this, and perhaps also better motivated. The table below ranks EU members according to the median per capita wealth. The scale on the vertical axis indicates the extent to which income has been redistributed through state transfers. The correlation is obvious and narrow. The wealthier the state, the more efficient in redistribution through transfers.

Income redistribution through state transfers
EU countries 1996

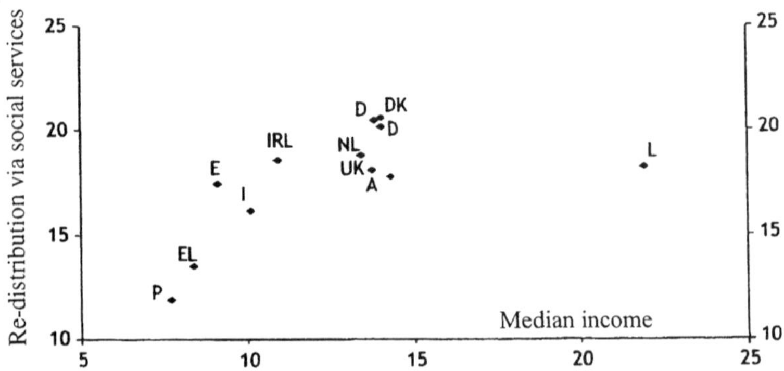

Source Eurostat

Yet another table provides proof of the efficiency of this redistribution. It shows what the level of poverty would be in the absence of these transfers; and what it actually is after these transfers.

Poor as a share of the total population before and after social transfers
EU member countries 1996; the poor are defined as the part of the population that has to live from an income that is less than 60% of the median income.

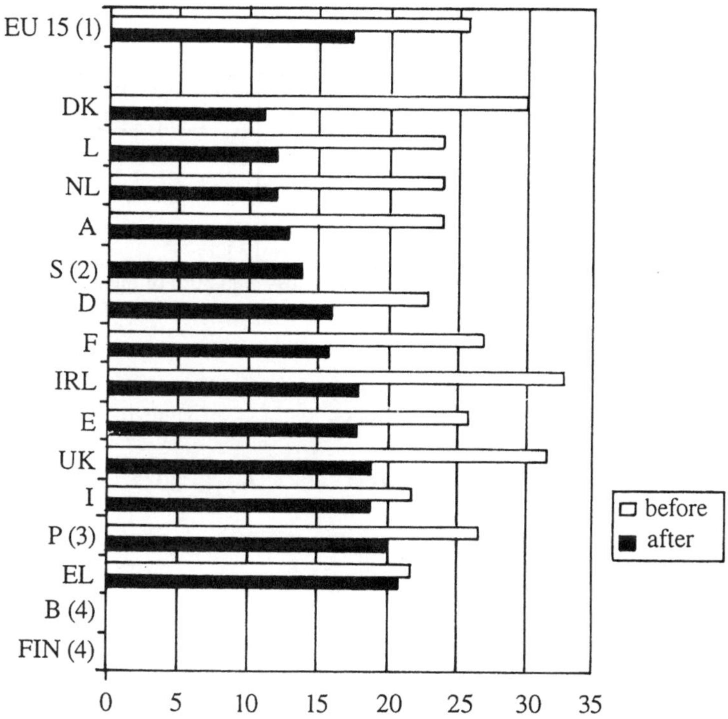

Source: Eurostat

In Denmark, for example, 30 percent of the population would live in (relative) poverty were it not for government transfers which are effective in reducing the number of poor to just 11 percent of the population. Note, however, that transfers do not have this effect in all of the EU countries. In Italy and Greece, for instance, this effect upon poverty is hardly noticeable (in World Bank parlance: transfers in these two countries are not very "targeted") .

The US differs from Japan and Europe in that the incidence of poverty is distinctly higher.

As we have seen, the present, very uneven distribution of after tax income in the United States is not just due to developments in gross (before tax) income but due also to changes in taxes and in state transfers. In the time between 1977 and 1999, the poorer fifth of the US population suffered a loss in after tax income; whilst the top fifth increased its after tax income by more than 40%.

Poverty in select OECD countries

State	percentage of population living in poverty
United States (1997)	17
Italy (1995)	13
Australia (1994)	12
Canada (1994)	11
United Kingdom (1995)	11

poverty is here defined as those living from less than 50% of the median income

Source: Smeeding 2000

Change in after tax income of US citizens
1977-1999, per quintile of the income group

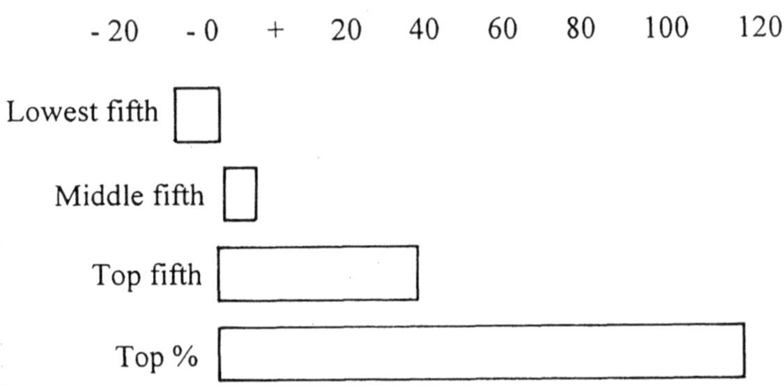

Source: Institute for Policy Studies

This stark inequality in income and wealth has become socially acceptable (at least in the United States). It is hardly an issue in US-politics. Those who try to make it an issue expose themselves to the charge of being fossils left over from pre-diluvian times of class-warfare. In fact, in mass culture and in the business sections of newspapers, the super rich are glamorised. In the US – and perhaps beyond – the wealthy and over-privileged CEO has become today's equivalent of the knight in shining armour. He has become a heroic figure. His high status is seen as well merited. It would reflect his courage and valour. In fact, the language used in describing him and his deeds does indeed connect to pre-modern, feudal times, when tales of roving bards were filled with accounts of evil enemies, bloody battles, glorious victories and their just desert.

It has become a taboo to raise, in the political discourse, the option of somewhat reducing the overly exalted position of the super-wealthy. Partly, this is because one might risk seeing the rich pulling up their tent and migrating to other places should they have to fear being treated less generously. But this option of evening out the wealth by reducing the wealth of the rich, has also been excluded from political discourse due to the simple lack of demand. Voters no longer call for it. Citizens admire the super-rich and vicariously identify with them. "He could just as well be me". Not the rich are seen as imperilling one's own status. This status is today seen as threatened by the poor. The resentment of the broad population, that once was directed at those above in the social hierarchy, this resentment is now being directed at those at the lower end of the social pyramid.

Occasionally, the political discourse touches upon the fate of the poor and excluded. If it does, it does so in terms that recall the 19th century with its notion of the "deserving poor" and the "lumpenproletariat"; with its notion that the poor can be redeemed by hard work; and that poverty is a consequence of personal failure and not something inherent in the very system.

In today's world, the gap between the rich and the poor is getting wider. The gap is getting wider between the rich and the poor states (we shall deal with that in another chapter). But the gap is also getting wider within states. In accordance with the "Kuznet law", it is getting wider within states that are in the early phases of industrial development. But it is now also again getting wider in most of the wealthy states. This development runs counter to the "Kuznet law" and it is mainly caused by the nature of economic development which has disadvantaged unskilled and semi-skilled labour and thus depressed its pay. In some countries politics have accentuated this tendency.

In wealthy countries, there are islands of exclusion and poverty. New York City is one of the wealthiest places on earth. But within this city, certain districts are definitely "Third World" according to statistics. In these districts in walking distance from obscene opulence, life expectancy is shorter and infant mortality is higher than it is in some places on the Indian sub-continent. Quite a few of those who no longer can, or who no longer wish to, participate in the life and life style of the general population now form an "underclass". Increasingly, this part of the population is beyond the reach of remedial social policy.

Economic development and globalisation has, on the other hand, created islands of the super rich in otherwise poor countries. There is little in lifestyle that separates the wealthy of Bombay from the wealthy of London. They both participate in globalisation; they share the same language, the same preferences, the same general philosophy and values.

Some decades ago, it was thought that the poor in the wealthy countries would unite with the vast armies of poor in the poor countries; and that these combined forces of the "villages of the world" would lay siege to and ultimately conquer the wealthy "cities of the world" (Mao Tse Dong). But this was not the case. In fact, the opposite happened. The poor in the rich countries resent the poor in the poor countries. They resent that these poor in the poor countries might further depress their own, already low wages. They fear that these poor from distant lands might turn up in their neighbourhood as poor immigrants or asylum seekers. In the rich countries it is the more wealthy part of the middle class that shows sympathies with the poor of the world; and not the declining class of blue collar workers; and even less so the new "underclass". Communists had once exhorted the poor of the world to unite – as they would have "nothing to lose but their chains". They have not done so and today such exhortation finds hardly any echo at all. Yet, without any such injunction, the rich of the world have been very well capable of uniting, so as to defend their high incomes and other privileges.

If open class warfare is out, the growing inequality and the clogging of the avenues of social advancement gnaws, nonetheless, at the woofs and warps of the social fabric. It weakens the capacity to adapt productively to the challenge of rapidly changing circumstances. It also weakens the capacity to co-operate in global governance. The rich withdraw into their isolated fortresses of wealth. The already disfavoured sink deeper into the mire of passive, resentful misery. Politicians become adept at exploiting, for easy gain, the fears of the rich and the poor. What is being lost is the principle of hope – the necessary base for all constructive efforts to change the world for the better.

The "Triad" and the Use of Economic Power

Seen in its totality, the world economy has grown rapidly. But in order to arrive at a more telling picture, we must disaggregate such global figures into those for the various countries and regions. The first thing to become obvious in such an exercise is the uneven distribution of wealth. This is reflected in the graph below. In this graph, countries are not depicted in their actual, geographic extension. The size of each country's territory is changed so as to make it equal to the volume of its economy. The picture thus created differs strongly from the picture presented in the usual topographic rendition of the world. In this rendering, the globe is mainly covered by just three states or regions: namely the "Triad" of the United States, Europe and Japan – with some of their neighbouring countries and regions clustering around them just as planets cluster around stars.

Three countries or regions dominate

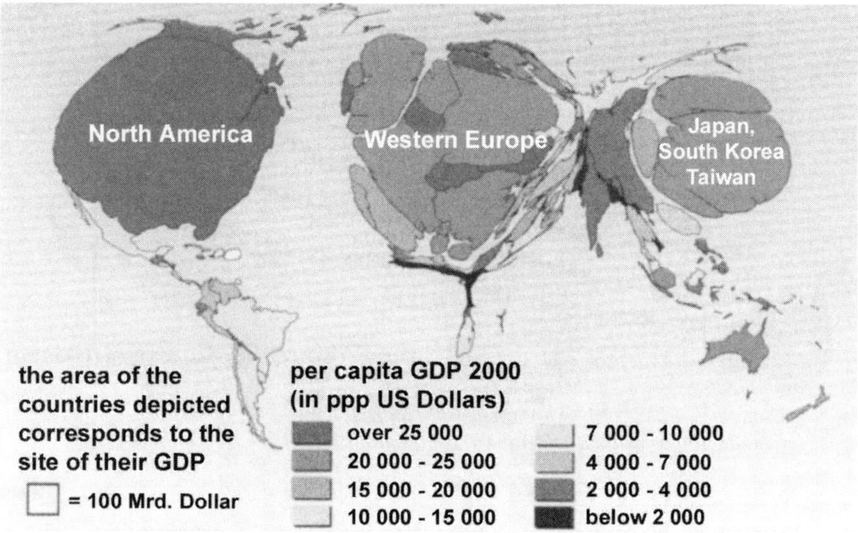

Source: Le Monde, Atlas of Globalisation 2003, based on Worldbank 2002

If one groups China, Korea and Taiwan and the ASEAN, together with the Japanese, in an East Asian cluster[1] the overall wealth of these three states or regions is not too different.[2]

Share of world output and population

	Output	*Population*
United States	22	5
European Union	23	6
Japan	9	2
Top three	*54*	*13*
Rest of world	46	87
Total	100	100

Source: European Economy (Brussels, no.66,1998), WTO, 1999.

GDP per capita in different areas 1950-2002
According to Maddison (in constant 1990 US Dollars)

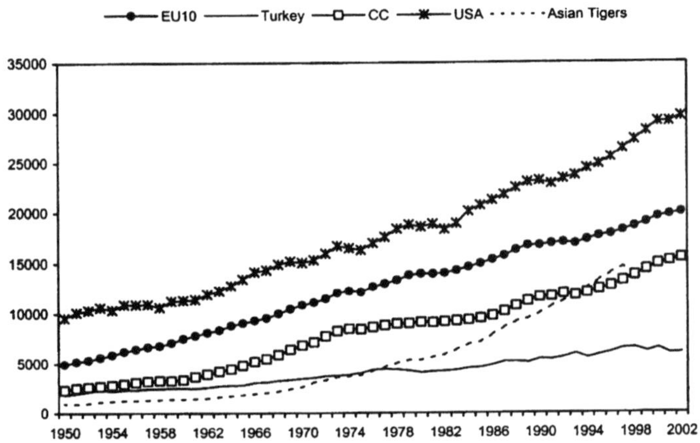

Source: Maddison as quoted by Aigner/Landesmann 2003

1 Something a bit problematic as this region is not (yet??) integrated very much and does not form a coherent economic unit; much less a political one.

2 If one takes Japan alone, its share drops to a bit less than half of the share of Europe or the US.

The US, EU-Europe, and Japan differ a bit in their (purchasing power adjusted) per capita wealth. The average per capita GDP of EU Europe is about 32% below the US. The Japanese purchasing power adjusted average per capita GDP is a bit higher than the European.

This is the picture that emerges from comparing average income.[3] It changes if, instead of average income, we compare the median income, that is, the income of the regular guy right in the middle of the income scale. Due to the very uneven distribution of income in the US, the average US income is much higher than the median income. And the median incomes in Europe and the US become roughly comparable. A Swedish family at the median income level has, for example, a standard of living roughly comparable with that of a median US family.[4] Comparing the wages of the average production worker, one finds that those in Germany and the Netherlands are higher than the ones in the US.[5] In Denmark and Sweden these wages are roughly the same as those in the US.

Relative hourly compensation of manufacturing production workers 1979-98
(using Purchasing Power Parities, US=100)

Country	*1979*	*1989*	*1998*
United States	100	100	100
Germany	86	111	132
France	66	86	87
Britain	62	76	81
Canada	81	92	107
Japan	49	61	78
Denmark	71	78	96
Netherlands	87	101	107
Norway	70	90	105
Sweden	78	88	97
Switzerland	75	87	96

Source: Economic Policy Institute

The members of the "Triad" are not just partners. They also compete against each other with their exports. They have a strong presence on the world markets.

3 The average between someone earning 10 million euros a year and someone earning nothing at all, is still an annual income of 5 million euros. This is an income few persons will reach.

4 Swedish families with children in the last percentile (the poorest 10% of the population) have incomes 60% higher than their American counterparts.

5 When calculated in Purchasing Power Parities.

Together they furnish nearly half of all world exports; with the European Union having the biggest share.

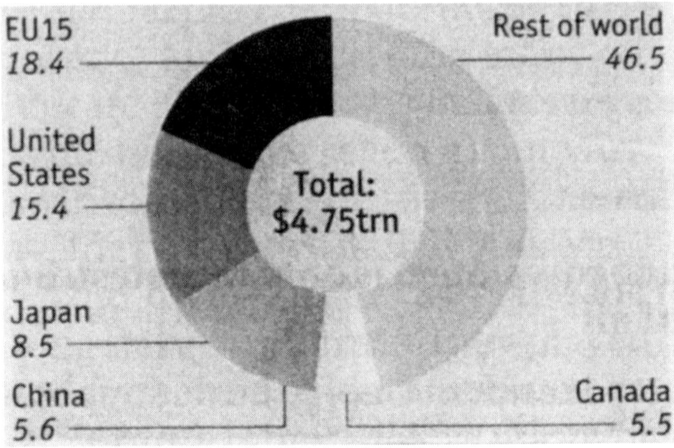

Source: WTO

Exports of goods and services
As a percentage of GDP averages

	1970-73	1974-79	1980-89	1990-99
US	6.0	8.4	8.5	10.6
EU-15	21.6	25.4	27.9	28.9
Japan	10.8	12.6	12.9	10.1

Source: Bessanini 2001

The three regions differ, though, in their openness to world trade. The economy of the European Union (EU-15) is more open[6] to international trade than the economy of the United States. Quite surprisingly, if compared to the EU, the Japanese economy is just as "closed" as the US economy; and while the US economy has at least opened up more or less steadily, the Japanese economy has again become even more closed in the 90's.

6 Attention – we do NOT count in this comparison the intra-EU trade; just the trade of all EU-countries with non-EU countries.

Yet, the competition of the three Triad members takes place within the confines of one global system, which induces conformity in many ways.[7] Due to the growing liberalisation and globalisation of the world financial system, European and US long term interest rates, for instance, are quite similar and have moved in parallel[8].

Interest rates on long term capital

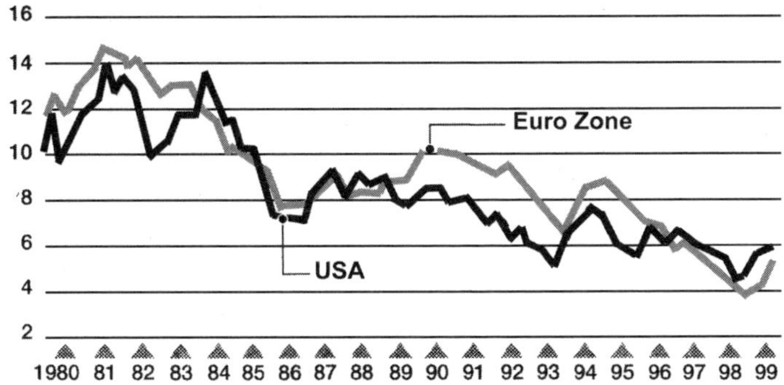

Source: Datastream

Between the three members of the "Triad", gross capital formation (that is the rate of gross investment) used to differ quite widely. It still does, with Japan investing proportionately more than Europe; and Europe investing a bit more than the US. Nonetheless, here too, the rates are converging, with a moderate decline of the investment rate in Europe; a more rapid decline in Japan; and a slow rise of investment rates in the US.

This also pertains to investment in human capital, that is, investment in education. A certain advantage of the US persists (especially as concerns university education). But, by and large, differences among the three members of the triad have become rather minimal in this respect too.

7 This does not hold true for all realms of social economy or political life. As we shall see later on, some even basic differences will continue to survive even a very intense "globalisation".

8 Interest rates in Japan are an exception; as the whole Japanese financial system is also still an exception.

Gross fixed capital formation; US, Canada, Japan and Europe
(in % of GDP)

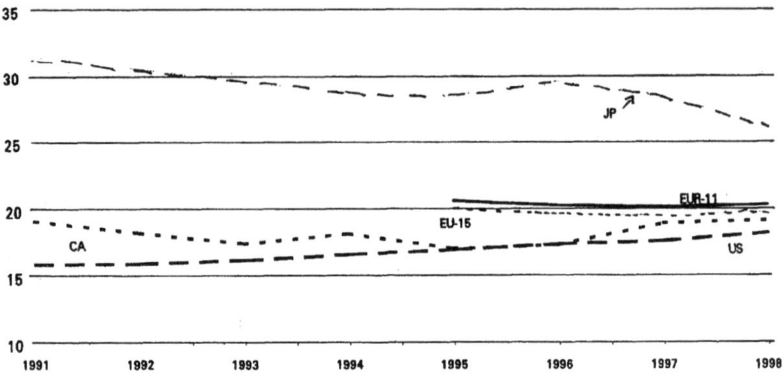

Source Eurostat

% of the population with at least an upper secondary education
(dark column = university education)

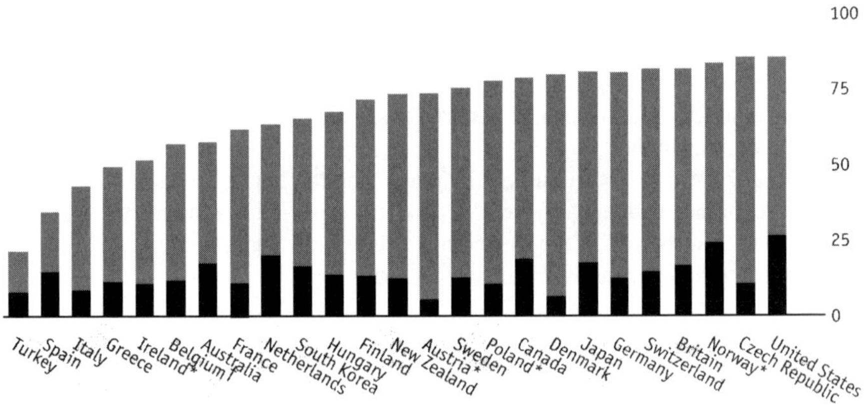

Source: OECD

Yearly number of scientific publications per million inhabitants

EU	US	Japan
609	739	480

Source: Eurostat

Rates of economic growth have also converged. In the more distant past they had been quite dissimilar. Between 1870 and 1950, the USA grew somewhat faster than Europe and Japan[9]. But, as we have observed, this was reversed in the period between 1950 and 1973, with the other two members of the Triad developing more rapidly. In the subsequent period between 1973 and 1992, all three evolved at roughly the same speed.

Average annual economic growth

	1870-1913	*1913-50*	*1950-73*	*1973-92*
USA	3.9	2.8	3.9	2.4
Western Europe	2.1	1.4	4.7	2.2
Of that: Germany	2.8	1.1	6.0	2.3
France	1.6	1.1	5.0	2.3
Great Britain	1.9	1.3	3.0	1.6
Italy	1.9	1.5	5.6	2.7
Southern Europe	1.5	1.3	6.3	3.1
Japan	2.4	2.4	9.2	3.8

Source : Maddison, 1995

Growth performance in the triad
Average annual GDP change

	Actual growth of GDP				Trend growth of GDP		Trend growth of GDP per capita		
	1970-80	1980-90	1990-98	1999	1980-90	1990-98	1980-90	1990-98	1995-98
United States	3.2	3.2	3.0	4.2	2.9	3.1	2.0	2.2	2.7
Japan	4.4	4.0	1.4	0.3	3.8	1.9	3.3	1.6	1.1
European Union [a]	3.0	2.4	1.7	2.3	2.3	1.8	2.0	1.5	1.7
OECD total [a, b]	3.4	3.0	2.3	2.7	2.8	2.4	2.1	1.8	2.0

Source: OECD

9 Much faster in terms of absolute GDP; just a little bit faster in terms of per capita GDP.

This changed again in the nineties. The latecomer, Japan, slowed into stagnation, while, since 1995, the US has pulled ahead again. The mood in the US changed from the "declinism" of the Carter years into the triumphalism of the Clinton-Bush era.

The recent, relatively fast, growth of the US is not due to greater capital intensity of US production. In fact, capital intensity (the ratio: capital/labour) has risen less in the US than it has in Europe and Japan.

Evolution of capital stocks and capital intensities
Average annual growth rates

		1980-90	1990-98	1995-98
United States	Capital stock	3.0	2.6	3.3
	Capital/labour ratio	1.1	0.6	1.0
European Union[b]	Capital stock	2.6	2.5	2.4
	Capital/labour ratio	2.8	2.7	2.3
Japan	Capital stock	5.7	4.2	3.6
	Capital/labour ratio	4.9	4.7	4.4

Source: OECD

During the last decade, the greater economic dynamism of the US was, therefore, not caused by the use of greater amounts of capital; but by the fact that capital was used more intensively. The lower European productivity per person was not caused by the dearth of capital invested in each work place; but mainly by the less intensive use of the existing pool of labour. In Japan, labour is used as intensively as in the US.[10]

The wider use of semi-qualified and non-trained labour[11] in the US is due to this labour being paid lower wages. In the US, incentives to replace such low-skilled labour by machines are thus fewer. The more intensive use of low skilled labour has tended to lower US unemployment (which, in the seventies, was still

10 But, notwithstanding this more intensive use of labour, overall productivity in the economy is still relatively low in Japan (if compared to Europe and the US) . This is due to the inefficiency, and thus low productivity, of protected sectors (like retail trade and agriculture).

11 Visitors to the US will be surprised to find that simple services like garbage removal or restaurant services are much less automated than they are – for instance – in France.

higher in the US than it was in Europe).[12] Nonetheless, the rates of unemployment now do not differ that much between the US, Japan, and Europe.

Employment rates
in % of working age population

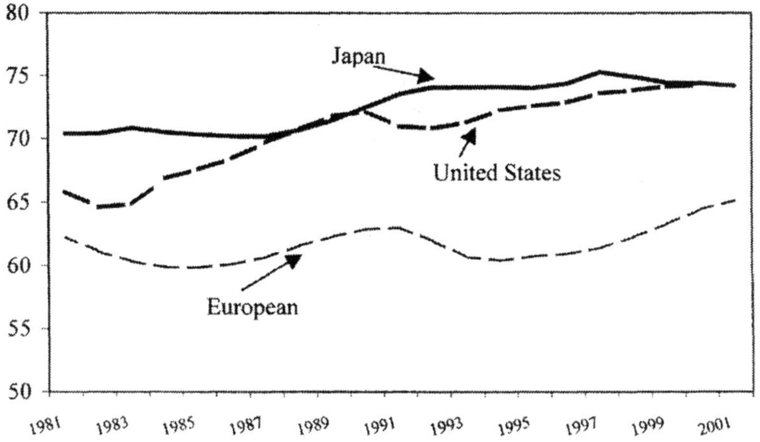

Source: OECD

Unemployment in the US, the European Union, and Japan

	2000	*2001*	*2002*	*2003*
US	5.7	6.0	6.6	6.7
EU	8.2	7.4	7.7	7.6
Japan	4.7	5.0	5.5	5.6

Source: IMF World Economic Outlook 2003

In Europe, on the other hand, the increase in production was due exclusively to an increase in productivity of the labour already employed. In fact, in Europe, there actually has been a decline in the percentage of the population still active in the labour force.

12 Note, though, that unemployment has been rising fairly rapidly again in the US over the last 2 years.

Growth in GDP per capita and its components 1990-1998
(average annual percentage change)

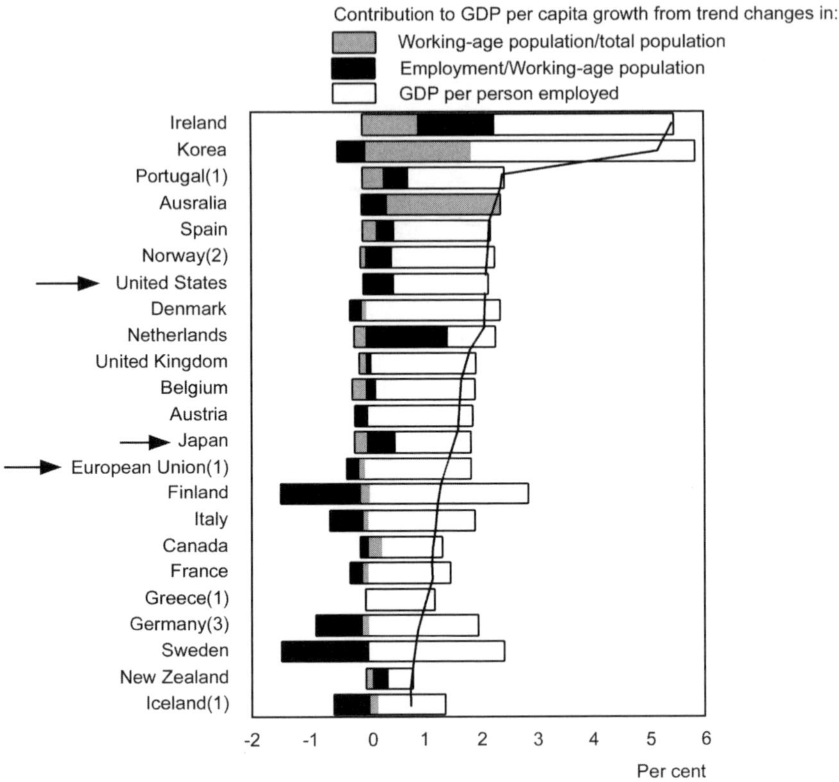

Source: OECD

In Europe, thus, the potential labour force is being used much less intensively than in the US. In the US, employees work longer hours, take shorter vacations, and retire at a later stage in life. The US potential labour force is also used more fully because of the higher labour force participation by US women.

Note number one: The US female participation rate in the labour force used to be below the European one up to the sixties. The change since has been dramatic. This rapid rise occurred even though, in the US, the support given by public authorities to working mothers is minimal if compared to Europe. Child day-care centres are few and often of poor quality.

Note number two: This is again one instance of many which prompt the ever same question: Do such differences between the US and Europe point to some underlying and profound differences in the very nature of European and US societies? Or is the US simply ahead of Europe and Japan in some economic and social developments; with the two laggards following sooner or later?

The special case of Japan

Japan's economy is in a stagnation. As of now, it has lasted for a decade. Growth has even been negative[13] on several occasions and the outlook now is even more gloomy than it was in the mid-nineties.[14] Obviously, this is more than a mere business cycle phenomenon.

Japan's GDP % change on a year earlier

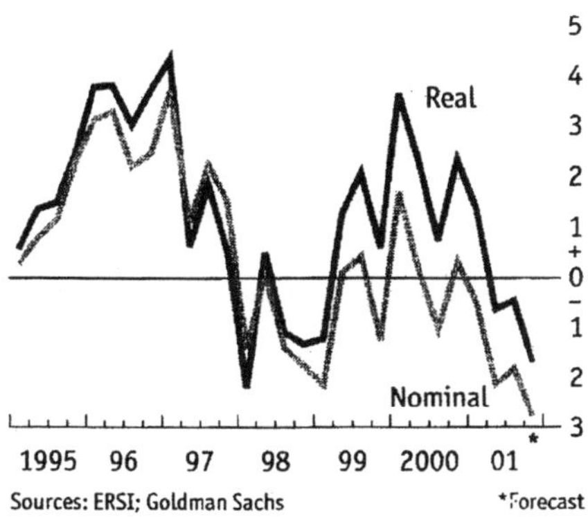

Source: ERSI; Goldman Sachs

13 One might object to this term as being an oxymoron. One can either have growth (positive) or decline (negative). But one cannot have "negative growth". Still, as this term is commonly used in economic discourse, we will have to accept it. It is not the only instance that makes us marvel at the world and verbiage of economics.

14 Some indicators remain strong though, and especially those that pertain to competitiveness on external markets: civilian/business research and development, business real investment; etc.

At last up to 2003, Japan was burdened with a true and self-perpetuating deflation: in the above graph, the nominal decline is stronger than the real decline in production. This implies that, instead of rising for each unit of GDP, prices are actually in decline. Such deflation is difficult to reverse with the tools of standard economic policy. It pulls the whole economy into going into reverse. The most immediate and biggest threat is directed at the financial systems as the value of bank assets diminishes and banks thus become insolvent.

Yet, this deflation is, in turn, but a symptom of deeper difficulties. The persistent sluggishness of the Japanese economy points to problems that seem inherent in the very nature of Japanese production, in Japanese politics and in Japanese society.[15]

The Japanese political and bureaucratic system gets its share of the blame. Its risk-averseness, its closed character, its escape from public scrutiny and control make it inconsistent with the ongoing rapid and unpredictable changes of an advanced mature economy. Its hierarchical, feudal political system has difficulties in adapting to the requirements and rules of competitive democracy. As a consequence, politics is not able to lead. It just passively follows the unfolding of the disaster; unable, especially, to effectively deal with the still spreading rot of the financial system.

One could speculate as to whether this failure might not reflect the reverse and negative side of "Asian values". The failure would be the price to pay for consensus politics and conformity; and for the fear of "losing face". Finding new solutions implies a break with the past and, thus, conflict with established interests and powers. Europeans have learned to accept and tolerate such ruptures. Americans even glory in them. The Japanese, though, seem different.[16]

All in all, the "competitiveness" of the three Triad members (as measured by the UNIDO Competitive Industrial Performance Index)[17] does not differ very much.

15 One might speculate whether this is connected to the ageing of Japan, which is more pronounced than the ageing of society in the US and even in Europe. By 2050, the median age in Japan will be 53; in Germany it will be 47; in the US 40.

16 Beware, though, of seeing "decline" as something irreversible. France was powerful at the beginning of the 18th century; and became powerful again 100 years later; Germany at the end of the 19th and at the end of the 20th centuries.

17 Manufacturing value added per capita, manufactured exports per capita, the shares of medium- and high technology products in manufactured exports.

Ranking and values according to the UNIDO industrial performance index 1998

Country	*Rank*	*Index Value*
Singapore	1	0.883
Japan	4	0.696
Germany	5	0.632
USA	6	0.564
Finland	8	0.538
France	11	0.465
Austria	12	0.453
Canada	16	0.407
Australia	23	0.211
China	37	0.126
Indonesia	49	0.054

Source: UNIDO 2002

But why is it important for each of the three partners/competitors in the Triad to stay ahead or pull ahead of the other two? One part of the answer was given earlier on, when we showed that we cannot do without continued economic growth. We would not know how to organise our personal lives and our communities in the absence of the drive to have more, consume more, and to work more productively. But this is only one part of the explanation. It cannot account for the sheer ferocity of the competition; the urge to outperform the other; the eagerness to use even small and temporary advantages as proof of the inherent superiority of one's own economic and social model. What is the motive behind this grandstanding and this shoving for first place? To be first is an aim in itself! It does not need an economic rationale. Being first in the pecking order implies having superior power. Power is also an end in itself. But what is power?

If, on the stage, the curtain raises on a royal drama, how does one recognise the king? If he is not wearing the crown, the king can be recognised by the way other actors treat him. If they treat him as king, he is the king. How does one recognise power? One recognises it by the behaviour of others who see themselves as subject to this power. If they act as if someone has power, this someone WILL have power. That state, which is regarded by others as already having economic power will become economically powerful or will at least add economic power. Of course, there must be a basis for this, their conviction (and an economic dwarf is not likely to evolve into an economic giant by such (mis-)perception). But the two things feed upon one another: the objective reality and the subjective conviction. The subjective conviction can re-enforce and augment objective reality. States profit economically from being considered economically powerful.

Yet this leads to another question. Power is usually defined as something that prompts persons or groups of persons to behave in a way they would not have chosen in the absence of such power. One state covets, for example, a certain piece of foreign territory and is ready to seize it. But it does not dare to do so because another state opposes this seizure. A state, which does have this capacity to prompt such change of mind of some other state, is considered powerful. We do not hesitate to ascribe "power" to that state when it was its military might that induced the other state to desist from enlarging its territory.

But is it justified to also use the term "power" in economic matters? Does someone hold "economic power" who, for instance, is in command of a brand with world-wide acceptance – like McDonald's or Coca Cola? By our definition, power is meant to imply that it could force a person or a state to do something which he would not have done otherwise. Certainly, there is some kind of power hidden in a brand name which induces a consumer to buy Coca Cola instead of some other soft drink. But then, on the other hand, buying Coca Cola is still a free decision (albeit one influenced by massive publicity). One can, therefore, not compare this kind of "power to persuade" with the "capacity to deter", that is inherent in military power. Economic power might, perhaps, induce someone to buy what he or she would not have bought otherwise. But, if this is power, it is certainly a form of power different from the power of physical coercion. Military power just leaves the choice between yielding or being killed.

The economic position of a state, therefore, cannot be discussed in terms akin to those used in a discussion of military power. Economic relations, both between individuals and states, are exchanges by their very nature. In the vast majority of cases, they are, therefore, based on mutual consent. Seeing an advantage in such an exchange cannot be compared to someone yielding to the threat of a gun pressed against his temples.

Yet it is difficult, on the other hand, to ignore that some sort of power is also present in economic matters. Clearly, those at the top of the pyramid of wealth are revered and they do expect such reverence. They expect (and not vainly) that their wishes are heeded in a way that wishes of those less fortunate are not heeded.

How then, exactly, does such economic power impact upon the global system? To no small extent, the answer to this question will depend on the categories and pre-conceived notions one applies in the analysis of the world. One may see the world, and especially the world economy, as a very fluid system with many constituent parts, each with changing roles and functions. In the framework of such a concept, it does not make sense to discuss the economic position of a state in a way one would discuss its military position. All states would be embroiled in an equalising mish-mash, with no one and no single state being truly powerful. Each would so very much depend on the other that even a big advantage in wealth or productivity would not translate into the potential to truly prompt others to act in a way in which they would not choose to act otherwise.

Or – on the other hand – one may come down in favour of viewing the economic world order as strongly hierarchical, with the Triad being on top; and within the Triad, the US being on top.

World output 1990-1998
Percentage change over the previous year (based on data in 1990 dollars)

Region/Country	1990-95*	1996	1997	1998**
World	1.9	3.3	3.3	2.0
Industrialised countries	1.7	2.9	2.9	2.2
Of which:				
United States	2.3	3.4	3.9	3.9
Japan	1.4	5.0	1.4	-2.8
European Union	1.3	1.6	2.5	2.7
Of which:				
Euro area	1.4	1.4	2.3	2.8
Germany	1.7	0.8	1.8	2.3
France	1.1	1.1	2.0	3.2
Italy	1.1	0.9	1.5	1.4
United Kingdom	1.2	2.6	3.5	2.1
Transition economies	-8.2	-1.5	1.4	-1.3
Developing countries	4.9	5.8	5.4	1.8
Of which:				
Latin America	3.3	3.6	5.4	2.1
Africa	1.1	3.9	2.7	2.9
Asia	6.4	7.1	5.8	1.6
Of which:				
China	12.4	9.6	8.8	7.8
Other countries	5.1	6.4	5.0	-0.3
Memo item:				
Developing countries excluding China	4.0	5.2	4.8	0.8

* Annual average
** Estimated

Source: UNCTAD secretariat

These are the two poles of the discussion. Probably, the truth does not lie with either of them. It also does not lie on some middle ground. Probably, things are much more complex. Economic power is not exercised by simply and overtly forcing others to do what one wants them to do. Economic power acts by setting the rules of the game. We will come back to that when discussing – in a later chapter – the role of the "hegemon". But economic might and a superior economic performance also relate to power in another way: they legitimise political power. Both conservatives and liberals, for example, have to demonstrate that their models are economically efficient. They could not claim such legitimacy for their models if they produced economic failure.

But, to return to the topic of the Triad and to its place in the global system: even if Japan does not recuperate soon, and even if economic growth in Europe remains relatively slow, the Triad will continue to dominate the world economy in the coming two to three decades. Underneath that dominance, change will progress, with the relative weights shifting and with the share decreasing, that the Triad countries hold in world production. China's rise will contribute most heavily to such a change.[18] But not just China, other still poor countries, too, will grow faster than the Triad. They have done so in the past. For decades already, some of the low and middle income countries have advanced rather rapidly. It is safe to predict the continuation of this tendency. But it is more difficult to predict the way this shift in relative economic weight will affect the world system.

1) The newly wealthy and economically powerful might cluster around existing poles of economic might. Central America might become connected more tightly to the northern part of the hemisphere. Africa, the Middle East and Russia might become attached more intimately to the European Union. And Eastern and South Eastern Asia might forge closer links to Japan and/or China.

2) In another scenario, old and new poles of economic power might fuse into one all-encompassing global system, with the world system, as such, then having become truly integrated and with the former three poles of the "triad" having lost their distinctness and their ability to gather their closer neighbours around them through special arrangements.

3) Or the Triad might change into a quartet, quintet, or sextet. New poles of economic (and political/cultural) attraction might arise. One obvious candidate is China. India is another one; as is – for Latin America – Brazil (as the driving force behind the Mercosur).

4) And finally, there is the ever present danger of everything going into reverse, with world wealth decreasing and nations again withdrawing into autarky. This would result in greater diversity – but certainly, also, in more frequent economic and political conflict.

---

18 Though one should not exclude the possibility of China's ascendancy being ruptured by internal turmoil – see chapter on China.

As concerns the “Triad”, though, we should note its failure to bolster its economic dominance by some more formal institutional arrangements.[19] It is both surprising and disturbing that the combined and overwhelming might of the “Triad” has no distinct political/institutional counterpart. The G-7 (now G-8) summit meetings have been perverted to mere photo opportunities. They no longer even pretend to actually wield the tools of serious “global governance”. The same holds true for the OECD. Instead of the G-8, the OECD could provide the alternate institutional back-up for the co-operation between the countries of the Triad. Such an institutional back-up would certainly be useful. But OECD cannot provide it as it has become marginalised. It has a rule setting function only in some rare and exceptional instances[20].

In a way, it should surprise us that the Triad lacks common, strong and efficient institutions that would permit a better coordination of policies and that would facilitate a joint approach to global issues. After all, the three members of the Triad are rather similar to one another. As we have seen, they have become more like each other in recent decades. This is, at least, the impression conveyed by economic data.

But perhaps we overestimate the political significance of economic data. For, in other than the economic realm, vast differences persist. These differences might even have become more pronounced recently. The three members differ when they define their respective positions in the world; and their strategic goals in foreign and security policy.

Japan acts as “Japan Incorporated”, with a tight meshing of political and commercial interests. It does not aspire to political leadership – not even in its very own backyard in the Western Pacific. In military and strategic matters, it defers to the US.

The US, on the contrary, has accepted with relish a role as the “sole surviving super-power” They have thus defined for themselves a world-wide mission. In their view, this not only permits them, but even obliges them, to act unilaterally on occasions, and in circumvention of existing multilateral organisations.

Europe’s strategic interests are clearly regional. It assigns priority to the completion of its own integration and institution building, which, in the end, might even result in the establishment of a true federal state (or something rather akin to it). Over and above that, Europe invests much effort in stabilising the immediate neighbours to the East and the South (such as Slavic successor states of the So-

---

19 The famous – or infamous – “Trilateral Commisssion of Nelson and David Rockefeller” can hardly be considered to be such a truly effective institution. Anyhow, it has since receded below the horizon of public perception or political relevance.

20 In fact, the OECD has lost much of its function as a discussion forum too.

viet Union; or the Arab countries on the southern shore of the Mediterranean). To the extent that Europe does recognise world-wide interests, these are pursued not through power projection, but by using the tools of multilateral diplomacy in international organisations.

Basic internal political institutions are widely different, too. Citizens of the United States distrust the state. The administration, as such and as a bureaucracy, carries little political weight. Yet the president is politically very prominent. He has to share power, though, with the members of Congress (which are elected on an individual basis). And power is also shared with the courts and with the media.

In Japan, little distinction is made in practice between economic and political power. The latter is vested with the administrative bureaucracy. The state is being trusted, yet the government remains politically weak and represents the bureaucrats more than it directs them. The political role of parliament is limited too, though it is dominated by one single party[21]. Media do not have a prominent political role.

In Europe, the parliamentarian political systems are (still) being dominated by political parties. Citizens are ambivalent about the state but ready to assign it important functions. The bureaucratic machineries of the state provide most of the input into political processes. The political clout of media has become more notable; that of courts is still minor if compared to the political role of courts in the US.

Similarly, social and economic policies of the members of the Triad continue to differ widely, too. In nearly all European countries, citizens have opted[22] for a very extensive – and costly – net of social protection including old age pensions, health services, quality public education, etc. Investment in public infrastructure, and frequently in public housing and urbanism, has been high.

Public social services in Japan are much more limited. They are more limited still in the US, where even public education is of poor quality in general; and where health insurance still does not cover all of the population.

Given these differences in strategic aims, in political institutions and in social policies, it comes as less of a surprise that there are no efficient organisations that articulate and represent the common interests of the Triad-members. Obviously, these differences in political values and institutions have not become more narrow over the last 30 years. On the other hand, earlier differences in economic in-

---

21 Creating a de facto one party system.

22 The "opted" needs to be emphasized. Contrary to what neo – conservatives would make us believe, those elaborate welfare systems were not imposed upon an unwilling electorate; but were requested by this electorate. Citizens in Europe want their welfare state.

stitutions and in economic performance did become smaller. This prompts a very general observation:

Up until now we have – openly or implicitly – argued on the basis of a kind of Neo-Marxist economic determinism. Economic development would set the pace and everything else would follow. As economies of the wealthy countries reach roughly similar levels, and as all of them will make use of roughly the same techniques, all wealthy countries would become similar to each other not just in their economic parameters, but also in institutions and values.

We now realise that increasing sameness in economic structures and data does not automatically make for cultural, social or political sameness. In fact, growing wealth might very well permit and facilitate greater differentiation.[23] We shall return to this argument at the end of this book.

23 At least in the short and medium term. In the very very long run it might be otherwise and all countries and societies might become alike once they have reached a similar level of wealth. But this is pure speculation. The experience of the recent past, at least, does not support this speculative conclusion.

The Myth of a "New Economy" and the US Asset Bubble

We have already dealt with some arguments that sustain the notion of economic growth rates becoming smaller as wealth rises. One such impediment to faster development was seen in the growing share of the service sector. One had also assumed that the marginal utility of capital would decline: A thousand units of capital added in an early phase of growth would boost production much more than the same amount of capital invested in a later phase, when much capital already is in place.

We have mentioned other facts that were assumed to lower growth rates. Life expectancy increases with wealth. The population ages. Not only would an older population be less dynamic. The higher share of transfers to those retired would also impose a drag upon the economy.[1] Furthermore, in the earlier phases of just catching up with the leaders, a country may rely on the use of technology already developed elsewhere. If, however, a country reaches a place near the top, it has to develop its own technology. That is both costly and time consuming.

One more complex but more powerful argument is based not on the physical ageing of a population or society, but on its social and institutional ageing. Unless having been shaken by a deep crisis recently, older and wealthier societies were assumed to become sclerotic. The grip of vested interests would harden. Change, the necessary companion of economic growth, would be met by ever more potent resistance.

Mancur Olson's theory on the ossification of wealthy societies

Economic development and modernisation bring a growing diversification of social and economic functions. Among these more numerous and more varied groups, those that express very specific and narrow interests may usually gain support that is more solid and emotional than the support that sustains groups which represent the vaguer interest of the broader public. It might, for instance, be in the interest of the broader public to see some important road pro-

1 A fact that certainly favours the US over Europe. Those over 60 make up 20% of the population of Europe; but just 16% in the US. This European handicap will increase markedly over the next 50 years. By 2050, 40% of the European population will be over 60; but just 22% of the US population (according to the US Census).

ject completed. But frequently such broader interest does not translate into a powerful and clear political mandate. Most voters will not base their choice at elections on whether the party they vote for supports or opposes a specific road project. But some more narrow groups do have a very strong interest in this question – groups of persons, for example, who would be forced to live next to this heavily travelled road. They have a strong interest in the road not being built. In this group, the decision to vote for a party or a specific candidate will be based exclusively on whether he or she does or does not join them in the fight against the project. Candidates will thus be advised by their counsellors and "spin-doctors" to also oppose the project. This will get them votes, while their support of the road project would sway very few voters. Stopping something is much more profitable politically than getting something done. The development of societies becomes "blocked".

We are thus faced with a host of powerful arguments which all purport to show that, by necessity, economic growth must become more sluggish the wealthier a country is. Nonetheless, in wealthy countries growth has kept up. It even has accelerated. This is due to two factors mainly. First, success breeds success and accumulated wealth and growing endowments provide favourable conditions for the creation of even more wealth. The second argument refers to the alleged stagnation and "ossification" of wealthy societies. It turns this thesis on its head. As all societies, wealthy societies, too, are shaken by unforeseen tragedies and disasters that break the routine and that deal a new deck of cards. But over and above that, they are rattled and blown apart again by the "gales of creative destruction" that originate in the economic system itself. The more wealthy a society, the more virulent these gales, the faster changing all collective human arrangements. Traditional societies are stagnant, but not the wealthy ones.

And indeed, the figures provided in the previous chapters have sustained this interpretation and have "falsified" all such theories on the inevitability of growing economic sclerosis and sluggishness. In the wealthy countries, average economic growth has accelerated over the last 150 years. Even the very "old" US economy experienced a sudden spurt of growth in the late 90s, that lifted it, once more, above its closest competitors.

US observers now claim that this spurt of growth was not a singular event. On the contrary, it signals that the US had entered into a separate and unique orbit, so to say, with growth rates being permanently higher in the US than they are in other wealthy countries. The US, thus, would have found a potent anti-dote against the forces of sluggishness and stagnation – an anti-dote not available to other wealthy nations. The era of more rapid US growth, therefore, would signal a permanent change and the transition to an information based "New Economy".

Its greater dynamics would be fuelled by the wide-scale and innovative application of computers.[2] This would translate into an above average growth of productivity in the US economy. The advance in productivity would provide to the US a permanent lead over the other economically advanced countries and regions.

Is there substance to this claim? In looking for an answer, we must disaggregate the figures on productivity and concentrate on the sub-element termed TFP or MFP (Total Factor Productivity or Multi-Factor Productivity). It is the residual that remains after discounting the use of additional labour and the use of additional capital. It thus measures the broadly defined technological progress we have described in chapter 3. It is the single most important factor making for economic growth.

To our surprise (and certainly to the surprise of the many that gloat about the alleged superiority of the US economic model), MFP growth did not differ that much between the three members of the Triad. In fact, if we look at the average of the complete period between 1980 and 1998, it even was more rapid in Japan and Europe than it was in the US.

Growth in multifactor productivity (business sector; skill adjusted)

	1980[1]-1990	*1990[2]-1995*	*1995-2000[3]*
United States	0.9	1.0	1.3
Japan	2.2	1.2	0.7
European Union[4,5]	1.6	1.1	1.0

1. 1985 for Austria, 1983 for Belgium, Greece, Ireland
2. 1991 for Germany
3. 1997 for Austria, Belgium, 1999 for France, Greece, Italy, 1996 for Ireland, 1998 for Netherlands
4. Excluding Luxembourg and Portugal
5. Growth rate for European Union is computed as a weighted average of country growth rates, using country trend GDP in business sector levels expressed in 1996 PPPs as weights

Source: Elmeskov 2002

2 It was also claimed that the new economy would no longer be susceptible to the ups and downs of the business cycle. It would be in a permanent "high". At least that part of the theory had to be discarded when, after an extraordinarily long phase of growth (1992-mid 2000), an economic slow-down set in in the US that finally resulted in a short recession in 2001/2002.

Those figures put narrow limits on the contribution the "New Economy" might have made to productivity growth in the US. Doubtless, productivity growth has been rapid in the industry that produces computers – that is, the hardware of computers. The share of this industry in total industrial production is somewhat greater in the US than it is in Europe. That is one reason why, in the time between 1995 and 1999, the increase of labour productivity in industrial production was a trifle higher in the US than it was in Europe.[3]

Labour productivity in manufacturing and in two ICT sectors 1999
(1995 = 100)

	Office, accounting & computing equipment	Radio, television & communications equipment	Manufacturing
United States	460	172	125
Japan	..	112	104
Germany	186	129	117
France	..	128	115
United Kingdom	160	..	103
Canada	97	141	105
Austria	116	134	130
Denmark	99	151	109
Finland	127	193	119
Korea	454	322	150
Mexico	117	144	119
Portugal	..	195	122

Source: OECD

But that is not the main issue. Because the proponents of the "New Economy" claim that it is "new" not because computers are being produced. It is "new" because of the contribution computers make to raise the productivity in other fields. This claim has been discussed widely. One of the sceptics is the Nobel prize winning US economist Robert Solow, who maintained that "you see the computer age everywhere these days except in the productivity statistics" (Solow Paradox). The OECD, too, has dealt with this claim. Its findings are reproduced below.

3 It does make a – bit of a – difference if one measures productivity of labour per person actually in the workforce; or if one measures it per hour worked (though the difference is not that great. People are more productive per hour worked if they work shorter hours). A rise of productivity was used to not just raise the compensation of labour and capital, but also to effect a reduction of weekly work time. In the present OECD countries, it shrank from 80 hours in 1900 to 40 hours at present. Remarkably though, this movement tended to slow over time. In 1931, 50% of the rise in productivity was still transformed into a shorter work-week, in 1956 just 36%; and in 1970 only 20%.

The contribution of ICT capital to output growth
(the bar stands for the percentage points of growth that can be attributed to the use of – new – ICT capital)

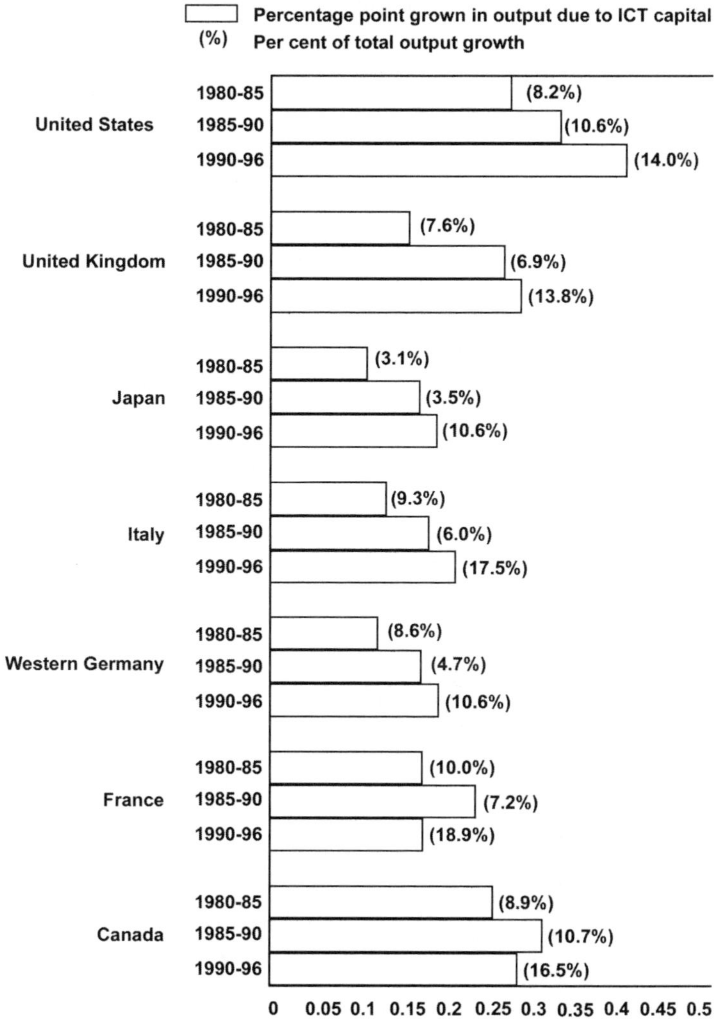

Source: OECD

The OECD finds that, in the time between 1990 and 1996, the application and use[4] of computers contributed about 0.45% to output growth in the US; as compared to 0.3% in Germany or 0.28% in the United Kingdom. The OECD thus contradicts Nobel prize winner Solow and claims that one could find a positive, causal relationship between the use of computers and output growth. But it concedes that this contribution, while visible, is not so significant as to justify the claims supporting the notion of a "New Economy".

Others are more sceptical than the OECD: One of the most notorious sceptics is Professor Robert Gordon. According to him, the contribution of computers was negative. The big contribution to multi-factor productivity would already have come from the use of the old "mainframe computers", when they were introduced decades ago for tasks like seat reservations on airplanes, or for tax and social security administration. A large part of the present computer use is just recreational. And indeed, on the INTERNET, most of the popular search terms are connected to one of mankind's oldest and dearest pre-occupations – sex.

20 most popular search terms at 10 leading portals and search engines

Rank	Search Term	Percent of All Searches
1.	sex	0.3289%
2.	hotmail/hotmail.com/www.hotmail.com	0.2131%
3.	yahoo/yahoo.com/www.yahoo.com	0.2044%
4.	porn/porno/pornography	0.1402%
5.	chat/chatrooms	0.1233%
6.	mp3	0.0935%
7.	horoscopes/horoscope	0.0800%
8.	ebay/ebay.com/www.ebay.com	0.0731%
9.	aol/aol.com/www.aol.com	0.0714%
10.	games	0.0659%
11.	map/maps	0.0585%
12.	pokemon	0.0549%
13.	nude/nudes	0.0541%
14.	music	0.0505%
15.	xxx	0.0473%
16.	travel	0.0470%
17.	screensaver/screensavers	0.0458%
18.	lyrics/song lyrics	0.0455%
19.	playboy	0.0430%
20.	free	0.0426%

Source: Alexa Research

Source: Alexa Research

4 NOT: production of computers

But whatever advantage the US might draw from its present leading position in the application of information technology, this advantage is likely to be shared soon by other wealthy countries. They are catching up with the US in the use of computers.

Personal computers per 100 inhabitants

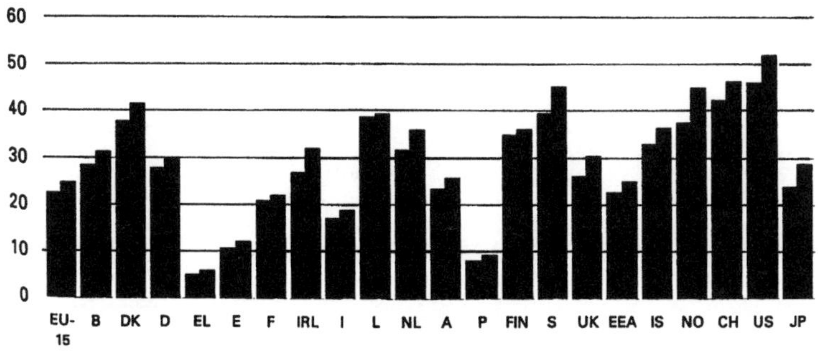

Source: Eurostat

Information Technology might have provided a small push to the growth of the US economy and might have enhanced – by a bit – the economic clout of the US in the Triad. But this advantage is not a permanent and strategic one.

This does not imply that the computer will not have long term and deep effects on the economy and upon the structure and organisation of the whole economy. But according to Peter Drucker, these effects will be indirect. They will arrive through changes of the business environment and they will be registered not just in the United States but also in other wealthier parts of the world.

While Information Technology will quickly permeate among the wealthy countries, it will do so much more slowly in the poorer parts of the world. The dawn of the computer-age will, therefore, accentuate the already wide gap that separates wealthy nations from poor ones. In that sense, information technology will act as a polarising, centrifugal force on the global order. On the other hand, it also is a unifying, centripetal force. It changes the structure of the global polity. It shifts, for example, power to the global "civil society" and to non-governmental organisations, thus diminishing the power of established global actors. These social and political effects of the "electronic revolution" are more important, by far, than the direct effect it has on the economy. As we have seen, this economic effect has not been very impressive; and certainly much smaller than was claimed by the proponents of a "New Economy".

Things other than information technology contributed more to pushing US growth in the nineties somewhat above the average of the other wealthy countries. The US had a more expansionary macroeconomic policy. It could have and sustain this policy because others paid for it. US savings by households and corporations had always been low. They became lower still in the nineties. These low savings were compensated for by the massive inflow of foreign capital. That permitted a spectacular rise in the US current account deficit. It now stands at about 5% of US GDP and amounts to no less than 82% of the current account deficits of all other countries of the world combined.

Current account deficits share of various countries and regions; 2000

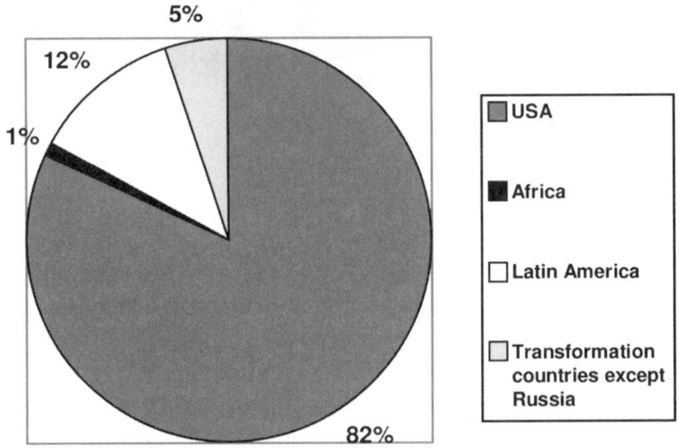

Source: IMF

This deficit is being financed by all countries of the world (and even the poor ones). Europe, Japan and China contribute the lion's share.

Part of the foreign capital that thus flows into the US does not come in the form of FDI – that is investment in the "real economy" –, but in the form of "portfolio investment"; that is investment just in financial instruments like stocks and bonds. All this money moving into the US had been propping up the value of the dollar, and had been driving up the price of shares at US stock exchanges. Foreigners were expediting their capital into the US because they believed that the US was "sound". Why did they believe that? The US was sound, they said, because the dollar then was still expensive; and US stocks then still were traded at a higher price than then comparable Japanese or European stocks. But why had the price of US stocks been at such dizzying heights and why was the dollar overvalued? Because foreigners bought dollars and US stocks. And why did they do so? Because they believed the US currency and US stocks to be "sound". And why...... etc. etc. etc.

Evidently, this had been a self re-enforcing process. It ceased in 2001/2002. There is a clear danger now of the whole process going into reverse. For much of the money that entered was not channelled into productive investment. It, therefore, did not make the US economy more productive. It merely inflated the price of assets, such as the price of stocks; the price of US real estate or the price of the US currency.

In the meantime, this bubble has been somewhat deflated. However, the process has been relatively slow[5]. Yet it still could turn into a true implosion. The consequences could be disastrous – not only for the US, but for the whole world. It took stock prices twenty five years to recover from the crash of 1929. A true collapse of the US asset bubble (coming on top of the collapse of the Japanese asset bubble) would affect the finance markets all over the world. It would depress and render sterile them over a very long period of time.

Dow Jones Industrial Average 1925-1954

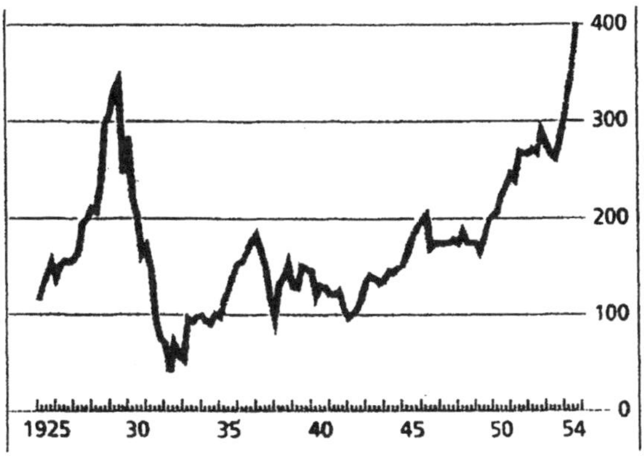

Source: Dow-Jones

A world financial crisis would trigger a global economic crisis. As we shall see, the existing institutions are not capable of thwarting such a development if it really were to become so massive as to lead to a deep dip in the prices of finan-

5 A so-called "soft landing".

cial assets. Such a financial melt-down would result in a true deflation – just as it did in Japan. If this were to happen, the US could certainly no longer claim to be the role model of economic efficiency and the prime engine of global economic growth. It would be seen as the dead weight to sink the floating vessel of the world economy.

Going Differing Paths – The Countries That Were Once Communist

Over the very long term, poor countries become wealthy and non-democratic countries become democracies. The formerly Communist countries should be no exception. Eventually, all of them should also become democratic and wealthy. These are their long-term prospects. But how have they fared until now? And how and when will they reach this final goal?

As we have learned since the demise of Communism in 1989, its legacy has been more onerous than expected. This will continue to handicap the political and economic development of ex-communist countries. But they fared less well too, when Communism was still intact. Southern European countries that, before World War II, were at the same or even at a lower relative level of wealth, pulled ahead of them by 1992, while they themselves have fallen back behind the relative position they still held in the pecking order in 1934.

Comparison in PPP Income 1934 and 1992

Select Communist and non Communist countries In 1990 USD; relative to the European average

	1934	1992
Germany	1,2	1,25
France	1,11	1,16
Austria	0,71	1,11
Finland	0,83	0,95
Italy	0,81	1,05
Ireland	0,75	0,76
Spain	0,51	0,81
Turkey	0,32	0,29
Bulgaria	0,31	0,26
Czech/Slova	0,72	0,44
Romania	0,48	0,31
Poland	0,48	0,31
Hungary	0,63	0,36
Yugoslvia	0,32	0,27

Source Maddison 1995

Communist countries did not just grow at a slower pace than the poor but "capitalist" countries of Europe. They also "mis-developed". Their modernisation was not the same as modernisation elsewhere. Communism had created disfunctionalities in their institutions, and in their economic, political and social culture. These had already impeded growth in the last and stale years of Communist rule. But these distortions had their effect also in the era after 1990, and they continue to have some negative impact even today.

The transition recession

Countries	*Consecutive years of output decline*	*Cumulative output decline (percent)*
CSB[a]	*3.8*	*22.6*
Albania	3	33
Bulgaria	4	16
Croatia	4	36
Czech Republic	3	12
Estonia	5	35
Hungary	4	15
Latvia	6	51
Lithuania	5	44
Poland	2	6
Romania	3	21
Slovak Republic	4	23
Slovenia	3	14
CIS[a]	*6.5*	*50.5*
Armenia	4	63
Azerbaijan	6	60
Belarus	6	35
Georgia	5	78
Kazakhstan	6	41
Kyrgyz Republic	6	50
Moldova	7	63
Russian Federation	7	40
Tajikistan	7	50
Turkmenistan	8	48
Ukraine	10	59
Uzbekistan	6	18
Output decline during the Great Depression, 1930–34		
France	3	11
Germany	3	16
United Kingdom	2	6
United States	4	27

Source: Maddison and IBRD

This is why the end of Communism did not result in an immediate spurt of growth. Time and inputs were needed to adjust institutions and behaviour to the requirements of a market economy. The old order and the old institutions had collapsed without new ones being readily available to take over. After 1990, the economies of the ex-Communist countries therefore shrivelled. In the Central European, Southeast European and Baltic countries (CSB), this decline was reversed from 1993 on. In the Commonwealth of Independent States[1] (CIS) the decline lasted much longer. Growth did not set in before 1998. But even thereafter, the process was not smooth. More often than not, the "first transition recession" was followed by a second recession (e.g. in Romania and Bulgaria 1996-97, or in Russia in 1998).

The economic decline that ensued is unprecedented both in its steepness and duration. The effect is much worse than the one created by the World Economic Crisis in the thirties of the last century.

After 12 years, some of the CSB countries still had not re-gained the level of wealth that had been theirs in 1990.

Real GDP in Central and Eastern Europe 1990-2000
1990 = 100

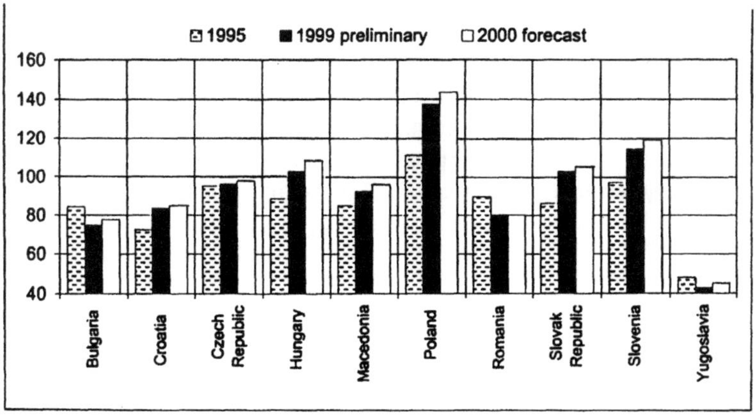

Source: WIIW

The decline in wealth was more dramatic still in the CIS where, in the year 2000, not a single state had regained the level of wealth it had in 1990.

---

1 The use of this term is problematic as the organisation that provides the common roof for this group of countries is hardly in existence any longer.

Real GDP in the CIS 1990-2000
1990 = 100

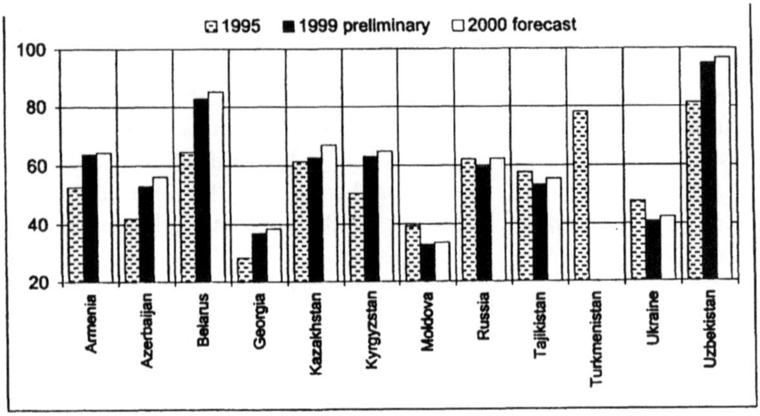

Source: WIIW

As we have seen in the first table of this chapter, a gap in wealth had always existed between the Eastern and the Western parts of Europe. Communism widened this gap. It became wider still in the years immediately following the demise of Communism.

When it set in, economic growth was not accompanied by a growth of the employed labour force. On the contrary, when economic reforms finally started to bite, the once overstaffed old plants shed labour in order to become competitive. With very few exceptions (e.g. Hungary) employment declined.

Manufacturing employment and productivity 2002
(1995=100)

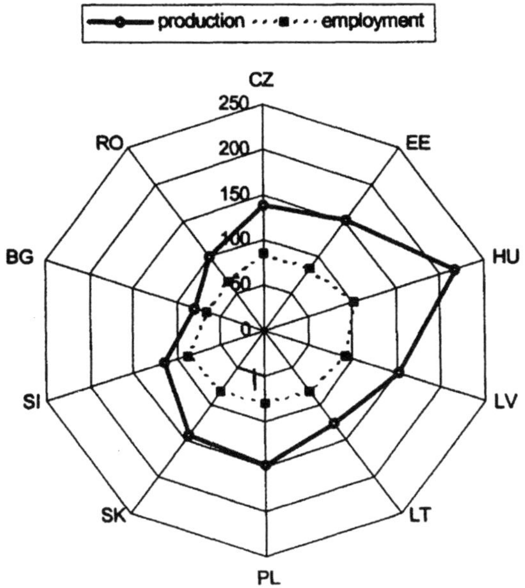

Source: WIIW

Unemployment grows. It reaches 20% in Slovakia and more than 40% in Macedonia. The ensuing social suffering and discontent is accentuated by an increasing inequality of income.

In this process, the formerly rather egalitarian countries of Central Europe have as unequal a distribution of income as the Western European countries; and, in many cases, an even more unequal one.[2] The CIS countries, however, have gone far beyond that. Inequality there is akin to the inequality in Latin American countries (which have Gini coefficients of around 50).

2 The **Gini coefficient** measuring inequality mostly stands between 25 and 32 in Western Europe.

Changes in inequality during transition

Countries	Gini coefficient of income per capita		
	1987–90	*1993–94*	*1996–98*
CSB	*0.23*	*0.29*	*0.33*
Bulgaria	0.23	0.38	0.41
Croatia	0.36	—	0.35
Czech Republic	0.19	0.23	0.25
Estonia	0.24	0.35	0.37
Hungary	0.21	0.23	0.25
Latvia	0.24	0.31	0.32
Lithuania	0.23	0.37	0.34
Poland	0.28	0.28	0.33
Romania	0.23	0.29	0.30
Slovenia	0.22	0.25	0.30
CIS[a]	*0.28*	*0.36*	*0.46*
Armenia	0.27	—	0.61
Belarus	0.23	0.28	0.26
Georgia	0.29	—	0.43
Kazakhstan	0.30	0.33	0.35
Kyrgyz Republic	0.31	0.55	0.47
Moldova	0.27	—	0.42
Russian Federation	0.26	0.48	0.47
Tajikistan	0.28	—	0.47
Turkmenistan	0.28	0.36	0.45
Ukraine	0.24	—	0.47

Source: IBRD

All this, and the decline in social services, has impacted negatively upon the general health of the population. While life expectancy has risen in Western Europe, it has remained stagnant in the CSB states. In the CIS it has declined. In Russia[3], male life expectancy has dropped by 5 years – something that has never been experienced before in an industrialised country; not even in times of war and crisis.

Not surprisingly, this has translated into social and political tension and unease. In the formerly Communist countries, the elites continue to preach the gospel of economic and political reform so as to meet expectations of their Western peers and of international organisations. The population, however, is not convinced. The vast majority is "not content" with the reform process. This disenchantment has grown over the years.

3 It needs pointing out, though, that this decline in average male life expectancy had already set in BEFORE the end of the Communist era; and is connected, to no small degree, to a worsening life style; and specifically, to **alcoholism**. But this scourge is in itself the symptom of serious social and consequently psychological tension.

Life expectancy at birth
Select CEECs and the EU average

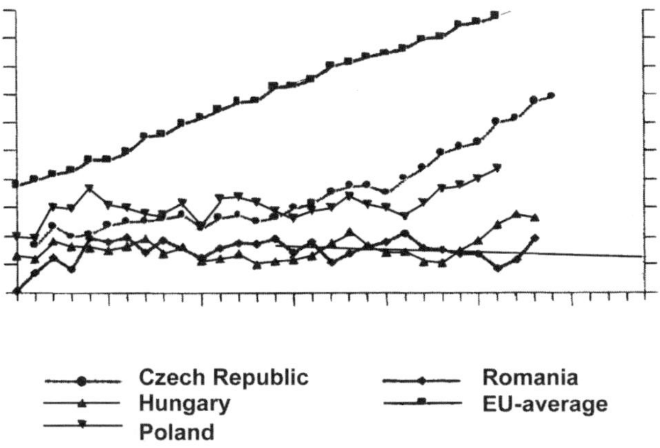

Source: WHO

Percentage of those answering in the affirmative to "I am not content with the reform process"

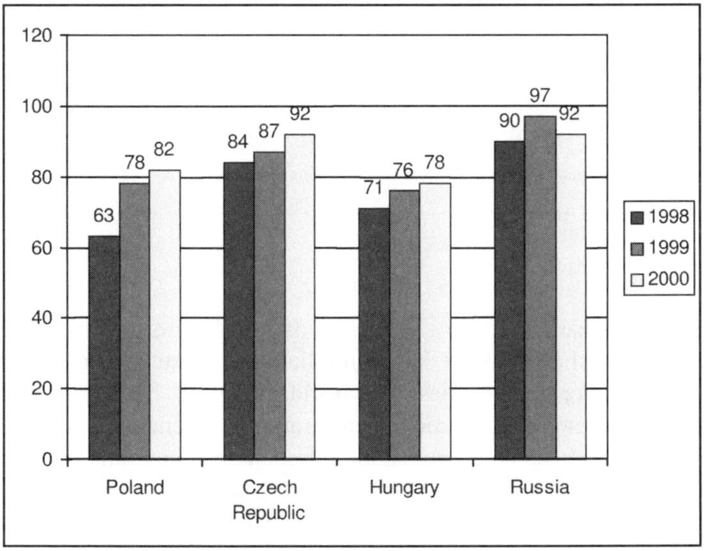

Source: Forschungsstelle für empirische Sozialökonomik

Disenchantment with reform translates into malcontent with democracy as such. In Russia, for example, the principle of democratic governance seems no longer to be based on the consent and approval of those so governed.

Percentage of those answering in the affirmative to " democracy just leads to chaos and anarchy in our country"

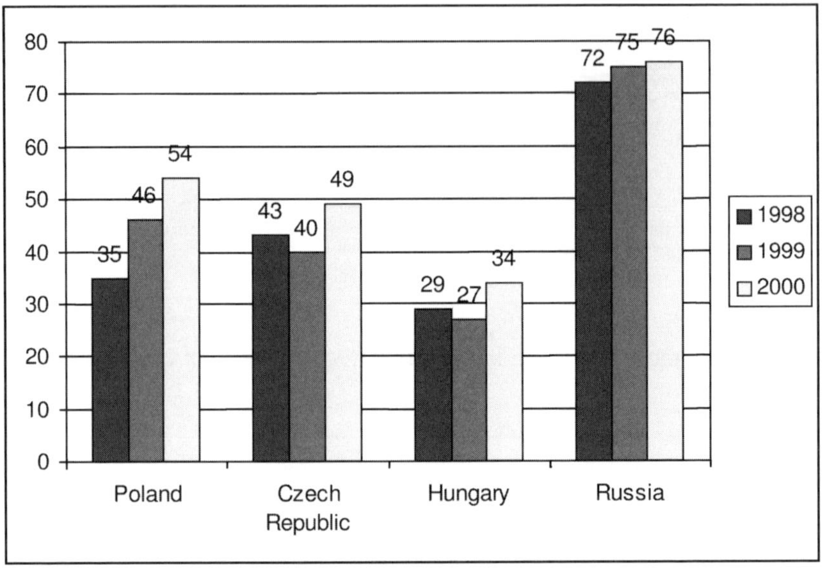

Source : Forschungsstelle für empirische Sozialökonomik

Political transition
Politics of transition

One hundred years ago, only a handful of states were governed democratically. By now their number has multiplied and more than one half of the world's states are democracies. The world, therefore, has experienced many transitions from non-democratic to democratic governance.

Political scientists have probed into these "transitions" and have attempted some generalisations. They have, for instance, found that the mode of transition is of great and enduring relevance. It would make a difference whether a transition is "pacted" between the old, outgoing political elite and the incoming, new political elite. "Pacted" transitions creates more favourable conditions for democracy.

Some support for this proposition of the "Transitologists" can be found in the switch to democracy as it occurred in the CSBs[4]. Nonetheless the transition from Communism cannot be compared to "transitions to democracy" as they occurred in other parts of the world. Two elements, in particular, made this transition unique:

First, the coincidence of a political transition with the wholesale transformation of the economic system; and, second, the effects of the break-up of the Soviet empire.

The loosening of the Soviet grip was certainly a precondition for democratisation in the CBSs. Till then, Soviet power had repressed all attempts of democratisation (Hungary 1956, Czechoslovakia 1968, Poland 1981). Unlike in other countries, the breakthrough to democracy thus did not just call for changes in the national environment, but for changes, too, in the international environment.

The second peculiarity is the co-incidence of wholesale political with wholesale economic transformation. Quite a few observers thought it impossible to combine democratic transition and democratic consolidation with economic reform. The former Polish Prime Minister and present head of the Polish Central Bank, Balcerowicz, for instance, believed that economic reform could just happen in a short phase of " extra-ordinary politics" immediately following the breakdown of the old system. Thereafter, economic reform would become blocked politically by the vast majority of voters who would suffer from reform instead of drawing immediate benefits from it.

Others pointed to the superior economic performance of China and pleaded for a "Chinese way" of postponing democratic reform until economic reform became consolidated.

This advice was not heeded – and for just reasons. As it turned out, far from being mutual impediments, economic reform and democratisation supplement one another. If one excepts China, those formerly Communist countries that lead the league of successful economic reformers are also those countries with the best democratic credentials. The ups and downs of democratic politics and democratic pluralism and multi-polarity have not impeded economic reform.

4 It was, for instance, easier in Hungary, where it was "pacted", and more difficult in Romania, where the old dictatorial ("sultanistic") regime simply collapsed.

Progress in (economic) policy reform, 1990s

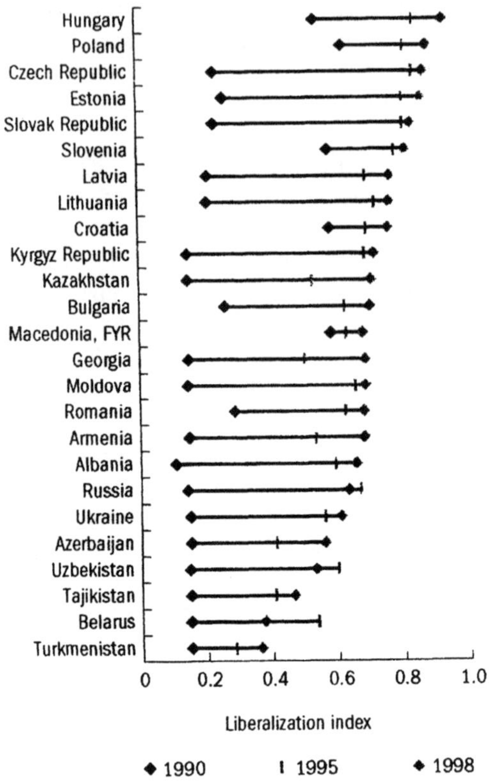

Source: de Malo, Denizen and Gelb 1996, EBRD 2000

Democratisation and economic reform thus are mutually compatible. At least in the CSBs, they even seem contingent upon one another[5]. Democracy can safeguard the transparency and the property rights that are essential for the functioning of a market.

When is political transition complete? And when can democracy be regarded as consolidated? The generally accepted definition for the completion

5 The social and political reality underlying these simple correlations is, of course, more complicated. The **direction of causality** is not clear. And it also seems likely that both democratisation and economic success are contingent upon the **same underlying social/ cultural mechanisms.**

of transition is the point at which the new institutions (like parliament, political parties etc) are firmly in place. According to one definition, "consolidation" would be completed after two freely contested elections. According to yet another definition, it would be complete after political power has shifted at least once from the incumbent to the opposition. Or, according to yet another definition, it would be complete when there is no longer any major political force that opposes[6] democratic governance.

What is clear, though, is that the formerly Communist countries differ not just in their economic performance, but also in the nature of their political governance. It ranges from pure democracy – like in Hungary – to pure, unadulterated dictatorship – like Turkmenistan.

We will neglect, for the moment, the CIS countries which tend to be in an altogether different orbit, and just look at the CSBs. Will the wide gulf in wealth narrow, that now separates them from the present EU member countries? The answer given in the table below is an – albeit modestly – optimistic one. Yes, the gulf will become more narrow again. But closing it will take time. Were the CSBs to pursue their recent average rate of economic growth[7], they could reach 70% of the EU average per capita GDP in (an average of) 47 years; and 80% of the EU average in 58 years.

An essential prerequisite for such a more rapid rate of economic growth is a high rate of investment. All over the world, robust growth is associated with high investment rates[8]. In East Asia, investment rates are all above 25% of GDP. The CSB countries that are candidates for adhesion to the EU come close to that; and – if one excepts Bulgaria and Romania – in all of them, the investment rates are above the EU average (of about 20%).

6 Note that according to this definition, some Western European democracies were not consolidated democracies for quite some time; given, for instance, in postwar France and Italy, the existence of powerful Communist parties that aimed at a revolutionary overthrow of the existing system.

7 The European Commission – EC – and others assume a higher growth rate for the CSB that is at 2% above the growth rate of the present EU members. Convergence to the 70% target of the EU average per capita GDP would thus happen earlier, according to this EC definition. This more optimistic assumption seems plausible in the face of the most recent data on relatively sturdy growth in the CSBs.

8 With the question being open as to whether high investment actually CAUSES more rapid growth; to a certain extent, at least, it might just be one of the consequences at the onset of rapid growth.

When will they catch up?
Time (years) needed to reach 70% or 80 % of the EU 15 average income

	$EU\ 25_{70\%}$	$EU\ 25_{80\%}$
BGR	123	139
CZE	8	17
EST	49	58
HUN	38	50
LVA	74	83
LTU	73	83
POL	40	50
ROM	42	48
SVK	30	42
SVN	-4	6
Mean:	47	58

Source: M. Wagner, J.Hlouskova, Real convergence prospects of the CEEC 10, manuscript

These investment rates have been boosted over what they would have been otherwise by a rather massive inflow of Foreign Direct Investment (FDI). In the Czech Republic, for instance, FDI has reached nearly 5% of GDP. FDI is important not only as a source of capital, but also as a mechanism for the transfer of know-how and in facilitating access to foreign markets[9].

Main recipients of Foreign Direct Investment, 1992-1999

	1992-95		*1996-99*	
Countries	*US$ millions*	*Percentage of GDP*	*US$ millions*	*Percentage of GDP*
CSB	*21,091*	*0.5*	*50,558*	*3.3*
Czech Republic	4,821	2.9	10,104	4.6
Estonia	647	3.9	1,050	5.2
Hungary	9,399	5.7	6,979	3.8
Poland	2,540	0.6	17,096	2.9
CIS	*8,272*	*1.0*	*22,001*	*2.5*
Azerbaijan	237	4.2	3,222	20.9
Kazakhstan	2,357	2.7	4,971	6.4
Russian Federation	3,965	0.3	8,412	0.7
Turkmenistan	427	3.5	334	3.0

Note: Shares of GDP are period averages of medians for the group
Source: World Bank staff estimates and country statistical office data

9 The exceptionally high level of FDI in Azerbaijan is due – exclusively – to foreign investment in oil fields; and has probably done very little to develop the rest of the economy; it might even have held back this development (see chapter on oil – "Dutch disease").

We may assume that the stream of FDI into the CSBs will continue and even widen, given the high growth potential of these countries.

Massive Foreign Direct Investment is being supplemented by grants and Technical Assistance of various forms. In 1999, these transfers amounted to 6 billion USD; that is roughly one tenth the volume of the development aid that was provided by OECD countries.

Official aid from OECD to "part II countries"[10]
1999, in 1000 USD, aid per donor country

	Total	Bilateral grants	Bilateral loans	Contributions to multilateral institutions
$ millions, 1999				
Australia	3	2	..	1
Austria	184	130	0	54
Belgium	82	6	..	75
Canada	165	165	..	..
Denmark	128	99	29	..
Finland	74	41	-4	38
France	550	148	-6	408
Germany	729	366	-124	487
Greece	11	8	..	3
Ireland	..	..	..	..
Italy	92	8	-1	84
Japan	67	72	-45	40
Luxembourg	3	3	..	..
Netherlands	22	22	..	..
New Zealand	0	0	..	0
Norway	28	28	..	..
Portugal	28	0	..	28
Spain	13	13	..	..
Sweden	99	94	0	6
Switzerland	70	62	1	6
United Kingdom	326	98	0	228
United States	3,521	3,204	240	78
Total	**6,193**	**4,568**	**89**	**1,535**

Source: OECD

10 Basically: ex-Communist countries; minus those ex communist countries that now clearly are developing countries.

The stabilisation of the CSBs is due, to no small degree, to policies of the European Union. The Union provides access to markets; grants technical assistance; promotes cultural exchange and political dialogue. It monitors institutional consolidation and grants financial support to investment in infrastructure. The Union has a dominant role in, and is the main financial contributor to, the quasi-protectorates in the Balkans (Kosovo and Bosnia/Herzegovina). However, the most precious contribution the EU provides is a positive perspective that stabilises expectations. In the CSBs, this perspective is identical with the perspective of ultimate EU membership. And, indeed, eight of these countries will join the EU as new members in 2004.

Yet neither technical assistance nor the inflow of money alone (either through FDI or grants) can guarantee self-sustaining growth. It might very well be that, after a period of more rapid development, the CSBs will still fail to catch up fully; and remain laggards of the type Southern Italy (the Mezzogiorno) has been in relation to Northern Italy. A warning that this could indeed be their future is being provided by the former German Democratic Republic (GDR) –now: "die Neuen Länder". After unification with the rest of Germany, there was a short spurt of growth. But its dynamics were shallow . This becomes evident in a comparison of the numbers of new enterprises registered in the Western part of Gemany and in the "Neuen Länder". Per head of population, fewer new enterprises are being created in the Eastern part of Germany. Although the Western "Länder" still spend about 4% of their GDP annually to support the transition and recovery of the Eastern part of now united Germany, the economy there has returned to a more sluggish performance. In many ways, Germany thus still is divided. Importantly – it still is not unified in the heads of its citizens. Politics, political attitudes and institutions still differ.[11]

Southeast Europe (the politically correct alternate name for the less acceptable "the Balkans") remains a special case. With per capita incomes of less than 2000 USD, these are "Low Middle Income Countries" according to the World Bank definition. They are thus separated by a wide margin from the "High Middle Income" ex-Communist Central European countries and from the "High Income Countries" of Western Europe. Also, most of the states of Southeast Europe are "young"; with no long tradition in administration and with quite some ethnic conflict across and within the borders that have been drawn so very re-

11 As is made evident by the strong position of the formerly Communist PDS party with its relatively strong presence just in the Eastern part of Germany.

cently[12]. Given these difficulties, one should perhaps wonder less at the violence that has erupted on occasions; and wonder more at the fact that it did not become much worse. There is clear resolve on both sides that "integration into Europe" is and should remain the prime policy goal of Southeast Europe. For the EU, probably no task is more urgent in its external relations.

Sooner or later, the countries of Central, Eastern, Southern Europe and the Baltic Republics will thus attach themselves to the European Union. The eventual place and course of the Slavic successor states of the Soviet Union, the future of Russia, the Ukraine, of Belarus and Moldova is less evident. In a sense this lack of clear perspective is but the prolongation of an historic dilemma. Throughout its history, Russia has always been a European power; and an important one at that[13]. But with its extension to the Pacific in the 17th century, it became an Asian power also. And in the perception and definition of its own identity, it has never fully and unequivocally embraced the European option. It claimed a specificity that would put it beyond – or above – other European nations. All through the 19th century, the battle waged to and fro between the Westernisers, oriented towards Europe, and the "Slavophiles", convinced of the uniqueness of "Holy Russia"[14] and of its duty and right to be left alone.

In its programme and dogma, Communism was a modernising, "Western" concept. But in the actual application of this dogma, in actual "governance", Communism translated into a distinctly non-Western regime[15] that continued with many of the institutions and practices of Tsarist "Holy Russia" (for example, with powerful secret services, over-investment in the military and with the distrust towards the capitalist bourgeoisie) .

The ambivalence continued even after the break-up of the Soviet empire in 1992. A brief period of identification with the "West" was followed by a period of greater distance and by the growing prominence (also in the strategic discussions) of those who prescribed for Russia an "Eurasian" way. It would translate, into foreign and security policy, Russia's unique geographic position on and between two continents. Now, under president Putin, the tide seems to have turned again and moved again in favour of the modernisers and "Westerners". But this is

---

12 An international "Stability Pact" is intended to respond to these challenges; the same is being pursued by the European Union through its "Stabilisation and Association Agreements". It takes a "regional approach" to prop up the region and to enhance contacts and co-operation between the Balkan countries.

13 For instance, in the concert of nations established after the end of the Napoleonic wars.

14 One important source of such sentiment being the orthodox church – always closely allied with the state.

15 Wittfogel would have termed it an oriental – despotic regime.

mainly due to the person of Putin himself. His preferences are not that widely shared, either in the administration or by common citizens.

The future place of Russia (and of the other Slavic successor states of the Soviet Union) will depend not just upon political choices. The development of their economy will also be relevant. As we have seen, the economy has started to grow again even in those countries. But the previous decline has been steep indeed. And much capacity and many capabilities have been lost in between. The countries have suffered massive de-industrialisation. They now start with a large disadvantage. The announced goal, that Russia will pull even soon in per capita income with the poorest of the EU countries (Portugal), seems overly ambitious. At present, the Russian economy is not bigger in volume than the economy of the small Netherlands.

Being surrounded mostly by poor and frequently unstable countries does not help. Furthermore, Russia's wealth in natural resources like oil, gas, gold, and bauxite might, in the long run, prove to be more of a draw-back than an advantage.

At present, Russia is certainly too weak to act as a player, as one of the "poles" in a multipolar[16] world. The vast geographic size and the possession of nuclear weapons do not compensate for its inferior economic status. Realism would thus oblige it to discard any notion of being on a par with either Japan, China or with Europe. Realism, on the other hand, should also oblige it to discard the notion or hope of soon becoming a full member of the European Union. Russia is simply too poor, anarchic, vast and too different to become integrated into the Union. That might change but it would take generations to complete such change. For the near and mid term future, the most plausible option is one of a close association with the EU, but one that stops well before full membership.

Economically, the states of Central Asia (the "-stans") and the Transcaucasian states (Armenia, Georgia and Azerbaijan) are even a rank below the "low middle income" countries of Southeast Europe. With per capita GDP of around 500 USD, they find themselves on an "African level of poverty". Politically most of the Central Asian[17] countries have ceased to even pretend being democracies. They hope to profit, though, through their "strategic location"; in the "heart" of the Eurasian continent; by their wealth in natural gas and oil; and by their present use as a base in the fight against Islamic/fundamentalist terrorism.

16 Notwithstanding its recent full integration into the "Group of 7", now extended to the "Group of 8", leading world powers.

17 It is different for the Transcaucasian countries, as these have become members of the Council of Europe, and thus are obliged to keep up appearances.

It is true that there are some very big oil and gas fields in the region. Some major new ones having been discovered east of the Caspian Sea. This has enhanced the relevance of states with such deposits; as it has enhanced the position of those states, the territory of which would be needed for the export of this oil and gas (e.g. Afghanistan).

Nonetheless – not too much should be made of that. The new oil fields pale in comparison to the oil reserves known to exist in the Middle East. In the end, wealth in oil and gas and the use as a base for foreign troops cannot compensate for the enduring inner weakness of these states; which finds expression in continuing de-industrialisation and in massive emigration; and which is made evident by the lack of democracy.

Central Asia, geopolitics, and the relation of centre and periphery

"Geo-politics" is a pseudo-science developed in a time when the mass of an army was decisive; and when transportation (also over oceans) was still costly.

They no longer are. Geography is no longer relevant, as a potential location of a battlefield or as a potential route for vast armies of marching soldiers.

In the time of the cold war, geography held importance for another reason. One held sway over a certain piece of the earth's surface in order to prevent the opponent from doing the same on the same spot (hundreds of thousands were killed in Vietnam for that reason). The "Non Aligned Movement" was created for the very purpose of containing and opposing such aspirations of the two superpowers. But with the cold war gone and with a new military technology in place (long range bombers and ultra precise ordinance), the urge to hold on to an otherwise unattractive place has disappeared.

Peripheral countries have also lost much of their relevance as exporters of raw materials, the (real) prices of which are in steady decline; and which make for an ever smaller share of inputs in the goods produced by wealthy countries. Geography counts now for other reasons: for embodying history; for the continuity of culture and institutions; and for tradition, especially, in the access to modernity. Geographic location thus counts as a vessel for cumulative social advantages or disadvantages in the process of necessary and ceaseless economic innovation.

Once, wealthy countries (the "centre") had solid reasons for extending their dominance as widely as possible. They no longer have. Once the poorer countries (the "periphery") had solid reasons to resist the imperialistic urges of the "centre". They no longer do. For them, the fear of being "exploited" has been replaced by the fear of having become irrelevant; the fear of being ignored. Witness the engagement of the former imperial powers of the UK and

France in Africa. It persisted after the break up of the empires; but has disappeared over the last decades. Witness the decline of the Non-Aligned Movement and the change in the economic policy of its former members. Instead of searching for maximum autonomy, they all (save perhaps, North Korea) search for a maximum of "connectedness" (see their support for the WTO).

To sum up: since the break-up of the Soviet empire, its former parts have drifted apart. The differences that have always existed between them have grown. Even among the non-CIS transition countries, the differences have opened into a yawning chasm. Measured in terms of nominal per capita GDP, the difference between Albania and Slovenia is one to nine; between Slovenia and Bulgaria one to five. The differences within the whole group of all the so-called transition countries are wider still.

Distance from the centres of early modernisation and progress in economic reform
(as gauged by the EBRD Transition Indicators)

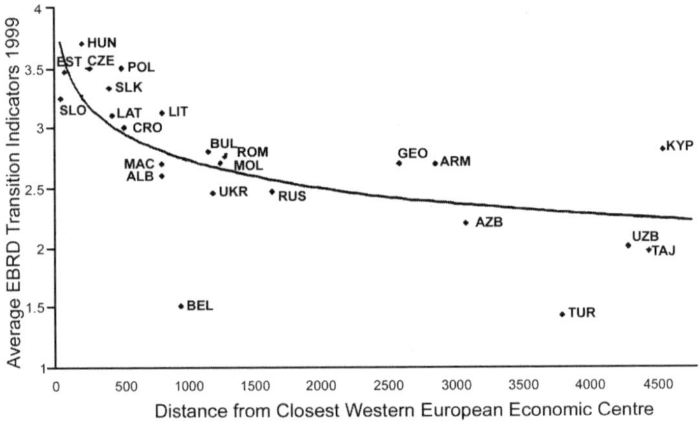

Source: J. Sachs, 1997. The paper of J. Sachs is based upon a complex, multifactor analysis and investigates the "weight" of several variables that have been used to explain the wide and growing divergence in the economic performance of the transition countries. J. Sachs finds that ALL such factors pale into near total insignificance against the sole factor of "geographice location" (which he measures not just by the simple physical distance from the "West", but by using a "gravity model" that multiplies this physical distance by the relative economic weight of each country or region)

A certain West-East gradient in wealth has always existed since the onset of modernisation. Generally, those were poorer that had been further removed from the traditional centre of modernisation (located somewhere at the triangle between Belgium, Southern UK and North-western Germany). But Communism and its legacy have made this gradient steeper. This gradient in wealth has as its counterpart a gradient in political culture and institutions. In the Western part of Europe, democracy has developed "from below". Central Europe remained stuck longer with rule by paternalistic elites. The Eastern part of the continent, however, had always been ruled and continues to be ruled "top down". This is a serious obstacle to modernisation – as modernisation has to be broadly based and has to be embraced not just by the ruler or the ruling elites, but by at least a sizeable part of the population.

What are the long-term prospects of the ex-Communist countries? Where and how will they fit into the global system? The Central/Eastern European states, and the Baltic Republics, will soon and fully integrate into the European Union. So will, eventually, the countries of South Eastern Europe. But, due to the poverty and inner fragility of these states, they will be kept in the waiting room longer, and still might cause some trouble in this ante-chamber.

At least two of the European successor states of the Soviet Union – Moldova and Belarus – are exceedingly weak and unstable. They might very well collapse or otherwise disappear. Should these states continue to exist they will seek (and obtain) a special relationship with the European Union; but one that excludes the prospect of ultimate membership.

The same prospect exists for Ukraine. It is more consolidated, certainly, than Moldova. But its internal political developments lead it away from Europe and back towards an authoritarian polity, which is – by necessity – something fragile. When too many politicians die from road accidents, it becomes difficult to find the cause in bad driving habits.

Ukraine – prominent road accident victims

Prominent road-accident victims	*When*	*Result*
Valery Malev, arms-export chief	March 2002, amid a scandal involving the president and arms to Iraq	Death
Yulia Timoshenko, opposition leader	January 2002, while fighting a travel ban before the general election	Injury
Alexander Yemets, parlamentarian	January 2001, at the peak of the "Kuchmagate" bugging scandal	Death
Yevhen Marchuk, former secret-police chief	February 2000, after returning to a powerful position as national security adviser	Injury
Boris Marusich, head of state second-hand weapons company	April 1999, during a revamp of arms exports	Death
Vyacheslav Chornovil, ex-dissident	March 1999, while gathering support for a presidential bid	Death
Alexander Veselovsky, deputy head of central bank	August 1998, during an investigation of dodgy deals with foreigners	Death
George Kuzmycz, US official dealing with nukes	December 1997, en route to an experimental military facility	Death

Source: Economist

A belt of insecurity formed by extremely fragile and corrupt states will separate Russia from those countries that will be members of the European Union in the near future. This belt extends from the Southern frontiers of the Baltic states down to the Black Sea. Not only are the inhabitants of these states condemned to continued misery. These states will also be heavy exporters of problems of various sorts – not least among them organised crime.

Russia is in a somewhat better condition; and for Russia, too, the European Union will become the most likely and most potent point of international attachment. But Russia is also likely to continue its special relationship with the United States. Both China and Russia will try very hard to keep their mutual relationship peaceful and on an even keel.

Central Asia and Transcaucasia will remain a troubled and poor region. Outsiders (China, Turkey, the US, Iran, the EU and, of course, Russia) will seek influence; but they will do so with limited investments and low stakes.

The Divide Between the Poor and the Rich Countries

The East-West divide that structured world politics so much has disappeared. What remains is the North-South divide – the divide that separates the world's wealthy from the world's poor. 40% of the world's population lives in countries with an average per capita GNI[1] of less than 755 US dollars. Another 35% live in countries with an average per capita GNI of less than 3.000 US dollars.

Distribution of world population among countries grouped by per capita GNI

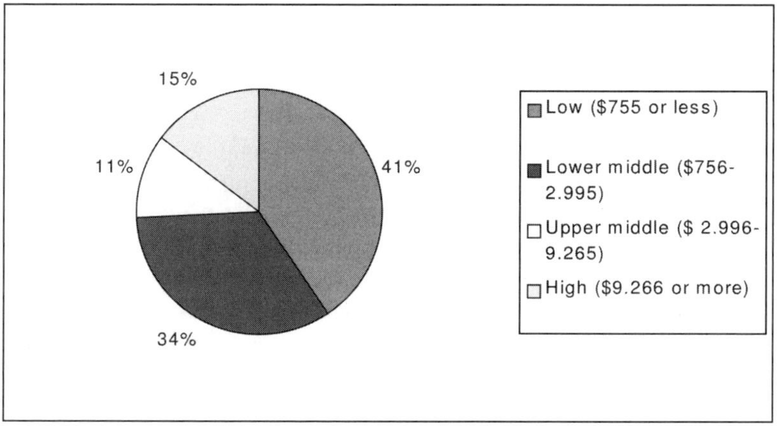

Source: World Bank Atlas 2002

This chasm has become deeper. If one juxtaposes the extremes of the world's twenty richest countries to the world's twenty poorest countries, the distance that separates these two groups has again doubled over the last 40 years.

1 GNI stands for Gross National Income. Unlike the GDP, it includes transfers like remittances from abroad; and is thus better suited to measure a country's true wealth; especially if it is a poor country.

Per capita GDP
In 1985 USD (PPP)

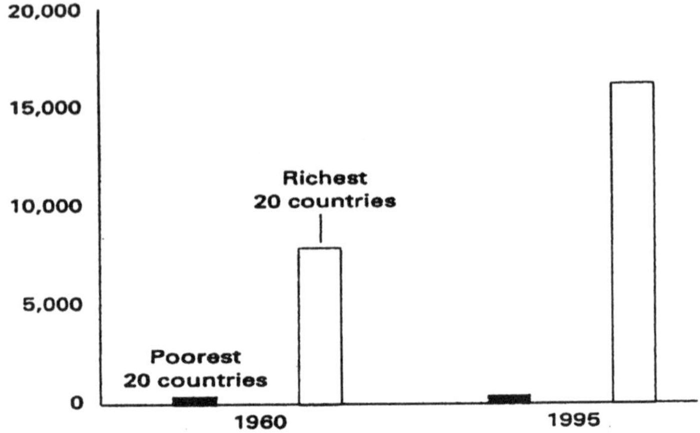

Source: IBRD

The wealthy countries form a rather compact group. In this group, per capita income differs at a rate of one to three at the maximum. These countries are fairly similar in other respects too. All of them have entered the "post-industrial age". All of them have more or less elaborate welfare systems. All of them are democratic. All of them are closely integrated into the world economic system .

The same does not hold true for poor countries. The best off have a per capita GDP 50 times higher than those worst off. Otherwise, too, this is not a homogenous group. One may divide it into at least five sub-groups, all of them with different functions and places in the global economy:

1) very poor countries with little to export
2) poor countries that rely on the export of a few, agricultural products
3) not so poor countries that have high, but widely oscillating incomes from the export of a single raw material (frequently oil)
4) countries in the early phase of industrialisation with huge internal markets, thus being less dependent upon international trade (India, China, Brazil)
5) countries past the first stages of industrialisation which already export a wide array of industrial products.

Given these divergent interests, the poorer countries find it difficult to agree on a common agenda if the discussion is, for instance, on the regime for the prices of raw materials; or on the regime for trade in industrial products. This weakens their capacity to impact on the global system and to change it to their advantage.

Will the gap in wealth continue to shrink, that separates them from the rich countries of the world? Will this distance become smaller and eventually even insignificant? Or will this distance to the wealthy of the world widen; or will it become first smaller and eventually turn insignificant? At first sight, the chances of poor countries catching up seem real. They grew at twice the rate of wealthy countries between 1978 and 1997. One should, therefore, expect the chasm between the rich and the poor to narrow.

Annual growth rate 1978-1997

world average	3,3%
developed countries	2,5%
developing countries	5,0%

Source : IBRD

Yet, this table discounts the growth of population. As population growth is fast in the poor countries, the economic growth measured by per capita GNI is smaller. Furthermore, these figures vary widely among the poor countries. Those that hold more than half of the population of all of these countries taken together, had their per capita GNI grow at an annual rate in excess of 3%. In 35 countries, on the other hand, which provide home to 14.6% of the developing world's population, per capita income even decreased in the time between 1990 and 2000.

Developing countries – Distribution of growth rates

Average annual per capita real growth rates	*Number of developing countries*	*% of all developing countries*	*Population (millions)*	*% of total developing world population*
Negative growth	48	35.0	727	14.6
Moderate growth	65	47.4	1606	32.3
High growth	24	17.6	2636	53.1
Total	137	100.0	4969	100.0

Notes: Negative growth implies an average growth rate of less than 0%, moderate growth a rate of 0-3%, high growth a rate in excess of 3.0%. Developing countries refer to lower and middle income countries in accordance with World Bank definitions.

Source: World Bank, World Development Indicators 2002

But even if these growth rates of per capita GNI were much higher than at present, the gap between the rich and the poor countries would still widen in absolute terms. They still would move further apart.

Simple math on how differences widen when they seem to shrink

Take country A and assume it to be very poor, with a per capita GNI of just 500 US dollars per year (there are quite a few of them).[2] Take, on the other hand, country B, with a per capita GNI fifty (!) times higher at 25,000 US dollars. Again, there are quite a few such countries. Now let us assume that the poor country A – due to a stroke of good luck and due to wise policies – grows at a rare annual rate of fully 20 percent. After a year, its per capita GNI would have increased from 500 to 600 US dollars. The performance of the wealthy country B is less spectacular. Its per capita GNI grows at a meagre 1.5 percent. It thus increases from 25,000 US dollars to 25,325 USD. Still, the difference that separates B from A would again have widened by 225 USD. In the very long run, of course, the country that grows faster will catch up. But for quite some time, the distance will become wider that separates it from the state that is wealthy but grows much slower.

To stay with the example just used: if we assume, for the poor country, a more realistic, continuous growth rate of 7 percent, and for the rich country, a growth rate of merely 1 percent (which would be quite below the historic average), the distance in absolute wealth that exists between them would still continue to become wider over the next 45 years.

But even with the distance to the wealthy still widening, poorer countries do reap tangible benefits from that growth, even at a very low level. Some of these benefits are quite spectacular. If the averages are taken again, a child born in a poor country may now expect to live 20 years longer than a child born in a poor country 40 years ago. 30 years ago, every other adult in the developing world could not read. Today three out of four can. The per capita intake of calories in developing countries has soared from 1.900 calories in 1960 to 2.600 in the year 2000. The growth in absolute wealth registered in many – but not all – developing countries thus has indeed improved the lives of billions. But even if life has improved for the very poor, the widening of the gap between rich and poor countries does have highly negative consequences; especially for global governance.

2 Some countries like Ethiopia even have a GDP of no more than 100 USD per capita.

A short note on the methods we have just applied in gauging the rich against the poor; and in ranking the poor among themselves. We have ranked one country against another; and have given equal weight to each, regardless of whether it is China with 1,3 billion inhabitants; or the Cape Verde Islands, with a few hundred thousand inhabitants. This does not make much sense. It seems more suitable in such a comparison to weigh countries according to the size of their populations.

Also – if we wish to inquire into the well-being of the population – it is more useful to use the yardstick of purchasing power parities, instead of comparing the average incomes valued at nominal exchange rates. Purchasing power comparisons measure what the citizens of two different countries can actually purchase with their incomes. So – in the table below – we move to the lower line (comparison of countries when weighted by population); and, in this lower line, we move to the right corner (comparison in using purchasing power parities). We find that – as measured by R. Wade – the income distribution between the world's rich and the world's poor countries has not changed very much over the last quarter of a century.

World income distribution movement over the past quarter century

		Income measured in:	
		market exchange rates	PPP exchange rates
Countries weighted by Population ?	No	Very much more unequal	More unequal
	Yes	Much more unequal	Little change

Source: R. Wade

Quoting a 1999 Word Bank Study, Björn Lomborg (the "sceptical environmentalist" we encountered before) even claims that, instead of merely staying constant, the gap in wealth has narrowed, if it is measured in purchasing power parities and if it is made to reflect the different size of population in each country.

Yet there are other IBRD studies[3] that lead to the opposite conclusion of the gap widening even if this gap is calculated in purchasing power parities; and calculated on a per capita basis instead of just taking countries as the unit to count.

3 Milanovic, B, 1999, comes to the opposite conclusion and sees the gaps in PPP adjusted per capita income widening.

Relationship between the richest and the poorest 20% and 30% in the world in terms of per capita GDP in PPP 1960-1997

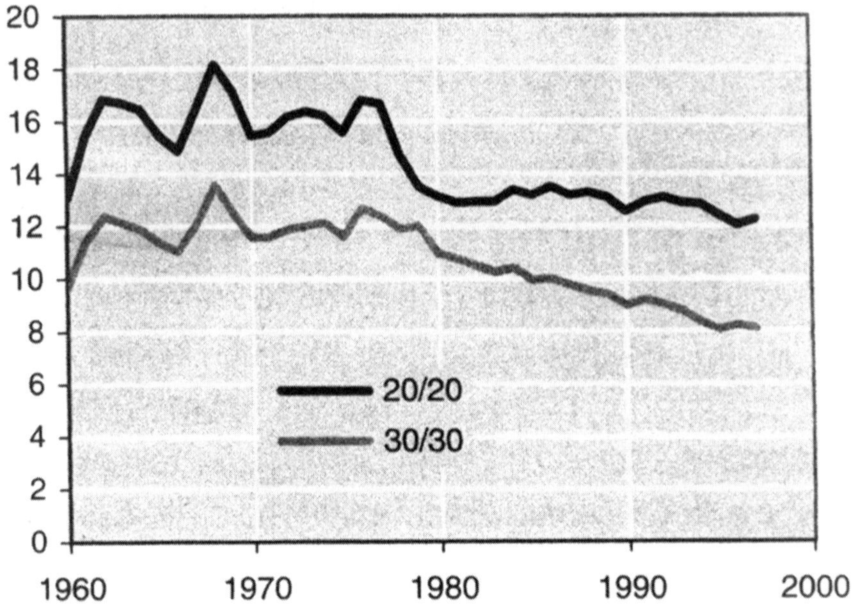

Source: World Bank as quoted by B. Lomborg 2002, p.74

Whatever their findings – none of these studies can make us ignore the yawning gap in wealth between the world's rich and poor. It has, and will continue to have, serious social, economic and political consequences. The situation is difficult to accept also in moral terms. In wealthy countries, citizens are becoming overweight while, at the same time children starve in some of the poorer countries.

Cumulative percentage of world income

Cumulative percentage of world population	*1988*	*1993*
Bottom 20%	2.3	2.0
Bottom 75%	25.9	22.3
Top 5%	31.2	33.7

Percentage of underweight children and of overweight adults in selected countries, mid-nineties

Country	*Percentage share of underweight*	*Country*	*Percentage share of overweight*
Bangladesh	56	United States	55
India	53	Russian Federation	54
Ethiopia	48	Great Britain	51
Vietnam	40	Germany	50
Nigeria	39	Colombia	43
Indonesia	34	Brasil	31

Source: FAO and WHO

In the process of modernisation, social status and with it identity and self-esteem cease to be ascribed by caste, gender, tradition or religion. They are ascribed by the place in production and by the level and pattern of consumption. The upper middle class consumption in the wealthy countries has now become accepted as a global aim and ideal. Needless to say, 99 percent of humanity fail to meet it. The experience of this failure translates into alienation and bitterness, which seeps into, and transforms, whole societies. It fuels alienation and aggression.

How have we come into this position of wealth being distributed so very unevenly. What has caused that inequality between nations? As we have seen, it is not a kind of natural state. It is historically recent. Two hundred years ago such differences were minor. At that time, India and China still had per capita incomes of half of the British[4] at worst.

Two mutually exclusive positions have informed the debate on this question. We term them the liberal one; and the neo-Marxist one:

a) According to the liberal theory, all nations were equally poor before industrial development set in. All were equally "non-developed". Later, economic growth began in some countries; but did not begin in others. This made for the difference in wealth. Poverty, thus, was simply the result of a failure to develop. Those that still have not developed, remain in the same poor state that has prevailed over centuries. Yet every country has the potential to escape the prison of

4 According to Maddison. According to Bairoch, the Indian and Chinese per capita income would even have been close to the British one.

poverty. Eventually, all countries will seize this chance. In the end, all countries will become equal again. All of them will be wealthy.

b) According to the neo-Marxist view, some countries are rich BECAUSE the others are poor. In a certain sense that is, of course, a truism. There would be no "poor" if there would be no wealthy ones compared to whom the poor are poor. But the real argument is not as trivial as that. It is argued that the accumulation of wealth is – largely – the result of the poor having been exploited as they were stripped of resources and assets which were siphoned off to the more powerful. That exploitation of the poor has permitted the now wealthy countries to set in motion the process of economic growth. Underdevelopment, therefore, is not natural (so to say the "state of nature" before development set in). Underdevelopment is the consequence of this exploitation of the peripheral countries by the rich and powerful ("the development of underdevelopment"). Furthermore, and after having themselves climbed up, those now on top would have pushed away the ladder on which others have otherwise been able to follow them.

Dependenzia

The dependenzia theory refines the Marxist/Leninist argument about asymmetric relations between wealthy and poor countries. Wealthy countries can effectively set the prices for their exports[5]. Poor countries cannot do that. Therefore, the terms of trade shift to the disadvantage of the poor exporters. Producing for the world market, the wealthy countries have their high industrial production runs and, thus, low unit costs. This advantage permits them to undercut any attempt of poorer countries to follow them on the path of industrialisation and modernisation.

What is exported from these poor countries is produced on some kind of "economic islands" connected to the rich "centre" and not to the poor local economy. The dynamics of these economic islands ("compradora economy") have no positive impact upon the economy of the poor host country.

Political/social dependenzia accentuates the economic one. In poor "peripheral countries", the local elites are not rooted in, and are not bound to, the local population. Instead, these elites are oriented to, and take their cue from, the elites in the distant "centre". In their consumption, in their self esteem, in much of their status, they are dependent on these far away elites. They depend

5 A more modern version: The industrial products rich countries export are still from the very first sections of the product cycle. They thus are relatively scarce. Selling them brings monopolistic / oligopolistic rent income.

on these elites in the centre much more than they depend on the masses in their own home country. Therefore, these masses are leader-less.

Which side in this debate has better arguments? Which of the two conflicting views is better supported by empirical evidence?

Dependenzia theory would instruct political leaders of poor countries to minimise – as much as possible – economic contacts to wealthy countries. Accordingly, those poor countries would be best off and would develop fastest, which had the least contacts with the wealthy "North". Obviously, this is not the case. Countries that heed that advice and that follow this strategy of a maximal "autarky" (like North Korea) have become very rare – and strange – exceptions. And have entrapped their citizens in poverty[6] and hopelessness.

On the other hand, economic growth has been most rapid in countries with an open economy.

GDP per person, 1990s annual growth rates in % (purchasing power parities)

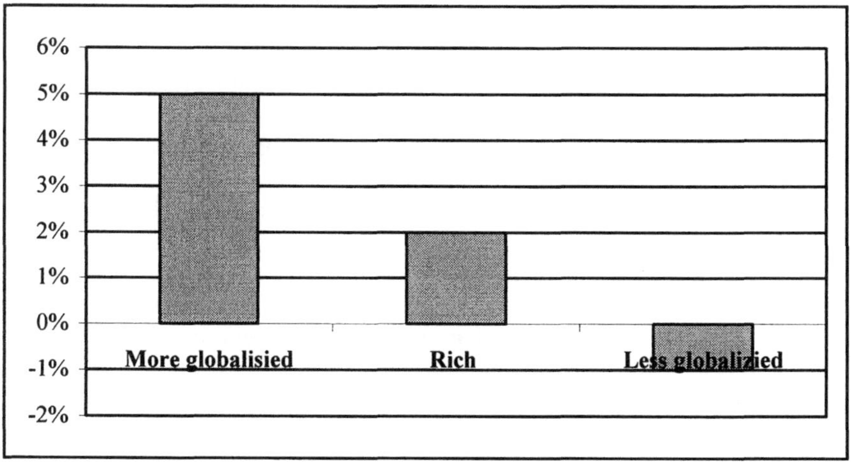

Source: World Bank 2002

6 In the case of North Korea, even in starvation. Two million (!) North Koreans have died as a consequence.

Export led growth does not automatically imply a liberal trade regime

Many countries that have profited from export led growth (prominent among them South East Asian and East Asian ones) have done so by ignoring parts of the dogma of economic liberalism. They followed at least some of the advice of dependenzia theory. They tended to offer some protection to their local markets. The higher profits their enterprises thus could realise were then used to penetrate into foreign markets. Nonetheless, conscious efforts were made to maintain stiff competition on the protected home markets, with always at least two local firms in place to fight for the local customer. This kept the competitors on their toes and dynamic.[7] So there is agreement on the necessity to maintain competition, even in the first spurts of growth and then during the catch-up. Internal competition is seen as a necessary prerequisite for also becoming competitive on the foreign markets.

There is, however, less agreement on whether it is legitimate and as to whether it makes sense to protect the home market during the first stages of industrial/economic development. The international financial institutions preach the virtues of full trade liberalisation. Some of the institutions close to the poor countries – such as the United Nations Conference on Trade and Development (UNCTAD), or the United Nations Industrial Development Organisation (UNIDO), do not fully support this recommendation of the financial institutions. They plead for a prudent, measured, tailor made trade intervention to favour nascent industries.

The issue is difficult to decide in an abstract manner. The size of a country certainly matters, with small countries simply not having the option of protecting an infant industry as their industry would have to produce for the world market right away given the minuscule size of the home market. Also, the quality of the administration is decisive. Trade intervention makes sense only if administered by highly competent and non-corrupt bureaucrats. In many poor countries, these are in short supply.

So there is uncertainty on how to transform poorer countries into competitive exporters. There is certainty, however, that this is happening. On average, poor countries are gaining ground in world trade.

According to dependenzia theory, the share of the poor countries in world trade should decline. But in reality their merchandise exports grew at an average annual rate of 12% in the time between 1970 and 1999; compared to a 10%

7 This is a feat of economic policy in East Africa that Latin America failed to duplicate.

growth of world trade as such. Their share in world merchandise trade increased from less than a fourth to almost one third.

The rising global integration of developing countries
(change in the ratio of trade to GDP from 1981-85 to 1997-2001)

Industrial Countries	3.9%
Developing Countries	15.4%

Source: IMF Economic Outlook

According to "dependenzia theory", exports from the poor countries also stay "primitive", or even become ever more "primitive". But again, this is not the case. Poor countries switched from exporting primary products towards exporting industrial merchandise. Overall, and on average, developing countries even were successful in upgrading the exports of industrial merchandise. Increasingly, they export products incorporating medium or high technology.

The the speed of this changeover to the export of high value and high technology products is indeed astounding. China, for example, managed to increase the share of high technology products in overall exports from a mere 1% in 1985 to 21% in just eleven years.

Composition of exports 1985, 1996
Select developing countries, percentages

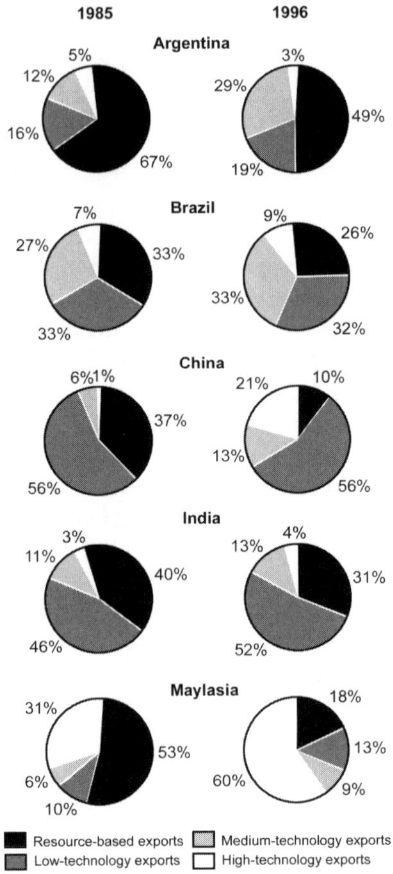

Source: Lall, 1998

Yet two caveats have to be applied. First, this development is due to the rapid advance of just a few countries. As is demonstrated by the table below, many were left behind. This table shows that quite a number of countries managed to turn from the export of primary products to the export of manufactures (upper left quadrangle – "new exporters of manufactures"). Yet the cluster of countries in the upper right quadrangle is even more dense ("traditional exporters of primary products"). Many countries that relied on just the exports of primary products thirty years ago were just as reliant on these exports thirty years later.

The second reason why the picture is not as rosy as it looks is that those industrial exports, and even all those exports of higher tech products, frequently incorporate little added value. Many poor countries act just as extended workbenches (for example, for the assembly of electronic gadgets), with the high value-added part of the production – such as research – remaining in the wealthy countries.

Share of primary products in developing countries' merchandise exports in the late 60s and the late 90s (percentage)

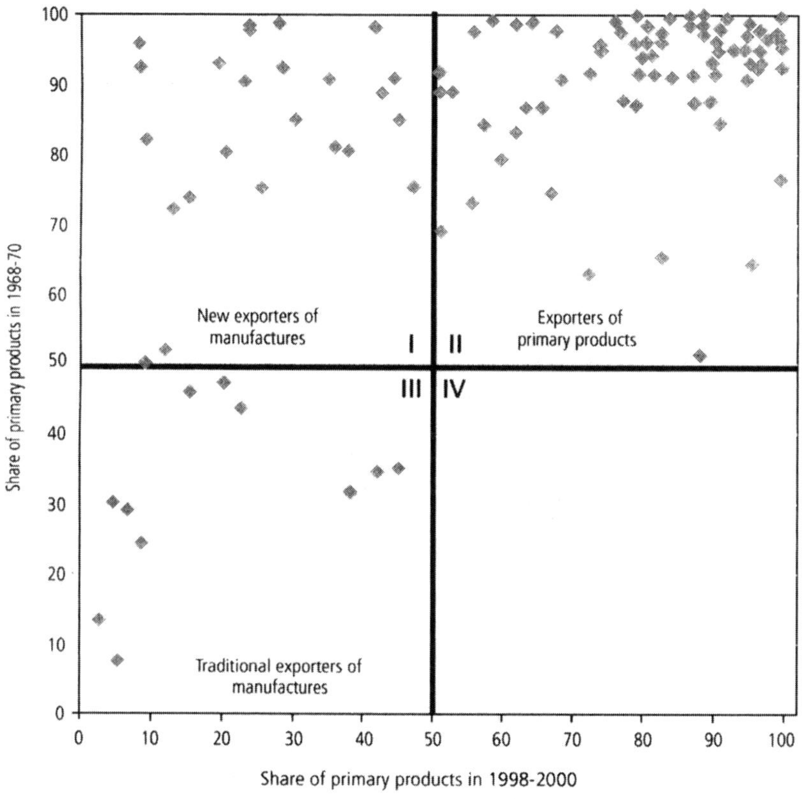

Source: UNCTAD 2002

Nonetheless, even with these qualifications, it is fairly evident that the poor countries gain from being more deeply involved in international trade. This explains their growing interest in open trade; and this is also reflected in the membership of the "World Trade Organisation" – WTO. There, poorer countries now outnumber the wealthier ones.

The deeper integration of – many – developing countries into the world economy is not just reflected by their membership in the WTO, but also by their reduction of external tariffs. In South Asia, for example, the average tariffs on merchandise fell from 65% in 1980 to 30% in 1996-98. In Latin America, they fell from 30% to 15% in the same period.

Number of GATT/WTO member countries

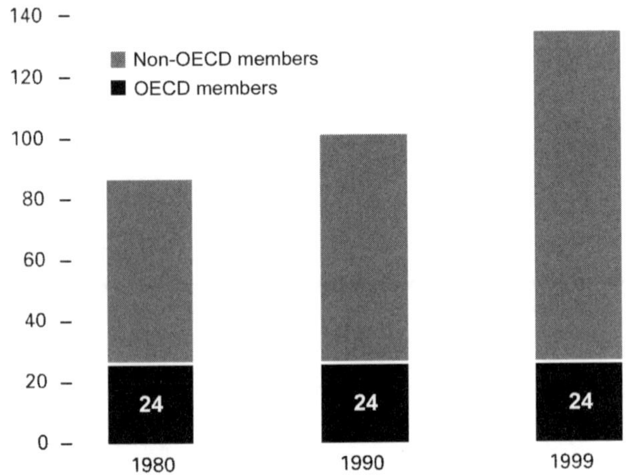

Source: WTO, Annual Report

Is there, thus, a kind of iron law that prescribes an ever closer integration also of poorer countries into the world economic system? In human affairs, there are very few such iron laws. As we have seen, North Korea has opted out. This is due to a clear political decision. North Korea (or its dictator) was willing to pay a very high price for that. Other countries – like many African ones – have opted out not because they wanted to. They have " de-linked" by "default". This too, came at a high price.

This de-linkage partly results from the failure of states to adapt, in their institutions and in their economic and political culture, to the requirements of an open economy. Their economies are being held hostage to pre-modern, feudal politics (as for instance to clientilism[8]). Public positions do not imply the obligation to serve the economy and the citizens. They imply the privilege to exploit them.[9]

Cost of business registrations
% of GDP per person

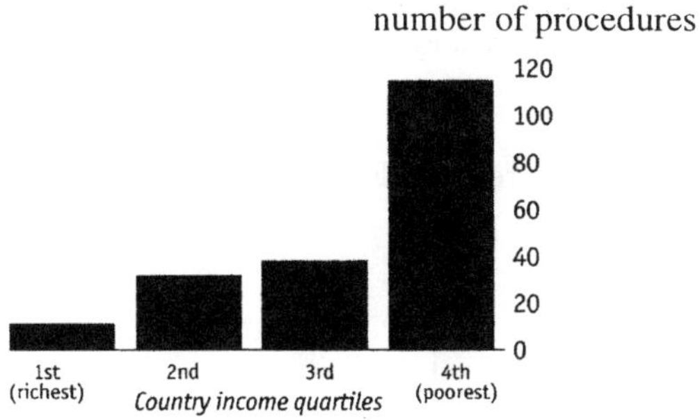

Number of registration prodcedures
by average GDP per person, $'000

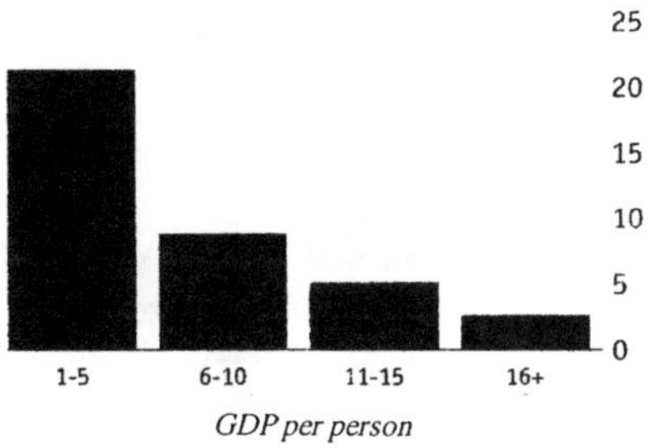

Source: World Bank

---

8 We do not preach the minimal state here; and are aware of the opposite also being a danger: namely politics being held hostage by economic forces.

9 Such impediments to development are now discussed openly. For just this reason "bad governance" has come to be seen as one very serious obstacle to development. Grants and credits to poor countries have, thus, become burdened with an ever greater number of "conditions" imposed by donor countries and creditors **("conditionality of aid")**. The aim is to, thus, impose upon recipients a change from bad habits. But one should doubt whether institutions and behaviour are susceptible to such a transformation by outside pressure. Ultimately, the aim must be to alter expectations and cultural norms. Indigenous peer groups can do that. Outsiders should not expect to have the same effect.

Some poor countries, thus, "de-link" from the world economy, either by default or by a conscious political decision. But, on occasions, the wealthy countries, too, chose to restrict their external commerce. Rich countries "de-link", for example, by erecting trade barriers against the imports from poor countries. On manufactured products that come from poor countries, the wealthy countries impose higher tariffs than they do on manufactured merchandise that comes from other wealthy countries.[10]

Tariffs on manufactured goods imported by high-income countries 1995 (tariff rates in %)

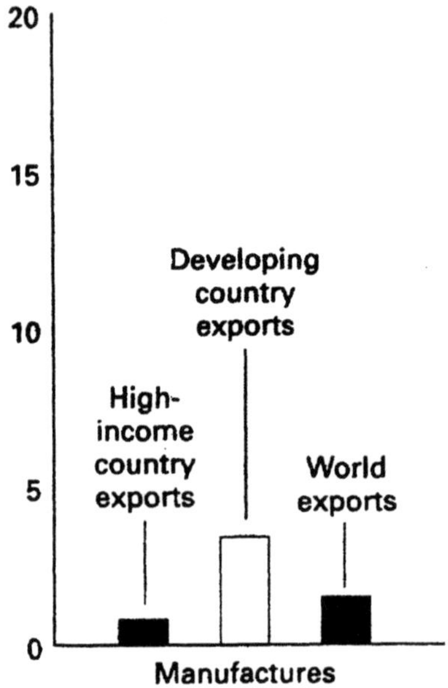

Source: Hertel and Martin 1999a

True and full world economic integration implies that the "factors of production" can move around freely. Capital, which is mostly held by the rich countries, can do so and wealthy countries and the wealthy providers of capital profit from it. But labour, which is abundant in the poor countries, cannot move freely across

10 In trade in agricultural products, the discrimination against poor countries is even worse. Poor countries incur more than 30 billion US dollars in annual export and income losses due to the agricultural policies of wealthy OECD countries.

borders. As we have seen in the chapter on world-wide migration, the wealthy countries have been effective, by and large, in curtailing the inflow of labour from poor countries. Among other things, this limits, for the poor countries, the potentially very important flow of income through remittances from nationals working abroad.[11]

Economic development is being impeded by still other hurdles:

- The prevailing technology is adapted to the needs of the rich and not to the needs of the poor.
- The consumption pattern imposed world wide favours the wealthy and the wealthy countries (preference is thus, for example, given in poor countries to imported beer over the traditional beer made from local tubers).
- The world financial system is geared towards those who are already wealthy. It puts a negative premium on poverty and upon the financial institutions of the poor. It protects lenders over debtors. It favours big transactions over the small ones; and the investment bank over the small savings and loan associations.
- As mentioned, world trade was liberalised in a fashion that facilitated the exports of the rich (e.g. financial services); but that still discriminated against many of the typical exports of the poor (vegetables, textiles).[12]

---

11 For Latin America, for instance, income from such remittances was four times as high as all income received as official development aid.
Workers remittances
For Latin America and the Caribbean, in billion USD

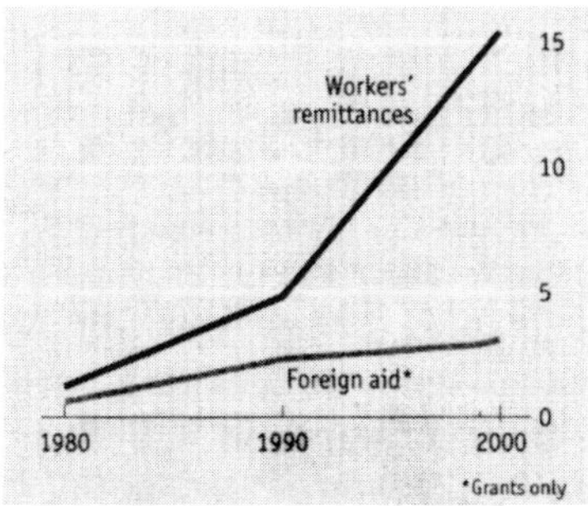

Source: IBRD

12 The most massive defence against the import of textiles from poor countries has been the "Multi-Fibre-Agreement" setting quotas for such imports. By 2005, these quotas will have been phased out under the Uruguay round ATC (Agreement on Textiles and Clothing).

It is also argued that in the future the path to wealth will become narrower and steeper than it has been in the past. Here are some arguments that lend credence to such fears:

- cheap labour is no longer that decisive in giving a competitive advantage in industrial production. Labour intensive industrial production used to shift to poor countries with their lower wages. This development might not continue as wages form an ever smaller share of the total costs of production.

- new technology is no longer sold on the free market but kept by the inventing firm for "strategic reasons".

- the production of some of the more modern goods call for inputs – like networks, reliable and cheap transportation, broad access to information, high level of tertiary education etc. – that are not that plentiful in poorer nations.

- financial liberalisation and higher mobility of capital exposes newcomers to higher costs of capital and to higher risks than have been borne by earlier industrialisers.

What conclusions to draw from these insights?

1) In the very, very long run, all countries may indeed become equal again in their per capita wealth. Yet this is a truly distant goal. In the meantime, the differences in wealth will widen. Now, and in the next decades, the gap in absolute wealth will be broader than it ever has been in human history.

2) According to Marxist-Leninist theory, "capitalist" countries could only survive in their wealth by becoming "imperialistic" and by thus exploiting their poorer colonies. This theory has lost all explanatory power. Imperialism and colonisation are no longer in fashion. The former imperial powers are better off for that. Instead of supporting their wealth, imperialism diminished it[13].

3) There is no proof either, for the claim that "primitive accumulation" (e.g. through slave trade or piracy) was the essential prerequisite for capitalist growth to set in, for instance in the Netherlands, the UK and in France. Incomes from such ventures only financed a rather insignificant part of gross investment. Economic development, thus, can do without imperialism and roguish/criminal exploitation. In fact, it is harmed by such ventures.

4) It is obvious, though, that even in the absence of imperialism, world economic relations are unequal and highly asymmetric. Poorer countries are at a clear disadvantage.

---

13 Joseph Schumpeter (1991) thus explained imperialism not by any economic motivation of its practitioners. Not search for material gain prompted the colonial adventures; but the pre-capitalist, feudal yearning for valour and glory.

5) It is obvious, too, that social, economic and political factors interact and, by doing so, re-enforce and stabilise such economic asymmetries. Not all claims made by "dependenzia theory" can simply be pushed aside.

6) Rapid economic growth does not, in itself, guarantee stability (and it might very well even be de-stabilising in the short run). But, on the other hand, enduring poverty and the widening gap between rich and poor will have consequences which are likely to be even worse.

7) Latecomers to development face some hurdles that those before them did not have to tackle. Of course, they also can profit from advantages that were not available to those before them. They might – for example – learn from the mistakes others have made. It is not clear which one of these two countervailing tendencies is the stronger one.

8) The majority of the world's population will feel unjustly excluded from what it assumes to be its proper position in life. It will blame the world system and those dominating it. This sentiment can cloak itself in various ideologies (like religious fundamentalism, aggressive nationalism etc.). What these ideologies have in common is an anti-modernist stance and the refusal to co-operate with those perceived to be the alien oppressors. These anti-modernist forces and sentiments fracture the base of a world order that, by necessity, must include tolerance and pluralism.

9) The poorer countries do not form a cohesive group. It is, therefore, unlikely that they will again join forces on the world scene as they did in the sixties – in the heydays of the "Non-Aligned Movement" – and under the banner of a "New World Economic Order".

In sum, and on the average, all these conclusions somewhat dampen the optimism that might have arisen from a first glance at the overall picture of the poor countries actually doing rather well; with their GDP growing faster than that of the rich countries; with their profiting from a closer integration into the world economy and their exports expanding even in the field of high technology products.

Looking back over the long period since the onset of industrialisation in 1820, we observe a long-term trend that remains unbroken till today. If measured against each other, that is, if measured in relative terms, the rich have become richer and the poor have become poorer since 1820.

Over the long run, (most) poor countries stay trapped in poverty; growth rates diverge between Rich and Poor 1820-1992

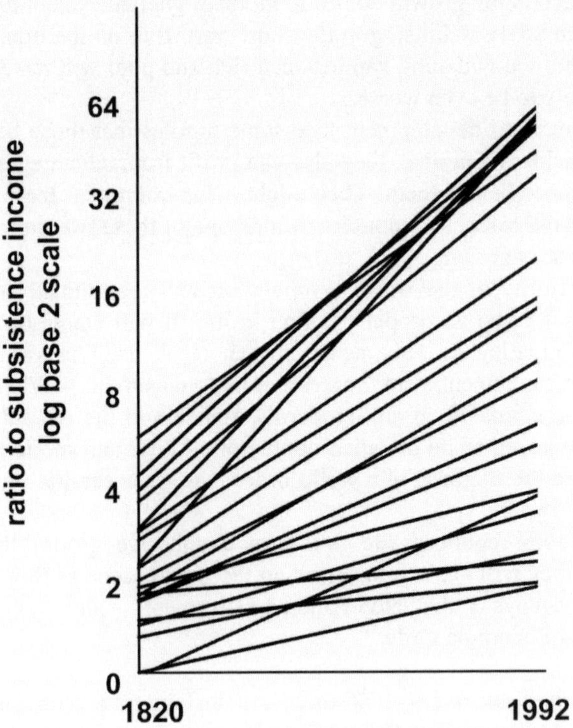

Source: www.worldbank.org/research/growth/images/ppt/povtrap5/sld026.htm.

The table is on a logarithmic scale. What, in reality, are growth curves thus become simple lines. They have the advantage of making the message clearer. Those countries grew rapidly that were relatively wealthy already at the beginning of the industrial age. Not only that. Their level of wealth also converged. In this group of countries that were relatively wealthy already two hundred years ago, the differences in wealth as they then existed became even more narrow. Those that were a bit behind in 1820 grew at a faster pace.

Those countries that were amongst the group of the poorer ones in 1820 remained poor and they have become poorer still if compared to the wealthy ones. Distances in wealth have not ceased to widen. Only rarely do the lines cross.

Only rarely has a country, that has been near the top, fallen back to a lower rank 200 hundred years later. Only rarely has a country, that was near the bottom of the list in 1820, managed to move closer to the wealthy ones, even in the time span of 200 hundred years.

Nor has the picture changed very much in the more recent past. In the 80s and 90s, economic growth was rapid in just a few of the poor countries (although in populous one like India and China), while the ones in the most miserable positions (especially in Africa) lagged behind. Within the group of poor countries, differences in wealth, thus, have become more accentuated.

GDP growth rates and per capita income levels in selected regions and countries

Area/Country	*1960-96 (% annual average GNP growth)*	*1980-90 (% annual average GNP growth)*	*1996 per capita income level in 1996 US $*	*1980 per capita income level in 1996 US $*
All Developing Countries	2.9	3.1	1350	985
UN least Developed Countries	2.2	2.6	228	227
East Asia and the Pacific	10.2	7.7	1190	
South Asia	5.6	5.7	380	
Latin America and Caribbean	3.2	1.8	3710	2334
Sub-Saharan Africa	2.0	1.7	490	594
Bangladesh	4.3	4.3	259	174
Tanzania	4.0	2.7	171	173

Source: UNCTAD 1998, World Bank 1998, IMF1997

Grand economic theory would have us assume that, in the end, and with full mobility of goods, services and capital[14], all such differences will disappear; with all factors of production becoming evenly productive in the end; and reaping an even reward, in the end; with Bangladeshi labourers earning the same as their counterparts in Denmark.

Neither the developments since 1820, nor developments in the recent decades support such optimistic conclusions. On the contrary, they substantiate the view that both economic success and economic stagnation are self sustaining, cumulative processes. Poor stay poor because they are poor. Rich become even more rich because they are rich already.

The graph above, thus, is a potent counterpoint to the graph we showed in the very first chapter of this book. The earlier graph depicted the growth path of the

14 Also – but necessarily – mobility of labour. According to theory, mobility of capital and the free exchange of goods and services could substitute for the transfrontier migration of labour.

already wealthy countries. It showed that the latecomers did better than the first ones; and that, among this group of the successful, wealth has indeed converged. This graph would indeed have supported the notion of classical economics that costs and the productivity of the "factors of production" would converge ultimately.

But looking closer, we have become sceptical about the whole notion of "factors of production"; with even the crucial contribution made by "technological progress" dissolving into the mist of non-economic, sociological and political speculation. Growth is certainly driven by things other than the simple accumulation of capital, or by a genius happening upon a path-breaking invention.

Convergence in wealth would also become more facile if economic growth were to become slower in the already wealthy countries. This slowdown, too, is stipulated by economic theory. But it has not occurred. On the contrary, over the last decades rich countries have grown faster than they did in the last century. This, too, impedes quick drawing even of presently poor countries.

Obviously, cumulative processes cause both the further growth of wealth among the already wealthy, and the continuation of misery among the already miserable. Nonetheless, we should not ignore the positive messages gleaned from this look at the past. Some of the lines in the above graph do cross. Some of the poor countries are on their way to escaping from the trap of poverty. These are very populous countries like China or India[15]. Like the previously successful Korea, Taiwan, and Singapore – they too, have cultures and political and social institutions that differ markedly from those of the "West". If they could enter a phase of self-sustaining and rapid growth nonetheless, why should other countries be unable, forever, to emulate them?

Why should the rich countries not be able to help them along? We shall deal with this question in the succeeding chapter.

15 A fact that tilts some global statistics on developing countries to the positive. If we exclude China and India, the picture would become more dim. But then – on the other hand – why exclude them?

Financial Flows to the World's Poorer Countries

In the early sixties, a large number of new and poor states emerged on the world scene. With the poor thus gaining a stronger voice in global affairs, the looming danger of a polarisation between the poor South and the wealthy North came to preoccupy the public. For a variety of motives – and self interest not being the least among them – the richer countries of the world resolved to address this issue.

The question was, however, what, exactly, could be usefully done. This question has been under discussion ever since. What, exactly, is the crucial bottleneck on the road to development? What, exactly, is the most important, the strategic element wealthy countries could add in order to see these poor countries off on a path of self-sustaining growth?

According to neo-classical economics (the "Harrod-Domar growth model"), lack of capital would constitute this strategic bottleneck impeding faster economic growth. At the birth of ODA, thus, stood the notion that a sufficiently large amount of capital would have to be invested to initiate sufficiently large changes in the economic structure and to, thus, start the process of growth with one "big bang".

It was assumed that – at the outset at least – incomes in the poor countries would be simply too low to permit savings that would create the amount of capital needed for the "big bang". Capital had, therefore, to be brought in from abroad. At that time, in the early sixties, it also seemed reasonable to assume that the global financial markets and private enterprise would not provide the sums required for the economic take-off in the poorer countries. Therefore, the capital would have to be provided by governments. It was under these assumptions that "Official Development Assistance" (ODA) got under way.

Fashions and fads in the theory on ODA

At the origins of ODA stood the belief that the mere addition of – officially donated – capital will provide the essential element still missing for economic take-off[1]. Such massive transfer of capital usually financed vast infrastructure projects – like dams, railroads, or basic industries (like steel or aluminium).[2] This philosophy also guided the work of the Development Banks (DBs).

Yet, the intellectual foundations of this policy have disappeared. One has come to doubt a clear linkage between economic growth and the rates of investment (share of gross investment in GDP). It is clear that fast growing countries do have high investment rates. It also is obvious that high growth cannot persist in the absence of high rates of investment. Historic experience also substantiates the assumption that in periods of rapid growth, not all capital comes from local savings. In such phases of rapid growth, a substantial percentage of invested capital had been provided from abroad. But it became clear that a massive first investment could not produce the "big bang" and then initiate the process of self-sustaining growth.Other things than capital have to be there to start such a process. If they are not, the impetus provided by the massive inflow of foreign funds will simply evaporate.

Policies based on the massive transfer of resources and on the financing of big industrial and infrastructure projects, thus proved to be misguided. They brought no lasting results. Attention, therefore, turned to the difficulties poor countries had in actually absorbing bigger amounts of external assistance. Such differing "absorption capacity" would determine – and limit – the good use a poor country could actually make of the inflow of capital provided by donors. Raising absorption capacity through training, education and other investment in human capital and institutional efficiency, thus became an important goal.

Later still, attention and emphasis shifted towards the transfer of technology. First one emphasised the transfer of existing technology such as it was used in the very wealthy countries. Later on, one came to appreciate that this was inappropriate in many cases; and that help should be given in finding and applying technologies specifically adapted to poorer countries with their ample supply of cheap labour and their dearth of capital.[3]

1 Probably, this conviction was also the result of the experience with the Marshall Plan in which this provision of capital had indeed been effective in jump-starting the European post-war economies.

2 There was a bit of Keynes in that. The purpose of such transfers was not just to raise productivity in the recipient country. The aim was also to simply raise the purchasing power by such transfers and thus to put into use present capacity that stood idle. Yet, such Keynesian notions do not fit the reality of poor countries. The idle capacities simply were not there.

3 Examples: ovens replacing open fire, hand pumps for lifting the water from wells, scythes instead of sickles and knives for harvesting cereals, or ball bearings for the oxen-drawn carts

More recently, the focus of attention has shifted once more. The crucial bottleneck is now defined as being the performance of (mostly public) institutions ("good governance") and as the lack of the proper incentives for productive engagement in the economy. This most recent fashion in ODA promises more sound advice. One has come to appreciate that development is contingent upon a change in behaviour. Any such change will depend on changes in the prevailing incentives. Proper incentives are needed, in particular, to have people prefer future gains to present gratification. There have to be incentives to save; and incentives to invest these savings in productive ventures.

The preferences that prevail at each instant of history are formed in a slow and long cultural process. In adopting a certain behaviour and harbouring certain expectations, people take their cues from past experience and from the peers that they wish to emulate. Even in the same country, and at the same moment in time, differences might exist as to which peer group favours which behaviour. In the central government in the distant capital, it might be fully acceptable among peers not to repay but to squander loans one has received for a specific purpose. But, in a small village community, everyone, and even the poorest, repays a small credit extended, for example, for the purchase of a sewing machine or of livestock. Due to the expectations of peers, everyone in a small village will follow this practice of prompt repayment at the price of otherwise being ostracised from this small community.

The key to economic development is thus seen in making prevail, in the limited circle of a smaller peer group, such rules and expectations that are conducive to productive investment in the future; and to use, in that endeavour, the greater cohesion and solidarity such as it exists on the level of more restricted, smaller communities, like villages.

So, in this latest turn of ODA philosophy, one has begun to prefer a "bottom up" approach, substituting or supplementing the "top down" approach of working with and via the governments of recipient countries. Local communities, non-governmental organisations, development banks, and transnational corporations increasingly join forces in by-passing central authorities in favour of decentralised initiatives. It is for these motives, that schemes of providing "micro-credits", for example, have become popular with donors. The money lent out by such "village banks" comes from the savings of fellow villagers. Not re-paying, thus, would be seen as a clear breach of time-honoured village solidarity. Outsiders and ODA just help in setting up such schemes. Their continued functioning is assured by those who will benefit. By and large such schemes have been successful. Helped by such credits, farmers, for example, could raise the productivity of their land sufficiently so as to be able to send their children to school.

But, notwithstanding these positive results, this philosophy of "empowerment" is just one other twist in the long story of the "philosophy of development". We should continue to greet all such generalisations with prudence and scepticism. In view of the growing differentiation of the so-called developing countries[4] there is no "one size fits all" recipe for development aid.

From the outset, it was evident that ODA would have to be complemented by other measures to make the lop-sided ("asymmetric") global economic relations between the rich and the poor countries more balanced . Here too, emphasis has shifted according to fads and fashion. Once priority had been accorded to the stabilisation of prices of raw materials. Later on, priority was accorded to a reform of trade policies both by poor countries and by rich countries. One such first instrument was one-sided tariff concessions by wealthy countries (GSP – General System of Preferences). Now, poor countries have gone on the offensive and are demanding the removal of trade barriers in those fields where their exports are most competitive. As of late, debt relief has come to figure prominently among the tasks that have to be tackled in order to permit poor countries to evolve economically.

Looking back on all these changing recipes, we have to conclude that the musings and injunctions of "development economics" have not provided much intellectual guidance to actual policies. Frequently they have even provided dysfunctional and misleading advice. Changes in actual policy were induced by feedback from actual experience; and not by intellectual speculation.

The volume and quality of ODA is being monitored by the OECD Development Assistance Committee (DAC). In 1999, the total volume of ODA provided by OECD member countries stood at 56,3 billion USD.

In the seventies already, wealthy countries had promised to earmark at least 0,7% of their GDP for development assistance. This goal is still binding in theory. A few Nordic countries have overshot this 0.7% target, but they are the rare exception. The US – as hegemon and thus as the international pacesetter – is even far below this target, with an ODA that stands at just 0.1% of its GNP.

The 0.7% target, thus, has become a very distant objective. The "UN Conference on Financing for Development" held in Monterrey, Mexico, in 2002, has therefore agreed on more realistic but more binding targets. ODA should be doubled by 2006. By 2006, the contribution of the European Commission and European Union countries[5] should have risen to 0.39% of the EU Gross National In-

4 A misnomer as some of those countries are not developing at all.
5 Which provided 25 billion US$ ODA in 2001 and, thus, more than half of all ODA.

come. The US committed itself to double its ODA by raising it by 5 billion US$ by 2005.

Official Development Assistance 1999
(in 1000 USD)

	Total	Bilateral grants	Bilateral loans	Contributions to multilateral institutions
$ millions, 1999				
Australia	982	730	..	252
Austria	527	381	-37	183
Belgium	760	454	-17	323
Canada	1,699	1,195	-23	527
Denmark	1,733	1,023	3	708
Finland	416	286	-45	176
France	5,637	4,320	-195	1,512
Germany	5,515	3,236	42	2,238
Greece	194	77	2	115
Ireland	245	149	..	97
Italy	1,806	551	-100	1,355
Japan	15,323	5,475	5,001	4,848
Luxembourg	119	89	..	30
Netherlands	3,134	2,359	-198	972
New Zealand	134	101	..	33
Norway	1,370	993	14	363
Portugal	276	273	-65	69
Spain	1,363	653	176	534
Sweden	1,630	1,143	3	484
Switzerland	969	719	..	250
United Kingdom	3,401	2,067	182	1,153
United States	9,145	7,638	-790	2,297
Total	**56,378**	**33,910**	**3,951**	**18,517**

Source: OECD

Share of ODA at the GNP in the year 2000 (at current exchange rates)

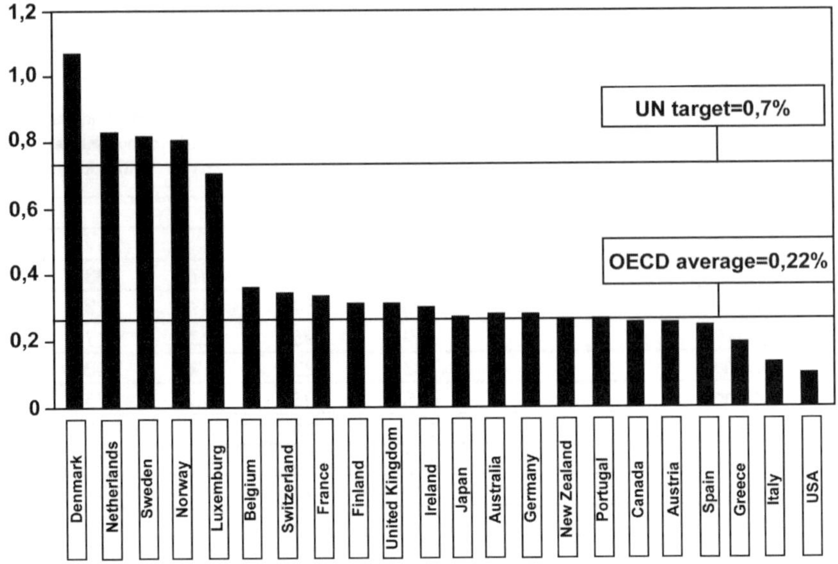

Source: OECD 2001

Over the last twelve years, the distribution of ODA among recipients has changed – but not very much. The lion's share still goes to Sub-Saharan Africa. ODA now has also become available to the poor ex-Soviet states mainly in Central Asia[6].

6 Only a few of the ex-communist countries are counted as "developing countries". Only transfers to those few countries are counted as ODA.

Average annual share of net receipts of ODA
(in percent of total ODA provided world-wide)

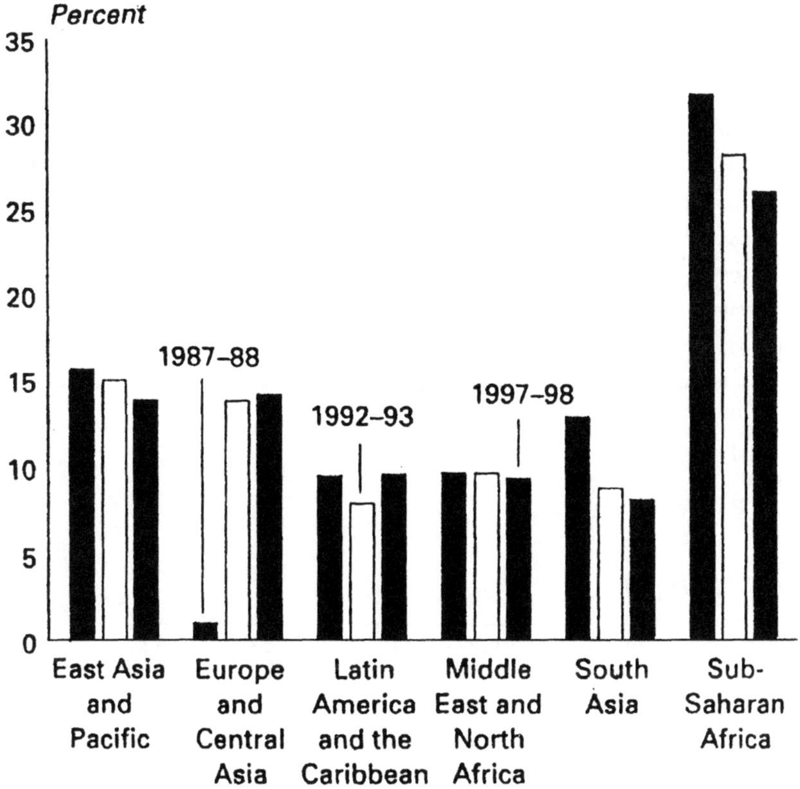

Note: Shares do not sum to 100 percent, as some aid is not
Source: OECD / DAC

Were the donor countries to live up to the promises made at the 2002 Monterrey conference, this would reverse a trend. For, up until now, the wealthy OECD member countries have not just failed to reach the 0.7% goal. They have been moving away from it. ODA has shrunk not just as percentage of their GNP. Since 1993, it also has shrunk in absolute terms.

Official and private flows from OECD to Developing Countries (DCs)
(in billion USD)

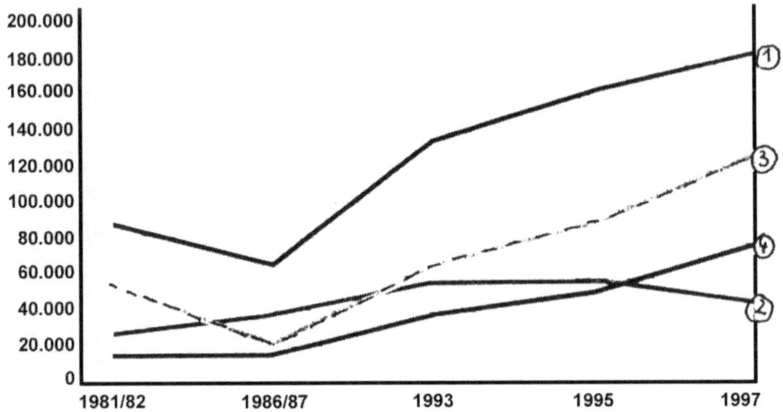

1 = Total
2 = ODA
3 = All Private Transfers
4 = FDI

Source: OECD / DAC

What reasons for the stagnation – and even decline – of ODA?

a) With the end of the East West conflict, the developing countries have lost the "strategic relevance" they had held in the Cold War era;

b) In most wealthy countries, public finances are under stress;

c) Economic growth in the main donor countries (Japan and Europe) is sluggish;

d) Doubts have grown as to whether ODA has been effective in meeting its purpose;

e) The rise in private financial flows, especially flows of Foreign Direct Investment (FDI), seemed to make public contributions less urgent.

There are cogent moral imperatives for development assistance. Helping those less fortunate is an obligation recognised in all societies. The future of humankind would be bleak indeed were it to become deaf to this moral imperative. Practical reasons, too, prompt the wealthy countries to fill the gap that separates the world's rich from the world's poor. But the rapidly changing fads and fashions that guide this aid testify to the fact that it is not that easy to truly and permanently improve, by outside help, the lot of the people in poor countries. Hence, this permanent search for alternate and better ways of helping.

In fact, when looking at the past record, we find no correlation between the economic growth of a country and the amount of development assistance it has received.[7]

Why this failure? As already mentioned, economic development is mostly about changing perspectives, changing incentives, changing behaviour. It can be argued – and is argued – that ODA has the perverse effect of impeding such change instead of promoting it.[8] ODA is routinely used by the powerful in the recipient countries to cement their elevated position; and to withhold economic power and assets from those who eventually might use it against them[9]. ODA also compensates for inadequacies in governance and removes the sanctions against inefficiency and corruption. If, for instance, a ruler in a country runs up large foreign debts, ODA will be used to write off these debts. The ruler thus might have no motive for avoiding the accumulation of new debt. As his unsound practices had not be sanctioned against before, he feels no need to change them. Or, if a ruler can rely on roads being built by foreigners and with

---

7 As measured in per capita of the population in the recipient country. This is a conclusion drawn from a simple correlation. One might object that a simple correlation abstracts from some salient factors. Those very poor are evidently those most in need of assistance. They thus get the lion's share of such assistance. Nonetheless, and at the same time, these very poor countries are also those countries where obstacles to economic growth are the greatest. So the relatively vast amount of ODA they have received might, at least, have prevented an even worse performance; and, thus, might have had a positive effect after all. It is for this reason that a simple correlation cannot tell us all of the story. We have to abstract from the other disadvantages very poor countries suffer from. And we have to ask whether ODA has made a difference. In order to answer this more complex question, also variables other than ODA have to be introduced into the calculations (the dependent variable still being economic growth). But even with the use of such more refined instruments of analysis, it is hard to discern a positive contribution from ODA.

8 "Zaire – now the Democratic Republic of Congo – has received 10 billion USD in Official Development Assistance over the past 40 years (most of that in the period under the rule of president Mobutu) while income declined by a factor of four between 1974 and 1996. Mobutu's Zaire also got 9 IMF adjustment loans." (Chief IBRD economist Nick Stern, Global Agenda 2002/2003)

9 Hence the spontaneous preference of the first generation of post – independence leaders for a state oriented economic policy, with "ministers of industrialisation" and "national plans". This assured them control over economic assets.

foreign funds, he will not feel obliged himself to search for ways of financing this and other basic infrastructure.

The 1998 World Bank Aid Effectiveness Study found that:

- in the past, countries with poor policies received as much aid as those making positive aid efforts
- aid has sometimes prolonged bad policies
- aid is fungible. Funds for schools may facilitate the acquisition of guns.

Narrow interests of donors may also make ODA inefficient and unlikely to truly affect and change behaviour in recipient countries. Many donors still tie their aid to the promotion of their exports. Or they send expensive experts to the field who dump volumes of unread and unheeded studies on the administrations in recipient countries. In their home countries, the success of the administrators of ODA is mostly being measured by how much money they have managed to disperse; and not by the ultimate effect of all that aid.

While ODA has stagnated or even declined, Foreign Direct Investment in developing countries has increased markedly. In 1994, already, FDI in developing countries equalled the volume of ODA. In 2000, it stood at twice its size[10]. Nonetheless, this FDI in poorer countries is just a part – and the smaller part – of world-wide FDI. World-wide FDI has also grown dramatically. It now stands at one trillion USD and is the most dynamic element in the world economy (and even in the world economic system as such). The lion's share of FDI is between wealthy countries.[11] Wealthy countries invest in other wealthy countries. The – much smaller – net flow to the developing countries stood at about 140 billion USD in 2000[12].

Latin America received much FDI in the time between 1975 and 1982. Later on, the already high share of the East Asian and Pacific countries increased even further. The formerly Communist countries have managed, by now, to attract between 15 and 20 billion US dollars[13] annually.

10 Note that the figures provided on the volume of such FDI vary considerably according to the source that provide them (investment houses, IMF, UNCTAD, OECD).

11 And their share is growing. According to the IMF 58% of the FDI stock was in wealthy countries in 1994. In the year 2000, that was up to 66%.

12 In 2001 and 2002, the volume of FDI shrunk; it being very sensitive to the ups and downs of the business cycle.

13 They are not shown on the following graph as most of them are not considered "developing countries".

Regional distribution of FDI inflows and outflows 1989-2000
(in billion USD)

Region/country	FDI inflows							FDI inflows						
	1969-1994 (Annual average)	1995	1996	1997	1998	1999	2000	1969-1994 (Annual average)	1995	1996	1997	1998	1999	2000
Developed countries	**137.7**	**203.5**	**219.7**	**271.4**	**483.2**	**829.8**	**1 005.2**	**203.2**	**305.8**	**332.9**	**396.9**	**672.0**	**945.7**	**1 046.3**
Western Europe	79.8	117.5	114.9	137.5	273.4	485.3	633.2	114.2	173.6	204.3	242.4	475.2	761.1	820.3
European Union	76.5	113.5	109.6	127.6	261.1	467.2	617.3	105.2	159.0	183.2	220.4	454.3	720.1	772.9
Other Western Europe	3.1	3.7	5.2	9.9	12.3	18.2	15.8	9.0	14.6	21.1	22.0	21.0	41.1	47.4
Japan	1.0	-	0.2	3.2	3.3	12.7	8.2	29.6	22.5	23.4	26.1	24.3	22.7	32.9
United States	42.5	58.8	84.5	103.4	174.4	295.0	261.1	49.0	92.1	84.4	95.8	131.0	142.6	139.3
Developing countries and economies	**59.5**	**113.3**	**152.5**	**187.4**	**188.4**	**222.0**	**240.2**	**24.9**	**49.0**	**57.6**	**65.7**	**37.7**	**58.0**	**99.5**
Africa	4.0	4.7	5.6	7.2	7.7	9.0	8.2	0.9	0.5	0.0	1.7	0.9	0.6	0.7
Latin America and the Caribbean	17.5	32.3	51.3	71.2	83.2	110.3	86.2	3.7	7.3	5.5	14.4	8.0	21.8	13.4
Asia and the Pacific	37.9	75.9	94.5	107.3	95.9	100.0	143.8	20.3	41.1	51.9	49.4	28.7	35.5	85.3
Asia	37.7	75.3	94.4	107.2	95.6	99.7	143.5	20.3	41.1	51.9	49.4	28.6	35.4	85.2
West Asia	2.2	-	2.9	5.5	6.6	0.9	3.4	0.3	-1.0	2.3	-0.3	-1.7	0.7	1.3
Central Asia	0.4	1.7	2.1	3.2	3.0	2.6	2.7	-	0.3	0.0	0.2	0.3	0.3	0.3
South, East and South-East Asia	35.1	73.6	89.4	98.5	86.0	96.2	137.3	20.0	41.8	49.7	49.5	30.0	34.4	83.6
South Asia	0.8	2.9	3.7	4.9	3.5	3.1	3.0	-	0.1	0.3	0.1	0.1	0.1	0.3
The Pacific	0.2	0.6	0.2	0.1	0.3	0.3	0.3	-	-	-	-	0.1	0.1	0.0
Developing Europe	0.2	0.5	1.1	1.7	1.6	2.7	2.0	-	-	0.1	0.2	0.1	0.1	0.1
Central and Eastern Europe	**3.4**	**14.3**	**12.7**	**19.2**	**21.0**	**23.2**	**25.4**	**0.1**	**0.5**	**1.0**	**3.4**	**2.1**	**2.1**	**4.0**
World	**200.1**	**331.1**	**384.9**	**477.9**	**692.5**	**1 075.0**	**1 270.8**	**228.3**	**355.3**	**391.6**	**466.0**	**711.9**	**1 005.8**	**1 149.9**

Source: UNCTAD, World Investment Report 2001

Regional distribution of foreign direct investment 1981-1984 and 1993-1997 (annual averages, US$)

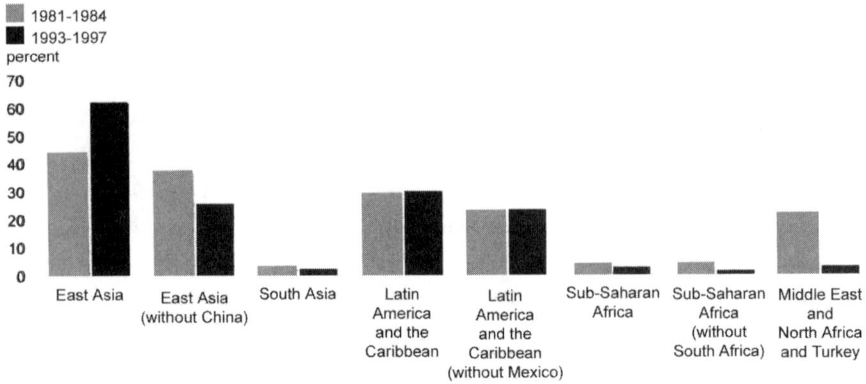

Source: UNIDO Scoreboard

In the poorer parts of the world, the lion's share of FDI goes to just a handful of countries, all of which are already well on the way of economic growth and/or already at an intermediary stage of economic development.

Net private capital flows per capita 1999 US$

	Economies	*GNI $ millions 1999*	*Population millions 1999*	*GNI per capita $ 1999*
Less than $1	28	479,258	691	690
$ 1-9	31	692,972	1,625	430
$ 10-49	29	1,712,106	1,793	950
$ 50-199	31	1,994,044	623	3,200
$ 200 or more	19	1,111,203	230	4,840
No data	69	24,005,020	1,015	23,640

Source: World Bank Atlas 2002

A third of all FDI benefitting developing countries (DCs) goes to China. A substantial part of this sum – and probably at least half of it – originates from ethnic Chinese living outside mainland China.

Footloose "portfolio capital" and loan capital is invested where short term returns are (or seem) highest. FDI follows other imperatives. Firms invest in production abroad for "strategic" reasons. What counts for them are the economic prospects of a country. That includes its capacity to provide a favourable institutional environment for business ("investment climate"[14]). Countries seeking to attract incoming direct investment thus usually attempt to improve this investment climate.[15] Frequently, too, they provide special incentives to foreign direct investors.[16]

Overall, there is a clear trend to make the climate for FDI more welcoming.

"Portfolio investment" – that is capital in the merely financial assets of developing countries – is much more volatile than FDI. This is proven by the complete drying-up of this flow in 1998 during and after the "Asian crisis", when – in net terms – no portfolio capital was made available to developing countries. Bank loans are still more volatile. The net flow of bank loans to poor countries even reversed in the year 2000. More capital of this type was exported, in this year, from developing countries than was imported by them.

National regulatory changes 1991-2000

Item	1991	1992	1993	1994	1995	1996	1997	1998	1999	2000
Number of countries that introduced changes in their investment regimes	35	43	57	49	64	65	76	60	63	69
Number of regulatory changes	82	79	102	110	112	114	151	145	140	150
of which:										
More favourable to FDI [a]	80	79	101	108	106	98	135	136	131	147
Less favourable to FDI [b]	2	-	1	2	6	16	16	9	9	3

Source: UNCTAD 2002

A profound change also occurred in the identity of those that borrow either portfolio capital or via bank loans. Private borrowers became more prominent than public borrowers. Notwithstanding the abrupt decline of private borrowing during the Asian and Russian crises, the trend towards increased lending private borrowers will continue.

---

14 There are several composite indices pretending to measure the quality of this "investment climate"; but use them with caution.

15 And all do, including those most developed.

16 The wealthier countries, at least, do not discriminate between foreign and domestic investors as they apply the principle of **"national treatment";** foreign investors are put on the same footing as national investors.

Capital flows to developing countries 1992-2001
(in billion USD)

	1992	*1993*	*1994*	*1995*	*1996*	*1997*	*1998*	*1999*	*2000*	*2001*	*2002*
Private capital, total, net	106.9	128.6	142.3	211.4	224.7	115.2	66.2	67.4	29.4	24.9	62.4
Direct investment, net	35.7	57.9	81.0	95.8	119.5	141.3	151.6	154.6	172.1	151.3	160.9
Portfolio investment, net	62.7	76.8	105.0	41.4	79.6	39.4	0.3	4.8	-42.6	-3.0	-4.0
Bank loans, net	8.5	-6.1	-43.7	74.2	25.6	-65.6	-85.6	-91.9	-124.3	-104.6	-85.9
Public capital flows, net	25.0	48.7	4.8	15.7	2.0	52.7	55.3	13.0	0.2	15.4	20.6

Source: IMF 2003

Countries that receive capital other than grants have to pay a price, of course. They have to pay interest. Interest rates on loans to "sovereign debtors" – that is, to states – vary according to the credit worthiness of that state, that is, with the risks connected to credits to that state[17]. The worse the reputation of that state as a debtor, the higher the risks associated to loans to that state; and the higher the interest rates (calculated in "base points", with 100 base-points for each percentage point). At the lower end of the risk scale is the most solid debtor who is being charged the lowest interest. Generally, US treasury bonds serve as such a benchmark for the least possible risk and lowest possible interest rate. What other sovereign lenders have to pay in interest over and above that benchmark is called "spread". For some of the poor countries such spreads can become exorbitant. When doubts about the future policies of Brazil climaxed in 2002, in the run-up to the presidential election, the country had to pay interest rates that were a full 1.700 base points above what the US Treasury had to pay in interest on its own bonds.

17 We can assume that these rates concern sovereign credits only.

Brazilian bond spreads over US Treasuries (basis points)

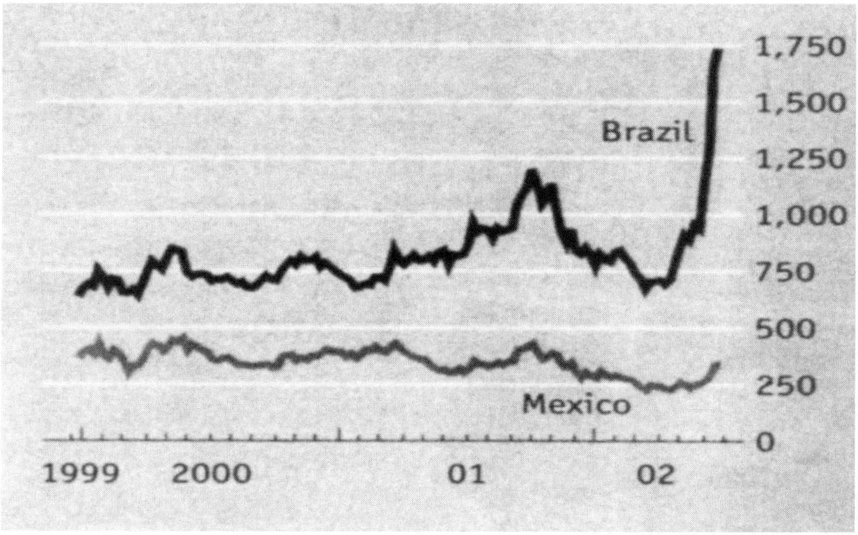

Source: J. P. Morgan

However, interest rates should not be, and ultimately cannot be, higher than the return on productive investment. Interest rates like those charged to Brazil, therefore, are far above what could be justified in terms of sound economic policy. Loans bearing such high interest rates impoverish the loan recipient instead of helping him along.[18]

18 For comparison: the Austrian government bonds trade at 30 to 40 base-points over the benchmark price.

Size of the foreign debt (in billion US Dollars) and volume of debt service

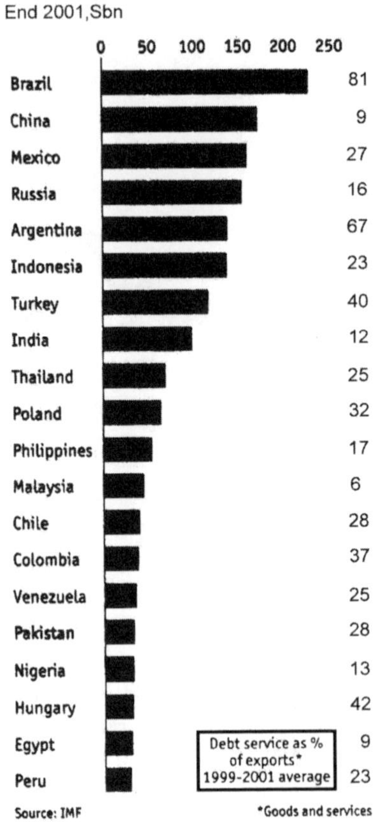

(as percentage of export earning; 1999-2001 average)

The issue is whether, in setting the price for capital, markets are as efficient and rational as they are made out to be. Obviously, in financial markets there is a clear tendency to overreact. This is so, in particular, in financial markets for poorer countries. Much short-term capital may come in. But it may exit as rapidly again and interest rates may fluctuate widely. De-regulation and the liberalisation of financial services have enhanced this potential for unpredictable and de-stabilising rapid changes in the flow of portfolio and loan capital and in the level of debt service. To this issue we shall return in a later chapter.

There is another burden and risk debtor countries assume: Their international debts are denominated not in their local currency, but in foreign currency. If they devalue (as most of them have to in times of crisis), the burden of debt becomes heavier still[19].

Debt service, thus, can become a very serious drag, not only on the official budget, but on the whole economy. In some poor countries, well over 20% of the export earnings are being spent on servicing the foreign debt. 20% of the public expenditures of Brazil and a full 81% of its export earnings go into servicing the debt. Sub-Saharan Africa is in an even worse position.

Clearly, the poorest countries are not able to carry such a heavy load for any length of time. In fact, in the Heavily Indebted Poor Countries (= HIPC), the burden of debt service increased while their per capita income declined. Only recently – since the mid-nineties – has this trend been reversed. This reversal of a pernicious trend is due mainly to debt re-scheduling and debt relief by the International Community.

19 Which prompts them to delay devaluation with the result that it becomes even more abrupt and costlier later on, after the reserves of the central banks have become depleted in the vain fight to preserve the external value of the local currency.

Heavily indebted poor countries

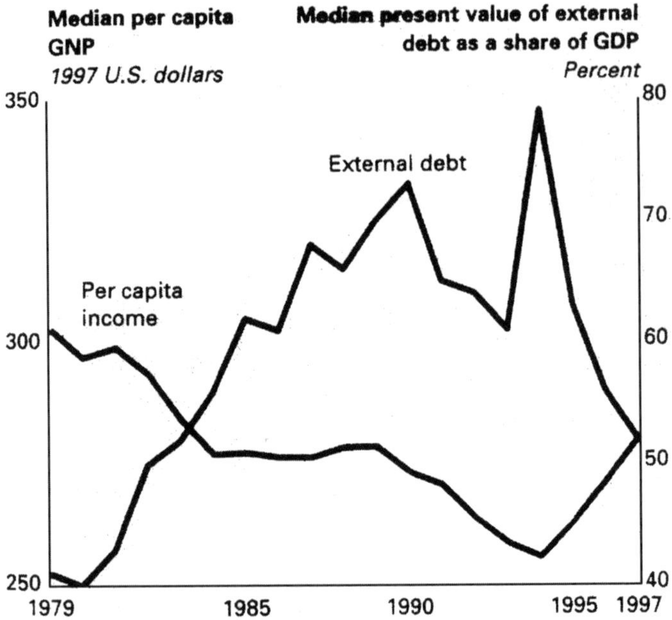

Note: The observed association between declining income and rising debt should not be viewed as implying that debt reduction will automatically result in higher incomes. Government policies are the key to growth and poverty reduction, and bad policies can lead to both higher debt and lower incomes.

Source: Easterly 1999c

After a slow start, the highly indebted poor countries debt relief initiative has made quite some progress. As it must be, this debt relief is tied to strict conditions so as to prevent debt from piling up again.

In the coming decades, and at least for the next fifty years, the growing inequality in the global distribution of wealth, and the growing inequality in the average per capita income of various countries, will pose the most profound and enduring challenge to global stability and global governance. These inequalities will sharpen. They pose a moral challenge and a challenge, too, to practical politics concerned with the immediate interests of nations.

Theoretical economics tries to soothe such concerns by pretending that the gap between rich and poor will be filled by the "invisible hand" of rational markets; and, especially, of financial markets. The financial markets will bring the optimal solution all by themselves. This will happen at a pace that could not be improved upon by the intervention of politics. Sufficient capital will flow to poorer countries. This flow will not only be broader than anything that could be mobilised by politics. It also will be more targeted; better suited to the true needs of poor countries.

Indeed, over the last decades, the international flow of private capital has widened. Yet, that broad flow mainly emptied into countries that were relatively well off already. The richest 20 percent of the world population received 88 percent of gross capital inflows. The poorest 20 percent received just 1 percent of gross capital inflows.

But there are serious drawbacks even to this trickle of resources to the very poor countries. First, this flow is highly erratic; being wide in one year just to dry up or even become reversed in the succeeding year. Second, that very erratic stream touches a very few countries only. And fewer still profit in any massive way from the kind of inflow of capital that is the most directly productive – namely from foreign direct investment.[20]

The erratic nature of these flows, and the fact that they run to a few countries, all re-confirm the rationale that led to the establishment of Development Banks and to the granting of Official Development Assistance. Though widening, the flow of private capital cannot yet substitute for the role of these public institutions and for the role of other public help. If their aim is to lift all from the bondage of poverty, one cannot do without special institutions and processes that have been created for that purpose and that are guided, not by the search for a maximum of profit, but by the search for a maximum of efficiency in eliminating the causes of poverty.

There is, thus, a case for continued Official Development Assistance (ODA). But, in looking back on the fifty year track record of ODA, one is led to the sobering conclusion that much money and much serious goodwill has been wasted in these five decades. ODA has been misled by changing ideological fashions and by the peripatetic short term international politicking.

Yet, both moral and sound "Realpolitik" would counsel rich countries to continue with efforts to deal with this widening gap in wealth and to at least smoothen some of the sharpest edges on this frontier between rich and poor. No patent recipe is there to guide such efforts. The vast and still growing differences between poor countries themselves condemn as illusory all such efforts to arrive at a "single size fits all" solution.

---

20 Though much capital is still being exported from poor countries either officially (for example as debt service) or non-officially as capital flight of vast proportions.

It is evident, though, that aid to poor countries has to be comprehensive, and should not just imply the transfer of financial resources and debt relief; but also technical assistance and measures that facilitate the integration of those countries into the world economic system.

Such assistance needs to be tailor made to the highly divergent nature of the recipient states. In some of them, it might be perfectly natural and effective to administer such assistance via the official channels of central government. In many other states, a "bottom up" approach might be appropriate, bypassing the central government[21]. Certainly, the approach will also differ according to the nature of the project in question. Nonetheless, there now is a distinct tendency to structure such projects in a way so as to directly "empower" the population it is designed to benefit; and to structure it in a way so as to enhance, among these persons, "social capital", that is, the capacity of constructive co-operation. It is also for these reasons and not exclusively out of humanitarian considerations, that the direct reduction of poverty has become a more prominent motive in development assistance.

21 In this distrust of central governments, leftists from a Trotzkite tradition now join the liberal conservatives persuaded by the opinion page articles of the "Wall Street Journal". Nothwithstanding the strangeness of this alliance, its case is a fairly convincing one. Rare are the cases where administrations in poor countries are not only supremely well organised and efficient, but also immune to the temptations of corruption or the temptations of nepotism and clientilism. In all of the countries not blessed by being so very exceptional, it seems wiser to entrust the future to the solidarity, as it exists, on a grass root level: instead of lodging it with anonymous bureaucracies, captive to their own narrow self interest and to the interests of their political masters.

Military Power and Armament

The evidence presented in the first chapters would make it seem that economic performance establishes the rank of a country in the world and its place in the international pecking order.[1] Has military power thus become irrelevant? There is much to support such a proposition. In the decades following World War II, Japan and Germany, for example, had hardly any military power. Nonetheless, the two countries rose into the first rank of nations. They are considered "powerful". The Soviet Union, on the other hand, had been armed to its teeth. It had been if not the first then certainly the second largest military power on the globe. This did not prevent its decline and eventual break-up.

Yet in today's world, wars and threats of organised violence still persist. As long as they do, writing off military power is premature. At the turn of last century, an English writer – Norman Angell – did exactly that. He wrote off military power and termed the belief in it an "illusion". He was wrong and caught in an illusion himself when claiming that just the economy counts and that global economic interdependence would automatically guarantee global peace.

Obviously, over the last 70 years, the world was shaped, to a large degree, by economic developments, by rising wealth, by new technologies, by the shifting economic weight of nations etc. But it also was shaped by military power.

What if Hitler had won World War II?

What if in 1945 the Soviet and the US armies had met at the Dnepr and not at the Elbe river?

What if the US had not decided to militarily "contain" the USSR after 1945?

What about the wars in the Middle East, on the Korean peninsula, in Vietnam, in Afghanistan?

As we see, military power and warfare are still important. They might not affect the very long-term global trends. But they do impact on the course of history. Military might may still cause enormous human suffering; or it might prevent it. Military power is still one of the factors that determine the international status of a state. It is mainly because other nations appreciate the military strength of the US that the US is being considered as the "sole surviving super-power".

1 It also would seem that this economic power has a direct effect. It does not first have to be translated into military power (as was maintained by Paul Kennedy) in order to have a discernible impact on the international scene.

Probably in the very, very long term, military power will have little bearing on the status and standing of a country. Military might has followed and not preceded the economic rise of Great Britain. And Britain's military might has not prevented its decline in the 20th century. As mentioned, military defeat has not thwarted the rise of Japan and Germany in the latter part of this 20th century. And one may safely predict that its present military might will not prevent the ultimate decline of the United States.

Yet the very long term trends are one thing, and at each succeeding moment of history the present is the present; and in each of these succeeding moments of history military power has been relevant – at least up until today. When looking back over the last two generations and on the impact it had on their own lives, people will certainly not be inclined to dismiss military power as irrelevant.

The human beast

In his often quoted article Francis Fukuyama predicted a prosperous and democratic world. He maintained that history – understood as the clash of opposing ideologies – would have "come to an end". This was understood to imply arrival in a world free of large scale wars. There would be no place and function for them in a world ruled by democracy and markets.

Markets and democracy depend on citizens being rational and being driven by rational self interest. Yet even Fukuyama conceded that humans are frequently motivated by other and darker things. He termed these forces "pride". Other writers gave them different names. Some call them the sense of belonging and identity. Others go back to the animal nature of the human beast and refer to an inborn aggression[2]; or to the territorial instinct which leads our genetic kin – the chimpanzees – into territorial wars and into killing (and eating) one another. Thomas Hobbes thought that this animal- and aggressive nature of humans could only be suppressed by an overpowering state (the "Leviathan"). Sigmund Freud juxtaposed the yearning for death ("thanatos") to the life supporting drive of the "libido". Elias Canetti, instructed by the wild roars from the nearby soccer stadium, also thought of massed human beings as having reverted to a beastly nature.

Success in the process of learning, success in ever closer co-operation and success in the process of learning co-operation is all that separates today's homo sapiens from his naked predecessor who entered the world scene 80.000 years ago. The complex nature of our man-made environment demands such

2 With Konrad Lorenz claiming that it would be blocked in animals by gestures of submission; but not in humans, these having "unlearned" such inhibitions.

constant learning. It puts a premium on enhanced co-operation. Were humans not to comply, the complex web would crumble that forms the base for their very physical existence. Yet, there are forces juxtaposed to this growing capacity to learn, to trust and to co-operate. Much negative energy seems to be present still in social relations, even if and where the process of civilisation is most advanced. Hitler Germany has provided the proof. The human beast will never be tamed completely.

In the 20th century, the two World Wars had amply demonstrated the destructive potential of military power.[3] Never before has killing been that efficient and large scale.

Deaths caused by wars

Period	number of deaths (in mio)	number of deaths per 1000 of population
0-1499	3,7	3,2
1500-1599	1,6	11,2
1600-1699	6,1	9,7
1700-1799	7,0	9,7
1800-1899	19,4	16,2
1900-1999	109,7	44,4

Source: W.Eckhardt 1991

Carnage on so vast a scale should have immunised humans against the temptation to repeat the experience. Indeed, it seems significant that both of the aggressors – Germany and Japan – are now those who have become the most pacifist in the group of wealthy countries. This does not only reflect a sense of guilt but also the fact that these aggressors had been punished most severely before their ultimate defeat and had been drenched deeply in the misery and horror of it all.

Still, there is flicker in the eyes of some elder Austrian men when they recall the battles, the hardships, the lucky escapes, the comradry and bravery on the frontlines of World War II. They still feel proud of having survived it all. So there are at least a few who actually like war. They see it as the ultimate challenge, the ultimate test. In the past, this group was more numerous. Popular en-

3 Not that such world-wide conflagrations would be without precedent. They had occurred before and one could,thus, have started numbering world-wars at an earlier date – perhaps beginning with the Thirty Years War in the 17th century. This conflagration, too, spread around the globe, caused much "collateral damage", and brought states to the brink of bankruptcy; or into bankruptcy.

thusiasm still greeted the outbreak of World War I in all countries that became involved. Five terrible years later, people had become ashamed of those, their first, sentiments. Abhorrence of wars should have been re-enforced in the experience of the Second World War; with the mushroom cloud of Hiroshima at its end so as to emphasise that now, at last, and once and for all, heroics have become vain and senseless.

And yet, it is still there: the notion that to suffer and to inflict death in war is something highly virtuous and praiseworthy; and that those who shy away from it are whimps and softies. Much of that has, for example, still coloured US attitudes towards Europe in the run up to the war in Iraq. For some, at least, war keeps its fascination. Some still might long for it. Some might even enjoy the experience of it as the ultimate proof of their manliness. The process of civilisation has only been skin deep. In many basic instincts, we still are awfully close to our semi-human predecessors, glorying in fights over females and territory.

So let us assume that the world is still the same; the human beast still untamed; with military force as the only means of international persuasion; as the only true "currency" to count in international transactions; with power, thus, still emanating (according to Mao) "from the barrel of a gun". Let us assume that this military power, in its turn, could be counted in numbers of soldiers and arms. What – in this perspective – would be the picture of the world? Is it one huge army barrack with an armoury attached?

Not quite! Out of the 6 billion inhabitants on earth, just 22 million (0.03 percent) are soldiers. In 2000, military expenditures stood at 0.8 trillion US dollars. That is a not negligible, but – on the other hand – not a really crippling, 4 percent[4] of the world GDP. These figures do not sustain the claim that the international system is basically about military power and about very little beyond that. Also, military expenditures have decreased over the last years. The end of the "Cold War" has resulted in a "peace dividend". In 1985, world wide military expenditure still stood at 1,25 trillion US dollars and took 6,7% of the world's wealth.

Arms and soldiers in the world 1985-2000

<table>
<tr><td></td><td colspan="6">Defence Expenditure</td><td colspan="2">Numbers in Armed Forces (000)</td><td>Estimated Reservists (000)</td><td>Para-military (000)</td></tr>
<tr><td></td><td colspan="2">US$m</td><td colspan="2">US$ per capita</td><td colspan="2">% of GDP</td><td colspan="2"></td><td></td><td></td></tr>
<tr><td>Global</td><td>1985</td><td>2000</td><td>1985</td><td>2000</td><td>1985</td><td>2000</td><td>1985</td><td>2000</td><td>2000</td><td>2000</td></tr>
<tr><td>Totals</td><td>1,253,517</td><td>811,452</td><td>399</td><td>219.3</td><td>6.7</td><td>3.8</td><td>27,953.5</td><td>22,237.4</td><td>34,761.3</td><td>7,669.0</td></tr>
</table>

Source: IISS 2002

4 Still more than ten times the total of all Official Development Aid.

The decline in world military expenditure has, however, levelled off between 1996 and 1998. Since then, expenditures have risen again – though at a moderate pace.

Global military expenditures*
(in constant 1998 US$ bn)

1992	*1993*	*1994*	*1995*	*1996*	*1997*	*1998*	*1999*	*2000*	*2001*
847	814	793	741	722	732	719	728	757	772

Source: SIPRI 2002

* the figures differ from those of IISS because SIPRI calculates in constant 1998 US$

High income countries have a three quarters share in world military expenditures. Yet, the poorest countries push above their weight. With just 3% of world income, they hold a 7% share in the world's military spending.

Global patterns of military expenditure, population and gross national income, 2000 (Shares of the world total)

	Military Expenditure	*Population*	*Gross National Income*
World Total	100	100	100
High income countries	75	15	80
Upper middle income	10	11	10
Lower middle income	8	34	7
Low income	7	41	3

Source: SIPRI 2002

The table below provides an overview on how military expenditures[5] have evolved in the various regions of the world.

As these figures demonstrate, the old bipolar system has ceased to exist. Russian military power has disappeared for all practical purposes. At best (or worst), Russia still might project some military power over its borders into its closest vicinity – towards unstable and troubled Central Asia and Trans-Caucasia. But it does not have the military capacity to do anything beyond that.

5 This table is in constant 1993 prices and constant 1993 x - rates, and thus differs from the previous table, with its current prices.

Evolution of military expenditures 1989-1999
(in billion USD, constant 1993 prices and exchange rates)

Regions/ Countries/ Country groups	*Military expenditures 1989*	*1994*	*1999*	*Percentage change 1989 to 1999*	*World-wide share 1999 in %*
World	995.4	714.0	686.5	-31	100
Industrial countries	842.7	561.8	520.2	-38	76
NATO	567.5	465.8	423.5	-25	62
USA	361.5	285.2	254.6	-30	37
EU	197.8	170.4	160.8	-19	23
Soviet Union/ CIS	179.3	20.4	21.0	-88	3
OSCE	797.4	511.3	469.1	-41	68
Middle East	49.7	40.9	38.2	-23	6
China	16.8	18.9	33.5	+100	5
Japan	37.8	41.2	42.5	+12	6
South Asia	11.5	11.8	13.9	+21	2
Africa	18.7	13.7	14.7	-23	2
South America	13.9	16.8	22.4	+85	3

Source: Bonn International Centre for Conversion (BICC) 2001

Contrary to what is often assumed, the US has reduced its military expenditure more than Europe has. But as the US started reducing from a much higher level, they are still far ahead of Europe by the volume of their military expenditures. With 254 billion US dollars, the US spends nearly 40% of what is being spent world-wide on the military. EU Europe is not that much behind with 161 billion US dollars. The problem for Europe is that it uses that money less efficiently.[6] Europe thus lags far behind the US in crucial military capacities like air transport, communication, smart weapons, and intelligence. The military might of the US is unrivalled and its lead in military technology unprecedented in history.

Military expenditures in the Middle East remain – relatively – high. They are also high in East Asia. If one discounts Latin America (with its puny 3% of the world's military expenditure), East Asia is the only region where the military budgets have withstood the general downward trend. Within a decade, for example, China has raised military expenditures by fully 100%.

US military superiority rests not only on the still high volume of military expenditure; but, as mentioned, also on how this money is spent. Less goes into personnel and more into equipment. Much again is spent on military Research and Development. In fact, the sums devoted by the US to this military R and D

6 Defence is not integrated by or in the EU; but remains a national affair, basically. A 60,000 soldiers strong "rapid reaction force" has come into existence in 2003. It could provide the core of a common EU defence, which – at the moment – seems far off yet.

are ten times superior to the next "big spenders" – the UK and France. And, whereas in France and the UK the budgets for military R and D have been cut, the military R + D budget has been augmented in the US. Military Research and development takes 54% of the total US Research and Development budget[7], while the figure for the UK is 39%; and for France 25%.

Government expenditure on military R and D, select OECD countries
Figures are in constant 1998 prices and exchange rates figures in italics stand for percentages

	Gov. exp. on military R&D				Change (%)			Share of R&D in mil. exp.	Share of mil. R&D in gov. R&D	
Country[b]	1981	1987	1995	1998	1981–87	1987–95	1995–98	1998	1981	1998
In US$ m.										
USA	33 050	56 200	39 870	39 800	*+ 70*	*– 21*	*± 0*	*15*	*55*	*54*
UK	5 670	5 320	3 730	[3 890][c]	*– 6*	*– 30*	*[+ 4]*	*10*	*46*	*[39]*[c]
France	5 010	5 750	4 570	3 550	*+ 15*	*– 21*	*– 22*	*9*	*38*	*25*
Germany	1 360	2 110	1 710	1 560	*+ 55*	*– 19*	*– 9*	*5*	*9*	*9*
Japan	. .	. .	1 210	1 110	. .	. .	*– 8*	*3*	. .	*5*
Spain	50	130	270	950	*+160*	*+ 107*	*+ 252*	*13*	*5*	*29*
Italy	290	490	300	180	*+ 69*	*– 39*	*– 40*	*1*	*7*	*3*
Australia	170	170	180	150	*± 0*	*+ 6*	*+17*	*2*	*10*	*7*
Sweden	310	650	520	140	*+ 110*	*– 20*	*– 73*	*3*	*15*	*7*
Canada	140	220	150	130	*+57*	*– 32*	*– 13*	*2*	*6*	*6*
Netherlands	80	80	90	110	*± 0*	*+ 13*	*+ 22*	*2*	*3*	*3*
Norway	50	80	60	60	*+ 60*	*– 25*	*± 0*	*2*	*7*	*6*
In US$ b.										
Total[d]	**46.2**	**71.2**	**51.4**	**50.5**	***+ 54***	***– 28***	***– 2***	***11***	***40***	***37***
OECD	**[46.7]**	**[72.1]**	**52.7**	**51.3**	***+ 54***	***– 27***	***– 3***	***10***	***36***	***31***
West Europe	**12.8**	**14.6**	**11.3**	**10.4**	***+ 14***	***– 23***	***– 8***	***7***	***25***	***17***

Source: SIPRI 2001

The result of this state of affairs has become evident in the wars over Afghanistan and Iraq. The technological gap between the Unites States and its NATO allies has become so very wide that Europeans have lost hope of ever closing it again. The impact of this upon the North Atlantic Alliance and upon all aspects of warfare and military strategy is momentous and we will return to this issue later on.

7 There is a hot debate on if, and to what extent, this military research "spills over" into the civilian sector; and thus also benefits the civilian sector. The "spill-over" is probably not as massive as is often maintained.

Arms production and the development of new military technology is boosted by the size of the market in which such arms can be sold. With world-wide military spending down, this world market for arms exports has shrunk from 92 billion USD in 1987 to 53,4 USD in 1999[8]. But the US was least affected by it. It has increased its share of the international market for (major) arms from 25% in 1987 to 49% in 1999. The UK and France have also increased their share on this market; but to a lesser degree[9].

Values of arms deliveries and market share 1987, 1999

constant US$m	*Total*	*USSR/ Russia*	*US*	*UK*	*France*	*Germany*
1987	92,494	32,444	24,987	7,656	8,291	2,246
1989	53,365	3,500	26,205	9,986	6,630	928
%						
1987	*100*	*35.1*	*27.0*	*8.3*	*9.0*	*2.4*
1989	*100*	*6.6*	*49.1*	*18.7*	*12.4*	*1.7*

Source: SIPRI

All three countries have reacted to their shrinking home market by exporting a greater percentage of the arms they produce.

Trend in arms exports in the USA, the UK and France 1990-1998

Country	*1987*	*1988*	*1989*	*1990*	*1991*	*1992*	*1993*	*1994*	*1995*	*1996*	*1997*	*1998*
Share of exports in total arms sales (%)												
USA	13	11	12	11	11	11	13	12	15	13	21	
UK	32	34	36	38	32	28	28	29	41	48	50	48
France	32	33	31	31	25	26	20	17	22	30	41	40

Source: SIPRI

The shrinkage of the arms markets is one of the driving forces behind the recent wave of cross border mergers in the arms industry. One other reason are the ever greater economies of scale. Arms markets, even of medium sized nations

8 These statistics concern major weapons systems only – like tank, aircraft, artillery etc. They do not include small weapons like automatic rifles and hand grenades, the international trade of which has expanded since 1995.

9 Note also the wide annual fluctuations in arms exports from countries like France, the UK or Germany. Therefore, arms dealers are in a very volatile market (this might explain the large mark – ups, and some rather strange practices).

like Germany and France, are simply too small to support an efficient production of more complex weapons. The move into the – shrinking – export markets cannot compensate for that. We, thus, must expect the concentration in the arms industry to continue with many producers leaving business and the fewer and fewer remainers becoming larger and larger.

Ever fewer producers hold an ever greater share of the world's arms market
Change in concentration rates (firms holding % of combined arms sales of the top 100 companies)

	1995	*2000*
5 largest companies	22	42
10 largest companies	37	58
20 largest companies	57	72

Source: SIPRI 2002

In 1990, the ten largest companies held 37 percent of the market[10]. In just ten years this share increased to 58%.

Where does that leave national autonomy – once a core value defended by every national security policy? Can nations still have an autonomous military security policy if they have ceased to be independent in the production – and maintenance – of major weapons systems?

Now to the importers of arms:

The Pacific Rim countries are the major importers; followed by the Middle East. Many and even most of the buyers are fairly poor countries. In the period between 1966 and 2000, Egypt imported major arms systems with a value of 3,6 billion US dollars; India imported arms for 4,2 billion US dollars. Altogether, developing countries imported between four to five times as much as the industrialised countries. This truly is a reverse net transfer of resources that benefits those wealthy countries that export weapons.

Europe is a major customer for US arms sales. In the period between 1996 and 2000, it bought arms worth 12 billion dollars from the US. This relationship is wholly one-sided. In the same period, hardly any European weapons were sold to the US.

10 formed by the 100 largest arms producers

Transfer of major conventional weapons to the leading recipients 1996-2000

The table includes countries and non-state actors with aggregate imports of $500 million or more for 1996–2000 from at least one of the five major suppliers. Figures are trend-indicator values expressed in US $m. at constant (1990) prices. Figures may not add up because of the conventions of rounding.

	Five major suppliers						
Recipients	USA	Russia	France	UK	Germany	Other	Total
Africa	**213**	**886**	**188**	**36**	**28**	**1 864**	**3 215**
Americas	**1 458**	**629**	**449**	**1 257**	**548**	**2 505**	**6 846**
Brazil	199	–	116	565	246	220	1 346
Others	1 259	629	333	692	302	2 285	5 500
Asia	**18 001**	**10 566**	**5 828**	**1 744**	**898**	**5 950**	**42 987**
China	31	4 793	122	26	–	259	5 231
India	–	3 286	91	134	114	603	4 228
Indonesia	61	–	91	709	274	63	1 198
Japan	3 495	–	–	27	5	31	3 558
Kazakhstan	–	648	–	–	–	–	648
Malaysia	348	14	42	546	–	495	1 445
Pakistan	344	86	611	–	–	1 585	2 626
South Korea	3 635	563	293	195	463	185	5 334
Singapore	1 507	28	15	10	–	314	1 874
Taiwan	7 700	–	4 548	–	–	33	12 281
Thailand	776	–	12	12	40	931	1 771
Viet Nam	–	643	–	–	–	89	732
Other	104	505	5	85	–	1 362	2 061
Europe	**12 117**	**1 677**	**839**	**610**	**1 790**	**2 371**	**19 404**
Finland	2 537	206	16	3	–	25	2 787
Greece	2 022	544	97	38	670	294	3 665
Italy	824	–	32	215	19	–	1 089
Netherlands	742	–	205	3	93	60	1 103
Norway	626	–	83	74	11	236	1 030
Spain	864	–	137	130	67	121	1 319
Switzerland	1 566	–	45	–	–	1	1 612
UK	1 286	–	37	..	12	359	1 694
Other	1 650	927	913	147	918	550	5 105
Middle East	**16 889**	**1 930**	**3 487**	**3 275**	**2 241**	**2 226**	**30 048**
Bahrain	554	–	–	–	–	11	565
Egypt	3 265	143	3	–	11	197	3 619
Israel	2 076	–	50	–	765	–	2 890
Kuwait	1 224	73	354	346	–	66	2 063
Qatar	–	–	704	270	–	36	1 010
Saudi Arabia	5 821	–	144	2 010	–	387	8 362
Syria	–	784	–	–	–	21	805
Turkey	3 295	100	406	69	1 464	330	5 664
United Arab Emirates	205	336	1 714	157	4	567	2 983
Others	449	494	112	423	6	603	2 087
Oceania	**588**	–	**2**	**100**	**90**	**846**	**1 626**
Australia	545	–	–	100	90	213	948
Other	43	–	2	–	–	633	678
Other[a]	**6**	–	**1**	–	**49**	**72**	**128**
Total	**49 271**	**15 690**	**10 792**	**7 026**	**5 647**	**15 849**	**104 275**

Source: SIPRI 2002

International arms embargoes

Target	Entry into force	Lifted	Legal basis	Organization
Mandatory UN embargoes				
Angola (UNITA)	15 Sep. 1993	–	UNSCR 864	UN
Iraq	6 Aug. 1990	–	UNSCR 661	UN
Liberia[a]	19 Nov. 192	–	UNSCR 788	UN
Libya	31 Mar. 1992	5 Apr. 1999	UNSCR 748	UN
Rwanda	17 May 1994	16 Aug. 1995[b]	UNSCR 918	UN
Rwanda (rebels)[c]	16 Aug. 1998	–	UNSCR 1011	UN
Sierra Leone	8 Oct. 1997	5 June 1998	UNSCR 1132	UN
Sierra Leone (rebels)[d]	5 June 1998	–	UNSCR 1171	UN
Somalia	23 Jan. 1992	–	UNSCR 733	UN
Yugoslavia	25 Sep. 1991	1 Oct. 1996	UNSCR 713	UN
Yugoslavia (FRY)	31 Mar. 1998	–	UNSCR 1160	UN
Non-mandatory UN embargoes				
Afghanistan	22 Oct. 1996	–	UNSCR 1076	UN
Eritrea	12 Feb. 1999	–	UNSCR 1227	UN
Ethiopia	12 Feb. 1999	–	UNSCR 1227	UN
EU embargoes (non-mandatory)				
Afghanistan[e]	17 Dec. 1996	–	96/746/CFSP	EU
Bosnia and Herzegovina[f]	5 July 1991	–	–	EU
China	27 June 1989	–	–	EU
Croatia[f]	5 July 1991	–	–	EU
DRC[e]	7 Apr. 1993	–	–	EU
Ethiopia[e,f]	15 Mar. 1999	–	–	EU
Eritrea[e,f]	15 Mar. 1999	–	–	EU
Indonesia[f]	17 Sep. 1999	17 Jan. 2000	–	EU
Iraq	4 Aug. 1990	–	–	EU
Libya	27 Jan. 1986	–	–	EU
Macedonia[g]	5 July 1991	26 Feb. 1996		EU
Myanmar (Burma)[e]	29 July 1991[h]	–	–	EU
Nigeria[e]	20 Nov. 1995	1 June 1999	95/515/CFSP	EU
Sierra Leone[f]	8 Dec. 1997	–	98/409/CFSP	EU
Slovenia[g]	5 July 1991	26 Feb. 1996[i]		EU
Sudan[e]	15 Mar. 1994	–	94/165/CFSP	EU
Yugoslavia[g]	5 July 1991	–	–	EU
Other international embargoes (non-mandatory)				
Azerbaijan[j]	28 Feb. 1992	–	–	OSCE
Burundi	6 Aug. 1996	23 Jan. 1999	–	8 African countries[k]
Nigeria	24 Apr. 1996	Nov. 1999	–	Commonwealth

Notes: FRY = Federal Republic of Yugoslavia; CFSP = Common Foreign and Security Policy; EU = European Union; OSCE = Organization for Security and Co-operation in Europe; UNITA = National Union for the Total Independence of Angola; UNSCR = UN Security Council Resolution.

[a] Does not apply to deliveries to ECOMOG forces in Liberia.

[b] The arms embargo was suspended on this date and formally ended on 1 Sep. 1996.

[c] Does not apply to deliveries to government forces in Rwanda. The embargo is also on equipment for persons in neighbouring states if the equipment is for use in Rwanda.

[d] Does not apply to deliveries to government or ECOMOG forces in Sierra Leone.

Source: SIPRI

Finally it becomes evident from the above table that regions of high tension and of potential conflict are the main importers (see, for instance, Taiwan with imports of 12,2 billion US dollars; or Israel, with 2,8 billion US dollars). As historic experience demonstrates, regional arms races tend to sharpen regional conflicts. It thus seems worthwhile to try to dampen such escalation by imposing an arms embargo. This has been done with increasing frequency. But such arms embargoes had no, or just very little, impact on these conflicts. If states or groups of persons are willing to go to war, they will find ways to get the necessary tools; or they might just use the tools at hand. Hundreds of thousands were killed in Rwanda with simple knives.

It is hard to predict what place and function military power will have in the future global system. We may assume that the nature of violent and organised conflict will change (and we will deal with these changes in the next, but one, chapter). We may believe that, in merely statistical terms, a secular trend might continue with wars between states becoming rarer still. All that would point to a future in which military power would impact less heavily on the standing of states and on the whole character of the global system.

But we cannot be certain about that. For, if nations become convinced that military power will become important again, it will become important again. Power is what is being perceived as power. If nations again start to believe that, ultimately, it is just military power that counts, it will be again military power that ultimately counts. Over the last fifty years, military power has become less relevant[11]. It's gaining added significance again would thus reverse this long trend. Nevertheless, such a reversal might occur. Some developments could be taken as symptoms for such a reversal taking place already:

- the end of the decline in world-wide military expenditure in the time between 1996 and 1998 and the subsequent slow rise of these expenditures

11 In the post war era, military power has certainly been instrumental in containing the Soviet Union. Yet, US neo-conservatives are mistaken in their belief that it was that military power (mainly of the US) that also caused the downfall and break up of the Soviet Union. Specifically, they claim that the Soviet Union would have been brought to its knees by president Reagan raising US military expenditures and by his decision to launch into the development of a missile defence system (SDI). This is simply not so. The main cause of the Soviet decline and break up was its inner weakness, caused by economic failure and cultural / political stagnation. The Soviet Union would still be alive and well, would it have continued in the 70s and 80s to grow at the pace it did in the sixties, when it could – credibly – threaten to overtake the US in wealth.

- the changed attitude of the US, which now scoffs at all efforts to limit armaments by international agreements and even glory in their resolve to ignore past commitments to do so

- the fact that the US – as the "hegemon" defining the international rules of the game – tends to impress upon the world the notion that even "pre-emptive" wars, and wars not sanctioned by the UN Security Council, should be considered legitimate

- the fact that the European Union has recently become convinced that just setting an example for peace through co-operation is not enough; and that, in addition, it would to have at its disposal its own, independent and efficient means to fight wars

- the continuation and slight acceleration of the arms race in Southern/Eastern Asia, with nuclear arms thrown in to raise the stakes and risks

- the escalation of the conflict between Israelis and Palestinians

Were these tell-tale signs for a true reversal of a long historic trend, and were military power again to become decisive, the nature of the present global system would become transformed, we would witness a return to the past. Not only would states continue to remain the most important "actors" on the global field. After having declined over the last decades, their status and prominence would grow again. They would regain the power and influence they had lost to other "actors". Bilateralism would again substitute for multilateralism in international relations. In global governance, human rights and democratisation would become relegated to a lower rank of priorities.

All that might happen: But, it just might as well be that all that has been portrayed above as symptoms of a true reversal and of a return to militarism, is actually nothing more than a short term and insignificant dint in the secular trend running against military power and its use. We do not know. And we do not know because it is humans that will decide between these alternatives. And their choices are open.

Weapons of Mass Destruction

Weapons of mass destruction – chemical, biological and, finally, nuclear arms – entered the scene in the 20th century. They are presumed to have thoroughly changed security policies and the nature of warfare. But have they?

The evolution of the nuclear doctrine; anyhow – what are nukes good for?

1) In the beginning, there was the simplistic notion of a "big bang for your buck": The atomic bomb would be just like any other weapon[1]. But it would be very cost-efficient. Relatively little money could buy a very big blast. This doctrine held only as long as the US had a monopoly on nuclear weapons and/or could not be touched by Soviet Union nuclear weapons.

2) After that, the doctrine was supplanted by one based on the notion that size and numbers count. Nuclear powers were like teenagers playing "chicken", who drive cars against each other on a single lane road. The less powerful car will yield to the more powerful car without having been actually hit by this more powerful car. Similarly, superiority in numbers and in the power of nuclear weapons would make yield the one with fewer or weaker nuclear weapons. Numeric superiority would, thus, directly translate into political advantage (without the weapons being actually used).

3) This was followed by the doctrine of "escalation dominance": one could and would reply – in a very slow escalation – to every move of an opponent. This would be done by planning to apply, in every reactive step, nuclear weapons a bit more powerful and devastating than the ones used by the opponent. The doctrine also provides for a "first use" of nuclear weapons in reply to an aggression with superior conventional forces[2]. If the opponent still was not deterred and continued his aggression, one could retort by increasing one's

1 Not a view shared by many of the scientists who co-operated in the "Manhattan-project" to rush the development of the first atom bomb. In their view, it was NOT a weapon like any other. They thought that it would permanently change the nature of war and of international relations.

2 This was NATO's doctrine in the time of the Cold War, when NATO-Europe was confronted with the numerically superior forces of the Warsaw Pact; and thus sought a way to deter a possible aggression by these superior conventional forces.

own dosage of nuclear destruction. The opponent, being rational[3], knows about this capacity and resolve and, thus, desists from all steps that could set in motion such a march on an "escalation ladder".

4) At the end of this ladder stands – aptly named – MAD; the capacity of "mutually assured destruction" – of inflicting unacceptable[4] damage upon an opponent.

Has MAD and escalation dominance worked? It is possible and even likely that mutual nuclear deterrence has contributed to the maintenance of peace in post-war Europe. In Europe, two highly armed powers or coalitions confronted each other for over half a century. Nevertheless, they did not go to war against each other. This is historically unique. One thus assumes that a factor was present in this period that did prevent the return to the historic pattern of open warfare. Quite naturally, many believe this factor to have been mutual nuclear deterrence.[5]

The big question for the future is whether deterrence will always work. In the future deterrence might fail simply because the number of states holding nuclear weapons will grow: the greater the number of states that possess nuclear weapons, the more likely an accidental development that might trigger a nuclear conflagration, even though none of the nuclear powers might actually wish for such a war.

Furthermore, some of these new nuclear powers like Pakistan, Korea or Israel differ quite markedly from the US and the Soviet Union. Unlike the US or the Soviet Union, they might face a situation where they justly will fear for their very survival. Or it might happen that some dictator under siege is ruthless enough to willingly take the whole population of his country with him to a final Armageddon.

In the US and the USSR, nuclear weapons were seen as a deterrent. Their sole – rational – function was to prevent an opponent from using nuclear weapons himself or from going to war with his superior conventional forces. But, for some of the new nuclear states, atomic weapons might not have the

---

3 It is not very rational to assume that humans will always act rationally. They are least rational in wars (the "fog of battle" – Clausewitz). There also is something highly contradictory in assuming nations to be irrational enough to start playing "chicken"; and then be rational enough to back off if the oncoming car is stronger; that is ,if the opponent has superior nuclear arms.

4 In the US, this was seen as implying about 20 million persons killed and half of the industrial capacity destroyed.

5 But it did not prevent the Korean war (where – it is true – the opponents of the US/UN were not nuclear powers at that time).

same function. Some of the new nuclear states might even fail to be deterred by the fact that the opponent has nuclear weapons too. Hitler would not have been deterred from using nuclear weapons had he had them and he would not have hesitated to use them, even when knowing that the other side would repay in kind. Also, there are situations in which just one side has such weapons and, thus, would not be threatened by nuclear retaliation. The side which has nuclear weapons might, thus, be tempted to actually use them.

Nuclear deterrence is based upon the capacity to inflict unacceptable damage on an opponent. This capacity to deter would only exist – so it is said – if a nuclear opponent could not strike first and thereby destroy, not only the country and its population, but all of its nuclear weapons, so that the one to hit first could not be hit in return. Therefore, it is maintained, only those countries can truly deter, that can keep their nuclear arms from being destroyed in a "first strike". Those countries which have the capacity to shelter the nuclear weapons have a second strike capacity. That is, they can strike back even after having, themselves, suffered a nuclear strike. The "second strike capacity" was seen as stabilising, as it reduces the incentive to launch nuclear weapons fast and first.

The best way to maintain such a capacity is by nuclear submarines (which cannot be eliminated by the opponent's atomic weapons). Using this criteria, we find that next to the US and Russia, France, the UK, China hes this capacity as they employ submarines armed with MIRVed[6] missiles.

Notwithstanding all efforts to stop such proliferation of nuclear weapons, quite a few countries will acquire them (and other weapons of mass destruction) over the next few decades. Two European countries – France and the United Kingdom – possess nuclear arms to deter the threat emanating from these new nuclear powers. But EU-Europe, as such, does not wield that deterrence. This raises the question as to the strategic significance of the French nuclear forces. Will the French nuclear weapons continue to serve France exclusively? Or could they – would they – come to serve EU-Europe as a whole? Might France be willing to make them tools not just of French but of European deterrence?[7] This is an open question. Yet the likely answer is negative. The likely consequence is that EU-Europe, as such, will have no tools to counter nuclear blackmail coming from non-European countries.

---

6 MIRV – Multiple Targeted Independent Re-entry Vehicles; that is: each carrier rocket launches several warheads, each of which is programmed to hit a different target.

7 We do not mention the UK, where such a possibility is even more remote.

European nuclear impotence could be compensated for, to some extent, by French "creative uncertainty"; with France being ostentatiously ambivalent as to the true functions of its nuclear arsenal; and as to whether it is meant to protect not just France alone but also the other EU-countries.

Nuclear warheads world-wide

Country	*Strategic warheads*	*Non-strategic warheads*	*Total warheads*
USA	6 480	1 120	7 600
Russia	4 951	3 380	8 331
UK	185	-	185
France	348	-	348
China	282	120	402
India	-	-	(30-35)*
Pakistan	-	-	(24-48)*
Israel	-	-	(~200)*
Total			~17 150

* By the number of deployed warheads. The stockpiles of India, Pakistan and Israeal are thought to be only partly deployed.

Source: Sipri 2002

Counting warheads only, one could assume that – contrary to our fear – the era of nuclear arms is drawing to an end. The number of nuclear warheads has declined substantially. But this is due – nearly exclusively – to the reduction in the number of US and Soviet/Russian warheads.

Not too much should be made of this development. It reflects nothing but the climbdown from a summit of irrationality when both sides had enough weapons to kill the other side completely and many times over. Even with these reductions, their arsenals are still stocked to blow the world into pieces.

Nor did this reduction in an over-supply of nuclear arms set a good example for others to follow. While the US and Russia were reducing the numbers of their nuclear warheads, others have been acquiring them. Next to the US, Russia, the UK and France, other countries have come to possess nuclear weapons. They have also acquired the means to deliver them (and other weapons of mass destruction) via medium range and/or long range missiles.

Why this interest in acquiring nuclear weapons and other means of mass destruction? After all, in purely military terms, those weapons have limited value only. Armoured personnel carriers and tanks can cross, within minutes after the explosion, a battlefield where nuclear weapons have been used. Hardened bunkers can withstand the blast of a nuclear bomb if it hits the ground just half a mile away. So it is not for their military value and use that some nations seek to acquire those weapons. They do so because possession of nuclear arms has psychological and political consequences.

Number of nuclear warheads world-wide

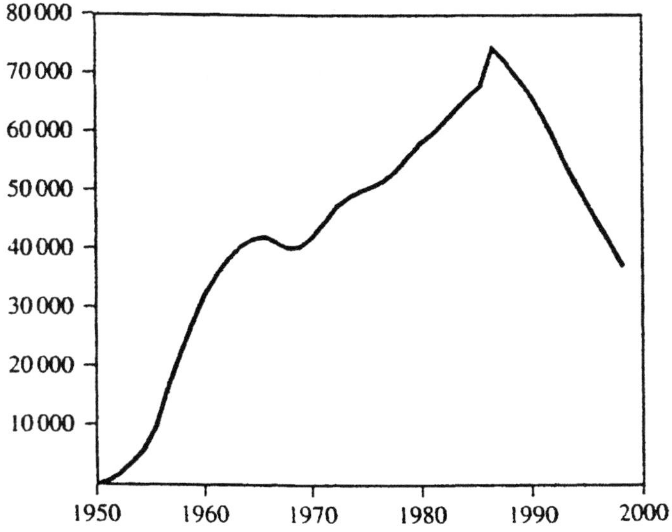

Source: NRDC

Even if nuclear weapons cannot inflict unacceptable damage upon the military of a hostile country, a few such weapons can inflict an unacceptable damage upon that country, as such. The psychological and political impact of such use would be deep; comparable, at least, to the impact the collapse of the World Centre Twin Towers had upon the psyche and the policies of the United States.

If nuclear weapons, thus, offer an advantage, those who possess them have solid reason to keep others from acquiring them too. If the existence of such weapons is inherently dangerous, the world, as such, also has an interest to limit the number of countries that possess nuclear weapons and other arms of mass destruction. Arranged against these two bigger groups is the smaller group of countries that has both the means of still acquiring such weapons; and the will and motive to do so. This has been an uneven match and the two stronger groups have united in fighting proliferation of weapons of mass destruction. This has resulted in a number of treaties and/or regimes which have, at least somewhat, slowed the process of proliferation.

International instruments to thwart the proliferation of Weapons of mass destruction

The most important is the Non – Proliferation Treaty, which, inter alia, bans the diversion of fissile material from civilian nuclear power stations to military use. This provision is being enforced by the International Atomic Energy Agency.

The Comprehensive Nuclear Test Ban Treaty seeks to ban all tests of nuclear weapons, and thus hampers the development of such weapons. The refusal of the US to submit this treaty to ratification is likely to prevent its entering into force.

A Chemical Weapons Convention entered into force in 1997. It provides for the – phased – destruction of all existing stocks of chemical weapons. This process is to be monitored.

The 1972 Biological and Toxic Weapons Convention not only provides for the end of all development, production and hoarding of such weapons. It also provides for the destruction of the existing stocks of such weapons. Unfortunately (and unlike in the field of chemical weapons), no mechanism has been put in place to monitor compliance with that treaty[8].

Frequently, agreements on the prevention of proliferation are of a more informal nature, and bind not all but just some of those countries that are capable of producing and exporting such weapons, their precursors, or equipment for producing missiles for their delivery.

One such group is the Missile Technology Control Regime, founded in 1987 and presently with 33 members. The Zanger Committee (with 35 members) and the Nuclear Suppliers Group (with 39 members) control the export of sensitive technology that could be used in the production of nuclear weapons. In the field of chemical weapons, the 34 member Australia Group has a similar function.

All these instruments, and the political resolve behind them, did have some effect. Till now, proliferation has not been as massive as had been feared in the

8 The recent Anthrax scare in the United States has given proof that the US still does work in this field or at least keeps some of the relevant material in stock. The same holds true for Russia

late fifties/early sixties[9]. The impediments to proliferation established by international co-operation and by these formal and less formal agreements had a dampening effect.

Nonetheless, "horizontal proliferation" seems to have accelerated again in recent years; especially with India and Pakistan breaking the taboo on further nuclear tests. They might have set in motion a chain reaction of such tests by other powers.

East Asia is the region most likely to become the theatre of further "horizontal proliferation" and new nuclear confrontation. Taiwan would have good reasons to acquire such weapons; as would Japan and South Korea; were they to doubt the reliability and/or political neutrality of the US nuclear guarantee, and come to fear the nuclear weapons North Korea has acquired already and will continue to acquire.

"Vertical proliferation" has also been set in motion again. Those already in possession of nuclear weapons are adding new layers to the system. They thus triggered an arms race as they are inducing others to follow their example. Indeed, several events or developments point in the direction of a renewed emphasis on nuclear weapons by those that already possess them.

1) The non-ratification by the US Senate of the Nuclear Test Ban Treaty, which is a cornerstone in the non-proliferation regime;

2) Proposals in the US to launch pre-emptive nuclear strikes against countries that have, or that develop, weapons of mass destruction.[10] Or suggestions to make use of nuclear weapons in conventional warfare for the purpose – inter alia – of destroying underground bunkers;

3) The renunciation by the US of the 1972 ABM (anti-ballistic-missile) treaty and the ongoing US effort to build a missile defence (NMD – "National Missile Defence System"). If it ever became effective, such a shield against incoming missiles would give the US a – destabilising – "first strike capacity". The US could strike against any opponent without them having to fear being hit by the enemy's missiles in return.[11]

---

9 Tom Lehrer's famous proliferation song:... "Luxembourg is next to go, and – who knows – even Monaco. We all will stay serene and calm when Alabama gets the bomb. Who's next?"

10 This was proposed in the annual 2002 "nuclear posture report" of the Pentagon (F.T.11.03.02).

11 The technical feasibility of the project continues to be doubtful. Obviously though, it is problematic also in its political implications. European allies of the US, for example, fear not being protected by such a shield. They fear that, without it, they might easily substitute for the US as a target.

4) The Russian switch from a "second strike" to a "first strike doctrine". This is a move one might expect from a state with now severely reduced conventional forces but still in possession of a vast array of nuclear weapons. Inevitably, a "first strike doctrine" brings less stability to the world than a "second strike doctrine".

Does the acceleration of "horizontal proliferation" and the renewed "vertical proliferation" imply that, eventually, a nuclear weapon will explode somewhere on earth? It would not be rational for any one to initiate such an event. But humans are not always rational. Some wish for a glorious suicide, taking their enemies with them. Or the use of nuclear weapons might be triggered by misinformation. This could happen, for example, if a meteorological rocket is mistaken for a military missile.[12] Erroneously believing the were under attack, a country could decide to launch its own missiles against its most likely opponent. Or nuclear weapons might be launched unilaterally due to a mere technical glitch. The greater the number of countries that own such weapons, and the more complex

12 As it happened once in Russia and brought a nuclear "red alert".

the systems become due to the ongoing "vertical proliferation", the greater the likelihood that, one day, calamity will strike.

Yet, even with proliferation speeding up again and with many states and many unstable states getting their fingers on the nuclear trigger, the main and most plausible threat to security will not come from missiles or from states that launch them. Nuclear bombs do not need to be transported by missiles. They can come in one of the many million containers shipped across the world. The hundred kilos of a small atomic weapon could even be transported in three or four suitcases. Also, it does not need states to expedite such shipments. Terrorists could do that too. Much fissile material has gone missing during the break-up of the Soviet Union. Instructions on the construction of bombs can be downloaded from the Internet. Terrorist organisations like al Qaeda could, thus, eventually assemble such devices. It also would be able to deliver them to their targets by very traditional means.

Countries with chemical or biological weapons (W) or research programmes (R)

Country	*Biological*	*Chemical*
China	W	W
Israel	W	W
Russia	W	W
USA	?	W
India	R	W
Pakistan	R	R
Iran	W	W
Iraq	W	W
North Korea	W	W
Egypt	W	W
Syria	R	W
Libya	R	R
Sudan	R	R

Source: "Deadly Arsenals" by Joseph Cirincione, Carnegie Endowment for International Peace 2002

The only time when nuclear weapons were actually used, in Hiroshima and Nagasaki in the summer of 1945, they certainly expedited the Japanese decision to surrender as they demonstrated US technological superiority and also the resolve of the US to go to the limit. This shows that nuclear weapons do indeed have a powerful psychological and political impact. But, in purely military terms, the US nuclear weapons were not decisive in changing the relative military might of the two opponents in the Pacific theatre of World War II.

The purely military case for biological and chemical weapons stands on even shakier ground. Though having been produced and stocked in large quantities, chemical weapons were never used after World War I.[13] The same holds true for biological weapons, which are even more difficult to apply than chemical ones, and more difficult still to control in their effects.

The one and undisputed function of these weapons is deterrence. They dissuade an opponent from using similar weapons first. But here, too, doubts are justified as to whether one may always rely on deterrence to function. Possibly it might not. It might not deter the "irrational" use of chemical or biological weapons by desperate pariah states or by terrorist groups.

Death and wounded civilians in 41 conflict zones of the 90es
(according to the weapons that had caused injury or death)

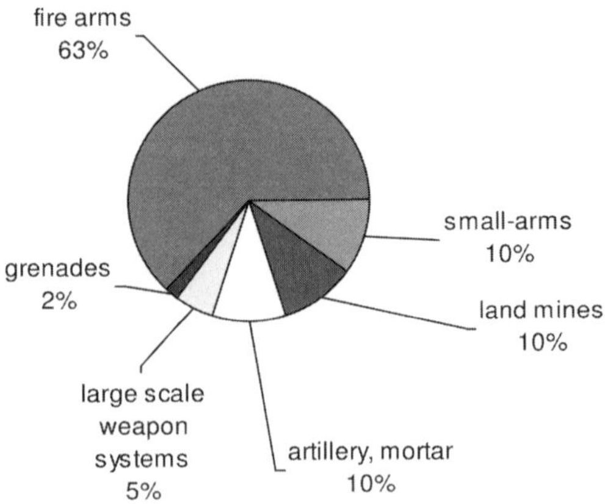

Source: ICRC

However, the true and effective weapons of mass destruction, those that have really destroyed masses are not nuclear; and neither are they chemical nor biological. They are assault rifles, hand guns, hand grenades etc. These are cheaply made and cheaply sold. It is impossible to stop or control their proliferation.[14] In

13 If we exclude the employ by the Iraqi dictator Saddam Hussein of chemical weapons against the Kurdish minority in his country – an example few military would recommend to be repeated.

14 Though efforts have been made, for example, by the 2001 UN Conference on the Illegal Transfer of Small and Light Weapons; or by the 1997 Ottawa Convention prohibiting the employ and the production of Anti-Personnel-Mines (APM)

the violent conflicts that took place in the 90s, only 5% of civilians killed or wounded may ascribe their ill fate to major weapons (like tanks or artillery). The remaining 95% of deaths and injuries among civilians were caused by simpler arms.

As in the application of new technology in the economy, in the production and application of weapons, too, the 20th century has been less revolutionary than it has claimed to be.

When, a hundred years ago, Norman Angell pronounced wars among nations to be a thing of the past, he was proven wrong by two consecutive World Wars. But perhaps his predictions were simply a bit premature. Perhaps he has been proven right now, a hundred years later. Or has he? That depends on what we define as "war". Do we define it the traditional way, as an armed conflict between two states? Or do we use a broader definition that pertains to all "sustained armed conflicts that cause more than one thousand deaths". Under this latter and broader definition, we would also have to include "intra-state wars" (as, for example, civil wars or wars for secession); as well as "extra-state wars" (states waging wars outside of their territory against an enemy that is not another "sovereign").

Using this broader definition, we find that, unfortunately, Norman Angell was mistaken. So defined, wars remain common. In fact – a record number of them was started in the nineties of last century.

War Onsets by Decade 1816-1997

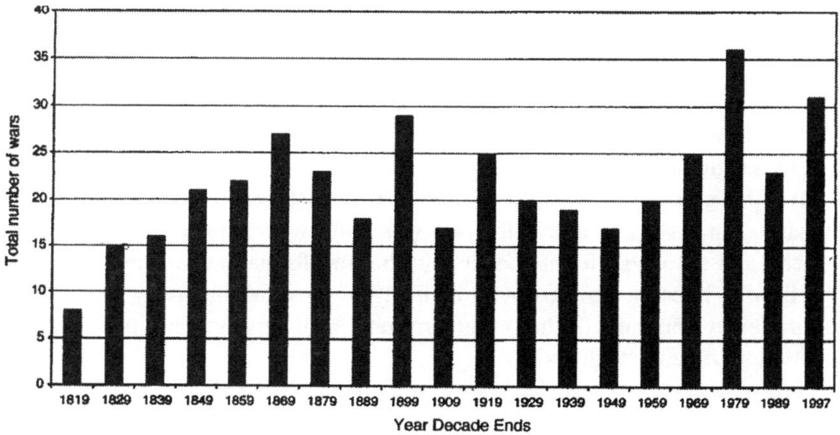

Source: Sarkees et al, 2003

Over these two hundred years, and up to the immediate past, the percentage of the world population that died in such wars has also remained constant (if one ignores the times of exceptional carnage in the US Civil War and in the two World Wars).

War deaths per Thousand Population

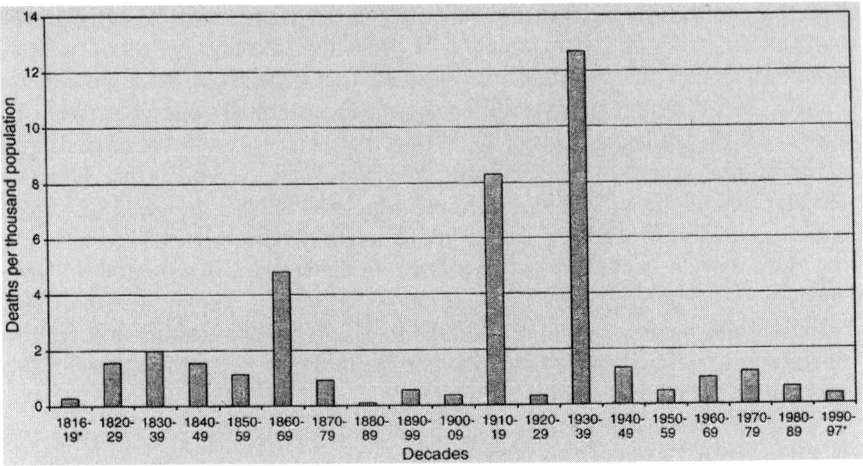

Source : Sarkees et al, 2003

These data would lead us to conclude that, even a hundred years after having been published in his book, the predictions or visions of Norman Angell still are off target. Wars have not disappeared. They remain with us and are as much a part of the global system as they were in the past.

But that conclusion is premature too. The persistence of wars is tragic and inhumane. But, over and above that, do wars, and wars mainly, define the global system, and are wars the main agents in the transformations of this system? For this is what is being claimed by quite many of those who actively deal in world affairs; or by some intellectuals who arrogate for themselves and their views the distinction of being "realists".

Were their views to mirror reality, wars would be routinely used by states as "continuations of (their) politics by other means". They would be the only truly effective tools to impact upon the global system. But the usage of this instrument has lost its attraction, as it seems. If inter-state wars are still with us, theiy are becoming less frequent.[1]

International and internal violent conflict 1945-1998
(cases per year)

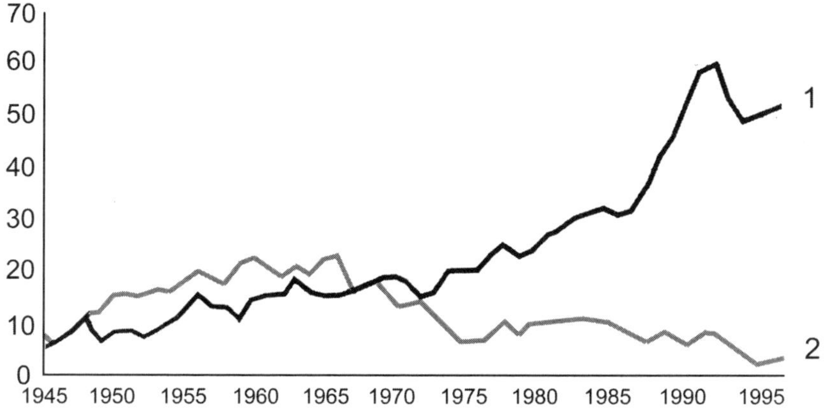

1 = internal conflicts
2 = international conflicts involving, at least on one side, a state as such

Source: Heidelberger Institut für Konfliktforschung

The number of wars between states has been declining; whereas violent conflicts within one state have become more frequent and deadly. According to the Human Development Report 2002, 220.000 persons were killed, in the 1990's, in conflicts between countries. Compared to preceding decades that is a drop of nearly two thirds. But in the same period, 3,6 million died in wars that took place within a state.[2]

---

1 This would not be the case if we use the same database that has been used in the compilation of the two tables above (which is the "Correlates Of War" database at the University of Michigan). Table three is, however, based upon a German database (Heidelberger Institut für Konfliktforschung").

2 This is the global trend. It hides some regional peculiarities. In Asia – the world's most populated continent, the danger of traditional war between nations has not receded as much as it did in other regions of the world: see the war potential of conflicts like the one between India and Pakistan, Iran/Iraq/Kuwait, or the People's Republic of China/Taiwan.

Intra-state conflicts are thus more common than traditional wars involving states on both sides. And even where such inter-state wars still have flared up, major powers have become less and less involved in them. This process of withdrawal of major powers from inter-state war has continued over centuries. It became more marked in the 19th century, when economic success instead of victory in war started to determine the place of a nation in the international pecking order. During 95 years of the 17 th century, there were wars that involved at least one major power. The number dropped to 71 years in the 18 th century; and to 53 years in the 20th century[3]. In the second half of the 20th century, this tendency has become even more pronounced. Big and wealthy states are loath to go to war against each other. And they are even less inclined to do so if both of them are democracies. Traditional wars that involve states on both sides are now fought not at the centre, but at the periphery of the world system. They thus have little impact upon this system.

With the end of the Cold War, the number of armed conflicts involving states has not gone up but declined. That defies dire predictions that, after the end of the East-West conflict this number would rise (J.Mearsheimer,1990). In the era of the acute East-West conflict, local wars had always had the potential of implicating the super-powers. With the super-powers involved, each of such small local conflicts could have developed into a full blown big and disastrous East-West confrontation. Therefore, the super-powers tried to keep such local conflicts under control. It was for this reason that there were fewer such conflicts than before.[4] Mearsheimer maintained that, with such restraints now gone, the number of smaller, armed inter-state conflicts would grow. Yet this is not what has happened. Since the nineties, armed conflicts involving states have become rarer still.

This does not imply that relations among states have become less conflict prone. In a world that is being woven together ever more tightly, interests and values are bound to clash more frequently. And indeed, the number of inter-state conflicts has risen. But most of these now more numerous interstate conflicts are being dealt with in a non-violent manner.

---

3 With the 19th century being even more peaceful: the respective number is 29 years.

4 We should note, though, that frequently the argument has also been turned on its head. Super-power-confrontation would have inflamed and incited smaller regional conflicts. With neither the Soviet Union or the US being able to advance against the opponent on a central front (e.g. in Europe) they would have sought gains in the periphery – for instance in Africa (Angola, Ethiopia) or Southeast Asia (Cambodia, Vietnam).

Predominantly violent and predominantly non violent inter-state conflicts
1945-1995, number of conflicts each year

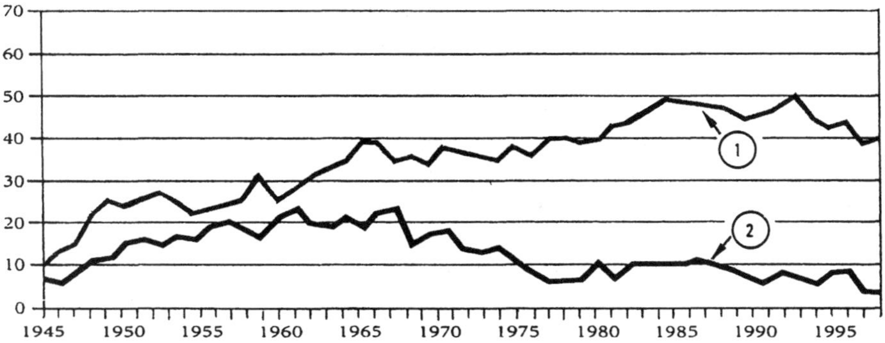

1 = non-violent
2 = violent

Source: Heidelberger Institut für Konfliktforschung

Violent conflicts (be they intra-state or inter-state) now mainly occur in poor countries.
Share of incidents of war, civil war and strife, 1990-95, %

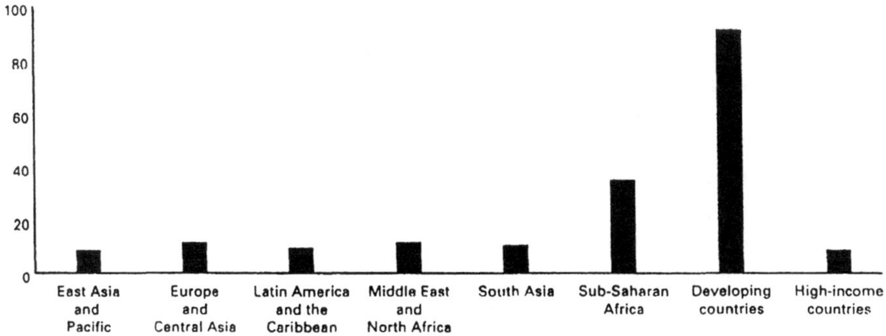

Source: USAID

Why do wealthy countries tend to refrain from war? First, because war has become a rather uncertain venture. Whoever starts a war intentionally should reflect on the fact that, in the 20th century, ALL wars between states had a different outcome than the outcome expected by the one who had started it. Second, if they exist at all, the rewards of war are few today. And while one may gain very little by war, one risks losing much. After both of the 20th century World Wars, even the victors were worse off by far than they had been before war started.

Wars used to be fought over possession of territory. But what use has territory today? Gaining a piece of real estate does not add very much to the power and wealth of the conqueror. At best, he will acquire additional agricultural land to augment unwanted agricultural surpluses. Today, what makes for wealth and power is not the territorial size of a state, but its place and function in the international exchange of goods. Tiny Singapore is a relevant global player. Vast Zaire is not. Other states might covet the economic potential of Singapore. But they cannot gain it by military occupation of Singapore. Such an occupation would destruct the factories and drive abroad its indispensable managers and engineers and thus would destroy the assets an aggressor would like to command. If one wants to profit from Singapore's wealth, one cannot do so by seizing it. One would have to co-operate with that city-state. Co-operation and not aggression is the way to greater wealth and standing.

Third, empirical evidence supports the notion of democratic peace. Democracies shy away from waging wars against each other. Fascists, Nazis and Communists were right. Democracies are not very heroic. The majority of states is now democratic; and, as such, diffident about the heroics of war.

In the previous chapters, we have dealt extensively with traditional military hardware: tanks, fighter aircrafts, battle-ships etc. This is hardware conceived for a kind of war that is becoming rare: namely the war between two powerful nation states. As we have seen, the nature of violent, organised conflict has changed and, with it, the tools used by the combatants. The confrontation between two forces of roughly equal strength and nature has yielded to confrontations in which opponents fight with different tools and are subject to different handicaps ("asymmetric conflicts"). On one hand, the traditionally stronger part has gained new strength; but he has also become more vulnerable. The same holds true for the traditionally weaker opponent. He too has become, at the same time, more powerful and more vulnerable. The events of 11th September 2001 and the following war in Afghanistan prove that.

The drawing below, taken from the New York Times, shows the US missiles vainly threatening an al Qaeda terrorist, victoriously brandishing a paper cutter as it was used on September 11, 2001 to highjack the planes later flown into the World Trade Center and into the Pentagon. Missiles were of little use in deterring persons anyhow committed to dying when carrying out their plans. The situation was asymmetric. Force did not match counterforce.

The attack also has underscored how vulnerable modern, wealthy nations have become. Which skyscraper – be it in London, Frankfurt, Tokyo, or Shanghai – could not be attacked by a kamikaze pilot steering a hijacked aircraft? And it is not just skyscrapers that are vulnerable. Much else is too: electric grids, electronic communications, water and transportation systems. All that could be destroyed or seriously impaired with using limited resources only. A handful of computer "hackers" sitting at their terminals could, for example, wreak havoc. According to one specialist, a concerted attack by just 20 talented hackers could very well immobilise the US. Such new offensive tools are at the disposal not just of governments (who are honing them), but also at the disposal of smaller, less structured groups of terrorists and criminals.

Wealthy and complex societies are now at the mercy of ill equipped opponents, provided these are sufficiently ruthless and resolved. For all practical purposes, wealthy and complex societies are not able to ward off all such threats. As US officials have not ceased to emphasise after September 11th 2001: "It could happen again. We will do our best to prevent it. But we cannot guarantee the success of such efforts."

In this "asymmetric" battle it is not just the terrorists, that here gained added power to inflict damage. So have formerly meek states or formerly powerless groups. New military technology used to provide a disproportionate military advantage to an economically advanced country. It thus could easily prevail over military opponents which, due to their lower wealth, did not yet possess such modern weapons[5]. This, at least, was the case in the past. But things have changed. By now the economically less advanced have gained access to quite some firepower and offensive capacity. It is not overly costly or otherwise difficult to obtain:

a) assault rifles that can be used to mortal effect even by the very untrained (child-) soldiers
b) grenade launchers
c) plastic explosives and home made explosives
d) land mines
e) shoulder held anti aircraft missiles
f) night vision goggles and GPS
g) cheap cross country vehicles.

Will wealthy countries and their useless heavy armour meet the same fate that met the mounted, armoured knights in battles with peasant infantry (battle between England and France at Acingcourt; battle of Moorgarten between the Austrian armoured cavalry and the Swiss pike-wielding foot soldiers)?

There is no clear answer. For contrary to such historic precedence, today's armoured knights have become light-footed again. The economically advanced countries have become not less, but more mobile, flexible and targeted in their war waging[6]. It used to be the case that guerrillas could hide in mountain and forest retreats for decades, playing cat and mouse with their enemies and wearing these enemies down until they capitulated. This has changed. In the Afghan war, the US could combine effective intelligence gathering with very light on-the-ground operations and with an ultra precise air war carried out mainly by long range bombers. Little Toyotas carrying Taliban soldiers became targets of US forces, as well as simple mud huts harbouring (or suspected of harbouring) al Qaeda or Taliban fighters. Guerrillas now can profit no longer from what they had profited before: melting into the population and countryside.

---

5 The battle of Königgrätz, for example, which substituted Germany for Austria as the predominant force in Central Europe, was won thanks to the higher efficacy of the newly invented rear loading Prussian rifles. The superiority of German tanks and airplanes gave Nazi Germany the edge and early victories in the first phases of World War II. One could also maintain that the late 19th century expansion of European colonial empires was based upon the efficiency of European machine guns.

6 We should not stretch the argument: in fact, it is just the US that has acquired this capacity.

Evidently, the small David has become stronger; but Goliath has become stronger too: The reverse side of the coin is that both have at the same time become more vulnerable. This has been termed a *"Revolution in Military Affairs – RMA – a change in the nature and conduct of military operations that either renders obsolete or irrelevant one or more competencies in a dominant player or creates new core competencies in some dimensions of warfare"* (definition by the RAND-corporation). The RMA implies more than a mere change in the military hardware used in fighting. It implies a change in the whole nature of armed conflict. One might term it a transition from "Industrialised Total Warfare" (which characterised World War II) to a "Spectator Sport or Post Heroic Warfare" (A. Catham 2002).

Next to this RMA, another major trend is under way. It is the privatisation of organised violence on one hand; and the privatisation of its opposite: the privatisation of services to maintain public security on the other hand. A step in this direction is already being taken by the ongoing transition from conscript armies to professional armies. A drafted soldier serves his country. A professional soldier does the job he is paid for. From a drafted soldier, one demands obedience and sacrifice. From a professional soldier, professionalism. This too, changes the nature of war.

Even countries with a long tradition of conscription (like France) are now turning towards professional armies. Obviously, they must have solid reasons for this break with an essential part of their history and tradition. Here are a few:

- there no longer is a need to thwart the invasion of a mass-army by another mass-army;
- massed soldiers have themselves become easy, inviting targets;
- today's complex military equipment can no longer be used and serviced by unskilled or semi-skilled conscripts;
- conscripts can be motivated – and usually will be motivated – to defend their home country. It will be harder to motivate them to risk their lives in establishing peace between waring tribes in a faraway country;
- much teamwork and co-operation is needed in modern armies and the necessary networks cannot be established and maintained in an ever-shifting mass of conscripts.[7]

---

7 Nonetheless, the end of the conscript army has profound political, economic and social implications. Not the least among them is the establishment and legitimation of a warrior class; separated from the rest of society by very distinct attitudes and values. In the US, nearly all of the – professional – soldiers do, for instance, vote for the Republican Party. The US professional Army thus no longer reflects the bipartisan structure of the general US public.

Conscripts and professionals in today's armed forces
Total active armed forces; 1000s,

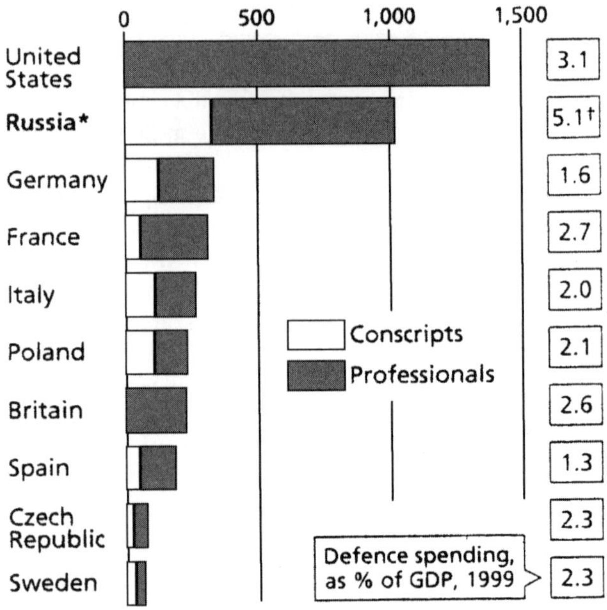

Source: IISS

The professionalisation of organised violence can even go farther, with professional soldiers being supplanted by mercenaries. These are not employed by the state, but by private entrepreneurs. Mercenaries can substitute for official armies, and they can be very successful at that. The legitimate government of Sierra Leone was safe as long as it was protected by the mercenaries of "Executive Outcomes". When these mercenaries left (and were replaced by UN forces), the rebels opposing the government advanced again.

"Privatisation" not only applies to the security provided by soldiers; but also to the internal security that, up to now, has mostly been provided by the state. This service, too, is becoming privatised at least in parts. What Max Weber has called the "state's monopoly of physical coercion" is being hollowed out. Private security services in the US now employ three times as many staff as the official police forces.

World market for private security services
(in billion USD)

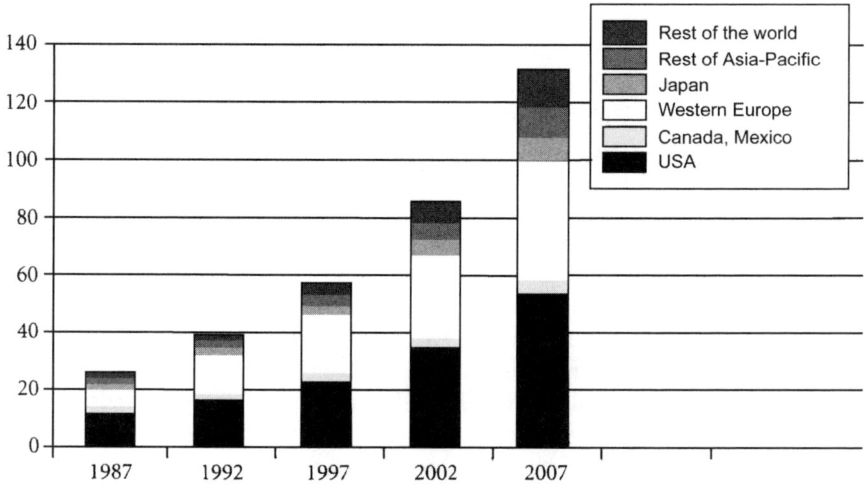

Source: Financial Times, 10 November, 2000

Not only defence against organised violence has become privatised; so has the use of this organised violence. Piracy, for example, had been a profitable private or semi-private business for centuries until it became extirpated two hundred years ago. Now it has made a come-back as a profitable private enterprise.

Privatised violence frequently takes the form of terrorism – with its acts aimed at crushing an adversary under the load of fear and insecurity. The task of fending off terrorists now tops the international agenda. That is proof – if proof was needed – that the terrorists have been largely successful in their endeavour. They have imposed their agenda upon the world. What al Qaeda or the IRA is and what it desires has become widely known as a consequence of their terrorist acts. Pressure is, therefore, on to accept such groups as valid interlocutors, notwithstanding their heinous crimes; or – possibly – because of these crimes. Terrorism works.

Hitler, Stalin and Mao still needed the power of state to create great evil... Now men and women...will be less bound by the state and need less industrial capabilities to create havoc" (Nye, 2002).[8]

In the past, much of terrorism was also state-supported. Such support has become less frequent. Today, most terrorism is the work of "diverse, free-wheeling transnational networks" that escape state control. The best known of them – of course – is al Qaeda. But there are others. In institutionally weak countries, even some sort of pseudo states have been created by brigands which gain their sustenance from the sale of raw materials that can be easily exploited and that have a high price on markets (like diamonds and cocaine).The government of Colombia, for example, has lost control over many of those patches of its territory where coca leaves are grown. These regions are now ruled by what are essentially criminal entrepreneurs who maintain their own army and police.

The borders have become fluid between such criminal groups and those terrorists who have things other than maximum income on their agenda. Columbia again can serve as an example with terrorists mixing commercial interests in drug trafficking with the political agenda of secession. This pattern is far from unique. It is, for example, repeated by some Albanian groups in Kosovo, where money from trafficking in drugs and prostitution finances secessionist terrorism. In Afghanistan, war-lords are, at the same time, entrepreneurs in drug growing and drug smuggling.

If the borders are fluid between state organised violence and non-state organised violence, the borders are fluid, too, between privatised organised violence and general non-organised violence, that is, anarchy. States can dissolve into anarchy. States can fail and such failures seem to have become more frequent in recent years. Contrary to what we were led to believe (by the so-called "realist" theory), more often than not, the danger of violent conflict arises not from the growing strength of states. Conflicts are now mainly due to the inner weakness of states; and frequently to the outright failure of states.

Many, if not most, of today's states are very young still. Many remain fragile[9]. Somalia, Sierra Leone, and Afghanistan serve as examples that such fragile new states can de-consolidate and crumble altogether. This can happen even in Europe, as was demonstrated in Bosnia and in Kosovo.

---

8 One aspect of the privatisation of violence is the widespread use of **children-soldiers.** Children are cheap (their death costs less than the death of an adult). And they can be ferocious as they have not yet learned fear and caution.

9 With artificial boundaries, for instance, imposed by colonial powers.

Being steeped in the optimistic vision of universal and irreversible progress, we have come to hold as inevitable the eventual consolidation of all states. Is this view basically correct and are "failed states", therefore, just an odd exception to a general and valid rule? Is such a decline of public order and institutions just an isolated and temporary set-back in a world-wide, unidirectional process that would make all states ever more robust?

Or might it be otherwise? Do these now more frequent failures signal a turn of the tide; a true reversal of the earlier trend? Have all states, even the most powerful ones, become meeker and more fragile? And are the poor and new states – states like Bosnia or Somalia – just the ones to feel the effects first?

Television pictures of obviously rampant and gratuitous violence; reports on the arbitrary shift of alliances between rival militias; the sheer strangeness of all might tempt us to not deal with this unpleasant question. We might prefer to believe that this problem is not ours. But there is no getting around it: the state's guarantee of internal security and its guarantee to protect against threats coming from abroad – these guarantees are becoming less credible even in places that have been havens of tranquility. Even well-run states now deliver less on their foremost promise: to quell violence within their borders.

Also, we have to accept that there are many stages of transition between fully consolidated, internally secure states and those where all public order has broken down permanently. Symptoms of an eroding authority and of a shorter reach of the state are fairly common. Crime rates soar. The police no longer enter certain districts. Corruption becomes accepted as normal and even necessary. Criminals no longer have to fear certain or even likely punishment. One no longer expects that all taxes are collected – and so on. Such common symptoms of eroding state authority may imply that quite a few live in states that are on their way to a very unpleasant future.

Outside intervention to remedy the failure of states cannot be limited to just the suppression of violence. It also has to deal with the broader social, political and economic issues, so as to break the chain of self fulfilling negative expectations in the population. This is a challenging task, as it is not easy to re-establish basic rules and security once these have disappeared completely. The twin task of assisting by humanitarian and economic aid on one side, and of assisting in establishing basic security and in creating viable institutions on the other, becomes daunting indeed.

A mor(t)al dilemma

It runs against all our instincts to concede that international humanitarian aid might become counterproductive when all order has broken down. Such assistance can fan and prolong conflict instead of dampening it. There is a distinct risk of such aid being appropriated or controlled by parties interested in pushing their side of a violent conflict. If they succeed, outside assistance will provide them with additional leverage and, thus, with less motive to end the conflict by a compromise with opponents. If threatened by starvation, a party in a violent conflict might consider negotiation and reconciliation. If fed and made comfortable through outside humanitarian aid, the party in such a violent internal conflict might be tempted not to give priority to securing a living for himself or his kin. He might prefer to oil his guns instead.

Outside intervention in crumbling states is difficult also because of the frequent lack of firm local partners and institutions. An outsider intervening in the chaos of a failed state cannot be "victorious" in the traditional sense of this word. In a situation where a clearly defined and coherent opponent does not exist, there is no one to be victorious against. When a country has dissolved as a polity, those that intervene in order to establish peace are frequently faced with a loose web of groups and warlords with uncertain and shifting alliances. Everything being fluid, there is no one outsiders can rely upon as partners in their endeavour to establish peace. Security, therefore, cannot be entrusted to someone already there. Security and order have to be created anew, bottom up. Intervention and the task of peacemaking, thus, automatically expands into the difficult and thankless task of nation building.

Whoever intervenes, therefore, must be aware of entering a costly and risky venture with no prospects of easy and early exit. Whoever enters will have to assume supreme responsibility. And he will have to do so for quite some time. Inevitably, thus, many of these interventions will, in fact, re-establish the institution of the "protectorate". It was considered a thing of the past, relegated to the dustbin of history by human progress and by the termination of colonialism/imperialism. But, in its substance, the institution of the "protectorate" has now returned and is alive and well – for example in Iraq, Afghanistan, Kosovo and in Bosnia-Herzegovina. The problem is that there are few volunteers for the role of the "protector" as this role involves high material and political costs and few rewards. As the US will come to appreciate, it will have to assume full responsibility in Iraq after having conquered the country. The expenses could be three to four times higher than the cost of the war that ended with the occupation of Iraq. In the worst case, the costs of a "quasi-protectorate" in Iraq could even reach 600 billion US dollars – or nearly 10 percent of the US GDP.[10]

Estimates of Direct, Indirect and Follow-Up Costs to the US of a War with Iraq (in billion US dollars)

		Low	High
Direct military spending		50	140
Follow-on costs	Occupation + peacekeeping	75	500
	Reconstruction, nation building	25	100
	Humanitarian assistance	1	10
	Impact on oil markets	-30	500
	Macroeconomic impact	0	345
	TOTAL	121	1,595

Source: W. Nordhaus, New York Review of Books, Dec.2002

Given the high costs and burden, it might very well be that no state or group of states is willing to shoulder them. It therefore might happen that some countries – like Congo/Zaire or Somalia – are simply written off and left to simmer in their misery with the international community just providing a minimum of humanitarian aid and trying to prevent such conflicts and their consequences from radiating into neighbouring states and regions.

Conclusion number one: The question of organised violence and of the defence against it remain on the agenda. The issue cannot be wished away or hidden behind the veil of overly optimistic assumptions about human nature and global order. Warding off organised violence remains a basic function of the nation state – indeed it still is its most BASIC function. But today, organised violence does not emanate mainly from states with effective and representative governments. And frequently, too, the ensuing problems can be dealt with only in cooperation with various other nations; or – on the other hand – by delegating the use of counterforce to a lower level. Thus, in this realm also, governments are yielding power either upwards – to a community of states; or downwards – to private or semi-private actors.

This poses problems for democracy; for, in this crucial field, who controls and legitimises these actors below and above the state level?

10 At present (July 2003) the cost of the military occcupation amounts to about 5 billion US dollars per month.

Conclusion number two: Changing technology and economic development have impacted upon, and changed, the advantages and disadvantages of both the powerful and the meek. As a result, both sides – the very powerful and the very meek – are now readier to use organised violence. And, while organised violence between consolidated, wealthy states has become very rare, we must expect it to remain common on the intra-state level, and in the confrontation of states with non-state groups.

Conclusion number three: threat – the declared willingness of an opponent to use organised violence – is but one element in a wider spectrum of risks a state has to ward off. These risks have increased with increasing wealth and with increasing globalisation. A security policy (be it on the national or on the international level) has to deal with all of them.

Main sources of risk

	Idiosyncratic	**Covariant**	
Type of risk	**Risks affecting an individual or household (micro)**	**Risks affecting groups of households or communities (meso)**	**Risks affecting regions or nations (macro)**
Natural		Rainfall Landslide Volcanic eruption	Earthquake Flood Drought High winds
Health	Illness Injury Disability Old age Death	Epidemic	
Social	Crime Domestic violence	Terrorism Gang activity	Civil strife War Social upheaval
Economic	Unemployment Resettlement Harvest failure	Changes in food prices	Growth collapse Hyperinflation Balance of payments, financial, or currency crisis Technology shock Terms of trade shock Transition costs of economic reforms
Political		Riots	Political default on social programs Coup d'état
Environmental		Pollution Deforestation Nuclear disaster	

Source: Adapted from Sinha and Lipton (1999) and World Bank (2000q)

But with this, let us return once more to the question of terrorism. Psychologically and in terms of strategic counter-measures, it was fairly easy to grasp the notion of another state having become the "enemy"; and fairly easy, too, to devise and politically "sell" the strategies against the threats emanating from this state. But how to react politically against the organised violence of terrorism?

If need there was, 11 September 2001 has convinced us of the vulnerability of complex modern societies. The collapsing twin towers of the New York World Trade Center have come to stand as a symbol for that. We have also come to realise that the same, or a very similar disaster could occur any time again[11]. Living with such fears and uncertainties is not facile. A heinous enemy could be everywhere: with other countries; with people of a different skin or creed; or even with the neighbours across the street. Obviously, such preoccupations heighten general distrust. They strain relations between states, religions, and even between the citizens of one and the same country. They thus weaken the international as well as the national polity.

Quite naturally, citizens will react. They will request a maximum of protection; and perhaps even pre-emptive action against potential evil doers. They will charge their states and their political representatives with reducing such dangers to the extent humanly possible. They will accept and even demand full social, economic and political mobilisation against these new forms of organised violence. Seeing such calls heeded by politicians will provide them with at least some comfort. They will accept and even welcome the notion of a "war against terrorism". And the politicians pandering such a notion will certainly gain in public approval and public standing. It used to be that politicians were charged by the electorate with keeping at bay their potentially intrusive state so as to preserve a maximum of liberty. This might now become reversed. Politicians might gain favour by making their own state much more intrusive.

But such a "war against terrorism" is not like any other war. In a war, the enemy is clearly defined. Not so in the so called war against terrorism. In a classical war, one usually knows the whereabouts of the opponent. This is not so in the "war on terrorism". Classical wars usually end with a clear victory of one side and clear defeat on the other. Not so in the war against terrorism. Has al Qaeda been vanquished? Does the term victory even have any meaning in this context? In a classical war, one state can go it alone, provided it is strong and resourceful enough. In the so called "war against terrorism", marked success is only feasible with the support of a very broad coalition of states and other international actors.

11 One has to credit US politicians with not sparing the public that unpleasant, tragic truth.

In a classical war, one or both sides usually have a rational, tangible goal: a slice of territory, the dismantling of the war machine of the enemy, or a change in the regime of the opponent; etc. Terrorists frequently lack such goals. Their fight might be a goal in itself – because it is glorious; leads directly into heaven; or, more mundanely, because it offers an exciting and well remunerated way of life. Such terrorists fight because the fight counts and not its results. If such is the case, one cannot terminate that fight by coming to an agreement about a possible end-result of the confrontation, as the terrorists are not motivated by the aim of achieving a certain end-result.

Or, alternatively, they might very well wish to attain certain tangible results. But such results could not be accommodated within the existing world order (as, for example, the desire to return to a religiously homogeneous, theocratic state).

It is therefore misleading to use the term "war" for efforts to contain and eliminate the threat of terrorism. This so called "war" is more akin to a vast and international police action. What it has in common with war, nonetheless, is a massive – also emotional – mobilisation. Quite a number of very different weapons will have to be thrown into this fight; and this fight has to be waged on many levels and in many locations. Such a mobilisation will be accepted and even demanded by citizens. But one should be aware of the connected costs. If terrorists were to stage two or three other spectacular actions, akin to their attack on the World Trade Center – the police would be granted far reaching powers everywhere. Fingerprinting would become common, remote control cameras ubiquitous and connected in one vast computer supported network. Electronic scanning for face recognition would become routine at places where masses gather. Most probably, the powers of police to detain and to interrogate would also be expanded. Non co-operating states would come under massive pressure; and borders would become much more relevant in the world which nowadays is often[12] perceived as having reduced the height of the walls separating one state from another. The prime task of any state is to provide physical security to its citizens. If the chips are down, other aspirations and political tasks will become sacrificed to this prime goal.

---

12 Quite erroneously though. Borders are still very important and probably more so than they were a hundred years ago.

The Notion of Progress; and How to Measure Progress

On the future of mankind dire predictions predominate. They have gained wider credibility and acceptance than more optimistic views. We have dealt with some of those sombre claims about what were alleged to be insurmountable hurdles on the future path of mankind: the explosive growth of the world's population; scarcity of water, of raw materials and of energy; environmental degradation; the decay and the disappearance of the communal; etc.

Since the beginning of the 19th century, the process of change and transformation has been frantic. Change has not only been massive in quantitative terms. It also transformed the quality of human society – the way communal existence on the planet is organised. But, in the course of our investigation, we have also come to appreciate that such developments are not blind forces that push and move along a passive human population. Such developments impact upon societies. But societies react and may influence, shape and direct these developments. If populations grow too fast, societies react by curtailing this growth. If too much energy is consumed, the price of energy rises and this then reduces the amount of energy being used. If the environment becomes degraded and if people suffer therefrom, the ecological errors and sins are being corrected and the quality of the environment is improved again; etc.

In the global system, and in the future evolution of this system, very little is truly inevitable. What is decisive, in the end, are less the physical constraints of limited space or resources. What truly makes a difference is the nature of the human reaction. And reaction there was. In that sense, a global governance does exist already. Societies have adjusted again and again to external constraints. They have effectively changed a good number of such external constraints. The first question we will therefore investigate is whether these attempts at governance – in its widest sense – have paid off? Was there "progress"?

As any concept, the notion of progress, too, is a social construct or discourse. "De-constructivists" suggest that any "discourse" is shaped and imposed by those who are in power at each phase of history. "De-constructivists" have a point. Indeed, they could demonstrate that the notion of "progress", too, has been coloured by the needs and preferences of the powerful. In the time of European imperialism, for example, the then prevailing notion of "progress" did accommodate the interest of the imperial rulers. As these rulers defined it, progress would demand the intervention of their countries in far-away colonies and in them shouldering "the white man's burden"; their accomplishing a "mission civilisatrice".

But, if a dominant and generally accepted discourse cannot be dissociated from power, neither can it be dissociated from reality[1]. For "discourse" is also and mainly a tool – a linguistic tool – to deal with this real environment. As all tools, it would be discarded if it were not useful in the completion of a task. A discourse becomes established because it responds, in a useful[2] manner, to reality.

As we mentioned before, it is not just an accident which can determine which of the various possible discourses becomes "dominant". Neither can it be determined solely by the group which is the most powerful at each instant of history. If the discourse about the sun circling the earth has disappeared, it is for other reasons. This discourse of the sun revolving about the earth has not been useful. To mankind, it has not provided a useful tool to deal with the practical problems it has to solve.

The notion of "progress" is widely accepted. It is tacitly implied in much of what we do. We become active because we believe that it is possible to improve our lot. And we become active collectively because we believe that it is also possible to permanently improve the lot of a political community. This implies that the notion of progress has been generally accepted; and it had been accepted because it has proven to be useful. Why is this so? Why has the concept been helpful in dealing with reality? In searching for an answer, we have to deal with two questions. The first one pertains to the notion that history follows a long-term forward and upward trend. The second question is on how we may define and measure this upward and forward trend that we term progress.

In a society that does not change, the notion of progress is pointless. In humanity's more distant past, the mode of production remained the same for centuries. Agriculture was the predominant activity. Life repeated itself unchanged. The future of humankind was, therefore, seen as the mere prolongation of the present. Or, as the repetition of the same cycle. At such times, and under such circumstances, the notion of history being flat or cyclical was an appropriate one. At such times and circumstances, it would have been in vain – and perhaps even dangerous – to uphold the opposite notion and to propagate the idea that soci-

1 Let us concur with the perhaps naive notion that such a thing as "reality" does exist.

2 One might perhaps ask: "useful to whom"; and might suggest that it would suffice if it were useful just to those in power. As mentioned, power relations certainly impact upon whether or not a certain type of discourse becomes generally accepted. But the claim strains credulity that it could be simply imposed in total liberty and irrespective of the perception of the general public, provided that those who impose it are sufficiently mighty (see also chapter 1).

ety's fate could be improved radically and permanently; and that each individual would be under moral obligations to contribute to such a broad transformation of the existing order. Such attempts would have run up against the wall of un-changed and un-changeable material circumstances. Under these unchanging circumstances, under the limits imposed by unchanged and unchangeable methods of production, happiness and self-fulfilment were not to be found in vain attempts to alter the system as such. Happiness and fulfilment resided in the passive acceptance of the circumstances as they were; and in accepting as immutable one's station in life and in the social pecking order. [3]

So, to put this graphically: in pre-modern times – history would be seen as being "flat"

time

Or it would have been seen as a repetition of the same cycle.

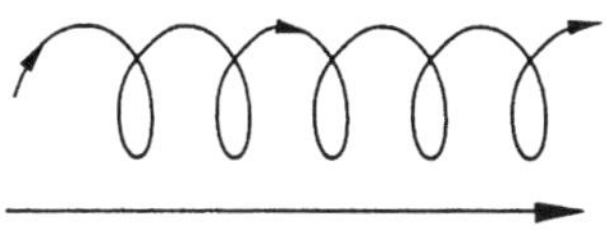

time

As mentioned – as all such notions – this notion of a flat or cyclical history was a "social construct" or a "prevailing discourse". It was accepted because it provided orientation in an environment that was basically stagnant; or that changed at a pace too slow for such changes to be perceptible to observers who could record just their own life experience; and that of a few generations that had preceded their own.

However, with the full onset of industrialisation, societies and their material base entered a phase of deep and rapid transformation. Under such changed circumstances, the notion of history being flat or cyclical lost its usefulness. Consequently, the "paradigm" of a flat or cyclical history was supplanted by the notion

3 This – in essence – is the main message that comes to us from oriental religions, especially from Buddhism and Hinduism.

of society moving forwards and upwards; with each technological innovation and/or addition of new productive capital being a step in a staircase leading towards a better world.

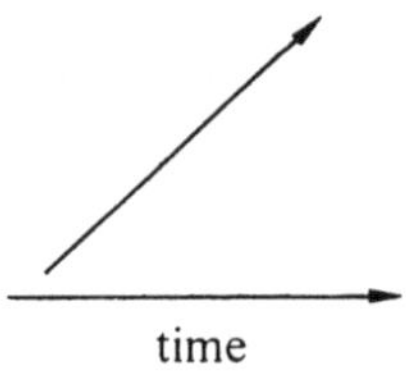

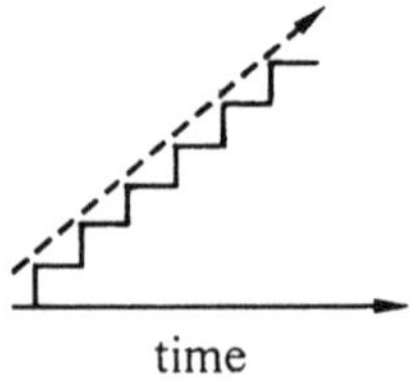

Later on, still, it became difficult to ignore the reversals, conflicts and contradictions that encumbered this "upward and forward" movement. Acknowledging them imposed yet another "change of paradigm". Conflict and contradiction was now assumed to be inherent in the process of "progress". Accordingly, the course of history was now seen as being "dialectic". Action would be followed by reaction; projects by counter-projects. But, ultimately, such conflicts and contradictions would become resolved by a new "synthesis"; with each succeeding synthesis being on a higher level than the previous one had been. This then was the "dialectic" version of "progress" as promulgated by Hegel and Marx.

Progress has been compared to biological evolution.[4] Indeed the two might be similar inasmuch as both are, in essence, processes of learning. Species "learn" by adapting their genetic material. Humans and human societies learn by adapting culture. This is a cumulative process. It takes the form of a "J" curve, as in societies the information contained in culture accumulates in a geometric and not in a linear fashion.

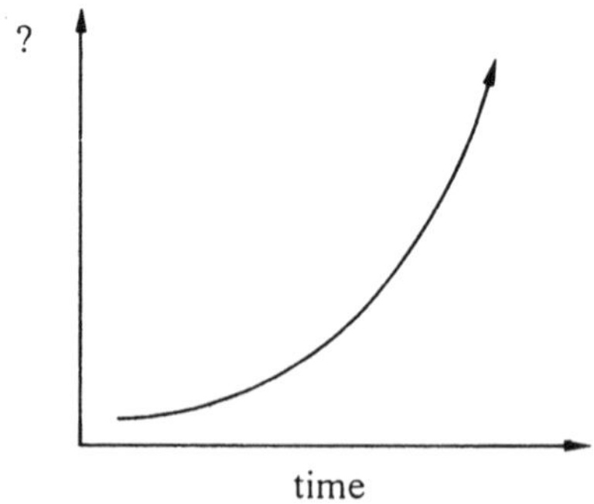

4 And this parallel with the evolution of species has certainly very much coloured the thinking in the late 19th century.

If we try to look into the very distant future, this perspective might change again. At the risk of becoming highly abstract and speculative, we may imagine that, instead of becoming ever more steep, the upward slope of the "J" might start to bend downward again; and – ultimately – the "J" might turn into an "S". This would occur when certain bounds are approached that limit developments in most spheres of biological or human existence. Nonetheless, and on the contrary, it might also be that the trajectory of the "J" transports us into new realms where totally new laws apply; into realms no longer endiked by physical restraints; where human freedom becomes the problem instead of the problems being posed by limits to this freedom. We will follow through on this argument – or speculation – in the last two chapters of this book.

One thing is obvious, though. However vaguely held and defined, the notion of "progress" is a broad one. It covers up, or fails to account for, failures and reversals; for very uneven developments among the many participants of the global system; and for very uneven developments in the many different spheres of this system. It is therefore not very useful to conceive of progress as a kind of straight and narrow path; or as one single movement. It results from many different movements that have added up to a pattern of the highest statistic probability. "Progress" becomes the net sum of numerous "progresses".

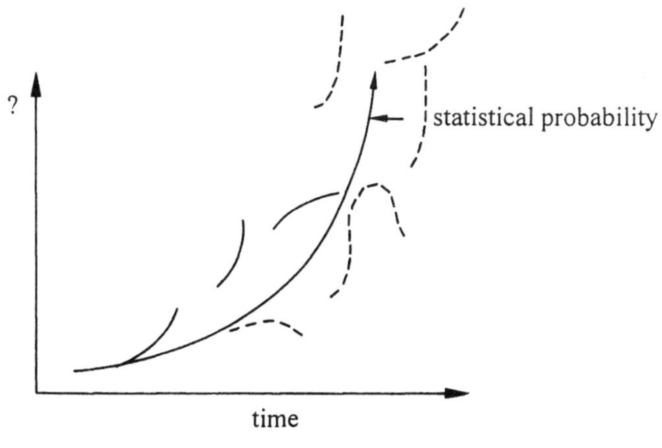

Or does it? Do we have to become more agnostic still? Is the variance in the movements of these many constituent parts so wide as to annihilate any clear pattern and clear line?

In the late part of the nineteenth century, "progress" had become the dominant metaphor, the dominant discourse. This had its counterpart in reality. As we have seen, in the second half of the nineteenth century, innovation and technological advance accelerated in an unprecedented fashion. Hence, this self-confidence. In the subsequent century, however, two World Wars and the holocaust eroded such confidence. After Auschwitz, can one still believe mankind to be set on a path of ever greater perfection? Can one still assume that the various "progresses" in all those different realms would statistically add up to an overall pattern of improvement in the human condition?[5]

Such sombre queries are, as it seems, the preserve of academics and intellectuals. Unlike them, the wider public retains a basic confidence in this seemingly outdated notion of human progress. It does so because of simple, solid and persuasive evidence. Living longer and being healthier is seen as being better than dying soon and being ill. Knowing more is seen as being better than knowing less. Being wealthy and having enough to eat is appreciated as a better fate than being poor and hungry; and so on.

Malnutrition falls as average income rises (Under-five malnutrition rate and per capita GNI, 2000)

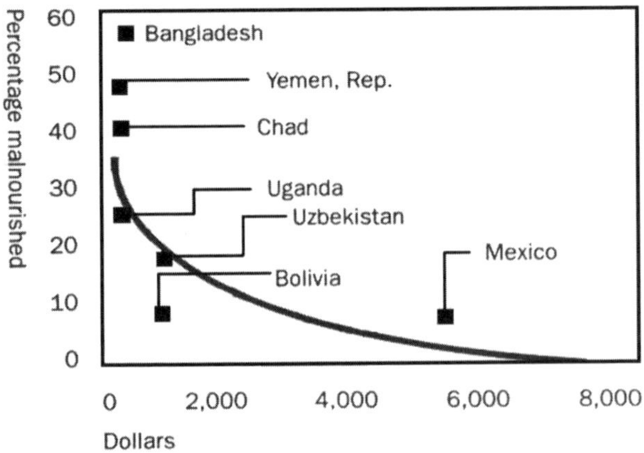

Source: UNICEF

---

5 One could argue that the notion of possible improvement is essential for human communities to survive, and argue that, if no betterment seems plausible, human action would become futile. There are two answers to that. One realistic – biological; and one philosophical – abstract. The biological is simple. We live because we live and do not want to die. We are active to support our own life and that of our community because we are genetically programmed that way. If it were otherwise, the species homo sapiens would have become extinct. The philosophical answer is that of stoicism: you do what you have to do, even if it is futile in the end.

It is simply impossible to ignore that – over the course of history – an ever greater share of humankind has been able to achieve such goals that are, more or less, automatically accepted as being worthwhile. That sustains this popular, if perhaps vague, notion of progress.

Nonetheless, recurrent waves of romanticism have discounted such gains as a sham and irrelevant. Instead they have cultivated the vision of a joyful return to an idealised past [6]. The notion of the noble, carefree and happy savage is usually part of such a romantic counter-world. But this world is the preserve of those privileged, coddled and bored by their good life; those that are sure that such excursions into the past would imply no personal risks – the return ticket for them being always assured. There is Queen Marie Antoinette, before being beheaded, impersonating a simple shepherdess at the fake hamlet (hameau) near their palace in Versailles. There is Thoreau playing the piano in his log cabin at Walden pond. There are also more violent counter-trends as, for instance, Nazism seeking salvation in a return of the German "Volk" to its roots in pre-medieval Teutonic tribes.

Such, more or less, periodic counter-trends point to unease and insufficiencies in our societies. But, till now, they have failed to rupture the persistent belief of the majority of humans who stick to the notion that, in the normal course of events, things will become better.[7] As it cannot be otherwise, the vague but all permeating notion of "progress" is socially defined. Yet, it is a notion and/or "discourse" not just established by those in power. It is widely accepted because it is deemed useful. The discourse has been accepted because the vast majority of humankind agreed on the basic message of past and possible future human improvement. It is convinced that such an improvement has indeed come about in areas it cares for.

With this we turn to the second part of our question: "if progress exists, how to gauge it?" What evidence exists for this still very general notion of "progress"? Against which criteria should one measure it? Should one measure it as progress in possessions; in culture; in wisdom; in morality?

Let us start with what is easy to measure: namely the amount of goods and services available for consumption. If measured by the volume of output of such

---

6 In no way does this imply a rejection of all criticism directed at modernity and at the post-industrial social order. And, of course, any such criticism of modern society does need to base itself on some notion of more "natural" human arrangements. What I am firm about, though, is the necessity of moving forward instead of yielding to the urge to move backwards into the presumed innocence of earlier times.

7 That holds true, too, for the "68-revolt". It has not broken the basic faith in progress; and, in fact, it has left few permanent traces; fewer certainly that the romantic revolution of the early 19th century.

goods and services, humankind has experienced much progress indeed (as shown in the tables in the first chapters on the growth of the world economy). Nonetheless, there might be a bit less to it than meets the eye. For what we measure in such statistics are the goods and services produced for the market. To a certain extent, the rise in the volume of goods and services produced for the market just substitutes for a decline in goods and services that had been produced by households and communities for internal consumption, without being sold and bought on markets. We therefore have to subtract these disappearing productions from what is produced for the market. The net is thus smaller than the gross.

"Das hat der Fortschritt so an sich,
dass er immer kleiner war als er
ausgschaut hat"

"Well that is in its very nature:
progress always seems greater than it actually is"
(Nestroy)

Over the last decades, the big political debate was over "state versus private":

The "big debate" state versus private

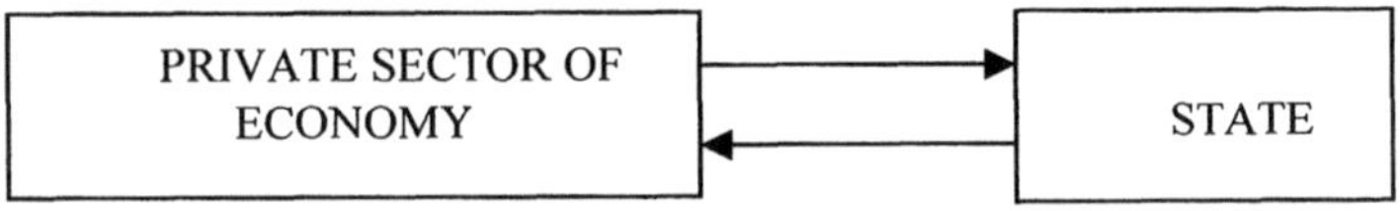

But that debate covers just a part of the ground. As mentioned, goods and services are not only produced by the state and the private sector of the economy. They were, and still are, also produced by the households and by the organisations of civil society. Originally, even the majority of economic activities was carried out in households and informal community groups.

The division of economic tasks before the onset of industrialisation

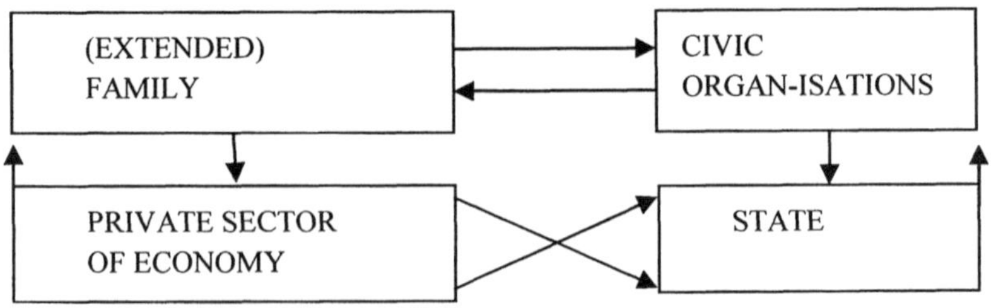

Modernisation brought a shift. Both the households and the organisations of civil society lost functions. These were transferred to the state and to the private economic sector. The state was to produce those goods and services which are difficult to rationalise (like education, health care, public order); whereas the private sector was to offer those goods and services, the production of which is easy to rationalise (like industrial production, financial transactions, trading).[8] The true debate should, therefore, not just concern the division of economic tasks between "state" and "private" but the division between all four of these entities.

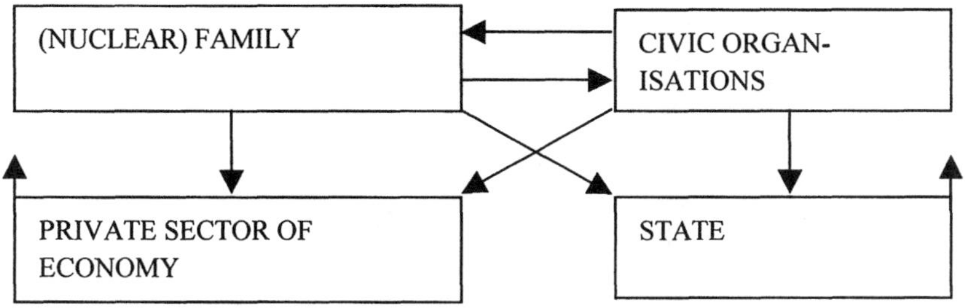

The table below catches a bit of that. In less "modern" societies, a non-negligible part of the income of the poor does not come from lowly paid work; or from state transfers; but from relatives and friends. The more "modern" a state, the more meagre, however, the material support provided by relatives and friends.

8 As a consequence, the services of the state are becoming costlier compared to the services and goods provided by the private sector. This is the "cost disease" of the public sector (Baumol). We shall return to this issue in the chapter on the future of the state.

Income share of the poorest quintile before and after having received private transfers
(mid 90es)

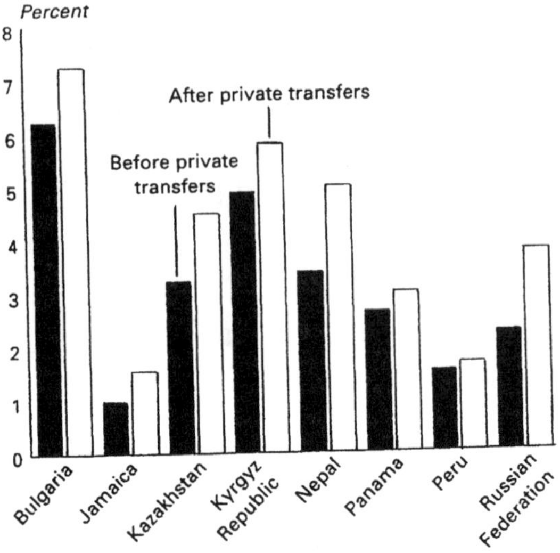

Note: Quintiles are based on per capita income distribution. Transfers are those accruing to the poor. Data are for most recent year available.

Source: Cox, Galasso, and Jimenez 2000

This shift of economic activity away from families and informal communities continues and shows no sign of abating. Services that two generations ago were still produced in households are now procured on the market or offered by the state. Retired persons that used to live with their families no longer do, but have settled in special quarters or homes that are either run on a "for profit basis" or by the state. In households of singles the oven is now mostly used for storage. Dinner is either ready-made and just heated in the micro-wave; or bought at a restaurant[9].

How have these shifts affected the individual, the quality of life and society as such? Overall, the increasing specialisation and division of labour has permitted a

9 My mother still used to bake the birthday cakes herself. My wife uses ready made cake mix; my daughter buys the cake – deep frozen – in the super market.

steady increase in productivity[10]. More is being produced at lower cost. More can therefore be consumed. But something has been lost in the process: not just the material value of the services and goods that had been produced in households and autonomous communities[11]; but also some autonomy, skill, and self esteem. Anarchists and conservative reactionaries join romantics in the belief that this shift away from households and from autonomous groups has diminished humans. A cleric – Ivan Illich – even thought it a mistake to have transferred the responsibility for education and health care from families and grown communities to the state. The quality of such services would have been better if they still were rendered in the traditional way[12].

As Nestroy has claimed, even if measured in purely material terms, progress has thus, indeed, been slower than it appears to be. If some non-material aspects are taken into account, it has been slower still. Nonetheless, I will argue that the growth in the world GDP has brought positive results overall; and I shall argue, furthermore, that – by and large – wealth, as measured by per capita GDP, is still useful in gauging all aspects of this progress. This is because growth in per capita GDP correlates with the attainment of many other gains humans wish to realise.

Health is certainly very important among these aims. Already in the 19th century, rising material wealth went along with significant advances in medical science and sanitation; and, thus, with it longer life.

10 Though – as we have seen – this benefit was unevenly shared between the public sector and the private sector; with the private sector reaping the main benefit.

11 Perhaps one should substitute the more modern – if not overly precise – concept of "civic society".

12 There might be a counter-trend in growing "self service"; in "homeworking"; in "doing it yourself", in gardening. Yet, these counter-trends remain isolated and less powerful, overall, than the general trend away from families and informal communities. By and large and on the average, we shall doubtlessly continue to exchange personal autonomy for greater material wealth.

Life expectancy in the UK

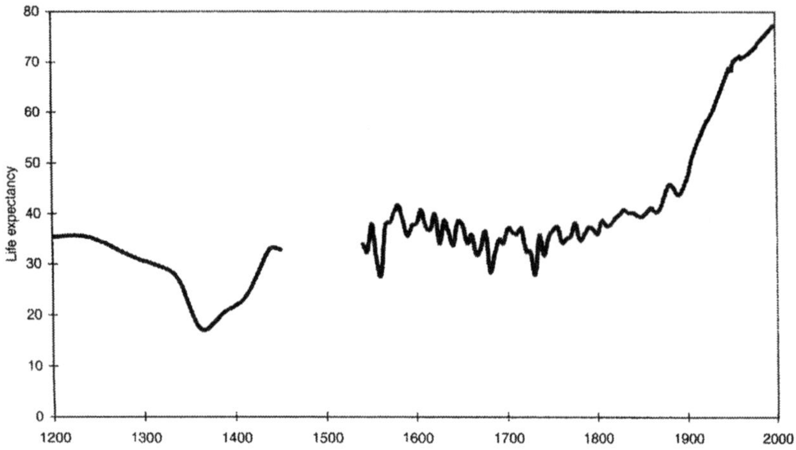

Source: Lomborg 2002

Growing wealth is based – of course – on a steep rise in the production of goods. The price to pay for this is a more intense use of resources; some of which are not renewable. These are, so to say, withdrawals from the stock of common endowment. One can subtract such withdrawals from the stock of monetary savings accumulated by economic growth; and arrive at "adjusted net savings". But, as the table below demonstrates, even the "adjusted savings" grow with higher wealth.

Adjusted net savings Percentage of GDP

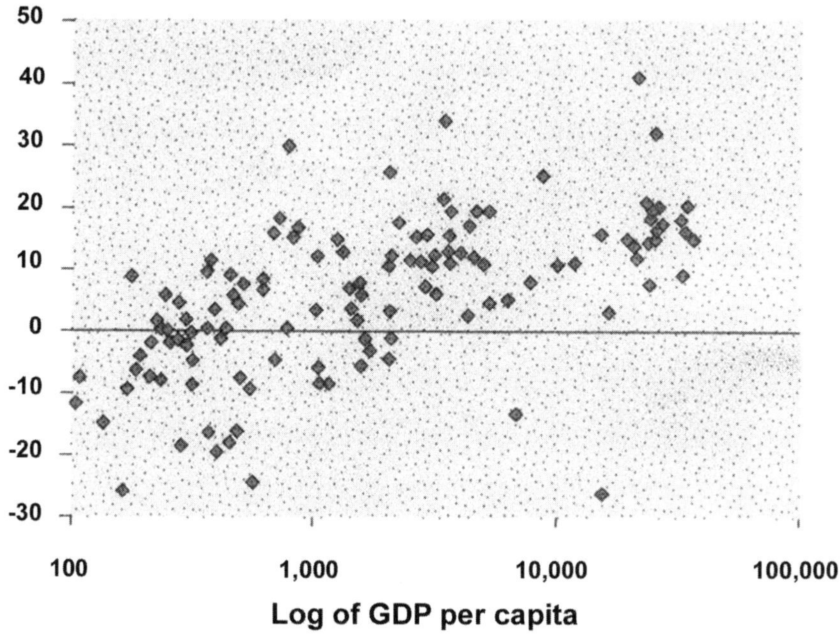

Source: World Bank 2001h

Greater wealth also coincides with the reduction of at least some noxious habits – like smoking.

Annual consumption of cigarettes by adults 1971, 1981, 1991

WHO-Region	*1971* *Number*	*1981*	*1991*	*Change in %* *1971-1991*
Europe	2,360	2,500	2,340	0.0
Western Pacific	1,100	1,610	2,010	3.0
North and South America	2,580	2,510	1,900	-1.5
South East Asia	850	1,140	1,230	1.8
Eastern Mediterranean	700	940	930	1.4
Africa	460	570	590	1.2

Source : WHO

Rising wealth created conditions that facilitate the emancipation of women.

Ratio of female to male literacy rate
Average, 1990-98

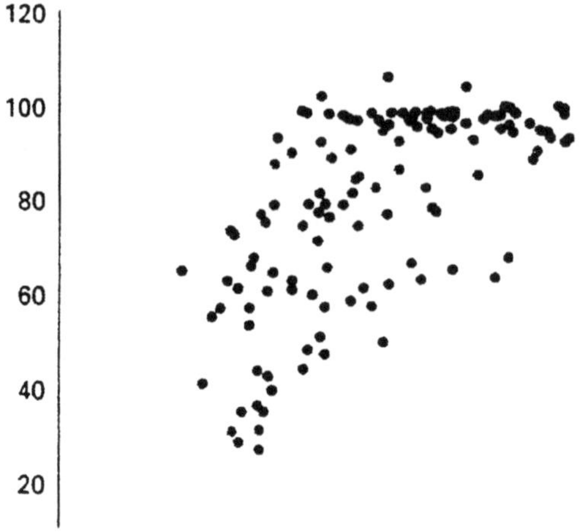

Source: World Bank

As wealth rises corruption recedes. The table below gives proof by relating the "Corruption Perception Index" to per capita income.

In the Corruption Perception Index of Transparency International, the highest grades go to those countries that are seen as being least corrupt. These are, at the same time and in general, those which are most wealthy.

Corruption and GNI per capita

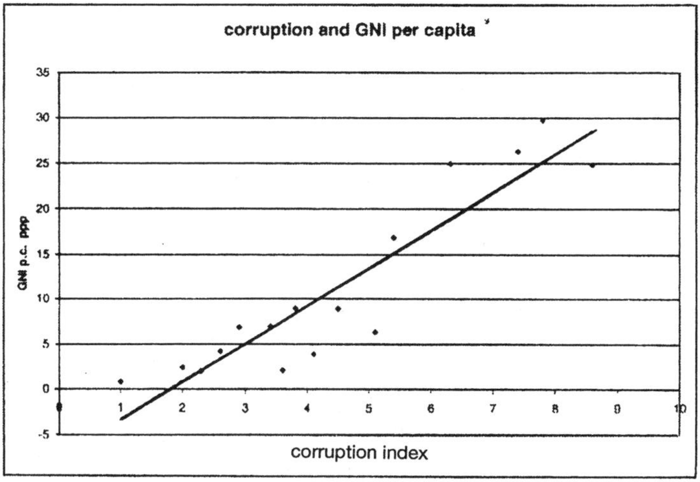

Source: Transparency International and World Bank

Wealth permits societies to secure for its elders well-funded retirement. It also enables societies to fund other measures of social protection. Poor countries do not have the money to pay for such things. Wealthy countries have.

Total social security expenditures as percentage of GDP
Selected regions; 1974-1992

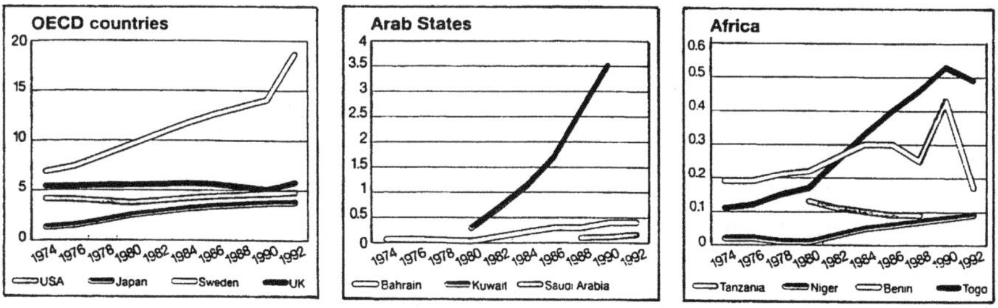

Source: IBRD

Other benefits of increased wealth and modernity[13] are less material. Here are examples of some not immediately material benefits. Rising wealth goes together with:

a) the decline of physical cruelty (intra family violence, infanticide, public executions);
b) democracy (more about that later)
c) personal liberty and scope for individual choice[14]
d) leisure
e) access to information and knowledge
f) tolerance
g) the luxury of being a child and of being young
h) the luxury of personal warmth in conjugal relations

Critics may concede that all this might be true. But it still would make little sense to measure "wealth" by GDP figures. The GDP (Gross Domestic Product) is the sum of all goods and services produced in a country. Everything that increases this volume thus increases GDP and with it – allegedly – wealth. But, obviously, the volume of goods and services is also being increased by things that contribute very little to true wealth: a car accident augments GDP – while avoiding accidents has no such effect. Wasting raw materials augments the GDP, saving on raw materials does not. Crime increases GDP; whereas law abiding behaviour does not. Critics thus have called for alternate gauges that avoid such absurdities and that should measure true wealth much better than the figures of GDP.

Several such gauges have been proposed and used:

One such index is the "Genuine Progress Indicator – GPI". Its aim is to measure "Sustainable Welfare". Unlike the index on the Gross Domestic Product, it does include the work and the products that are made in and by households and by various voluntary organisations. It also subtracts from material wealth the costs of destroyed natural habitats and costs of other environmental degradation. It includes, as mere costs and subtraction from wealth, crime, family breakdown and an unequal distribution of income.

---

13 The two movements are NOT identical; yet, while they might diverge in the short or medium term, they still are mutually contingent and usually run parallel.

14 Those who yearn for a return to the rural innocence of some "Walden pond" would do well to explore how rural life had been portrayed by those that suffered it; like, for instance, the Spanish writer Llorca; or the Austrian writer Innerhofer: its pettiness combined with ruthlessness and brutality, its wallowing in prejudice and willed ignorance. Thoreau had a piano at Walden pond. Very few rurals do.

According to this "Genuine Progress Indicator" (GPI), and if measured in its terms, "true wealth" has not grown in the US. Genuine progress has co-evolved with rising wealth up to the seventies only. Since then, the GDP has continued to rise, while well-being, as measured by the GPI, has declined.[15]

Another indicator also purports to show that – at least in the US – things have gone downhill since the seventies, instead of always becoming better. This is the "Index of Social Health" by Fordham University. It puts a heavy, negative weight on developments like family break-ups, crime rates, inequality etc.

Index of Social Health and Gross Domestic Product 1959-96

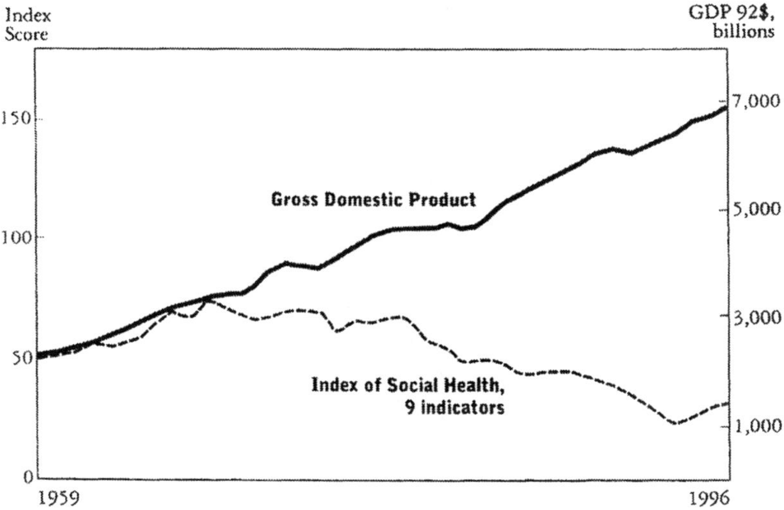

Source: Fordham Institute of Innovation on Social Policy

Alternatively, one can compose an index that just measures the ecological sustainability of the actual behaviour and the actual policies of various countries. It prominently neglects all other aspects of poverty or wealth and just reflects the effectiveness of policies in preserving and restoring the environment. This is done with the "Environmental Sustainability Index".[16]

15 This result of the GPI is probably due to the very high negative values it assigns to the use of natural resources and especially to the depletion of Carbon Dioxide "sinks". As we have seen in preceding chapters, this high emphasis is probably not wholly justified.

16 The index suffers from the lack of reliable data for many environmental indicators.

Environmental Sustainability Index

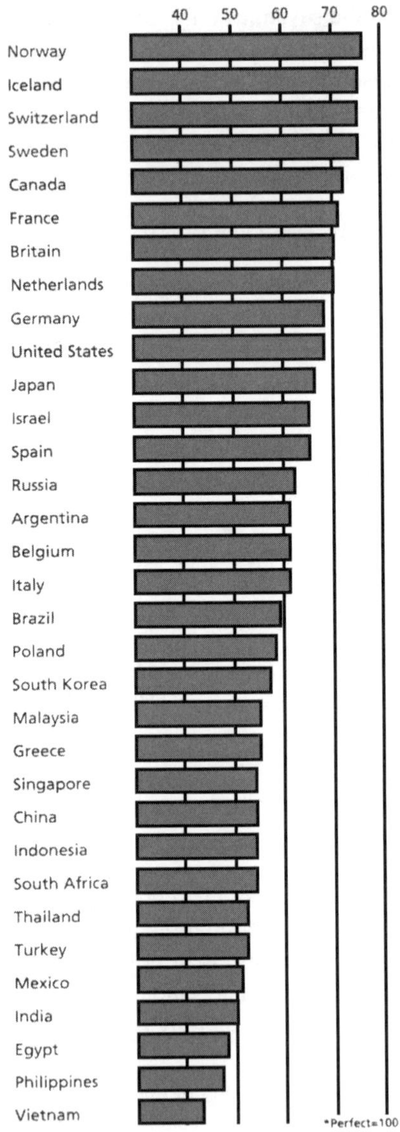

Source: Yale Centre for Environmental Law and Policy

The ranking in this Environmental Sustainability Index is surprising. One would assume that the poorest countries, those least touched by modernity and industrialisation, have the most unspoilt and least endangered environment. But the opposite is true. The wealthiest countries do best in this respect.

The most commonly used Index for measuring "true" wealth and progress is the HDI - Human Development Index published in the annual Human Development Report of the UNDP. Unlike the Environmental Sustainability Index it does count material wealth. But it counts wealth not in nominal terms (that is converted at the official exchange rates), but in purchasing power (PPP) terms. That drastically improves the position of poor countries, as – generally – most goods and services necessary for daily life are much cheaper in poorer than in richer countries. But next to PPP gauged wealth, the index also includes the data on life expectancy at birth, adult literacy and enrolment rates in primary, secondary, and tertiary education.

If one compares the wealth as traditionally measured by (nominal) per capita GDP with the "true" wealth as measured by the Human Development Index, one will find that countries with the same nominal per capita GDP can be quite a distance apart in true wealth as measured by the HDI; and vice versa.

Thailand, for example, has the same HDI value as has Saudi Arabia, which, however, is twice as wealthy as Thailand in terms of nominal per capita GDP.

The table below gives the HDI country ranking:

Human Development Index

HDI rank	HDI rank		HDI rank
High human development	Medium human development		Law human development
1. Norway	54. Mexico	99. Jordan	138. Pakistan
2. Sweden	55. Cuba	100. Cape Verde	139. Sudan
3. Canada	56. Belarus	101. Samoa	140. Bhutan
4. Belgium	57. Panama	102. Kyrgyzstan	141. Togo
5. Australia	58. Balize	103. Guyana	142. Nepal
6. United States	59. Malaysia	104. El Salvador	143. Lao Peoples Dem. Rep.
7. Iceland	60. Russian Federation	105. Moldova	144. Yemen
8. Netherlands	61. Dominica	106. Algeria	145. Bangladesh
9. Japan	62. Bulgaria	107. South Africa	146. Haiti
10. Finnland	63. Romania	108. Syrian Arab Republic	147. Madagascar
11. Switzerland	64. Lybian Arab Jamahirya	109. Viet Nam	148. Nigeria
12. France	65. Macedonia FYR	110. Indonesia	149. Djibouti
13. United Kingdom	66. Saint Lucia	111. Equatorial Guinea	150. Uganda
14. Denmark	67. Mauritius	112. Tajikistan	151. Tanzania
15. Austria	68. Colombia	113. Mongola	152. Mauritania
16. Luxembourg	69. Venezuela	114. Bolivia	153. Zambia
17. Germany	70. Thailand	115. Egypt	154. Senegal
18. Ireland	71. Saudi Arabia	116. Honduras	155. Congo, Dem. Rep. of
19. New Zealand	72. Fiji	117. Gabon	156. Cote d'Ivoire
20. Italy	73. Brazil	118. Nicaragua	157. Eritrea
21. Spain	74. Suriname	119. Sao Tone and Principe	158. Benin
22. Israel	75. Lebanon	120. Guatemala	159. Guinea
23. Hong Kong China SAR	76. Armenia	121. Solomon Islands	160. Gambia
24. Greece	77. Philippine	122. Namibia	161. Angola
25. Singapore	78. Oman	123. Marocco	162. Rwanda
26. Cyprus	79. Kazakhstan	124. India	163. Malawi
27. Korea, Rep. of	80. Ukraine	125. Swaziland	164. Mali
28. Portugal	81. Georgia	126. Botswana	165. Central African Republic
29. Slovenia	82. Peru	127. Myanmar	166. Chad
30. Malta	83. Grenada	128. Zimbabwe	167. Guinea-Bissau
31. Barbados	84. Maldives	129. Ghana	168. Ethiopia
32. Brunei	85. Turkey	130. Cambodia	169. Burkina Faso
33. Czech Republic	86. Jamaica	131. Vanuata	170. Mozambique
34. Argentina	87. Turkmen-istan	132. Letsotho	171. Burundi
35. Hungary	88. Azerbaijan	133. Papua New Guinea	172. Niger
36. Slovakia	89. Sri Lanka	134. Kenya	173. Sierra Leone
37. Poland	90. Paraguay	135. Cameroon	
38. Chile	91. St.Vincent and the Grenadines	136. Congo	
39. Bahrain	92. Albania	137. Comoros	
40. Uruguay	93. Ecuador		
41. Bahamas	94. Dominican Republic		
42. Estonia	95. Uzbekstan		
43. Costa Rica	96. China		
44. Saint Kitts and Nevis	97. Tunisia		
45. Kuwait	98. Iran, Islamic Rep. of		
46. United Arab Emirates			
47. Seychelles			
48. Croatia			
49. Lithuania			
50. Trinidad and Tobago			
51. Quatar			
52. Antigua and Barbuda			
53. Latvia			

Source: UNDP

Or, one may turn the HDI on its head and measure the absence of symptoms of true poverty. This is done by the "Human Poverty Index" HPI (also published by the UNDP). It, too, is a composite index, taking into account illiteracy, the percentage of population that will die before becoming 40 years of age, the percentage of population with no access to safe water or to basic medical services, etc.

The table below gives the HPI values for developing countries.

Ranking of developing countries on the human poverty index

1. Urugay	23. Paraguay	45. Swaziland	67. Uganda
2. Costa Rica	24. Turkey	46. Indonesia	68. Pakistan
3. Cuba	25. Peru	47. Viet Nam	69. Malawi
4. Chile	26. Ecuador	48. Botswana	70. Bangladesh
5. Trinidad and Tobago	27. Bolivia	49. Guatemala	71. Haiti
6. Fiji	28. United Arab Emirates	50. Tanzania, U. Rep. of	72. Cote d'Ivoire
7. Jordan	29. Thailand	51. Kenya	73. Senegal
8. Panama	30. China	52. Zimbabwe	74. Benin
9. Bahrain	31. Iran, Islamic Rep. of	53. Myanmar	75. Gambia
10. Gyana	32. Syrian Arab Republic	54. Congo	76. Yemen
11. Colombia	33. South Africa	55. Egypt	77. Mauritania
12. Mexico	34. El Salvador	56. Iraq	78. Guinea-Bissau
13. Lebanon	35. Sri Lanka	57. Comoros	79. Mozambique
14. Mauritius	36. Tunisia	58. India	80. Nepal
15. Venezuela	37. Cape Verde	59. Ghana	81. Mali
16. Jamaica	38. Oman	60. Sudan	82. Central African Republic
17. Qatar	39. Honduras	61. Rwanda	83. Ethiopia
18. Malaysia	40. Lesotho	62. Nigeria	84. Burkina Faso
19. Libyan Arab Jamahirya	41. Nicaragua	63. Togo	85. Niger
20. Dominican Republic	42. Algeria	64. Zambia	
21. Brazil	43. Maldives	65. Morocco	
22. Philippines	44. Nambia	66. Cameroon	

Source: UNDP, Human Development Report Office

Just as in the case of the HDI, the ranks according to nominal per capita GDP do not correspond to the rankings according to this HPI. For example, most European countries rank ahead of the US, according to this HPI, while most of them rank below the US in terms of their per capita GDP.

Comparing two rankings: nominal per capita GDP (left column); and ranking according to the HPI (right column)

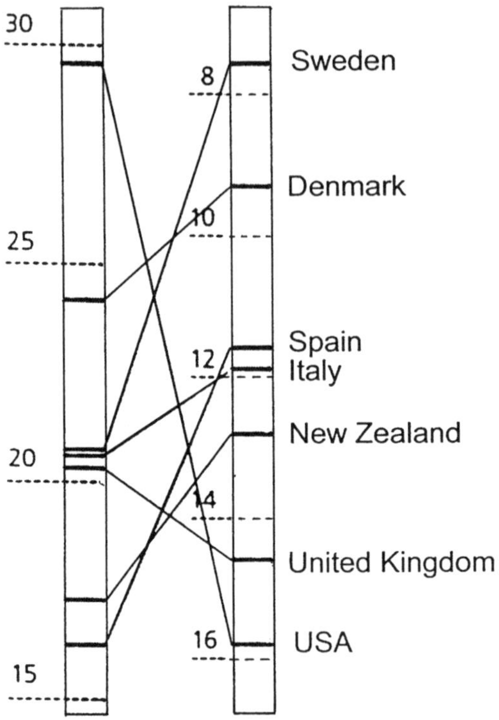

Source: Human Development Report Office

The World Health Organisation (WHO) has come out with yet another index – one for the disability adjusted life expectancy (DALY). Rather than just estimating how long a child can expect to live, the WHO has tried to calculate how much of the child's life will be spent in good health. World-wide, the average "healthy life expectancy" of babies born in 1999 is 7 ½ years less than their total life expectancy. Japan, Australia, France and Sweden all have DALYs of more than 73 years. At the other extreme, the countries with the worst DALYs are in sub-Saharan Africa. Thus, in this field too, there is a close connection between well-being (as measured by DALYs) and wealth (as measured by GDP per capita). DALYs in rich countries are higher by far.

But, if there is a close correlation between high wealth and a high DALY, the correlation is not rigid either. Poverty is a powerful ally of illness; but greater wealth does not necessarily buy a proportionate amount of better health, even when much is being spent on health. America is famously the world's biggest spender on health care, but with a DALY of 70 years, it still falls behind Japan, which forks out far less for health services.

Altogether and in their sum, these various indices hold some important lessons:

First, by any indicator we use, humankind has progressed over the last hundred years. It has progressed in the sense that more persons were able to reach goals humans generally aspire to.[17]

Second, if measured in nominal per capita GDP, the differences between the various states are staggering and reach a rate of one to twohundred. These differences shrink somewhat if we use gauges other than nominal GDP to measure well being.

Third, using other gauges than that of nominal per capita GDP, the gap disappears that separates (EU-15) Europe and Japan from the US.

Fourth, policies count. Proactive health, social and environmental policies leave their imprint (as becomes evident from the top rank of Scandinavian countries in most of these alternate indices for "true" wealth).

Fifth – that being said – we still find that all these indices bring fewer surprises than we might expect. Those on the top of one index are usually also very close to the top on another index. The same holds true for those at the bottom. And within a certain range, the ranking on all of these indices still follows the ranking established by the index on per capita GDP.

Sixth, this does not imply that the only thing truly relevant is the increase of GDP; and that all of the rest would follow. What it implies is that the development of per capita GDP portrays a very complex, not just material process, that permits (but does not assure) progress also in many realms beyond the realm of personal wealth and consumption.

Seventh, and as mentioned under point five, there is a clear correlation of per capita GDP growth with many of the indicators that measure the true quality of the human condition. Nonetheless, this correlation becomes more tenuous the higher the level of average per capita wealth.

17 Mozambique's present HDI score is thus distinctly above the level of the HDI achieved in some parts of Europe – for example in Spain and Italy – in 1870.

Change of the values of the Human Development Index 1975 to 1988, low income, middle income and high income countries

		1975	1998	Change
High income countries	Australia	0.841	0.929	+0.088
	Denmark	0.859	0.911	+0.052
Middle income countries	Tunisia	0.511	0.703	+0.192
	China	0.518	0.706	+0.188
	Zimbabwe	0.519	0.555	+0.036
Low income countries	Indonesia	0.456	0.670	+0.214
	Nepal	0.291	0.474	+0.183
	Mali	0.248	0.380	+0.132

Source : UNDP

The above table shows that added wealth brings fewer other added benefits in the quality of life the higher the level of wealth already attained.

Eighth, some of the indicators of "true progress" attach greater importance to developments and problems that are peculiar to wealthy countries. This holds true, for example, for the "Genuine Progress Indicator" that includes figures on family breakdown and crime; and which counts as negative the disappearance of unpaid services rendered in households and in civic organisations. Such indices that concentrate more on the issues arising in already wealthy countries, tend to present a more sombre conclusion than do indices that concentrate upon what becomes better at an earlier phase of economic development (such as rising literacy and life expectancy).

Ninth, happiness as a subjective feeling is difficult to define and to measure. But, if measured, it correlates but loosely[18] to wealth. It does relate strongly though, to the overall social conditions of a country; with people in egalitarian societies being much "happier" than people living in societies that are strongly, hierarchical. As it seems, in countries already wealthy, the addition of even more wealth counts for less than the conditions under which this wealth is produced; and it counts less than the experience of an even or uneven distribution of that wealth.

18 The correlation is positive but very weak.

If we abide by the traditional view of the world being shaped by big powers rising and falling, and by alliances gathering and unravelling, attention should focus on three developments which will have a major impact upon the global system over the next fifty years.

a) the future policy and future status of the United States;
b) the future relationship between the US and Europe;
c) and, finally, the future status and policy of China and of the other rapidly rising countries in its vicinity.

Let us address the last question first.

Population forecasts for China and India

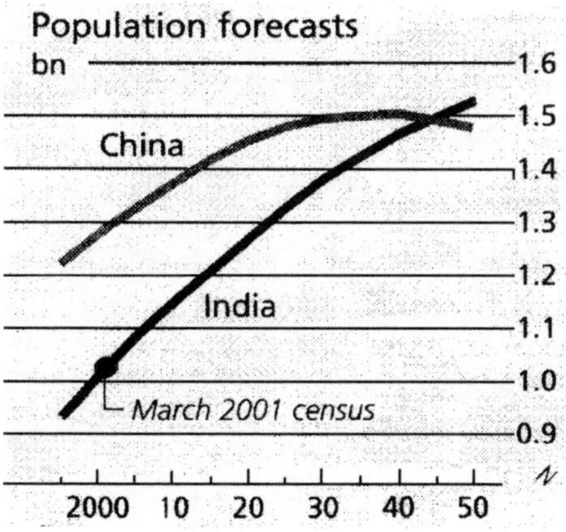

Source: Indian census, UN

It is a simple but, nonetheless, elementary fact that China is the most populous state on earth. It is home to one fourth of the world population. In terms of population, India is catching up though. Due to its less stringent policy on birth control, it is growing more rapidly. By 2040, it will have more inhabitants than

China. At that time, population growth in China will have come to a standstill[1] and China's population might even start to shrink from that time on.

But while the growth of China's population is being reigned in, its economy continues to expand rapidly.[2]

CHINA – GDP growth rates (real GDP, % increase on a year earlier)

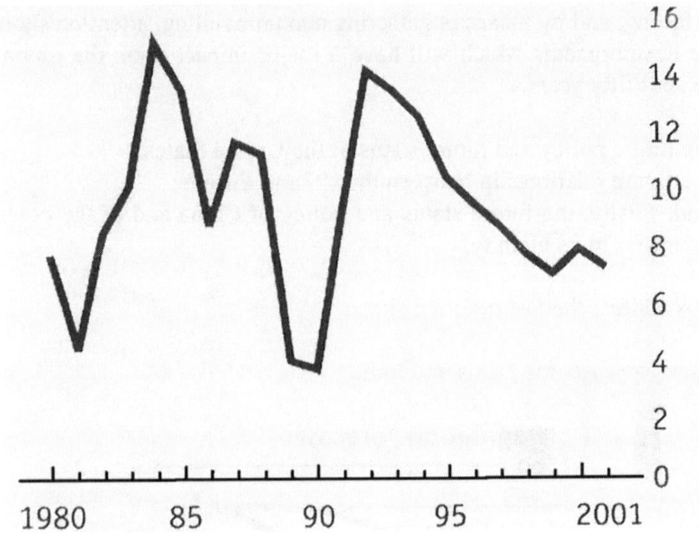

Source: Economist Intelligence Unit

As was to be expected, in the course of catching up, the rates of Chinese economic growth have decreased somewhat over the years. But they still are high in international comparisons. At the time of the "Asian crisis", when the economies of other Asian countries like Thailand and Korea fell into a recession, growth in China continued to advance at a pace of 7% to 8% per year.

---

1 The exceptionally rapid drop in population growth rates will pose acute problems for China from 2020 on, as the percentage of persons reaching retirement age will rise very abruptly. Building a sustainable old age pension system is one of the most urgent political and economic tasks now facing China.

2 Some foreign observers suspect that the actual growth rates are lower than rendered in official statistics. But they cannot be that much off track given the export performance of China.

The size of the Chinese economy is thus expanding rapidly. If measured in purchasing power parities, it has already surpassed the size of the Japanese economy.

China, USA, Japan, Germany, UK and Russia nominal GDP; and GDP adjusted for purchasing power (in trillion US$; 2000)

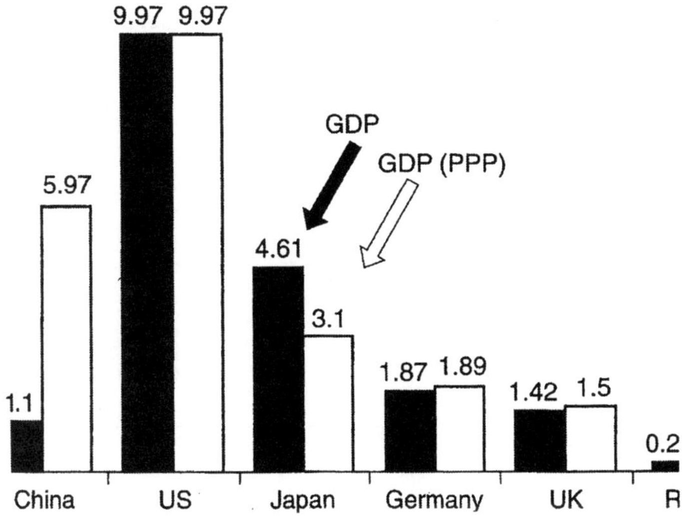

Source: Standard and Poor's

As has been explained before, purchasing power parities are useful in comparing true wealth, the true living standard, in various countries. However, if it comes to measuring economic might and power, the nominal GDP[3] is the better gauge. If measured in these terms of nominal GDP, the gap between Japan and China is very wide still, and China's economy has just approached the volume of the British economy.

Economic growth was possible only because China had slowly and quietly discarded the Communist economic system. The share of the output that state-owned enterprises had in overall industrial output peaked in 1992 and has been in

3 In poor countries, nominal GDP is always much lower than GDP measured in PPP. The local currency is thus "undervalued"; which, in turn, reflects the fact that the country in question is not yet very competitive on international markets and has to compete via prices (and not via the nature and quality of the products it exports).

decline ever since. The greater part of industrial production now comes from private enterprises. Many other enterprises are owned by villages and towns. They too have a higher share of industrial production than the state owned enterprises (though a smaller one than private firms).

Industrial GDP by Yuan 1980
by state owned enterprises (SOE) community owned enterprises (COE) and privately owned enterprises (other)

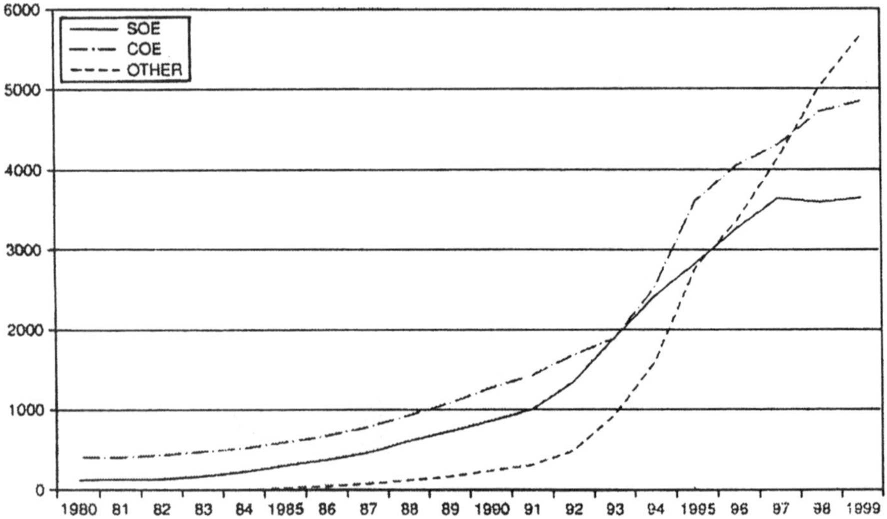

Source: Gabriele, A., 2002

In 40 to 50 years the volume of the Chinese economy will have become equal to the volume of the US economy. But, in order to rank as a world economic power, a big nominal GDP alone does not suffice. Market and product leadership also counts; as does having a cutting edge in technology; or being atop the financial system. Is China on the way to acquire such assets or can it be confident to acquire them in the not too distant future?

The example of Taiwan can provide an answer to this question. Originally, conditions there were similar to those prevailing on the mainland. But today, the Taiwan province of China has already acquired many of the trappings of a mature and even of a leading economy. Taiwan produces 39% of the world's disk drives, 54% of its PC monitors and 95% of its scanners. So, if Taiwan can acquire this sort of economic assets, we should assume that mainland China can do the same.

Indeed, the mainland is advancing very fast in the technological content of the goods it produces and exports.

Nonetheless, such progress is not preordained and inevitable. Much will depend on political choices. And these are difficult. Obviously, the rise of private enterprises and the decline of state owned enterprises has put a serious strain on the political system. While the political system remains Communist, the economic system is now mainly capitalist. Hard choices therefore have to be made. Hard choices will also have to be made in foreign and in security policy. Where will China turn? Will it integrate into the global system without much fuss and friction. Will it insert itself into the concert of big powers by taking the fourth seat next to the three present members of the "Triad"? Or will it become an adversarial power? Will it assume the role that once had been the role of the Soviet Union? Will China become the focal point and support of all of those nations and groups that oppose and wish to destroy the prevailing system?[4] Will the second half of the 21st century thus become a re-play of the second half of the 20th century, with a new bi-polar system?

Chinese nuclear forces, 2000

No. deployed	Year first deployed	Range (km)[a]	Warheads x yield
120	1965	3 100	1–3 bombs
30	1970	400	1 x bomb
40	1971	2 800	1 x 3.3 Mt
20	1980	5 500	1 x 3.3 Mt
20	1981	13 000	1 x 4–5 Mt
48	1985–86	1 800	1 x 200–300 kt
12	1986	1 700	1 x 200–300 kt

Source: IISS

4 This had been the ambition of Mao who saw himself as the leader of the "world's villages" (of the poor and disadvantaged) against the world's cities (of the rich and privileged). He did not shy from the notion of seeing nuclear weapons employed in this contest; with the poor surviving the holocaust better, due to their much greater numbers.

China's present security and defence policy is one pointer as to the course it is likely to choose. It has acquired strategic nuclear weapons and also the missiles to deliver them over vast distances. This points to an ambition to eventually reach traditional great power status.[5]

As we have observed in the chapter on arms and arms trade, China's military expenditures and arms purchases have expanded, while they have shrunk in most other regions of the world. Howerer, as China's economy has expanded at a pace faster than its military budget – the share of GDP spent for military purposes has decreased. It now stands at 1,9% of GDP (according to official counts even at a mere 1,1%). That is quite low in international comparison; and this is not a burden that would slow economic expansion. Clearly, China gives priority to economic development over military development. According to the CIA, even by 2015 its military forces will not yet have become fully modernised.

China's military burden, 1989-98

Military expenditure				
Official (b. yuan, current prices)[b]	Official (b. yuan, constant 1989 prices)	Total[a] (b. yuan, current prices)	Total[a] (b. yuan, constant 1995 prices)[c]	Military expenditures of GDP Official (%)
2	3	4	5	6
25.147	25.147	43.9	82.9	*1.5*
29.031	28.153	49.3	90.1	*1.6*
33.031	30.980	53.7	95.1	*1.5*
37.786	33.315	69.2	115.1	*1.4*
42.580	32.731	73.1	106.1	*1.2*
55.071	34.117	87.2	102.0	*1.2*
63.672	33.687	104.5	104.5	*1.1*
72.006	35.906	124.0	114.4	*1.1*
81.257	39.415	138.7	124.5	*1.1*
91.710	44.045	155.6	141.1	*1.1*

Source: IISS

5 Already now, its missiles are capable of reaching the US. China is also one of the five countries with nuclear arms that have a "second strike" capacity.Only four other nations have this strategic nuclear capacity; namely the other four permanent members of the UN-Security Council.

Given its vast size and its rising wealth, even this low percentage of GDP spent on the military does, however, add up to a substantial volume. Nonetheless, if present trends continue, it would take one quarter of a century for China to outrank Japan in military spending.

Actual and projected 2025 military expenditures for China, the US and Japan (in billion USD)

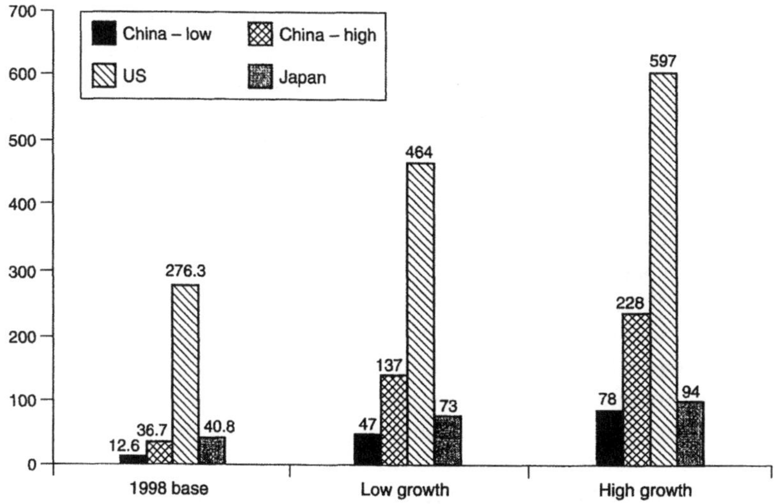

Source: IISS

But in the foreseeable future, neither of these two states will have the key role in setting the terms of military security in the region. This will continue to be the role of the US – provided the US does not opt to withdraw into a new isolation[6]. In the North Pacific, and even on its Western rim, the US will thus dominate in military terms for quite some time to come.

Notwithstanding the present regional military preponderance of the US, and notwithstanding the still limited size of China's military machine, the security policies of China raise questions as to its ultimate aims. Some of the arms purchased by China are clearly offensive ones (like, for instance, submarines or the

6 This is a serious issue: the security of this region – which is ripe with dormant or otherwise potentially violent conflict – is dependent on the engagement of an outside power. Were this power to lose interest or to disengage for other reasons, there would be nothing there (in terms of power, networks, institutions) to fill the vacuum.

semi-finished aircraft carrier[7] bought from the Ukraine). The acquisition of such offensive weapons points to a Chinese resolve to be able to escalate the military confrontation with and over Taiwan. Were it to explode into war, such a war could very well escalate beyond the confines of the region. The US has promised to support Taiwan if it's being attacked from the mainland. China, in its turn, has not excluded the offensive use of military power in the case that Taiwan declares its independence from the mainland. Unlike the first two World Wars, World War III could start in Asia.

Obviously, China's material interest should prompt it to seek deeper integration into the world system; and to co-operate with the other leading powers. Its material interests should dissuade China from aiming to become the crystallisation point and advocate of all of the discontent of this world. Indeed, there is little in its recent behaviour that would reflect a desire to assume such an adversarial role. On the contrary, China's co-operation with the US in the fight against Islamic fundamentalist terrorism points in the opposite direction; as does its recent membership in the World Trade Organisation.[8]

Chinese economic growth has been export led. Its continued economic development, therefore, depends upon its main export markets remaining open. Prominent among these markets are the US and Japan. China exports much more to the US and to Japan than it imports from them. China would be in serious trouble were the Japanese or the Americans to close their markets to Chinese exports for political reasons. This, however, would be bound to happen were China to opt for confrontation in the region or on a world wide scale.[9]

China is also dependent on Foreign Direct Investment. Foreign investors dominate, especially in the crucial field of high value-added exports.

---

7 It is not very plausible that it was bought and towed across oceans to serve as nothing more than a tourist attraction.

8 With far-reaching consequences for its internal economic and political regime.

9 The tables can be reversed. Chinese sometimes argue that, in view of their economic interests, the Japanese and Americans could not afford relations with China turning hostile.

Exports of high-technology from China by ownership of production, 1996-2000

	State-owned enterprises (Per cent)	*Foreign affiliates (Per cent)*
1996	39	59
1997	..	..
1998	25	74
1999	23	76
2000	18	81

Source: EIU

China will be able to grow enough grain to feed its population only if it exploits all of its agricultural potential; if it does so in an optimal way; and if it applies much additional irrigation. With current methods, and without more irrigation, just 492 million tons of grain can be produced. Against this stands a grain demand that is likely to reach 650 million tons by 2025. A substantial amount of grain will therefore have to be imported. It is similar with oil. Demand is rising rapidly. It cannot be covered from Chinese wells. Much of the oil will have to be imported both from Russia and from the Middle East. China thus depends on the outside world not only because it provides a market for its exports. It also depends on the outside world for essential inputs like grain and oil.

Its material interests should therefore prompt China towards a liberal and world-open policy. They should also prompt China to assume, next to Japan, a leading and constructive role in the region. But such material motives are one thing. Irrational emotions are something else. History provides many examples of emotions running counter to, and overriding, the rational in the behaviour of states. Nationalism is one such strong emotion and Chinese nationalism is pervasive and virulent.[10] Surprisingly, it is strong especially amongst the younger generation.[11] The explosive force of nationalist emotions could inflate smaller international incidents into full-scale violent conflicts which, by their very nature, would escape political control.

Nonetheless, the future course of the Peoples Republic of China will depend less upon these developments in foreign and security policy. It will depend mainly upon its internal situation. China suffers from some serious cleavages and from great inner diversity. Such differences have grown. The table below provides a glimpse of the vast gap in wealth that now separates the well endowed Eastern coast and its cities (Shanghai); from the poorer Western provinces like.

10 As shown by the nationalist outpourings on private Chinese internet sites.

11 Chinese nationalism seems a belated reaction to the degradations and humiliations the "Middle Empire" (the longest continuous culture and state on earth) had to suffer at the hands of foreign powers.

Even when measured in purchasing power parities (which tend to downplay such inequalities), the gap in wealth corresponds to an astounding 1: 6 relationship.

Regional differences in China according to various HDI indicators, 1997

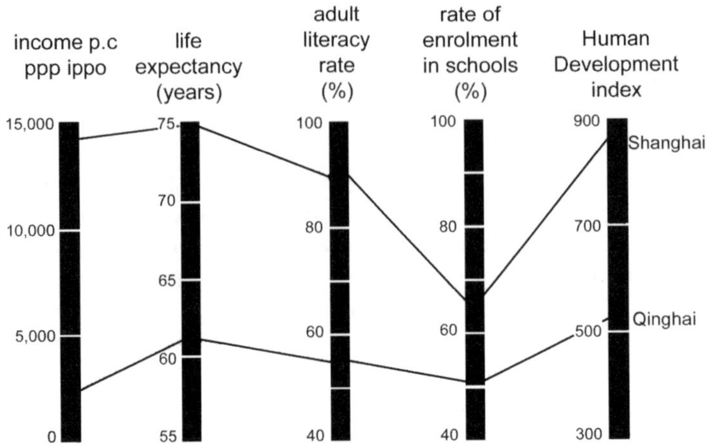

Source: UNDP

The resulting potential for inner conflict is accentuated by simmering conflict between the Han and the non-Han population. The latter are a minority and tend to live in the poorer, Western and Southwestern parts of China.

And then there is the issue of democracy. If it wants to secure its future, China will have to become democratic eventually. Wealth and a dynamically growing economy cannot be secured in the absence of democracy. Democracy and greater wealth are contingent upon each other. As we have seen, the Chinese economic system can no longer be considered Communist. Large parts of the economy are privately owned and function according to capitalist principles. But the private sector can flourish only under conditions of greater transparency, the rule of law, the protection of ownership rights, etc. These are conditions that only democratic governance can guarantee. Even more basic – there is the issue of how to transfer political power from one leader to his (or her) successor. In the absence of democracy this process can become very traumatic and destabilising.[12]

China's society is more liberal and less fear-ridden today than it has ever been in recent history. Yet the country is still far removed from meeting even some of the more basic criteria of democracy. Obviously, Chinese leaders are loath to push in the direction of true democratisation.[13] They fear that, once launched, the process of democratisation might escape control and that the country might plunge into anarchy[14]. This fear is not wholly in vain, as a certain amount of conflict is already inherent in the very concept of democracy. This potential for conflict becomes higher still in the uneasy transition from authoritarian to democratic governance.

Inevitably, too, democratic governance will make surface the tensions resulting from the stark socio-economic inequalities; the estrangement between ethnic groups; the despair of millions of homeless migrant workers and the unemployed; and all the unease resulting from the general turmoil of a country in the grips of ultra-rapid change. Nobody can guarantee that the surfacing of such tensions and conflicts will but enliven democracy; and that democracy will quickly mitigate and solve them. The opposite might happen. China might slide into chaos and anarchy. In its long history, China has repeatedly experienced such "periods of trouble" and Chinese leaders fear their repeat more than anything else. Outsiders preaching the virtues of quick democratisation should be aware of such dangers too. They, too, would not escape the consequences of a failure of the Chinese state. If, as a consequence of such anarchy, agriculture collapsed together with all other things, who, for example, could then feed l, 3 billion Chinese?

Yet, sooner or later, but inevitably, democracy and democratisation will have to be risked. Some first prudent steps have been taken already – for example by competitive elections on the village level and by a – selective – liberalisation of the media. But further progress is required for China's success to continue. Democracy may create turmoil in the short run. But, in the long run, it is the only form of governance that can assure stability and continuity. Only democracy can assure, for example, the peaceful change of leadership; the control of the powerful; and continuous adaptation to new circumstances. It is, in the end, also the only true remedy against the most immediate danger facing the PRC. This danger is

---

12 Though the transition from the "third" to the "fourth generation" of power-holders went quite smoothly in 2003 and followed pre-determined, quasi-constitutional procedures.

13 A slow, step by step transition to democracy would conform to the "East Asian pattern". It is in such a way that Taiwan and South Korea turned democratic.

14 According to a hearsay I cannot verify, in the Chinese language, the meaning of the word "democracy" is identical with "disorderly discourse" or "mutual haggling".

is rampant corruption. Corruption can hollow out a state. Endemic corruption can even make it collapse. Yet, in present day China, corruption seems to be systemic. Therefore, it takes a change of the system, as such – the transition to democratic control and rule – to prevent this cancer from metastasising into a terminal illness of the polity.

The best one can hope for is, thus, for China to follow – with a certain time lag – the Asian way of democratisation. There would be no sudden break as it occurred in the countries of the former Soviet empire. Democratisation would be introduced step by step; and the authoritarian character of the government would change but slowly. This is how Korea and Taiwan changed into democracies. Most likely, democracy will arrive in China in the same manner.

Barring serious internal disorder, or serious problems in relations with the rest of the world, China's global position is bound to become prominent[15]. The problem is that this rise, and the ensuing massive shift in economic and political ranking, occurs in a region where co-operation has not yet become routine and has not yet become institutionalised. It also occurs in a region that is marked by many unresolved conflicts.

China's future global position and role will thus be defined largely by its role in the more immediate region, and by how the region re-arranges so as to accommodate this rising giant.

But, is it reasonable to view and treat East and Southeast Asia as one coherent region, in the same manner as we treat Europe as one coherent region?[16]

Elements and trends exist that would permit us to do so. Such trends are evident at least in the economic realm. While it is true that regional intra-trade is still less intense than intra-trade within the European Community, this intra-trade is growing rapidly.

It is true that the region basically lacks the formal and official institutions that could promote and safeguard economic integration. But there are powerful informal networks and institutions that compensate for that.

There are the Japan-led production networks (with Japanese enterprises outsourcing certain tasks to countries of the region in a "flying geese pattern"; with the poorer countries receiving the more labour intensive production). There are

15 It is difficult to predict what will happen in a final phase of a catch-up. 25 years ago, it was generally assumed that Japan would overtake the US as the leading economic power. This has not happened; and for reasons still ill understood, Japan suddenly ran out of steam. The same fate might befall China the moment it is about to close the gap that separates it from the members of the cartel of the economically mighty.

16 We have done so in a few lines of the chapter on the "Triad", when we remarked that the volume of the East and Southeast economies together are equal, at least, to the volume of the US and to the volume of Europe's economy.

sub-regional, cross-border economic zones (like the economic zone around the Straits of Malakka). And there are the dense ethnic Chinese business networks. Sizeable minorities of Chinese live in all countries of Southeast Asia. In terms of wealth and economic impact, they push far above their weight in demographic terms.[17] They are the prime promoters of – also cross-border – investment.

Overseas Chinese

Host country	ethnic Chinese as share of the population; %	share of Chinese owned market capitalisation; %
Indonesia	3-4	73
Malaysia	30	69
Philippines	2	50-60
Singapore	78	81
Thailand	14	81

Source: EIU

Yet informal arrangements can only go so far. From a certain stage on, more formal institutions are required even in the economic realm. Yet few such institutions exist and those that do exist are weak:

In the aftermath of the Asian financial crisis of 1997/1998, East and Southeast Asian central banks have made some attempts to somewhat emancipate themselves from the tutelage of the International Monetary Fund.[18] They agreed on a system of mutual stand-by swaps in the event that, once again, a rapid exit of capital should come to threaten one of them.

Another institution in place is ASEAN (Association of South East Asian Nations) – the common institution of Southeast Asian countries. But, up to now, the plans have not materialised to advance free trade among the ASEAN states by some more resolute moves to lower tariffs and other trade barriers.

The very unequal distribution of economic and military power is one of the reasons for the failure to put regional co-operation on a more firm footing. Giants

17 Perhaps also because of this, their economic dominance, ethnic Chinese have frequently become subject to discrimination and even persecution in their host countries. This might be one of the motives for them maintaining lively contacts to their places of origin in China; and for their being prominent investors in these places. A good part of Foreign Direct Investment in China comes from such overseas Chinese – most prominently from Taiwan.

18 Which rightly had been criticised for ignoring the specifics of Asia in its intervention, thus aggravating the crisis (at least in its first phases).

co-exist with dwarfs. This is not going to change. The distribution of power will remain very uneven also in the future. While declining in relative terms, the power of Japan will remain prominent. And this preponderance will continue to fuel distrust and resentment. East Asia still carries the echo of the traumas caused by the Japanese aggression and cruelty during World War II. The post-war rise of Japan to world-power status has kept those fears alive[19]. This complicates the attempt at true partnership, which was difficult already given the fact that Japan used to tower far above the other nations of East Asia. In Europe, France and Germany, two medium-sized countries of roughly equal strength, could form the core of growing intra-European co-operation. In Asia, no such balance existed. Japan simply was too powerful. It prompted others to search for a balance to this power instead of seeking security by inter-linkage and interdependence as was the case in Europe.

Instead of being its promoter, Japan, thus, was an obstacle to regional co-operation. This negative function of being an impediment to regional co-operation is now being transferred from Japan to China. In four to five decades, China will be more powerful than Japan could ever aspire to be. Other nations will be as hesitant to attach to China as they have been hesitant to become closely joined to Japan. Distance in power between the number one and the rest is simply too wide to permit true partnership.

The region differs from Europe, furthermore, by the number and the severity of open or potential inter-state conflicts. In after-war Europe, borders were uncontested[20]. This is not the case in East Asia. The border between North and South Korea is still a de facto one, established by a truce and not by a peace treaty. Japan and Russia were unable to resolve the question as to whom some islands north of Hokkaido should belong. Several states lay claim to the same patches of the South China Sea (said to harbour undersea oil deposits). The border between India and China is contested too; and China and Vietnam even went to war over border questions two decades ago. North Korea is being ruled (if that is the term) by a paranoid and unpredictable tyrant. He commands the fourth largest army of the world and has, at his disposal, several nuclear warheads, together with the missiles to deliver them (something he threatens to do at irregular intervals). As mentioned, the potentially most dangerous conflict is over Taiwan. It might escape political control and it could escalate, by some dynamics of its own, even against the express wishes on both sides of the Taiwan strait.

---

19 One added reason of the still prevailing unease over Japan is its refusal to come to terms with this dark part of its past and to acknowledge its having been guilty of cruelty and aggression. Germany has managed to do that. The Japanese prime minister prefers to honour the soldier who carried out this aggression.

20 Except the question of German (re)- unification.

The great economic and political divergence of the countries of the region also hampers co-operation. Some, like Myanmar (=Burma), are unreformed dictatorships. Some are corrupt autocracies. Some are halfway on the path to democracy; and some have arrived there. Some, like Laos or Cambodia, are among the poorest and among the most self-enclosed countries of the world. Some, like Singapore, are among the wealthiest and the most world-open. Cleary, interests and values are bound to vary among these nations in the same way as their wealth and their political systems. Finding common ground is not easy. Regional integration enhances mutual interdependence. Given this large number of conflicts and these diverging security interests, one should doubt whether interdependence is really something the nations of East Asia long for.

Co-operation in East and Southeast Asia will thus grow only in step with and because of the integration of these states into the world system; and not via some specific and powerful institutions of regional co-operation. But even that is contingent on two things. First, the world economy must indeed continue on its present trajectory, with no basic breaks in trends, rules and institutions. Second, the region must be able to avoid its conflicts escalating into open warfare or into a prolonged intra-Asian Cold War.

East Asia cannot emulate Post-World-War-II Europe. One should fondly hope though, that at least it does not emulate Pre-World-War-I Europe; where rising wealth was accompanied by an escalating arms race and by virulent nationalism, ultimately making the outbreak of war a self-fulfilling prophecy.

That being said, it is true, on the other hand, that not only China, but the region as a whole, is and continues to be evolving rapidly in economic terms. Many of the improvements in the global indicators on the reduction of poverty, illiteracy, and the improvement of health are due largely to this rapid progress in East and Southeast Asia; the "Asian Crisis" of 1998 having been but a simple road accident that has not affected the basic trend.

Quarrelous Relatives – The Atlantic Relationship

The US political scientist Kenneth Waltz predicted that NATO would dissolve and that the historic quarrels between European states would resume. That return to the past would be caused by the disappearance of the Soviet Union. It had been the common and powerful enemy, which had prompted otherwise disparate countries to join – against their natural instinct and inclinations so to say – in an alliance intended to balance and deter this powerful enemy.

Obviously, the second part of the prediction has not come true. European integration has not become reversed. On the contrary: the introduction of the common currency, the completion of the single internal market, and finally the massive expansion in the number of Union members projected for 2004, all that shows that European integration has continued to move to the direction of an "ever closer union".[1]

So what about the second prediction of Kenneth Waltz on the weakening and likely demise of the US-European Alliance? Has this prediction also been proven wrong? At first sight, this seems not to be the case. One could even come to believe that NATO has become not less but more relevant – given the adherence of new members in two successive waves and given the numerous "Partnership for Peace Agreements" with many of those still outside.

But under the gloss of this new veneer, the substance of NATO has thinned out. This is so for several reasons:

1) The enemy it was designed to oppose no longer exists. If another common enemy should appear, it would be very different from the Soviet Union. Therefore, the organisation and equipment of the NATO-European Command is no

1 Should one say: not become reversed yet? For about three years, the efforts seem to have stalled. The lack of forward momentum implies the danger of reversal (bicycle theory of integration: if you do not move ahead, you fall). The EU-summit of NICE was certainly a serious set-back; as it failed to bring the reforms necessary for an enlarged Union to function smoothly, effectively and with democratic legitimisation. Unfortunately, this failure might not be accidental. It might reflect a changed "anti-integrational" mood in the European population at large. It seems no longer that much interested in, and concerned about, the building of a Federal Europe. A further and very serious set-back came with the deep intra-EU split on whether or not to support the US war against Iraq. Which way Europe will go will become clearer by the failure or success of adopting a "EU-constitution" in 2004.

longer functional. Should there be another major war, it would not be fought over a vast land mass with millions of soldiers, battle tanks and artillery. What European allies once were able to offer to the US – strategic depth, soldiers, traditional heavy weapons – has lost much of its military value.

2) It used to be that wars could not be won from the air. Even with bombs raining down on Germany and Austria in 1944, the Third Reich was still able to increase arms production and, especially, the production of aircraft. Germany was vanquished not by bombing raids, but by the Allies marching in[2]. The first Gulf War already brought a change, with air power and precision bombing having become more decisive. This change was subsequently confirmed in the war over Kosovo; and finally and beyond doubt, in the war over Afghanistan.

3) With the US being able to substitute bombs dropped and drones and missiles fired for soldiers fielded, the assistance of allies becomes less urgent. The US even came to see them as a bother.[3] Why mess with troublesome foreigners when acting alone is much more expedient?

4) In military technology the US has always had an advantage over its European allies. But, with the US now outspending the Europeans by 1:10 in the field of applied military research, this gap has widened dramatically. Europeans doubt whether they will ever be able to close or even narrow it. Also, it seems unlikely that Europeans will soon be in a position to replicate the unique US combination of advanced technology, broad and powerful logistics, pin-point intelligence and the innovative combination of ground and air power that stands behind the – widely unexpected – fast US victory in Afghanistan. The US on one side, and its European allies on the other, no longer fight on the same battlefield, so to say.

5) The victory in Afghanistan highlights another important consequence of these changes in military technology and tactics. The US can attain victory with no, or with very few casualties. In that sense, wars have become much "cheaper" for the US. But they have not become cheaper for the European allies which cannot avail themselves of these modern technologies. Wars remain more risky for Europeans[4].

---

2 The lesson of the insufficiency of air power was repeated in Vietnam. Saturating the country with more bombs than had been dropped in World War II did not prevent US defeat.

3 Particularly after security leakages by Allies damaged war efforts in Bosnia and in Kosovo.

4 These differences certainly also arise from other sources. They are, for example, also sustained by cultural differences, that is, different perceptions of the merit of using organised violence. Obviously, the barrier against the use of violence is lower in the US than it is in EU-Europe.

In the past, high technology was of little use against an enemy that used just simple, primitive military technology. The US war machine could not cope with bare-footed Vietnamese soldiers. This has now changed. After having been re-made by modern technology, the US war machine can now cope very well with Afghan tribesmen. As mentioned, this is likely to make the US more ready and more confident to take recourse to the organised violence of war also against such weak opponents.

On the other hand, the tribesmen and their allies have become more confident too. The collapsing World Trade Centre is a symbol of how powerful they, in their turn, have become. The collapsing World Trade Centre demonstrates to them and to others the heavy damage they, the weak, might inflict, provided that they are determined and clever enough. September 11th 2001 also demonstrates to the world how very vulnerable the mighty have become and how exposed they are to hostility emanating from the very weak.

Until a decade ago, history had instructed us on the ultimate futility of war. This lesson might now become unlearned; as both the very strong and the very weak have become equally confident that they can heavily damage the other side without themselves suffering unsupportable costs.

Call the situation: new uncertainty and instability.

6) Militarily, the US does not need Europe. But Europe needs the US. Even the 60.000 person strong European Intervention Force will not very much change this situation. In order to become effective – especially in faraway countries – this force still needs US support (for instance in the field of intelligence and logistics). The military relationship is thus asymmetric.[5]

If one defines security in military terms only, and if one sees international relations largely determined by military power[6], the Atlantic Alliance seems to

---

5 This one-sided dependency has come to be reflected in European policy and demeanour. Swedish prime ministers and French presidents, who, twenty years ago tended to high-handedly lecture the US on security matters, are now all humility and understanding, even with the US stepping on the toes of some of their closely held national interests. Compare the wild and wide ranging discussion over the instalment in Europe of medium range missiles in the seventies, with the muted response to, at least equally, far reaching US decisions (abrogation of the ABM treaty, and the decision to employ a "Strategic Missile Defence"; discussion on the resumption of testing of nuclear weapons, preparation for war waging against satellites, complete side – lining of the European Allies during the Afghan war, etc.)

6 And for many that is, indeed, the only force that shapes and determines all international relations.

have run into serious trouble. Having lost its strategic role[7], it would persist as a mere phantom and cloak of no more than ceremonial value. New tasks defined for it (for example at the 2002 NATO summit in Prague) seem to serve only the therapeutic value of keeping the organisation employed.

Between the US and Europe, problems exist in realms other than the realm of military security. Conflicts over trade even have a certain tradition. They have cropped up ever since the Common Market came into existence and, with it, a common European stance on questions of external trade. It might be that such controversies, nonetheless, have become a bit more tense in the last two-three years, as several more weighty issues were added one atop of another. This might have given a sharper quality to such controversy: There is controversy over tax support for US exporters; over the unilateral imposition of a 30% US tariff on imported steel; on the still unresolved question of the import into Europe of US-"hormone treated beef"[8]; there is conflict, too, over the international regime concerning air traffic; etc.

Frequently, such disputes have been called "trade wars". Yet the metaphor of "war" is misleading: US-European trade relations have been mostly co-operative. That did not change with the end of the Cold War.[9]

The problems between the US and its European NATO-partners thus have causes other than conflicts over trade. They stem from growing differences in the approach to international problems and issues of world governance. Not just in the military field, but in others too, the US now seems resolved to go it alone. Obviously, they believe they no longer need partners. They call on some nations on occasion and when they have specific needs (as, for instance, in the fight against terrorism). But, evidently, they wish for nothing beyond. This diffidence towards a more permanent, stable and institutionalised international co-operation stands in stark contrast to European attitudes. European countries are small or medium sized. They have learned that they can have an international impact only when acting together. Also, they are still very much aware of the high price they had to pay in the past for confrontation and hostility. They thus have learned to co-operate and to appreciate institutions that facilitate such co-operation. They project such experience in their approach to the world outside – witness, for example, their strong and steadfast support for the United Nations and the International Criminal Court; their substantial Official Development Assistance; or their resolve to stick with the Kyoto agreement on the reduction of CO_2 emissions.

---

7 Except perhaps as a US tool to prevent Europeans from building parallel capacities independent from the US.

8 With the WTO supporting the US in this case.

9 E. Frey, 2003, even claims that trade policy has become more accommodating to the other side at this time.

Those differences in the basic approach and in political philosophy thus translate into different definitions of priorities in the field of foreign and security policy. The tone in the conflict over such differences has become shrill. It is a tone of willed disregard, of conscious demeanment and gratuitous hostility – stronger now on the US side than on the European one. This estrangement runs its course while, economically, the two sides of the Northern Atlantic have actually become more similar to one another than they have ever been in the past.

As we have seen, the two sides have moved rather close to one another in actual wealth. The US has some advantage in modern technology. Also, at the end of the nineties its economic growth was more dynamic (albeit by a very small margin not wide enough to support triumphant US claims of having transited into a superior and altogether "New Economy"). Both sides hold roughly similar shares in world trade. Europe is ahead of the US in its share of world industrial production – though, again, by a small margin; while Europe has surpassed the US – by quite some margin – as the source of capital for directly productive investment.

As shown in the chapter on the "Triad", long-term interest rates have moved in tandem and are now converging. Investment rates that correlate with economic growth have also become more similar. These rates dropped in Europe, while the US rates moved up to the EU level.

In the European Union, economic growth now creates more jobs than it did before; and in the US, it now creates fewer jobs than it did previously. In this respect, too, the US and Europe have moved closer together.

Job creation per percent of growth in the Euro 12 and in the USA

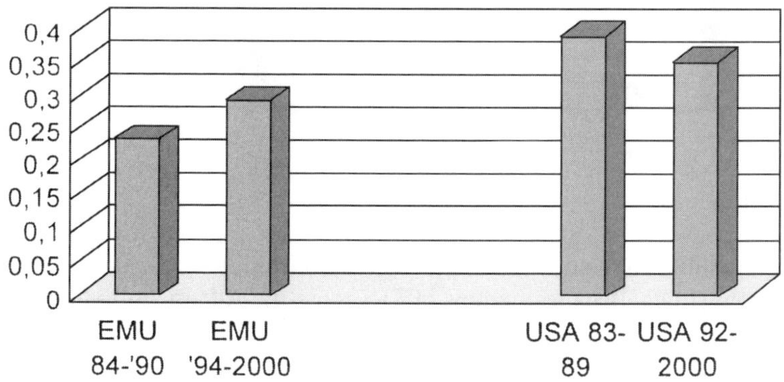

Source: Belgian Trade Union Congress, Dec 2000

In business culture, differences obviously continue to exist, for example, in the financing of enterprises – with Europe preferring financing through bank loans; while the US gives stronger preference to financing through equity.[10] But even these differences in business culture are becoming more narrow. Within just two years, Europe has expanded risk and venture capital financing by 100 percent.

In a way, the economies of the US and of Europe are merging rapidly. In the confines of the global system, the two economies together form a distinct subsystem; with the relations between the two parts being more intense than the relations of either part to the rest of the world.

The share of the Triad in World FDI
flows and stocks, 1985 and 2000

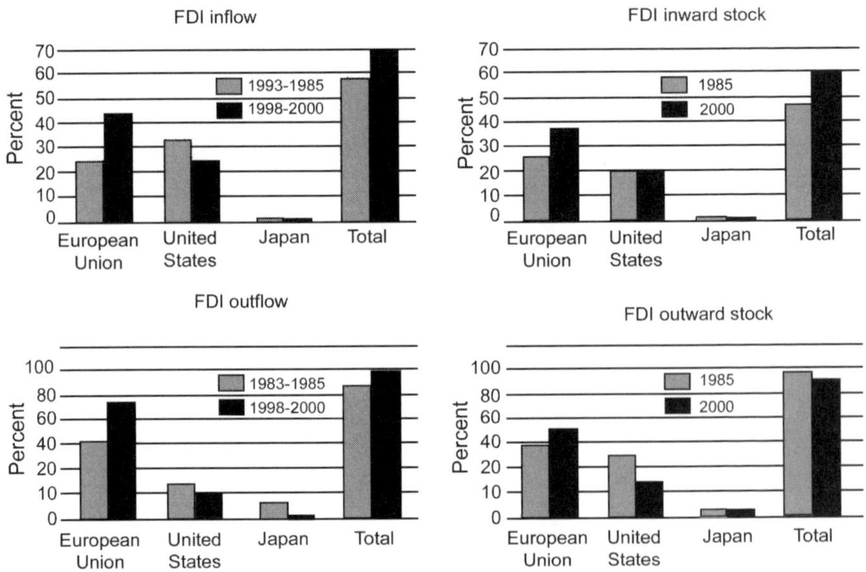

Source: UNCTAD

The graphic above demonstrates this relationship in the field of foreign direct investment (FDI). Broader streams of FDI cross the Atlantic in both directions[11];

10 Not necessarily to the disadvantage of Europeans.

11 Note that the flow going from Europe to the US is much broader than the one flowing in the opposite direction. In the 60s, there was fear that the US would simply

while just a trickle of FDI moves to the rest of the world; and very little FDI goes to, or originates in. Japan (after all, the third partner in the "Triad").

In a speech often quoted since, Lord Acton once remarked that "nations do not have friends, they just have interests". That sounds hard nosed, cynical and thus rather credible. But does this remark by Lord Acton actually fit reality?

For what are "national interests"? How are they defined? Henry IV of France and Emperor Rudolf II of Austria would have maintained that the prime national interest was to preserve or to restore the predominance of Catholicism. Three hundred years ago (in the age of the so called "physiocrats") national interest demanded the acquisition and fruitful employ of a maximum of agricultural surface. A hundred years ago, the most prominent "national interest" would have been seen in the acquisition and expansion of a colonial empire. By now, such goals seem quixotic.[12]

National interests are, therefore, not immutable and eternal. Obviously, they are more spurious and shifting than the friendship among countries which Lord Acton had so readily dismissed as irrelevant. Friendships among countries are based on a similarity of public institutions, on common goals and values, on common historic points of reference. These things are formed over centuries, and thus change but slowly, if at all. Friendships among countries are, therefore, more long-lived than what each country believes to be its "national interest". And indeed, the US and Europe do have many institutions, goals and values in common. Even while they defined themselves as something wholly unique in their Declaration of Independence in 1776, the US founding fathers still did so with reference to the ideas of the European Enlightenment and to writers such as John Locke or Montesquieu. Later on, in the second half of the 20th century, it was Europe's turn to become the receiving part in the realm of culture and ideas; in the field of mass culture, the arts, in hard sciences and social sciences.

Much, therefore, in the stock of cultural heritage and in the stock of belief and values is common to both Europe and the US. There is instant recognition on what is actually going on in the other part of the Atlantic, on what is actually implied with an utterance or action. Both societies thus seem carved out of the same wood.

---

buy up Europe ("le defi Americain" - Lecanuet). Now the opposite seems to be happening.

12 Just a bit less so than the prime national interest Hitler had envisaged for Germans: namely, the preservation of the purity of the Aryan race.

Notwithstanding this commonality, there is a long tradition in Europe portraying Americans as uncultured, violence prone, ruthless and domineering. Both the extreme right and the extreme left in Europe are in full agreement about the moral inferiority of the American social model.

On the other hand, there is a certain tradition in the US of defining oneself primarily by being different from Europe. One cannot understand the actions of the new US administration, for example, when abstracting from this need to define themselves as true, heroic, valorous, fearless Americans, who rightly mistrust European cant. Just as one could not understand the French president Charles de Gaulle or the Swedish prime minister Olof Palme, if one abstracted from their desire to emancipate themselves from the US "father" and to show themselves as superior to Americans in empathy or in political acumen.

There thus is a tradition of "Anti-Americanism" in Europe, just as there is a tradition of "Anti-Europeanism" in the US. Both of these two traditions are broadly based and both run deep. But, if that has been so over centuries, why do these sentiments echo so much more loudly today? Why have they come to actually swerve and even define policies?

Part of the answer lies in the uniqueness of the present US administration of George W. Bush. The nature of this administration is difficult to describe in terms that are used to describe European politics. There is no European counterpart for the mixture of Christian fundamentalism, missionary zeal, old fashioned imperialism, belief in the military and glorification of the market (and especially of financial markets).[13]

We do not know whether, in historic retrospect, this administration will be seen as a rare exception; as a singular accident, so to say. Or whether it will be seen as having been the bellwether for other US administrations to follow. While we may only speculate about the answer, we may, nonetheless, look at some developments that at least could give some credence to the second, not very pleasant, interpretation.

If we look at nothing more than some basic economic data, Europe and the US have become more akin to one another. Since the beginning of the 20th century, and up to the end of World War II (and perhaps even up to the Johnson era), they also had moved closer to one another in their political institutions, structures and beliefs; in their social policies; and in their outlook on the world.

13 Clearly though, this administration is extreme, and extreme also in its complete break with past US administrations. Foreign and security policy is now exclusively in the hands of persons with strong ideological convictions, but with little exposure to the realities of other countries. This is truly unprecedented.

In retrospect, it is obvious by now that the American public had difficulties to follow. Some fundamental values that underlie politics and institutions differ profoundly from those that prevail in Europe. The US public is strikingly traditional and this much more so than the public of any other country with a similar level of wealth. This shows, for example, in the broad US acceptance of the death penalty. It becomes evident, too, by religion permeating US life[14] in a way that has no parallel in any other wealthy country. In this respect, the US is closer to Turkey or India, than it is to Europe.

Secular-rational values versus traditional values

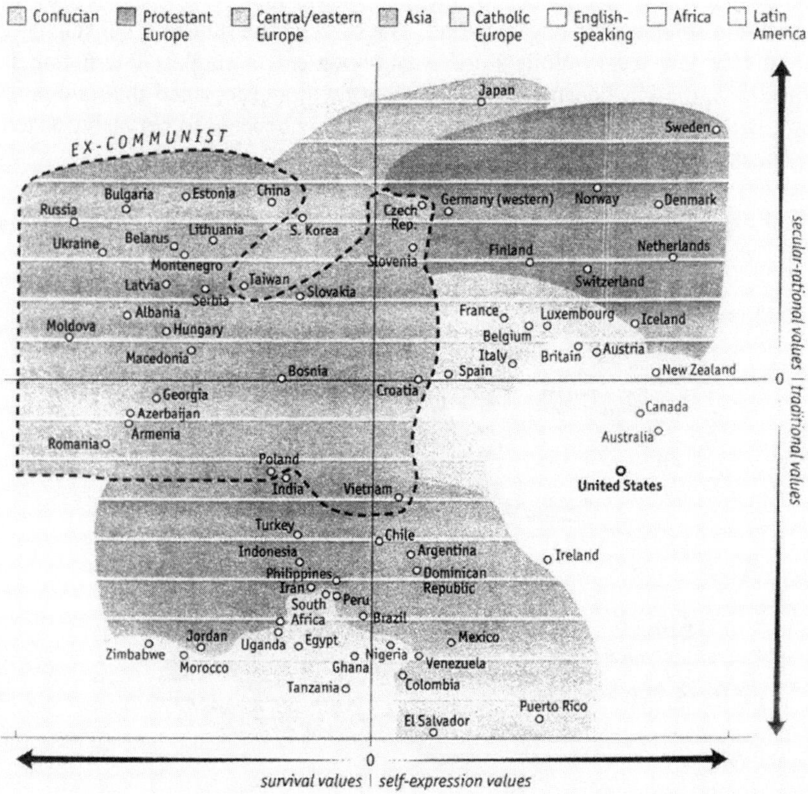

Source: The World Values Survey, University of Michigan

14 Where else on earth but in conservative Muslim countries and the US could a national currency be imprinted with “in god we trust”.

Social policy was always a bit different in the US and in Europe. But, for a long time, these dissimilarities had narrowed. Now they are widening again. The US Social Security system was established a bit after it had been established in Europe. It is less comprehensive (and does not include public health insurance). But it is roughly comparable to the European system. Public housing was introduced also in the US, as was public radio and television (that still predominate in Europe). US Trade Unions were powerful. The share of the state in GDP rose rapidly not just in Europe, but also in the US; and so on.

Yet thirty years ago, social policy started to diverge again. While the welfare state was being expanded in Europe, it was reduced in the US. Public housing has disappeared nearly completely in the US. Public radio and television have retreated into small niches of the market. The share of the state in GDP stagnated at a relatively low level. While Europeans continued to support international organisations, the US became estranged from them and lessened their support for them. Differences in these arrangements have now become so pervasive as to justify speaking of two different socio/political models.

Social expenditures and the level of wealth (1998, social expenditures as % of GDP; wealth in ppp)

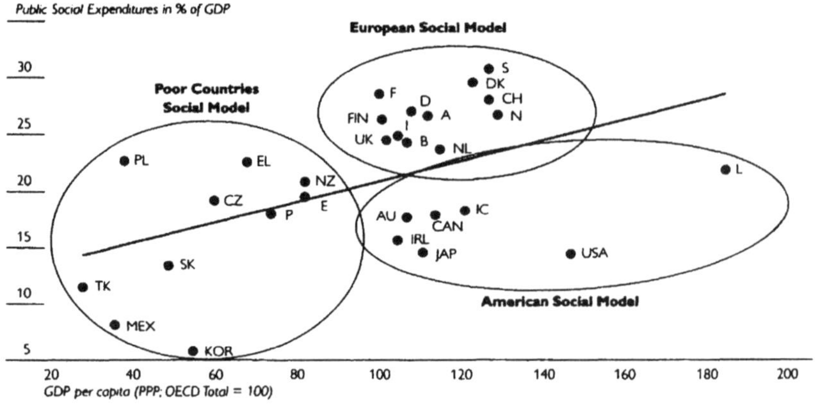

Source: OECD

All these were long term developments. The present US administration has just accentuated them. As the US is a democracy, we must assume even this acceleration of development to reflect the mood and preferences of the US population. If we believe that policies are based on such values and preferences, we must also accept that the estrangement within the US is something more than temporary; and that it will outlast the present US administration.

We might, however, also take the view that ultimately the policies chosen by a nation will have to be practically useful. If we start from that proposition, the future of the Transatlantic relationship is less bleak. True, the common task of warding off the spread of the Soviet empire has disappeared. But numerous other common tasks have appeared; tasks that also call for close co-operation between the two sides of the Atlantic.

The US and Europe basically live in the same economic realm. If they wish to effect true changes in the world, the US and Europe can do so only by acting in common. Yet, being absorbed and fascinated by the contemplation of its superior military strength and success, the US seems to have become oblivious of this simple truth. Maintaining a free world trade; promoting democracy; stabilising global financial and monetary affairs; warding off the perils of environmental degradation and disaster; offering the prospect of economic betterment to the poor of the world; sustaining international organisations – all these are tasks that the US – with its mere quarter of world production and a mere 4 percent of the world population – cannot accomplish alone.

Population growth and economic growth are fast in the countries that are not partners of the Atlantic Alliance. Even with Europeans and Americans joining forces, the two together will face increasing difficulties in making their values, interests and views prevail. The chances of success will be lower still for both Europeans and Americans, if each of them ignores the other. Joining forces across the Atlantic becomes even more necessary as time advances and the more both Europe and the US together lose weight and influence in the world.

With 1914, the European century had drawn to its close.[15] The rest of the 20th century had indeed been an "American one". Yet, a hundred years from now, the curtain might well have been drawn on both Europe and the United States. The time in between should be used to establish the world order on another and more solid basis than the one of military power and economic dominance.

> *"The chief long-term strategic challenge facing the United States [...] is the decline of five centuries of North Atlantic military dominance over the world and the rise of Asian nationalist regimes."*
>
> Paul Bracken, 1999. Fire in the East – the rise of Asian military power and the second nuclear age. Harpers, New York.

15 Followed – it must be said – by a very remarkable European revival between 1955 and 1980.

Globalisation and Countertrends

We have started out with reflecting on how it has become possible to buy strawberries in winter, even in northern latitudes. Indeed, this is one aspect of globalisation. Provided one has the means, one may purchase goods that come from all over the world. We have followed through with a look at the production of goods. Much of this production has also become globalised. Much merchandise is produced not just in a national market. It is assembled from different places of the world.

Many problems are of a global scale and have to be tackled on a global level. This holds true for many tasks of environmental protection; for financial/monetary crises; for terrorism; for drug abuse; for contagious diseases; etc. The list of things, events, developments, problems that have become global – this list can be prolonged easily. Everybody can do so, as in our daily lives we are in routine and constant contact with many aspects and consequences of globalisation.

But what has driven globalisation? What has made for this matter of fact presence of global interdependence? The obvious reply to that question is that globalisation has been brought about by the economy.

Economic connections across the globe are not unprecedented. Even in ancient times, some economic activities had joined parts of the world that are quite distant from one another. In the Neolithic age already, long distance trade in Baltic amber reached Central and Southern Europe. In the Bronze Age, Phoenician sea-going vessels plied the Mediterranean. In search for tin, they even reached Southern England. The empire of Alexander the Great covered a large part of the then cultivated Eurasian land mass. The discoveries of new continents in the 16th century had a profound impact on Europe, for example, via the "import" of syphilis and of potatoes; and by providing an ample supply of silver and gold. This mining of silver and gold in the new world was backed by bankers and merchants with a global reach. In their visions and motives they did not differ very much from present day CEOs who rule the vast transnational companies[1]. The

1 These early transnational capitalists seem to have been very efficient: in the 12th and 13th centuries (!) Genovese bankers operated with interest spreads of 2% - something few modern bankers would care to do today in international transactions.

trading companies of the 17th and 18th centuries also operated on a world wide scale.

Nonetheless we should beware of treating the early 21st century just as a mere prolongation of the past. The global system has changed. So have its constituent parts. A "state" today is not what a "state" was in the early 16th century. "Trade" does not have the same meaning and impact. Communication now is much broader and has a different effect. The very volume of what can be considered "global" has expanded dramatically; and, with it, the interface that connects this "global" to the "national", to the group, or to the individual. To use a Marxist term, the massive "change in quantity has resulted in a change in quality".

Globalisation is powerfully promoted by the shrinking price of covering distance. Costs of transportation have plummeted. The cost of air traffic has decreased by 60 percent since 1950. The costs for communication are even close to disappearing.

Transport Costs
(Constant US Dollars; 1950=100)

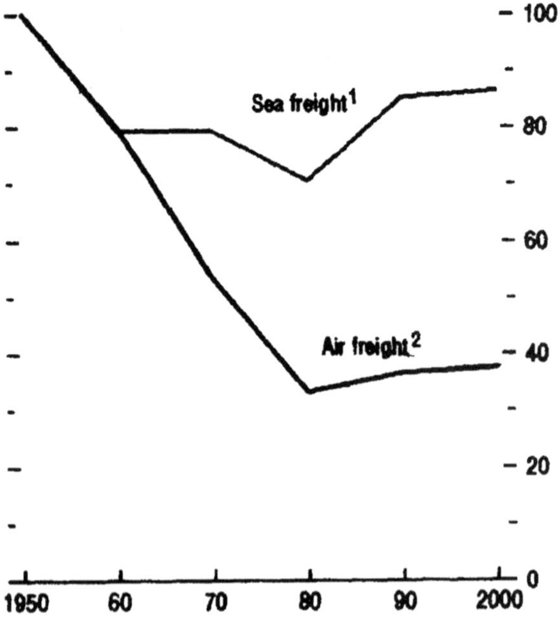

Source: IMF 2003

A deep reduction has also occurred in what economists call "transaction costs", that is, the costs of concluding a business other than the costs of communication and transport. The biggest of these transaction costs is the cost of gathering relevant information – such as information on potential markets; on alternate sources of input; or on potential partners in an economic venture. Thanks to the advance in information technology, such costs have been very much lowered. Producers now find it easier to optimise inputs and outputs on a global scale.

The consequence of all this is a vast expansion of international trade. It grew faster, by far, than the World GDP. In real terms, trade has expanded twenty-fold since 1951.

Growth of world production and world trade 1951-2000
(Index 1951 = 100)

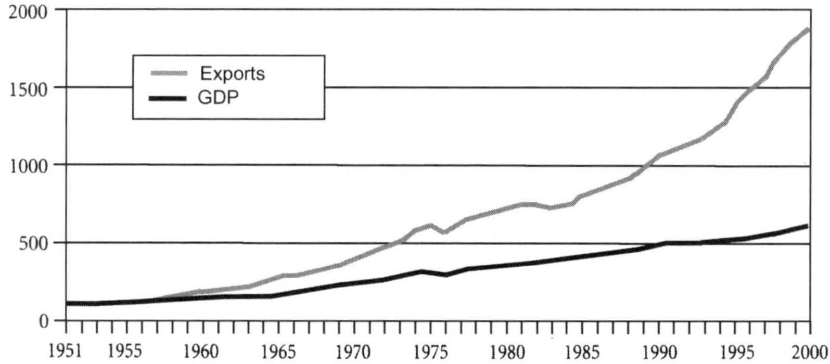

Source: WTO

As world trade grows faster than the world's wealth, an ever greater share of what is produced is being exported. For many products the market is no longer a national or regional one, but a global one. On the other hand, much of what is consumed (or used for further production) is being imported.

The organisation of production has adapted to these new conditions. Frequently, the optimal "economies of scale" now are realised in a production for this global market. Therefore firms that produce for the national market only, produce on too small a scale. As a consequence, their products become too expensive and therefore non-competitive. This has rendered useless, if not noxious, trade policies aimed at economic self sufficiency and import substitution[2]. Today, such policies just promote inefficiency and insufficient competitiveness. Governments, thus, no longer push for import substitution, but emphasise policies that result in an "export led growth". Not taking this option and choosing autarky or even the full withdrawal from the world economic system carries a heavy price. At present, only North Korea seems willing to pay it[3]. Other nations aim at fuller integration into the world economy. As a consequence, tariffs have been lowered and trade barriers have been removed.

Trade policy indicators 1988-1996

	Average tariff rate, all goods*			*Non-tariff barriers, import coverage ratio*		
	1988/89	*1993*	*1996*	*1988*	*1993*	*1996*
United States	4.4	4.7	5.2	16.7	17.0	7.7
European Union	8.2	8.4	7.7	13.2	11.1	6.7
Japan	4.2	3.6	3.4	8.6	8.1	7.4
Canada	8.7	8.4	12.1	5.7	4.5	4.0
Norway	5.3	4.0	22.3	13.8	11.1	3.0
Switzerland	4.8	4.5	3.2	13.2	13.2	9.8
Australia	11.2	6.6	4.2	8.9	0.4	0.6
New Zealand	10.6	5.7	5.1	11.5	0.2	0.2
Mexico	11.0	12.9	18.0	18.6	17.4	6.9

*Production weighted

Source: OECD 1997

Foreign direct investment is even more potent than trade in promoting globalisation. Enterprises themselves are globalising. The world has become not just one single large market to sell products and services on; but also – and increasingly so – it has become one vast productive unit. The rise in Foreign Direct Investment corresponds to this need to globalise production. The expansion of FDI is, therefore, more rapid still than the already rapid growth of world trade. In some smaller, wealthy countries with an open economy – like the Netherlands or

2 Save, perhaps, if applied in very special cases, to very specific productions and in sufficiently vast markets/countries (like Brazil, Korea and Japan).

3 Or to be more precise: the very strange but ruthless dictator ruling this unfortunate country is willing to accept the suffering of his subjects as the price for pursuing his whimsy about absolute national independence. 2 million North Koreans are said to have died from starvation in recent years.

Finland – incoming or outgoing FDI now already makes up more than one quarter of the gross capital formation. [4]

FDI inflows
in billion USD

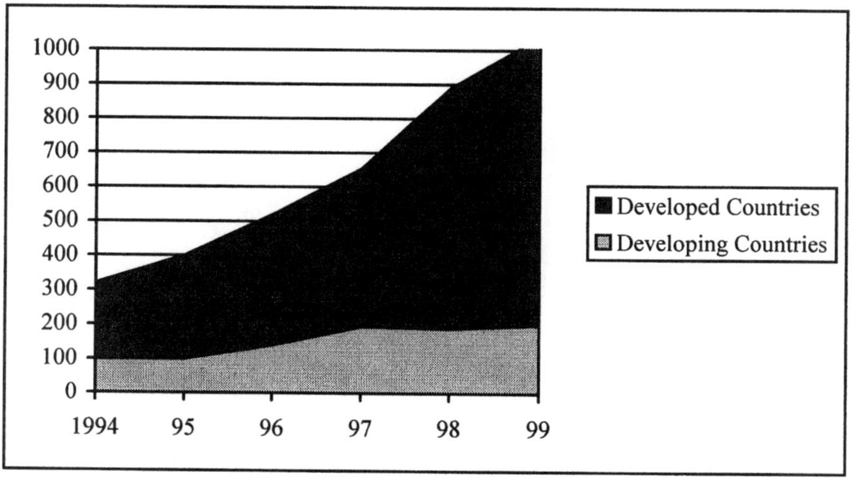

Source: UNCTAD

All these developments have an aura of inevitability. They look like something humans have to accept passively, like pre-ordained good or bad fate. Looking back, as we just have done on the last 50 years, would seem to confirm such a fatalistic vision of globalisation. It seems that people have no choice but to accept it. After all, not many will wish to emulate North Korea and to opt instead for a maximum of independence at the stiff price of starvation, isolation and poverty. We thus tend to believe that people will always prefer globalisation to its alternatives.

The late 19th century already had seen a drop in the costs of communication and transportation (brought about by the telegraph, the transatlantic steamer and the railroad). Proportionally, this drop was as dramatic as the decrease of the cost

4 The globalisation of the economy had the effect of lowering the prices of internationally traded goods. They have shrunk compared to most of the prices of goods and services that can just be produced / and or consumed locally. Consumption being price-elastic, this lowering of import prices further promotes international trade.

of long distance transportation that happened over the last 50 years. In the late 19th century, already, a good part of GDP was exported and imported. At that time, capital markets were as international and as liberalised as they are today.

Capital mobility

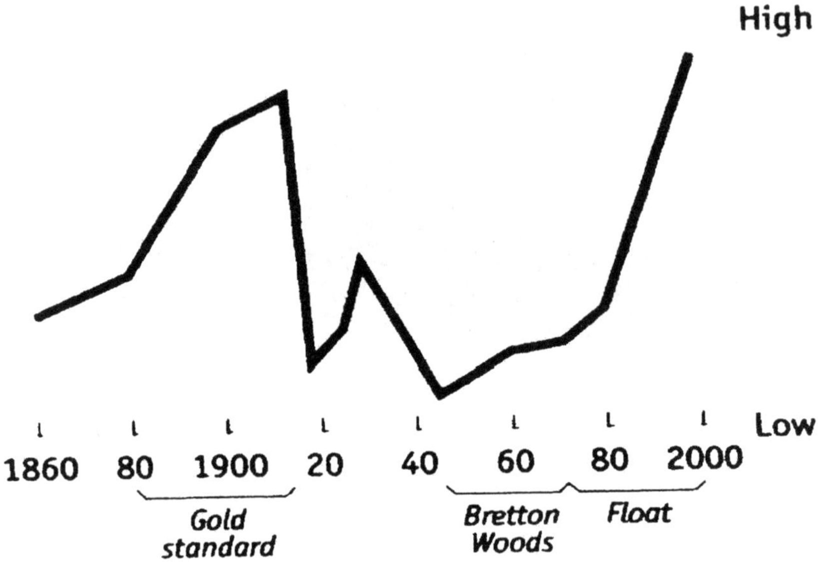

Source: Obstfeld & Taylor

As concerns the freedom of persons to move around and migrate, it was certainly greater in the second part of the 19th century than it is at the beginning of the 21st century.

Nonetheless, the globalisation of the 19th century became reversed. At first, this happened but slowly. From the end of World War I on, the process accelerated.[5] Only after World War II has this trend towards greater autarky become reversed. Only then did the economic interface between nations start to widen again. Still, it was only in the 1970s that globalisation became as intense as it had been before World War I.

---

5 Looking at the data in the thirties, the German economist Werner Sombart even maintained that growing autarky, and not growing globalisation, would be the wave of the future.

Merchandise trade as % of GDP[6]

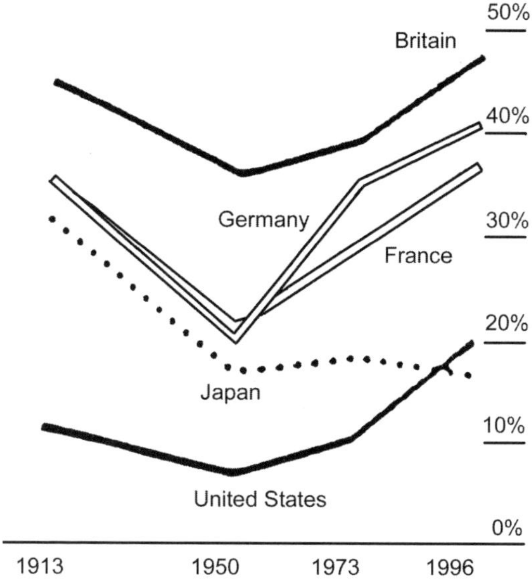

Source: A.Maddison 1997

There are differences, of course, between this first, 19th century wave of globalisation, and the present, second wave.[7] The first wave was driven by the expansion of trade in merchandise. Only a few services were traded. Also in that first wave of globalisation, international trade had not been "intra-industry". Goods of one type were exchanged against goods of a completely different nature – as, for example, cotton against guns. Nowadays, on the other hand, trade tends to grow in the direction of an intra-industry exchange. Auto-components, for example, are being exchanged against other auto-components or against complete automobiles coming from other countries. Accordingly, an increasing share of in-

6 Note the exceptionality of Japan. Unlike in other big countries, the international exposure of its economy did not grow after WWII; but it shrank. Japan's present deep economic crisis might be partly explained as the price it had to pay for this exceptionality.

7 Some authors claim that the 1850-1914 wave of globalisation was preceded by an even earlier one. The first half of the sixteenth century was also marked by global economic interconnectedness and liberalisation; a situation that drew to its end when conflicting nations expanded their claims so as to obtain a maximum of global resources (and so as to be better able to wage war against each other.)

ternational trade is in more complex products, a good part of which serve as inputs in the production of other complex goods.

Share of medium- and high-tech products in global exports 1980-1997

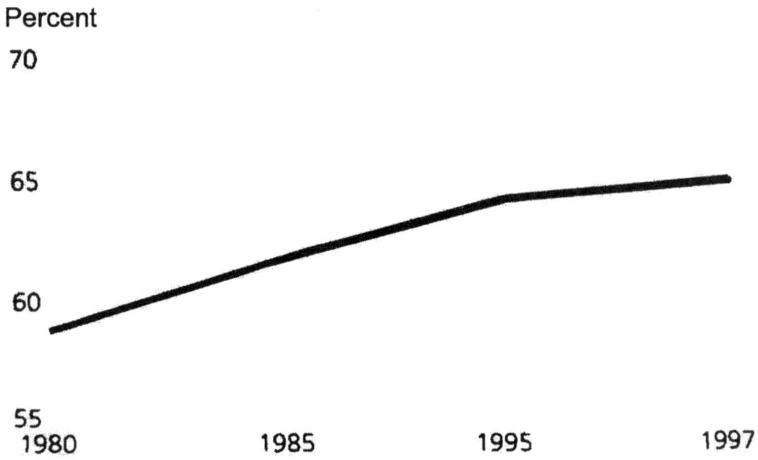

Source: UNIDO 2002

This growth of intra-industry trade is related to the fact that today at least one third of world trade is actually trade that takes place within the same firm. Trade is being carried out between different plants of the same firm, but located in different countries.

Media also have a more prominent place and function in globalisation. They act globally in a way they could not act in the 19th century. The international financial system has also become more complex. Some financial products are, in fact, being assembled from constituent parts from all over the world. A sovereign loan to India could thus become hedged by a derivative created independently by a big American investment house. Such complex financial products did not exist in the late 19th or in the early 20th centuries.

All that might tempt us to assume that this time globalisation will be more difficult to reverse than a hundred years ago. That might be the case. Nonetheless, one cannot exclude such a reversal coming about. This might happen even as – in general and on the average – the people of the world benefit from globalisation. Globalisation brings a more rapid diffusion of new technology, greater economies of scale, better use of scarce resources, more competition and lower prices.

Globalisation has thus contributed to keeping world economic growth at its unprecedented high level.

Doubtlessly, thus, the world economy, as such, has gained from globalisation. But did all countries of the world also profit from it? When we were looking at the poor countries of the world, we noted that not all of them have profited in such a way. Some have been left in the wake of economic progress. This failure is self-inflicted to a large extent. But, on the other hand, and in addition, globalisation has not opened the chance and prospect of economic advance to all of these poor countries. For some of them it has, on the contrary, created new hurdles that now make it more difficult for them to follow those already successful on their way to economic improvement.

In their past, many of the countries that now are rich started their economic growth not with a full opening to the world economy, but by a wise and targeted sheltering of some of their nascent industries. Since then, globalisation (and the political/economic forces behind it) makes it more difficult for countries to avail themselves of such a strategy. Also, and as mentioned, the economies of scale have changed in the meantime. Today, they are such that only a very few and very big countries would be able to develop competitive industries were these industries to produce for the national market only[8]. Such industries could become competitive only if they were able to produce for a market of a wider region or even for the global market. Now – effective regional integration has not advanced very much in the poor parts of the world. No wider regional markets have been created for their new industries. The markets for new industries thus remain the old and narrow national ones that impede a cost-efficient production run. The option of more efficient production for the global markets is not always open, because on the world markets the newly established industries of poor countries will face well entrenched competitors. These have deep pockets. For a certain time, they, therefore, are able to sell even below costs, if that permits them to kill the unwelcome competition from poor newcomers.

This is one reason why not all countries have profited evenly from globalisation; and why some have not profited from it at all. However, in those countries that did profit, did these benefits reach all of their citizens? And if so, were these benefits distributed evenly to all these citizens?

This is a hotly contested question. The most likely answer is as follows: In poor countries some groups of persons will lose out in the short run. In the long

8 I remember the Egyptian minister of industry remarking that Egypt – after all, a middle income country of no less than 70 million – would be too small to support an automobile industry. The output of one single modern car assembly plant would be superior to what the local market for new cars could absorb.

run however, all citizens of poor countries will profit from globalisation. It is different for wealthy countries. There, globalisation might disadvantage some parts of the active population more permanently. This is true, in particular, for low-skilled labour.

In one of the prior chapters, we looked into the growing inequality in rich countries and we tried to establish the causes of this rising inequality of income. We found the main culprit to be technological change that makes redundant low- and semi-skilled labour as well as many routine office jobs. But, doubtlessly, deeper involvement in international trade also contributes to the sharpening of this inequality.

Labour intensive products are no longer produced locally, but are being imported. This lowers the demand for low-skilled labour. As a consequence, wages drop. But globalisation contributes to rising inequality also in other ways. Business might decide not to just simply import labour intensive products from abroad. It might decide to move labour intensive production to poorer, low-wage countries. Or business will hesitate to invest in countries where labour is expensive. All that contributes to a slackening of demand for low-skilled labour in rich countries and all that, thus, makes for lower wages in that part of their labour force.

Globalisation implies the liberalisation of global capital markets. As a consequence, capital became footloose. In order to keep capital from exiting, countries think it expedient to lower taxes on capital.[9] As we have seen in the chapter on inequality, this has accentuated the inequality of income.

In the rich countries, rewards and burdens of globalisation are therefore distributed unevenly. The advantages go mainly to those already rich. The burdens fall mainly upon those who are already poor. This is reflected in politics. Trade Unions that represent labour and low skill office workers now have become protectionist. They wish to reduce the economic interface between their country and the world. Professionals and other wealthy parts of the population, on the other hand, support globalisation. They profit from it.

Yet, it is less those material aspects that fuel the debate on globalisation and that stir opposition to it. Less tangible things are more important. Humans are moved by still other motives than the yearning for material possessions. It is both condescending and unrealistic to term such other motives irrational. They might seem so to the narrow group of economists who acknowledge as "rational" only the quest for material rewards. But humans are moved by other motives too.

---

9 The fear of prompting an outflow of – productive – capital is mostly unfounded. According to Garret G. 1998, globalisation has not resulted in a "race to the bottom" in the taxation of wealth and capital.

These other motives have as much a function in assuring human survival as the quest for material comfort.

Humans wish to be free to decide on their own fate – they long for this freedom. They also desire to be familiar with their surroundings and circumstances and they wish to know the challenges they are likely to face. Humans also yearn for being imbedded in a group. In this group they wish to hold a firmly assigned function and status.

Globalisation might bring a greater abundance of material possessions to at least a vast majority of humans. But, for a vast majority such abundance is bought at the price of moving away from such other goals: globalisation brings a growing frustration over the failure to remain in charge of one's own fate. It increases a fear of things and developments that are not familiar and which, therefore, seem strange and threatening. Globalisation uproots humans from their accustomed social habitat. It deprives them of the identity they have acquired by having been given a clearly defined place and function in the social order.

Not so long ago, economies were not even organised on a national level but within more narrow geographic confines only. Smallish districts, grouped around towns, were largely self-sufficient. Trade across the divides between these units was in a few items only (like salt, spices or metals). It was only in the 18th century that, thanks to the new roads and canals and through a more efficient public administration, these smaller units became merged into the larger unit of one coherent national market. This development has advanced further and now has reached its limits. The smaller units of these national markets are now being merged into the single and largest unit: namely into a global market. Globalisation implies interdependence on a global scale.

Within nations, mechanisms had been developed to guide and control the forces of the market and to compensate for their deficiencies. The motive behind such efforts was, on one side, the wish to compensate for the malfunctioning and irrationalities of markets. But, the other and powerful motive was the wish to accommodate these needs of humans for things other than material possession and for material comfort. There is, for instance, this need for basic security; the necessity of lifting the fear for ones own physical survival by being sheltered against aggression and famine. The need for a clear status in the community and the need for clear procedures for resolving conflicts or for finding solutions to problems that have to be tackled jointly. Confidence needs to be sustained in the capacity of political communities to remain in charge and to be able to steer those developments that impact upon the existence of individuals or on the community of citizens. In order to meet these needs, democratic political institutions have evolved. Binding legal procedures and effective courts were instituted. Social security systems were built so as to protect citizens against risks they could not ward off themselves.

Few of these instruments of national governance have a parallel on the global level. Few institutions exist on the global level that could effectively balance, guide and control markets that have become global. And even where such global institutions exist, they are perceived as remote and alien by the average citizen they purport to serve. Ordinary citizens do not feel that these remote institutions are theirs to use to impact on global events.

Globalisation therefore creates strong countervailing forces. Once again and as they did in the first part of the 20th century, such countervailing forces might overwhelm and reverse globalisation. Such a reversal would come at the price of reduced wealth. As the markets cease to be global, the economies of scale become smaller. Productivity decreases and products become more expensive. But this is a price people might be very willing to pay if, in turn, they would gain greater autonomy and self determination and/or preserve more of their traditional way of life.

The historic precedent should warn us, however, against assuming that such a renewed reversal of globalisation would come only at the price of lower wealth; and that such a reversal would open the way to a return to primeval innocence, to straightforward democracy, and to greater solidarity between the different groups living in one state. The consequences of such a reversal would be noxious both for the national and for the global polity. Opposition against globalisation is usually connected to a gut reaction against things unfamiliar. It is fed by an insecurity that triggers hostility towards foreigners and that seeks solace in conformity. It is a powerful agent in making the atmosphere of politics "reactionary" in the true sense of the word: reactive to perceived or imagined threats and injustices; and incapable, for that reason, of tolerance or of the optimism that is needed to provide a reformist, forward-looking twist to politics.

If globalisation is driven by the economy, it nonetheless has also other than merely economic/material consequences. We have mentioned some negative ones that make people insecure, fearful, and apprehensive. But that is just one side of the coin. The wider interface with the wider world is also enriching. It widens the intellectual horizon. It teaches the relativity of firmly held national beliefs. It thus tends to induce greater tolerance. It could teach world-wide solidarity and responsibility. It could prompt us to listen to reason more than to emotions. But these positive reactions and lessons may very well lose out to the negative ones; with fear being always stronger than hope; and with uncertainty likely to be perceived not in terms of chances opening up, but in terms of threats likely to arise.

Just as in the first part of the 20th century, national politics might once more become infected by this negative emotional reaction against globalisation. This would destroy the psychological/social/political base for world-wide solidarity and for global governance. Once again the world would be caught in political fragmentation and in an antagonistic polarisation among nations. Were this to happen, the 21st century could very well become as fertile in murderous conflict as the 20th century was.

> Globalisation is frequently depicted as a cultural steamroller, bringing everything down to a similar low and even infantile, Mickey Mouse level. The Disney figures and the golden McDonald's arches are pervasive indeed. They are an element of a globalised culture. But they do not define it exclusively. Take the world literary market. Like the US McDonalds in gastronomy, US authors figure prominently on this global literary market. But, next to them, countless writers from other nations have gained world-wide recognition; as, for instance, Latin American and Indian writers. McDonald's hamburgers that are sold world-wide have, nonetheless, retained their character as a typically American product. Likewise, the Latin American writers that are being read world-wide have still maintained in their writing a distinct Latin American style. In that sense, globalisation of culture has expanded – and not narrowed – cultural options and experiences.
>
> The issue is not one of some "global culture" crushing into oblivion all that is worthwhile and precious in a local culture. The issue is whether this local culture dares to open up to the outside, and dares to participate in world-wide exchange; and – yes – competition[10].

A dangerous twist is added to this opposition to globalisation, when globalisation comes to be seen as a weapon of "Western culture", used with the intent to exterminate all other cultures different to, or opposed to, Western culture. Globalisation advances rapidly. Cultures, patterns of behaviour, belief systems change but slowly. Globalisation will, thus, not make disappear these differences in culture; and major confrontations would thus become inevitable if globalisation is seen to impose one specific culture upon the other.

This potential for violent conflict is augmented when such clashes of cultures become clashes of religions. By their very nature, religions must be absolute.

10 Measures taken by the European Union to protect its audio-visual production have not been legitimised by appeals to cultural protectionism; but by the claim that the cultural competition was not fair; as the playing field was not level. English language films are, for example, dubbed into other European languages. In the US, however, no "dubbed" films are being shown. The US film industry claims that the US public would not accept "dubbed" films.

They must uphold the notion of being the sole and only true creed; and of their opponents being ignorant and non-enlightened at best, and tools of Satan at worst.

Obviously, globalisation will push cultures close to each other and atop of one another, even those that are incompatible or hostile to one another. It is argued that this would become the prime fuel of international conflict. That, at least, was predicted by Samuel Huntington. In his notorious "Clash of Civilisations" he saw the future world as being defined by such clashes.

The world according to Samuel Huntington

Source: Economist (1.9.1990)

It is easy to criticise Huntington and many have done so. The point most frequently made is on the near absence of empirical proof for his far ranging conclusions. Nonetheless, there is something to his claims. Culture – or what he calls "civilisations" – matters. Globalisation puts cultures or "civilisations" in direct and stark competition. Conflicts are bound to ensue. They might turn violent and be carried out by other than cultural means.

But will such conflicts become central to, and even come to define the future of the global system?

a) As mentioned, there is no evidence to prove the claims of Huntington that, after 1950 (that is after the full onset of globalisation), or after 1990 (after the end of the bipolar system that might have suppressed them), cultural-civilisational conflicts have increased. They have not. The reverse is true.

b) the gaps between cultures (or "civilisations") have narrowed. At least, some of the sharp edges have been cut and some of the things have been removed that would have altogether impeded any meaningful intercourse. 18th century China and 18th century UK literally lived in different worlds. They had no common points of reference. This is no longer the case.

c) There still is much that is "Non Western" in "Western Culture" (left-overs from pagan times, for instance, like some Christmas or Easter rites). Much of what is considered typically "Western" is, on the other hand, also present in non-Western cultures – including the Islamic cultures[11].

> When accepting the Nobel prize for peace in November 2000, the Korean President Kim Dae Jung drew attention to such similarities and parallels in the world's great cultures:
>
> "In Asia, long before the West, the respect for human dignity was written into systems of thought, and intellectual traditions upholding the concept of the "demos" took root. [...] Mencius, disciple of Confucius, said: "The king is son of heaven. Heaven sent him to serve the people with just rule. If he fails and oppresses the people, the people have the right, on behalf of heaven, to dispose of him." And this, two thousand years before John Locke expounded the theory of the social contract and civic sovereignty."

d) The modern globalised economy (or "capitalism") is tolerant of quite some cultural diversity. Japan is highly developed economically. In fact it is one of the three partners in the "Triad". Over large stretches it has, nonetheless, preserved its cultural uniqueness. Cultural differences endure even in Europe in the integrating Union. They do not seem about to disappear. Economic efficiency does not require a sameness of culture.

Some basic values have to be accepted by all major global actors so as to keep the global system functioning (as e.g. a certain amount of tolerance, or the principle of non-discrimination and much else from the Universal Declaration on Human Rights). But, over and above that, differences might persist and will persist. Such differences might even persist in the "core" area of economic organisation and of economic institutions. Japanese and Chinese business culture has withstood the competition from other and different business cultures. And while

11 Both the economist Amatya Sen and the former President of Bosnia-Herzegovina Izetbegovic have pointed to the democratic and liberal tradition in Islam.

the European business culture has, of late, integrated a few more US elements, it nonetheless stays distinct too.[12]

Huntington thus erred in seeing clashes among civilisations or cultures as the main causes of violent conflict. Violence is prompted less by the differences in long established cultures than by the opposition to globalisation. This opposition will be directed against globalisation irrespective of the cultural garment it will appear in. Globalisation brings more material possessions. But, of late, organised violence has rarely been about material possessions. It had its causes in insecurity; loss of identity. Globalisation that enriches us in material possessions will, thus, not make disappear conflict that arises from such non-material motives and it will be fought in the name of such non-material motives.

Religious affiliation in Mexico

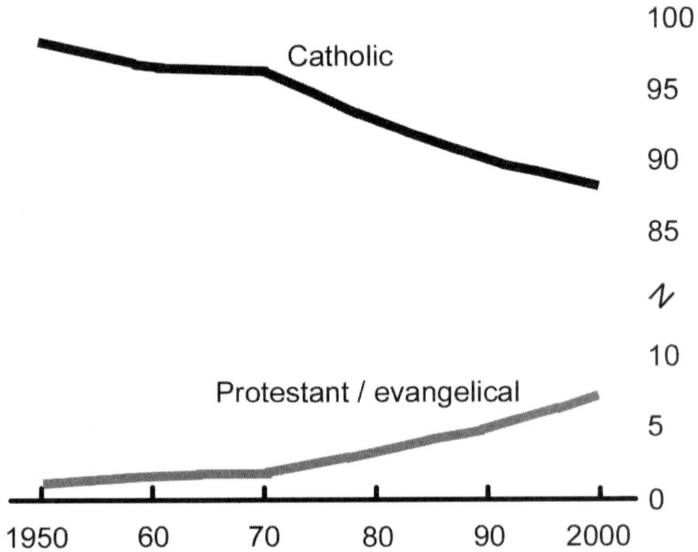

Source: Mexican government Census

12 In the long term, however, will any one of these **different cultures** win out, nonetheless? Will, for instance, education in US business schools and will the pressures of New York based stock analysts make **disappear** any other than the US business culture? If the past offers any instruction the answer would be a: **"probably not".**

Economic rationality, the search for maximal "utility", or "modernisation", never has reigned supreme. It will not reign supreme in the future either, even after having proven useful in raising the material well-being of a majority of the world's population. Increased material wealth might even strengthen opposition to globalisation. It might be that, after being freed from the shackles of daily toil and from the daily confrontation with hard reality, humans feel free to unshackle from this reality and to transit into shangri-las of irresponsibility and irrationality. California is one of the most "modern" places on earth. Nonetheless and perhaps even because of that, it has also come to stand for the wild foibles of a "new age". Another pointer to a "new age of irrationality" is the fact that fundamental religions like the Jehova Witnesses, Mormons, ultra orthodox Jews and – certainly – xenophobic, fundamentalist Islam are those social movements that have known the fastest expansion.

Fundamental religions are connected to, and feed from, a "common reaction against the disruption of cultural certainties and family support networks...and the loss of identity and meaning...Fundamentalism is a reactionary retrieval of traditional beliefs" (M. Marty 1991). As such, it is the natural ally of anti-globalism and is part of the cluster of attitudes that cannot be reconciled with global interdependence.

The irrationality of the "New Age" that is a creature of modernity and globalisation thus joins forces, in a certain way with the irrationality of religious fundamentalism that has its origin in a reaction against globalisation and modernity. This is not a pleasant prospect, especially as the defence of the rational middle ground seems to lack vigour and broad support. Some people are willing to die in order to become martyrs to their fundamentalist brethren and sisters. Some seem willing to float off the surface of the planet into the never-never land of a "New Age". There are those who disengage from any responsible reaction to globalisation by withdrawing into the self-sufficiency of an utterly private life. They even withdraw into the irrationality of a New Age and thus withdraw from any productive connect to the real world and the real issues that need to be tackled by politics. Then there are those who oppose globalisation and wish to return to the past and the past dominance of nation states politics over the forces of the market.

They would do this, however, at the risk not only of lower overall wealth; but at the risk, too, of a return to all the conflicts that this regime of nation-states had brought to the world in the 20th century. And then there are those with whom the onslaught of globalisation has raised nothing but fear and loathing and, with it, aggression and the wish to destroy.

Not all of these groups may be hived on board for a more rational approach to globalisation. A more rational approach to globalisation might however limit the power of such antagonistic forces to persuade and mobilise. Such a rational approach would aim to consolidate governance on a global level; just as governance was consolidated on a national level three hundred years ago.

Much attention has been devoted to the problems and implications of globalisation. The number of publications on this topic has expanded tenfold in the nineties. Less attention is still devoted to the question of global governance. The number of publications dealing with the legal aspects of globalisation has expanded much less rapidly. Much is being said and written on what globalisation is and what it implies. Less is said and written about how we should deal with it.

Frequency of "globalisation" in publication titles

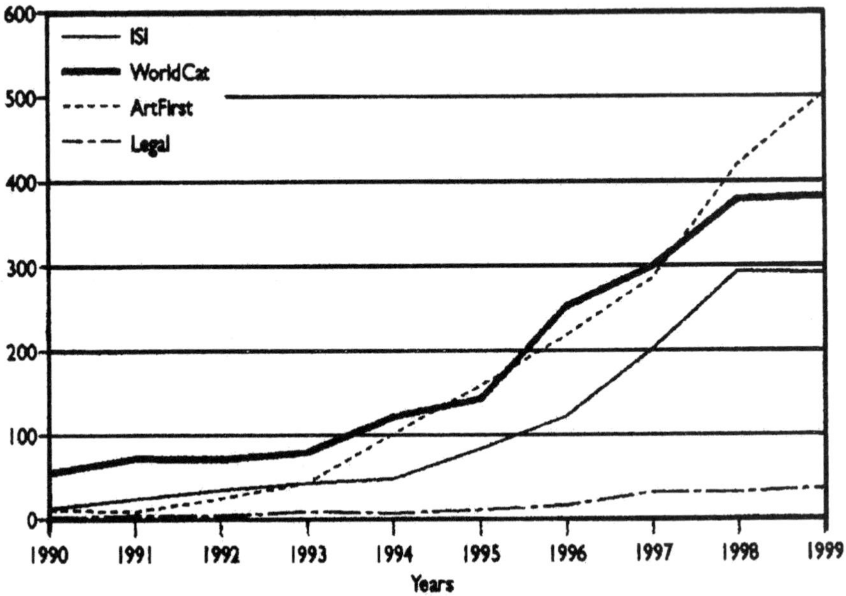

Source: World Development Report, 2003

Globalisation will endure only if sustained by global governance. We will thus address the issue of global governance in the succeeding chapters.

Who Rules? Markets? Financial Markets?

If globalisation sets the pace and if globalisation rules supreme – who then rules globalisation? Who sets the norms and defines the rules of the game in and for this era of globalisation? One answer frequently provided is that nobody does. Globalisation would be a self-regulating process. No outside intervention in this process would be warranted.

As we have assumed, and as seems plausible, the economy is the engine that drives globalisation. The economy is the dynamic element. Developments in other spheres would just follow whatsoever has been determined by the economy and its laws and requirements. If the economy needs more genetic engineers, the university curricula will be changed so as to produce more genetic engineers. If it becomes economically feasible and profitable to expand the reach of utilities beyond national frontiers, the markets for the services of utilities will become "liberalised". If costs for air travel shrink, international travel will grow; and so on.

In this view, states and politics would basically follow the economy, and the direction and pace of the economy, in its turn, would be determined by markets. As a concept, this is rather attractive. Ultimately, markets are driven by the wishes and preferences of the consumer. In a way, markets thus embody a daily practised, direct democracy: if, in the end, consumers prefer product B over product A, those who make product A will cease to do so. So – seen from that perspective – anything would be noxious that interferes with the preferences of the consumers being translated into changes in the economic structure; and ultimately translated into changes in the global system.

There would be no need for politics to intervene. On the contrary, politics should be kept out, as they would do nothing but distort the working of this everyday democracy of consumer preferences. Politics would just interfere with the daily referendums exercised by consumers through their spending money on this and not on that product.

It is claimed, furthermore, that the intercession of politics would not just negatively affect consumers. Politics would also make for a less efficient production. The economy is driven by entrepreneurs seeking profit. Profits can only be made through innovation. Profitable innovations cannot be predicted (for if they could be predicted, profits would be discounted and would tend towards zero). Rule setting, however, is based on the predictable. It is based on past experience. It cannot anticipate, or provide room for innovation. World rule setting by the state, therefore. limits the productive and innovative role of the entrepreneur. It reduces wealth.[1]

This has indeed become a political credo of quite many voters: there is little need for political rule making and direction. Both within states and on a global level, the function of politics should remain minimal. In essence, it should be restricted to two tasks:

a) the establishment of "property rights"
b) the safeguarding of the freedom of and in markets.

Everything else could then be left to the markets. And why not?

There are – and there could be – markets for this and that: markets for textiles, cars, houses, stocks, money, news and other information, culture, education, transportation, health, social services, addictive drugs, rendering of justice, contract murder, nuclear weapons.

But should there really be free markets for nuclear weapons and for contract murder? Can one conceive of a system of justice where judges are bought by the highest bidder? Evidently, things are not as simple as the dogma of the free market would make us believe. The dogma ignores some things that are at least as plausible as the gospel of unlimited free choice:

a) the freedom of one person has to be balanced against the freedom of the other person

b) some things can just be purchased by the community as such, that is, via politics (as for example: an efficient judicial system)[2]

c) among the things that cannot be purchased on the market are those that one does not desire. One cannot purchase the preference for not being murdered; or the preference for the air not being polluted.

d) many things can only become meaningful consumer items if they are produced under conditions set by politics (the production of meaningful news demands, for instance, preservation by political intervention, of the plurality of sources of information)

---

1 Therefore the mantra of economic liberalism: "de-regulate".

2 Over the course of economic/social development, the relative volume of these purchases will probably increase. That can be done only by and for the community. This is a consequence of the growing volume of inter-personal relations. It is bound to grow faster than the volume of the economy.

e) people do not act the way economists assume that they act. Economists assume that they act "rationally" in the sense of maximising their "utility" (whatever that is). But that is not how people behave in real life (or in experiments simulating real life). In real life they prefer, for example, group cohesion to personal gain (by choosing to punish deviant behaviour in preference to realising some personal gain). And, of course, their rationality is also bounded by their less than perfect information.

Finally – and this is the most important point – markets are not something that exist like air and water; something that has been there forever, and something that just waited to be used by humans. On the contrary, markets are human creations. They do not just co-evolve with human polity. The existence of a human polity is even a pre-condition for the coming into existence of markets.

As we have noted in chapter 11 ("damage to the social environment"), in a "state of nature" and in the absence of a polity, each human will be inclined to grab whatever he or she can grab. In a "state of nature" and in the absence of a polity, markets, therefore, do not exist; but just the conflict of all those that wish to "grab" a piece of something that is, so to say, laying on the ground. Markets can only emerge after communal life has been put on the basis of co-operation instead of conflict. This new communal order must be able to guarantee the social functions of "making", "exchanging", "preserving" (World Development Report 2003). The making of the polity thus precedes the emergence of markets. Thereafter most markets will have to be controlled or otherwise supported by the polity. As the last point is central to our subsequent argument, two examples will make it less abstract.

Trade is of course, essential to the economy; and trade is, of course, no longer being carried out on a barter basis. Goods or services are not exchanged against other goods and services but against money. What is money? In a sense it is confidence. A ten euro or ten dollar note is not a slip of paper, but something of value because you trust that it is valuable and because this trust is confirmed by experience. It has not happened to you recently that, when buying a bagel, the vendor has refused to take your money and has demanded something valuable instead.

This trust in money is a social product. It is the product of a social /political process. If the trust disappears (as happens during hyper-inflation), people will again revert to barter; and large parts of the economy will thus become blocked and/or collapse. The base of the economy is trade. The base of trade is money, the base of money is trust; and this trust does not pre-exist like air and water. It has to be created. And it has to be sustained by politics and institutions (like Central Banks).

Take another example from recent history. There are markets for stocks. In terms of capitalisation, the most sizeable of these stockmarkets is the New York Stock Exchange. After the end of the Communist era, Central European countries aspired to also establish such stock exchanges, not least because they were considered flag-ship institutions, giving visible proof of their success in having become truly "capitalist".[3] The Czech Republic was especially ambitious in this respect, being led by a prime minister who truly believed that the sole function of the state would be to guarantee property rights and the freedom of markets. In this vein, he thought it sufficient for stocks to be issued (property rights), and for them to be traded freely (at the exchange). No institution was charged with effectively controlling transactions. During the reign of this prime minister, the Prague stock exchange languished and did not attract much foreign (portfolio) capital. One main reason was the lack of transparency, which would have been assured by effective state regulation and supervision. In the meantime, the New York Stock Exchange boomed ahead. The New York exchange, and the papers traded there, are controlled by the powerful and intrusive SEC (Securities Exchange Commission).[4]

Evidently, the two things are connected. The New York exchange could boom (also) because it was controlled and because the customers, thus, could have confidence in papers not being fraudulent. No such guarantee could be provided at the Prague exchange. A market for stocks, in order to be effective, demands control and surveillance. Otherwise it fails.

What markets deliver also depends on the kind of socio/political systems these markets are imbedded in. Let us again provide an example. As we have seen in the chapter on the "new economy", the market for INTERNET services has expanded dramatically. Originally, this market had been conceived as the "agora", as the meeting place of free and high minds. But society being organised as it is, and humans being as rapacious and dirty as they are, the INTERNET market came quickly to be dominated by commercial interests and by the providers of lurid excitement. If it had developed in a martial/feudal society, the nature of this INTERNET market would have been different; different not just by the products bought and sold on it; but different, too, in its very structure.

In this and in the subsequent chapters we will, therefore, attempt to answer the following question:

3 Tellingly, the Warsaw stock exchange was established in the building that once provided headquarters for the Central Committee of the Communist Party.

4 Still not powerful and intrusive enough to prevent wide-spread stock manipulations by corporate crooks and greedy investment bankers.

As markets expand beyond the nation state and even become global, who, or which institution, controls these globalised markets? Who provides the rules for them, or even provides the basis for their continued existence? Also, which kind of socio-political order[5] will these markets become imbedded in?

As we shall see, the answer is not easy and obvious. All we can say with some certainty is that – though essential – markets alone and in themselves cannot sustain and provide stability to the global system.

But, after having established that markets need governance, and before going on to how such governance may come about, we should pause and give its due to the power of markets. It is true that markets cannot exist without polity. But it is equally true that a polity cannot exist without markets; at least not a polity that co-exists with a wealthy and complex society and economy. The polity reflects the communal; while markets reflect private choices. They are contingent upon another and both have their function in organising society.

And in today's world, the function of markets is broad indeed. Markets connect the cocoa growing farmer on the Ivory Coast to the child chewing a Mars bar in Cleveland, USA; they connect a secluded researcher at some university to the red neck steel worker probing the temperature of molten metal; markets direct the giant container ships plying the seas, the satellites in outer space, just as they direct communal taxis in Istanbul. The fact of markets having become global is actually the main characteristic of globalisation. It is markets more than anything else that structures this globalised world.

Yet, all that still does not obviate the need for these global markets to have a counterpart in global governance.

Financial Markets

Could it be that the global markets are ruled and governed by another market that would be a notch above them? They could be governed by financial markets. These would sit, so to say, atop all other markets.[6]

---

5 To provide yet another example: The market might be defined via the lowest possible prices on the one hand; or by the preference for "environmentally sound" products on the other.

6 This view comes naturally, of course, to those who hold – or administrate – financial assets. For who does not want power; or does not want to be seen as holding power? But power is ascribed to the holder of financial assets also by the harshest critics of capitalism, who also are convinced that capital reigns supreme – although as a cruel and unpleasant king.

And indeed, capital and money[7] do have a special position and function in the world's economic/political order. Financial markets are indeed strategic as they distribute savings[8] and permit these savings to be transformed either into consumption or investment. Savings are "leftovers", so to say. They are what is left over from the wealth that has not been used up in a prior phase, either for investment or for consumption[9]. The size and use of this "leftover" has a deep impact on the rest of the economy of a single country or of the world, as such. Too much savings not re-invested might pull down the economy into depression. Too high savings and too few solid investment opportunities might result in too much money chasing assets of doubtful value. "Asset bubbles" might form and later burst with noxious consequences (as they did in Japan). Too little savings might curtail investment and thus lead to sub-optimal economic development.[10] A high price on savings – that is high interest rates on capital – might impede investment and growth. Furthermore, high interest rates will dramatically re-distribute income and wealth to those who are already rich. Too low interest rates, on the other hand, might prompt a flight of capital.[11]

Those who hold financial capital have vast power to decide how it is used; where it will be invested; what for; and under which conditions. To a large extent, this is a sellers market with the providers of capital being in a much stronger position[12] than those who wish to make use of this capital.

---

7 The two terms overlap in their meaning: money is very short term, very liquid capital.

8 And in addition, as Schumpeter pointed out, investments are also financed from the receipts of a kind of tax imposed on the public by inflation which is caused by an expansion of credit.

9 In that sense one could call savings "derivates" of the sum total of investment plus consumption in a prior phase.

10 Or into debilitating deficits in the balance of the current account.

11 Something interest rates do NOT do is impact upon the volume of savings. The volume of savings by households does NOT depend upon the level of interest rates.

12 A good argument can be made for this sellers' market being an artificial creation and not the result of a quasi natural constellation. It is obvious that the holders of capital and their political allies push for measures that increase demand for capital; and thus increase the price of capital (i.e. the interest rates or return on equity). They insist upon a reduction of taxes even when it is not, or cannot be, balanced by a reduction of public expenses. The resulting deficits in the official budgets have to be financed on the capital market. Or they push for mergers and acquisitions that do not create new capacity, but that are very expensive and have to be financed by huge debts. They insist on the sale of public utilities – something that again creates new investment demand and offers new investment opportunities without increasing the capacity in the real economy.

Financial markets thus are powerful. They and those active on them have quite some impact on national and international politics. Swedish Prime Minister Persson tells a story of his encounter in New York with a room full of mostly junior financial analysts. The encounter he describes took place at a time when he still was minister of finance and when Sweden had suffered an economic downturn and had to seek external financing. Sweden, thus, was dependent on the goodwill of international financial markets and on the judgement of the analysts who were assembled in the room. If Persson had disappointed these analysts, either no credits would have become available; or such credits would have become burdened with much higher interest rates. So here was the minister of finance of a sovereign state, of a very well run and modern state, which never had defaulted; and this minister was faced with the suggestion or even the demand by some supremely confident (or arrogant[13]) youngsters to discard the traditional Swedish political system by abolishing at least a good part of the extensive schemes of social care and welfare. He somehow managed the situation but drew the lesson that never, never again should a Swedish government have to suffer the same experience. The budget is now in surplus and the Swedish state no longer needs to borrow on foreign capital markets. But few countries are in this lucky position. Witness the sorry spectacle of countless ministers of finance who, when trying to sell their countries' bonds on various "road shows", have to stick to a narrow script. Even if they do not believe in them, they have to mouth those pieties which financial analysts are apt to be pleased with.

Very well, one could say, that is how it is. One ruler has simply been dethroned by another one. Financial analysts have taken over the function of public

13 A counsellor of former US President Carter is quoted with this view on the power of financial markets: "When I was young, I wanted to become President of the United States. I changed my view after having been assigned to the president's office, and thought that to become the Pope would be a better choice. After all, the Pope has the enormous advantage of being infallible. But then, after a few months, I changed preferences again. After all, even devout catholics frequently do not do what the Pope wants them to do. So I decided that I should aim at becoming the "financial markets". Everybody trembles and obeys when being told that the "market" has arrived at this or that judgement; or "believes" this to be right or wrong. And, like the Pope, the "markets" cannot be second guessed". Or, as Robert Rubin, chief economic advisor, told president Clinton shortly after his inauguration, "Your success or failure lies in the hands of a bunch of bond-traders".
The arrogance – and basic ignorance – of and in financial markets is also reflected in several of the indicators used by big investment banks to classify countries according to their "competitiveness". Frequently, these rankings relate in no way to the actual economic performance of countries. With poor UK and poor and underperforming New Zealand outperforming – according to these indices – dynamic Finland or Denmark.

officials. And anyhow, these financial markets are essential. The modern economy could not do without them. While that is true and evident, there are several drawbacks: not only do financial markets lack democratic legitimisation; they also are not very efficient as rulers. They might solve some problems. But they create a host of other serious problems. And lastly: they, in themselves and without outside support, cannot fulfil the tasks they are supposed to fulfil.

Financial markets lack the democratic legitimisation for the kind of role they claim for themselves and that is assigned to them. In the financial markets it is wealth that votes. But the distribution of wealth is more unequal still than the distribution of income (which already is very unequal – as we have seen).

US-ownership of corporate and business assets (1992)

	Business assets	*Stocks*	*Bonds*	*Trusts*
The top 1%	61.6%	49.6%	62.4%	52.9%
The next 9%	29.5	36.7	28.9	35.1
Everyone else	8.9	13.6	8.7	12.0

Source: Phillips 2002

Popular capitalism US households

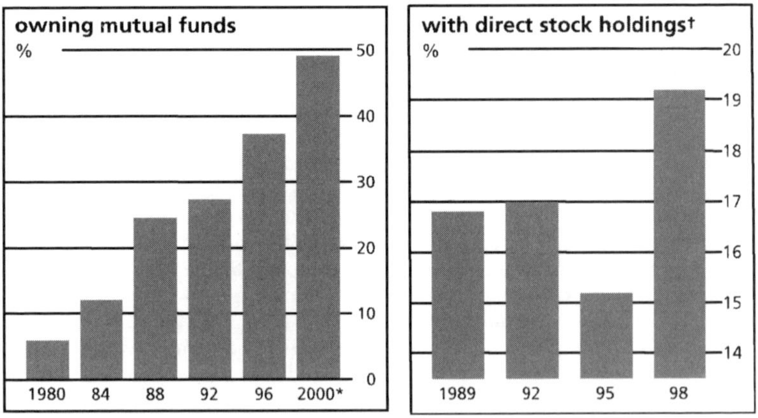

Sources: Investment Company Institute; Federal Reserve Board

And while, in the US, a large and growing number of households own shares, they mainly own them indirectly and via funds (with the managers of funds having their say at the shareholder meetings and on boards; to the exclusion of those that have invested in such funds).

The governance of the financial markets would not become more democratic if more of these shares were held directly by households and not by funds. The voices of small shareholders are mostly ignored. In the republic where capital votes, most citizens are disenfranchised.

A countertrend

Recently, however, small shareholders have become more active. Small stockholders of some companies have become organised. Some managed to, become a serious bother to management. There are two kinds of motives for this activism. One is simply material. Small stockholders may feel damaged in their material interest (for example by executives who grant themselves seven digit dollar salaries even when dividends drop). Other activists, however, use their voting rights at stockholder meetings to raise issues of a political nature (why, for example, has the company invested in a country that massively violates human rights; or why does it still damage the environment, etc). Some of this activism has been effective. It has – for instance – made some bigger US companies very circumspect in environmental matters; or loath to deal with unsavoury states or statesmen.

If the republic of capital is not very democratic (with power in the hands of relatively few), it is, nonetheless and increasingly, a truly global republic. Stocks of listed companies are increasingly dispersed amongst owners from many different nations.

Trans-frontier transactions of the purchase and sale of stocks
(in % of GDP)

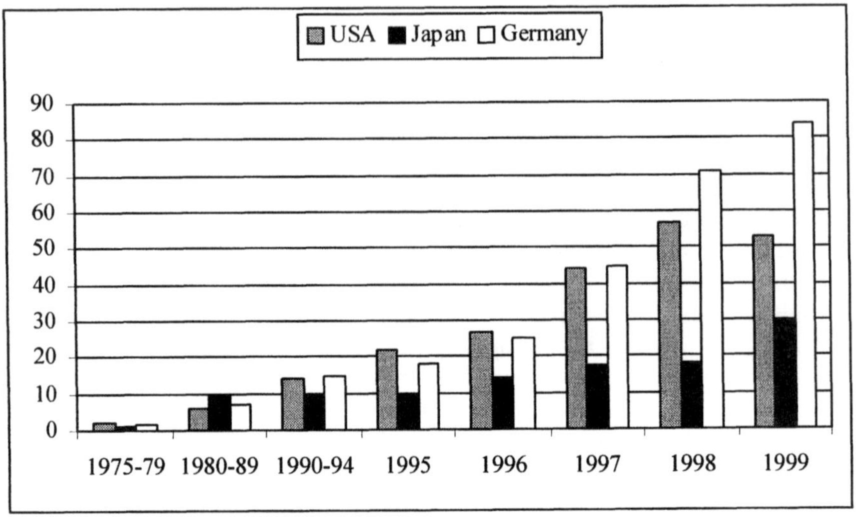

Source: BIS

It is rather obvious that the rules, the "culture", of this international republic of capital are mostly American (with a sprinkling of the United Kingdom thrown in, reflecting the role of London as the prime centre of money-trade). But the main stakeholders are by no means exclusively American. They are the wealthy from all over the world.

The lack of a broad and efficient democracy in this republic of capital is one of the reasons for its inefficiency. In addition, this republic of capital frequently produces "not the solution but the problem"[14]. In an efficient democracy, power is tightly controlled. In the republic of capital, that is not always the case. Take the example of ENRON, which used to be one of the world's major companies and was rather self confident in demeanour and in throwing around its might (for instance, in India, where it built a generating station; or on Capitol Hill and the White House, where it impacted upon US energy policy). Within half a year, ENRON'S stock market capitalisation of 90 billion US dollars evaporated. It

14 To invert the famous R. Reagan quote of the "state being the problem and not the solution"

went bankrupt. Obviously, those who owned the ENRON stocks had not been able to efficiently control the behaviour of the company.

ENRON capitalisation in current share value

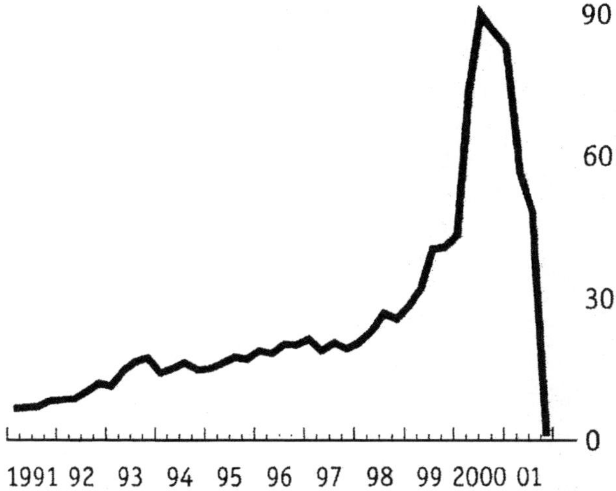

Source: Datastream

Anyhow, the notion is somewhat scurrilous that those who hold the shares of an enterprise actually own it in the sense of being able to direct, preserve, and evolve it. They do not have the information relevant for that purpose; nor do they have enough time and incentives to acquire such knowledge.[15] Small wonder then, that the valuation of stocks rarely corresponds to the long-term performance of the respective enterprises.

In fact, a deep gap separates the world of finance from the real economy. This gap is reflected on the front page of "Business Week" reproduced on the next page: It poses the question: "Volkswagen is one of the world's best car companies; but will it ever be a good investment?" (for people buying Volkswagen shares). How can that be? How can a company be considered supreme in performance; and, nonetheless, be not worth investing in?

15 The situation improves when employees become stock owners. In the US, such ownership is promoted by ESOP (the "Employee Share Ownership Plan"). ESOP companies perform better than other stock companies. (www.nber.org/"conter/2002/ISS02/kruse.pdf)

Being dissociated from the real economy implies, amongst other things, that prices of financial assets are less determined by the performance of the companies that stand behind them; and more by the mood and whimsies of the financial markets themselves. These depend on expectations on where the market will move. The shares of a certain company thus become valuable not because the company in question is suddenly doing so very much better. The share prices of the company go up because the participants in the financial markets believe that the other participants will believe that the prices of these shares will go up; with the second group, in its turn, justifying its optimism by watching the behaviour of the first group eagerly buying up the stocks and thus driving up their price. The classical bubble ("asset bubble").

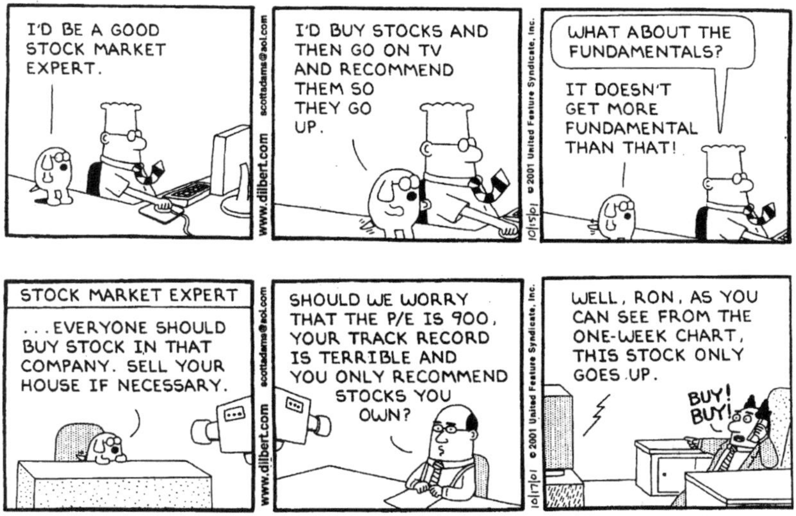

Source: Nex York Herald Tribune

Nonetheless, it is true that financial markets do, in a way, sit atop and dominate the real economy. And while they can do little to enliven it, they can do a lot to damage it. According to the US economist Charles Kindleberger, of the twenty eight economic implosions he recorded for the time between 1720 and 1975, twenty one originated wholly or partially in stock market bubbles in Holland, Britain and in the United States.

The real economy and the financial world come apart because of the sheer volume of capital that now divides the two realms. The daily turnover on the international money markets is well over one trillion (!!) US dollars[1]. Only between two and six percent of these movements[2] are connected to transactions in the real economy. The rest is not.

On the money markets too, profits are to be found in moving with the herd. If everybody believes that the external value of a currency will fall, fall it will. And if everybody believes in its external value rising, rise it will, even if objective data do not justify such a rise. There is enough free floating money around to hike up the external price of a currency for a long period of time[3] even when this is done against all traditional odds.

An example is provided by the euro/dollar exchange rate. Since its introduction in 2000, and up to the end of 2001, the euro had lost about 15% of its value against the US dollar. This was quixotic because Europe's current account balance was even, whilst the US current account balance was and still is massively negative[4]. Spendthrift US consumes more than it produces[5]. It imports more than it exports. In a like situation, one should expect money markets to speculate on the external value of the US currency going down. But up to the end of 2001, money markets continued to speculate on the price of the dollar going up. Why? Because one money trader believed that the other money trader believed that the other money trader believed etc. that the dollar exchange rate would appreciate. Therefore it appreciated and it did so against all laws of economics.

---

1 In 1973, when the fixed exchange rate regime was abandoned, the volume was a mere 20 billion USD. At that time, most of those transactions were still connected to transactions in the real economy.

2 These estimates vary widely.

3 Just as there is enough money around to force a currency into devaluation, even if this is not justified by objective data. Defending the Austrian schilling against an attack for just a few hours cost the Austrian National Bank about 20% of its reserves a few years ago. Had the attack persisted, for a few hours more the National Bank would have run out of ammunition and would have had to capitulate.

4 Something the US would not fail to criticise very harshly, if the culprit were on the other side of the Atlantic.

5 see the following chapter on the role and function of the "hegemon".

With the monetary and financial system having become detached from the real economy, crises are bound to occur. Given this high liquidity and volatility of financial markets, one should even wonder why there are so few of these crites. This relatively benign outcome is due to controls, rules, and regimes. Some of them become effective on a global or regional level; many of them just on a national level[6]. In the national regulation of capital markets and of money markets, two tendencies have become more prominent recently:

First, there is a clear tendency towards tighter supervision.[7] This is in response to the increasing complexity of financial markets. The new and ever more elaborate financial products that have been introduced call for a parallel heightening of supervisory vigilance.

Second, there is a tendency for some of the rules and institutions that were purely national before, to have an impact on a regional or even on a global level. This applies mainly to US rules. Many big transnational firms feel constrained, for example, to register with the New York Stock Exchange. This implies compliance with the detailed rules of the US Securities and Exchange Commission – SEC. The rules of the SEC thus gain global reach.

Central Banks, on the other hand, have clearly lost much of their function and their capacity to actually impact the economy. By now, they have largely lost control over the volume of money in circulation in a country. They still have some say in setting the interest rates for short-term capital (that is for money). But, even on these money-markets, they now are rivalled by other, frequently powerful players. They have hardly any influence at all on the pricing of long-term capital. The much publicised decisions of the US Federal Reserve or of the European Central Bank (ECB) refer to short-term capital, to inter-bank money only. For investment activity and thus for the real economy, what is more important by far are the interest rates on long term credits. These are set by the markets, by the laws of supply and demand and not by Central Banks.

The joint institution of the world's Central Banks is the "Bank for International Settlement – BIS" in Basel. It does have a certain co-ordinating function and even has been able to set some effective rules for banks across the globe. Several years ago, it established the requirement for the founding capital of a

6 Now, in the European Union, such rules are increasingly also on the EU level; see, for instance, the "Lamfalussy Report" on the integration of the market for financial services.

7 These controls are not foolproof, as shown by the downfall of the Barrings Bank as a consequence of the dealings of some "rogue trader" in faraway Singapore. Neither had external auditors detected the large scale fraudulence at the Bank Burgenland in Austria; and external auditors might have been a bit blinkered when going over the books of the US energygiant ENRON.

bank having to reach 8% of the bank's assets – as a minimum (Basel I). The BIS is now about to require further and more targeted precautions against the exposure of banks to risks (Basel II)[8].

Financial institutions frequently call on outside expertise for assessing such risks, such as, for example, the risk of buying the treasury bonds of a specific country. Such risk assessments are carried out by "rating agencies" (like Moodys, or Standard and Poor's). How effective are such agencies in completing this task and in providing guidance to financial markets? For an answer, let us look at how they have done in the Asian crisis of 1997/1998.

Development of the ratings by Standard and Poor's for long term debts denominated in local currencies

	Rating	*Date*
Indonesia	BBB- ↓	20.7.92
	BBB ↑	18.4.95
	BBB- ↓	10.10.97
	BB+ ↓	31.12.97
	BB ↓	9.1.98
	B ↓	27.1.98
	B- ↓	11.3.98
South Korea	A+ ↓	1.10.88
	AA- ↑	3.5.97
	A- ↓	24.10.97
	A- ↓	25.11.97
	BBB- ↓	11.12.97
	B ↓	22.12.97
	BB+ ↑	18.2.98
Thailand	A- ↓	26.6.89
	A ↑	29.12.94
	A- ↓	3.9.97
	BBB ↓	24.10.97
	BBB- ↓	8.1.98

Note: Ratings are from AAA downwards, BBB- is the limit for "investment grade". The arrows pointing upwards and downwards indicate an appreciation or devaluation of the local currency.

Source: BIS, 1998

8 "Basel II" is to enter into force in 2007. It is intended to enforce upon banks a closer scrutiny of credit risks.

As we can see, Standard and Poor's started warning about the looming crisis in East Asia only when the difficulties of these countries had become common knowledge. Korea had even been upgraded by Standard and Poor's a few months before the crisis broke.[9] The rating agencies had thus failed in their prime function to provide early warning[10]. They did, however, a further downgrading in the very trough of the crisis, thus sharpening and prolonging it. By December of that year, Korea had been downgraded to a mere "B". This prompted fund managers to withdraw investments from South Korean assets, thus imposing an added burden on the struggling Korean economy.

In view of such data, it becomes difficult to give credit to rating agencies for providing a meaningful contribution towards stabilising global financial markets. They seem to follow and not to lead the herd of portfolio investors. In crucial moments they seem to reinforce disturbances instead of calming them. Had rating agencies been up to their assigned task, they would have given early warning about likely difficulties in Asia. They would have downgraded these countries well ahead of the crisis. In the depth of the crisis, they should, however, again have taken the long perspective. They should not have assessed Korea with a ridiculous "B" – proven to have been wholly unjustified by the later rapid recuperation of the Korean economy.

But one cannot really blame rating agencies for this failure. The simple truth is that crises as well as profits cannot be predicted with precision.

In the end, predictions are impossible; and risks remain risks

To appreciate the point, take a look at the crisis triggered by the near-default of "Long Term Capital Management – LTCM". LTCM had to be bailed out by the US Federal Reserve and by US banks so as to prevent a "financial super melt-down", which would have caused serious difficulties all over the US economy. LTCM dealt with derivatives. This is riskier than dealing with more mundane stuff. But it is also more profitable. To be on the safe side, and to contain the volume of such risks, LTCM hired two US professors who had

9 The Asian crisis surfaced with the Thai decision on 2 July 1997 to devalue the baht.

10 Everybody agrees on the usefulness of "early warning" . After each major financial crisis, ministers of finance and presidents of central banks are apt to call for this kind of closer monitoring. They are asking for the impossible. An IMF study has analysed all more recent financial crises. Using all indicators that could be gleaned from this study, the IMF found that – at best – only half of the crises could have been predicted beforehand. Early warning is a phantom, a mirage. The overall behaviour of the financial system will remain unpredictable (and, as I believe, it cannot be otherwise).

won the Nobel prize in economics for their models of calculating and discounting risks. To do that, one has to have a base. And this base was the totality of risks that had become known until then. Risks that had not become obvious up to then were thus ignored. The model therefore did not deal with the consequences of a very sudden drop in US share prices. Such a sudden drop had not occurred before. But it occurred, for a short time, in 1997. When this happened, the whole strategy of LTCM became unstuck.

One may generalise: only those things are truly and highly profitable that are without precedent and not fully proven and not fully certain. For, if something is certain and proven, profits will be discounted by the markets. When everything has become certain, profits will have disappeared.

There are very elaborate schemes for risk assessment[11]. Benchmarks do exist that allow for separating into groups of lower or higher risks. The above mentioned Basel II Accord will make the use of such schemes obligatory. But that should not make us oblivious to the simple fact that future profits are always uncertain; and that high expected profits imply high uncertainty.

That leads us to the institution that is central to the maintenance of stability in the world monetary system: the IMF – International Monetary Fund. Its creation coincided with the end of the last World War. The Fund was given the task to prevent a repeat of the developments that had caused the world-wide economic crisis of the thirties; a crisis that had doubtlessly contributed to the rise of fascism and to the outbreak of the war. At its creation, two major tasks had been assigned to the Fund:

a) to establish and maintain stable exchange rates so as to prevent a recurrence of "competitive devaluations", which were characteristic of the pre-war period

b) to provide, as "the lender of last resort", liquidity to the world economy should it become threatened, once more, by deflation and, thus, by a deep downturn.

Both of these essential functions were lost. The regime of fixed exchange rates was abandoned in 1973. Like Humpty Dumpty it is not likely to be put together again. This is not only due to a lack of international political resolve and consensus. This is also due to the fact that the combined reserves of the IMF and of all the Central Banks are just a small fraction of the amount of money sloshing

11 I myself worked on a few of them. Beware especially of what is called "political risk assessment". Its predictive power is zero.

around freely on the euro-dollar market and on similar markets[12]. If speculators decide to attack a currency, neither the Monetary Fund nor associated Central Banks would have the reserves necessary to fight them off for any lengthier period of time. Better not enter a battle one is likely to lose. If one lacks the tools to defend fixed exchange rates, one should not envisage re-introducing them.

As the IMF could no longer guarantee fixed exchange rates, the major economic powers of the world decided to take the lead in preserving at least some continuity and rationality in the world monetary system. The world (economic) summits were intended to take over parts of the former functions of the IMF.[13] In the beginning, these meetings had some limited effect; witness the example of the so called "Plaza Agreements" of February 1985:

The German mark / US dollar exchange rate

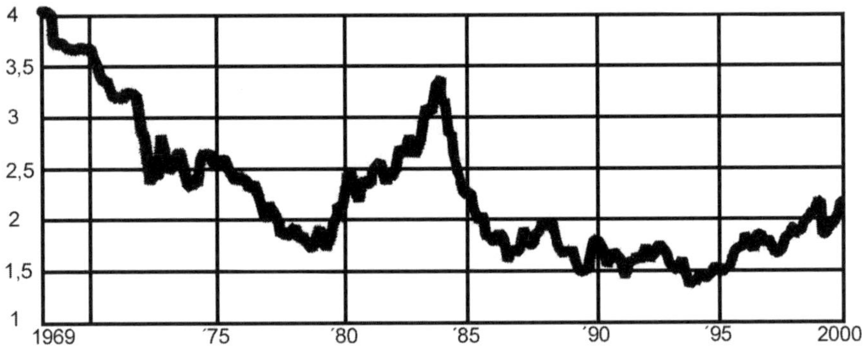

Source: Datastream

For reasons not really evident (or perhaps just because the financial and monetary markets liked US President Ronald Reagan), the US dollar started to surge in the early eighties and did so in a de-stabilising way. For a while, the representatives of the G-7 succeeded through this "Plaza Agreement" to "talk down" the US currency. But this feat could not be repeated. In late 2000, Europeans and Americans attempted a similar coup when the dollar again had risen against the

12 The "Tobin Tax" would put a price on such transactions. It would make them costlier and, therefore, less frequent. This would reduce the volatility of the world monetary system. The fact that this very sensible proposal has no chance of being accepted and even no chance of being discussed seriously, says quite a lot about this global system; and about the interests prevailing on and through it.

13 As of summer 2002, expanded through the inclusion of Russia into the G-8. These summits have lost much of their prior function of setting policies.

European currency (this time already the euro). This was to no avail[14]. The dollar remained high, the euro low.

This demonstrates that the G7 (now: G8) is no viable substitute for the functions the IMF has lost. But even after this loss, the IMF still does provide at least some essential support for the world monetary system. If it could not halt the wild gyrations of monetary markets, it could at least dampen them. It has been able to smoothen the cycles of booms followed by busts to which many markets, and financial markets in particular, are prey.

Leading a consortium of International Development Banks (IDBs), of governments and of private banks, the IMF has certainly reacted rather forcefully to the Asian crisis. Acting together under the leadership of the IMF, these institutions have provided substantial liquidity to Asian economies at a time when this needed liquidity would not have been provided via other channels. Without the IMF, and in absence of this co-ordinating role of the IMF, the crisis would have certainly been worse. As it was, the IMF and the IMF-initiative was able to compensate (at least to a large extent) for the capital flight from these countries that accompanied the crisis.

Standby credits provided under the leadership of the International Monetary Fund during the Asian financial crisis 1997/98
(in billion US $)

Country	*Year*	*Credit sum*	*IMF*	*World Bank*	*Regional Development Banks*	*Bilateral credits*
Indonesia	1997	42.3	11.2	5.5	4.5	21.1
South Korea	1997	58.2	20.9	10	4.0	23.3
Thailand	1997	17.2	4	1.5	1.2	10.5
Sum	1997	117.7	36.1	17	9.7	54.9
Brazil	1998	41.5	18	4.5	4.5	14.5
Russia	1998	22.6	15.1	6	-	1.5
Mexico	1995	51.6	17.8	1.5	1.3	31

Source:IMF

The IMF is criticised less for this role in supplying liquidity than for its policy prescriptions. In the Asian crisis they were clearly counterproductive. As can be gathered from the table below, the macroeconomic situation of the Asian Crisis countries had been basically sound before the onset of the crisis. Unlike in some

14 Which could prompt a more general observation: joint actions are bound to be more efficient if not done on an ad hoc basis; but when rooted in, and backed up by, institutions.

South American countries that experienced crises earlier or later, spendthrift governments were not the problem in Southeast Asia. Budgetary deficits were low, and anyhow compensated for by very high saving rates. Given the fast economic growth, the deficits in the current accounts could not be considered excessive.[15]

Macroeconomic situation in the Asian Crisis Countries before the onset of the crisis (i.e. 1996)

	Indonesia	*Malaysia*	*Philippines*	*S.Korea*	*Thailand*
Rate of inflation	7,9	3,5	8,4	4,9	5,9
Deficit state budget % of GDP	1,4	4,2	-0,4	-	1,6
Current account deficit % of GDP	-3,3	-4,9	-4,7	-4,9	-7,9
savings as % of GDP	28,8	36,7	19,7	33,3	33,1

Source: IMF

Nevertheless, the IMF treated the Asian crisis as if it was just one of the recurrent crises in Latin America; and as if it, too, had been caused by exploding deficits in the state's budget, by low savings rates and unsustainable deficits in the current account. In fact, however, the Asian crisis was the result of an asset bubble that burst.

The liberalisation of the foreign exchange regime and of banking was one important cause of this asset bubble. Yet the IMF (and related institutions) had pressured the Asian countries to open their capital markets. They prevailed and, as a consequence, much short term (portfolio) capital entered into these Southeast Asian countries. Southeast Asian citizens and corporations could, in their turn, henceforth invest freely abroad. This prompted Southeast Asian Banks to hike up the still low interest rates on deposits so as not to lose such deposits to banks in foreign countries. To balance the rising costs of these deposits, Asian banks were forced to seek assets promising high returns. Vast amounts of money therefore came to fuel speculative ventures (like stocks and commercial real estate) that – ultimately wrongly – promised [16] such high returns.

15 Except in Thailand with a deficit in the current account of –7,9% of GDP.

16 It is always a signal of imminent danger if, in a poor country, real estate prices explode. Here is my golden rule: a country is the more financially solid, the lower, in relation to its overall wealth, the prices for choice real estate.

When the bubble burst, capital fled the region. This created a credit crunch that depressed the economy.[17]

Such failures do not imply that the IMF has become irrelevant. On the contrary, it has remained quite powerful[18]. For many countries it holds the keys to access to external financing. Few creditors are prepared to lend to a country (or to lend at a reasonable rate) if that country is de facto blacklisted by the IMF – which happens when the IMF refuses to extend or to prolong a "stand by credit". Even countries fairly well off and not in need of a stand-by credit are queasy about the so called Article 4 IMF examinations of their macroeconomic policies. Should the IMF find too much to criticise, this would damage their reputation in financial markets and would make it more expensive for them to raise capital when they need it.

One (not so secret) source of the IMF's power is steadfast support from the United States. In the IMF, the US holds the largest block of voting rights[19]. The US uses this privileged position to protect their (political and economic) interests. If the IMF speaks, everyone is thus conscious of the fact that it is also speaking with the authority of the United States (even though, and in order to keep up appearances, the managing director of the IMF is always European). The perception of the IMF as being an instrument of US policy is sustained by its policies. It intervenes fast and decisively when US interests are at stake – as they were in Mexico. It becomes more diffident when European interests are at stake (as they were in 1998/99 in Romania[20]).

---

17 On a grander scale, the same thing had happened in Japan before. There, the bursting bubble of stock and real estate prices even had set in motion a deflationary spiral. Until now, Japan has not been able to extricate itself from this self-reinforcing trend downwards.

18 In Lithuania, for example, the IMF representative has his office right next to the office of the prime minister. The IMF also ranks high in the pecking order of international organisations. Certainly, the IMF itself is convinced of being at least as important as the United Nations.

19 The Euro 12 block acting together would have more voting rights. But for reasons difficult to fathom, and notwithstanding their common foreign and security policy, Europeans did not vote as a block on the IMF Board; not even the Euro 12 did that (save in exceptional circumstances when the euro, as such, was at stake): They now have promised to co-ordinate their voting (as they do at the United Nations). But it remains to be seen if and how that promise will be implemented.

20 Far from sheltering Romania from bankruptcy, the IMF made strong efforts to force it into bankruptcy; so as to teach careless lenders a lesson. This motive did not, however, prevent the IMF (and/or the US) from quickly coming to rescue when trouble threatened again in Mexico. It has to be noted, though, that the IMF did not interfere to prevent the default of Argentina.

Transnational constituencies

We should take note, at this place and when dealing with the IMF, of something that we will encounter also in other international organisations. The IMF has its own constituency of ministers of finance and of presidents of central banks. They meet twice a year, at least. Many thus know each other personally. They share the same pre-occupations. In many instances, they therefore are closer to one another than they are to their ministerial colleagues in the government which they are part of. Also, congregating on an international level, they reinforce in one another the sense of a special mission. Decisions taken in such gremia[21] might, thus, deviate quite widely from the overall policy of a specific IMF member country. The IMF/IBRD constituency of ministers of finance and of central bankers are thus all very close to what is called the "Washington consensus": the gospel of deregulation, privatisation and liberalisation.[22] They hold such positions at least while in Washington and while not under immediate pressure from their national constituencies.

Notwithstanding its power and prestige, the IMF is far from meeting its original purpose. As mentioned, it cannot safeguard the stability of the foreign exchange rates of the major economic powers. Neither does it have the tools to combat a truly serious world economic recession. As the Asian crisis has demonstrated, these tools are barely sufficient to cope even with a relatively short-lived regional crisis.

Also, its policies have come under quite some criticism. It emanates from two sides. The political Left sees the IMF as a stooge of US capital and criticises its narrow ideological focus and its "one size fits all" policies. Criticism coming from the conservative side is more fundamental still. Conservatives pose the more basic question as to what the institution is good for and why one should not abolish it altogether. Both the Left and the Conservatives agree on one point: the IMF mainly serves the interests of creditors. It protects them from the consequences of their own bad judgement and their recklessness in lending. Both the political Left and the political Right question why it should become the task and the function of the IMF to "bail out" imprudent lenders. These should be made to

21 The same tendency can be observed in the EU Economic and Financial Council – ECOFIN.

22 According to John Williamson, who created the term "Washington consensus", its ten rules of structural adjustment could be applied universally.

suffer for their own mistakes. That would teach them a lesson and would make them more circumspect in the future.[23]

The question thus posed is certainly relevant. This has been recognised by the IMF and, as a consequence, the organisation has tried to somewhat change its course. It now wishes not to just "bail out", but to also "bail in" foreign lenders. The IMF would now like to see lenders suffer a bit when a country fails to repay debts that they had extended. Under discussion is a new mechanism that would serve this purpose of "bailing in" private creditors. The "Sovereign Debt Reduction Mechanism – SDRM" would create, for indebted states, a mechanism which would resemble the "chapter 11" mechanism used for illiquid firms in the US.[24] Under the supervision of the IMF, all creditors and the debtor would together negotiate a debt reduction and a schedule for the servicing of the remaining debt.

Another former IMF policy has also been abandoned after having been shown to be counterproductive and misguided. The IMF used to recommend (perhaps even: impose) that the currencies of "weak" countries be firmly tied to currencies of "strong" countries; either via a fixed peg; or even via a currency board. Argentina had heeded that advice to its own bad fortune. The IMF has drawn the lesson, too, and now favours more flexible exchange rate regimes.

One other change in IMF policy comes in reaction to the criticism over its complex, intrusive, and detailed policy prescriptions. Critics demand that the IMF be less generous in giving good advice on how countries should be governed. According to Horst Köhler, the managing director, the IMF will therefore restrict such advice[25] to a few basic recommendations on macro-economic policy.

The IMF has also moved away from its prior, intransigent insistence on the opening up of national capital markets. There are some interesting studies on this done for or by the IMF itself. They show that the vast majority of recent financial

23 In 2002, the IMF refused to bail out Argentina, which drove the country into default. This was the first time that the IMF has failed to come to the rescue of such an important debtor; and that it thus has "bailed in" those that had provided the credits to Argentina.

24 Or to the "Ausgleich" provided for by German commercial law.

25 Less euphemistically: "conditions for its support".

crises had been caused by "pre-mature" liberalisation[26] of the capital account.[27] The evidence is there for all to see. Not just countries in Eastern Asia but many ex-Communist countries, too, started to run into difficulties from the moment they opened their capital market to outsiders. The conclusion is also supported by the two graphs reproduced below. The first compares the "openness of markets" for goods and the openness of the financial markets across various regions of the world. Most poorer parts of the world are more open to trade than to capital flows. But the reverse is true for Latin America.

26 Capital controls were maintained by some of the wealthiest countries – like Sweden and France – up to the early nineties. This should counsel prudence on demanding from much weaker countries that they open their financial markets immediately.

Restrictions on capital flows – Index

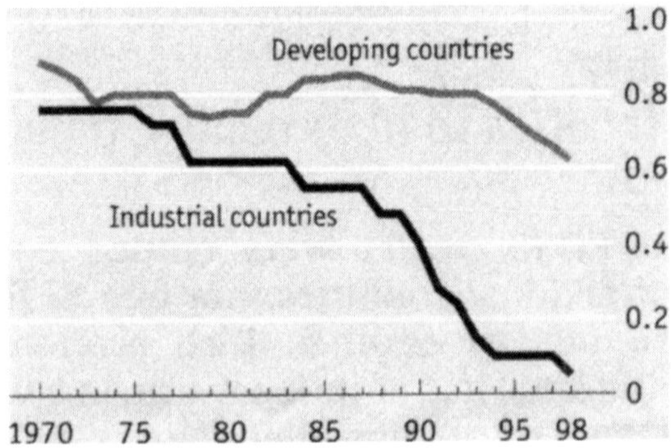

Source: IMF 2003

27 Liberalisation of the capital account led to such crises, if and when such liberalisations of the capital account, and of the financial system, coincided with what the IMF believes to be inappropriate macro policies. But it is not too difficult to find faults with a country's macro – policies.

Trade and financial integration across developing regions 1975-99

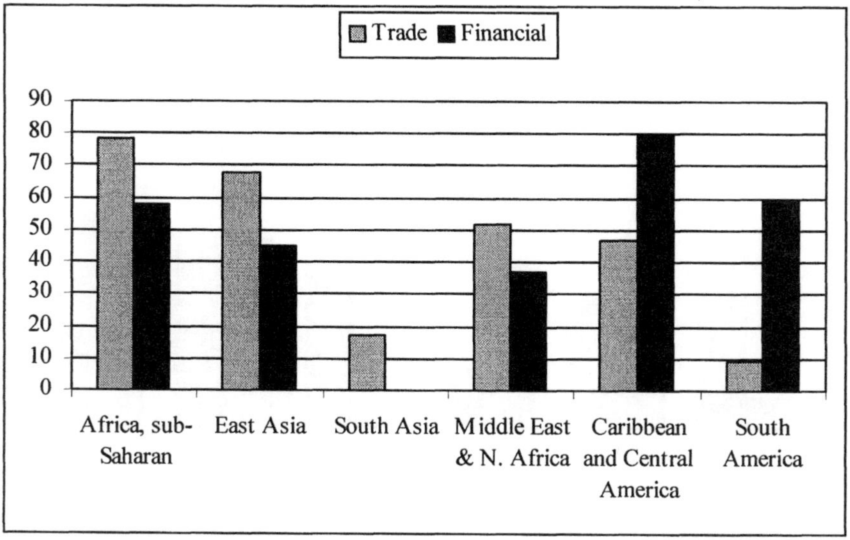

Source: IMF 2003

But Latin America is also the region to have experienced the greatest number of financial crises.

Frequency of external financial crises in Developing Countries
(the black column stands for the frequency of crisis; the grey column for the openness of financial markets)

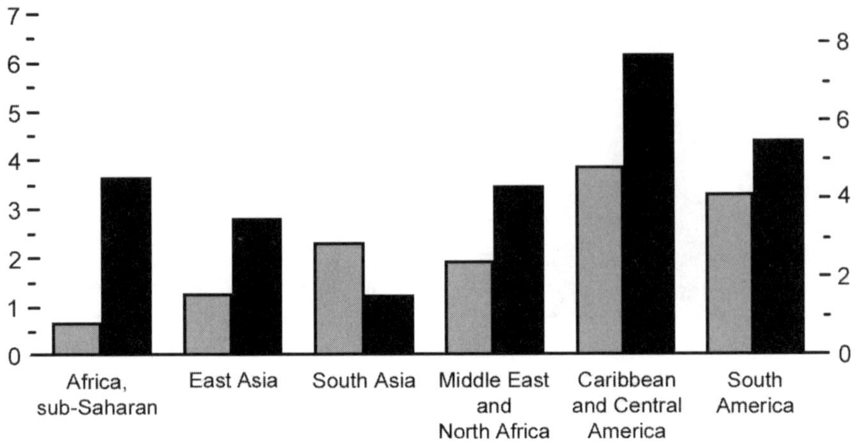

Source: IMF 2003

As mentioned, the IMF has drawn conclusions from such statistics. It is changing track. It very much has softened its prior stern demands that even poor countries open their financial markets and that they do so as rapidly as possible.

Unease persists about the functioning and function of the two Bretton Woods sister institutions (World Bank and IMF). It has translated into off/ on /off proposals for a wholesale transformation of the "architecture" of the world financial system[28]. But such calls will not be heeded. No one has the resolve and power to effect such wholesale transformation and those who do call for it do so for widely diverging, and even incompatible, motives. One side (let us call it the "Left") wants to strengthen the two institutions and to focus them more clearly on their core tasks (for the IMF: managing the world monetary system; for the World Bank: fighting poverty). Conservatives, on the other hand, wish to more or less abolish the two institutions. They are convinced that, by intervening in the world economy, these Bretton Woods sisters have done more harm than good.

Let us thus sum up this and the previous chapter:

28 with such debate usually dying down half a year after the last crisis has passed

1) Markets are not just useful; they are essential. Financial and monetary markets form the roof over other types of markets. Their behaviour has a deep impact upon the rest of the economy. But, by their very nature, these financial and monetary markets are especially volatile;

2) Strong regulatory efforts correspond to this volatility. Such regulation is attempted on the national, the regional, and the global level;

3) Nevertheless, national or global regulation will never completely eliminate the strong fluctuations and recurring crises of financial markets. The optimum one can realistically hope for is the dampening of such crises;

4) In these efforts, the IMF still has a central role. But notwithstanding the high prestige and the visibility of the IMF, this function remains a limited one. Certainly, it is minor compared to the function originally conceived for it. No global institution is in place to perform two essential tasks: limiting the wild swings in the external value of currencies; and standing by as an effective lender of last resort in the case of a global deflation. Discussions on changing that through a new "world economic architecture" are likely to be aborted.

5) Nonetheless, up to now, financial and monetary governance on a global scale could score some success. It has, as one must assume, prevented regional crises – like the Russian or the Asian crises – from growing into a world financial crisis.

Two points, finally, to reflect at a greater distance on the issue of the dominance of financial markets:

a) If, at the time Jesus was born, just one "drachme" had been invested at a real interest rate of just 2%, and if the gains from the interest would have been added to the original account, this account would, by now, be larger in size than all capital presently available world-wide. We therefore have to conclude that interest rates should be lowered drastically to near zero. Should that not happen, one will have to accept that capital will be destroyed from time to time. Actually, this is what has happened throughout history. Capital was destroyed by inflation, wars and the wholesale default of entire countries.

b) In a mental experiment, one may discount the value of major investments usually done by states. The further in the future and the less certain the pay-off, the higher the discount. Seen from this point of merely financial return, little money should be invested in some basic infrastructure, in much of the human capital, in the beauty of cities, or in the protection of the environment. Frequently, the pay-off for such investments would be too uncertain and too far in the future. Fortunately, societies still invest in such things.

Transnational Corporations – TNCs

Big and powerful firms existed in the past. In the past, too, some of them operated in faraway places and a few even had activities the world over. In the sixteenth century, the German trading houses of the Fugger and the Welser had mines not only in Central Europe but in South America too. The Dutch and the British privileged trading companies assumed the role of imperial powers. The Rothschilds created a world financial empire. Rockefeller's Mobiloil produced and sold the world over. The notorious American "United Fruit" held economic and political sway in Central America.

In the last fifty years, the number of such companies with a presence not just in a single country, but in many different countries, has very much increased. Once, such firms were called "multinationals". This term might suggest that they were composites of equal contributions coming from many different nations. But this was not so. The capital of such "multinationals" still used to come from one country only; and so did the top-managers. Most core business activities were also retained in the original home country of those companies. Their subsidiaries were present in other parts of the world for two reasons mainly: either to better serve the local market; and/or to provide, from local sources, low value-added inputs into the main production, which was carried out, not in a decentralised fashion, but, basically, just in the home country of the "multinational" firm.

In many cases, the connection between the local branches of such "multinational" firms and the local economies was but a loose one. At worst, such subsidiaries remained some sort of an economic island, staffed from abroad, purchasing their inputs from abroad and: either again exporting the total of their output; or, on the other hand, selling the foreign goods on the local market with nothing being added from local production; and with all of the profits from sales being repatriated back to headquarters[1]. To the extent that they were subject to effective political or legal control from public authorities, this control was mainly exercised by the original home country of that company.

Today, "Transnational Corporations – TNCs" have largely replaced the former "multinationals". This implies more than a mere change in name. "Transnationals" are a new species of enterprise that did not exist before. Their presence

1 Creating a so called "compradora" economy, termed after the early colonial Spanish trade stations, perceived as having been parasitic on the local economy.

on the world scene is massive. Together, the 100 biggest TNCs have sales of 4,6 trillion US dollars – that is more than half the amount of the GDP of the United States (which – as the world's biggest – stands at 8 trillion US dollars).

The world's 100 largest TNCs, 2000
Billion US dollars, number of employees and %

Variable		*2000*	*1999*	*Change 2000 vs. 1999 (Percent)*
Assets				
	Foreign	2 554	2 115	20.8
	Total	6 293	5 101	23.4
Sales				
	Foreign	2 441	2 129	14.6
	Total	4 797	4 318	11.1
Employment				
	Foreign	7 132 946	6 057 557	17.8
	Total	14 257 204	13 385 861	6.5
Average index of transnationality		55,7	52.3	3.4

Source: UNCTAD/ Erasmus University

Assets and sales of the TNCs are increasing faster than the volume of the world economy. This implies that the place and function of the TNCs in the world economy is growing.

The United Nations Conference on Trade and Development (UNCTAD) measures "transnationalisation" of companies with a special "Transnationality Index"[2] (TNI). According to this index, transnationalisation has progressed unevenly over the last decade. It slowed, for example, in the phase of economic stagnation in 1993-94. Overall, though, there is a clear trend upwards. Transnational companies are becoming even more transnational.

2 Another and related UNCTAD index measures the "Network Spread" of TNCs. (Network Spread Index ; NSI)

Average transnationality index for the world's 100 largest TNCs, 1990-1999

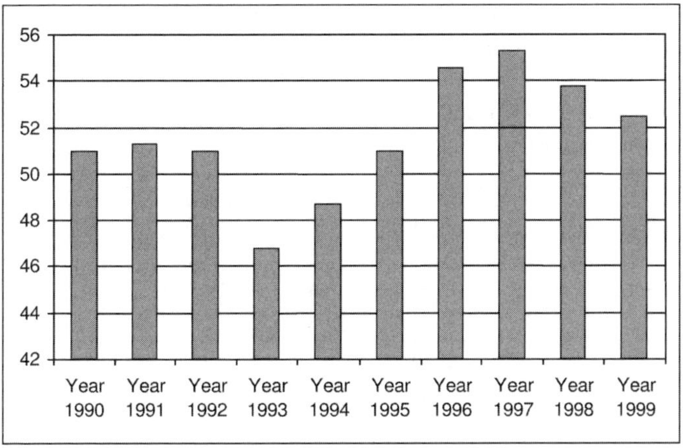

Source: UNCTAD

Their financing no longer comes just from one single country. It is done on the world financial markets. The treasuries of these corporations also distribute the assets over the entire global financial market.

Numbers of companies listed on the New York Stock Exchange[3] – NYSE

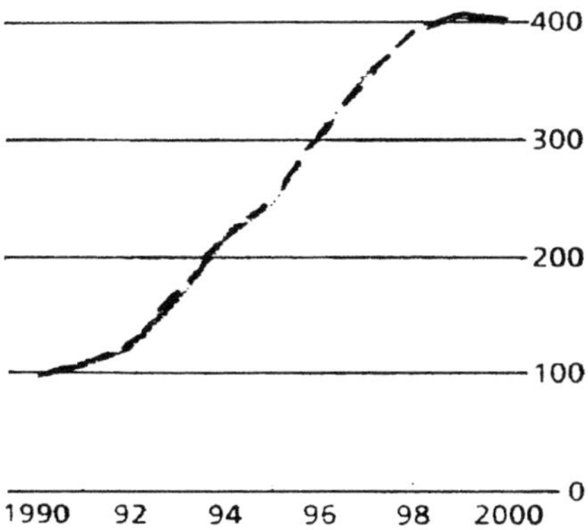

Source: NYSE

3 A sure prediction: with globalisation proceeding, the numbers of stock exchanges will shrink quite drastically.

The expansion of the TNCs is intimately connected with Foreign Direct Investment. Its volume exploded from 57 billion US$ in 1982 to 1.271 billion US$ in 2000 (!!). This latter sum amounts to one fifth of the world's gross fixed capital formation (= 6.466 billion US $).

Selected indicators of FDI and international production, 1982-2000 (Billions of dollars and percentage)

	Value at current prices (Billions of dollars)		
	1982	1990	2000
FDI inflows	57	202	1 271
FDI outflows	37	235	1 150
FDI inward stock	719	1 889	6 314
FDI outward stock	568	1 717	5 976
Cross border M&As	-	151	1 144
Sales of foreign affiliates	2 465	5 467	15 680
Gross product of foreign affiliates	565	1 420	3 167
Total assets of foreign affiliates	1 888	5 744	21 102
Export of foreign affliliates	637	1 166	3 572
Employment of foreign affiliates (thousands)	17 454	23 721	45 587
GDP at factor cost	10 612	21 475	31 895
Gross fixed capital formation	2 236	4 501	6 466
Royalties and Licences fees receipts	9	27	66
Export of goods and non-factor services	2 124	4 381	7 036

	Annual growth rate (Per cent)					
	1986-1990	1991-1995	1996-1999	1998	1999	2000
FDI inflows	23.0	20.8	40.8	44.9	55.2	18.2
FDI outflows	26.2	16.3	37.0	52.8	41.3	14.3
FDI inward stock	16.2	9.3	16.9	19.8	22.3	21.5
FDI outward stock	20.5	10.8	16.4	20.9	19.5	19.4
Cross border M&As	26.4	23.3	50.0	74.4	44.1	49.3
Sales of foreign affiliates	15.6	10.5	10.4	18.2	17.2	18.0
Gross product of foreign affiliates	16.4	7.2	11.0	3.2	27.2	16.5
Total assets of foreign affiliates	18.2	13.9	15.9	23.4	14.8	19.8
Export of foreign affliliates	13.2	14.0	11.0	11.8	16.1	17.9
Employment of foreign affiliates (thousands)	5.7	5.3	7.8	16.8	5.3	12.7
GDP at factor cost	11.7	6.3	0.7	-0.9	3.4	6.1
Gross fixed capital formation	12.2	6.6	0.6	-0.6	4.3	-
Royalties and Licences fees receipts	22.1	14.1	4.0	6.1	1.1	-
Export of goods and non-factor services	15.4	8.6	1.9	-1.5	3.9	-

Source: UNCTAD, World Investment Report 2001: Promoting Linkages, table I.1, p. 10

Next to the rise in "greenfield" Foreign Direct Investment, there is also a rise in cross-border mergers and acquisitions (=M&As). It used to be that mergers and acquisitions were mostly between firms of one and the same country[4]. But in recent years such mergers and acquisitions have increasingly jumped across national confines.

Number of world-wide mergers and acquisitions 1990-1999

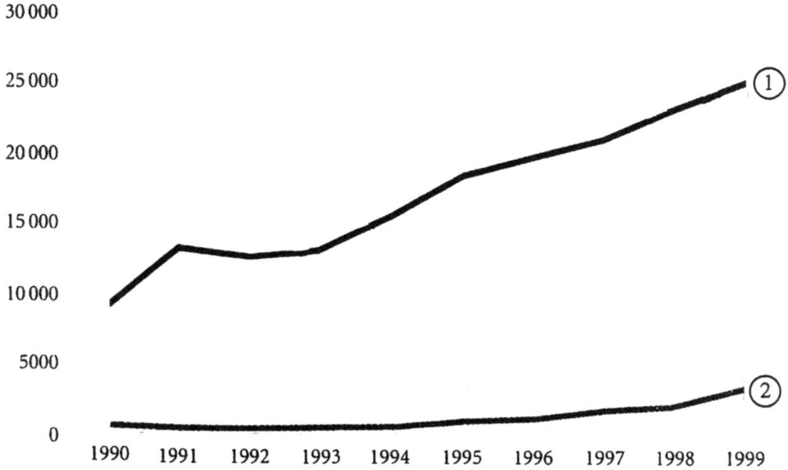

1 = MA worldwide

2 = transfrontier MAs

Source: Houlihan Lockey, Fortune, Securities Data,

Transnational companies acquire financial resources on a world wide scale. The same also holds true for technology.

4 That was true even within the European Union. Until very recently, there were very few mergers between firms of different EU member countries.

Share of patents[5] of the world's largest firms attributable to research in foreign locations 1969-1995 (percentage)

Nationality of parent firm	1969-1972	1973-1977	1978-1982	1983-1986	1987-1990	1991-1995
United States	4.96	5.89	6.40	7.53	7.91	8.62
Germany	12.77	11.05	12.07	14.47	17.05	20.72
United Kingdom	43.08	41.24	40.47	47.09	50.42	55.79
Italy	13.39	16.03	13.85	12.59	11.14	16.47
France	8.16	7.74	7.17	9.19	18.17	33.17
Japan	2.63	1.88	1.22	1.26	0.92	1.08
Netherlands	50.40	47.37	47.65	53.99	53.96	55.69
Belgium-Luxembourg	50.36	51.11	49.28	58.15	47.53	53.25
Switzerland	44.36	43.63	43.78	41.59	42.99	52.47
Sweden	17.82	19.90	26.20	28.94	30.60	42.42
Austria [a]	5.06	16.76	19.84	11.82	8.00	-
Norway [a]	20.00	1.67	12.31	32.50	37.14	20.22
Finland [a]	18.87	27.11	26.89	18.67	27.94	39.49
Canada	41.19	39.30	39.49	35.82	40.12	43.96
Others	28.21	22.22	26.37	30.34	7.54	3.94
Total	10.04	10.53	10.50	10.95	11.28	11.27
Total excluding Japan	10.52	11.59	12.25	13.87	15.76	16.53
Total European countries [b]	28.01	25.19	24.52	26.95	29.99	34.78

Source: Cantwell and Janne, 1997

With some TNCs the share of such patents based on research in another country[6] is now above 50%. The tendency to make use of foreign research has become stronger over the years. This is remarkable in view of the frequently voiced fear that even truly "transnational companies" would reserve the very high value added and strategic activities – like research – to the country they are most attached to (the country they could be considered the primary "citizens" of).

It is widely suspected that the highest positions in such companies will remain reserved for nationals of this very country of their original attachment. To a large extent, that is still the case. But increasingly even the top management of TNCs is now truly "transnational". Increasingly, leading positions are being filled by candidates coming from all over the world.

5 Patents registered in the US (as the US has the most comprehensive of all patent registers).

6 A country other than the one the parent company is a "national" of.

Top positions in some of the companies listed on the London stock exchange

Company	*Name*	*Position*	*Place of birth*
Amvescap	Charles Brady	Chairman	United States
Billiton	Brian Gilbertson	Chairman & CEO	South Africa
BOC Group	Danny Rosenkranz	CEO	Kenya
CGU	Bob Scott	CEO	Australia
GKN	C.K. Chow	CEO	Hong Kong
Granada	Gerry Robinson	Chairman	Ireland
Orange	Hans Snook	CEO	Canada
Pearson	Marjorie Scardino	CEO	United States
Rio Tinto	Leon Davis	CEO	Australia
Royal & Sun Alliance	Bob Mendelsohn	CEO	United States
Sema Group	Pierre Bonelli	CEO	France
SmithKline Beecham	Jan Leschly	CEO	Denmark
South African Breweries	Graham Mackay	CEO	South Africa
Standard Chartered	Rana Talwar	CEO	India
Unilever	Niall Fitzgerald	Chairman	Ireland

Source: Company reports

The office culture, too, is no longer determined exclusively by the country of the original attachment of a TNC. English has become the lingua franca in some major transnational corporations that had their original attachment to a country where another language is spoken. This is true, for example for "German" companies like Siemens and Mercedes/Chrysler. But English is now being used for internal communication even in transnational corporations that have their main attachment to France.[7]

Michael Porter (1990) maintained that a "corporation's home is where the core product and core process technology is created and maintained". Were we to follow this definition, we would have to conclude that many important corporations no longer have a clearly defined "home". They have become truly "global".[8]

7 And though a French law passed 10 years ago (lois Toubon) prescribed the use of French in French companies and for other purposes; 10 years after its passage, it is quietly ignored. Strolling through Paris recently, I was struck by the fact that many of the billboards were in English; and in English only.

8 It therefore was proposed to use the term "ecumenical" for such companies that no longer have a clearly defined "home" and that obtain what is useful for them from all over the world.

International brands – a new form of exploitation?

We will argue that host countries usually benefit from the presence of transnational companies. There is some controversy, though, on whether this holds true also for a group of transnationals that mainly sell their name; that is, those transnationals in possession of an internationally recognized brand. Questioning might become especially acute if the brand-product is not high-tech; but a simple consumer item like T-shirts (Lacoste) or a carbonated beverage (Coca Cola). Brands are valuable to their owner because they create rent income.[9]

The owners of brands are usually wealthy and usually live in wealthy countries. Those that buy their "branded" products, do, however, come from all over the world including from very poor countries. The ensuing "negative transfer" is being criticised. But obviously, there is little one can do about this negative transfer. Few governments would be prepared to forbid their citizens drinking Coca-Cola or wearing Lacoste T-shirts.

Successful global brands are one example of what has been termed the "winner takes all economy". The winner in a field (like Microsoft) can reap huge benefits and simply leave no room for any competitor to come up. The "number one position" provides an economic advantage that makes it very difficult for competitors to mount a serious challenge.

Attention is commonly fixed on the very big transnationals. Two of the most dynamic aspects of transnationalisation are thus ignored. First, the still relatively small but rapidly growing share of TNCs having their main attachment in developing countries. Second, the equally dynamic growth of TNCs that are just medium sized.

Whereas the world's 100 largest TNCs have sales of 4,3 trillion US$ altogether, the sales of the 50 largest TNCs from developing countries make up no more than 8% of that sum. This figure is not impressive, but it is not negligible either. It is worth noting that the sales of the first group (of 100 of the world's largest TNCs) grew by a mere 5,3% in 1999; whereas sales of the 50 largest TNCs from developing countries grew by 27%.

9 That is income not balanced by actual inputs into production.

50 largest TNCs from developing countries
(billion of US $, Number of employees; percentage)

Variable		*1999*	*1998*	*Change 1999 vs. 1998 (Percent)*
Assets				
	Foreign	129	109	18.3
	Total	531	449	18.4
Sales				
	Foreign	122	109	12.0
	Total	367	449	27.1
Employment				
	Foreign	383 107	400 475	-4.3
	Total	1 134 687	1 546 883	-26.6
Average index of transnationality		38.9	36.6	2.3

Source. UNCTAD

UNCTAD now counts 60.000 transnational corporations with 800.000 affiliates abroad. Necessarily, many of these 60.000 companies are just medium sized. Austria offers a good example of the dynamics of such medium sized transnationals. In some very narrow segments of the market, such medium sized Austrian firms have come close to holding a world-wide-monopoly (as, for instance, in automatic rail-track maintenance; or in the production of leather bands for wrist watches).

The "transnationalisation" of medium sized firms, and of firms from developing countries, has been made possible by the drastic reduction in the costs of international transport and of international communication; and by the reduction of transaction costs in trans-border business. These costs used to be high, so that only very big firms in very big and wealthy countries could shoulder them. Only big companies from big countries were able to compensate for the high costs of being transnational by their big production runs and by the ensuing better economies of scale. Today, the big firms have lost this unique and privileged position.[10] Today, becoming transnational does not add disproportionally great expenses.

10 I cannot suppress recording personal encounters with the transnationality of even small firms. My carpenter, an accomplished craftsman, could not finish in time a piece of work I had ordered. This was because he had been kept busy completing the interior furnishing of a house a fashion designer had had built for himself in Long Island, New York. The carpenter and his crew commuted to New York on a weekly basis; and the semi-finished pieces of furniture were transported to New York via aircraft. Nonetheless, the price of the furniture thus produced was not substantially

The cost-reduction in "going transnational" is also reflected in changes in the methods used to run an international business. Being transnational previously implied having big offices and much of the staff permanently abroad. These arrangements are now being replaced by cheaper, more cost-efficient short term assignments; by simple business trips; or even by international commuter travel[11]. Thanks to globalisation, all types of international assignments have grown in numbers. But permanent assignments abroad have grown least.

% of companies experiencing an increase in each type of international assignment

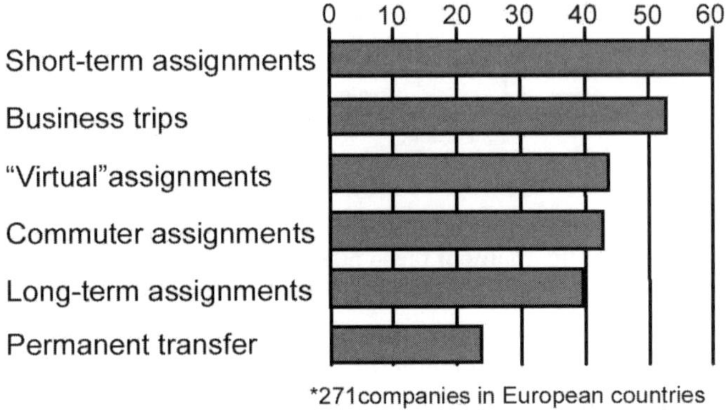

Source: Pricewaterhouse Coopers

The "transnationalisation" of production has transformed the world economic system and the world political system. Much of that is due to the fact that transnational corporations are footloose. They have a deep impact on the economy of any host country. Nonetheless, many of them can simply move somewhere else if

above the price a New York craftsman would have charged. The Austrian firm, by the way, has its office in a village in Burgenland; still the poorest part of Austria. Another example: One of my German friends inherited, from his father, a medium sized, run of the mill glass shop. He now holds what amounts to a near world-monopoly for glass display cases in art museums.

11 I experienced this shift with my former employer – the Austrian Ministry of Foreign Affairs. When I entered the diplomatic career, those abroad stayed abroad for the time of their assignment, and those at the home office in Vienna stayed there till posted abroad. That has changed very much. On each day of the week a good percentage of the Vienna based Austrian diplomats is away on some mission abroad. On the other hand, and thanks to EM and FAX, some of the embassies are now functioning as de facto extended departments of the Ministry of Foreign Affairs.

they are no longer satisfied with conditions at their present location. Governments, on the other hand, are permanently fixed in geographic space. So are – to a large extent – the employees of that corporation. There is an inbuilt asymmetry in this situation that works to the disadvantage of the state and to the disadvantage of workers. In that asymmetric relationship, the transnationals have the stronger cards. It used to be that companies lobbied governments for favours. Nowadays, it often is the other way round. An anecdote to put that into relief:

The Austrian government had spent quite some money to re-structure a high-end Austrian tire manufacturer. That having been done, the firm was sold to a German tire company. This sale was under the condition that the new owner would maintain production for a pre-determined period of time. That time having lapsed, most of the production in Austria was promptly terminated.[12] Obviously, that move was bound to create ill feeling among Austrian taxpayers. They were bound to ask why and to what end they had been forced to bail out a firm, if, after a few years, that firm was going to disappear anyhow. Such questions are politically inconvenient and the Austrian Chancellor felt compelled to intervene and seek a meeting with the new owner of the tire factory. But that gentleman was very busy and simply had not enough time to come to Vienna to meet the Chancellor. But if the Chancellor would, nonetheless, like to see him, they could meet at the lounge of a small airport 400 kilometres south of Vienna, where his private jet would touch down on the way home to Germany. The private jet would certainly also have been able to make a small detour and land in Vienna, instead of landing at some small provincial airport 400 kilometres south. But, that would have been an inconvenience; even though a very small one. The Austrian head of government was not able to impose this inconvenience on the German CEO of a transnational company. Instead, he had to hop in a car and travel 400 kilometres for a talk with the CEO. To no avail – by the way. The factory in Austria was closed, nonetheless.

Two small footnotes to that anecdote:

a) the tire company in question had high profits that year;

b) the CEO of this company has a private jet; the Austrian Chancellor does not.

By now, transnational companies have acquired many of the trappings of nations; and their chief executive officers (CEOs) have acquired many of the trappings of sovereigns. They have their private planes, their security guards or mili-

12 Though the production in Austria was profitable. But given the world-wide overcapacity in tire manufacturing, plants had to be shut down. Evidently, the German TNC chose to close production in Austria instead of closing those in Germany.

tias, they rule in towering and glittering office buildings that dwarf the old government buildings. And all of that is not just empty posturing. There is substance behind those symbols. The turnover[13] of some of the major global companies now equals the GDP of even medium sized countries like Sweden or Turkey.

GDP and turnover of some of the major transnationals
in billion US $

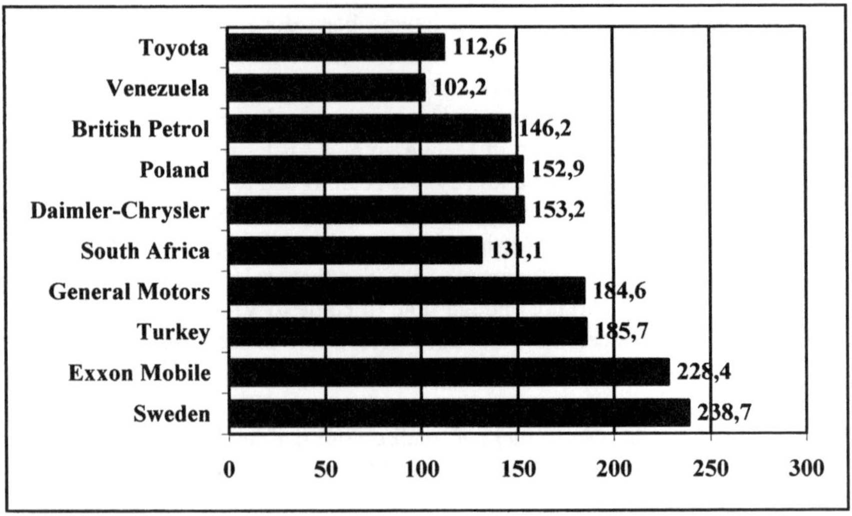

Source: Der Standard

One of the charges raised against TNCs is that they tend to dislodge from high-wage to low-wage countries; and thus are able to force down wages with the threat of otherwise pulling up stakes. Indeed, in a few instances, this was the case, with firms seeking ever new locations with ever lower wages. That is how the production of shirts, for instance, moved from Italy to Portugal, from there to Turkey, from there to Thailand and now, finally, to Bangladesh.

The production of shirts is labour intensive and calls for no great investment in machines, nor for great skills or much education on the part of the workers. But, with automatisation increasing, and with the ever costlier and complex ma-

13 One should note though, that the comparison is somewhat misleading, as the GDP just accounts for the net worth of production; while many things are counted twice or thrice in the figure on turnover.

chines being necessary for other productions, this advantage of low wage countries[14] is now confined to just a few sectors of the economy (as textiles, footwear, simple furniture, or plastic flowers). In the actual assembly of an automobile, wages for workers now amount to just 15% of its complete production costs. Wages amount to roughly the same percentage of costs in the production of microchips. Whether a worker producing cars or microchips earns 10 or 30 euro per hour is therefore much less relevant in cost calculations than other factors. More important than the relative level of wages is whether one may expect deliveries to arrive on time; whether the infrastructure at the chosen place of production is well maintained and efficient; whether the supply of electricity is constant and secured at all times; whether labour relations are confrontational or consensual.

Even the quality of the local schools for the children of expatriate staff (and the quality of the golf courses for their fathers) can rank quite prominently among the factors that make a transnational company decide to locate in one country and not in another one instead.

Minimising the costs of production is just one of many motives that prompt a firm to produce in another country. Firms may also wish to exploit some unique skills and know-how that is available just in that location. They might wish to "cluster" with other similar firms so as to benefit from mutually useful networks (for instance in the Silicon-Valley or on the French Cote d'Azur). Or they might wish to get better access to local markets by producing in these markets. They might wish to produce in several locations so as to spread risks; etc. Many of these motives discourage investments in poor, low income/low wage countries. And, as we have seen, most Foreign Direct Investment, and indeed the lion's share, is done in highly developed countries.

Transnational companies not only provide jobs, they provide jobs that are better paid.

Such higher wages reflect a higher level of productivity. This higher productivity has a pace-setter function as it may percolate through the economy of the host country. Local supply chains that deliver to the local affiliates of transnational companies function as the "transmission belt" for this spread of higher productivity. TNCs and host country governments are usually eager to develop such local supply chains.

---

14 Even then, low wages alone do not provide an advantage if the productivity of labour is very low. What counts is the wage level multiplied by the figures for the productivity of labour. Only this sum, and not the level of wages, determine the wage costs of production.

Average wage paid by foreign affiliates, and average domestic manufacturing wage
(by host country income, 1994)

	All countries	*High-income*	*Middle-income*	*Low-income*
Average wage paid by affiliates $'000	15,1	32,4	9,5	3,4
Average domestic manufacturing wage $'000	9,9	22,6	5,4	1,7
Ratio	1,5	1,4	1,8	2,0

Source: Edward M. Graham, Institute for Economic Research

For all these reasons, attracting foreign direct investment has become a major preoccupation of governments – not just of national governments, but also of regional and local ones. More often than not, specialised public agencies have been created for that purpose. And – again in most cases – the offers such agencies submit to potential investors are embellished by subsidies of various sorts: free building sites or even free buildings; ready to use infrastructure; the training of workers; favourable tax treatment, etc. Such open or hidden subsidies may cover as much as 25% to 30% of the total costs of a new investment by a transnational company.

Competition among these public agencies is fierce, and potential investors certainly relish dangling a deal in front of such agencies; with these agencies outbidding one another in what they would do to lower, for the transnational company, the cost of the investment and the costs of the subsequent production. These investment agencies thus negotiate away tax income of their states; and they burden tax payers with subsidies they provide to international investors. But their behaviour is rational in the sense that the winner in this competition usually does reap a net profit.

The old "multinationals" tended to produce in just one location (or in a very few locations); and just to sell on a global scale. The modern "transnationals" not only sell, but also produce on a global scale. Supply chains are global. Windshields for cars come from one country, gearboxes from another, the upholstery still from another; and it might be that, in the final stage of assembly, little additional value is actually added, so that it becomes difficult to define where, in which country, a car has actually been produced.

That makes for a dramatic change in the nature of international trade. As has been mentioned before, in connection with Foreign Direct Investment, it is estimated that already more than one third of all international trade is carried out between the various branches of the same company; between various affiliates of the same firm that are located in different countries.[15]

US and European Affiliates Sales US Trade

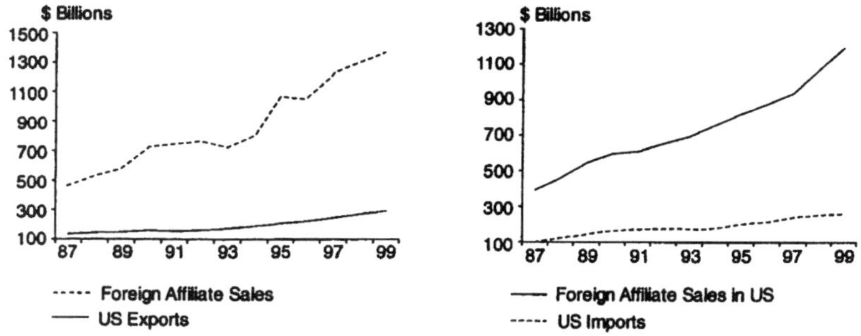

Source: US Bureau of Economic Analysis

This internationalisation of production has impacted upon, and has changed, traditional trade policy. A few decades ago, a country could still be tempted to raise tariffs so as to protect and safeguard the development of a nascent national industry. Now, with industrial production becoming imbedded in transnational supply chains, such a policy becomes rather tricky as the advance in "transnational production" calls for a policy that facilitates free foreign trade. With products of one country serving as an input in the production of another country – and vice versa – obstacles to trade would hamper the integration of a country into the transnational supply chains.[16] Transnational companies will hesitate to locate in a country that ignores the global market and that promotes production just for the local market. What is true for tariffs is true too for Non Tariff Trade Barriers (NTBs). It is also true for the monetary regime. A premium is put on the fewest possible NTBs and on the monetary regime that does not impede trade and which, thus, is stable, with a convertible currency whose external value does not oscillate too much.

15 For the US, intra-firm trade amounted to 47% of total imports in 2001 according to the US Department of Commerce.

16 Very sound arguments used to support the notion that nations in their first stages of industrialisation were well advised to shelter their nascent industries. Today, and for the reasons mentioned, such policies are, at the same time, more difficult to implement and more problematic in their usefulness. Powerful arguments support the opposite strategy of "export led growth" and the aim of full and fast integration into the world economy.

This limits the freedom of a state to decide on a specific trade policy or on a specific monetary policy. The state is no longer in a position to simply dictate its terms to national (and even less to international) firms. It has to accept them as partners in its decisions.

Today, international trade is, to a large extent, the result of decisions taken within companies; and taken on the basis of their own strategic considerations on where to locate production. Policies that tend to impede the transfrontier movement of goods and services can damage, not just transnational enterprises, but also the material interests of the citizens of the country that passes such restrictive rules. In the sense of having the potential of becoming a serious nuisance and obstacle to trade, states are still relevant today. But, in the positive sense of augmenting the volume of international trade, the power of states has become rather limited. They cannot accomplish what has been one of their most important tasks in the past. Today, states by themselves can do but little to create or promote international trade. Transnational enterprises, however, can. They are efficient at that.

The internationalisation of production impacts upon national politics also in a more indirect way by weakening identification with the state. Citizens certainly continue to identify with their state. The state will even remain the main pole of identification for quite some time. But the workplace, the firm one works for, its inner culture, is a very potent source of identity too. For a politician, a policeman, a civil servant, a farmer or a hairdresser, this does not create a problem. The source of employment and of professional identification is national. But it is different for those who work for transnationals (or even for national firms with a strong engagement in the international realm). For them it might not always be so certain that the ultimate allegiance is to the national state and the national state only; and that a firm could make no claim on a similar allegiance; and that the allegiance to the state should be unconditional under the principle "my state – right or wrong". We cannot be sure that, for such persons, the formal and informal rules of the state will always take precedence over the formal or informal rules that govern behaviour in the professional world of a transnational enterprise.

Transnational corporations, thus, have come to have quite some impact on the international system. They exercise this influence by lobbying national governments and international organisations[17]. This has always been the case and should

17 Labour is free to do the same; and indeed and like business, labour too has formed international groups to do some lobbying on an international level (eg International Confederation of Free Trade Unions) . But, all too obviously, labour is less efficient in this lobbying, than the employers, by far.

not surprise us. What is new though, is that big firms are now in a position to establish effective rules by their own authority and without the intercession of a state giving its approval and/or legitimising such decisions by processing them through the mill of formal law making.

Transnational companies, assembled in a committee, have, for example, agreed among themselves on the standards for E-commerce – that is commerce carried out over the Internet. This is no trivial matter. How E-commerce is regulated has a deep impact upon government (excise and value added taxes); and on citizens (precaution against fraud, adequate consumer protection; etc).

Another conspicuous example for this rule-making capacity of TNCs is provided by the "Sullivan principles"[18]. These were to be applied by transnational corporations active in South Africa, then still under the Apartheid regime. Major transnational companies had come under quite some political pressure from African governments, but also – and mainly – from NGOs (Non Governmental Organisations) who warned them about being accomplices of a racist government. Reacting to these pressures, the vice-president of General Motors, Sullivan, drafted a code of conduct for transnational corporations active in South Africa. These rules were intended to secure, within factories, the equal treatment of black and white workers. No major company active, at the time, in South Africa and in the rest of the world could afford NOT to apply the Sullivan principles. A rule invented by one transnational company thus gained, in effect, the force of a law for all other transnational companies.

"Unilever" provides another example of TNCs creating global rules that come close to having the impact of "strong" international law. Unilever joined with the "World-Wide Fund for Nature" (an important International Non-Governmental Organisation) to found the "Marine Stewardship Council (MSC)" in 1997. "Through negotiations with key fisheries stakeholders around the world, the MSC developed a set of strong environmental standards." (IBRD World Development Report 2003).

Not only have TNCs created internationally binding norms. Through an extensive system of international commercial arbitration, they have also established a judicial system that is independent from states.

The evolution of this norm-setting activity of corporations can be carried even one step further. Corporations can, in fact, take the place of governments – at least on the communal level. In the US, some communities are already directly owned and governed by corporations. One specimen is "Celebration", owned and run by Disney.

---

18 Named after a vice – president of General Motors.

Mouse and Garden

"Celebration [is] an experiment in "New Urbanism" in Disney's entertainment megalopolis near Orlando. Like the handful of theme parks that surround it, Celebration is itself a theme town, trying to recreate the small-town American life of a bygone era. Most of Disney's marketing effort appealed to a desire for escape from the trials of modern urban living: crime, troubled schools and broken-down communities. Living in the town means obeying the rules of the Celebration company, a Disney shell firm created to run the community in lieu of elected officials. Many rules govern the town's exterior appearance: any house colour other than white, for example, cannot be duplicated within three houses on the same side of the street. Hedges in the front garden can be no higher than three and a half feet (1.07 metres), and at least a quarter of the front and side gardens of each house have to be planted with something other than grass." [19]

(See also chapter 11)

Even in the US, very few towns, though, are owned and operated by corporations. More frequently, US corporations just provide services that were once considered purely public/governmental functions. US corporations are running prisons, schools, hospitals, and even courts (if one considers arbitration to be a kind of court). The markets for those services by corporations is still mostly a purely national one. However, some of these corporations, (like health providers or security services) now also operate beyond the US on a global level.

The obvious question is why corporations could invade such fields which were once considered purely "governmental" or communal? This question is less acute in the field of utilities or transportation, or services like garbage removal. In these fields, private enterprises usually outperform public ones in terms of cost efficiency. They deliver these services at lower costs.[20]

Private enterprise and private corporations have, however, recently advanced also into sectors that once had been considered purely public. This prompts questions as to the limits of that process. As mentioned, corporations

19 It is worth pondering the question as to why US citizens are ready to accept deep intrusions into their private sphere if the intruders are companies; and why they are allergic, even to some minor intrusions, if the intruder is a governmental agency.

20 A "halfway-house" between the public and the private are the "public-private partnerships" that use inputs from both realms for the completion of a project.

might be more efficient in running things.[21] But this cost advantage may be compensated for by the cost of having to remunerate the owners of the private capital that has been invested in a certain venture. These owners demand a return on their capital that is significantly above what public authorities have to pay when raising capital on the financial markets. So, from the point of view of the costs of capital, it is cheaper to finance, for example, a road project from the public budget, instead of having it financed by a private corporation.

Other problems and objections arise when corporations invade fields like health care, internal security, education. In all such fields, the quality of the service delivered also depends on other than purely material criteria. Teachers have to be trusted by parents and children. They must have a professional ethos that drives them to engage in the advancement of pupils. They must feel part of, and be seen as part of, the community they are engaged in. A similar thing holds true for police personnel, for judges, for doctors etc. The framework set by profitoriented enterprise does not sustain such attitudes and the services rendered by such private enterprise will thus lack one essential ingredient.

The issue of democratic governance is automatically raised with this advancement of corporations into realms that were public ones in the past. This holds true as much for the national sphere as it holds true for the global realm. One could argue that corporations are controlled by shareholders and customers. One may argue that these two groups are as efficient in controlling a company as voters are in controlling their elected officials. We will return to this argument in a later chapter when we deal with the future of the state. But, we should signal doubt, already, as to whether stockholders and consumers are indeed surrogates for democratic control, exercised by citizens and their political institutions. An international system controlled by corporations instead of states and/or voters is likely to be a less democratic one.

Let us sum up some of the findings of this chapter:

The global system is increasingly shaped by transnational corporations. They are the driving force behind the rapid growth of foreign direct investment; and they have transformed the rules that govern international trade. The realm is no longer reserved for big firms. Medium sized firms, too, are becoming "transnational"; as are companies from poorer countries. The economic effect of this transnationalisation of firms is mostly positive. Problems arise, however, in the

21 Though that is not always the case. The public administration is sometimes more cost-efficient in running hospitals. The administration of public old age pensions is usually more cost-efficient that the management of private pension schemes.

political realm, with such TNCs taking over functions that had traditionally been reserved to states and that had thus been under political control. This shortens the reach of democracy.

The United States as "Hegemon"

Transnational corporations create and enforce rules that have a global impact. But while these rules are significant, their volume and reach will remain circumscribed. Transnational corporations will never become the sole masters of the global system. This is because they themselves need someone or something that positions them in the global environment and helps them to survive in it. Transnational corporations may rule over a distinct and expanding realm. But they themselves need guidance and norms. The question is as to where this guidance and these norms are coming from.

What is true for transnational corporations is true also for states and for the other actors on the global scene. They too need guidance and orientation. They need someone or something that shapes for them the environment they are active in. They need someone or something that stabilises expectations and establishes the basic rules of the game.

Evidently, no supreme world-ruler can provide that. A dwindling but still prominent group of scholars thus maintains that, in the absence of such a global rule maker and rule enforcer, anarchy is what prevails in the world. If this anarchy does not result in daily bloodshed, rape, theft and murder, it is because anarchy is tempered by mutual fear; by the meeker fearing the more powerful, and by states threatening each other with war if some of their basic interests are violated.

These scholars boast that their view is the only truly "realist" one. Their school of thought is thus termed "realism". Beyond the confines of a state, no stable rules would prevail. If there is some sort of stability, it is because the power of even the mightiest state is balanced by the power of one other state or by an alliance of other states. Such precarious calm would be shattered if the balance of power changes. All such changes would be associated with conflict and war. International rules would thus be few, not very effective, and always subject to quick reversal.

Yet, if we look at the actual world, we find that it does not correspond to this gloomy picture painted by the so-called "realists". The millions of transactions taking place each day between firms and citizens of different nations would not be possible in a state of anarchy. Those transactions are possible only because of the shared expectation that a large number of formal and informal rules will be respected.[1] Were it otherwise, most of these transactions would simply cease. It is difficult, for example, to imagine how massive foreign direct investments would be made, if it were not for the expectation of continuity in international economic affairs; and for the expectation that, in these affairs, certain rules are observed.

Evidently, a substantial stock of informal and formal rules exists that maintains the necessary steadfastness and stability in world-wide transactions. The stock of these formal and informal rules is termed "REGIME". Political Science defines "regime" as a set of "*formal and informal rules on which the expectations of the (international) actors converge* ".(Gilpin 1987)

The question is how such a "regime" comes into existence and how it is kept in existence. Sure enough, these rules, patterns, regularities were not created by some kind of world government – because such a world government does not exist. Some rule-making has been done by international organisations. Some rules are made by transnational corporations. But their rule-making is still limited; and more limited still is their power to actually enforce the rules thus made. We are, therefore, faced with a paradox. There is no superior rule maker that could legislate for the world as such and that could enforce such rules on a global scale. Nonetheless, rules exist and they are being observed even in the absence of such higher authority. We thus have to assume that rules emanate from the very same actors who are subject to these rules; namely, from the many different actors who participate in the global system. We are tempted to assume that the international actors themselves have agreed upon a set of formal and informal rules; and that they have done so because that was to their obvious advantage and benefit. We assume that they continue to observe these rules because defecting and ignoring them would automatically entail serious disadvantages.

This is, of course, a very pleasing vision of all participants automatically doing what is best, not only for each one of them, but also for the community of all of them. We are tempted to compare this self-regulating system to biological systems which are also complex, self-regulating, and evolving. Nobody, for example, is "in charge" of evolving the brain from that of an infant into that of an adult. Nobody is "in charge" of an evolving eco-system. These systems are self regulating. They evolve by trial, error and success; and by integrating the feedback from these trials, errors and successes. These systems are the result of adaptation, of selective growth and selective elimination. They are the product of continuous feedback, of continuous learning[2].

---

1 A yawning gap thus separates the world of the "realist theory" from the actual daily experience of statesmen, entrepreneurs, and civil servants. This "cognitive dissonance" is in itself worth some reflection.

2 Robert Jervis (1997) System Effects: Complexity in Political and Social Life, Princeton University Press, Princeton.

If seen from this elevated, abstract perspective, the prevailing global "regime" may indeed be perceived as one such complex, self regulating and evolving system. There would be nothing specific about this global regime that would make it differ from other complex, evolving and self regulating systems.

As we have mentioned, "feed-back" is an essential part of any such system. The global regime differs, however, by the fact that this feed-back comes as a collective and purposeful action, intended to influence and shape the system. Human perceptions and human preferences intervene. In biological complex systems, the nature and effect of a feed-back is pre-determined.[3] This is not so in the political realm. Different perceptions on what is relevant intervene as do different wishes on what the final shape of things should be. These human perceptions and human preferences make a crucial difference. Were it otherwise, and would things simply run their course, the global system would certainly have collapsed already under the weight of 6 billion members of the human species.

So we need to learn more about the nature of this political feed-back; about how it is produced; about how humankind arrives at collective action, and how it establishes the institutions or arrangements that have to underpin this collective action. As mentioned, there is a riddle to solve. A powerful global regulator (or "Leviathan") does not exist. We should assume that, in its absence, each international actor is guided by his or her most narrow and immediate self interest, even if and when he/she knows that this might be damaging to the community of all of them; and sub-optimal even for her/himself (see chapter 11 on the so called "prisoner's dilemma").

Persons, states, could very well become entrapped in the expectation of others behaving badly, of others disregarding what would provide the greatest overall benefit to the community of all of them. If others misbehave, they would be prompted to misbehave too. If, for example, others cheat on free trade, they would be motivated to do the same. If others start to arm, they should better follow suit. If others spoil the global ecosphere and reap profit therefrom, they should not be prudish about copying this misbehaviour.

If there is no certainty or likelihood that reasonable rules are being respected, international actors would be tempted into a "negative sum game". All of them would be worse off in the end, as long as no one is there to cut this damaging sequence of action and reaction; this self-re-enforcing downward trend towards ever worse outcomes.

The history of international relations offers many such examples of negative sum games: wasteful arms-races; trade wars; short-sighted over-exploitation of the world's "commons"; escalating national rivalries over questions of prestige;

3 Although, due to the complexity, a great number of different outcomes is possible.

etc. But this bad part of the record makes us ignore the simple fact that in today's world, international actors are more likely to co-operate in a positive manner. By and large, the present global system is more shaped by co-operation and "positive sum games"; than by each one speculating on the worst possible outcome and thus opting for a "negative sum game". Such negative sum games will not be played when international actors can be rather certain that others will also stick to those rules which are seen to benefit all of them.

Obviously, stable and reasonable rules and the continuity in the global system are to the benefit of most of the many different "actors". But the salient question is how such rules have become established in the first place; and as to how these rules are maintained even in the absence of a global political institution (like a world government) that could enforce them. For these rules have to be maintained and enforced. The stability of the global system might survive a few "defections" of actors disregarding the rules. The stability is not endangered as long as such defections are seen as rare exceptions. If these defections become more numerous, however, they will change expectations of the other "actors" in the international system. They will motivate them to defect too. The system would crumble.

The salient question is, thus, the question of getting from here to there; to move from general mistrust and from the fear of others disregarding the common good, to the trust that few will "desert", and that most will stick to the rules of a "regime" that ensures the common benefit. The question is on how international actors will acquiesce into such a development and support it, even though that might entail some short term costs here and there; and even if this or that player could reap some short-term benefit from disregarding the rules others wish to have accepted.

According to a rather plausible theory, it would be up to a "HEGEMON" to assume this crucial role of stabilising expectations; of preventing international actors from defecting from a "positive sum game". Such a "hegemon" would function as a kind of catalyst that permits the realisation of the full potential for global co-operation; a co-operation that – in its sum and overall – is beneficial to all.[4]

For a "hegemon" to play this role, three conditions have to be met. A "hegemon" must be

a) powerful
b) willing to assume this function

4 We could also put it in other terms: the "hegemon" facilitates, through his weight and example, the production of public goods; such as the maintenance of peace; of free trade, of global monetary stability; etc.

c) ready to forgo – at instances – its own immediate benefit if this is necessary to sustain the global "regime".

The hegemon in today's world is the United States. They are supremely powerful and thus meet criterion a). Until quite recently, they also met the other two criteria of being willing to exercise this function; and of also being willing to forgo narrow selfish interests, if this was required for the maintenance of the international regime. It will be argued that the US is less likely to do so in the future. But let us look first at criterion a) of the United States being powerful.

Power is the capacity to make others do what one wishes them to do. There are two ways to achieve that result. One can either force someone into obedience against his will and instinct. This is seen as the exercise of what is called "hard power". Or one can persuade or seduce others to do what one wants them to do, so that they follow in the belief that this is to their own benefit. This is termed the exercise of "soft power".

The position of the United States is unique and without historic precedents in two respects

a) because they can combine "hard" and "soft" power

b) because of the size of the gap that separates their military power from the military power of their next closest competitor

This unique position has tempted Americans to define themselves as the "sole surviving super power". It has tempted them to see the world system as having become "uni-polar".

It is clear that the United States is truly without rival in the military realm. This is not just a question of the volume of military expenditures; but also, and even more so, a question of military technology. The United States have the capacity to combine, with devastating effectiveness, military dominance in several fields[5]: high capacity in long range logistics; a vast network of intelligence gathering (both by conventional means and by electronic eavesdropping); "smart ammunition"; unmanned aircraft; helicopter transported small commandos working in stealth on the ground; long range bombers and cruise missiles; etc. The gap in both capacity and technology that separates the United States from others, and especially from their European NATO-allies, has, in fact, become a yawning abyss, with both sides being aware that the situation will persist for quite some time.

---

5 As proven by the wars in Afghanistan and Iraq.

Paul Kennedy has claimed that such military superiority has always come at a heavy price. Hegemonic nations tend to overspend on the military, with their economy being less and less able to support the heavy load of an outsized military machine. This burden stunts economic development and the military hegemon thus falls behind economically, making a place for a new hegemon to rise. But the US has not fallen into this trap of military over-expansion. They do not overspend on their military. In fact, since the end of the "Cold War", the US has cut their military expenditures more deeply (in percentage points) that their European NATO allies. At present, the US does not devote more than 4 percent of its GDP to military purposes. This is not a burden to cripple an economy.

The US also wields economic power. In terms of their GDP, they are the world's second biggest economy. As we have seen (chapter 13 on the “Triad”), in the late nineties, economic growth was also a trifle faster than growth in the European Union, feeding the claim that these dynamics are due to some US uniqueness that Europe could not copy.[6] Compared to other wealthy countries, the US certainly is advantaged economically by

- a broad and homogenous mass market with high purchasing power
- excellent infrastructure
- the more intense use of labour (with higher female participation in the labour force, with people working longer hours, with fewer vacations, lower unemployment, and with people working longer in life)
- during the last decade, a more accommodating macroeconomic policy, with massive public deficits in the first half of the nineties, and low real interest rates in the second half
- the massive inflow of foreign capital from abroad that compensated for the private saving rate declining towards zero[7]
- ease in the financing of newly founded and high tech firms (venture capital)
- close (working) relations between universities and the economy
- a policy favouring the immigration of “the best and the brightest” from all over the world

6 The more rapid growth of the US is indeed a bit surprising, because one should expect economic growth to become the slower, the wealthier a country becomes; and one would thus suppose that Europe – with still some catching up to do – should have grown faster than the US.

7 US commentators claim that this inflow is proof of the superiority of the US economy. Capital streams in because the US economy is superior. And why would it be superior? How could one prove that? This would be proven by the capital coming in. Of course, this is a circular argument. This is a reasoning that usually underlies the build -up of asset bubbles.

- a continuing growth of population; compared to the declining population of Europe

Saving rates of private households in major economies,
year 2000; in % of disposable income

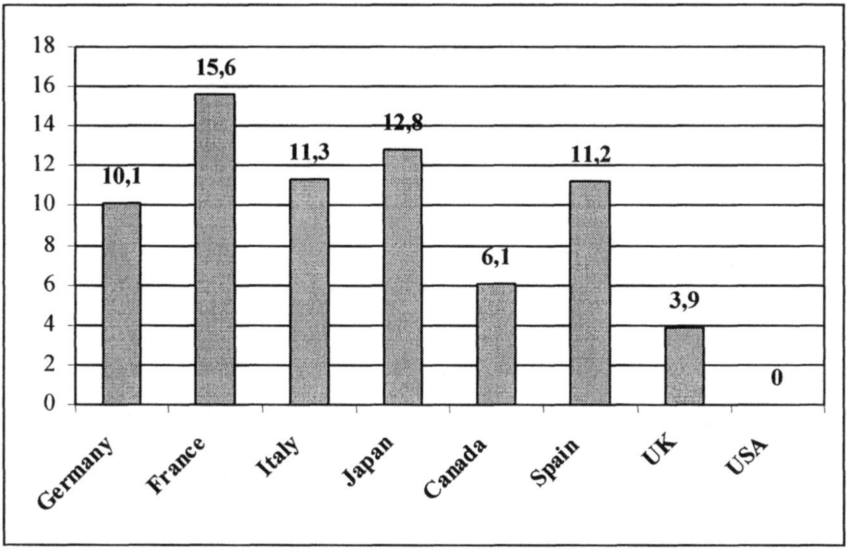

Source: OECD

Current account deficit[8] of the US since 1989 in billion US $

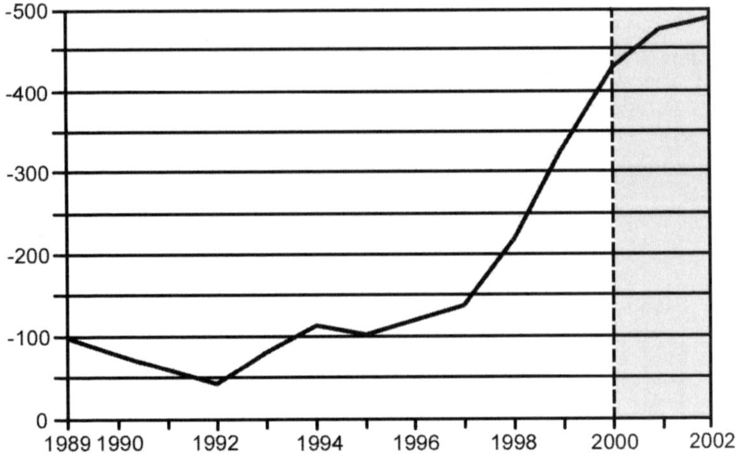

Source: OECD

- Let us note at this place, already, that it is not compatible with the function of a world economic hegemon to import capital on such a massive scale. This makes the hegemon dependent upon, and vulnerable to, the whims of the capital markets and to the political whims of the countries that export capital. The logic of the global economic system, which the hegemon has to sustain, also demands that a wealthier country exports capital instead of importing it.

Further economic advantages accrue to the US thanks to the dominance of the dollar. World-wide, most of the reserves of central banks are still being held in US dollars and the euro has not yet made a very big dent into that dominating position.

The US is thus – basically – still the only country that can pay its debts by simply printing money (seignorage). Others, still, will buy these printed papers as part of their reserves.

Furthermore, nearly half of the international bond issues floated are still denominated in US dollars.

8 The US current account deficit amounted to more than 4% of GDP in 2000. If the European Union had registered such a deficit, it certainly would have come under heavy criticism from the US and from US dominated institutions like the IMF; which goes to show that – to no one's surprise – some nations are more equal than others.

Share of various currencies in the reserve holdings of Non-US central banks (1998)

End of period	*US-Dollar*	*German Mark*	*Yen*	*Pound Sterling*	*French Franc*	*Swiss Franc*	*Dutch Guilder*	*ECU***	*Rest****
1975	78.2	8.8	1.8	2.8	1.8	2.2	0.9	-	3.5
1980	69.7	14.8	4.2	2.9	1.7	3.2	1.3	-	2.4
1985	66	14.1	7.4	2.9	1.2	2.2	0.9	0.5	4.9
1990	56.4	19.1	9	3.1	2.1	1.7	1	4.6	2.9
1995	58	14.2	6.9	3	2.1	1	0.4	2.2	12.2
1998*	60.8	12.9	5.1	3.4	1.2	0.8	0.3	1.7	13.8

*March 1998 **Reserves of central banks in European currency (ECU) ***Other currencies and statistically non-divisible reserves

Source: IMF

The US dollar is also the currency most frequently used in international trade. Unlike the debtors and unlike the enterprises in other countries, US firms and debtors, therefore, do not have to hedge against currency risks. This provides them with a massive competitive advantage.

Notwithstanding all these assets, the US claim to economic superiority over any potential rival is less well founded than the US claim to military superiority. Unquestionably the US has quite some economic clout. Doubtlessly they act as a hegemon also in the global economy. Evidently they profit from this role. Yet this, their economic power, is less permanent than their military power. Europe certainly is a very close competitor.

Finally, there is the cultural and intellectual dominance of the United States. One obvious, and yet big, advantage lies in speaking English[9]. In the INTERNET age, this advantage becomes amplified as English is the dominant linguistic vehicle on the INTERNET: 80 percent of the web pages are in English.

9 This is a big advantage, of course, for the US audio-visual industry, which is indeed dominating world-wide. US films shown abroad have to be dubbed. But, in its turn, the US refuses to dub films that come in a foreign language. The US thus has the advantage of a big and protected home market for its movies. By the way: the US uses a more Shakespearean version of English than the one used, at present, in the country of Shakespeare.

Language used on Internet web pages, 1999

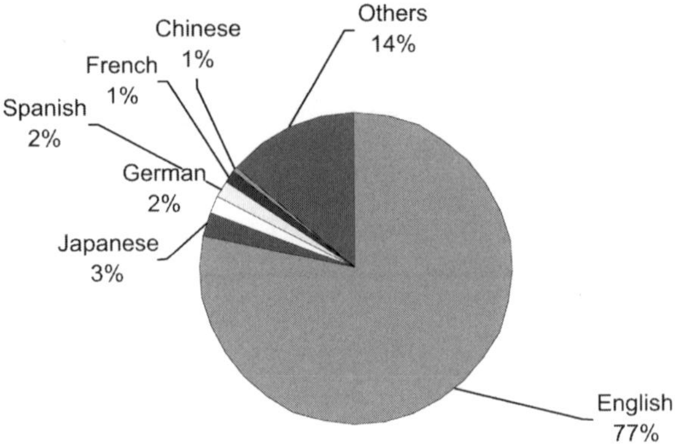

Source: OECD

But it is not just the English language (in its US version) that dominates; it is, to a large extent, US culture in its widest sense. It sets the pace world wide. The cultural dominance of the US is evident in:

- the world's reading diet. US authors dominate the best-seller lists, even in countries with proud and strong cultural traditions like France and Germany;
- trends in the arts, in architecture, in design, in new forms of consumption, etc., usually start in the US;
- the global mass and youth culture has been largely formed by the US. The trousers of the American cow-shepherds have become the unsightly and not very comfortable standard wear for teens and twens all over the world;
- the terms of the debate on global issues are mostly set in the US and by US authors nearly exclusively.[10] US social scientists are the pace-setters, too, in the realm of international studies. They define the methods and the issues. American International Relations journals have no real rivals. In these journals, US authors dominate;

10 Take, for example: "The Rise and Fall of Great Powers" by P. Kennedy; "The End of History" by F. Fukuyama; or "The Clash of Civilisations" by S. Huntington.

Average distribution of authors by affiliation in American IR journals, 1990-1997

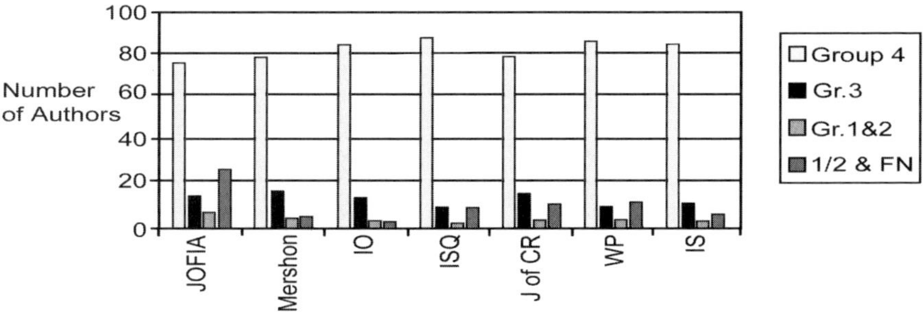

In group 4 are just US authors
In group 3 authors from the US "periphery", that is Ca, EU, Australia, Israel
In group 2 India, Russia, Japan, China, Eastern Europe
In group 1 the true periphery – the rest of the world

Source: E.Aydilini, J.Matthews, Intern Studies Perspective

- the benchmarks for an optimal economic and social policy (and the discussions in fora like the "World Economic Forum", the IMF or the OECD) are defined by the US.[11]

Cultural dominance is in itself a form of "power". But it also carries economic advantages[12]. The same holds true for the field of education, and especially for tertiary education. Both the greater width and the superior quality of US tertiary education are impressive. In this respect, some European countries (like Germany) have even fallen further back behind the US, instead of catching up.

11 With Europeans being incapable of making a counter-point, even where it would be fully substantiated by their own experience and success.

12 Consider the simple fact that MBA courses usually will tend to follow US textbooks and US examples. This puts US students – and US managers – at a clear advantage.

Years of education per person aged 15-64
1950-1992 (USA=100)

	1950	*1973*	*1992*
Belgium	87	82	84
France	85	80	88
Germany	92	79	67
Italy	49	52	62
Netherlands	72	70	74
Sweden	84	72	79
UK	96	80	78
Portugal	22	32	50
Spain	46	43	64
USA	100	100	100
India	12	18	31
Japan	81	83	82
Korea	30	47	75
Taiwan	32	50	77

Source: Maddison 1995

Obviously, thus, the US meets the first criterion for being a "hegemon". They are powerful. They even are uniquely powerful, in as much as they can combine, in an unprecedented way, cultural, economic and military power. So let us look at the second prerequisite of being an effective "hegemon": the willingness to actually assume this function.

> What is "the US"? Who acts as "the US"?
>
> Until now, we have talked a bit loosely about "the US" as if it would be a single person; motivated by a single will; acting with full coherence and unity of purpose. For convenience's sake, we have thus seriously distorted reality. Even a smallish and rabid dictatorship would find it difficult to subordinate, to one single goal, all that which connects it to the rest of the world. In a vast democratic country with a modern and pluralistic society this is clearly impossible. The US government cannot order its publishing houses and literary authors to dominate the global literary market. It cannot order Hollywood to dominate the visual media; and its accounting firms and business consultancies to hold a global quasi monopoly in their field.

In judging whether there is the will to assume this role of a "hegemon", we therefore must look beyond the official foreign and security policy and beyond the official US international economic policy; we must include in our analysis the multitude of US institutions which are active in international affairs and which are also able to set the "global tone", so to say, even if they are not part of the top US administration.

US courts, for instance, do have this potential to set the global tone in certain matters. US courts are in the habit of interpreting very broadly their right to be seized in matters that touch on foreign interests. They are ready to pass judgement even where the connection of a specific case to the US is a very loose one, and where not they, but other courts in other nations, would seem destined to be seized to rule on a case. It suffices, for instance, for a company to simply have assets in the US, or of having sold in the US, in order for a US court to declare itself competent to render a verdict on a matter pertaining to that company. There are very few transnational companies that thus could avoid becoming subject to the jurisdiction of US courts. If they become subject, the outcome can be extremely costly to them. The verdicts are usually passed by juries. What these juries award is frequently way beyond the mere compensation for actual damage. The verdicts become clearly punitive. As the US legal system is being based on case-law; one such punitive judgement is setting the precedent for similar judgements in the future.

US jury verdicts – top awards
Million US Dollars

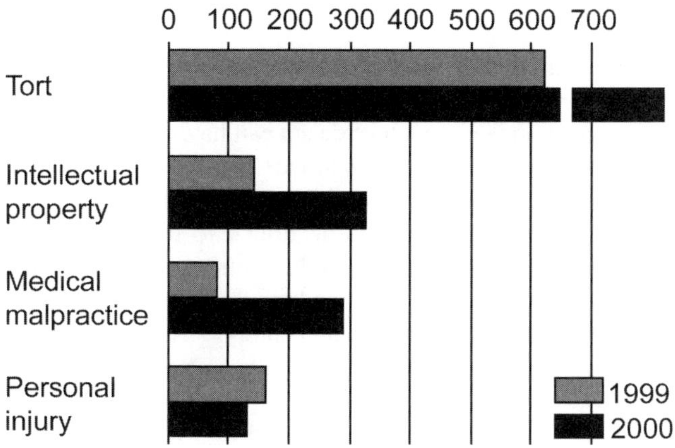

Source: National Law Journal

Companies from all over the world thus have to adjust their practices to the smaller or greater likelihood of becoming subject to a judgement rendered by a US jury. In this manner, the US juries have assumed a de facto legislative power[13] and that power extends beyond US frontiers. Globally active corporations must calculate the risks of becoming subject to US "class action suits", with enterprising US lawyers assembling a group of plaintiffs who might have reason – often a rather precarious one – to feel damaged by one event or another. Verdicts rendered in such cases do, in fact, establish international norms, more binding frequently than formal international law. Prominent examples are the class-action suits against tobacco companies or the litigation against companies that used asbestos.

Other US institutions have a similar function as "international quasi-legislators". We have already mentioned the "rating agencies", that rule on the financial respectability of firms and nations; or the US "Securities and Exchange Commission – SEC" which becomes involved when a foreign company enters the US securities market – as most major transnational companies will have to.

So, the role of a hegemonic rule-setter fell to various US institutions and not just to US governmental institutions alone. In the era after World War II, the international system, the international norms, the expected behaviour were, to a large extent, the ones that had been defined and sustained by US governmental and other institutions.

"The American Century"

It is a fortunate human trait to wish to improve upon things; and, therefore, to criticise what exists in the hope of thus contributing to the emergence of a better alternative. And, indeed, much criticism can be directed against the way the US has acted as hegemon in the second part of the 20th century. Nonetheless, if seen in the historic perspective, the role of the US has been a rather positive one overall; and certainly one more beneficial to the rest of the world than what had been in earlier periods when other countries acted as "hegemons". In its second half, the 20th century has been "the American Century".

What will come after the "American century"? As we will argue, there is a real chance of the US abdicating from its role as hegemon. In the absence of

13 One of the consequences being that with all their preaching on "de-regulation", the US is today and de facto regulated in a manner that would be considered unacceptable and overly intrusive by citizens in other nations. In order to avoid law suits on sexual abuse, for instance, very detailed instructions are provided to employees; inter alia advising them to avoid dating a colleague; or even giving support when he or she stumbles on the stairs.

US leadership, the evolution of the global system could very well become reversed, with international co-operation becoming thinner and conflict and national rivalry more common. The way events unfolded in the run-up to the war in Iraq in 2002/2003 points in this direction.

But it might also be that this lapse of US-leadership and responsibility will have just been a troubling but limited episode, and that the US will, thereafter, continue to assume the function it had in the last 6 decades. In that case, the era of the American hegemony could still last another 50 years. But what would come after that? The answer to that question, and for the period from 2050 onwards, will be provided by the developments in East Asia and, to a smaller extent, by the success or failure in building a European Federal State.

If, in the second half of the 20th century, the US has been successful in its role as "hegemon", this is due, to no small degree, to the fact that the US was generally liked. Some resented, of course, the elevated position of the US. But these were a minority. Even statesmen who espoused Marxism-Leninism sent their children to US universities; or they called on US hospitals when seriously ill. When they wanted to air their opinion, they asked to be interviewed by US journalists. In short, the US way of life was attractive; and this attraction is a form of soft, but very potent power. The US is about to lose at least some of it.

This might be due to the arrogance[14] towards other countries that has become so very obviously part of the US discourse. It puts others at distance and thus makes it difficult for them to identify with the US and its way of life. The US way of life is, however, also seen as having become less enticing. The US was perceived as the land of equal and great opportunity. The dramatic rise in economic and social inequality does not sustain that good reputation.

14 Nicely captured in the Westpoint speech of President George W. Bush., claiming that “America is the single surviving model of human progress”.

The US leads in inequality:

How many dollars those in the richest fifth earns for every dollar earned by the poorest fifth

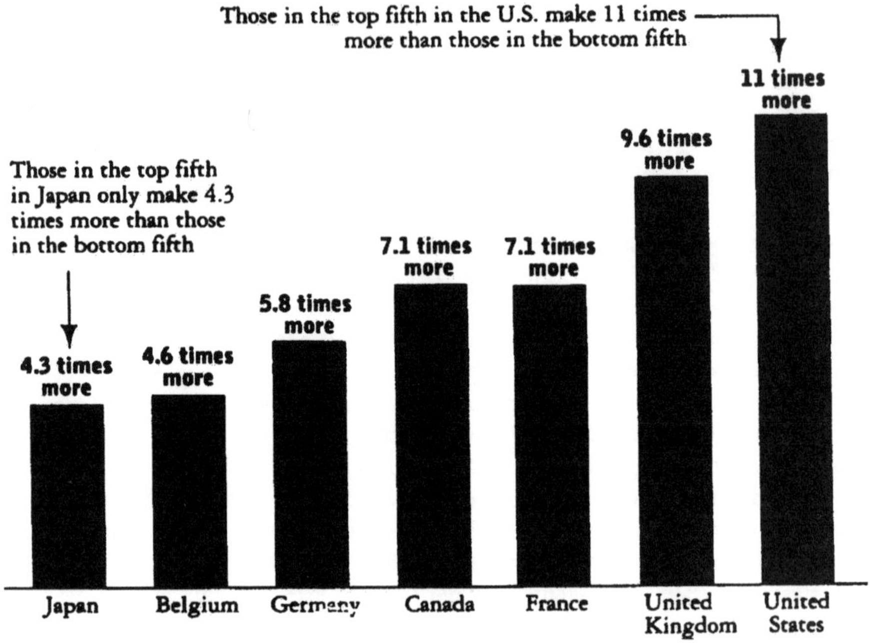

In a similar vein, would-be imitators and admirers of the US have been put off by the US penchant for violence, as it becomes evident in the cult of guns and in the wide spread application of the death penalty.

Such cleavages were amplified by the US reaction to September 11th 2001, with the US declaring war on terrorism. Flags went up everywhere. Such flag-waving implies a hidden warning to all those who have other flags. It is a warning to everything non-American. Dangerous and misguided emotions are also fed by the use of the term "war" in the fight against terrorism. To fight terrorism no "war" is needed, but the widest possible international co-operation. Following that logic, the US would have had to seek international consensus on some very intrusive police actions. The US also would have to make better and fuller use of those international institutions that back up this co-operation. Instead, the US chose to go in the opposite direction. A new US defence doctrine claimed for the

US the right to intervene unilaterally; to do so with the tools of warfare; to do so with breaking international law; by ignoring the UN Charter; and to do so even with using nuclear weapons. It is clear that this doctrine is not compatible with the world order as it has been built since 1945. It is clear that this doctrine bids farewell to the international function the US had held up until now.

As hegemon the Unites States have shaped the global institutions: the International Monetary Fund and the World Bank; the United Nations; the World Trade Organisation[15]; the universalisation of human rights; the rapid de-colonisation; the notion of development assistance: all that would not have come into existence if the US had not seized the initiative. In this shaping of the global order, the role of the US has been crucial, and the role of other countries or regions of the world has been minimal indeed[16].

The question is whether the US will continue to provide this input into the global system. If the answer to this question is to be provided by the recent past, one should doubt that they will. Since some time already, the US has been less and less willing to support the global system in a role as a responsive and responsible hegemon. The US is, in fact, gradually withdrawing support from those very international institutions which it had done so much to establish in the first place. Such waning of support is evident in the US relations towards the linchpin of the post-war global order – namely, towards the United Nations.

US support has become weaker even for institutions that have been more direct instruments of US policy. There is serious discussion in the US of reducing support for the IMF. The IMF is not only central to managing and stabilising the world monetary and financial system. It also has served, very well, immediate US interests. In fact, the IMF has sometimes been denounced as a "mere extension of the US Treasury". Frequently it has bailed out countries where US banks had been the main creditors. The US even uses the IMF in its "fight against terrorism". But, notwithstanding this use of the IMF for its own purposes, the US no longer feels obliged to actively support and enhance the role of the IMF.

Equally startling, difficult to comprehend and ominous is the recent "benign US neglect" of the Atlantic Alliance. This new US attitude has already become evident in the run-up to the war in Afghanistan. The Alliance had reacted to the

15 After a lengthier transitory phase when it existed just as "GATT".

16 With the exception, perhaps, of the immediate post war era, when the UK still had some influence and some input in these decisions.

terrorist attacks of 11 September 2001[17] by engaging – for the first time in its history – under article 5 of its charter.[18] The US reply to this has been a "very nice of you, but thank you. We wish to act alone and do not want to be bothered by allies. Do not call us. We shall call you in the unlikely case we need you".

The move away from international engagement and from the obligations of a "hegemon" has been accelerated in the last decade and especially under the presidency of George W. Bush. But it has been in the making for a long time. This trend has different causes. Some of them have existed before; some of them are more recent.

One cause of long standing is the US sense of uniqueness and exceptionality. It has characterised the American identity ever since the first community of settlers vowed, in the seventeenth century, to establish a "shining city upon a hill"; a beacon to the rest of humanity; a token of god's grace bestowed on true believers. This sense of exceptionality found expression again in the US Declaration of Independence, and, ever since, it has defined the US view of its function in the world. This basic sentiment[19] can inform two radically antagonistic attitudes. It can either induce a missionary zeal to save the world by making it conform to US standards. Or it can lead to isolationism – the resolve to cut to a minimum the ties that bind the US to the rest of the world with all its depravity and hopelessness.

Historically, the US has tended to follow the one alternative for some time and then to switch to a policy informed by the opposite sentiment. Phases of very

---

17 European countries have co-operated very effectively in the fight against Islamic terrorists

Notable arrests of suspected al Quaida terrorists in Europe

Country where arrested	Number of known arrests	Main nationalities of those arrested	Known number charged with terrorist offences
Belgium	2	Tunisian	2
Bosnia	7	Algerian	none
Britain	37	Algerian/ unspecified North African	24
France	29	Algerian/ French	7
Germany	8	Algerian	7
Italy	33	Egyptian/Moroccan/ Tunisian	17
Malta	1	Tunisian	1
Netherlands	12	Unspecified	6
Spain	47	Algerian	24

Source: Economist

18 An aggression against any one of the NATO members is thus defined as an aggression against all NATO members.

19 Inevitably, it contains a fair dose of Anti-Europeanism. Right from its beginnings, the US defined itself as the alternative to a Europe that, in turn, was seen as arrogant, imperialistic, morally decayed, irresolute or weak.

active international engagement were followed by phases of withdrawal into self sufficiency. The time immediately after World War II was a phase of active international engagement. The tide then turned with the looming defeat in the Vietnam war and with the US being forced to abandon the gold standard in 1971. US development assistance started to decline. The originally very strong support for the United Nations became weaker. During the Reagan presidency it changed into outright hostility. Narrow national interest came to dominate the US Middle East policy; etc.

The end of the Cold War – unilateralism instead of a "new world order"

The collapse of the Soviet empire seemed to offer the prospect of a "new world order" that would replace the bygone order of a "bipolar system"[20]. President George Bush (sen.) promised that such a "new world order" would become established upon initiative and with the prodding of the hegemonic United States. Vastly strengthened international organisations would constitute the pillars to support this construct; and especially a vastly stronger and more effective United Nations. This remained rhetorical flourish. In real life, the end of the Cold War did not stop the US withdrawal from internationalism. It accelerated the process.

In retrospect, it seems clear that – at least from 1947 onwards – the US international engagement (support for the UN, for European integration, founding of NATO, assistance to poor countries; etc) had been motivated to a large extent by the need to contain the Soviet Union. With the Soviet Union gone, the motives for a stronger international engagement also seem to have dwindled.

The second prerequisite for the role of a hegemon is a willingness to exercise this function. This will of the US is waning. Ad hoc efforts – as the ones connected to the building of an alliance against terrorism – are no substitute for a persistent, long-term, and broad engagement required from an effective hegemon.

Third, in order to be effective a hegemon has to be credible in this role. Other nations will only be willing to forgo short term interests and profits if the leader of the pack does the same. They will support the common good and will not "defect" if the leader of the pack sets a good example. This example of the powerful hegemon makes it plausible that all will stick to the rules.

20 If it ever was truly bi-polar. It might have been so in purely military terms; but it never was so in the economic sense or in the cultural-intellectual realm. The US led alliances were always vastly superior to the Soviet block in these two spheres.

The US is losing this credibility. This is most clearly the case in the area of trade. Free trade is central to the maintenance of the present global system. In each country, however, powerful lobbies exist that wish to curtail free trade. They are rather resourceful in finding plausible arguments to support such wishes. As long, however, as the hegemon is seen to ignore its own lobbyists, leaders in weaker nations are also well placed to do the same. They always can point to the good example of "big brother". If, however, the "big brother" himself yields to these lobbyists, meeker nations are ill placed to resist them. If this happens, protective measures will escalate. Free trade will become restricted and will finally become more the exception than the rule.

Unfortunately, the big brother is less and less willing to set the good example. US support for free trade has become reserved for those areas where the US has strong competitive advantages (audio visual production, financial services, agriculture); whereas new barriers are being set up by the US in places where they fear international competition (textiles, lumber, steel).

It is not necessary for a hegemon to forgo all of its own interests in favour of a common, long term good. Quite on the contrary. Usually the hegemon will define the international regime in such a manner as to put his most potent assets to a maximal advantage. A hegemon with a powerful navy and merchant marine will emphasise the freedom of the seas as a core element of an international regime.[21] A nation with a strong position in media and in audio-visual production will emphasise the free exchange of information and of audio – visual products. A hegemon with a potent financial system will establish a world regime in which the freedom of financial flows is central; etc. For other states and international actors to accept such regimes it is not necessary that they benefit from them[22] in the same manner as the hegemon. For them to accept the regime it is only necessary that the regime is better than the absence of any regime. This will be the case more often than not.

The international regime supported by the hegemonic United States has certainly, and over all, benefited the hegemon. This makes it the more quixotic that the US no longer seems willing to even carry the relatively light burden such a role imposes on its freedom of action.

Nor is free trade the only area in which the US now fails to exercise the leadership expected from a hegemon. Next to free trade, another important element of

21 As did Britain in the 19th century.

22 Europeans have even accepted the US spying on them through the "Echelon" system of electronic eavesdropping. Only the European Parliament has protested.

the present regime is limits set to competitive armaments and especially to a competitive race to arm with weapons of mass destruction. There is a common interest, for example, to stop, or at least to slow, "vertical" and "horizontal" nuclear proliferation. Banning nuclear tests is a necessary part of such an anti-proliferation strategy. Nonetheless, with the tacit approval of the US administration, the US Senate has permanently shelved the ratification of the Nuclear Test Ban Treaty, which is the key element in any strategy to prevent horizontal proliferation. Neither has international criticism stopped the US from developing an anti-ballistic missile system and thus to advance vertical proliferation. Notwithstanding an international ban, the US is also prepaing for warfare in space.

One might object that the US administration under President George W. Bush is far from withdrawing from international engagement. One could argue that, on the contrary, it has given proof of its willingness to engage the United States all across the globe in a world-wide fight against terrorism and against those rogue states that constitute the "axis of evil". The US administration even plans to re-establish a true protectorate over Iraq, so as to bring democracy and peace not just to this country but to the Middle East as a whole. No other nations would seriously entertain such a grandiose scheme. Does this prove that – after all – the US does still act as a leader and effective hegemon even today?

One should question that. What the US wants to achieve with such schemes does not correspond to what other nations define as their interests. These US plans are not apt to translate into a project that they can share and support. They will not be able to agree to the US acting alone when projecting its "power" across the oceans and into a conflict-prone area. They will not accept as legitimate the US claim that they are right to occupy a middle sized country and right in their aim of ruling it alone, without a prior war and that occupation having been legitimised by the United Nations.

The US war against Iraq and the US occupation of Iraq does not bring an advance over the existing international order. On the contrary, it implies the negation of the multilateral order as it has been built, with the help of the US, in the years after World War II. It implies a return to the imperial policies of the 19th century. After all, this is how imperial powers justified their empire building a hundred and fifty years ago: to weed out evil, and to bring "civilisation" and, ultimately, democracy to countries in the prey of malevolent and inept rulers.

Some US authors that are close to the US administration (like Kagan, Krauthammer, or Boot) are very frank in their reference to this 19th century pattern of imperialism. They encourage the US government to summon courage to openly embrace it.

This US return to imperial politics based on military power prompts us to return once more to the theories of Paul Kennedy and his view on the inevitable decline of hegemons and empires. He maintained that military over-expansion has always caused their ultimate demise; while their rise would have been associated with superior economic performance. In the final phases of imperial rule, the economic performance would have become inferior, while their military might was still intact and even rising.[23]

Does that hold true also for the US of today? One should not over-stretch historic analogies. All parameters used in such comparisons have changed over time and these changes have been particularly deep in recent decades. Also, and as we have mentioned the US is very well capable to still shoulder the economic costs of their strong military power. In that sense, they are not as over-extended as Spain or the Netherlands had been in the 16th and 17th centuries.

Nonetheless one cannot fail to note that at the turn from the nineteenth to the twentieth century, the US still produced 35% of the world's industrial output. A hundred years later they produced but 25%.

Comparative national shares of world manufacturing value added

Period	*Britain*	*Germany*	*US*
1870	31.8%	13.2%	23.3%
1881-85	26.6	13.9	28.6
1896-1900	19.5	16.6	30.1
1906-10	14.7	15.9	35.3
1998	4.4	8.5	25.4

Source: Phillips 2002

Was Paul Kennedy right after all? is the US already in decline, with that decline just being hidden by a short spurt of economic dynamics in the 1990s and by their fabulous military superiority?

If that should be the case, this demise would be bound to be slow. But even while retaining an elevated position, the US would still need the co-operation of other states, both in pursuing its own interests and in filling the function of a hegemon that structures and stabilises the global system. Over the next decades, this need for the US to seek the support and co-operation of other states will even grow, as, in relative terms, the economic power of the US is bound to decline further.

23 It thus is ominous that those intellectuals that have set the course for the US administration of president George W. Bush rely on military power primarily as a base for their ambitious project of making the 21st century yet another "American Century". See http://www.newamericancentury.org

Unfortunately, present US politicians do not see it that way. They believe not in co-operation but in unilateralism. They believe the US to be unique, with other states being unable to share US aspirations and tasks. The dilemma is not that the US lacks the wherewithall for a hegemon. What bodes ill for the future is that the US refuses to act as a hegemon.

This failure to live up to their task as "hegemon" is also made obvious by their active opposition to the International Court for Criminal Justice[24]; or by their refusal to implement an (already signed) agreement to limit the emission of the so-called greenhouse gases (Kyoto-protocol); the failure to sign the UN Convention on the Rights of the Child; the failure to ratify the (signed) Nuclear Test Ban Treaty; the refusal to envisage a control system for biological weapons.[25] All these US actions signal the withdrawal from the role of a responsible hegemon. The US no longer provides the leadership and the example that would be required for others to adhere to a system of mutually beneficial rules and standards.

To sum up: the present global system has been shaped, to a large extent, by the United States. The US thus has acted as a "hegemon" that catalysed the potential for international/transnational co-operation. In this, they had been successful. The peacefulness of the second half of the 20th century is to be credited to the US mainly. But the US is now withdrawing from this role as constructive hegemon. This withdrawal creates a dangerous void as no credible replacement, no new hegemon, is in sight[26]. There is a growing risk of the positive sum game of co-operation and of rule based behaviour giving place to an anarchic free-for-all, with each international actor pursuing its most immediate and narrow self interest to the detriment of the global community, as such. If the 21st century threatens to be more fraught with conflict and trouble, it is because the US now fails to live up to its former role; and because no one is in sight to take over the function the US no longer seems willing to exercise.

---

24 While at the same time insisting upon the extradition of foreign war criminals.

25 With the US president declaring the Kyoto agreement "dead".

26 I have argued in another place (Nowotny 2001) that the European Union should take over where the US leaves off. But I do realise that this is a wish more than a realistic expectation.

International Organisations – IOs, International Non-Governmental Organisations – INGOs, and the Global "Demos"

Universal International Organisations have existed since the mid-19th century – with the International Telecommunications Union and the Universal Postal Union being the first ones established. The growth in the numbers of such organisations has been spectacular and has accelerated further after 1945. In this process, the focus of activity has shifted. While the old international organisations dealt with narrow, technical issues, many of the new international organisations have a broad agenda. International organisations now cover nearly all those political issues that also are being dealt with on a national level.

The graph below describes this development since 1909. The lower line depicts the rise in the number of "International Governmental Organisations – IGOs". The upper line depicts the rise in the number of "International Non Governmental Organisations – INGOs". That rise was truly explosive, and it reflects the emergence of a global "civic society". We will look at the implications later on. As to the official International Governmental Organisations, there were 37 of them in 1909 and 251 ninety years later.

Growth in the number of international organisations 1909-1999

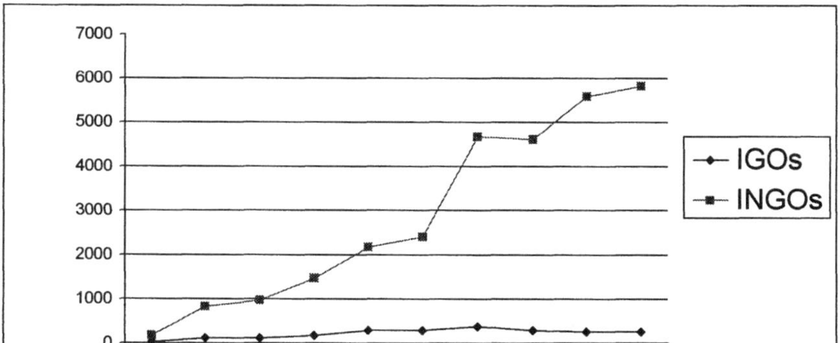

	1909	1951	1956	1964	1972	1978	1985	1991	1997	1999
IGOs	37	123	132	179	280	289	378	297	258	251
INGOs	176	832	973	1470	2173	2420	4676	4620	5585	5825

Source: Union of International Organisations

This development has transformed traditional diplomacy. "Multilateral diplomacy" – that is, international politics carried out in and via these international organisations – has largely replaced "bilateral" diplomacy – that is, political transactions between no more than two states.

Changes in the global system are reflected in changes in the diplomatic apparatus

If bilateral diplomacy is increasingly yielding place to multilateral diplomacy this is due to the fact that, nowadays, few international issues are bilateral in nature and thus can be resolved on a purely bilateral basis, with just two states interacting. Ministries of foreign affairs used to be organised according to the desk system, with officers assigned to monitor and shape relations with one specific country or with one specific group of countries. These desk officers tended to be generalists. They dealt with all issues open in relation to that specific country. But it became less and less plausible that one single person would be able to judge and deal with all of the widely different strains of international problems. In the ministries of foreign affairs (even of smaller countries) diplomats now are forced to specialise in some specific field of international relations. They no longer specialise in dealing with certain countries. They specialise in dealing with certain issues.

The relationship between the foreign office and its embassies has also been transformed. Embassies used to be central in the process of foreign policy decision making. They and the ambassadors no longer are. Embassies and ambassadors had a decisive role only as long as travel and communication was still tedious and expensive. With travel expenses and costs of communication down, the central foreign office and its specialists have taken over most of the truly substantial work. Embassies have largely been reduced to ceremonial functions and to public relations ("public diplomacy").

One may analyse international governmental organisations from the perspective of international law, that is, according to their legal nature; according to their founding text or "constitution"; or according to the nature of their output ("hard" international law; "soft international law"). But such legal analysis carries us only so far. It does little to advance understanding on the place and the function IGOs have in the global system. In this context, the core question is about the political base of international organisations; and specifically about their relation to nation states.

We can easily dismiss as utopian one interpretation. IGOs are not the substitutes for nation states. They are not tools of some world government – tools of some kind of super-sovereign throning above the nations of the earth.

The other extreme interpretation is more widely accepted though. According to this interpretaion, IGOs are but empty shells, without a proper identity of their own. Their activities are defined – and completely so – by their members. With decisions usually requiring unanimity (or at least consensus)[1], any member can block a decision. The final decision would thus reflect the "lowest common denominator" as it exists among the nations participating in this IGO. In that sense, international organisations would even be less than the mere sum of all of their parts (i.e. of all their members).[2]

Another school of thought would concede to international organisations at least some proper identity, independent of the political identity of their members. In their decisions and actions, IGOs could move beyond the smallest common denominator. They may become, and usually are, the catalyst for defining and implementing common goals. They could not have this function if they were to provide nothing more than the venue for the meeting of fully independent and fully autonomous nations; with national representatives not being able to do more than articulate the most narrow self-interest of their home country. Moving beyond, to an agreement on common goals is a step by step process. It involves a give and take that can be carried out in a broader framework only where trade-offs are possible. Trade-offs between nations; or inter-temporal trade-offs are possible only under the roof of an appropriate institutional framework. Such institutions permit one nation to forego some present advantages for future ones. They facilitate the decision to shoulder the risk involved in trusting others. They can make it likely that others will at least try to stick to their word and to actually implement joint decisions. If these conditions are met, national representatives may move beyond the stage where any of the participants might be welded to a narrow and immediate national interest where they think it prudent not to trust others. In such a case, international organisations cease to be the lowest common denominator of their member nations. They assume a life of their own.[3]

---

1 "Unanimity": everyone has to give positive approval; "consensus": nobody actively objects.

2 "There is no such thing as the United Nations" – US Under-Secretary for Arms Control and International Affairs, John R. Bolton, as quoted in the New York Review of Books, 26 September 2002, in an article by Francis Fitzgerald.

3 Generally, it seems that sociological theories and methods should be used more prominently in exploring how IGOs impact upon those working in them; and immediately with them. Or, one may use the tools of economics. Expressed in terms of economics: IGOs lower transaction costs.

Other interpretations or models of IGOs enlarge on this idea of IGOs having a proper identity. The so called "functionalists"[4] provide this more positive and ambitious definition of the nature of IGOs. According to functionalists, IGOs are endowed with superior problem solving capacity. This gives them a special and growing role in the global system. Administrative elites from member countries, specialists in their field, congregate in specific international organisations. Their joint decisions and actions bring visible benefit to citizens in their home countries. This enhances the legitimacy of the specific international organisation. In view of this superior performance in service of their interests, citizens transfer to the international organisations part of the trust and legitimisation that, up until then, had been vested with national governments exclusively. Thus supported and legitimised, IGOs may enter into related and new fields of activities ("spill-over"). Decision making power thus gradually shifts from national governments to such international organisations.

Obviously, the theory does not match reality. Contrary to what "functionalists" assume, loyalties of citizens have not been transferred from the nation states to international organisations; at least not in any significant way. Contrary to the predictions of "functionalists", little or no "spill-over" has occurred. Most IGOs have stuck with their original mission. Rarely have their constitutions been enlarged so as to expand the legal base to support new activities.

If not by "functionalism", how may we otherwise explain this increase in the number of IGOs? Three answers to this question have the merit of being rather obvious:

a) There is a growing number of problems that need global solutions;

b) National peer groups of professional administrators interact with their foreign counterparts. They do so more intensely than before. They, therefore, find it expedient to provide this co-opertion with a firmer base by anchoring in international organisations;

c) Certain types of global issues that are being dealt with by IGOs have attracted a rapidly growing global constituency (for example: the need for protecting the environment on a global scale).

Point a) is self explanatory: In several of the past chapters we have provided examples of growing global interdependence and of the need to manage it politically:

---

4 Even further up this scale of increasing autonomy of IGOs are the models provided by the "**institutionalists".** According to their view, the IGOs shape the actions of nations instead of being shaped by the actions of nations that are their members.

- global "commons" like the high seas, or sweet water resources
- global environmental problems (greenhouse gases)
- migration, transport , communication
- threats to health (AIDS, strains of bacteria that have become resistant to antibiotics)
- terrorism, collapse of states
- turbulences in the world monetary system; etc etc.

As to point b), it is obvious that various peer groups which congregate in IGOs have become more solid in their coherence[5]. At the same time, the allegiance of each of these peers to their own home state becomes a bit weaker. Ties to, and identification with, like-minded persons in other states becomes more prominent among the things that define self-esteem and social rank. This also pertains to high ranking officials in the national administrations. Their identity and self-esteem used to be based on the recognised place and function they held in the administrative bureaucracy of their home country. Step by step that self-esteem and claim to social rank now also comes to depend on their place and function in the group of international peers. All of those who are part of such an international group will gain in standing and prestige if their joint enterprise succeeds. Furthermore, they do, of course, benefit in a very direct and practical manner from their being part of an international group. They learn from each other and keep each other abreast of salient developments.

Coming together on an international level, these higher civil servants form transnational groups with very specific identities and agendas. Top national health officials meet at the WHO; top national labour officials at the ILO; central-bankers at the BIS; top trade officials at the WTO; and so on. Such encounters strengthen the group coherence and the pride of being part of a prestigious community. National and international standing thus enhance one another. IGOs are essential in this process.

Point c), finally, refers to the emergence of a global "demos" – to the emergence of global constituencies for various issues and policies. This is in parallel with the emergence of a global "public sphere". Increasingly, public opinion aggregates in dis regard of national boundaries. It no longer refers to this or that national institution or political goup. It has became free floating and it is the transnational counterpart to a transnational coverage of world events. In that sense, a public sphere has emerged that is potentially global in scope; but that is certainly wider than the public sphere that forms the counterpart to national politics.

5 In part, this explanation parallels the one provided by the functionalists; but it adds a sociological twist.

IGOs differ widely[6]. They differ according to the issues they address; according to their constituencies; according to the professional groups that operate in and through such organisations. It therefore makes little sense to deal in the same vein with – lets say – the IMF on one hand and the World Meteorological Organisation on the other.

Notwithstanding this diversity, we may draw some more general conclusions from this brief look at the IGOs:

- The trend towards multilateral diplomacy will continue.
- Increasingly, therefore, diplomats will become replaced by specialists.
- The number of IGOs will continue to increase, as will their diversity.
- IGOs are more than mere extensions of national governments and administrations.
- IGOs have a firm and distinct place in the global system and its governance. Most of them have a proven record in problem-solving.
- States have ceased to be the exclusive counterparts of IGOs. Increasingly, IGOs co-operate with INGOs (more about that later); but also with business corporations; and even with individuals.[7]
- Nonetheless, their scope of action will remain circumscribed by nation states preserving the last stretches and, for still quite some time, their dominant role in the international system.

With that, let us return to the emergence of a global "public sphere", to the parallel emergence of a global "civic society"; and to the concomitant and exponential growth in the numbers of International Non-Governmental Organisations – INGOs. We have already remarked on the rapid increase in their number in the time since 1909. Now let us look more closely at this development as it has occurred in the more recent past, since 1956.

The number of INGOs has grown rather steadily from 1956 on, with a five-fold increase in the time to 1990. This implies that, already in that earlier period, the number of INGOs grew much more strongly than the number of the official international governmental organisations. From 1990 on, however, this growth in the number of INGOs became very rapid indeed, with yet another five-fold increase occurring in the time span of just ten years.

6 The European Union is an altogether different animal; and more of a nascent federal state than a mere IGO. We will look at it more closely in a subsequent chapter.

7 See, for example, the 1 billion US dollar foundation set up by Ted Turner for the United Nations.

International non-governmental organisations; in thousands

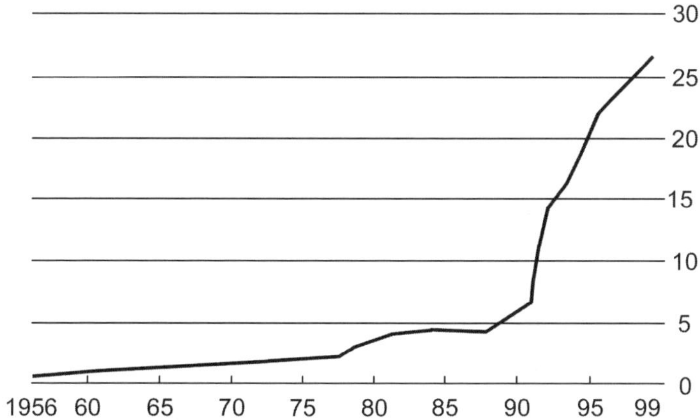

Source: Union of International Organisations

> The INGOs – a bridge between the realm of national politics and the realm of international politics
>
> In theory – and to a large extent in actual life, too – governments and their administrative machines (like the diplomatic service) used to provide the link between politics carried out on the international level and with what happened, on the other hand, in internal politics (they were "gatekeepers").
>
> Of course, the border between internal and international politics has never been as watertight and as controlled as was assumed under this traditional model. Undoubtedly though, this border between internal and international policy has become much more porous over the last decades. One wide sluice has been opened through the growing number – and growing political prominence – of INGOs. They by-pass the traditional gatekeepers that stand guard at the official passageways between the international and the national realms. A Dutch branch of "Greenpeace", for instance, will not ask permission from the Netherlands Ministry of Foreign Affairs if it wishes to protest with the French government against the resumption of nuclear tests. Nonetheless, such a protest will have a political impact in both France and the Netherlands.

INGOs are effective not only politically. They also can be effective operationally. They may mobilise resources that official governmental agencies cannot mobilise (like compassion and charity); or they might be more flexible and nimble in the execution of certain tasks. This is being recognized by public administrations. They use INGOs, for example, in administering assistance to poorer countries.

NGOs and development assistance, 1998
in billion US $

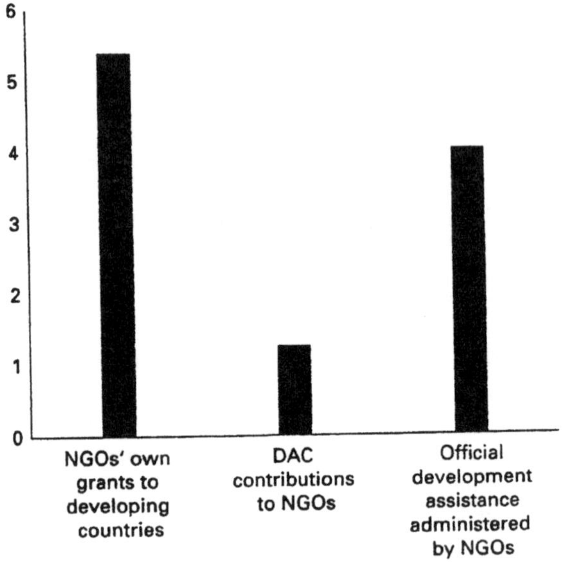

Source: OECD/DAC

Not only did NGOs provide (about) 5 billion dollars[8] of their own money for development assistance in 1998. They received – roughly – the same amount from donor governments that used these NGOs as channels, administrators or agents for their development assistance.

Activities of INGOs thus mix with the activities of regular International Organisations and with the activities of governments. They inter-penetrate and can mutually support one another. But they also may collide.

8 OECD / DAC warns that these estimates are very rough ones. Many NGOs do not report to national or international monitors their DA contributions.

Several years ago, OECD attempted to draft a Multilateral Agreement on Investment – MAI[9]. This was done the traditional way with just the usual administrative elites – diplomats and higher civil servants of member countries – being involved. It was not least this customary lack of transparency that raised suspicions with INGOs about the likely outcome of the negotiations. A massive wave of protests and massive lobbying with OECD member governments was the consequence. Finally, under pressure from INGOs, the effort to conclude such a treaty had to be abandoned.

OECD seems to have learned and heeded the lesson. Negotiations on the renewal, adaptation and reform of the OECD code of conduct[10] for transnational firms could have raised similar suspicions and apprehensions with INGOs. This was avoided by OECD making the negotiating process transparent to INGOs; and by consulting them on questions these INGOs deemed crucial. This example shows quite clearly that, in many cases and fields, INGOs have become effective "international actors".

INGOs might either cooperate with the official state administrative machines; they might oppose them; or they might simply by-pass them. They can by-pass them by lobbying with politicians who have the final authority to make decisions; or – alternatively – INGOs might appeal directly to public opinion and voters (as, for instance, via demonstrations or by spectacular activities, like affixing banners to soot belching smoke-stacks) . They might also make use of the courts – and in the future this might become a very effective way for INGOs to make their impact. Consider the implications of a gathering of INGO lawyers that the New York Times reported on:

---

9 It would have "multilateralised" the hundreds of bilateral investment agreements as they exist between OECD members. But the project became fraught with supplementary wishes – especially from the US, which pleaded for a maximal freedom of investors and for quite some protection against eventualities that might impair profits of those investors.

10 A "code of conduct" might seem a particularly "soft" form of international law. But actually, some "soft" law can become quite stringent. Before Anglo – Saxon courts, the disregard for a code of conduct might have the same effect as the disregard for a formal law. Also, it might be highly detrimental to transnational firms to disregard such codes. Doing so might seriously impair their image; and "image" (and the related concept of "brand") is of increasing relevance in international business. Note, for instance, the damage done to the image of the footwear producer Nike by tolerating abysmal working conditions in Indonesian plants producing Nike shoes; or the damage to the image of "Shell" through its neglect of the local population in Nigeria

"Environmentalists Plan Legal Attacks From Afar on Nations or Firms

Last month, two dozen lawyers from around the country met in Washington to explore the avenues they might pursue to force the United States or corporations to reduce emissions of heat-trapping greenhouse gases, which scientists say are already warming the planet and posing serious risks to human health, property and even entire nations.

The lawyers, representing groups like Greenpeace, the World Wildlife Fund and the Natural Resources Defense Council, envision winning damages for people or whole countries that have suffered adverse effects of global warming.

"Those who are directly injured in a very concrete way by the impacts of climate change are concluding that they will not get the remedy they need through the political process, whether it's the international or domestic process."

Suits could be brought, for example, on behalf of Tuvalu, a tiny nine-island nation in the South Pacific. [It could] vanish within 50 years because of rising sea levels caused by the earth's warming."

INGOs may have considerable impact, too, by simply making things transparent and known. "Freedom House", for instance, makes transparent and widely known how, and to what extent, nations limit civic and political freedom. "Transparency International" makes known the level of corruption as it is perceived to exist in various countries.

Frequently, INGOs will be more effective politically than IGOs

A minister of finance might sign off official pamphlets about the excellence of the investment climate in his country. He might distribute them – for example – to and via the European Bank for Reconstruction and Development – EBRD. If, at the same time, "Transparency International" gives very bad grades to this country in its index on corruption, Transparency International, and not the minister of finance, will have the greater credibility; and greater impact, thus, on investment decisions by foreign enterprises or banks.

If an official report on conditions in jails paints a fairly rosy picture of the situation in a particular country; and if, at the same time, a report by "Amnesty International" paints a picture that is less rosy, the latter report will be credited with higher credibility.

Any minister of justice or of finance is thus well advised to take this into account. It is better to receive emissaries from "Amnesty International" and from "Transparency International". Treat them as what they are: important international "actors".

There is a widening interface and growing co-operation between INGOs and IGOs. Major UN-conferences, for instance, now regularly provide a special forum for INGOs; and INGOs, in their turn, frequently provide inputs in the preparation of such events. INGOs also contribute substantially to various IGO publications (as, for example, to the UNDP Human Development Report mentioned in an earlier chapter).

National non-governmental organisations may have quite some impact internationally; and international non-governmental organisations may have quite some impact on national politics. Altogether there can be no doubt about the growing national and international political weight of non governmental organisations. As mentioned, this growth in strength corresponds to public opinion having become globalised on certain events and issues. Today, public opinion aggregates not just on the national but also on a global scale.

But, as on the national level, on the international level too, this aggregation is now mostly around very specific and frequently narrow issues. Just as on the national level, on the international level too, some pressure groups, interest groups, or non-governmental organisations are more determined and vociferous than others; and all of them are more vociferous – of course – than the far larger group of citizens that are not engaged in any of these groups. As on the national level, on the international level too, it would be the task of politics to establish consensus and to arrange for compromises among divergent groups; and to correct for some being too loud and pushy by giving added consideration to those that have not spoken out as loudly.

National politics (still?) has the tools for doing that. Most citizens participate in periodic elections, and these elections, thus, bring the day of reckoning, when each pressure group, interest group, non governmental organisation is reduced (or more rarely: enhanced) to its proper size by the simple fact that all voters have equal weight. At the same time, views and wishes expressed by such groups are given their democratic legitimisation.

But there is no international electorate to vote on – lets assume – decisions of the UN Security Council or decisions taken at G-8 summits. Who, thus, in the end, can decide on what has been more legitimate: the decision of the G-8 summit; or the violent protests of those INGO-groups assembled in the streets around the meeting place that oppose what had been decided by the G-8 heads of state and government?

In a sense, a still very fractured and partial "global demos" has come into existence. But, whereas in democracies the "demos" is held together and identified by its support for, and its support in democratic political institutions, no such institutions exist on a global level. The representation of the global demos is still a very indirect one. Governments retain the monopoly on legitimately representing the public. On occasion, they are being by-passed by INGOs. But ultimately, and in the absence of global government and global elections, it will remain incumbent on national governments to accept or reject the postulates of the "international civic society" represented by the INGOs.[11]

Furthermore, most people living on earth will not be included in a "demos" of any kind, and, least of all, in a global one. They are either not informed on, or interested in global issues. Or they have no access to international public opinion, nor to persons active in the realm of international politics.

Finally, a "demos" must have inner coherence. A political community can only arise and become effective if all members are sufficiently similar to one another; and if there is sufficient contact and intercourse between them. "Humankind" is no such community. As we have seen, the differences in wealth and in quality of life have never been greater, with the income in the wealthiest country being two hundred times higher than the per capita income in the poorest country; and with little else in common between the two groups of countries.

Nonetheless, there are certain sectors, certain issues where the interest of even such disparate groups converge; and where problems and issues are seen as common ones. A transnational "demos", therefore, can exist as something sectoral; as something that may be fractured according to the issues being addressed; with the possibility of a truly global and all-encompassing "demos" coming into existence only where truly universal issues are at stake.[12]

This is the moment to somewhat question the belief that political actions can gain legitimacy on the national level only; and that international actions, thus, lack democratic legitimsation. After all, the majority of countries are democracies by now. The more powerful countries certainly are. Their representatives on the international scene, therefore, remain accountable to the national electorates; which – by the way – are not as ignorant on international matters or as unin-

---

11 This question parallels the one posed in the discussion on the merits and functions of the so-called "civil society". This discussion brought the issue of democratic legitimisation forward on the national level. If something has to be done that affects all or many in a polity, it should be done by those common political institutions that are under common democratic control. Delegating such tasks to outsiders withdraws this specific field of activity from democratic decision making and scrutiny.

12 One could maintain that the UN "Declaration on Human Rights" does represent the consensus of a global demos. No country openly dares to defy it.

formed as is often assumed[13]. If we accept representative democracy, why not accept it in the international realm – with the foreign ministers, for instance, acting as some kind of parliamentary deputies – although ones elected only indirectly?

Components of a Democratic Process

ACTORS PROCEDURES	Individuals	Organisations (territorial or sectoral)
Deliberative	Direct deliberative democracy *("Schwatzbude")*	Associative democracy (expertocracy)
Aggregative	Majoritarian democracy ("telecracy")	Bargaining democracy (Eurocracy)

In: European Journal of International Relations 6/2

That being said, it is clear, nonetheless, that there are problems in the democratic legitimisation of politics on the international, or on the global level. Many institutions and procedures of democratic government have no international or global equivalent.

A "global government" does not exist and will not exist for quite some time. We are well advised, therefore, to avoid taking such a hypothetical global government as a benchmark against which to measure the perfection or imperfections of democratic politics on a global scale.

> "Governance"
>
> New forms of political participation, of public administration, of providing public services, of organising the political process have arisen on the national level. Traditional, clear and strict structures no longer fit this fluid, fuzzy, pluralistic nature of modern politics and administration. The notion of "government" (conceived of as a top down process along hierarchic lines) has thus yielded to the notion of "governance" which describes a more complex pattern. If the use of this word "governance" is justified in the realm of national politics; it is justified even more and is more fitting as a description of the political attempts to impact upon and steer global developments.

13 The interest in international politics is – roughly – on the same level as the interest in national politics: only a minority is "very" interested in politics; be they internal or international.

If a coherent global "demos" exists, it does exist in some narrow fields only; and it connects to just a few select issues. Over and above that, the global demos is highly fractured. There simply is not that much common ground. Citizens of the world are not just separated by yawning gaps in wealth, but also by profound differences in basic values, by widely divergent cultural conditioning, and by differences in their political institutions. Within separate regions of the world, however – within Western Europe, Sub-Saharan Africa; Latin America, the Caribbean for example – such differences are smaller as a rule. Also, one should assume that states geographically closer to one another have more intensive contacts with one another. These closer contacts facilitate a joint approach to common problems.

Intra-regional exports, 1985-1997
share in %

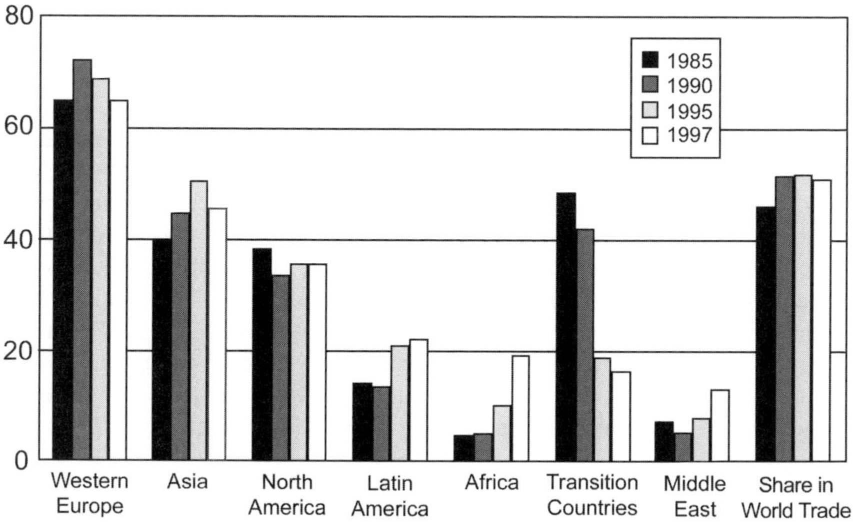

Source: WTO

If we measure the intensity and facility of contacts by the volume of trade, the figures we find would – on the average –confirm this hunch about contacts being more intensive among neighbours. Roughly 50% of world exports are within just one region.

But, at the same time, it is obvious that the density of intra-regional trade is dependent not only upon geographic proximity, but also, and more so, upon the stage of economic development. Intra-regional trade is on a very high level in Western Europe. But it is on a low level in less developed peripheral regions like Latin America or Northern Africa; and it becomes minimal in Sub-Saharan Africa[1].

Politics can make a difference in boosting or limiting the volume of intra-regional trade. Politics have boosted the volume of intra-regional trade in North America (through the creation of "NAFTA" – North American Free Trade Agreement). On the other hand, after 1989, the crumbling of the "Council for Mutual Economic Assistance – COMECON" had the effect of dramatically lowering trade among the formerly Communist countries.

And indeed, there are reasons to promote intra-regional co-operation. As we have seen, a low volume of intra-regional trade is a token of poverty and of a "peripheral status". Most of the external ties of a poor and undeveloped country are not to its kin next door; but to some distant, wealthy "centre". But such a low volume of intra-regional trade is not just the consequence of economic under-development. It is also one of its causes. The promotion of intra-regional exchange is, therefore, a tool in the policy kit for economic development.

Intra-regional exchanges should be intensified not just for narrowly economic motives. A host of other than economic problems also need solutions that are on a broader scale and, thus, more effective than solutions effected by just one single state. Regulations on emissions, on food and drugs, on financial products, on migration, are examples. The list is long. Of course, one may wish to address like issues not just on a regional level but on a global level. But frequently, it will be difficult or impossible to forge the necessary consensus among all nations of the world. Consensus is more readily found among states which – due to their geographic closeness – have much of their interests and values in common.

Intra-regional co-operation may come in forms that differ in their legal nature. Some of these arrangements can be very binding legally, and such binding ar-

---

1 Intra-regional trade is quite substantial in Asia, though the region is not that wealthy overall, and is not as consolidated politically as North America or Europe. This stronger inter-linkage is due – mainly – to strong intra-industry trade; which again is the consequence of much FDI done by one Asian country (Japan, Taiwan) in another one (PR China, Thailand).

rangements may be supported by some quite complex institutions[2]. Or, on the other hand, such arrangements may be very informal and may be only supported by some very ad-hoc institutional back-up. Regional co-operation might be over many and very diverse issues like culture, traffic, information, human rights, etc. Trade, nonetheless, remains central in all attempts to enhance the co-operation within one region.

In fact, the number of regional trade arrangements has risen steadily.

More intra-regional trading arrangements (IRTAs) came into force in the 1990s than ever before;
numbers of IRTAs entering into force

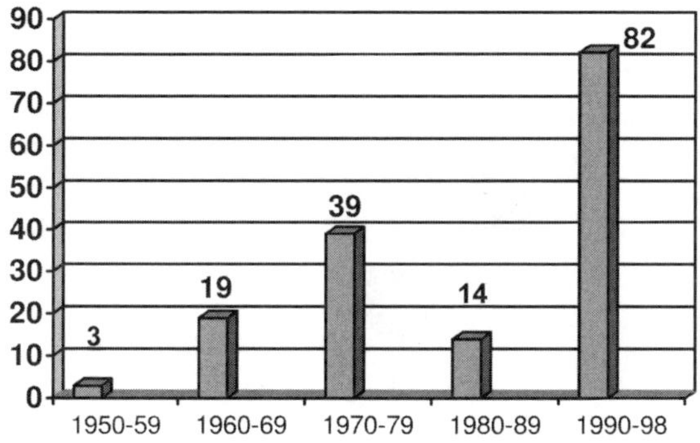

Source: WTO

These efforts resulted in (or ran parallel to) a rise in intra-regional trade.

Intra-regional exports in some regional trade arrangements 1990 and 1997 share in %

	1990	1997
EU (15 members)	64,9	60,8
NAFTA (3)	42,7	49,0
Mercosur (4)	8,9	24,4
ASEAN(9)	18,9	23,6

Source : WTO

2 with the three-tier form of organisation characteristic of most international organisations: assembly, council, secretariat

Mercosur is a customs union that joins the countries of Southern Latin America, with Argentina and Brazil as its most prominent members. The level of intra-Mercosur trade is still rather low (but this has to be judged against the fact that this group is not a very large one, so that its small size automatically lowers the share of intra-trade in the overall trade). Nonetheless, this trade has tripled within less than a decade, with intra Mercosur exports expanding from 8% to 24% of all trade of its members.[3] As concerns the external trade of Mercosur, the European Union is the most important partner by far, taking 25% of Mercosur's exports with just 18% going to the US.

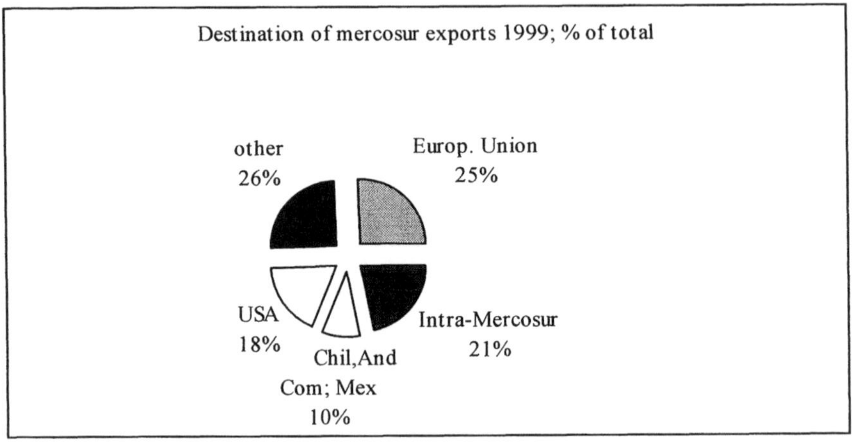

Source: WTO

Three countries on the North American continent – Canada, Mexico, and the US – are joined by the "North American Free Trade Agreement – NAFTA". The Agreement is on more than free trade only; but falls short, by far, from being a customs union or even an economic union. In 2001 talks were started to launch negotiations on the ambitious project (promoted by the US) to link all of North and South America in a "Free Trade Agreement of the Americas – FTAA". Mercosur would become part of that arrangement as would the free trade area of the CARICOM in the Caribbean and CACM in Central America. The chances of success for this project seem less than even.

3 Recently, however, the dynamics of this evolution stalled, when crisis hit the Southern part of Latin America in 1998.

The "Association of Southeast Asian Nations – ASEAN" is not, in first line, a trade agreement, but a grouping that is mainly political in nature (and a rather feeble organisation at that). As we have noted, membership in this group includes countries that are widely different in their level of economic development – from wealthy Singapore to dirt-poor Laos. A free trade regime is envisaged for the future. It is not yet in place.

As we have remarked before, the European Union is the most coherent block, by far, if measured in terms of its intra-regional trade. The expansion of intra-trade seems to have levelled off at the end of the eighties; and even seems to have declined a bit since. But that drop was due to the opening of the East and to the subsequent rise in trade between the Union and the formerly Communist countries. When, in 2004, many of these ex-Communist countries will have become members of the Union, the percentage of EU-intra-trade will revert to the higher level it had in 1990.

Regional co-operation can be very loose, or very stringent; it can cover many different fields, or just a few ones. It can be carried out by just one common institution; or by many different ones. Regional co-operation is on a high level and is very dense in Europe. This level and density does not have a counterpart in any other region of the world. Co-operation in Europe is not just based on, and founded in the European Union. Although the Union provides the strongest pillar sustaining European co-operation, other organisations also have important functions in this regard. Membership in these organisations is diverse but – over vast stretches – overlapping. Next to the EU several other European institutions deal, for example, with the issue of external security: NATO, OSCE, Partnership for Peace.

Other European organisations work on other issues and problems:

- the Council of Europe – COE – deals mainly with parliamentary democracy and human rights
- the Economic Commission for Europe – UN/ECE is mainly engaged in support of trans-European transport and in the promotion of pan-European action to safeguard the environment
- the Organisation for Economic Co-operation and Development – OECD serves as a venue for discussion on economic and social policies and for analysing problems common to the most advanced countries[4]

4 The organisation has its origins in the Marshall Plan assistance, provided by the US to Europe after WWII. The Non - European members, like Australia and Japan, joined only later. OEEC – the precursor to OECD – laid the foundation for the unification of Europe, with the multilateralisation and liberalisation of trade (achieved in

- the European Space Agency – ESA has successfully established the European presence in outer-space.

Next to these organisations with a very wide membership (frequently including non – Europeans), there are those with a more restricted membership that promote and support what is called "sub-regional co-operation". Here again, some deal with trade exclusively as, for instance, the European Free Trade Agreement – EFTA, the Central European Free Trade Agreement – CEFTA, the customs union between the Czech Republic and Slovakia, and numerous other intra European free trade agreements (like the ones among most of the successor states of Yugoslavia).

Other such sub-regional organisations also have things other than merely trade on their agenda: the Baltic Sea Council, the Baltic Council[5], the Black Sea Economic Co-operation, the Central European Initiative (CEI), the Southeast Europe Cooperation Initiative (SECI), the Southeast Europe Stability Pact, the Nordic Council (grouping the Scandinavian countries); etc.

Even when ignoring the unique experiment of the European Union, the density of intra-regional co-operation in Europe remains remarkable. This density of co-operation sets Europe apart from other regions of the world where intra-regional co-operation rests on a more narrow base. It sets Europe apart, in particular, from East Asia. No East Asian institution exists to deal with even the most pressing of the problems of the region: which is external security. The OSCE or the "Partnership for Peace" have no counterpart in East Asia. This void is troubling because, next to the US and Europe, East Asia is the third "strategic" region of the world. As we have noted, it is furthermore a region whose relevance of which is bound to grow.

Political institutions do, of course, impact upon their environment. This is their very purpose. But, on the other hand, they also must be supported by this environment. They do not exist, and cannot function, in a political/social/ economic void. Obviously, post-war Europe has provided such an environment for intra-regional co-operation to flourish.

European co-operation was certainly motivated and enhanced by the need to face the common threat emanating from the Soviet Union. Co-operation was also facilitated by the fact that, with the victory over Germany, and with the

the mid-fifties) from whereon the European Economic Union took over as the main promoter of European integration.

5 The Baltic Council provides for free trade among its three members. But it deals with non-trade issues too.

division of Germany, no single state was there to overpower and overshadow all others. Finally, the deep shock of the break down of civilisation in World War II seems to have provided a lesson that has been heeded (at least by the war generation, and by the first post-war generation).

That being said, it is clear, however, that the European Union stands at the core of European intra-regional co-operation. It is equally evident that its political base, its aim and its track record make it differ from other organisations that promote intra-regional co-operation.

We cannot go into the details of the political processes that underpin the Union. What interests us here is the question as to whether Europe will be able to impact the future of the world and contribute in a positive way to shaping it. To do so, the European Union will have to act as a single unit and with a single purpose. Can it do that?

Let us try to answer the question by using the tools of social science. A social scientist will set the following conditions for a group to become a coherent political actor:

a) its members must not be too dissimilar from one another

b) the members must have more intense relations between one another than they have to outsiders who are not members of the group

c) a group identity must emerge. Members must become aware and positive (perhaps even proud) about their membership in this group

d) co-operation in the group has to be propped up by institutions that facilitate common action

With this in mind, let us look at the co-operation and integration as carried out in the European Union.

Are the countries of Europe sufficiently similar to one another to form a coherent entity? The answer is positive. Notwithstanding the obvious diversity and notwithstanding all that separates a Sicilian farmer from a Swedish miner, the member nations of the European Union do resemble one another more closely than countries in other regions of the world. In Latin America or East Asia, for instance, the differences between the various countries in these regions are much bigger.

Countries may differ by wealth and this differentiation is a crucial one, of course. Yet, in Europe that differentiation is rather muted. The wealthiest EU member country (Luxembourg) has less than double the income of the poorest (Greece). This gap is not wider than the one that used to separate the wealthiest state of the United States (Connecticut) from the poorest US state (Mississippi).

Furthermore, this gap in income is shrinking. In EU-Europe, per capita GDP is converging.

GDP per head from the date of entry
EU = 100

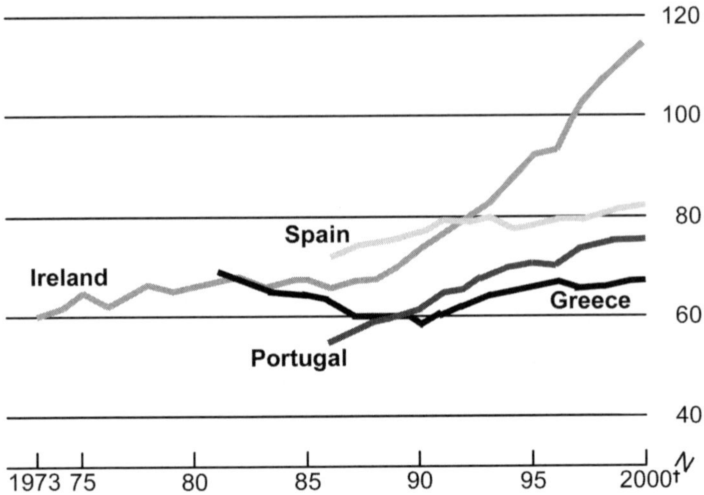

Source: EC

In part, this convergence is just the result of the emergence of a single economic space, in which differences tend to level automatically. But in part, this convergence in wealth also results from political action, from the conscious transfer of wealth to the poorer regions as is practised via the EU structural funds.

Like the differences in wealth, the differences in social structures are minor. The income distribution differs among EU member states, with it being more equal in Scandinavia and less so in Latin countries. But these differences in "equality" are not extreme. Differences in the rates of (relative) poverty are also not very significant.

Poverty rates in the EU

EU average	17
Belgium	17
Denmark	11
Greece	21
Spain	18
France	16
Ireland	18
Italy	19
Luxembourg	12
Netherlands	12
Austria	13
Portugal	22
United Kingdom	19

Source: Eurostat

Macroeconomic data are also converging among EU countries. This is partly due to the emergence of a single economic space; partly it is due to conscious policy and to the resolve to establish economic and monetary union and to use but one single, joint currency – the euro.

European capital markets are melting into one. This development, too, has been accelerated by the introduction of the euro among 12 of the 15 EU members.

A company's share price might be affected by the company's individual performance; by the performance of the industrial sector it is part of; or by the economic performance of its home country. Over the past years, the country effect has come to count for less within the euro area. Since the introduction of the euro, the prices of shares move less in line with the prices of shares of the same country; and more in line with the prices of shares in the same sector (in all member countries of the euro-zone).

EURO POWER

Correlation between euro-area sectors and countries over time

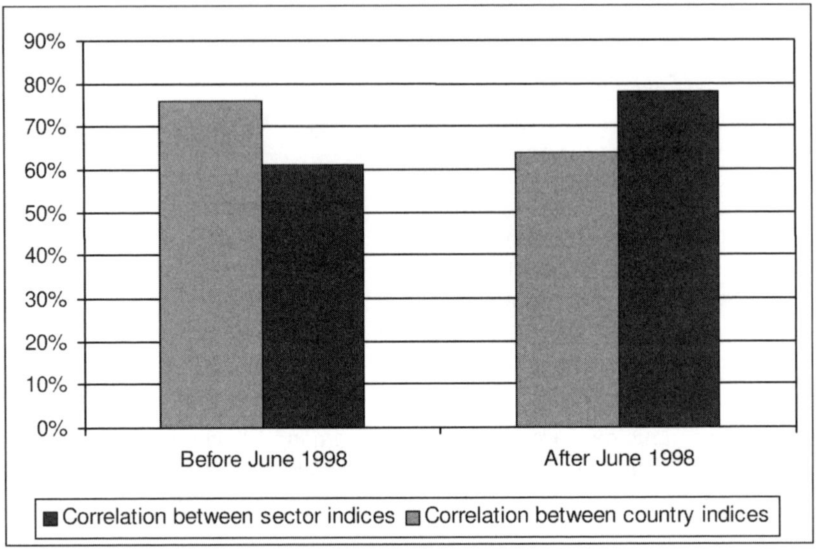

Source:

In order to become one coherent entity, communication and transaction within a group must be intense; and more so than transactions and communications with those that are not members of the group. A very useful gauge for the intensity of this economic interaction are mergers and acquisitions of enterprises.

Number of mergers notified to the European Commission

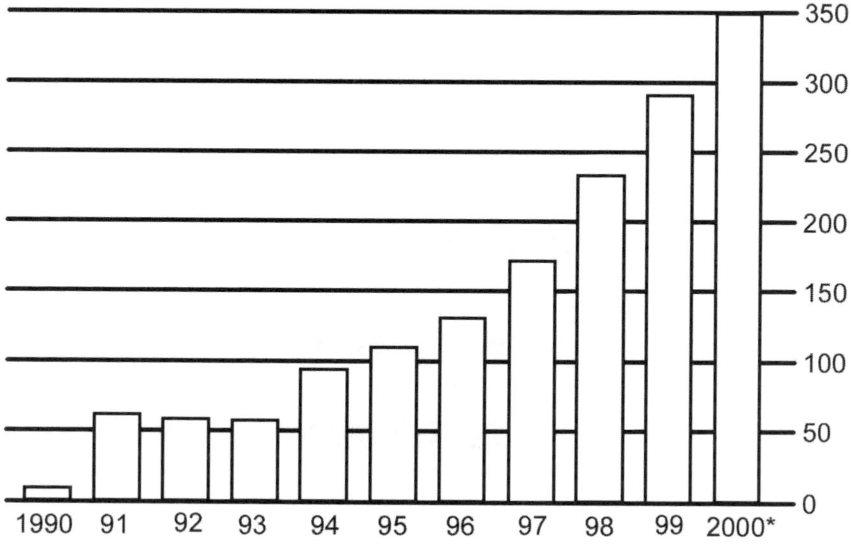

* To Aug 13st, annualised

Source: European Commission

The strong rise in intra-EU mergers in 1998 and 1999 is a consequence of the completion of the single internal market and of the impending introduction of the single common currency.

For a group to become a political actor it is necessary that this group does indeed conceive of itself as a specific and distinct[6] entity. Voting patterns in the European parliament support the notion that such a sense of identity is emerging.

Members of the European parliament might see their primary task as representing their country of origin. Or, alternatively, they might see it as their primary task to represent a certain EU-wide political-ideological group, like the Christian

6 A parallel might be drawn here to Karl Marx and his notion of a class "an sich" and of a class "für sich". For the proletariat to come into existence in the political sense, it is necessary that proletarians convince themselves of indeed being proletarians; and as something distinct, something that differs from other classes of society. They have to become "eine Klasse für sich".

Democrats, the Socialists, or the Communists. In the first case, they will align their votes with the votes of other deputies from their home country. In the second case, they will align their votes with those of their ideological kin, even though these come from other countries.

Party cohesion in the European Parliament
% of MEPs voting according to party lines

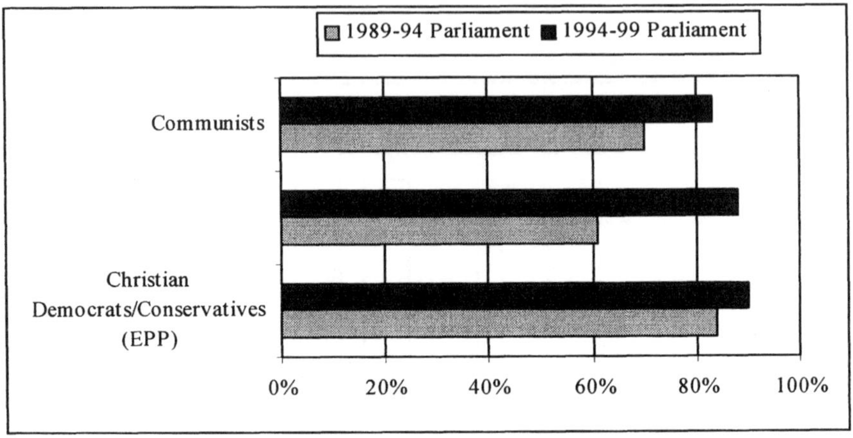

Source: Simons, London School of Economics

Increasingly, members of the European parliament tend to vote as representatives of Europe-wide movements[7] and not as representatives of their original home country. One has to conclude that the members of the European Parliament gain their political identity primarily by representing an EU-wide agenda; and only secondarily by representing this or that EU member state.

Yet, if we put that question to regular EU-citizens of the EU, the answer tends to be different. And indeed, this question is put to them via the "Eurobarometer". In this poll, they are asked whether they see themselves as being European or, on the other hand, as being French, Italian, German, or Austrian. The overwhelming majority still responds with confirming their traditional national identity.

7 Or nascent all-European parties.

One might explain that by "consciousness" always lagging behind reality; and by "masses" being less alert than elites to profound changes in their external circumstances. Yet this explanation is not very satisfying.

The more likely explanation is that "Eurobarometer" simply asks the wrong question. The question presupposes, as given, a simple dichotomy. One could either feel oneself being a citizen of Europe; or, alternatively, as a citizen of this or that EU member state. There also is the option of replying that one believes oneself to be a little bit of a European and more of a citizen of this or that state; and there is the option of evenly distributing one's loyalty and attachment. These possible answers might be strung along one line; of which, at one extreme end, we find full identification with the EU only; and on the other end, the full identification with the nation/state only.

This uni-dimensional view of the issue is misleading, and the underlying notion is simplistic and outdated.[8] In such a view of the world, there is no place for persons that have a split loyalty, that might feel themselves partly German and partly French, for example. And there is no place either, in this world-view, for persons who are loyal in different ways both to Europe and to their nation/state.

Alas, it might very well be that, emotionally, someone sees him or herself primarily as French; or as Austrian. But that does not exclude that, for specific questions and on specific issues, he or she attaches prime responsibility, and thus prime loyalty, to European institutions. One may, for instance, trust and proudly use the new euro currency; and bestow confidence in maintaining its value on the European Central Bank. The fact that the same person remains emotionally attached to Austria or France, therefore, does not automatically condemn him or her to distrust the euro or the European Central Bank. It does not condemn him or her to being a bad European.

One should move the discussion from the emotional issue of "identity" or "nationality" towards a discussion of the political concept of "citizenship".[9]

---

8 This is the notion of the state having a claim to unconditional and exclusive loyalty. This notion might be founded on a view of the international system as being shaped by the ever present threat of war. Such a system calls on states and their citizens to be ever ready to go to war against each other and to kill each other. As a true Frenchman, you would have to be ready to kill a German. A true German would have to be ready to kill a Frenchman.

9 Citizen entrusts certain political institutions with certain tasks. And they feels bound to these institutions and they support them, because they are efficient in accomplishing the task they had assigned to them.

Europeans are perfectly willing to entrust the Union with certain important tasks, feeling confident that the Union is the political organisation best equipped to deal with them. What better proof of the viability of the Union than the fact that even the French are perfectly willing to grant it greater authority in "making food safer"?

Should the EU have bigger powers to…
(% of yes minus no)

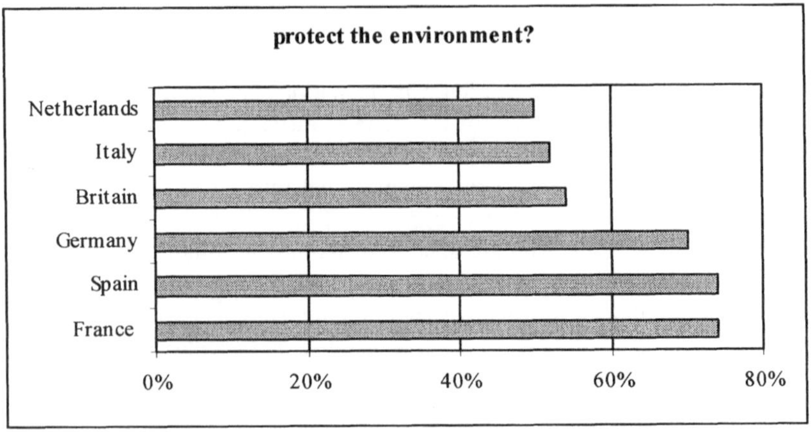

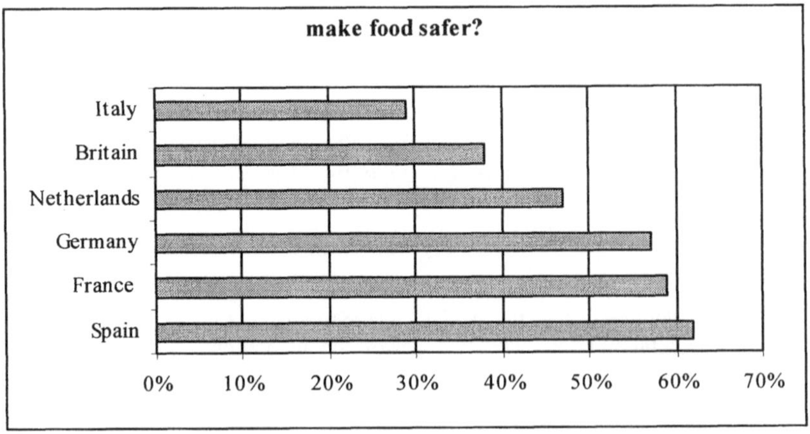

Source: The European Barometer

Finally, if it wishes to act as a group and to be recognised as a coherent group, any such group will have to establish institutions that facilitate common action. The instruments at the disposal of the European Union for common regional/European action are vastly more powerful than the instruments that could be used by any other regional organisation on any other continent. The number and efficiency of these EU instruments has grown over time[10].

The question is, however, whether these instruments are yet plentiful and potent enough to permit Europe to actively shape the global environment, to defend its interests and to preserve its specific model of political/social/economic organisation. Obviously, many of the tools that would be needed for such a task are not (yet?) there. Tools do not match ambition. This is also because, with each succeeding step in European integration, the need and ambition have also grown even further. Nor is this ambition vainglorious. It responds to real challenges.

Taxes and social security contributions as percentage of GDP, 1998

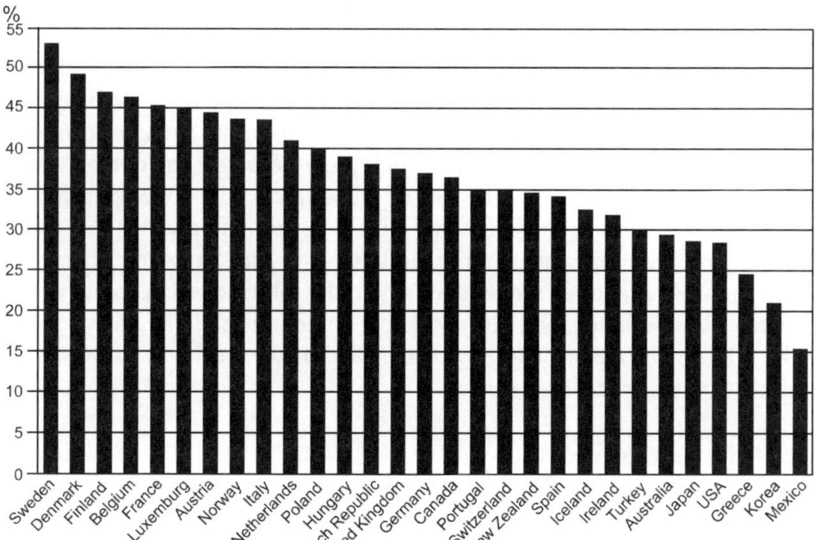

Source: Eurostat

As mentioned, one of these is the need to defend and evolve the "European socio-economic model". But is there truly such a thing? Is there a distinctly "European model" of organising politics, society and the economy? The US,

10 The process has not been steady and even. At times there even have been retreats.

Europe and Japan – that is, all three members of the "triad" – have much in common. The United States and Europe have even more in common still – from their ideological base to their dietary customs. So, in a certain sense, we can speak of a North-Atlantic socio-economic model. On the other hand, within Europe itself, there is quite some diversity. Various socio-economic "sub-models" co-exist: the Scandinavian model of the welfare state; the German-Austrian ("Rhenian") corporatism; the "statism" of France, the syndicalist traditions in Southern Europe; etc.

Notwithstanding this variety; and notwithstanding many similarities with the United States, some social and political arrangements are, nonetheless, distinctly European. One such specificity is a large public sector. Whereas in Japan and the USA, taxes and social security contributions constitute just a little bit more than 30% of GDP, they constitute around 45% of GDP in Europe. That European specificity has major implications for the entire way public and private life is organised.

Notwithstanding the common roots in protestantism and enlightenment, and though they might be obscured by a superficial "Mc-Donaldisation", there are also profound cultural differences that separate US society from European society: attitudes towards work differ; attitudes towards religion; towards leisure; towards gender relations; towards the family. Obviously, the attitudes towards public violence are not the same[11]. The commonly accepted balance between risk and security is different on both sides of the Atlantic with Americans being less risk-averse. Definitions on what constitutes a "good life" diverge. All these differences find their way into politics. Indeed, it is hard to ignore that a distinct European socio-economic model does exist. The ultimate test: step out of the hotel in any European city, and you will know without much telling that you are not in the US; nor in Japan or in any other place of the world. A European city is immediately recognizable as such.

The British exceptionality

Notoriously, the British attitude towards the European Union and/or to the rest of Europe is ambivalent. There is something very defensive about this attitude, as it seems to betray lack of self confidence more than any unshaken belief in British superiority. Britain's lack of self-confidence is very likely a reflection of the sharp decline in relative power it suffered in the first half of the 20th century. Britain evidently tries to compensate for this trauma by upholding the

11 Reflected in attitudes towards gun control and the death penalty.

notion of having been assigned some specific and unique role, apart from and superior to the role of other European nations.

On occasions, British policy even conveys the impression of an ambition to prolong the traditional British role towards what is termed "the continent", and to prevent any "continental" power from becoming dominant. That policy now seems to be extended to the European Union which is perceived (and pictured at least in the tabloid press) as a Franco-German conspiracy to threaten the UK's position and its capacity to tip the balance between contending powers. Somewhat unrealistically, the UK hopes to be able to back up this stance by leaning upon the US and by being some sort of in-between for the two continents.

In a crisis, which of these – Europe, the Commonwealth or the United States – do you think would be Britain's most reliable political ally?

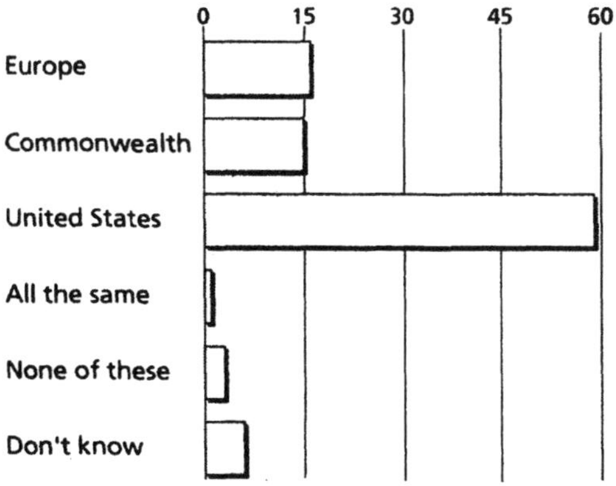

Source: MORI

The UK thus acts as a brake on the process of European integration, without being able to stop it altogether; and always being forced, some years later, to make the concessions it had refused to make at an earlier date.

As a defender of common interests and as a protector of the European socio-economic model, the Union is clearly attractive. It has grown as, in succeeding waves, new members have been admitted. The next such expansion will occur in 2004, when 10 new members (among them 8 formerly Communist Central European countries) will join. This, the 5th EU enlargement, will increase the EU population by about one third[12]. The increase in wealth will be a more modest nine percent.

Impact of successive enlargement upon the EU*

Enlargement	Increase in area, %	Increase in population, %	Increase in GDP (at PPP[1]), %	Change in GDP per person, %	GDP (EU 6=100)
EU 6 to EU 9, 1973	31	32	29	-3	97
EU 9 to EU 12, 1986[2]	48	22	15	-6	91
EU 12 to EU 15[3], 1995	43	11	8	-3	89
EU 15 to EU 26[4]	34	29	9	-16	75

*Based on 1995 data 1 Purchasing power parity (PPP) seeks to equalise the prices of identical bundles of goods and services in each country 2 Greece joined in 1981 3 Including German unification 4 excluding Malta and Turkey

Source: European Commission

Some argue that this enlargement will put an end to the quest for an "ever closer union". The Union will not be able to make the necessary changes in the rules on voting, and in other organisational/constitutional arrangements that would be needed to keep the Union functioning, even with such a vastly expanded membership. Also, the new members will differ too much from the old ones in wealth and in political traditions. Decision making will become extremely onerous. The process of integration will stall and will even reverse.[13] Instead of progressing towards a federal state, the Union will become divested of its political substance and will revert to being a simple customs union. Such a development – so it is claimed – will be likely for yet another reason. In the past, integration was pursued with the goal mainly of balancing Soviet power on the European continent. This was a very cogent motive. With the Soviet threat having disappeared, this strong motive for further integration has also ceased to exist.

These arguments are certainly weighty. Yet, one should note that similar apprehensions also greeted earlier expansions of the Union. Subsequently, they were shown to have been ill-founded, as each wave of expansion was followed by a wave of reform that "deepened" integration. "Deepening" and "widening", thus, have not been the mutually exclusive alternatives they had been pictured to be. On the contrary, they were mutually contingent.

12 Bulgaria and Romania are counted in the table, but shouldn't be as they will adhere to the EU later – probably in 2007.

13 Calleo David, 2002, Rethinking Europe's Future, Princeton University Press, Princeton

As we have shown, the disappearance of the threat that emanated from the former Soviet Union has certainly affected US-European relations. It certainly has weakened the North Atlantic alliance. Yet, up until now, it does not seem to have weakened the Union. This is because thwarting the Soviet threat had only been one – and not the most potent – motive driving integration. This is proven by the fact that integration has progressed even after the Soviet threat disappeared. In the nineties, the Amsterdam treaty vastly expanded the competences of the EU; the Lisbon summit brought a co-ordinated strategy for greater economic dynamics; and the introduction of a common currency has sealed the merging of national markets (especially in the strategic area of finance).

What about the future? It is clear that Europe's place and function in the global system will depend upon the success or failure to pursue integration; to establish not only a common foreign and security policy; but, also, as its necessary counterpart, a truly common defence. Europe's place and impact on the world will, furthermore, depend on its capacity to keep the economy dynamic and to keep its markets open and flexible (which can be done by joint efforts only). It will depend on its capacity to preserve – by its own means – peace in Southeast Europe and on its success in helping nation building in this troubled region. It will depend, last but not least, on its being able to integrate – in succeeding waves – the countries up to the Ukraine-Russian border.

In order to meet all those targets the European Union still has some way to go: in military capacity; in some areas of high technology; in reforming the EU institutions; in tackling new challenges and threats to democracy, etc. But why shouldn't it succeed? Why should integration that has progressed in the past, cease to do so in the future? Why should we refrain from projecting into the future this trend that has been so distinct in the past?

Why should we become sceptical about the continuation of European integration? There is some reason for fears that the future will be unlike the past; and that integration will not only cease to progress; but will even reverse. One cannot ignore that, over the last three years, the process has stalled and has been punctured by repeated and serious failures. The 2001 Nice summit should have adapted the EU procedures to the larger number of members. The most urgent change would have been the switching (in crucial areas where it still holds) from the requirement of unanimous decision-making to decision-making by a majority. This reform has become more urgent as, among 25, unanimity is even more difficult to arrive at than in a group of merely 15.

A more serious set-back came in the run-up to the war in Iraq, with an intentional US assault on EU unity. In this crucial question, the EU splintered with some important members yielding to the US and defecting from a common European stand.[14] That split has – for a time – poured water on the hope of fast progress towards a common foreign and security policy. It also has seriously impaired the ongoing work on the draft for a new EU constitution which would have to be completed by the end of 2004.

The EU is, of course, decisive for the future global role of Europe; and recent developments make it less certain that the Union must progress in the future as it has done in the past. If we assume, however, that it will master its present crisis, as it has mastered crises in the past, we may also assume that Europe will be able to maintain its role as one of the three pillars of the "Triad". Economically, it might even become the sturdiest of these three pillars. The future rise in productivity is likely to be a bit faster than it had been in the rather sluggish 1990s; with the negative effect of an ageing population being compensated for by faster growth in the Eastern and in the Southern parts of the continent[15]; and by a more supportive macroeconomic policy[16]. At the March 2000 Lisbon summit, the Union did, in fact, set for itself the target of becoming – by 2010 – "the most competitive and dynamic, knowledge-based economy in the world". It has established benchmarks and a process (Lisbon process) to monitor progress towards that goal. Given the present sluggishness of the world economy and of the European economy, many of these targets will be missed; as, for example, the ambitious target of an average annual 3 percent growth rate.

But, whatever might happen to this Lisbon process; and whatever might happen to the larger process of EU integration, it is certain that EU countries will not jettison their common currency or destroy the coherence of its single internal market, which have become essential for the economic well-being of each of the EU members. As the Union will be expanded from 15 to 25 members its demographic size will increase by 30% and – as mentioned – in these new member countries, economic growth will also be more rapid.

Most probably, thus, the Union will at least equal the United States in the mere volume of production[17]. The position of the two entities will remain differ-

---

14 This US-intervention in inner-European affairs marks a strategic shift in US policies. Since its inception, European integration had been supported by the United States. It even was initiated by the US. Now the US policy has changed towards "disaggregating" the EU. This is in line with the new 2002 US security doctrine which calls for pre-empting the emergence of any power that could rival the US.

15 And in the adjoining rim regions of Russia, the Ukraine and the Southern shore of the Mediterranean.

16 It would need quite some resolve and demand quite some energy to repeat, in the coming decades, the deflationary aberrations characteristic of European macroeconomic policy in the 1990s.

17 Concentrating on the ever interesting spectacle of US – European competition; and of the competition between all three members of the "triad", we should not lose

ent, though, at the cutting edge of production. Europe is likely to preserve – and perhaps even expand – its lead in the field of mechanical engineering, civilian aircraft, and pharmaceuticals. But it will probably find it difficult to challenge the US world dominance in certain key services – like audio-visual services, software production, investment banking , and the management of information.

Its economic clout would, therefore, assign to Europe a future role equal to the role of the United States. But the potential European impact upon the global system is likely to be diminished by its failure to reach the assigned goals in the realm of traditional security- and power politics. The thinning out of NATO's political and military substance has alerted Europeans to the necessity of rapid progress in their Common Foreign and Security Policy; and especially to the need to arrive more quickly at some truly common defence policy. Some progress has been made over the last years. The 60.000 person strong European intervention force has become operational in 2003. Co-operation in arms production has intensified[18]. Nonetheless, there is neither the political resolve nor are there the financial resources that would be needed to permit Europe a more than secondary role next to the US in the field of traditional power politics and power projection.

Looking back, one even has to register a steady decline of Europe's capacity and role in this field of traditional military security. In the years immediately following World War II, both France and Great Britain still aimed at – and maintained – a global military presence. Both developed nuclear weapons at a pace roughly equal to the pace of these developments in the US and the Soviet Union. Challenging the US, both France and Great Britain still intervened militarily in the Suez war of 1956. In the 1990s, however, Europeans were no longer capable of even backing up, by proper military means[19], their policies in their very backyard in former Yugoslavia. Until the 1980s, Europeans still assigned some secu-

---

sight of the simple fact that, over the next fifty years, the relative total global economic weight of all three triad members together is bound to decline. This is mainly due to the rapidly growing relative economic weight of East-, Southeast- and Southern Asia.

18 Work has now started, for example, on the joint European military air transport plane.

19 Early on, the European "founding fathers" decided to start European integration not in the economic field but, by the "European Defence Union". The plan foundered in 1954 in the French parliament (upon the joint resistance of French Communists and Gaullists). Thereupon the tack was changed and integration was sought via economics, with the precursor of the Union – the European Economic Community – coming into existence in 1957. Institutions, procedures and informal rules became adapted – of course – to this economic approach. It is obvious that it is not that easy to implant upon these basically economic structures the wholly different structure of a joint security and military policy.

rity interest to a presence in Africa. This no longer is the case and Europe mostly leaves it to Africans to deal with security problems on their continent.

But on the other hand, Europe does make a sizeable contribution to a less traditional version of global security policy. It is a major player in what may be termed "world-order-politics". Europe is the main donor of Official Development Assistance. It is mainly Europe that pushes for the evolution and tighter application of international law. Europe spearheads the movements for disarmament and arms control, and against the proliferation of weapons of mass destruction. It leads in all humanitarian intervention; and carries more than its share of burdens in UN peacekeeping operations.

Unlike the US, Europe does not dominate world audio visual production. Also, the European contribution to world wide mass culture is less prominent[20] and certainly less visible than the US contribution made – for example – by jeans and fast foodchains. As it seems, the US is destined to continue to dominate the world with this very soft form of power. And the US seems destined to retain its social dynamics by being open to the world, and to immigration; and by being able to thus build the model of what could – eventually and in different versions – become a world culture.

But with a role less spectacular, Europe is a player in this game too. Like the US, many nations of Europe have been "melting pots", integrating a multitude of diverse immigrants and other ethnic groups. At the same time, most European nations have learned to live with that diversity that cannot be amalgamated into one all encompassing national culture. Both the capacity to integrate and the capacity to live with diversity is as much a source of strength for Europe as it is a source of strength for the US. European societies are not closed societies, and Europe is not a closed continent. It is open to the world economy; but also to the cultures of other parts of the world. At its frontiers are not walls but bridges: Spain and Portugal link to Latin America; France to Africa; Greece to the Arab world; Poland to the Ukraine; etc.

So all in all, Europe has the wherewithal to defend its values and interests on a global level and to impact upon and co-determine the global order. Whether this potential will be used, this is – however – contingent upon further progress in European integration. Such progress is far from certain. As we have seen, the process of integration has slowed over the last years and in some crucial fields there have been setbacks; as, for example, the failure of the Nice summit; or the failure to arrive at a common position when the US was pushing towards war in

20 Among the European contributions: designer clothes, mass transportation, wine, soccer, outdoor activities like skiing, public broadcasting, the pub and the bistro, pasta and schnitzel; etc.

Iraq. These failures make obvious the extent to which present European politics are still mired in pettiness. None of the present political leaders is capable or willing to look past last week's opinion polls or past the last day's headlines and TV news. None of them is willing to contemplate the inconvenience of being seen to sacrifice an ever so small national benefit for the common European good. Leaders would behave differently and act more as "Europeans" if voters were to revolt against such indolence and short-sightedness. But voters do not revolt. They share the smugness of their political leaders. According to opinion polls, European citizens are still quite willing to charge the common European institutions with this or that chore. But only a tiny minority of European citizens is prepared to fight in order to equip the common European institutions with the tools needed to accomplish such new tasks. Very few citizens are resolved to make progress in European integration the core demand addressed to their elected representatives.

The statistics presented on the last pages have testified to the growth of intra-European coherence and cohesion. Yet, we have noted that this progress was not something quasi-automatic. To a large extent, it resulted from conscious political resolve to move ahead with integration. In no small part this resolve was founded in the desire to have Europe play its role in the shaping of the global order it is imbedded in; and which, in turn, will impact upon Europe; and will do so ever more deeply as global interdependence grows. Obviously, the political foundation is becoming weaker upon which such past success has been based. This puts a big question mark behind all projections on the future place of Europe in global affairs.

But, with these observations on the specific case of intra-regional co-operation in Europe, let us return to the wider subject. Regional governance is an obviously useful "in-between" global governance and national governance. Yet the conditions to make it effective are more limited on other continents than they were in Europe. The world scene is, therefore, littered with failed attempts to imitate the European example in other parts of the world[21].

Regional arrangements seem especially useful in two realms:

- external security; and
- external trade.

In these two areas, the simple economies of scale severely limit the effect of purely national efforts (except efforts of giant countries like India or China). No-

21 As is demonstrated, for example, by the many failed schemes for regional co-operation in the Arab world or in Africa.

body will invest in an automobile factory that serves a market of just ten million or so. No army of a country with just ten million inhabitants or so will be capable of mustering all the military technology and all the complex equipment needed to prevail on the modern battlefield.

We therefore should expect continued interest in finding solutions for such and similar issues on a level above that of the nation state, but below a global level. Such efforts at regionalisation would also encompass governance and rule making.

And indeed, in the field of trade, at least, the last years have seen an advance in regional co-operation. Yet not all continents have profited from it; least of all Asia and Africa. In the field of external security, regional co-operation is scarcer still. This is a bit surprising given the evident benefits of nations delegating some of their tasks of governance upwards to regional organisations. Vested interests have certainly done much to prevent such a delegation of tasks. But one other cause is equally evident: the regionalisation of government presupposes the existence of functioning nation states. Where nation- and state building is incomplete still, regional co-operation and regional governance will have no firm base either. Regional co-operation can complement what national governments do. It cannot compensate for what national governments fail to do.

Regional co-operation could be especially useful to peripheral countries; but it is also especially difficult among peripheral countries as, in most cases, the contacts between them are anaemic, while at the same time they frequently differ from one another quite markedly and have fewer things in common[22] than adjoining wealthier countries.

22 In addition, in many of the peripheral countries, political power is an important source of income and there might be reluctance, for that reason, to delegate any of this power to a political entity "above".

"Localisation" – Politics on a Sub-State Level and the Enduring Relevance of Geography

We have claimed that, in the global context, location has become less important. The costs of transport both over land and over the seas have dropped. It is now less expensive to ship a car from Osaka in Japan to Los Angeles in the United States, than to transport it from Los Angeles to mid-America Chicago. Even more dramatic is the drop in the costs of communication[1]. The massive amount of information contained in the INTERNET is available for the low price of a local telephone call. Jet airplanes have reduced the price of long-distance travel to the extent that quite a number of persons now use them to commute to work. It has become quite common to travel up to a thousand miles for a business appointment in the morning; and to return on the same day in the evening. All this has permitted a decentralisation and globalisation of production. American-based companies maintain call-centres in Ireland and even in India. Cars are being assembled in one country from parts that arrive from all over the world. On the other hand, these cars are then also sold on a world-wide market.

In that sense, geographic location has indeed become less relevant. In that sense, the advertisements of cell phone companies are not mendacious, that show some tanned business person doing his or her office work at the poolside of some hotel on a tropical island. But such freedom and luxury is accessible to only a very small segment of the working population. The enticing picture of establishing an office in a tropical island might hide an altogether different truth. For, if we reflect more closely on the issue, we even might come to suspect that geography has not become less relevant today. Probably, it even has become more important.

Two hundred years ago, the life of someone born in the United States and of someone born in India did not differ too much. Both of them could expect to reach roughly the same age. Both used writing to communicate with persons they could not contact personally. Animals were used in both countries to draw carts and carriages and to ride on. Both had only limited means to fight against the rig-

1 When I started work in the Austrian diplomatic service in the sixties, prior authorisation was still required for any overseas telephone call so as to curtail and control the telephone fees. To colleagues now entering the service this must seem a stone – age practice. Much of their working time is spent on the phone; and many of their calls are overseas. Of course, since long ago, no prior authorisation is required for such calls.

ors of the climate, or to cure ailments and to numb the pains of decaying teeth or ageing bones. At that time, two hundred years ago, geography did not make that much of a difference. If someone happened to be born in India, his or her personal life experience did not differ that much from the life experience of someone born in the United States.

Today, the poorest country – Ethiopia, has a per capita GDP of 100 US dollars; the wealthiest – Luxembourg, has a per capita GDP of 40.000 US dollars. The luck of a favourable geographic location thus makes the population of Luxembourg 400 times as wealthy as the poor Ethiopian population. That yawning gap in wealth translates into a host of other stark differences: life expectancy, health, education, access to information, personal comfort, goals in life; etc. In that sense, geography still matters and in that sense it even matters more than it ever did before[2].

We already touched upon that issue when dealing with the poor countries of the world. In doing so, we have already pointed to one cause of this blatant inequality, and to one important reason why some countries move ahead while others remain mired ever deeper in poverty and hopelessness. Both economic growth, and economic stagnation are cumulative processes. Economic growth creates and strengthens conditions for further growth; just as economic stagnation reinforces the causes of backwardness[3]. Such virtuous and vicious spirals wedge apart the group of the successful countries from the group of failing countries.

Wealthy people can acquire skills, create institutions, accept values, behaviour and incentives that promote further growth. Poor people, having to fight for sheer subsistence, accent incentives and mores that are detrimental to economic growth. It is deeply ingrained in humans to adjust to persons and circumstances surrounding them. Poor are surrounded by poor. This breeds a culture of poverty and this culture is best adapted to the prospect of hopelessness as it helps to survive in hopelessness. Economic growth and success create a culture of hope conducive to saving and investing, conducive to risk taking, and to economic growth. Poor people reinforce in one another those traits, norms and behaviour that will continue to hamper lasting economic development. The reverse is true for the successful and wealthy.

---

2 And due to the ease in the spread of information, those vast differences have certainly become more visible than they were a few decades ago. To those poor Ethiopian subsistence farmers who have access to television, the standard, US-based, globally-distributed television series presents the image of a level of consumption and ostentatious well-being that his grandchildren will fail to attain even under the most favourable circumstances.

3 It is similar with democracy: the practice of democracy strengthens democracy further; the absence of democracy makes it even harder for democracy to flourish.

This is clearly shown by the economic impact exerted by groups of migrants. Those that came from wealthy countries into more backward and poorer ones, frequently brought with them not just tools and skills; but – more importantly – such values, attitudes, expectations and institutions that favoured economic success. They thus created islands of greater wealth and economic dynamics; and – again frequently and over time – their success prompted imitation by the indigenous population. Frequently too, groups from poorer countries migrated to wealthier countries. There they acquired new skills, attitudes and values. With those in their back-pack, the groups returned to their original home countries. This again had a positive impact upon the rest of the population. Migration thus was an instrument for prying open the self-perpetuating circle of poverty. But, doing so, it did underline the permanence of this cycle where it was not broken open by migrants. As Easterly (2002) maintains, poor are poor because they live next to poor people. And successful people are successful because they live next to successful people.

Both poverty and wealth thus tend to "cluster". The later frequently in very narrow parts of the globe. Those are the economic powerhouses that provide the energy for the global economic machine. More often than not (and save, perhaps, in small nations like Switzerland or Luxembourg) , the limits that geographically circumscribe those clusters of higher economic energy are not identical to national frontiers. Just a very few and rather small regions, for instance, endow the United States with those assets that underpin its global economic presence: a 50 mile wide strip along the Pacific coast, some locations on the upper Mississippi and in other parts of the Midwest, and the counties along the Boston-Washington corridor in the East.

Those regional clusters that hold such assets will wish to manage and control them. That applies to internal control as well as to control of their outside relations. It is for this reason that even in some of the formerly centralised states – like Italy, Spain or France – political power has become more decentralised. Part of the power of the state has shifted downward to such regions. For the same reason, such regions have also entered as actors on the global scene.

Obviously, there is a tendency opposed to the centrifugal equalising and centralising force of globalisation. This opposing centripetal is the force of "localisation". It is fed not just by economic forces and motives. It also responds to human preferences and to the need for effective governance.

Co-operation among states is based on the expectation that benefits will ensue from co-operating with other states and from moving closer to them. One expects that some tasks will be tackled more easily in such a co-operation, while a single state alone would have difficulties in addressing them effectively. Frequently, such hopes will materialise. Yet, the opposite might also be true, on occasions.

Sometimes benefits might ensue from moving away from others and by disengaging from them. This suggestion runs counter, of course, to the whole notion of globalisation. It runs counter to the – basically sound and well founded – conviction that globalisation will demand enhanced co-operation. Globalisation, therefore, should not facilitate a withdrawal into the cosiness of the smaller political unit.

Globalisation has made some seemingly local problems and conflicts have world-wide, negative repercussions. But these negative effects vary. On occasion, they might not be that serious or immediately obvious. Also, some such local conflicts and problems might be difficult to solve by outsiders. Outsiders intervening thus might have to do so at great costs and with little hope for success. In such cases, prudence would counsel outsiders to remain aloof and stay away as far as possible; so as to avoid – so to say – contagion from a dangerous disease.

One example to prove the case is the horrendous genocide of the Tutsi population at the hands of the Hutu population of Rwanda. At least several hundred thousand persons were killed. The world followed with moral anguish and abhorrence. But these emotions were not sufficiently strong and persuasive to prompt those nations that had the means, to actually intervene. United Nations soldiers on the spot were not reinforced in numbers. Instead, those that had been there were withdrawn. The effect in those countries that remained distant and aloof was some bad conscience (at best). But these distant countries were not affected otherwise.

Various motives are behind this abstinence. The rewards for an intervention in Rwanda would have been few. There might have been some recognition for having done the proper thing; for having saved human lives, for having sustained the hope for general human improvement or for a better new world. But such rewards are short lived. As my former boss, the Austrian Chancellor Kreisky once remarked, "gratitude is not a currency with enduring value in politics".

On the other hand, the costs of intervention are rather high. Sending soldiers to a battle field and doing so knowing that some of them will be killed – that is not an easy decision for any elected official to take. It is even harder to take when these soldiers are not professionals, but come from a draft army (as many in Europe still do). Then there are the purely material costs. Military interventions are expensive. Maintaining the military peace-keepers in Bosnia Herzegovina costs – roughly – five times as much as all civilian aid that has been rendered to that country in the post-war era.

The most potent cause for the lack of an effective reaction to the Rwanda killings is, however, the conviction of not really being touched by it in any serious way. Interdependence is not universal and all-encompassing. If such a tragedy should have any repercussions in faraway and wealthy countries, such repercussions would not be felt immediately or in the near future; and they might have to travel over complex, twisted pathways. In the absence of an electorate roused by gory CNN pictures of the slaughter of Tutsis, the ruling politicians in wealthy countries thus could shrug of the bad news as being of no immediate relevance to their state and to their chances on winning the next elections.

But, whatever the causes, it is a fact that the last decades have indeed been a time not only of growing international engagement. They also have been a period of much disengagement and withdrawal:

- The US has very much lowered its engagement in Latin America.
- Europe has withdrawn – to a large extent – from Africa.
- Russia has withdrawn from Central Europe.
- In the Middle East, the engagement of Russians, Europeans, and Americans has become less intense.

Whenever a void opens today in any of the more troublesome and crises-prone regions, it does not suck in distant foreign states and powers like a vacuum sucks in air. On the contrary – with such faraway powers, the first, spontaneous reaction usually is one of marking distance.

If foreign powers come in after all and in the end, it is not because they are driven by the enticements of power, wealth or glory. They come from some vague sense of duty. Or they may become involved because they are not that certain that some distant conflict might not, after all, have negative repercussions on themselves. Or an intervention might be prompted by very long-term concerns over "world order politics" – the conviction that in the very long run, a free and prosperous world would not be compatible with large-scale, bloody violence.

Countervailing forces, therefore, are at work in today's world:

engagement – withdrawal
co-operation – isolation
globalisation – localisation

This is the place for a more general observation. Globalisation implies greater interconnectedness around the world. That much is obvious. But that does not imply that interconnectedness is all encompassing and universal. Issues, persons, groups, and states might be bypassed. The broader connections to the rest of humanity brought about by globalisation might even permit and encourage a certain amount of withdrawal that would not have been feasible in earlier times. This is as true for the personal realm as it is for national and international politics.

To be entertained, one does not have to go to the movie-theatre or to the stadium. One can watch the TV screen at home. Instead of commuting to the office, one can work at the computer in the living room. Instead of being surrounded by a large family, more and more persons live in single households. There now is a chance that the thinning out of remote peripheral parts of a country might stop. But till now this has not been the case with persons migrating into the populous the agglomerations. Or – to argue on another level: shouldn't we reflect on the fact that some of the wealthiest countries[4] in Europe – Switzerland and Norway – are also those most sceptical about membership in the European Union? Might their wealth permit these countries to stay aloof and to disengage from a joint, historic European enterprise?

As mentioned, globalisation thus has a counterpart in "localisation". We might loosely define it as the closer attachment to some (often geographic) specificity. This trend has shifted power to the smaller political unit.

Technological developments stand behind both globalisation and localisation. In the past, two potent constraints mainly had strengthened centralising tendencies and had put a premium on the largest possible size. First, there was the ever present danger of war. To gain victory, to fight off invaders, or to conquer an opponent, a state had to be mighty. The more unified, the more homogenous and bigger that state, the better. Today, the threat of war between states is receding. Wealthy countries no longer consider war a viable option in their mutual relations. This lessens the need for them being big, for their inner coherence and for their homogeneity. If a state does not have to fear that a mighty neighbour would attack and conquer its own territory, the size of this state becomes irrelevant for the preservation of its external security. Even small states with small armies may feel secure.[5]

A vast territory has also ceased to be prerequisite for wealth and economic success. This too is something new. Markets used to be national. The bigger these national markets, the greater the economies of scale, the cheaper and more competitive the production. Today, commercial exchange is based on the principle of free trade. Quantitative restrictions on foreign trade have largely disappeared. Tariffs are very low[6]. Whatever is needed for local production may be imported without great difficulties. Equally-whatever is being produced locally can be exported freely, provided that such products are demanded in other countries.

4 Except Luxembourg, which is a EU member.
5 Or they could, like Costa Rica, do away with their army.
6 That holds true, at least, for most industrial products.

In the time sinceWorld War II, the number of states has increased vastly from about 70 to about 200. Most of these new states are small. That development must be seen against the background of changes in the global system. Smaller states are no longer at a serious disadvantage in comparison with bigger states. Today, smaller states might even have an advantage over larger ones. One of the advantages is that they are easier to govern; and that they are easier to govern democratically, efficiently and honestly.

The table below ranks various OECD countries according to the quality of their "governance" (with the best possible grade being a +2,50; and the worst possible grade a –2,50.) Keeping other things equal, it seems that smaller countries generally do better than bigger ones in providing good "governance".

Quality of governance – a composite index

	Account-ability	Political stability	Effective-ness of imp-temcutation	Quality of regulations	Rule of law	Corruption
Austria	**1,34**	**1,27**	**1,51**	**1,19**	**1,86**	**1,56**
Belqium	1,24	0,87	1,29	0,58	1,34	1,05
Canada	1,33	1,24	1,71	1,07	1,70	2,05
Denmark	1,60	1,34	1,62	1,09	1,71	2,09
Finland	1,69	1,61	1,67	1,42	1,83	2,09
France	1,11	1,04	1,24	0,59	1,22	1,15
Germany	1,42	1,21	1,67	1,08	1,57	1,38
Greece	1,12	0,79	0,65	0,71	0,62	0,73
Ireland	1,57	1,24	1,79	1,33	1,54	1,16
Italy	1,10	0,82	0,68	0,59	0,72	0,63
Japan	1,03	1,20	0,93	0,64	1,59	1,20
South Korea	0,98	0,50	0,44	0,30	0,55	0,37
Luxemburg	1,41	1,48	1,86	1,49	1,86	1,78
Mexico	0,12	0,06	0,28	0,58	-0,41	-0,28
Notherlands	1,61	1,48	1,84	1,50	1,67	2,09
Norwan	1,58	1,32	1,35	0,73	1,70	1,76
Portugal	1,42	1,41	0,91	0,81	0,94	1,21
Spain	1,15	1,01	1,57	1,08	1,12	1,45
Sweden	1,65	1,38	1,51	1,08	1,70	2,21
Switzerland	1,73	1,61	1,93	1,21	1,91	1,91
Turkan	-0,55	-0,75	-0,15	0,04	-0,16	-0,48
United Kingdom	1,46	1,10	1,77	1,32	1,61	1,86
U.S.A.	1,24	1,18	1,58	1,19	1,58	1,45

Source: World Bank, Jan 2002

The tendency towards smallness might, however, be carried one step further and lead to a level below the level of central state authority. It might lead to sub-regions of a state. Frequently, such regions tend to have a political identity of their own. This becomes evident from looking at a map of Europe on which the national borders have been eliminated, but on which the borders of the regional administrative sub units of states have been preserved. We may colour these sub-regions according to their level of wealth; shading the wealthier sub-regions with a darker colour; and the poorer ones with a brighter colour. It become obvious in this rendering that the national borders do not coincide with the lightly or darkly coloured patches that exend over several of such sub-regions. Fictive "nations of greater or lesser wealth" cut across national borders. They tend to ignore these borders. A broad swatch of wealthy regions extends, for example, from Southern England, via the Southern Netherlands, the Rhine valley, Western Bavaria and Western Austria down to Northern Italy. These regions from, so to say, the economic spine of Europe. They are part of a coherent "nation of wealth". Other sub-regions of the same state, as for example Eastern Germany or Southern Italy, are not included in this fictive nation of the wealthy. They belong to the fictive nation of the poorer sub-regions.

The regional sub-units of states differ, of course, by their legal/ constitutional status. But there is a clear tendency to grant them more political/administrative autonomy. States that once had been very centralised (like Spain, Italy, the UK, and France) have moved very close to becoming federal states, with their newly established regions having gained quite some power to run their own affairs.

But whatever the legal/constitutional dress they might wear, these sub-state regions are certainly distinct entities in the socio-economic sense. And they compete against each other economically[7]. They do so very visibly in the quest to attract outside, direct investment. There is a certain danger that such competition could reinforce cumulative tendencies, with the successful regions becoming even more successful; and the less attractive regions even less attractive.

It is difficult to judge whether such fears will prove well founded. If they do, it would signal a break in a trend. For, up until now, such polarising forces had been more than compensated for by the stronger forces of economic integration and globalisation, which tended to level out the differences within states. Over the last half a century, wealth has thus become more evenly distributed among the 50 US states. As we have observed, a similar development has also taken place in EU-Europe.

7 Nearly all of them have special offices for that purpose. These offices become active on a global level. They seek to address investors wherever these might reside: from Taiwan to Switzerland.

In the above arguments, we have defined regions by their economic characteristics. But things other than level of wealth can also define a region; different ethnicities, for instance[8].

There is an obvious tendency for multi-ethnic states to break up, with the inevitable consequence of ethnic cleansing and/or the vast exchange of populations. Greeks were driven from Turkey; and Turks from Greece, Muslims from India and Hindus from Pakistan. Jews were expelled by many countries and four to six million of them were simply killed. Ethnic Germans were expelled from Central and Eastern Europe; French from Algeria, Indians from Uganda; and so on.

The increase in the number of states we have remarked upon is also a consequence of this tendency to form ethnically "pure" states, and some claim that the right to do so is guaranteed to ethnic groups by the principle of "self-determination" (enshrined in some UN texts). But can such a principle be fully implemented? Should we wish it to be implemented? There are 6.000 languages spoken on earth. Should there be 6.000 states?

Granting some form of autonomy to various ethnic groups seems to be a necessary and inevitable step in eliminating actual or potential ethnic tensions. But, more often than not, such ethnic groups do not live on one coherent territory. More often than not, they live interspersed with other ethnic groups. It therefore might become very difficult to grant autonomy on a territorial basis; and to define the reach of autonomy in territorial terms. The better alternative would be to base autonomy on a "cultural basis", that is, to grant it to a group of persons wherever the members of this group might live.[9]

Whether based on an ethnic identity, or based on economic/social specifics, sub-state regions have clearly become actors on the international scene. Many have acquired the appropriate attributes with some still smallish kind of "foreign offices" attached to the main administrative unit; and with their direct dealings also with full blown states and with international organisations.[10]

One specific form of such "international" activity is co-operation with similar regions that are on the other side of a national frontier. This sort of co-operation tends to make national borders more permeable and compensates for the economically stifling effect of such borders ("dead border"). A much quoted exam-

---

8 It is exactly because of the existence of such ethnic differences that some of the European states (like France or Spain) became very centralised so as to thwart the danger of a violent disintegration of the polity.

9 Such solutions to the dilemma could be patterned after the early 20th century settlement between the German speaking and Czech speaking groups in Moravia = "Mährischer Ausgleich"

10 Most major European sub-state regions have offices in Brussels to deal directly with the European Commission.

ple for such a successful trans-frontier co-operation is the "Euregio" which ties together Swiss, French and German communities in the area around and north of Basel.

With the dramatic lowering of costs of transportation; and the near disappearance of costs of communication, the costs of covering distance have become very small indeed. Production has become dispersed all over the world. The same information is accessible with the same ease (nearly) all over the world. Like minded persons from wide apart nations stay in permanent contact with one another and thus form global communities with their specific community spirit and identity.

All that – it is said – has made distance and geography irrelevant. "Geography has disappeared". In a certain sense it has. But, in many ways it has not disappeared and has become fraught with even heavier consequences. It is the different location in geography that determines that one child that is born into the state of Sierra Leone, with a per capita income of 200 US dollars; and another child that is born into Switzerland, with a per capita income of 30.000 US dollars. Countless obstacles then prevent the grown up child to move from Sierra Leone to Switzerland. Even after it would have managed to make such a move, other obstacles would still make it difficult for her or him to integrate into Swiss society. Seen from that perspective, geography has never been more important than it is today; because the socio-economic differences between different geographic locations on the globe also have never been as wide as they are today.

Where one lives and where one works makes a difference, even if the choice is not between two countries, but within two locations in the same country; or even within the same city. Being born in Manhattan north of 96th street makes for a difficult life and high chances of remaining poor and in a low status. For those born, growing up or doing business in the Manhattan area below 96th street, life chances are much better.

In the past, differences between poor and rich regions have tended to even out – at least in the wealthier countries and at a later stage of economic development. But the new ease in travel and communication might have brought a reversal of the trend. At least in some instances, it has accentuated the advantages and disadvantages of geographic locations. The poor congregate where the poor live. The rich and successful congregate where the rich and successful live. Thus, a tendency to geographic polarisation. Inevitably, this translates into politics; with the rich location devising strategies to remain rich and keep the poor out; and the poor locations devising strategies for tearing down the walls around the bastions of wealth. This is true as much for internal politics[11] as it is for international politics.

11 See the new political North-South divide in Italy.

The State – Here to Stay

The English 17th century political philosopher Thomas Hobbes perceived the state as a tool to prevent, with its draconian powers, life from becoming a battle for mere physical survival with everyone fighting everyone. A century and a half later, Wilhelm Friedrich Hegel assigned a more noble mission to the state. He maintained that states are the ultimate achievement in the march of human progress. After that, nothing basically new and better would be brought forth in the mode in which human society was organised. With the creation of states, history would thus have come to its end[1]. And indeed, history seems to have vindicated this claim. To become a state turned into a global aspiration. Since the mid 19th century, the number of states has risen more than fivefold.

Number of states 1850-1990

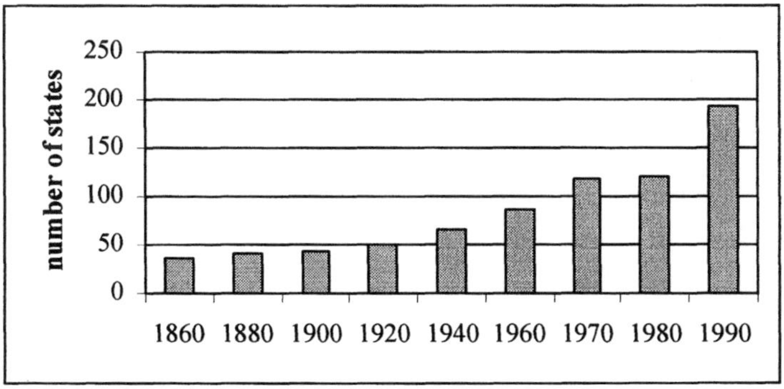

Source: R.Dahl, 1999

As claimed by Hegel the state still is and remains the most prominent, encompassing, and expedient polity. No viable alternatives are in sight. It is difficult to conceive of some populated region of the globe NOT being part of a state.

1 He was to be corrected by F. Fukuyama who put the "end of history" at a later date: namely at the time when Communism ceased to be a viable alternative to democracy.

This corresponds to human wishes. No democracy has opted for an alternate institutional framework for its politics.

This dominant order is being questioned only by a tiny minority of radicals both on the left and on the right. Both Marxists on the left, and economic liberals on the right consider the state not only useless, but even a stultifying and oppressive burden. It should be done away with as speedily as possible. Both Marxists and ultra-liberals, therefore, dream about the "withering away" of the state. They hope that the state might eventually be supplanted by groups that organise spontaneously around common interests – be it the interest of the "proletariat" or the interest of "maximising economic utility" through unfettered markets.

Until now, their incantations have been in vain. But might "globalisation" now bring this world they were dreaming about? Will globalisation effect the "withering away" of the state that had been postulated by extreme conservatives and extreme leftists? Outward appearances do not seem to sustain their radical vision. The old order still seems to hold up well. It even seems to flourish with the number of states still rising.

But, perhaps such outward appearances are misleading and, perhaps, behind this re-assuring facade the old order is being hollowed out? For when looking closer, we do find that states have lost quite some of their prior functions. Some of their traditional tasks have now become tasks of entities bigger than and above the state. They now are incumbent upon international financial markets; upon big transnational firms; or upon world-wide international organisations. On the other hand, some traditional tasks of the state have been entrusted to entities that traditionally were "below" the state – to civic organisations, to commercial enterprises, or to geographically more narrow political units like districts, regions or cities.

But how massive was this shift of tasks? Was it massive enough to sustain the claim that the state is dissolving into irrelevance and becoming a mere shell, devoid of political or social substance?[2]

In tackling this question we have, however, first to become clear about what we imply when speaking about "the state". What is the true nature of this "state" we are supposed to see wither away?

---

2 As a rule, one is well-advised to retain some scepticism towards claims of unprecedented and total changes in the way humans tend to arrange their affairs. "Natura non fecit salta"; and neither should we expect such sudden jumps in the complex and "path-determined" social arrangements that constitute the political world system.

A state is not a state, is not a state

The nature of the institution "state" has changed over time.

Less than a handful of states – like China or Ethiopia – have a long and continuous history. But even in these rare cases of historic continuity, the state that existed one or two thousand years ago is not the same as the present state, with its present tasks and functions. States have been reborn and redefined continuously.

Historically, they have started out as loose confederations of tribes. Later on, they transformed into either a kind of personal property of one ruler who combined religious and secular functions, or they became feudal states with the sovereign sitting on top of a rather fragile pyramid of mutual loyalties and obligations.

States in the modern sense only came into existence with the demise of feudalism and with its being supplanted by governance through professional bureaucrats. In Europe, that innovation coincided with the end of the Middle Ages and with the ruler assuming unchallenged authority by becoming the "sovereign". This new world order is termed the "Westphalian order" (after the Westphalian peace arrangement that terminated the 30 Years War and which, in the midst of the seventeenth century, eliminated the last vestiges of the fuzzy medieval political order). The basic conceptual and legal structure of this "Westphalian" system has remained unchanged up until now. We still retain the notions of "sovereignty" and accept that states are administered by vast bureaucracies. But, if the legal and conceptual frame for this order has not changed, the core tasks of states have.

The original and prime task of a state was war – the prevention or the waging of war. States were organised in a way so as to maximise this war-waging or war-deterring[3] capacity. Other tasks were added later on:

- the production of sufficient food (physiocrats)
- the development of trade and of early manufacturing (mercantilism)
- support for the more rapid growth of industry (developmental state)
- providing the institutional base for a mature market economy (regulatory state)
- the taming of brute capitalism and the provision of social services ("welfare state")[4]

---

3 Not that there was that much difference between these two organising principles according to the traditional view of security and on how it was preserved.

- making a country more competitive in the globalised economy ("competition state")

As we see, even the core functions of the state have become more numerous and varied. At present, the functions of the state would be best compared to those of a conductor of an orchestra. Like a conductor, the state has been assigned the task of bringing together and harmonising many different actors.

So – if we speculate about the demise of the state; its withering away; and its dissolving in the web of globalisation, we have to question which kind of state we purport to see disappearing: The welfare state? The war state? The regulatory state? And we also have to ask whether other and new functions might come to replace those tasks and functions the state is losing at present.

The office at the United Nations Secretariat that registers international treaties will greet with incredulity the rumour about the demise of the state. This office has seen nothing of it. On the contrary, if measured by the number of treaties they conclude amongst themselves, states have never been more active and vivacious on a global scale. The UN has registered a stock of 55.000 such treaties.

4 The German term "Sozialstaat" is usually translated into "welfare state". But these two terms have widely differing meanings; which is one of the reasons that makes for difficulties in the transatlantic dialogue.

Number of trans-frontier treaties

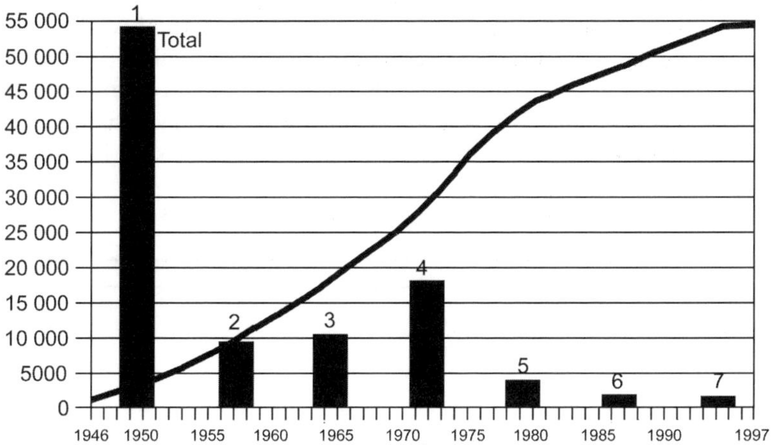

1=total; 2=administrative, diplomacy; 3=development co-operation; 4=economy, telecommunication, transport; 5=culture; 6 =environment, agriculture; 7=labour, health, social development

Source: World Treaty Index; University of Washington

International treaties are just one aspect of, and indicator for, a strong presence of states in the global realm. These treaties demonstrate that states participate in global rule-making and in the enforcement of such rules. One other indicator for the prominent function of states in global governance is the increase in numbers and tasks of "official inter-governmental organisations" (mentioned in Chapter 30) and the fact that most of the "line" ministries of national governments feel obliged to add special administrative sections that deal with international affairs. This reflects the fact that, even at a lower level of administration, the "international" now has a prominent presence (e.g. in the police, in the labour market administration, in regional planning, etc.). It shows, on the other hand, that even lower level state bureaucracies now impact quite substantially on developments beyond the borders of their own state.

States would "wither" away, if they had fewer and fewer resources at their command and, in the end, would command hardly any resources at all. But this is not what we observe. In the wealthy countries, the state has command[5] over

5 If that is the proper term.

roughly 40% of all that is produced. As the table below demonstrates, this share of the state has not been declining but rising.

Generally, the wealthier a country, the higher the share of wealth that is administered by the state. There are exceptions, of course. Both Japan and the US[6] are very rich, yet the share of the state is lower than should be expected in view of the high per capita income. Overall and on the average, though, there is a clear correlation between higher wealth and a greater share of the state in this wealth.

Tax income as share of the GDP of wealthy countries 1965-1998

Country	*1965*	*1980*	*1998*
Sweden	35.0	48.8	53.0
Denmark	29.9	45.5	49.3
Finland	30.3	36.9	46.9
France	34.5	41.7	45.2
Italy	25.5	30.4	43.5
Austria	33.9	40.3	44.3
Netherlands	32.8	45.2	41.1
Poland	.	.	40.0
Hungary	.	.	39.0
Czech Republic	.	.	38.3
Germany	31.6	38.2	37.1
UK	30.4	35.1	37.6
Portugal	15.8	24.7	34.9
Switzerland	19.6	28.9	34.8
Spain	14.7	23.9	34.2
Australia	22.3	27.4	29.6
USA	25.0	27.6	20.8
Japan	18.3	25.4	28.8
Korea, Republic South	.	17.5	21.1
EU (15)	27.8	36.9	41.0
OECD-Europe	26.4	35.4	39.7
OECD total	25.8	32.8	36.6

Source:OECD

6 Note another exceptionality of the US. Not only is the share of tax income low in comparison to other countries; but instead of growing, this share has even shrunk substantially between 1980 and 1998. This is because many of the services (like transportation and higher education) that are being provided by the state in Europe, are being provided by private firms in the US. Also, transfers (via health and pension system, e.g.) are low in the US.

Tax revenue as percentage of GDP and (PPP) per capita GDP

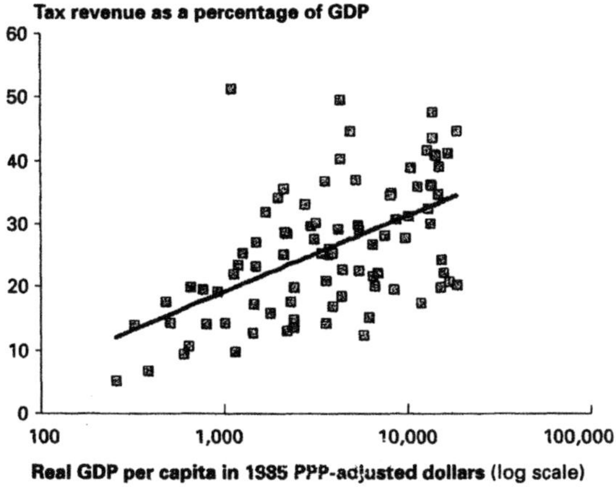

Source: IMF

Contrary to widely held prejudices, the growth of the public sector has not been detrimental to economic performance[7]. Both the OECD and the IMF have studied the issue repeatedly. Some of these studies find no correlation between the level of the tax burden and economic performance.[8] Some other studies conclude that, on the contrary, such a correlation between weaker economic growth and rising taxes does exist. But even these studies show this negative impact of higher taxation to be minimal. If rising taxes do impair economic performance, this performance is raised, on the other hand, by some essential state services that can be financed with higher tax income. State investment in education, research, infrastructure, and internal security clearly has a positive, growth-enhancing effect. Even social spending does. According to a study of the IMD business school in Lausanne, Switzerland, the "competitiveness" of a nation is higher, the higher the share of public social expenditures in its GDP.

7 This conclusion is based upon the comparison of countries on a similar stage of economic development.

8 Neither is there a strong correlation between the rate of economic growth and the rate at which the tax burden was increasing.

World competitiveness and public social expenditures

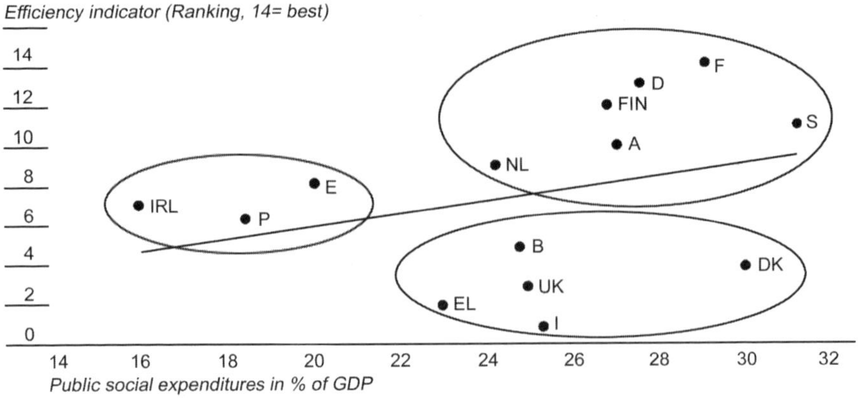

Source: IMD The World Competitiveness, 2002, Consanne

This is not to imply that there are no economic limits to the relative size of the public sector. Certainly, it cannot grow to take a hundred percent of all that is produced.[9] Generally, and on the average, it should not reach more than 50 percent of GDP. One could guess that over and above that threshold, an added tax load might come to seriously distort and impede the working of the economy. But, if such a threshold exists, it is one that is specific to specific countries. The economy of Scandinavian countries, for instance, can more readily support a large public sector without the ill effect such a large public sector would have in other European countries. Due to "clientilism", the public sector is rather inefficient, for example, in Italy and Greece. It therefore does not add to, but lowers the dynamics of the economy. In these countries, the public sector is inefficient.

One may measure this efficiency. Social transfers, for example, can be assessed according to how much they contribute to economic efficiency ("economic efficiency of social spending"). The European Commission has done so in the table reproduced below. It shows that some European countries have a high but "inefficient" social spending[10], while others, with the same level of social expenditures, spend this money with greater beneficial effect on the economy.

9 As has been demonstrated by the failure of the Communist system.
10 E.g. for pension transfers.

Efficiency of public social expenditures

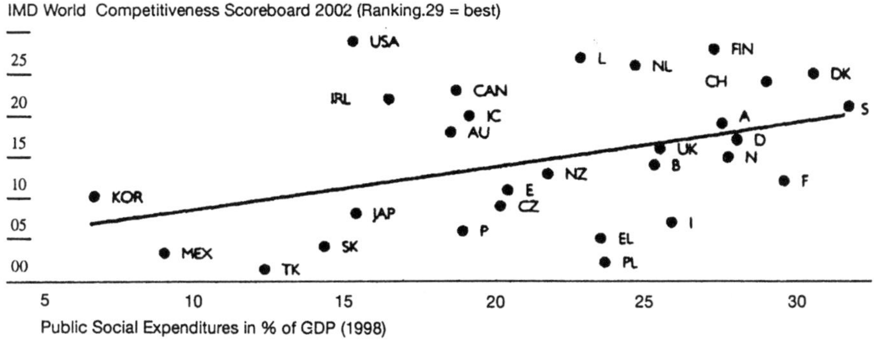

Source: EU 2002

Politicians sometimes garner votes by presenting the state as a rapacious reptile beyond public control, with the inherent drive to devour a maximum of wealth and to amass a maximum of power over its subjects. It would tend to expand its services beyond what citizens actually need and desire.[11] Some elements of truth might be hidden in this accusation. As all bureaucracies, public administrations wish to expand; as all bureaucracies, public administrations seek opportunities for doing so; and as all bureaucracies, state bureaucracies also try to evade external control and to work for their own selfish needs and not in the service of tax payers and citizens.

Nonetheless, at its core, the expansion of public service does conform to the wishes and interests of the public. The wealthy countries listed in the above tables are, after all, democracies. If citizens wished to cut back the state and reduce its tasks and services, they could do so by electing politicians that see this as their task. But that has not happened on any grand scale. It is hardly conceivable, therefore, that the public opposes the expansion of public services. In fact, most citizens expect and wish the state to provide a wide range of services; and citizens cast their vote accordingly. Electorates react furiously when essential but expensive state services like old age pension or health support are cut. Politicians in the US are warned "not to touch Social Security" or Medicare. In the UK, the Labour government came under pressure for not investing more in its – nationalised – health service.

11 As, for example, the British prime minister M. Thatcher and the US president R. Reagan. According to them, "the state is the problem and not the solution". They preached the gospel of the state being a dead load; a nuisance at best and an evil at worst.

A German turn of the century economist – Adolph Wagner – had already observed this connection between rising wealth and the rising share of the state in this wealth. This correlation has thus been termed "Wagner-law". As we have seen, when wealth increases, there is an ever stronger inclination or need to consume not via private purchases, but to consume via public services, that are being paid for by taxes.

Factors behind the Wagner-law on the rising share of the public sector

1) externalisation of costs from the private to the public sector. One notorious example is road transport, where the trucking firms make the profits and the rising costs of building and maintaining roads are being shifted to the state.

2) transfer to the public sector of tasks earlier borne by households, as, for example, the care for the elderly, which is no longer done by families but in old age homes.

3) the so-called "cost disease" in the public sector: by their very nature, most of the services usually incumbent upon the state (education, hospital care, defence, law enforcement) need much human labour. They therefore cannot be rationalised the same way one may rationalise industrial production. These services thus become more expensive in relation to the goods produced by industry (see chapter 21).

4) with rising levels of wealth, citizens desire more of the goods only the state can provide (urban amenities, national parks; thorough environmental protection).

5) changing age structure. An ageing population needs more of those services that are mostly provided by public authorities.

Notwithstanding this tendency to increase the volume of services rendered by the state, citizens are not that eager to pay for them via increased taxes. This is a plausible reaction inasmuch as nobody likes to part with money. But it is difficult to understand why someone is eager to part with his money for the purchase of – let us say – a dress or a fancy car; while he is less eager to part with his money, if this money is siphoned off via taxes to fund more essential things – like public education and infrastructure.

As it seems, resistance against paying taxes is even growing. Several facts may explain this phenomenon:

a) As the tax load is being shifted from the fewer wealthy to the more numerous middle class, it becomes even harder to maintain the fiction that public services are something "others" (e.g. the super-wealthy) pay for.

b) The public sector frequently is seen – and frequently is, in effect – not very cost-efficient in delivering services. In the private sector productivity has been honed by constant competition. This has not been so in the public sector.

c) The ideological drumming of conservative ideologues has left its mark. The population has thus become persuaded that a large public sector and high taxes are detrimental to economic performance (though such claims cannot be verified, as we have seen).

d) There is a glaring imbalance in the publicity for public goods and in the publicity for private goods. The publicity that promotes the consumption of private goods has become a monstrous, ceaseless, tasteless, dumbing presence that we have come to accept, fatalistically, in the same way our elders accepted famine and the pest. It had its impact, nonetheless. It has succeeded in conditioning us to the notions that beauty, longer life, more exciting sexuality, honour and esteem can only be gained by purchasing something from the private sector. The public sector does not and cannot compete with this incessant propaganda for private consumption. Goods and services produced by the state, thus, are assigned a lesser value.

Two tasks on the agenda of governments are especially costly; and will become costlier still: these are the costs of

- the pension systems
- and the health systems.

In both realms, governments have tried to contain costs. In both realms such efforts have had but a limited effect.[12] As we have pointed out in the chapter on the ageing of societies, life expectancy has grown, and it is likely to continue to grow. This implies that fewer persons of working age will have to support more numerous retirees. In the OECD countries the situation will be at its worst around the year 2030, when – in OECD average – 100 persons in the 15 to 64 year age group will correspond to 66 non-working persons; most of them in the age group of "65 and more".[13]

12 There is a distinct danger that rising expenditures for health and pensions will eat into expenditures for even essential public functions.

13 If one would keep all other things constant in the Austrian pension system (level of benefits = replacement rate; rate of subsidy from the budget in terms of the percentage of the state budget; contributions from employees and employers) one would have to raise the effective retirement age (now at 58) by ten years to keep the system solvent.

Older persons consume more health services. Wealthy people consume more health services. Medical technology is becoming more expensive; and medical services (like those provided by nurses) are also becoming more costly as there is little scope for rationalising the personal care for the infirm and ill. The wealthier a country, the higher, thus, in general, the percentage in private and public expenditures devoted to health care. The US already spends a full 14% of their national product on health services. But, while there is a clear tendency of these expenditures being indeed higher the wealthier a country, the costs of these health services still differ more than wealth itself.

The mode of financing health services also differs. In some countries – like the US – the greater part of these expenditures is financed not from the public sector; but is being financed privately. Nonetheless, even in the US, 45 percent of the costs of health care are being paid for by public money.[14]

With all possible savings in the health and pension system realised, pension and health expenditures of states will rise, nonetheless. The same holds true for other essential – if less costly – services like the courts and the police. But the needed parallel rise in taxation meets growing resistance. On one hand, the pressure on states to increase their services will continue. But, at the same time, it will become more difficult to finance this expansion of tasks by raising taxation. At a certain point – different in different countries – voters will veto such a rise. These limits to the share of taxes in GDP are therefore less of an economic nature. They are mainly defined by politics. The level of taxation is contingent upon the demand of voters for public services; upon the efficiency of the public sector to provide such services; and upon the willingness (or the lack thereof) to pay for such added services with higher taxes.

14 More money does not automatically translate into greater effect. As mentioned, the US spends 14% of its GDP on health care. The UK spends but 6%. Nonetheless, life expectancy in the UK is higher than in the US (by one year for males, female life expectancy is even in the two countries). In that sense, the fully public health system of the UK is at least as efficient as the – mostly private – US health system. These divergences point to the scope for making national health care systems more cost-efficient.

Health spending as % of GDP,1997

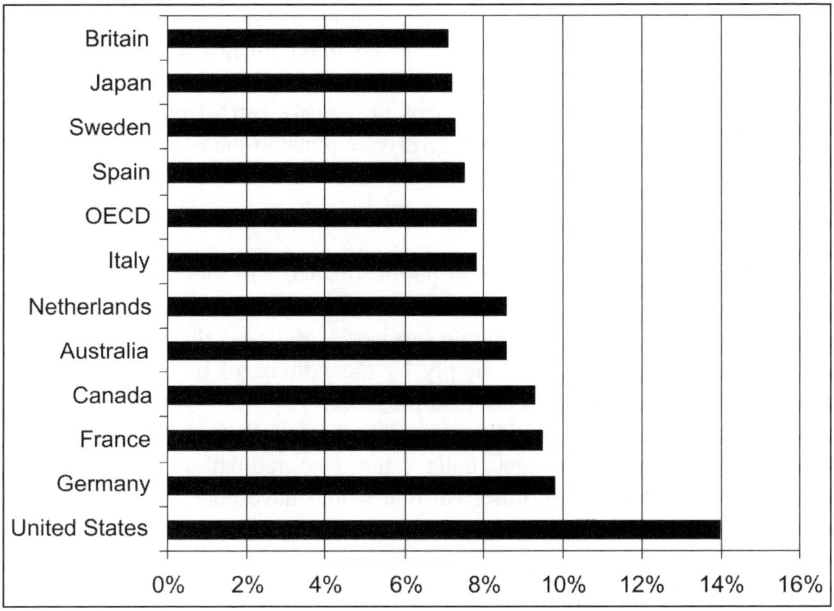

Source: OECD

There is a growing demand for public services. At the same time resistance to higher taxation is growing too.

What ways out of the dilemma?

Privatisation
Public private partnerships
User fees
Rationing of public services
Restructuring of the public sector through internal competition
Cut back in services; targeting of services

It is safe to assume that the public sector and the private sector will increase co-operation. On occasion, the two sectors might even merge (with some problems for both sides). One thing likely to suffer therefrom is the universality of public services.

Also, it is in no way assured that the transfer to the private sector; or the participation of the private sector will always make for greater efficiency and lower costs. "British Rail" offers an example as to how privatisation may make both worse and more expensive services previously carried out in the public sector. Also, the cost of administrating private pension funds or private health insurance are *substantially* higher than the cost of administrating public health and pension schemes.[15]

Some solutions to the dilemma of public finance will inevitably weaken the state. "Public-private partnerships" will, for instance, give quite some say to private investors in the running of public services[16]. Yet even that would not make the state "wither away". Judged simply by the volume of its expenditures, the state will certainly maintain a prominent presence.

Next to the burden of taxation, states also impose the burden of regulation. Some purists among economists[17] believe that such regulations are detrimental, whatever their nature and purpose. No one would have better information than the economic agents themselves. Any intervention by the state would just result in a loss of information. It therefore would bring outcomes worse than the ones we should expect had the state not intervened.

From the point of view of pure economics, this view might be consistent. It is not consistent with actual experience. The theoretical model stipulates for every economic agent perfect knowledge and information; complete rationality[18]; total command over the resources he "owns"; complete flexibility in the use of such resources; etc. Economics also stipulate that the human quest expresses itself exclusively in the search for a maximum of such possessions that can be reproduced and purchased on this or that "market". Obviously, these stipulations have no

15 In every category of costs, the investor-owned US hospitals incur higher costs per patient per day (except operating the facility). The differences in the cost of administration are especially high. Private hospitals thus charge 22% more per patient than comparable public hospitals.

16 Substantiating the adage that profits tend to become privatised, while losses tend to become "nationalised".

17 Economics are – basically a – very elaborate and formalised – normative science. In my view, economics does not deal with the world as it is; but with a world as it should be.

18 In terms defined by economics. In that sense, economic rationality would demand that expected risks always balance expected profits. But millennial experience has taught prudence to the human species. Humans consistently err on the side of prudence and – wisely – prefer lower risks to higher profits.

counterpart in real life. As we have shown in chapter 26, markets have to be created. They come to exist through collective political action. Neither can markets continue to operate without control and regulation by states.[19]

Northern California electricity prices ($ per megawatt-hour, peak hours)

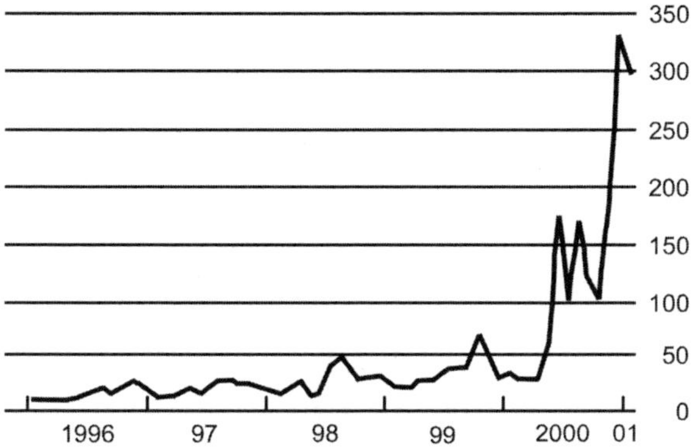

Source: Cambridge Energy Research Associates

State regulation and state intervention in markets might become necessary for many reasons. They are needed to create the necessary transparency and credibility in the accounts of publicly owned companies. Or they are needed so as to prevent "overshooting" of markets with wild and destabilising swings in prices. This danger of "overshooting" is especially acute where demand is inelastic and where the products sold on these markets provide essential, irreplaceable input. Such is the case, for example, with basic food-stuffs; or with electric energy. California[20] paid dearly for ignoring this rule, when, due to inept deregulation, the supply of electric energy became insufficient, with the price of electricity suddenly tripling within just one year.

19 Inept and even fraudulent accounting in major companies listed on the US stock exchanges has, for example, triggered a major crisis of confidence in the financial markets in 2002. Even the former "true believers" in the virtues of unregulated capital markets suddenly came to discover the need for regulation and better and closer supervision.

20 Though one should not ignore that the very inept form of deregulation (and not just simply deregulation as such) contributed to the enormity of the disaster in California.

There are many other examples to falsify the claim that the absence of the state and of state regulation would enhance economic performance; and that states should therefore largely cease regulatory activities. It is claimed, for instance, that state intervention and regulation would make labour markets less "flexible". UNIDO has found no such linkage.

Unemployment, regulation and alleged labour market "flexibility" (Source: UNIDO1999)

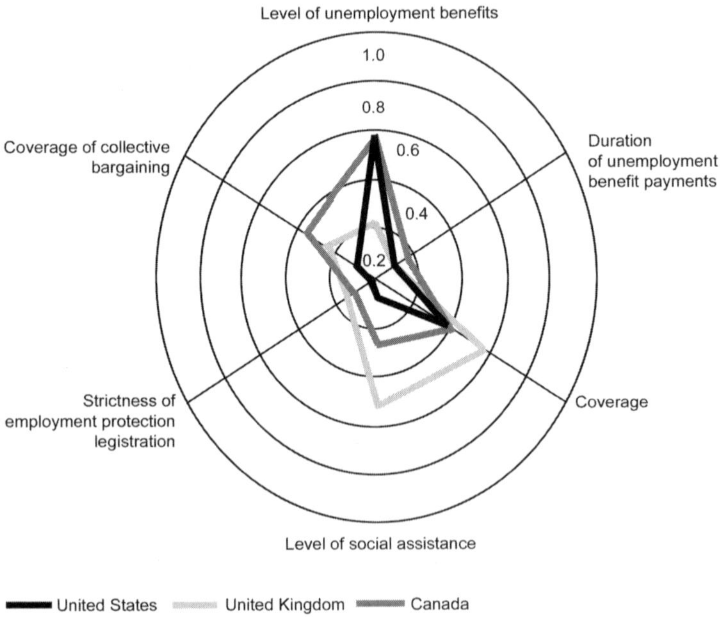

Unemployment protection indicators - selected high-level systems

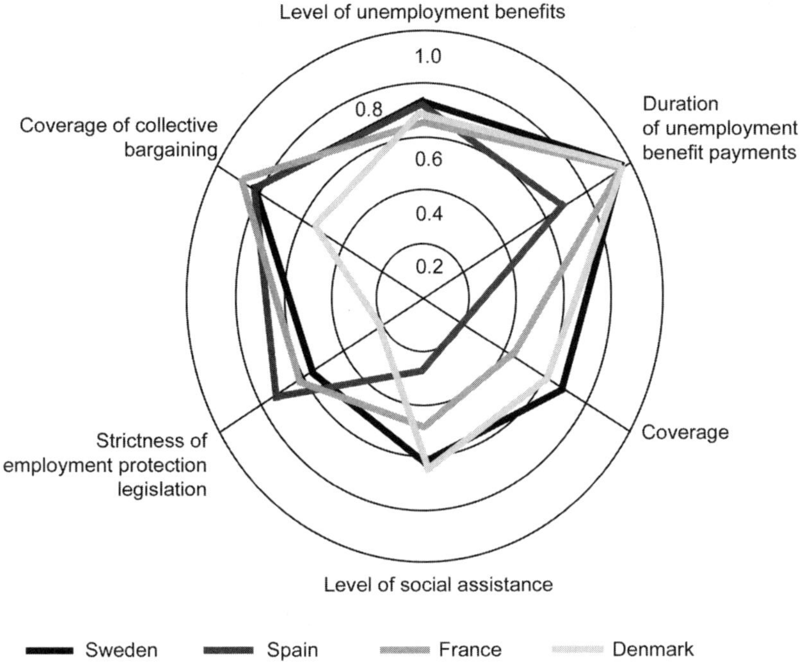

Source: UNIDO

The first graph depicts the regulatory density in countries with allegedly "flexible"[21] labour markets. These are countries like the US, the UK and Canada. The second graph depicts countries with a high regulatory density of their labour markets. Some in this latter group, like Sweden, Spain and France, have done quite well economically, and – if the last 25 years are taken as a gauge – have certainly outperformed the UK.

A state very active in regulating the labour market does not thereby depress productivity of labour. It might even enhance it. The US economist Dan Rodrik argues that a higher level of protection (and thus alleged inflexibility in the labour market) is a price wealthy countries have to pay exactly in order to keep their economies flexible and dynamic. Greater economic dynamics imply greater

21 The adverb "allegedly" is not being used in a polemic way. It should signal that there are many different forms of flexibility, so that the allegedly "inflexible" Japanese labour market, for instance, might, in fact, be very flexible.

risks. Risk averse behaviour, on the other hand, depresses economic growth. As people shy away from added risks more than they value potential benefits, they will be willing to engage in necessarily risky new economic ventures only if and when, by doing so, they do not incur some truly important, existential danger (e.g. of dying of hunger). Unemployment insurance provides such a guarantee and thus encourages people to move into new jobs and ventures even if these are uncertain. In that sense, an unemployment insurance would not diminish, but would enhance labour market flexibility.

Regulation is thus not a dead weight upon the economy. Occasionally, its drawbacks might outweigh its economic advantages. But generally, the density of regulation will grow together with the growing complexity of production and with the growing interdependence through globalisation. It thus will increase together with rising wealth; just as the share of the state will also tend to grow with rising wealth.

Neo-conservatives charge that some public services and state enforced regulations frequently have the perverse effect of heightening the evil they intend to cure. On occasion, that might be so. Transfers to the indigenous might indeed make some of these indigenous less eager to escape their situation. Jailing large parts of the population might indeed enhance criminality instead of reducing it, etc. But such failures to meet the original purpose seem the exception. By and large, public services and public regulations will have the intended consequences. They can, for example, effectively reduce poverty.[22]

Different traditions and cultures become visible in this discussion on the role and function of the state, on its effectiveness and efficiency; and on a need to politically regulate economic and social life. Each side in this discussion tends to pontificate on the superiority of its own tradition and culture. Japanese preach the superiority of the Japanese model of relationship between state, economy and society. The US praise their model and seek to impose it on the world. And the Europeans (with a bit less insistence and with a self confidence less robust) hope for the universal acceptance of their specific way of arranging this tri-lateral relationship. Such grand-standing can be explained with the desire to have others adjust to one's own way of doing things; instead of having to adjust under pain and with stress to the models of other regions or states of the world. Remaining what one is; preserving one's identity is, after all, one of the most basic aims of both individuals and of societies.

22 See table on poverty before and after state transfers in chapter 11 on poverty within states.

But such a missionary drive of Americans, Japanese or Europeans will not accomplish very much. The triangular relationship between economy, state and society will remain distinct in each of the three members of the "Triad". Countless other such distinct patterns will also continue to exist in other parts of the world.

And why shouldn't they? The modern economy (or "capitalism") is a very flexible arrangement. Different versions of it can be effective. All of them can be – roughly – equal in their efficiency. Corporations can be managed either by consensus of all "employees" (the Japanese model); or by all "stakeholders" (the European model); or by the shareholders and their representatives (the US model). On occasion, one economic model might have the advantage over the others. But such advantages are ever shifting, and they are minuscule anyhow.

There is a second reason for all missionary efforts to convert the world to follow but one single socio-political-economic model being in vain. It is difficult to transfer such a model from one region or state to another region or state. Take, for instance, the model of insuring against unemployment. In some cases, the state pays persons that become unemployed the rough equivalent of what they had earned when they still had a job (a high "replacement" rate). In a Scandinavian country, a high replacement rate might indeed – and as argued by Rodrik – make for added flexibility in labour markets. With high replacement rates, Scandinavian workers would have less reason to fear unemployment. Scandinavian employees would, therefore, find it easier to switch jobs or change qualifications. In a Southern European country, however, with a tradition of clientilism and a track record of persistent underemployment, the consequence of a high replacement rate might be the reverse. In such countries, a high replacement rate could decrease labour market flexibility, as jobless workers would be content to draw unemployment insurance without searching for new jobs.

Nor is there any sign of state regulation having become less necessary. Quite on the contrary. The experience with the badly regulated market for electric energy in California; and the experience with the failure of control and regulation in the case of the US energy giant ENRON, have recalled the virtues and necessity of good and close regulation. As regulations are still needed for the economy to function, and as the state still is the foremost producer and enforcer of such regulations, the state will continue to be needed for that end.

But perhaps some other services and functions of the state might become reduced for a simpler reason. The rich, at least, find it easier to do without them.

The rich might be able to escape from under the state, having come to depend less on the services provided by the state; and finding it easier by now to escape from taxation through the state. As we have seen (chapter 12), there is a clear tendency to shift the tax burden to the poorer parts of the population. Capital and the wealthy may migrate to other parts of the globe if not treated gently by a state. Fearing that eventuality, governments have lowered the tax burden on corporations, on capital, and on high income.

But the ensuing pressure on the state to lower taxes on corporations, on wealth, high income and capital is probably less acute than it is made out to be. Various "cantons" of Switzerland, for instance, tax wealth and income very differently, with such taxes being three times higher in the canton "Jura" than they are in the canton "Zug"[23]. Not all wealthy persons have left the canton of Fribourg – the one with the third highest tax rates in Switzerland.

Index on the taxation of wealth and income in Switzerland (Switzerland as a whole= 100)

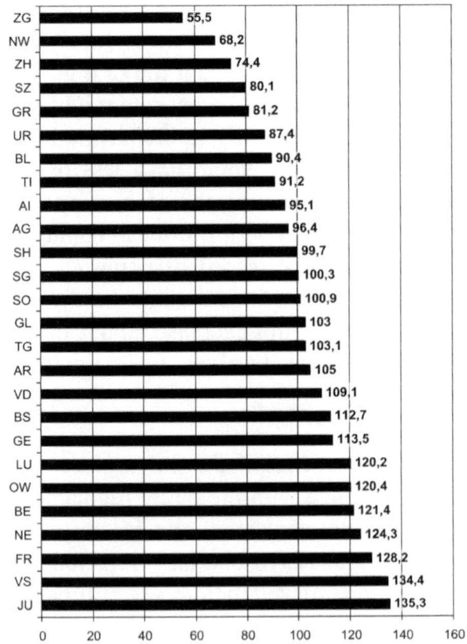

Source: Gesellschaft zur Förderung der Wirtschaft

23 A notorious tax haven.

Equally, income tax rates are comparatively high in the US State of New York and relatively low in the US State of Delaware. There are still a lot of wealthy people living in New York. Only a few have emigrated to Delaware. The pressure to unify the tax rates and to generally lower the average level of the taxes on income and wealth cannot have been that strong in Switzerland and the US.

Nonetheless, it is clear that, by and large, the wealthy now find it easier to escape from the duties states impose. It is equally obvious that they are less in need of the state and of its services. Obviously, too, they find it easier to opt out of the community that ties them to the other citizens.

Household income of public and private nursery school enrolments
(% October 2000; % of three and four year olds enrolled in school)

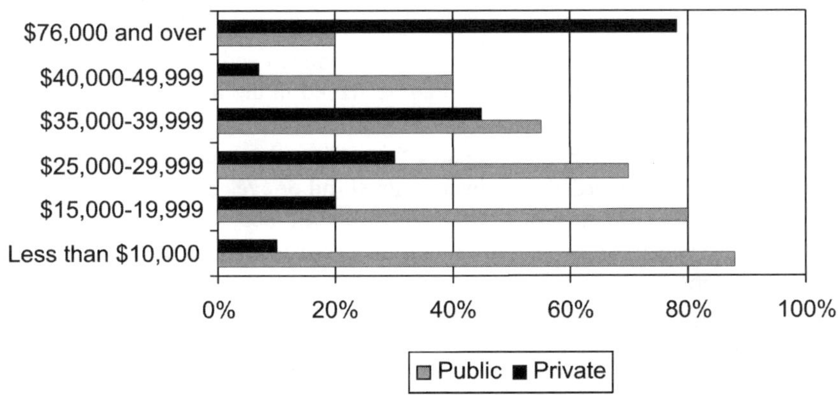

Source: US National Institute for Early Education Research

This is part of a more general phenomenon. A profound change seems to have taken place. Since about a century ago and up to quite recently, the different classes and groups of the population had been moving closer to one another. The distinction and deep cleavage between the nobleman and the commoner had disappeared even before. Contrary to what has been predicted by Karl Marx, the cleavage that separated proletarians from entrepreneurs and capitalists has also failed to widen. A broad middle class has emerged. Mass media, broad education, and industrial mass production created mass wealth and a mass culture. Up to quite recently, citizens of one and the same state therefore had much in common. But now the still distinct groups of society are drifting apart again; and the wealthy are drifting away from the state. Inevitably, this will weaken states.[24] In a way, we therefore may turn Marx on his head and claim that, instead of being an instrument of the wealthy and of the owners of capital, the state has become more of an instrument of the poorer classes.

The state is still the only institution to effect large scale transfers of wealth. This power or monopoly has been eroded somewhat; with the wealthy being less and less willing to part with some of their income; and with the wealthy being better able than before to make this resistance effective. This holds for wealthy individuals as well as for wealthy regions. Resistance to transfer of wealth to the poorer parts of Italy, for example, stands behind the electoral success of the "Northern League" in Italy. The same motive also informed – in large parts – the decision of the wealthy republics of former Yugoslavia to secede in 1992. But notwithstanding such resistance, and notwithstanding the growing tax-privileges of the rich, the state now transfers more income than it ever did before.

Traditional societies were stratified. Distinctions according to profession, descent, function, creed, gender, wealth were recognized and accepted as providing the necessary structure to the polity. People stayed in the life's station they were born into; and they were expected to do so. This social order was regarded as natural or god given[25]. Rebelling against this politically sanctioned inequality and discrimination was regarded as unbecoming, sinful or even as a crime.

Nowadays we hold it to be "self-evident that all men were created equal". In democracies, constitutions or bills of rights expressly forbid discrimination, be such discrimination based upon race, gender, descent, religion or wealth. These rules against discrimination are being enforced by the state. But, at the same time, the state enforces the one discrimination that weighs heaviest in today's world. It discriminates between those who are citizens; and those who are foreigners. It cannot do otherwise. Would a state fail to make that distinction, it would lose an essential prerequisite for being considered a state: namely the prerequisite of ruling, and ruling exclusively over a distinct group of persons.

In a world order largely based upon the prevalence of democratic norms and the notion of non-discrimination, the state retains the privilege of insisting upon

24 There are exceptions. In some respects the wealthy still are even more in need of the state than are the poor (e.g. by their need to secure their wealth in well regulated capital markets).

25 Both natural and god given, according to a catholic dogma that prevailed in the thirties. The "corporate state" propagated by the papal encyclica "rerum novarum" was based upon the notion of such stratified societies of unequals. The person's equality in dignity before god was to recompense for the inequality that had to be accepted humbly as upon god's own order down here on earth.

and enforcing the heaviest discrimination of all. But were it not for that privilege, which youngster of sun starched and dirt poor Central Africa, for instance, would not prefer pulling up tent stakes and moving to where the grass is greener? Which CEO or international tennis star would not prefer to move to a location where no income taxes fall due; which criminal not to a place where judges and their verdicts can be bought and prisons keep their doors open?

In a world of stark inequality, it is the necessary and inevitable task of states to safeguard the props that support global inequality. Notwithstanding all efforts at development aid; and notwithstanding all efforts of multilateral diplomacy to find global solutions to global problems; notwithstanding the attraction of the concept of "one world", we could not do without states keeping watch over the uneven status and the uneven life chances of the people of this earth. They have the – perhaps morally repugnant – task to divide between the "ins" (their own citizens) and the "outs". No one and no other institution can substitute for this role.

States have always had and still have an important role to play in the promotion of economic growth. In 19th century US, federal and state governments provided between a quarter and one half of all investment (for example, contributing to investment in rail-systems). The tasks that states shoulder in promoting economic development have changed since. The goal as such remains. Colossal efforts by public authorities underpin research and development; the building of infrastructure; investment in human capital; the penetration into foreign markets; the search for high-value-added incoming Foreign Direct Investment; etc.

Notwithstanding the advance of terrorism and of organised crime on one side, and of private security services on the other, the state still retains large parts of its prior "monopoly of organised violence". If states break up in ethnic strife, it is not because of underlying ethnic tensions that they fail. They fail because they are weak as states and, thus, fail to effectively enforce their "monopoly of organised violence". Weak states cause ethnic violence. It is not the other way round. Where the quality of state institutions is high, inter-ethnic killings are not state sanctioned. They are, however, state sanctioned where the quality of the state institutions is low. This is the case even where ethnic tensions are not very acute. If well constituted, a state thus can maintain this "monopoly of organised violence" even under the adverse conditions of inter-ethnic tensions. It is essential that it does. For if it fails to do so, there are no ready substitutes to take its place and to provide physical security.

Ethnic diversity is associated with violence where institutional quality is low

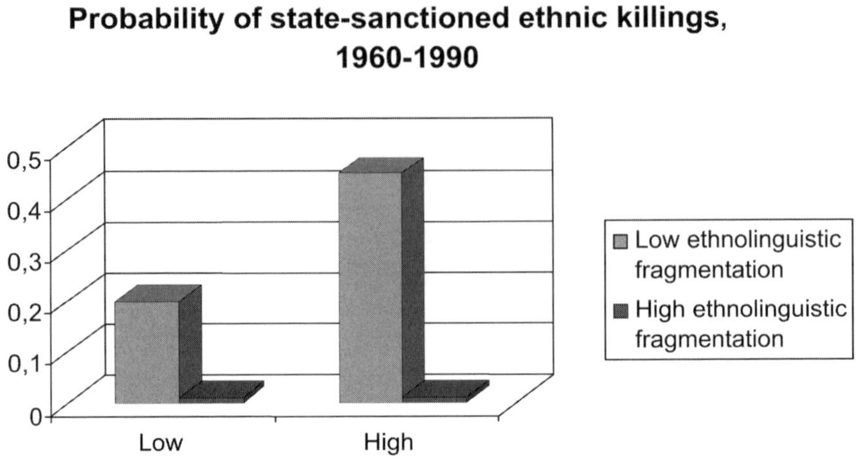

Source: Easterly 2000

The worst possible scenario for any place in the world is still the complete break-down of a state. Where and when it occurs, the international community is hard pressed to step in; sometimes to the extent of creating a "surrogate" state in the form of a "protectorate"[26].

At least in the more "modernised" parts of the world, humans still define themselves primarily as citizens of this or that state.[27] They highly relish things that only states can provide: such as a sense of physical security, of continuity, of commonality and of practised fairness in sharing risks and rewards.

26 A designation not "politically correct"; but fairly accurate nonetheless. Bosnia, Kosovo, Afghanistan are protectorates for all practical purposes, even if they are not called so.

27 Equal in importance at least with their professional status.

Austrians cling to their state
Do you find these terms sympathetic or non sympathetic? % of those Austrians replying "sympathetic"

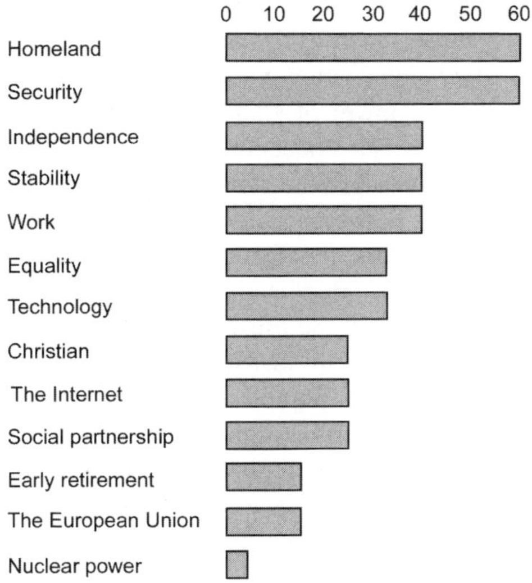

Source: IMAS

The belief has spread that, thanks to globalisation, states will no longer be central in the new world order. States will be replaced by new forms of social and political organisation. Unlike the old nation states, these new units will no longer have any fixed geographic base. They will aggregate persons and institutions from all across the globe that share common interests and values. And indeed, such groups have come to exist. Some of them have become quite powerful, as we have seen in our peregrinations amongst transnational corporations and International Non-Governmental Organisations.

It is also clear that these new players have limited the political reach of states, and that they have succeeded in breaching the former monopoly of state as actors on the global scene. Nonetheless, states do remain central in the global order and in global governance. In a certain sense and in certain fields they have become weaker. They have lost some of their former tasks either partly or completely. But other tasks have accrued to them over time, that now substitute for the tasks they have lost to other actors. If measured in terms of the volume of resources states may mobilise, their position has even become stronger both inside their own borders and in the realms beyond.

In looking at the issue, we may not neglect its normative aspect. We should not abstract from what we wish the world order to be like. The old order with states having a monopoly as global actors has had its serious draw-backs. It was marked by endless warfare. Generally it had been marked more by competition than by co-operation. New global actors now provide some sort of checks and balances against the exclusive power of states. These new actors, therefore, have changed the rules of the game. This became obvious, for example, when we looked at transnational corporations. Unlike states, they have a distinct and big interest in a world order not marked by conflict, but marked by co-operation.

But that should not lead us to wish for a world order in which the function of states would become negligible. There is no guarantee that such a "new world order" would be more peaceful than the present one. It certainly would be less democratic. States still remain the main instrument of collective political action. A reduction in the role of states thus implies a reduction in the scope and reach of politics and of democratic co-determination. This will hold true, at least, as long as other actors who impact upon the global system (like international organisations and transnational corporations) have not become subject to a more consistent and broad democratic control and co-determination.

Being free and poor is a miserable condition. But being enslaved and wealthy is more miserable still. Freedom and democracy are valued not just because they are associated with wealth. They are valued as such. Those sitting jubilantly atop the Berlin Wall on 9 November 1989 did not just celebrate the prospect of becoming part of wealthy Western Germany. They celebrated their liberation from dictatorship.[1]

Type of government
number of countries

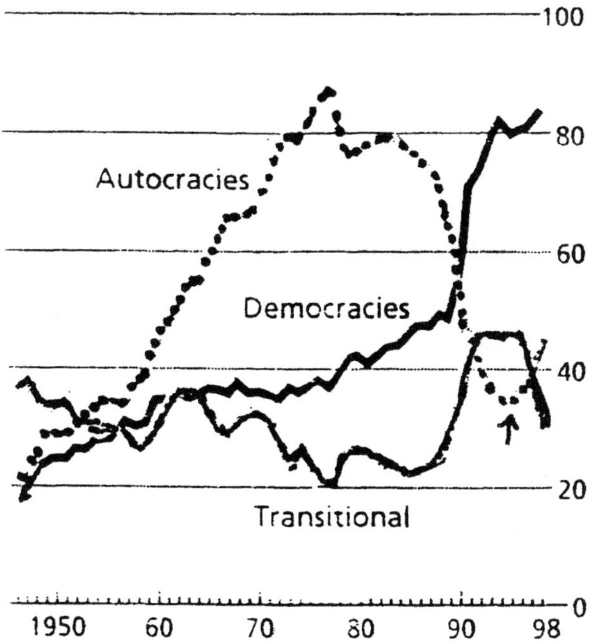

Source: Centre for International Development and Conflict

1 Ignoring that obvious fact is one of the many failings of "political economy".

The number of democracies has grown and a majority of countries is now ruled democratically.[2]

One of the virtues of democracy is that it facilitates change. An essential function of both democracy and of markets is to integrate continuous change into the political and economic system. What will be produced by the politics of a state or by a market economy is not pre-determined. It will depend on the wishes and preferences of voters and of consumers. If voters desire improvements in their public schools, the political system will deliver improvements in the public school system. If one political elite fails to deliver such improvements in the school system, it will be voted out of office and replaced by another political elite. If consumers prefer supermarkets to Mom and Pop corner shops, the Mom and Pop shops will disappear and will be replaced by supermarkets.

Both markets and democracy thus embody and facilitate permanent revolution. It is exactly because of this, their function, that they themselves seem irreplaceable. The two institutions support and supplement each other. Democracy can only function if there is a true chance of someone other than the ruling elite coming to power eventually. For this to happen, the elite that is opposing the present rulers has to be economically independent from these rulers. Were it otherwise, the present ruler would, of course, try to squash the opposition by impairing its economic base. Democracy, thus, can only thrive in states where private property is not likely to be seized or unduly intruded upon by those in power. Such secured property rights, on the other hand, are also essential if a market economy is to operate properly.

And indeed, if we look at the world, we find that democracy and rising wealth are linked.[3] All of the wealthy countries are democracies. Most of the very poor countries are not. The trend to greater overall wealth is accompanied by the trend towards democratic governance.

---

2 The development is not limited to the process of developing a central government. Democratisation has also progressed at the lower, local level.

3 The relationship between rising wealth and democratisation is not uni-directional. Rising wealth permits democratisation. Democratisation, in its turn, facilitates a reduction of material deprivation and suffering. Since 1995, 2 million people – a staggering 10% of the population – have died of famine in ruthless dictatorial North Korea. Between 1958 and 1961, nearly 30 million people died of famine in the, then still totalitarian, Peoples Republic of China. India, which is equally poor but a democracy, has not known a single famine, even in years of severe crop-failure. (UNDP Human Development Report 2001)

Democratic freedom in the high income countries

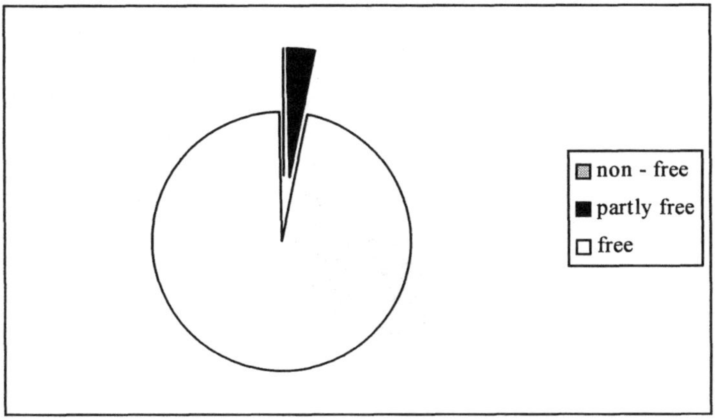

Democratic freedom in higher middle income countries

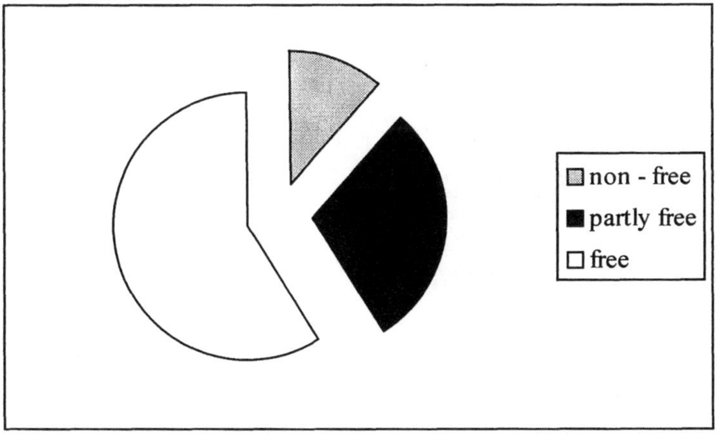

Democratic freedom in lower middle income countries

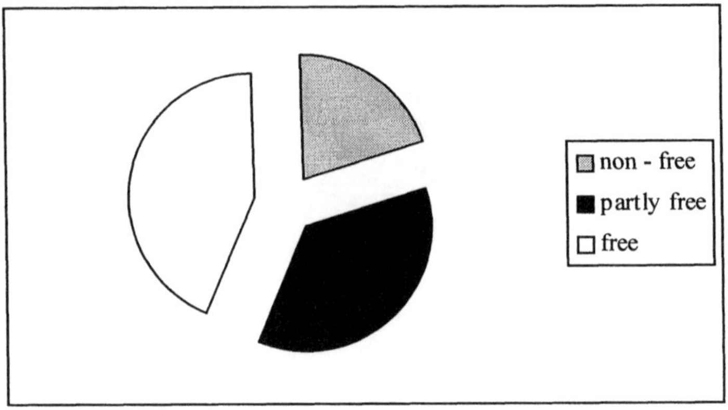

Democratic freedom in low income countries

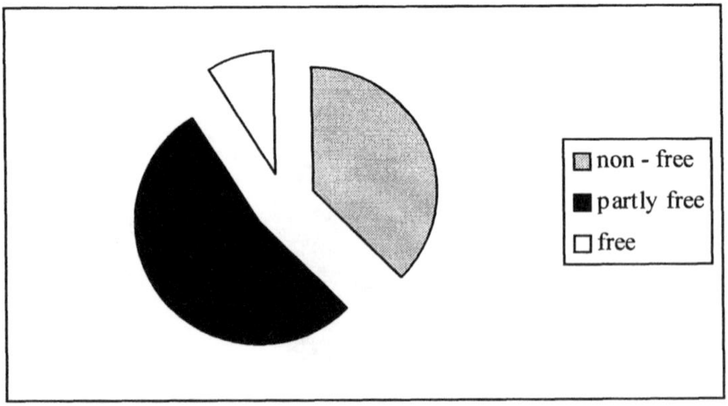

Source: Freedom House 2001

Democratisation has come in historic waves. The first wave touched only a handful of core countries[4] like the UK, the US and France. The second wave carried along the other countries in Western and Central Europe. The third wave encompassed Southern Europe and much of Latin America. Now we seem to be at

4 I always find it a bit annoying and a sign of the Anglo-centrism prevailing in social science that the world`s two oldest democracies are usually being ignored in such broad historic presentations: Switzerland and Iceland.

the end of the last, and fourth wave that brought democracy to Eastern Europe, the Balkans and to a few countries in East Asia and Africa.[5]

Reversals have followed each of these waves. The present fourth wave is no exception. The wave crested in the early 90s. Since then, there has been regression in some of the poorer parts of the world, for instance, in Africa. Serious setbacks have also occurred among some of the countries that issued from the former Soviet Union. None of the Central Asian Republics (the so called "stans") can be considered democratic; and democracy has broken down or become seriously impaired in ex-Communist states closer to the centre of Europe – for instance in Albania, Moldova, Belarus and Serbia.

Democracy may even become reversed in economically more advanced countries. In the not so distant past, in the period between 1930 and 1945, fascism became the vogue in all but a few parts of Europe. We still have to live with the trauma of a full-scale breakdown of civilisation in the barbarity of the Nazi horrors. That happened in a country that was considered, and that did consider itself, as being among the leaders of the "civilised world". We therefore have to wonder whether democracy is really as universal an ideal as it is made out to be, given the fact that two generations ago even relatively wealthy countries with democratic traditions reverted to totalitarian rule. Have we truly become immune to a repeat of such reversals. Could they "happen again"[6]?

Today, democracy has certainly become universal in the sense that nearly everyone, even bloody dictators, pay lip service to democratic ideals. Such bloody dictators may secretly despise democracy. But most of them dare not say so openly. On the contrary, many of them claim to embody with their reign not just democracy, but a more advanced and truer form of democracy. Their mendacity is obvious, but so is the absence of any ideal or big ideology that they could confidently oppose to the ideal of democracy.

In that sense, Francis Fukuyama is wholly to the point. If, as he claims, history has to be understood as a combat of opposing ideas, history would indeed have "come to an end". There is no valid alternative to the idea of democracy as

---

5 Some authors include democratisation in Central-Eastern Europe in the "third wave".

6 Some controversy has arisen recently over the abundance of literature, research, monuments, museums, etc. all dealing with this breakdown of civilisation under Nazism. A self-promoting "holocaust industry" is said to have come into existence working, in the end, against its professed purpose. One should wonder. For this "industry" (if it is one) does provide us with a constant reminder of what was possible in a country (countries) that saw itself to be at the pinnacle of civilisation. Such a reminder is of continued relevance. Investing in this "industry" is thus a solid investment in the future.

such. If we stick to a minimal definition of democracy, we would thus have to agree with Francis Fukuyama. There is no other feasible and generally accepted blue-print for organising a modern polity. All alternatives one could think of would be dangerously expensive, risky and inhumane.

According to these minimal criteria, any country could qualify as a democracy where mechanisms are in place that provide for one governing elite being replaced by a different elite through free competition for votes at regular elections. If no such mechanism exists, one elite – or one person – could cling to power until replaced by force. Such violent ruptures are exceedingly costly to the community. These costs are avoided by democracy.

But if that is all that defines democracy, democracy would provide no more than an institutional arrangement, a frame that can be filled by any picture. As we have shown, this openness has its advantages and is one of the strengths of democracy. If it permits the free selection of rulers, it also grants freedom in the selection of political contents. If voters yearn for security first, and for harsh discipline and a maximum uniformity of society, this would be provided by those who win the election. If voters prefer a flexible, pluralistic and liberal society, this again would be produced by a democratically elected government. Just as markets permit changes in consumption and production, the political market of democracy also permits changes in the production of public goods. Just as industrialism would crumble if it were not adjusted continuously to the changes in technologies and preferences; so would democratic governance crumble if it would not adjust in a similar vein. Democracy is not just an "open system" (Karl Popper) . It is a tool to keep the system open (just as markets are a tool to keep the economic system open) .

Yet, upon closer reflection it becomes obvious that the functioning of democracy – even if defined according to these minimal criteria – is, nonetheless, contingent upon a number of further preconditions. In elections, different elites must be able to compete against each other freely. This freedom implies, inter alia, that voters must be able to learn what the competition is about. They must be able to inform themselves about candidates and about political programmes. That implies the existence of media that advise them about that. In order to be credible and to fulfil these functions, the media have to be free, which again implies a pluralism among media. Freedom at elections also implies that voters do not feel threatened when openly confessing their political preferences. This implies that they must be permitted to associate so as to form parties; etc.

Democracy is now universally preferred as a mode of defining – in a non violent way – who governs. But, as demonstrated, this implies the acceptance of a set of rules and values.[7] Certain conditions thus have to be met for democracies to function. These conditions are universal. Universal yardsticks thus can be used in assessing if, and to what extent these conditions are present in the various polities of the world. But over and above that, over and above this minimal sameness, democracy may vary. It might vary in intensity. It might vary in the values it embodies.

Democracy is not just a mode of governance. It also is an ideal. It is a principle juxtaposed permanently to the equally permanent inclination of power to concentrate and accumulate. It is an ideal and principle that seeks expression not just in periodic elections; but also in other realms of politics; and that seeks expression even in realms other than politics (for instance in culture, or in the organisation of paid work). Put simply, this principle demands that those affected by a decision should have a say in decision-making. Countries vary according to their capacity or willingness to move closer to such an ideal. Quite naturally, they also vary by the nature of values citizens wish to see realised through democracy.

The discussion on the so called "Asian values" puts the issue into relief. If Asian countries wish to be considered democracies; and wish to function as democracies, they will have to respect universal, minimal preconditions for a functioning democracy. They could not be considered democratic if they seriously curtailed the freedom of media, or excluded opposing elites from entering the political arena. But over and above that, there is room for a specific "Asian" form of democracy. It might rely more on arrangements arrived at by seeking consensus. Asians might also wish to uphold the family as the core of their social system. They might be utterly strict in sanctioning deviate behaviour. They might establish their own and very specific form of balancing the economic with the politic; etc.. In that sense, a democracy can certainly be also based on "Asian values[8]".

If "democracy" can come in such different models, we also should expect these models to compete against each other. And they do[9]. There are neo-corporate models of democracy, there is the model based on mass parties; or – alternately – based on a smallish group of dignitaries. Presidential and parliamen-

---

7 These rules and values are indeed not unique to the "Western World". We have already mentioned the tradition of liberalism in Islam (e.g. exemplified by the Indian Mogul ruler Akhbar the Great); as well as the concept of popular empowerment in Confucianism.

8 Against the values of accentuated individualism and competition that are considered typically "Western".

9 A fact perfectly obvious except, perchance, to a few ethnocentric political scientists, who claim universal significance for just one model – which is the one of their own home country.

tary systems of democracy co-exist. There is democracy marred by clientilism; and there is democracy marred by the dominance of big finance; etc. In that sense, Fukuyama is wrong. Even if "democracy", as such, is now accepted more or less universally, there are still different forms or models of democracy. They are mutually exclusive and thus compete against each other as ideologies or ideals. In that sense, as a competition of ideals and models, "history has NOT come to an end".

How does democracy and how does the growing number of democracies impact upon the global system?

1) Analysing the data banks with information on those violent international conflicts that have occurred within the last 200 years, one concluded that one democracy had never waged war against another democracy[10]. The expansion in the number of democracies therefore makes wars less likely.

2) Democracy makes porous the dividing lines which separate national from international politics. This might "democratise" international politics. But it will also make them more complicated. The democratic "nationalisation of international politics"; and the "internationalisation of national politics" provide greater leverage to national lobbies of various sorts; like ethnic minorities, environmentalists, large enterprises, etc. It makes it easier for them to impact on the global scene.

3) As international issues become issues of internal politics, citizens expect that these international issues are amenable to the same treatment as issues of internal politics. On a national level, citizens expect to be listened to. They expect policies to be adjusted to their preferences. But on the global level, the population of one specific country constitutes just a small section of all the citizens of the world who are interested in or touched by a certain question. The weight of public opinion just in one democratic country, therefore, might not weigh much on a global scale. But, in this specific democratic country, citizens have come to expect that their political wishes are not ignored. If they are, they will become frustrated. This is likely to feed a polarisation between the global sentiment on

10 Many scholars have since dealt with the question; have refined the analysis; have conceded some exceptions or near exceptions. But generally, the original finding still holds. There is such a thing as "democratic peace". This runs counter to the widely held view of ordinary citizens being violent, emotional and war prone; and thus being in need of restraint by an authoritarian and supremely rational and prudent elite. Polls done in the US show, on the contrary, that the "masses" are much more diffident than elites about entering war. For, if given a choice (as they are given under democratic governance), ordinary citizens are usually very cautious. They spontaneously shrink from the risks entailed in warfare.

one hand, and national sentiment and preferences on the other.[11] The much commented "backlash" against globalisation may be caused by such resentment over national preferences not being heeded in a global context.

4) Within states, democracy is sustained by the politically active citizens – the demos. Democracy cannot exist without a "demos". As of now, no true "demos" does exists on a global level. Yet, as has been pointed out in the description of International Non-governmental Organisations, democracy and the porous nature of national frontiers has nonetheless permitted transnational alliances to emerge on certain issues of interest to citizens of more than one single country. Such alliances can be formed, for example, around economic interests, around moral interests; humanitarian interests or out of concern for the protection of the environment, etc. Democratisation has thus facilitated the – still partial – emergence of a – still very fractured and not very comprehensive and all-inclusive – global "demos". But these are fleeting occasions. The global "demos" still lacks coherence and permanence.

5) National politics and politicians now frequently attempt to directly impact public opinion in other countries. For instance, by bribing[12] or otherwise influencing the media in this other country; or by addressing opinion leaders; or by establishing direct contact with legislators – bypassing the ministries of foreign affairs. ("public diplomacy"[13]).

The democratisation of governance has, therefore, changed the international system. In investigating or guessing the likely future of this system, we thus have to also make some informed guesses about the future of democracy. This is not that easy. The track-record of democracy is still very young.

---

11 Some of the backlash against globalisation might be explained that way; as well as a good deal of the complaints about the lack of democracy within the structures of the European Union.

12 To bribe obstreperous journalists was the instruction given by the Austrian chancellor Metternich to his ambassador in the UK, already 200 years ago. In the meantime, open bribing has become too dangerous and mostly counter productive. More subtle methods are now being used.

13 When I was ambassador in the UK, my wife once explained to the Queen her being engaged in "public diplomacy". "Oh – the Queen replied – has it come to that".
It is increasingly common – at least within EU Europe – for politicians of one country to help like-minded politicians in another country in their campaign. Mostly still under some faint pretext – like attending a congress. But there is an obvious tendency to be less bashful about such interventions. A generation ago they still would have been considered illegitimate interference in internal affairs.

	Date all adult[1] men granted the right to vote in national elections	Date women gained equal voting rights with men
New Zealand	1879	1893
Australia[2]	1901	1902
Norway	1898	1915
Russia	1917	1917
Germany	1867	1918[3]
Denmark	1920	1918
Canada	1920	1918
Netherlands	1917	1919
United States	1870[4]	1920
Sweden	1909	1921
Britain	1918	1928
Spain	1869[5]	1931
Brazil	1889	1932
Turkey	1924	1934
Philippines	1936	1937
France	1848	1944
Italy	1919[6]	1946
Japan	1925	1946
Venezuela	1946[7]	1947
Argentina	1912	1947
Belgium	1920	1948
India	1950	1950
Mexico	1909	1953
Colombia	1853	1957
Iran	1906	1963
Switzerland	1848	1971
South Africa[8]	1994	1994

1 Aged 25-plus 2 Aboriginals enfranchised 1967 3 Women gained equal (but property-restricted in two provinces) rights in 1918. Full adult franchise 1920. 4 Vote extended to blacks 5 Abolished after 1874 coup, restored 1890 6 1912 for men aged 30-plus 7 1858 for lower-tier bodies; national ones were indirectly elected till 1946 8 Full adult franchise for whites only 1931. The few black and Indian voters lost their rights in 1936 and 1946 respectively.

Sources: "Democracy and Elections" by Richard S. Katz, Oxford; The Economist

Even "old, established democracies" are not really that old. In Britain – the country that created the "mother of all parliaments" – universal male suffrage was introduced not before the end of World War I; and universal female suffrage only ten years later. In France, universal female suffrage was introduced after World War II only. Even in its short period of existence, democracy has proven less robust than we wish to assume. We already have mentioned the reversals after the "second and third wave" of democratisation. What is especially troubling, though, is that among the first countries to introduce universal (male) suffrage, there are some (like Brazil, Colombia and Spain) in which the hold of democracy proved to be very tenuous, and where democratic governance had been interrupted by dictatorial rule for long periods.

But what about the future? May we truly assume it to be a kind of iron law that modern and wealthy societies cannot be governed in any other manner than a democratic one? May we truly assume the trend to democracy to be irreversible; with relapses being bound to occur; but with no basic break in this long-term trend?

Aristotle (and Machiavelli) thought that democracies tend to self destruct. Aristotle saw political history as a re-enactment of ever the same cycle. As citizens lost their republican "virtue" and became pampered by politicians seeking their favour, democracy would falter, to be replaced by tyranny, which would be replaced by oligarchy; which would be replaced by democracy; which again would yield to tyranny – an so on, in a never ending sequence. The question posed by Aristotle remains relevant. Is there indeed something in democracy that drives it to self-destruct? And, in addition, are there specific dangers to democracy that emerge now at this particular moment at the beginning of the twenty first century?

The demise of mass parties is one such development that needs to be scrutinised for its long-term consequences and for its impact upon democracy.

Membership in political parties
grey column = inscribed party members as percentage of all voters
black column = changes in party membership between 1980 and 1999

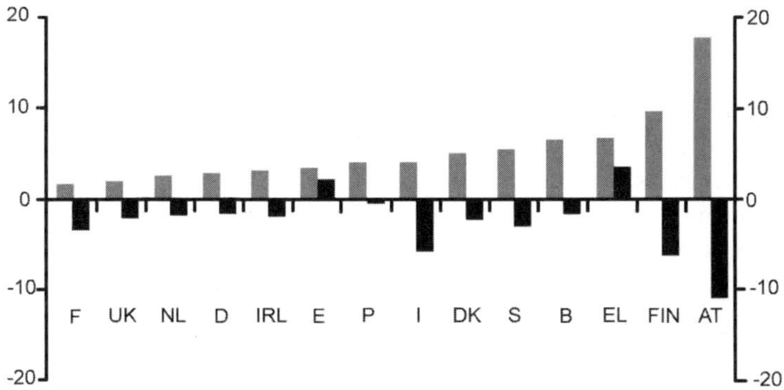

Source: Sociaal en Cultureel Planbureau, Nederland in Europea, 2000

The demise of mass parties might be seen as a necessary by-product of modernisation; as the result of a move towards greater freedom and personal choice. It would permit and empower self-confident citizens to escape from old, semi-feudal tutelage in mass organizations to the freedom of a purely personal choice. But there are some less positive and troubling aspects to this development. Mass parties have many essential functions. They recruit, select and train persons for political positions. They facilitate participation of citizens in politics. Most mass parties have succeeded in channelling potentially disruptive emotions into constructive civic engagement. Mass parties structure the political agenda by providing broad and internally consistent political projects that can compete with one another on the political stage, etc.

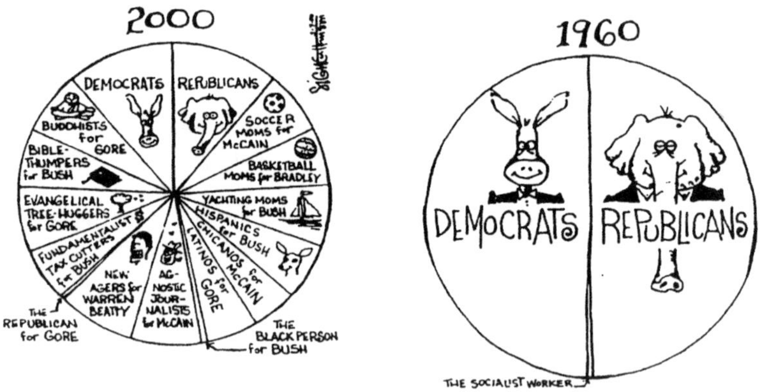

New York Herald Tribune

Mass parties wither. In the US, politicians have become unattached entrepreneurs who organise their campaigns on an individual basis. The party hardly enters the picture as provider of campaign funds or by setting the programme of a candidate for office. In the US, mass parties, therefore, can no longer provide comprehensive and mutually exclusive political programmes. If broad based political parties still have any function in the US, it is by being loose associations that spring into existence at election time only. At elections, they provide the umbrella that shelters a multitude of diverging interests, groups and lobbies. Each of these groups has its own narrow agenda. There is no one and no institution in place to tie all these wishes and interests into the coherent whole of one comprehensive and cohesive programme. In this, the US most probably has set the pattern for other countries to follow. In other mature democracies, too, mass parties lose appeal and members in a similar manner.

If other institutions would have now assumed the functions that the old mass parties have lost, we would not have to worry about their demise. Unfortunately, no institutions are in sight that could substitute for the functions mass parties have lost.

This is true – in particular – for the media. The rise of the mass media has accompanied the rise of democracy. For a long time, the two developments were perceived as being mutually supportive. The danger in the mutual relation was mainly seen in politics invading the realm of media and in thus curtailing their freedom and colouring their judgement. But today, the reverse is the more acute danger, by far. Instead of just accompanying politics, media substitute themselves for politicians and for politics[14]. They set the political agenda. They transmit information from "below" to "above"; and from "above to below". They monitor and control the performance of the executive much more efficiently than elected parliaments.[15] They have a strong hand in the selection of candidates – especially for top offices. Frequently now, media persons even promote themselves into elevated political positions – as, for instance, the US president and former movie star Ronald Reagan; or the Italian prime minister and media-mogul Silvio Berlusconi.

Yet, this too should not cause concern if media would thereby sustain and promote democracy. But this is not the effect of their heightened prominence. They follow other than democratic rules and incentives. Their main interest is commercial[16] and not political. They must sell copy or – in television – advertising time. This is better done by selling politics as scandal; or as a kind of sports competition; or as just some sort of entertainment. They do not sell political content as political content does not tickle the raw instincts of viewers or readers and, therefore, does not augment the readership of newspapers or the numbers of people watching a TV channel.

This noxious tendency is exacerbated by television having substituted itself for other media as the most important carrier of information. The vast majority of citizens receive the vast majority of their information (or what they erroneously

---

14 In Austria, the mass circulation tabloid "Kronenzeitung" has, in fact, begun to act as if it were a political party, going to the extreme of claiming for itself the right to decide on the continued survival, or the end of a government.

15 See, for example, their role in ending the Nixon presidency and the Vietnam war.

16 As shown by the media tycoon Rupert Murdoch caving in to Chinese pressure and curtailing the freedom of one of his satellite television chains in order to obtain, in exchange, the permission of PRC authorities to broadcast from his satellites into China.

believe to be information) via the television screen. Yet, television has notorious difficulties in delivering true information as its appeal is through style and emotion. This holds true especially for political news. Accordingly, the "handlers" and "spin doctors" of competing political candidates no longer go for true information in the very brief, paid for spots they have inserted into television programmes. These spots (or "sound bites") appeal to the irrational and they intend to stir emotion. Sound bites are not about political programmes. They are not part of the rational discourse democratic politics need in order to function.

These short spots of political advertising are similar to those that advertise detergents or chewing gum. They have the same appeal to the viewers. They tell viewers to purchase this, or to vote for that person; and then persuade viewers that doing so will bring immediate and effortless gratification. Gratification is therefore seen as something owed by politicians to the citizens who had voted them into office. The mature, responsible citizen, aware as much of his duties as of his rights, this mature citizen disappears just as the mass parties do. Politics become infantilised[17] with voters wailing at each little inconvenience they have to suffer. They do not relish appeals to civic virtue and duty; and they have become unaccustomed to being confronted with harsh reality.

"And above all, I said, and as a result of all, see how sensitive the citizens become; they chafe impatiently at the least touch of authority and at length, as you know, they cease to care even for the laws, written or unwritten; they will have no one over them.

Yes, he said, I know too well.

Such, my friend, I said, is the fair and glorious beginning out of which springs tyranny."

(Socrates to Adimatus as quoted by Plato in "The Republic", Book VIII)

Wealth and leisure produced by highly evolved economies have heightened the dilemma that Socrates pointed to. Life in mature capitalism is bifurcated. One part is being spent in the workplace where each person is but a tiny cog in a supremely complex machine which would break down were each participant not to observe the rules of rationality and strict discipline. The other, and increasingly larger part of life is spent in the realm of consumption with the style of consumption now frequently defining a person more than does his

17 The language used by media accommodates and promotes this trend; with every minor traffic disturbance being called a "traffic chaos"; and with every stronger wind that fells a few trees becoming a "disaster"; every small rise in taxation an "assault on property".

status in the productive process. In this growing part of life, rationality does not reign supreme. On the contrary, the ceaseless chorus of advertisements encourages citizens to be selfish, impulsive, hedonistic, improvident. Yet such attitudes are hard to reconcile with democracy, which can function only if citizens behave rationally and responsibly.

Consumption now often serves to signal and project a distinct life-style. One defines who one wishes to be by the product purchased. Politics now offers the same fare. Someone pleads for this or that cause so as to establish his or her own identity and his or her image with other citizens. Politics is no longer about moving, changing anything. It is about posturing and about the proper posture. The main thing is to show the proper spirit. The consequences of such posturing – or the absence of any positive consequences – are not that important.

Democracy needs a "demos" – the base of citizens that identify with the institutions of their state and that feel responsible for its general well-being. Such a "demos" must be based on a sense of shared fate; on the experience of commonality. Yet common space is shrinking. Arenas and platforms for the mutual encounters of citizens are disappearing: Sunday service in church; the city square; serving in the draft army; massively attended sports events; public schools, common health services; travel by mass transport; etc.

Space common to all citizens might shrink even more dramatically in the future. After the age of the television screen, we now have entered the age of the computer screen. Each one sitting before his PC screen will consume just the information that has been pre-selected to correspond to his "profile". While sharing the same planet, people would literally live in different worlds. It would become perfectly feasible for someone to be but faintly aware of the latest presidential elections; but be much moved by the discovery of a new species of beetles; or by a new record set in baseball. What is deemed central by one is being ignored by the other. If important information is no longer shared, democratic politics loses its very base, as it cannot function in the absence of citizens that know what has happened and what is likely to happen.

This negative consequence of the spread of personal computers and of the INTERNET was not foreseen. On the contrary. There was hope that the computer and the INTERNET would open the doors to a more participatory and full democracy.[18] This hope was not wholly unfounded. Computers and the INTERNET have sustained the stronger role of non-governmental organisations. They may have added some transparency and thus may have enhanced the accountability of

18 In a similar vein, radio and television broadcasting were thought to have the same effects

those in power. But they have certainly not basically changed the nature of the democratic process. And their positive contributions have to be balanced against those negative ones that have eroded public space instead of widening it.

The political rise of television and the decline of mass parties has made campaigning very expensive and dependent on private financing.

Expenses for the year 2000 campaign for the US Senate and the US House of Representatives
in US dollars

	Senate	House
expense per campaign for each seat	4,967.676	639.892
expense by challenger	2,146.166	278.819
expenses by the incumbent	3,561.481	628.396
expenses of all campaigns	360,810.990	440,472.400

Source: US Federal Election Commission

The year 2000 campaign between Hillary Clinton and Ric Lazio for the Senate seat of New York cost both contenders together the sum of 80 million US $. Billionaires invested huge amounts from their own fortune. Michael Bloomberg spent 65 million US $ in the campaign to become mayor of New York. Jon Corzine spent 63 million US $ in his campaign for the New Jersey Senate seat. Both were successful. Money works.

Obviously, this cost explosion impairs democracy. Politics becomes either the playground of the super-rich, or candidates for political office come to depend on the generosity of wealthy business and of wealthy pressure groups and, thus, are constrained to implement the agenda of their benefactors. Or – and that is another solution – politicians will have to recover their investment in the campaign by taking in money through illegal means, such as bribes.

Efforts of various sorts have been made to tackle the problem.

- limits to the amount of money a candidate may spend in her/his campaign;
- limits to the duration of the campaign;
- limits to the amount of money an individual or company might donate to a candidate or to a political party;
- substitution of public subsidies for private donations;
- some countries have forbidden paid advertisements on television.

The efforts to reign in costs of campaigning and to limit the role of private campaign contributions show that the problem has been recognized in its serious implications of posing a threat to democracy. But, it also is evident that no single remedy will provide a solution. This looks like another continuous battle that will have to be fought to keep democracy from becoming a sham.

More than fifty years ago, the British author George Orwell predicted in his novel "1984", that in that year, and with the help of advanced technology, public authorities would have gained complete control over the population. Citizens would have been reduced to a cowed, angst ridden existence at the mercy of "big brother", who could manipulate them at will. It has not been so. A good case can be made for technology having had the opposite effect of diluting the power of central authorities, and of widening the realm of free choice and of self-determination.[19] So far so good. But might the predictions of George Orwell become true, nonetheless; and might they come true just a bit later than Orwell assumed? Do we still have to fear the arrival of "big brother"?

Substantial progress has been made in technologies that permit the exact tracing of humans and the collection of data on all their habits, preferences and vices. Plausible, even convincing, arguments will always be at hand to support the development and use of this intrusive surveillance made possible by modern technology. After 11 September 2001, heightened security at airports with their bothersome checks are accepted passively and patiently. In some airports, such checks now include automatic face recognition. The use of this latest method of screening humans is no longer restricted to airports. It is about to be applied in other venues too – for example, at major sports events. Such technology and its use tilts the balance against the claim of individuals for a private sphere sheltered from outside intrusion. The power derived from a constant surveillance of the population will, on the other hand, accrue to those already powerful: namely to the state or to private corporations.

Up until now, democracies have been able, as it seems, to circumscribe and reign in the power the state could gain from such technologies (laws exist that severely limit the use a state may make of personal data available to it through its own activities). At least up till now, the democratic state has shown no sign of evolving into big brother. But it might be that – in response to new threats and risks – the state will become (and will have to become) more intrusive and less concerned with the privacy of citizens. For how, otherwise, would it thwart the

---

19 Computers (and especially their connection to the internet) have had the effect of vastly de-centralising information; and with it, power. This effect can be compared to the effect book printing had as of the 16th century. Parishers could themselves read the (now printed) bible and did not have to rely on pompous clergymen to read it aloud to them. Increased mobility has also loosened central control.

very real danger of – for instance – suitcase nuclear bombs[20] being brought into the country? Or the risks of some suicide bomber entering a big stadium or shopping mall?

At present though, the major problem is posed not by an intrusive state. It looms in the use of private data stored in the private sector. The volume of such data has multiplied. They inform corporations about the consumption habits, preferences and inclinations, whereabouts, income and financial situation of practically all citizens. Trade with such data has become big business (direct mailing). These data can no longer be considered under the control, and as property of the person they concern.[21] Not politics determine what can and should happen with such data. Commercial interests do.

This is just one example of a broader trend, which is the shrinkage of the political realm; of the realm subject to the rules and procedures of political democracy. City councils rule on the budget for public schools and they (or the elected school boards) decide on how this money is going to be spent. No such procedures govern the funding of private schools and their decisions on finance. In the US, private schools have expanded at the expense of public schools. Very likely, the same will happen in Europe (especially if and when European societies become less homogenous). Security guards replace police. There are formal rules that permit one to lodge a complaint against a policeman. No such legal and democratically sanctioned rules exist to guide, channel and process a complaint against a private security guard.

Or to take the example – already mentioned in chapter 11 – of the growth of communities owned and administered by corporations. It is the board of such a corporation[22] that may pass strict rules, some of which will impact heavily upon the lives of the residents. Such decisions are therefore not made by an elected

20 More likely still: nuclear weapons hidden in the millions of containers that move around the world with little inspection of their content. Only 2% of them are screened.

21 A number of European countries – as well as Japan – require persons on their territory to signal to police authorities any change of permanent residence. Anti-state Americans would never grant that right to public authorities. Nonetheless, there is a private US website that permits one to find the addresses of most persons living in the US. Paying a few dollars more, one may even obtain information on the finances and the banking records of the person. There are rules that prohibit the collection and publication of such information. But obviously they are not heeded and not enforced. Americans distrust the state and shield their private sphere against the state. They fail to shield their private sphere from the intrusion by commercial interests.

22 It needs to be stressed that in a large part of these communities, decision are NOT taken by a company board, but by an association of property owners who – in the legal sense – are the representatives of the community.

City Council responsible to voters. But even when corporations do not own and administer whole towns, they may own and administer communal services. They do so with increasing frequency. Citizens living in towns used to have some say on the organisation of services delivered to them by: power-stations, streetcars, postal services, garbage removal, etc. Many of these services – and the mode of their delivery – have a deep impact upon daily life. Nonetheless, the delivery of many of them has now become incumbent upon private firms. These firms have to subordinate the wishes of their customers to the wishes of their stock-holders. This too shrinks the political realm.

As we have seen in the chapters on the national and international monetary systems, monetary policy has become shielded from any democratic scrutiny and has been entrusted (if that is the word) to those that represent the interests of financial capital. With that, yet another and vital part of the economic/social system has been lost to political/democratic steerage and control. In all wealthy democracies, independent courts have assumed quasi-legislative functions and are expanding them. Like independent central banks, independent courts also do not have to answer to voters. Democracy can only exist if citizens have reason to believe that their votes in elections have an impact on their life. Doubtlessly, the field has expanded that is not subject to control and co-determination by citizens.

Percentage of eligible US voters actually voting

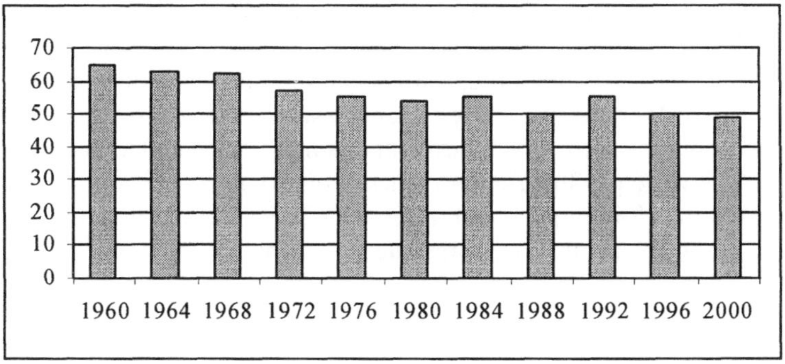

Source:

All of these challenges to democracy are fairly evident. But there seems to be something more sinister and ill-defined that eats at the roots of democracy. One symptom of this creeping disease is falling participation in elections. Even in presidential elections, only half of eligible US voters went to the polls. The situation is not as bad in Europe; but here too, fewer and fewer care to vote[23].

Decline in voter participation is not the only sign of disaffection with democracy. With one or two rare exceptions, trust in politicians and in political institutions is in stark decline in all of the long established democracies. Politicians and political institutions, like parties or governments, are no longer seen as serving the common good. They are perceived as serving the selfish interest either of bureaucrats of a narrow minded political class that has become estranged from those that have put them into office through their votes.

There are two possible explanations; both of them plausible:

A. = there is something inherent in the recent development of societies that makes democracy less attractive.

B. = there is something inherent in the very process of democracy that makes it less attractive.

It seems that the percentage of those in society that feel disaffected, wronged and resentful has grown. Necessarily, some feel hopelessly left behind in the competitive race towards ever higher and more prestigious consumption. A growing number of persons experience difficulties in defining their place in modern society. They fail to retain some sense of identity and continuity.

These difficulties are especially acute for the unskilled and semi skilled, blue collar workers. They used to have history on their side – so to say. Their income moved closer to the average income. They became wealthy enough to buy their own homes. They experienced upward social mobility. Now they experience the reverse trend. There is less demand for unskilled and semi-skilled labour; and even for labour, as such. Unemployment among the blue collar workers is growing; as is the wage gap that separates them from white collar[24] workers. Blue collar workers thus join other social groups that have become insecure about their position in society and that feel threatened by anonymous forces.

---

23 Some have claimed that to be a sign not of an imminent danger, but of democratic maturity: voting would no longer be seen as a state imposed duty, but as a right that might be exercised or not exercised. This argument is not very convincing, especially to one like me, and to my generation in general, who is woefully aware of alternatives to democracies, and who experienced democracy as liberation and a gift; not as a natural given, or even as a bother.

24 A trivial remark: The term "white collar" is no longer truly adequate. Those who had worn white collars in the past now wear mainly blue collars (bankers), grey collars(media) or black collars (priests and architects).

Rising classes are optimistic. Declining classes are pessimistic. They also are deeply resentful. The political energy of the rising working class used to be targeted against those that held the higher positions they themselves wished – and hoped – to hold. Today, the political energies of the declining working class are directed against those even weaker than themselves and that constitute the "underclass" of society; an underclass blue collar workers fear to join eventually.

> As we have observed, in most of the advanced countries, the trend towards a more equal distribution of income has been reversed in the last decades and inequality is growing again and is doing so at a rapid pace. This is more than a social inconvenience; or an obstacle to faster economic development. It also becomes a threat to democracy.
>
> "The disparity of fortune between the rich and the poor had reached its height, so that the city seemed to be in a dangerous condition and no other means for freeing it from disturbances seemed possible but despotic power." (Plutarch on Athens, as quoted by Phillips 2002)

The experience of an obscure threat to one's position translates into suspicion of everything foreign or distant. And finally it turns into the conviction of the "whole system" being corrupt, and either irrelevant or possibly even hostile to one's own interests. Parties that give voice to, and thrive on such resentment are on the rise everywhere. And while in earlier times they used to recruit adherents among the disaffected bourgeoisie, they now can fish in the larger pond of disaffected blue collar workers.

But disaffection with democracy rises not just because of recent shifts in the social structure of wealthy societies, it is also because of the working of the democratic mechanism itself. With the old ideological bearings gone, there is nothing to structure or guide the strategies of candidates and parties. They are therefore free to find ways to maximise the number of votes they hope to obtain. Following these strategies, they obscure issues, hide unpleasant realities, pander to foibles and fashions of the populace, and generally think it expedient to appeal to the lowest common denominator and to the lowest instincts.

This brings not just a change in style but it affects the very base of democratic governance. The democratic system is transformed and is less and less capable of dealing with reality. Voters and citizens are also affected. They must sense and resent the low opinion politicians have of them; and they must resent the mendacity of political life.

In the graph on the first page of this chapter, we have pictured the world-wide evolution of democratic governance over the last 50 years. On this graph we see the rising line of countries governed democratically; and the declining line of countries governed autocratically. But there is also a third line labelled as "transitional" regimes. This term suggests a uni-directional development. Such semi-democratic or "illiberal" democratic regimes would emerge in the final stages of an autocratic regime and would ultimately evolve into democracies.[25] In the end, more and more countries will join the ranks of full-fledged liberal democratic states. In view of all that has been said above, we may no longer be that certain about this "uni-directionality". We have to face the real possibility of developments turning the other way, with full-blown democracies turning illiberal. They would turn into some hybrid form of governance halfway between autocracy and democracy. They would become less liberal than they are today.

Is this a terminal illness, or something that can be healed in a new bout of reform?[26] Should we assume that being an open system, democracy might also find the means to overcome its present deficiencies? We do not know the answer. What is certain though is that a weakening of democracy would have serious repercussions on the whole global system[27]. The concern is less with the – temporal – failure of some of the new democracies such as the Central Asian republics. The concern is more with the democratic core states that set the tone and define the political climate world wide. It need not be pointed out that xenophobic nationalism, for instance, is incompatible with the world wide co-operation demanded by the tightening of mutual interdependence.

None of the big democracies is likely to fail in the near future. But we cannot be that certain about the medium and the long term. This perspective of democracy failing is very unsettling – especially in view of what happened in Europe in the twenties and thirties of the last century. But it might also be that democracies simply deteriorate without failing outright. That is not a pleasant prospect either, with global co-operation crumbling under the assault of nationalism and xenophobia.

To a large extent the global system has been shaped in the recent decades by the major powers trying to live up and move closer to the democratic ideal; and by their aim to have democratic ideals accepted universally. Were key powers to defect from that line, the global system will be bound to change for the worse.

---

25 "140 of the world's nearly 200 countries had multi-party elections, but only 80 of them, with 55% of the world's population, are fully democratic." (UNDP Human Development Report 2002).

26 Such a bout of reform transformed an indifferent and corrupt political system in the US at the turn from the 19th to the 20th century.

27 Just as the rise of nationalist xenophobic populism has already left its trace in slowing and endangering the process of European integration.

The long, secular trend has favoured democracy until now. Even though that happened in waves, and even though there were reversals, the number of democracies has expanded. Democracies have also been "democratised". The suffrage became universal. Internally they tended to become more liberal and tolerant.[28] Democratisation is a cumulative process. Living in functioning democracies makes people more democratic. Yet we cannot really be certain that this trend will continue forever. There are ominous signs that in modern societies, basic attitudes and values become eroded which are needed to keep democracy vivid and functional. Vigilance is called for.

28 As shown in succeeding opinion polls.

The Evolution of the Global System

Politics are intended to impact upon the social and economic reality and change it. But, of course, politics and also rest upon a social and political base. That includes the base of common interests and values. Communication and a multitude of contacts are necessary to develop this commonality of values and interests. The nature and scope of such contacts is circumscribed by the state of technological and economic development. Contacts and communication will be more limited under the condition of poverty, with a low level of technological development. The horizon for contacts and communication will widen with increasing wealth and with more modern technologies becoming available. The scope and nature of contacts and communication is, thus, different at each stage of history.

When humans lived as hunters and gatherers, contacts and interests were shared just within a small horde of two hundred persons or so. Contacts beyond the realm of the horde were sparse. If they occurred, they were mostly hostile, taking the form of fights over territory. Within the horde, however, hostilities were repressed, since peace was required by one person being dependent upon the other for its survival. But if co-operation in this small group was necessary it would, nonetheless, pre-suppose dense and constant inter-group communication. This communication created the trust necessary to maintain internal peace. Within a group, intense communication is thus one pre-requisite for the absence of violent, bloody conflict.[1] The commonality created by joint interest and dense communication also provides the foundation for political institutions.

With technology evolving, the scope for communication and co-operation widened. As a consequence, political communities grew in size. They changed from hordes, to tribes, to petty kingdoms and city states, to full fledged states. Today some forms of co-operation and some joint interests have become worldwide. We therefore have to ask if and how this globalisation of contacts and interests has impacted upon the political organisation of society. Should we expect the frame for political organisation to become wider still? Should we expect the two hundred states of the world eventually to merge, first into vast regional super-states (the United States of North and South America, of Eastern Asia,

1 What the Czech/American political scientist Karl Deutsch called "peace community".

etc[2]); and then, ultimately, merge into one single all encompassing global state? Projecting past trends into the future, we should expect political communities to become wider and wider; and, in the end, encompass whole continents, and finally even the whole world. Why, thus, do we assume so very readily that the trends of the past will not continue and that the width of political communities will basically remain at its present level for now and forever?

For it is indeed a break with a millennial trend if increasing contacts and growing common interest no longer correspond to a geographic extension of the polity. World-wide contacts and world-wide interdependence grow. Yet states do not become bigger any more. The tendency to ever bigger polities had reached its pinnacle, as it seems, with the creation of the vast colonial empires at the end of the 19th century. Since then, the tendency has been reversed. The number of nations is not declining but growing. Empires have disappeared.

Global interdependence is nothing new. In some ways, the parts of the globe have always been interconnected. Humans migrated over the globe and technologies diffused among them. But that happened at a very slow pace.[3] Things then accelerated with the invention of sea travel in sheltered waters (Mediterranean); and then with the invention of long distance sea travel across the oceans. In the 16th century, for example, Portuguese had already come to depend in their protein consumption on cod caught several thousand miles away on the great banks off the American coast. Politics also expanded in its geographic reach. Already in the 18th century, the war over the Spanish succession and the Seven Years War were fought all around the globe. But just as in the times of primeval hordes, the organising principle of politics still was territory and competition over territory.

As mentioned, at first this resulted in the expansion of the average size of the territory covered by a polity. As the trend to territorial expansion has become reversed, however, we should wonder whether a new organising principle for politics has been introduced; supplementing and perhaps even replacing the principle of territoriality. After all, we have found that mere size of states no longer provides much advantage; and even seems to be a drawback in some instances.

At this place, a word of caution is necessary. The flow that carries societies and polities forward is uneven. It dashes ahead in places. In other parts it forms eddies or becomes stagnant. One thus should doubt the usefulness of subsuming all political entities under one same category. One should question the usefulness

2 The European Union is an exception and it might indeed merge into one federal state eventually. But world-wide, the European Union is a rare exception in this respect.

3 Agriculture was invented in the Middle East in 6,000 BC. It took 3,000 to 4,000 further years for this technology to become accepted in Western Europe, a place more than 4,000 kilometres distant from its place of origin.

of models stipulating a sameness of "states" as if states were alike one another, at least in their essential characteristics. Societies and polities based on subsistence agriculture were still very much alike all across the world. It therefore was legitimate to count them as members of the same species. That has changed. Today's Burkina Faso, Canada and Luxembourg have little in common. It is questionable whether subsuming all three of them under the notion "state" will enhance understanding of what the global system is about.

Within the global system there is a growing differentiation. Instead of merging into ever greater sameness (and eventually, perchance, into one or several super-states) , the polities of the world have become not more similar but less so. Or – to be precise – they have become less similar in many essential characteristics such as their wealth, their productive base; their demographic make up; and in their tasks and in the tools available to accomplish them.

In the most archaic and orthodox version of political theory, states are still portrayed as being the exclusive "owners" of whatever sits on their territory. The state is portrayed as a unitary actor as if it were a physical person, driven by a single will and purpose. This archaic image still informs a good part of the discourse on global politics. When pondering the question as to the nature of the present global system, the predominant and ready argument still is that the system has ceased to be "bi-polar". The question then usually being dealt with is as to whether the global system now has become "uni-polar; or whether it has become "multi-polar". These simple models imply that only states form such poles. How states and their satellites group around each other on issues of external security is the sole variable that defines the nature of the world system. Similarly, when speculating about "international actors", one still assumes, more often than not, that these could be states only.

The following graph attempts to translate into the visual this traditional view on the nature of the global system.

The triangles represent the actors that impact upon the global political system. In this archaic vision of things, these actors are states exclusively. The scope of their political interaction is limited. Furthermore, this interaction remains fully under the direction and control of those who are at the top of the political hierarchy in each of the countries. Each sovereign would be free to upgrade or downgrade relations to another country. He is free to form an alliance; start a war; create or discontinue trade; etc. He could do so with a wave of his hand; by dispatching his ambassadors to transmit the corresponding diplomatic note to the sovereign on the other side.

The traditional view of the global system

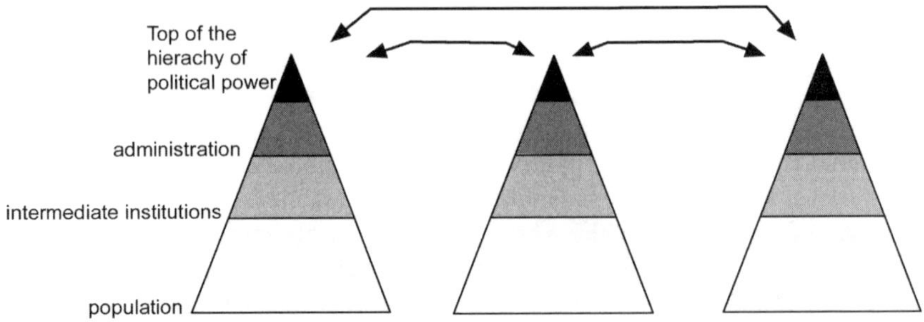

This global order would have provided for unequivocal and undiluted sovereignty. It would have provided to the sovereign absolute power to rule over his subjects as he saw fit. And it would have liberated this sovereign from all constraints and obligations in his behaviour towards other "sovereigns", his freedom being retained by the sheer military weight of an actual or potential opponent only.

This is, of course, an over-interpretation and even a myth. Such a global system has never existed in pure form. In the idealised form, this order would have called for the sovereign to have full control over his own territory and to hold, in this territory, the "monopoly of legitimate violence" (Max Weber). In many and even the advanced states of Europe, this had not been the case up to the beginning of the 19th century. It was contested till that time, inter alia, by roving gangs of robbers. In England of the late 18th century, these gangs made travelling hazardous even in the immediate vicinity of London. Effective rule over all of the claimed territory was impeded by the lack of adequate and reliable transport. In France (the most advanced country at that time) this was remedied in the 18th century only by the building of roads and canals.[4]

4 States were always constrained in their external relations; and they were **constrained** by more than just the military power of another state. None of the sovereigns was ever in a position to shape external relations as he liked. They were influenced not just by their fancies and preferences. They were constrained by the stage of economic development, by the geographic location of their country, by past economic linkages. External behaviour of states even remained constrained by some sort of supranational political institutions: weak though it was, the "Holy Roman Empire", for example, continued to exist in Central Europe until 1806. It continued to, at least somewhat, limit the nominal sovereignty of German princes.

In order to comprehend the changes underway since, we must de-mystify and separate the various elements that together have been assumed to make a state the exclusive global actor. These elements are[5]:

1) Authority: that is the recognized right to rule[6]. This authority had never been held by the sovereign exclusively. Banks, for instance, have, and continue to have, recognized authority in their realm. Mayors had and have authority in their towns. Most importantly, property owners had authority over their property (a fact that differentiated European from non-European polities and a fact which – very likely – had been an essential prerequisite for the "take-off" of economic development in Europe) .

2) Sovereignty: is the right to make the ultimate decision in the political realm. The sovereign may rule on conflicting claims of several subaltern authorities. In Europe that power of the sovereign had been limited by the "estates" (proto-parliaments of clergymen and nobles). But from the 16th to the 18th century, the power of these bodies had become curtailed. The sovereign therefore did indeed hold the uncontested monopoly on top political decisions for a while.

3): Territoriality: refers to the political organisation of space. Sovereignty is seen as the right to exercise supreme authority and decision making power over a slice of territory. The reach of the highest political authority is spatially identical with the official state boundaries. Territoriality excludes other principles of political organisation.

4) Citizenship: each person is assigned to a certain state; and has political rights only as a citizen of that state.

Sovereignty has never implied full autarky. Sovereignty is a legal/political concept. Autarky is a social/economic one. But it is clear that, while not limiting sovereignty in the legal sense, economic interdependence, as it has always existed, had also always limited sovereignty in a practical way. India never had a chance of conquering England. It was the other way round. Due to interdependence, and due to asymmetric interdependence, the "sovereigns" have been independent and have been one another's equal in the fiction of international law only. It is evident, though, that 200 or 300 years ago, a global system had come into existence that tended to enlarge the sovereign's freedom in international af-

5 Here I follow Karen T.Litfin, Mershon International Studies Review (1997) 41, 167 – 204.

6 "Authority" is a concept broader than the concept of "legitimacy"; the latter being too strongly connected with the concept of rule by consent. Therefore, it does not cover the whole historic experience.

fairs[7]. The very same system also worked to suppress the former diversity in the internal organisation of states and made them more homogeneous.

Clearly, both of these aspects of sovereignty have become blurred in the course of globalisation. Diversity within states can no longer be suppressed that easily; and the freedom of action on the global scene has certainly become more restricted. But even before that, the base for undiluted "sovereignty" had crumbled. At least since the onset of industrialisation, the notion has become less convincing that states relate to one another via their "sovereigns" only.

The second phase – "transnational" relations complement or replace "international" relations

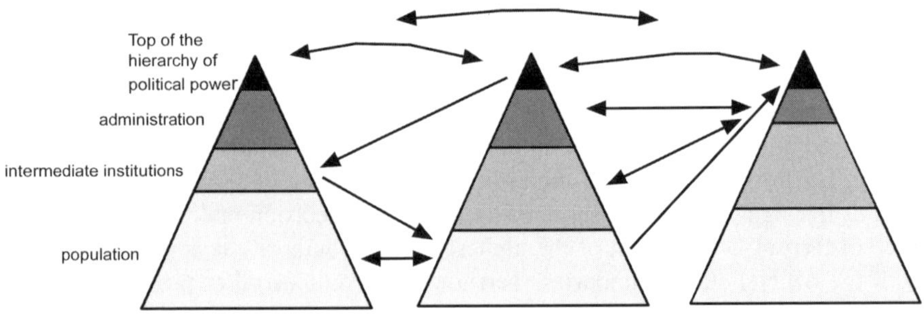

At the top of the pyramid, the highest political authorities still communicate with their kin in other countries, using the official channels of diplomacy. But, in another country, they now may also contact layers of political power below the one on top (and vice versa) . Furthermore, the layers below the top ones now can also interact with one another directly and without the intercession of the "sovereign" or of his bureaucrats. Administrators in one country interact directly with the administrators in another country, without using the channels reserved for the top political communication. Coming from different countries, experts on – let's say – foot and mouth disease – will encounter one another and will decide on what has to be done, without calling for the service of diplomats.

This new image of international, or transnational relations is already a bit closer to present reality. But even according to this rendering, states remain the only political unit on the scene. In one of the prior chapters, we have shown that the state does not "wither away". It retains a central function in ordering politics

7 Or even the "anarchy" that traditional scholars claim to be the "non rule" prevailing in relations between states.

within its borders. States are also those global actors that remain most powerful in impacting upon the behaviour of other global actors. But, nonetheless, they have lost their prior monopoly as the sole political agents.

The fuzzy web of the new global order

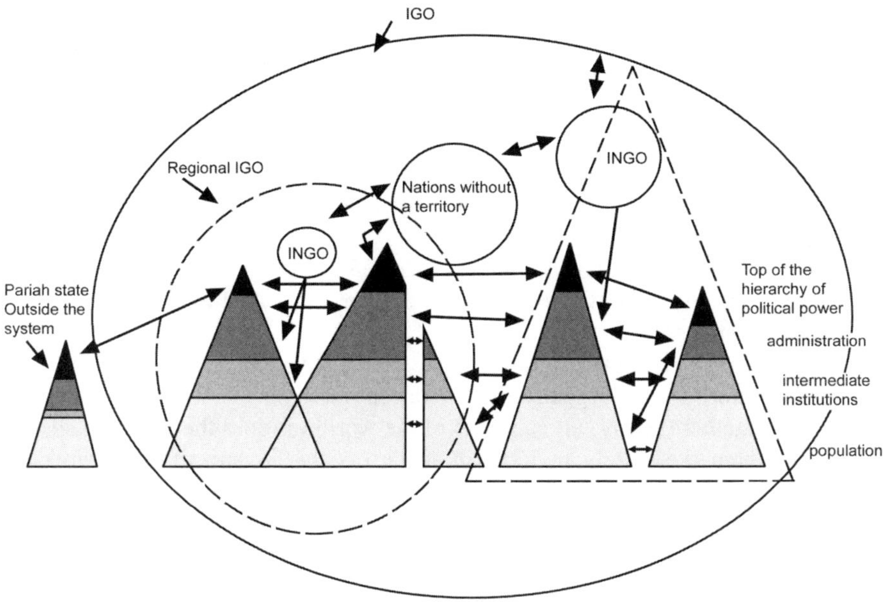

The above graph attempts a visual presentation of today's global system. In this graph we still find the triangles that were used in the two previous graphs. These triangles, representing states, are still prominent in this third picture. As in the previous rendering, the administrations and societies of the various countries interlink directly. But these linkages have now become stronger and more regular.[8] One triangle has split in a peculiar way. The top has remained intact but

8 Something that might colour, transform and occasionally block the usual "top down", or "bottom up" communication between the political leadership and the population, by interposing the layer of an administration that is listening to "a different drummer" and is following its own whims and instincts. One aspect of the process of European integration is the confrontation between two groups. On one side there is an international peer group of high level professional administrators which wishes to promote further integration; on the other side there is an alliance

what is below has become divided. On this lower level, the population and the intermediate institutions of this "split-away" are tied very intimately to their opposite in a state other than their own.

Two triangles have merged at the base. This indicates that the population in the area covered by the overlapping triangles feels loyal to both states, though they are being administered by different bureaucracies.

Something else has changed with the triangles representing states. They are no longer of even size. Their different heights reflect wider or smaller political functions within the global system. It also points to a certain hierarchy among states. Some are prominent and effective as international "actors". Others are less so as they lack a strong voice in the "concert of nations".

Two triangles are contained within the – still-faint – outlines of a larger triangle. This larger triangle could be a nascent federal state – perhaps the "United States of Europe".

One smallish state has more or less dropped out of this web representing the global system. Its relations are just to one other state. And even these relations are "top to top " only[9].

What is new in this third graph are the oval shapes. Those with faint outlines represent International Organisations of various strength and stringency. Some of these tie together (nearly) all countries of the world (as does the United Nations), some of them are merely regional in scope (as the Organization of American States – OAS).

The smaller ovals contained in sharper outlines stand for politically active "nations without a state". These could be either ethnic groups (like the Sri Lanka Tamils, or the Basque separatists). They could be terrorist or criminal organisations like al Qaeda. Or they could be highly active Non Governmental Organisations with a quasi-governmental agenda (like "Amnesty International").

The "nations without states" we have mentioned are not really replica of existing states, though they have assumed and effectively exercise some functions that earlier on were the tasks of states exclusively. These "nations without states" can command much of what a state can command. They have amassed "sufficient power, wealth and shared purpose to acquire vast resources for those functions performed by the traditional state... defending its citizens, protecting their health and well-being and implementing a monetary system..." (Dillard/ Hennard 2003).

Unlike a state, they have no territorial base. Yet they have their own "subjects" that are loyal to them and that are under their direct authority. They also

---

between rulers and the common voters, both of which have special motives to be sceptical of yielding too much power to the authorities in Brussels.

9 This might aptly describe the situation of North Korea.

deal as equals with the traditional sovereign – the state. Furthermore, they have quite some leverage to back up such dealings with sovereigns. They might not command aircraft-carriers and army divisions. But they command other powerful weapons like press releases. They can organise protests, or initiate political campaigns. Denying such organisations a personal meeting can have worse consequences for a prime minister than being unwilling to receive an ambassador of this or that country.

All that does not transform agencies like Amnesty International into yet another state and make it behave like a state in the web of global relations. These "nations without states" are something new and different. Yet, however we define their true nature, they clearly have become relevant in today's world.

It is impossible – of course – to squeeze this complex picture into the fiction of an "equality of all nations", of unfettered "sovereignty", or into the fiction of states being the sole shapers of the global political system.

We have wondered why the vast historic trend towards ever bigger and fewer states came to an end quite some time ago already. The answer lies exactly in this appearance of a new principle that has come to structure the global order and that now stands side by side with the old structuring principle of territoriality. This is the principle of a functional differentiation of authority, sovereignty and loyalty (or citizenship).

If we compare the last three tables on the evolution of the global system we will find that three states were pictured on the first two of them; but five on the last table that shows the present situation. There is a reason for this change in presentation. It should alert us to the increase in the number of states. Between 30 to 50 of them existed a hundred years ago. Now there are about 200 of them. This trend is likely to continue. In the last decades, some larger states – like Yugoslavia or the Soviet Union – have splintered into several smaller states. The motives that prompted that, and the conditions that permitted it, are still present and effective today. We thus conclude that not just the number of "non state actors" will grow, but, most likely, also the number of states themselves.

The last table could, of course, not replicate the full extent of this proliferation of states. But, it is insufficient, and in other aspects too. The table is two-dimensional. It just shows the scope of the constituency of states and of other international actors; and the relationships that exist between these constituencies. Yet, that is only part of the reality we would have to present. To the two dimensions shown we would have to add others. One such added axis would measure the amount of resources each actor is able to mobilise. One other axis would measure the power to sanction co-operation or non-co-operation of other global actors that are in intercourse with this specific global actor. Legitimacy among its constituents and among the other global actors would be a further dimension that would have to be explored and measured; etc. The ensuing complex, multi-dimensional picture would be even harder to describe than the already complex two dimensional table reproduced above.

But notwithstanding this complexity, one thing is immediately obvious. The difference in the nature of global actors has grown not just by "non-state-actors" now having joined the group of the traditional actors, that are the states. Differences have also grown in the nature of states themselves. States have become very uneven in all those qualities that used to define the essential prerequisites of statehood. Territoriality and citizenship are two such elements that were crucial to the old global order. States were assumed to exercise supreme and exclusive control over a piece of territory delineated by their frontiers. They no longer do so. Even with powerful armies, they can no longer protect their territory from foreign organised violence – might it come by missiles expedited by foreign states or might it come from international organised crime or terrorism.

Given global economic interdependence, they are no longer free to impose on their inhabitants any taxes they want. States used to hold the monopoly in law enforcement. They no longer do as arbitration supplants commercial courts, and as private security services take the place of public police. States cannot prevent being spied upon by foreign powers eavesdropping on electronic communication. Citizens used to "belong" to one state only and to owe to this single state their ultimate and supreme loyalty. Such exclusivity is now gone as citizens are also entangled in identifications and obligations other than the one owed to their own state.

The notion of states being the sole lords of the world, and the notion of states all being similar to one another in their basic characteristics, these notions were the foundation of the by-gone "Westphalian" order. These notions have lost explanatory power. States are not all the same. They are not the sole masters of the globe.

We have mentioned that a hundred years ago, just 30 to 50 states were in existence, while today there are 200 of them. If we go further back to the year 1500, however, we will find that, at this much earlier time, a larger number of politically organised units could claim to be counted as some sort of "international actors". In Europe and its close vicinity, there were about 200 of such units. Just as in the Middle Ages, there now again exists a large number of politically organised territorial units. In that sense, we have returned to the bygone, Medieval order.

There are other and even more compelling parallels between today and that more distant past. In the Middle Ages, too, things were fuzzy and overlapping. Supreme authority was exercised by the emperor in some fields, and by the pope in others. Below the emperor were the kings; and below them the dukes; and below them the counts; Each of them could claim to possess elements of "sovereignty". But the writ of all of them did not extend (or only partly so) to the free cities which were proto-democracies. Different rules pertained to different groups: to nobles or commoners; to the clergy or to the lay-persons; to traders or to farmers. This whole complex web was suspended between the poles of two different political/ideological philosophies anchored in two competing power bases: namely the church and the state.

The global order has become as fuzzy again as it was in the Middle Ages[10]. Just as in Medieval times, the population of a political entity might be independent and sovereign in some respects[11]; yet subject in other respects to a sovereign higher up in the hierarchy. Small polities might be powerful in their economic wealth and economic function just as some free medieval cities were powerful. Big polities might be vulnerable due to their military weight and over-expansion just as some medieval kingdoms had become vulnerable for the same reason. Loyalties of subjects may be divided, as one and the same person might belong to different polities or be existentially tied to different global "actors". This web of complex relations might be very densely woven in some places and it might be very loose in others.

Obviously, we have moved far away from any order that would correspond to the simple one described in the first table of this chapter, with "sovereigns" being fully in charge and with states being the sole global actors. We have arrived at a new global order and, as mentioned, it resembles the Medieval order in many ways. Yet, this is, nonetheless, not a return to something that already existed in this more distant past. It is a change into something wholly new. It is a step in an evolution; an evolution that can be compared to biological evolution. Like biological systems, social and political systems, also, evolve. Like biological systems, they do so by adapting to changes in their environment. With animals and plants, genes are the carriers of the information that is being adapted. In societies, this information is imbedded in culture and in institutions. Just as the genetic material changes in the course of biological evolution, political institutions and culture change in human societies so as to adapt them to new circumstances and to assure their survival under these new circumstances[12]. The institutions and the culture of the global order also evolve.

---

10 Prompting commentators and political scientists to speak about a "New Medievalism".

11 In some European Federal States, regional political sub – units are even legally entitled to negotiate directly with "sovereigns". De facto, nearly all of them do, as we have seen.

12 We have used this metaphor already once in the discussion of reproductive human behaviour.

We can plot this development as a graph, with one axis representing time, and the other, vertical axis, representing the complexity of the world system(s).

The development of the world system(s) as an evolutionary process

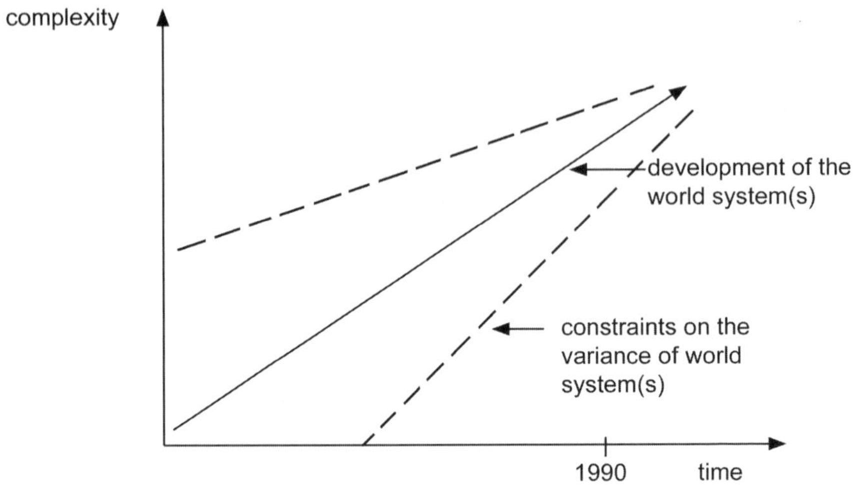

What tentative conclusions are suggested with this graph?

1) as biological systems, the economic/political systems have become more complex in the course of evolution[13]

2) the constraints on the global totality of these systems have become more narrow, thus limiting the scope of evolutionary discretion

The present global system is the product of evolution. It depicts how political institutions and culture have adapted to the external constraints imposed by greater wealth, modern technology, and an unprecedented growth in the world's population.

It is evident that, with the dramatic increase in world population and with increasing wealth, the various societies and systems press more tightly against each other. For each of them, the survival within the system becomes more difficult.

13 Defying the second law of thermodynamics, which would stipulate that, over time, complex systems decay into simpler ones and, in the end, into chaos (entropy).

The competition for survival of a specific culture and of a specific set of institutions becomes harder. The process of the evolution therefore becomes more selective. For each of the subsystems, and for the global system, as such, the limits to variance set by external constraints have become more narrow.

Projecting Trends and the Vagaries of History

If the constraints on the development of the international system have become more narrow – as we have claimed – this would imply that the future will hold few surprises. We therefore should feel free to project into the future the trends we have observed in the past.

Given the assumption that things will evolve in the manner in which they have evolved until now[1], what would the world look like in forty years?

1) The global population will have increased by another billion, with all of that increase having happened in the poorer countries. Most of the wealthy countries, on the other hand, face a hard to manage decline in their population. In the poorer countries, a youngish population, with no prospects of finding adequate jobs, will be tempted to seek employment in the wealthier northern part of the world. South-north migration (both legal and illegal) will expand. While actually in need of immigration, some of the rich but ageing countries, like Japan or some North-European states, will be ill-prepared, nonetheless, for their new function as haven for immigrants. The issue will impact[2] heavily upon internal and external politics.

2) Eventually, a shift in wealth and political influence will follow the changes in the demographic weight of various parts of the world. The relative economic and political weight of the present Triad countries will decline in line with their declining share in world population.

3) The depletion of oil reserves in other parts of the world will make the Middle East the most prominent source of oil supply (and to a lesser degree: also of natural gas). This will enhance the strategic relevance of the region which, at the same time, will remain politically volatile. This is an ominous combination. Due to a rising demand, and due to the reserves being slowly drawn down, the

1 In its projections for the year 2015, the CIA sees the following as the "key drivers" of trends: 1) demographics 2) natural resources and environment 3) science and technology 4) the global economy and globalisation 5) national and international governance 6) future conflict 7) the role of the United States. This last point might tell us something about the present US state of mind. No other state or group of states may aspire to the role of a "driver" of global trends.

2 Just as the massive increase of immigration into the United States, that happened in the last decades of the 19th century, had deep and lasting impact upon US politics.

price of oil will increase; and – as a consequence – prices will also rise for other forms of primary energy. But this rise will be gradual and modest. Shortages in raw materials other than oil will be temporary at worst.

4) Water shortages will plague some of the countries that are, at the same time, arid and poor. Such shortages might interlock with and/or cause inter-state conflict.

5) Environmental problems will be acute in some densely populated low income states. In high income countries, a good many of the environmental problems will have been eased. The world's "commons", such as the open ocean or pristine nature, will have become either strictly regulated; or their use will have become commercialised and privatised to a large extent.

6) Wars in their classical sense will have become even rarer. But other forms of organised violence will be more common and they will merge or overlap with ordinary, organised crime. This also applies to large scale terrorism. Terrorism and other forms of organised violence will frequently be motivated by economic/commercial reasons[3] as such activities can provide high[4] income to groups that otherwise would be marginal. In that sense, organised violence will have become "privatised"; just as the defence against this threat will also become "privatised" to a large extent. This defence will be organised solely via politics and public institutions; but also via private, commercial institutions.

7) Proliferation of weapons of mass destruction will continue. Concerted efforts by states and other international actors will somewhat slow this process of proliferation. No such slowdown is to be expected for the rapid proliferation of very "cost efficient" small weapons. They will become accessible to an ever wider circle of persons and even to very poor ones.

8) In the absence of US political leadership that could promote co-operation between the three pillars of the "Triad", competition between these three poles of power will become more marked. The members of the "Triad" will draw into a closer relationship with some but not all of their neighbouring countries like Ukraine or Mexico.

9) Within the "Triad", the US will continue to dominate. But US policy will continue to be torn between the opposing forces of international (even missionary) engagement and isolationism. The latter sentiment is likely to prevail and the US will cease to invest in the maintenance of a stable world system. This will leave a vacuum that will not be filled by any other state or combination of states. International co-operation will suffer from this lack of a supportive "hegemon".

3 As for instance piracy, which is increasing quite rapidly at the moment.
4 If not solid.

10) As measured in per capita income, the wealth of Europe will remain rather even to per capita US wealth. The bigger size of the population of EU-Europe will be compensated by the decline in its population. Overall and in economic terms the two shores of the Atlantic will retain the same relative weight they hold now. Within these limits, Europe will remain a significant global player. Such a role is contingent, however, upon further progress in European integration. It is also contingent upon Europe being willing and capable of managing some of the crises at its doorsteps (in the Transcaucasian countries; in the Southern rim of the Mediterranean, or in the Middle East). The euro will equal the US dollar as international currency. Europe will maintain its role as chief supporter of the United Nations and as the main source of development assistance. Primitive Anti-Americanism will have disappeared from Europe. Serious concerns about US-European political differences will have taken its place.

11) Transatlantic relations will become thinner and conflict between both shores of the North Atlantic will become more frequent. Overriding common interests should impede such a development, but different world views, values and political philosophies will drive this estrangement.

12) A withdrawal from Europe and all of the "West" would not serve Russia's objective interests and Russia is, therefore, likely to continue on a basically "pro Western" course. Its (not very impressive) potential will thus be added to the potential of Europe. But Russia's inner weakness and backwardness will prove a severe handicap not only on its own future and on its place in Europe. It also will impair the standing of Europe.

13) The Transcaucasian and Central Asian countries of the Southern rim of Russia will revert to the state of low income, developing countries. They will be relevant only by the trouble they might cause and not by any positive contribution they will make to world order.

14) Continued bad governance, the failure to fully embrace modernity, and the failure, especially, to evolve the institutions of secular, civic society will prevent the high potential of the Arab world from being realised. Some of the Arab rim-countries (like one or two of the Gulf emirates, Oman or Tunisia) might be the positive exceptions.

15) China will have become a major power in both economic and military terms. The main question is how it will use this power. Were it to follow its immediate, material interests, China will opt for full integration into the world system. But strong nationalist tendencies, the unique structure of its polity and the still existing potential of war with neighbours (for instance, and most prominently, with Taiwan) might tempt it away from this course. In such a (less likely) case, China could form the core of a group of "negating powers" that oppose the

prevailing global order (thus replicating the role of the Soviet Union in the time between 1945 and 1990).

16) Together with the rise of China, the rise of far North Eastern Asia will continue. This rise will bring the single most important change in the architecture[5] of the global system. It will redistribute relative power around the world. If these Asian countries were a unit, and a unit including, next to China, also Korea and Japan, this unit would be the world's most powerful economic entity already now. The problem is that such unity is far off. Co-operation between these states remains underdeveloped. They lack common political institutions that could sustain such co-operation. The most serious deficiency in that context is the absence of a multilateral security arrangement that might contain the numerous actual and potential conflicts of the region. If there were a "World War III", it could originate in Asia.

17) Next to China and other North East Asian states, a number of other countries will gain prominence too, most notably India, Indonesia, Mexico, and Brazil.

18) A fair number of "low income countries" will have changed their status into that of "high middle income countries", or, at least, into that of "low middle income countries". But even among those that remain in the "low income" group, social conditions will improve.

19) Whereas differences between the wealthy countries will continue to be minimal, differences will remain staggering and even grow among the countries that are not "high income". These will be differences not just in wealth and social conditions; but also in governance, in inner coherence and in culture. The tensions created by such stark divergence will radiate into the global political and security system and it will do so with a negative and destabilising effect.

20) Several poor and fragile states will "fail". So as to deal with such eventualities, the international community will formally re-establish the institution "protectorate". Some of these crisis spots might, nevertheless, be left to simmer on, without outside help or intervention.

21) Global interconnectedness will have the strange consequence of some areas and countries simply being left out of the loop, as these countries have neither the potential to add something to other countries or societies; nor the means to seriously damage them.

22) Institutionalised international co-operation will become still more dense in a wild, unplanned growth of international organisations and agencies. These will be supplemented by international non-governmental organisations. Both

5 If this architecture is defined the traditional way, namely as being created by the interplay of mayor powers.

governmental and non-governmental organisations will frequently by-pass public administrations to directly deal with citizens, transnational enterprises or civic organisations. Even official international organisations might derive at least parts of their income from other than purely governmental sources. Declining US support for international organisations will, however, seriously handicap their actual effectiveness.

23) Within the next quarter of a century, overall global wealth will have doubled at least. Recurring regional economic crises will have been dealt with in an ad-hoc manner. As in the past, this will be done by combining efforts of the private sector, of governments, and of international financial institutions. The latter will not have undergone any drastic reform. These tools are not sufficient, however, to deal with a serious, world-wide crisis such as the one that depressed the world economy and world politics in the thirties of the last century. It might emerge from the imbalance of the world economy caused by US politics. The huge US appetite for capital inflow will even grow with the US current account balance deficit and with the federal budget ballooning due to increased expenditures for war and armament; and decreased federal income due to a lowering of US taxes. No international remedy can compensate for such gigantic imbalances. They create a very fragile situation. It might collapse, as sudden shifts in moods and perceptions might set in motion a deflation in US assets. This would result in a world-wide economic crisis.

24) The power of international finance will persist, though the pinnacle of its prestige and influence had already been passed at the turn from the 20th to the 21st century. Main street economy (that is the real economy) will again take first seat and thus demote "Wall-street" (that is the power of mere finance) from this place. World-wide, the political and the economic will merge even more intimately.

25) Private enterprise will become more deeply engaged still in global rule setting and in the enforcement of such rules.

Is that what will actually happen? We cannot be sure. Such predictions may be wrong simply because our analysis is wrong; because we have concentrated on changes and variables which – in retrospect – might not have been that crucial. We thus might have ignored other variables that truly make the difference. The trend we thought was there did not really exist. Looking back on some of such forecasts made over the last century, one should become prudent indeed in proclaiming as certain (or even plausible) some specific development.

Some famously wrong forecasts:

1897 – Lord Kelvin: "the radio has no future"
1901 – Gottlieb Daimler: "the world-wide demand for automobiles will not exceed 1 million"
1932 – Albert Einstein: "there is not the slightest indication for us ever being able to develop nuclear energy"
1950 – The US officials on an aid mission to Japan (as quoted by Easterly): "Japan will have trouble competing on world markets. It might try selling "knickknacks" to other developing countries."
1965 – Batelle Institute: the last buses will have been withdrawn from city traffic by 1990
1977 – CEO of Digital: "I see no reasons for individuals having their own computer"

That well known and knowledgeable persons have erred so miserably[6], should make us more prudent in predicting this or that.

The predictions just provided could be wrong for the simple reason that the systems we have analysed are very complex. As all complex systems, they are inherently "chaotic". Even small and accidental causes can have vast effects (see chapter 1). Who would dare to predict that a piece published on the opinion page of a low circulation daily would ultimately force a basic political change of course? Who could dare to ascertain that a minor change of mood would escalate into a breakdown of the world financial system? Who could have predicted that some hundred voters in Florida having punched their voting cards in this way and not another in November 2000 have, thereby, toppled the Post-World-War-II global order?

Evolutionary processes like economic and technological developments are random by their very nature. Inevitably, we will get things wrong if we just stick to projecting into the future the trends of the past and do not allow for the unexpected and unpredictable.

6 The biggest, and latest, collective error in forecasting concerned the future of information technology. A revolutionary, massive transition to a new age was predicted. It did not happen. The bubble created by unrealistic expectations burst in the year 2000, when it became evident that no "new economy" had emerged, and that the stocks issued by some of the IT firms were highly over – rated.

We might be wrong in our forecasts because human action impacts upon the global system. It does not function like clockwork or any other algorithmically programmed machine that automatically runs a set course. The global system is self-reflective. Humans react to changes in their environment. Their actions are guided by certain perceptions, values and goals. In the realm of politics, and even in the realm of global politics, events and developments are, therefore, not the result of some blind forces that are as remote from human influence as are wind and weather. To a large extent, events and developments are what humans wish them to be.

And indeed, until now, we have carefully avoided predicting, with absolute confidence, some very specific technology that might come to prevail; or some very specific markets that will develop; or some very specific event that will occur. We have only looked at major trends as they have emerged over longer periods of time. We have dealt just with those trends and vast developments that have withstood the vagaries of this or that accidental turn of history. Looking, for instance, at the development of the world economy in the 20th century, we have remarked that neither the two World Wars, nor the terrible economic crisis of the thirties, have left any lasting imprint on the steep upward curve of world-wide economic growth. So, even if we are not able to predict world wars and world economic crises, we still could have greater confidence in making forecasts based on such secular, vast trends as the development of the aggregate world economy; or on the likely development of the global population. Or so it seems.

For chaos theory instructs us not only on the fact that small events can indeed have disproportionally large consequences. It also instructs us that a complex system can "flip" and that "catastrophic" discontinuities[7] and breaks are bound to happen and cannot be foreseen. It therefore is not that easy to distinguish between secular trends that will persist, irrespective of such major reversals; and those trends that will be broken in such reversals. Frequently, what we assume as likely to happen, will not occur at all. And what will occur will be unanticipated. The future is not "surprise free".

The scenario technique is used to confront policy makers with the unexpected. A scenario, therefore, is not a description of the most likely future. It is a mental experiment to teach policy makers about the vast range of possibilities in future developments. Here are some possible futures that deviate from the "surprise free" scenario we have presented at the beginning of the chapter:

---

7 One such catastrophic discontinuity – and the worst one possible – would be a collapse of the whole world ecological system. Such collapses happened – as mentioned – on some small islands. A recurrence on a world-wide scale does not seem likely. But still, we cannot be utterly confident about that.

What if:

The US turns completely isolationist and withdraws from engagement in the world
The United Kingdom and the Netherlands join the US as 51st and 52nd states
European integration is reversed
Some European countries become ruled by authoritarian/ nationalist regimes
Russia continues to decline and ultimately disintegrates
The UN and, with it, other major international organisations lose all their legitimacy
World War III erupts over a confrontation between the PRC and Taiwan
In China, a fight over political succession leads to "war-lordism" and, ultimately, to a complete breakdown of order. Starvation threatens 1,4 billion humans
The rich take to the habit of purchasing states
The poor take to the habit of destroying states
States dissolve into islands of commercially organised "walled communities", surrounded by spaces of anarchy and poverty
A serious world wide economic depression defies any counter-measure and endures for a decade with record unemployment and a deep drop in production
World-wide free trade collapses or slowly withers away
Religion, instead of work and consumption, becomes the structuring element in society
Break-throughs in genetic engineering result in a tripling of the world food production
Accidents in genetic engineering lead to some mortal strains of bacteria becoming immune to all sorts of antibiotics
Little green men from a planet close to Alpha Centaurus land in front of Buckingham palace

The above list points to the vast differences in "possible futures". Each of these developments might indeed occur. None of them can be excluded beforehand.

Increasing wealth, more ample resources, slower growth of the population, a vast increase in knowledge and the very targeted use of technology have provided humankind with much freedom of choice – a freedom not known to previous generations. Humans may now work less. They may, thus, either shorten the work week, take longer vacations, or seek earlier retirement. We may, however, also use the enhanced productive capacity to consume more of the things we want.

We may send persons to the moon; we may construct nuclear shelters instead; or purchase drugs to drift off into Nirvana; we might donate to the poor; support philharmonic orchestras; or develop the most sophisticated and powerful weapons ever known to humans; we may purchase the last surviving tropical hardwood; or create national parks and natural preserves.

The whole, complex global system that produces all that wealth and choice is running on a very tight schedule. We now have unprecedented power to change things. Such changes might, however, have deep repercussions throughout the whole world. Many of them might be very negative. The freedom of choice is thus more apparent than real. And the power to effect far reaching change must, therefore, be brought in line with the requirement to preserve, intact, the complex system of world-wide interdependence. The capacity to change has to be controlled. But we do not yet possess all instruments for such a control, not even on a national level. Fewer tools are still available to address the issues on the global level. It is as if automobiles had been invented and produced; but no traffic rules and traffic police to keep cars on the roads safely.

Global governance is still deficient. We act without any institution being in charge of evaluating the consequences of such actions and of restraining choices and developments to those that will not be damaging in the long run. Unfortunately, humankind frequently finds itself in the position of a sorcerer's apprentice; having called the spirits, it then lacks the tools to handle them. Looking at the implications, one may wonder, for instance, whether it was wise to discover nuclear fission. Eventually, and somewhere in the future, a nuclear bomb is bound to explode. All efforts to prevent that from happening would have been in vain. Humankind is simply not equipped to control all of the consequences of this one fateful discovery. Technology that has such a fateful impact on all our lives escapes political, democratic control. Nuclear fission has brought home already the dreadful prospects resulting from this failure. Possible disastrous developments in the world financial system provide one other prominent example for this, our wont to master our own fate. We have already mentioned the very real possibility of a recurrence of a world economic crisis like the one that had destabilised societies and polities in the first half of the 20th century. Seventy years after that disaster, we still lack tools to cope with a similar event.

Human procreation provides another example for our collective failure to steer our collective destiny. Demography used to be determined by facts beyond human control, such as the availability of food, the occurrence of plagues; etc. Only a small part of demographic developments was due to human decision and intervention: like celibacy, or late or early marriage. This has changed. Demographic developments now depend on culturally defined human preferences. In modern societies, adults are socialised in a culture that no longer discriminates against remaining single; and/or being childless. Fertility is below the replacement rate. Populations shrink.

But such culturally defined preferences might change. Perhaps it might become fashionable again to have many children (just as it became fashionable in the post WW II baby-boom)[8]. Perhaps people in wealthy countries will become fed up with the competitive race for ever more expensive consumption. Were this to happen, one would have to revise the forecast of world population growth coming to an end by 2150 with 11 billion humans populating the planet. Instead of 11 billion, the population could thus amount to 17 billion persons. Who knows? And, of course, a world of 11 billion inhabitants does differ substantially from one with 17 billion inhabitants. Whether we will have the one or the other depends on human choice.

Yet this is merely the quantitative aspect of human procreation. Until now, the qualitative aspect was not accessible to human influence. One could not decide on the nature of the offspring one was to have. One may do so today, even by using just those technologies that are widely available already.

Today one may come to know the gender of an embryo and, thus, of a future off-spring at a very early stage of its existence. The relevant technology is widely accessible. In all countries of the world, there is a preference for children being male. In some poorer countries (like India, China or Egypt) this preference is pronounced. As abortions are available too, female embryos tend to be aborted much more frequently than male embryos. In poorer countries the result shows in statistics. It is a widening deficit in the number of female infants. In the future, this imbalance between male and female offspring will make it difficult for males to find spouses. This could prove destabilising. Unattached young males are a prominent and notorious source of trouble.

Artificial insemination is yet another technology already at hand and widely practised. Yet, we still know very little about the long-term consequences of its wider use. What is certain is that it will further weaken the already very tenuous line between sexual activity and procreation. Shopping around for suitable genetic material, either in the form of egg cells or sperm, might become more common. Not only personal preferences and fads might guide the selection, but eventually, politics might intervene too.

It has become possible to enhance bodily growth. Just as there is a preference for male children, there is a universal preference for being tall. Most human needs, however, grow exponentially with human height: apartments and houses,

8 There are signs of this happening already. In the wealthiest countries that are bellwethers so to say, fertility rates are on the rise again. This is the case for example in the United States and in the Scandinavian countries (see chapter 4).

food, textiles to cover the body, cars and buses, etc. Maintenance of humans is thus more expensive the taller these human beings are.[9] Should governments wish to prevent such disproportionate rise in consumption? Would they feel tempted, therefore, to forbid growth enhancement of children? Or might they even go further and come to insist on a general height limit for children in view of the savings that could be realised by such a policy?

In fields other than the one of human procreation, no socially or politically acceptable rules are available, either, for dealing with the consequences of some new medical technologies. Human lives can be prolonged by various implants and machines. Some of these gadgets and interventions are very expensive. Should society accept that such technologies become available just to those wealthy enough to pay for them? If, on the other hand, everyone would become entitled to use these technologies for the prolongation of human life, who would then cover the vast expenses that are bound to ensue?

Traffic in human organs is against the law in all states of the world. Yet there is a steep demand in wealthy countries for the implant of kidneys. Thousands of patients are on the waiting list for such an operation. They are willing to pay large sums for jumping the line. As a consequence, there is a thriving market for the illegal donation and the illegal implant of kidneys. In very poor countries, a donor may receive the equivalent of a life's earnings for having one of his kidneys cut out and sent to a recipient in a far away and wealthy country. How is one to deal with this problem? Can one accept that a market has sprung up and continues to function notwithstanding the violation of basic moral principles?

As mentioned, all of these technologies are at hand, and are already being used widely. Technologies still in the pipeline present us with even more troubling prospects.[10] The human genome will become the object of manipulation. This is inevitable. Hard to dismiss motives will justify the crossing of this dangerous threshold. Once it becomes possible to eliminate, via genetic manipulation, a gene that causes a hereditary disease, who could justify or demand not manipulating genes in such a way that this disease is not transmitted from parents to children? If the insertion of a gene can heal insulin insufficiency, who would stand in the way of this being actually done so as to save persons otherwise condemned to death or the miserable existence of a lifelong diabetic?

But once this threshold is crossed, and once one has started to manipulate the human genome, where is one to stop? If it becomes possible to eliminate heredi-

9 Short people are discriminated against. SHRIMPS (=~ severely height reduced individual male persons) have worse professional chances and are less favoured by potential sexual partners.

10 Many of the things that genetic engineering is feared to do, might be done by neuroscience first.

tary disease in one's future children, why should it be forbidden to equip them with special desired traits; such as higher intelligence, red, dark or blond hair, greater height, or a pleasing physiognomy?

What can be done, will be done
Consider these articles from the November 28, 2002, New York Times:
1) A group of American...biologists debating whether to create a human/mouse hybrid...animals born...would be chimeras...the outcome of such an experiment cannot be predicted.
2) An Italian doctor announced... that a woman would give birth to a clone in January 2003

Humans have become empowered to change the biological base of their existence.[11] In doing so, seemingly innocuous and reasonable individual decisions can add up to a common disaster. Why not have a boy instead of a girl as the first child? Why forgo artificial insemination if the partner cannot reproduce? Why not pay for a kidney if one has the money to do so and when there is someone willing to provide one of his or her own at that price? Yet, as we have seen, such individual acts might, in their sum, very well result in problems we are not able to cope with. To do so, we would need a powerful and efficient political authority which could rule effectively on the use of genetic engineering. Yet, at present, even states cannot cope with the issue. What leverage they had in this field, has been eroded and it is being by-passed thanks to globalisation.

No amount of money, efforts and vigilance has permitted the US, for example, to curtail the flow of hard drugs entering its territory. The traffic of hard drugs has become a global problem and it, thus, would have to be tackled on a global scale. Yet there are no authorities in place to do so. The United Nations Drug Control Programme is certainly not up to that task.

But, even if international organisations could acquire such authority they still would lack political direction on what to do. The problems involved in genetic engineering may, once again, illustrate that point. Genetic engineering will cer-

11 "Political freedom has meant the freedom to pursue those ends our nature has established for us. Those ends are not rigidly determined. Human nature is very plastic... But it is not infinitely malleable... elements remain constant... particularly our species-typical gamut of emotional responses ... the safe bastion that permits us to connect – potentially – with other human beings." (Francis Fukuyama 2002, Our posthuman society).

tainly have a vast impact. Nonetheless, it will be hard to control politically. Genetically engineered living things like plants, bacteria and animals have been and will continue to be patented. This patented genetic material therefore no longer belongs to humankind, as such, as did other genetic material. It belongs to a company which will decide on its price and uses. This company will try to create and expand the markets for the products it has developed. And it will be politically difficult to interfere with that market-mechanism. Just as hard drugs will be sold (illegally) as long as there is a sufficiently strong demand, such new genetically engineered products will have their market, regardless of whether this is desirable and adds to the overall well-being of society. These negative overall implications could become the more severe, the more specific and targeted the effect of drugs will become – as it will. Who would still work if the same satisfaction derived from work can be obtained by popping a pill? Which general would refuse feeding courage enhancing pills to his soldiers? Which prison would resist mixing material that enhances passivity and obedience into the food?

Genetic engineering, much more than information technology, will determine the future of society. But, while these prospects which have been opened by biological science are the most spectacular and unsettling ones, in other fields, too, developments will outpace our capacity to cope and to guide via politics. As mentioned, we already are at a loss about what to do with nuclear fission. The technology has been with us for half a century. It still threatens our survival. We still have not managed to contain this threat. We have failed to cope with even more simple technology. We do not even know how to handle the proliferation of small arms, and do not have the political/administrative tools to slow it down. We are not, and will not be, able to efficiently deal with the threat of global warming; or with the phenomenon of mass migration from poor into wealthy countries.

Lest the picture painted is too dismal, we should not ignore the other side of the coin; the prospects of radically positive changes in the circumstances of human existence: bringing to life the barren and frozen regions of the world; using information technology to weld a truly global community; applying high tech to thwart crime and terror; producing more with less inputs; reversing environmental degradation; transforming slimy, torrid slums into liveable cities; expanding education and the appreciation of arts; and so on.

But all of these positive and negative options thus opened transgress the present traditional capacity of social/political control. Up to now, no tools have been available to squeeze the scope of options back into a band within which we have learned to manage things.

Possible options transgress the boundaries of political and social steerage

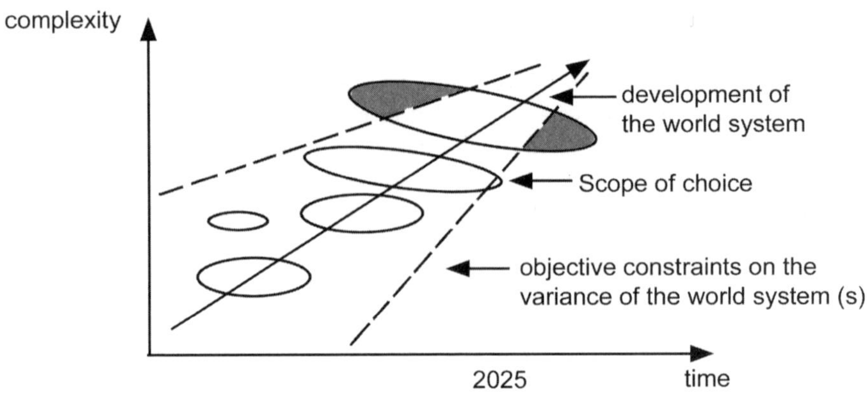

The base for even long term trends will thus have changed. Greater caution has therefore to be applied when projecting into the future the trends we have gleaned from the observation of the past. The surprise would be if the future would be surprise free. All we can surmise with some certainty is that – as it is – global politics (in its many incarnations and on its many levels) is ill equipped to deal with many of the consequences of this widening of human choice.

Even before having been transformed by homo sapiens, the earth had been a very complex system. Adding six billion humans with a rapacious appetite for all sorts of things has made it more so. The question is how such a complex system can be kept stable and evolving. Who or what will do the necessary steering and will effect the necessary changes and adjustments?

One may, perhaps, see things from a very remote perspective and not bother about such details. The whole earth might be defined as nothing but a complex, self-regulating system. As long as the human species persists, the system has functioned. It has adjusted and learned from this or that disaster, and adjusted and learned from this or that success.

But we are not permitted such an Olympic view of things. For the minor details neglected in such a detached vision implies the question, for instance, of whether the adjustment would include, or would have included, five of the six billion human inhabitants of earth being wiped out. There is an even more basic reason why such a view of things is inappropriate: The feed-back loop of adjustment passes through human brains. The global system adjusts and evolves because humans reflect upon what they experience, and because they can arrive at decisions as to how to shape the system according to their wishes. In particular, they may, through their collective resolve, reverse many of even the long term trends that, at first sight, seemed irreversible[12]. In short, politics intervene and the issue, thus, is the one of the future place, function and form of political governance on a global scale.

In its 2003 "World Development Report" the IBRD has reproduced, in the form of two graphs, the institutions and processes that are needed for effective governance to come to exist.

If we scrutinise the two tables below, it becomes obvious that the values, processes and institutions needed for effective governance are still largely absent on a global scale.

Over the last centuries, this issue of political direction and governance has gained prominence. In the early Middle Ages it was not that important. Politics were about who could kill whom in order to appropriate this or that parcel of the earth's surface. The outcome of such contests did not change the global order of things. It did not make much difference whether this or that tribe, this or that petty kingdom had prevailed in a battle.[13] This did not very much reduce or augment the food available for each head of the worlds population. It did not decrease or increase very much the pool of knowledge; it did not affect the level of technology used in the production of everyday goods. In that distant past, the feed-back loop of conscious political intervention was not that relevant for the actual shape of the global system.

Now it is. Let us assume – for instance – that in view of the many risks and uncertainties involved in this technology, humans resolve by a collective political decision to forego the use of genetic engineering. This would certainly have a deep impact upon the global order. Or we might, on the other hand, in the vein of science fiction, project a "dystopic" scenario of an evil ruler, deciding to make all of the world population, except his own subjects, extinct by a genetically engineered disease that results in infertility.

---

12 One prominent example we have examined is environmental degradation.

13 "Europe had dominated world affairs from the end of the 15th century to the end of the 20th century. What form of world order will come in next place is not a "natural state" of humankind; but a – late – child of the European-liberal order. (Michael Howard 2000).

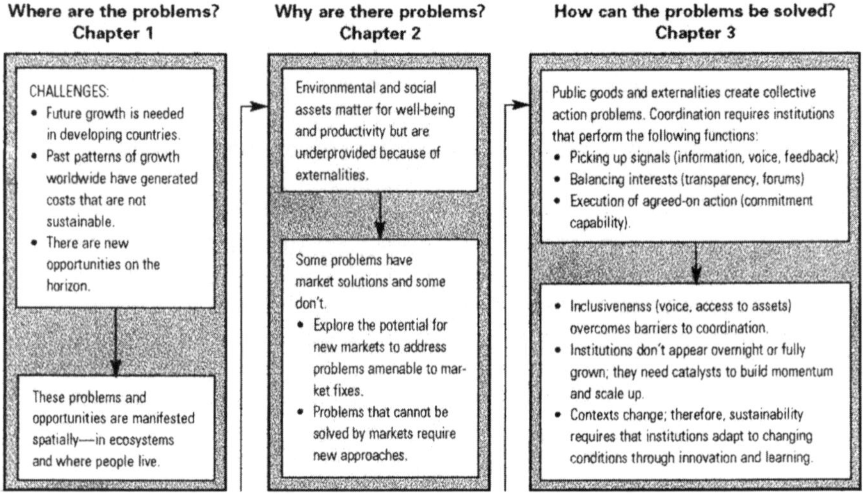

Source: IBRD 2003

Social norms, values and organisations for co-ordinating human behaviour

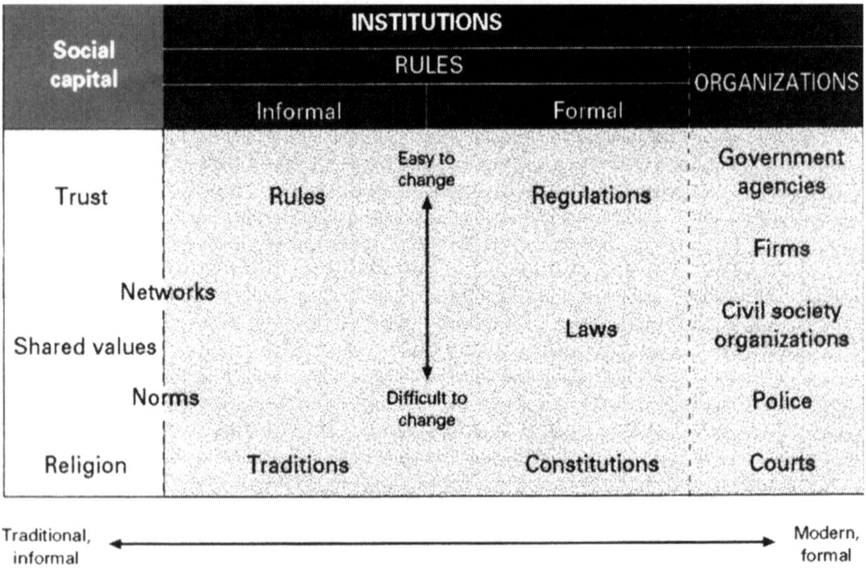

Source: IBRD 2003

Global political governance might result in – or be based upon – a world-wide competitive arms race involving all kinds of weapons of mass destruction. Or it might be based upon, and guided by, the aim to reduce the vast gap between rich and poor nations. Or it might be mainly guided by the aim to optimise the ecological foundation of human existence. On the other hand, it might be informed by the ambition of each "global player" to appropriate the maximum of scarce resources and to deny their use to a competitor.

Obviously, all these options can be taken. Some of them, though, would disrupt the continuity in the global evolution. One may hope, perhaps, that in the very long term, humans will have learned from past failures. One may hope that they will correct for noxious options taken in the past; and that they might have come to conclude, for example, that competitive arms races are not a suitable instrument for building a global order. But one cannot be that certain that this conclusion would be actually drawn.[14] In complex systems and in human affairs too, many processes are "path dependent". Once a specific path has been chosen, it becomes difficult to turn back and decide on an alternate option. And even if such corrections could be made in the end, much could have been lost in the time in between.

The world is a highly complex system based upon past efforts of humans that have permitted the species to multiply by six; and to double life expectancy within just one century. This complex system is very vulnerable (and will become even more vulnerable the more people that inhabit earth; and the wealthier these inhabitants)[15]. Therefore "wrong" choices can have disastrous consequences.

The "right" choices are, however, not predefined; neither in their substance nor in the way they are made. They are, to a large extent, the outcome of a political process. They result from the interplay of the various "actors" in the global system. We are far from having the tools to prompt, facilitate and guide such a common action.

---

14 As seen from the European perspective, the US has failed to draw such lessons from the past; as – at the dawn of the 21st century – they now aim to reform the world order to what it had been at the pinnacle of the imperialist era at the end of the 19th century.

15 The breakdown of the Roman Empire, often used as a metaphor, remains, nonetheless, a valid warning about what could be at stake; though fifteen hundred years ago, the losses of such a breakdown were still minor compared to what they would be today.

Bibliography

Abramovitz, M., 1986, Catching Up, Forging Ahead, and Falling Behind, Journal of Economic History, vol 36, pp 385-406

Abramovitz, M., 1993, The Search for the Sources of Growth: Areas of Ignorance, Old and New, Journal of Economic History, 53: 217-43

Abramovitz, M., and P. David, 1996, Convergence and Deferred Catch – Up: Productivity Leadership and the Waning of American Exceptionalism, in R. Landau, T. Taylor, and G. Wright (eds.) The Mosaic of Economic Growth, Stanford, Stanford University Press, pp 21-62

Acemoglu, D., S. Johnson, J. Robinson, 2001, The Colonial Origins of Comparative Development : An Empirical Investigation, American Economic Review 91, December 2001

Adams, R., 2003. Economic Growth, Inequality, and Poverty: Findings from a New Data – Set, WP 2972, World Bank, Washington DC

Adler, E., P. Haas, 1992, Epistemic Communities, World Order and the Creation of a Reflective Research Programme, International Organisation, 46 (1), pp 367-390

Aglietta, M., 1976, Régulation et crises du capitalisme : l´experience des Etats Unis, Paris, Calman & Levy

Aiginger, K., M. Landesmann, 2002, Competitive Economic Performance: USA versus EU, Wien, The Vienna Institute for International Economic Studies, WP 291, November 2002

Akerlof, G., Social Distance and Social Decisions, Econometrica, September 1997

Alyson, J., K. Bailes, 1996, NATO – towards a new Synthesis, Survival, autumn 1996, pp 27-39

Andreas, P., R. Price, 2001, From War Fighting to Crime Fighting: Transforming the American National Security State, International Studies Review, 3/3, Fall 2001, pp 31-52

Andreoni, J., A. Levinson, 1998, The Simple Analytics of the Environmental Kuznets Curve, National Bureau of Economic Research, working paper 6739, Cambridge, Mass.

Angell, N., 1910, The Great Illusion: Study of the Relation of Military Power in Relations to Their Economic and Social Advantage, London, Heinemann.

Arbeitsgemeinschaft für Kriegursachenforschung (AKUF), 2002, das Kriegsgeschehen 2001 – Daten und Tendenzen der Kriege und bewaffneten Konflikte, Opladen, Leske & Budrich

Art, R., and K. Waltz (eds.) 1993, The Use of Force: Military Power and International Politics, Lanham, University Press of America

Asam, S., 2000, Poverty from the Wealth of Nations: Integration and Polarization in the Global Economy since 1760, New York, St Martins Press

Atwood, M., 2003, Oryx and Crake, London, Doubleday

Auty, R., (ed.), 2001 Resource Abundance and Economic Development, Oxford, Oxford University Press

Badie, B., 1995, La Fin des Territoires : Essais sur Désordre International et sur l'Utilité Social du Respect, Paris, Fayard

Bairoch, P., 1981, Disparities in the Economic Development since the Industrial Revolution, London, Macmillan

Bairoch, P., 1993, Economics and World History: Myths and Paradoxes, London, Harvester Wheatsheaf

Bassanini A., S. Scapetta, 2001, The Driving Forces of Economic Growth: Panel Evidence for the OECD Countries, OECD Economic Studies, No 33, Paris

Baumol, W., 1986, On the Possibility of Continuing Expansion of Finite Resources, Kyklos, 339:167 –79

Baumol, W., 2002, The Free Market Innovation Machine: Analysing the Growth Miracle of Capitalism, Princeton, Princeton University Press

Beck, U., 1994, Risikogesellschaft – Auf dem Weg in eine andere Moderne, Frankfurt, Suhrkamp

Beck, U., 1998, Was ist Globalisierung: Irrtümer des Globalismus – Antworten auf Globalisierung, Frankfurt a M., Suhrkamp

Beck, U., 2000, What is Globalisation? Oxford, Polity

Bell, D., 1973, The Coming Post – Industrial Society, New York, Basic Books

Bell, D., 1979, Cultural Contradictions of Capitalism, London, Heinemann Educational

Berger, P., 1994, The Gross National Product and the Gods, McKinsey Quarterly, No 1

Berger, P., S. Huntington, 2002, Many Globalisations – Cultural Diversity in the Contemporary World, New York, New York, Oxford University Press

Bergsten, C., America and Europe: Clash of the Titans, Foreign Affairs, 78/2, pp 20-34

Berman, P., 2003, Terror and Liberalism, New York, Norton

Bernauer, T., C. Achini, 2000, From Real to Virtual States? Integration of the World Economy and its Effects on Government Activity, European Journal of International Relations 6/2 pp 223-276

Bernstein, S., et al, 2000, God Gave Physics the Easy Problems – Adapting Social Science to an Unpredictable World, European Journal of International Relations, 6(1),

Bertrand, G., A. Michalski, L. Penck, 2000, Five Possible Futures for Europe, European Commission, Forward Studies Unit, Brussels

Betts, R., 2002, The Soft Underbelly of American Primacy: Traditional Advantages of Terror, Political Science Quarterly, 117/1, Nov 2002, pp 19-36

Betz, HG., 2002, Rechtspopulismus in Westeuropa: Aktuelle Entwicklungen und politische Bedeutung, Österreichische Zeitschrift für Politikwissenschaft 2002 2/3, pp. 251-264

Bhagwati, J., 1998, The Explanation, The New Republic, May 25, 1998, pp 32-35

Birdsall, N., A. Kelley, S. Sinding (eds), 2001, Population Matters: Demographic Change, Economic Growth and Poverty in the Developing World, Oxford, Oxford University Press

Blaney, D., N. Inayatullah, 2002, Neo-Modernisation? IR and the Inner Life of Modernisation Theory, European Journal of International Relations, 8/1, pp 103-137

Boot, M., 2003, The New American Way of War, Foreign Affairs, July/August, 2003

Botcheva, L., L. Martin, 2001, Institutional Effects of State Behaviour: Convergence or Divergence, International Studies Quarterly, 45, pp 1-26

Bobbitt, P., 2002, The Shield of Achilles: War, Peace and the Course of History, New York, Knopf

Boeri, T., 2001, Does Europe Need a Harmonised Social Policy ? Paper at the ANB – Volkswirtschaftliche Tagung, Vienna, June 2002

Boswell, J., 1988, The Kindness of Strangers, New York

Bourdieu, P., 1996, Le mythe de la mondialisation et l'état social européen, http://sami.is.free.fr/oeuvres/bourdieu

Bowles, P., 2002, Asia`s post – crisis regionalism : bringing the state back in, keeping the (United) States out, Review of International Political Economy, 9/2, summer 2002, pp 230-256

Bracken, P., 1999, Fire in the East: The Rise of Asian Military Power and the Second Nuclear Age, Harper, New York

Braudel, F., 1982, Civilisation and Capitalism ; 15th – 18th Century, New York, Harper & Row

Brown, E., H. Phelps, 1968, A Century of Pay. The Course of Pay and Production in France, Germany, Sweden, the UK and in the USA, 1860-1960, London, Macmillan

Brown, L., 1992, Vital Signs : The Trends that Shape our Future, New York, Norton

Bundesministerium für Finanzen, 1987, Staatliche Verteilungspolitik in Österreich, Bericht an den Nationalrat, 2e Auflage, Juni 1987

Burstein, D., 1991, Euroquake: Europe's Explosive Economic Challenge Will Change the World, New York, Simon &Schuster

Buzan, B., R. Little, 1998, What World History Tells us about International Relations Theory; manuscript, IRA Conference, Vienna, Sept 1998

Buzan, B., R. Little, 2000, International Systems in the World History: Re-Making the Study of International Relations, Oxford, Oxford University Press

Calleo, D., 2002, Rethinking Europe's Future, Princeton, Princeton University Press,

Canetti, E., 1960, Masse und Macht, Hamburg, Claassen

Cantwell, J., G. Santangelo, 2000, Capitalism, Profits and Innovation in the New Techno – Economic Paradigm, Journal of Evolutionary Economics, 10, 131-157

Cardoso, F., 1972, Dependency and Development in Latin America, New Left Review, 74, July-August 1972

Carlson, M., L. Hernandez, 2002, Determinants and Repercussions of the Composition of Capital Inflows, IMF WP No 86/ 2002, Washington DC

Carson, R., 1962, Silent Spring, Boston Houghton Mifflin

Chandler, T., 1987, Four Thousand Years of Urban Growth: A Historical Census, Lewiston NY, Edwin Mellen Press

Cirincione, J., 2002, Deadly Arsenals, Washington, Carnegie Endowment for International Peace

Clark, A- M., 2001, Diplomacy and Conscience: Amnesty International and Changing Human Rights Norms, Princeton, Princeton University Press

Clausewwitz, G., 1915, Grundgedanken über Krieg und Kriegsführung, Leipzig, Insel Verlag

Coleman, J., 1988; Social Capital in the Creation of Human Capital, American Journal of Sociology, 1988/89 supplement, pp 94-120

Cohen, D., 1997, Fehldiagnose Globalisierung, Frankfurt, Campus

Cox, M., 2002, September 11th and the US Hegemony: Or Will the 21st Century be American Too? International Studies Perspectives (2002) 3., pp 53-70

Crafts, N., 1998, Forging Ahead and Falling Behind: The Rise and Relative Decline of the First Industrial Nation, Journal of Economic Perspectives, 12(2), pp 193-210

Crafts, N., 2000, Globalization and Growth in the Twentieth Century, Washington DC, International Monetary Fund, WP/00/44

Dahl, R., 1971, Polyarchy, Participation and Opposition, Newhaven, Yale University Press
Dahl, R., 1998, On Democracy, Newhaven, Yale University Press
Dahl, R., 1999, Can International Organisations be Democratic? A Sceptics View, in Shapiro, I., C. Hacker-Cordon, (eds), Democracy's Edges, pp 19-36 Cambridge, Cambridge University Press
Dahrendorf, R., 1997, An der Schwelle zum autoritärem Jahrhundert die Zeit, vom 14.11. 1997
Daubon, R., H. Saunders, 2002, Operationalising Social Capital: A Strategy to Enhance Communities "Capacity to Concert", International Studies Perspectives, 2002/3, pp 176-191
Dawkins, R., 1986, The Blind Watchmaker, New York, Norton
Dawkins, R. 1996, Climbing Mount Improbable, New York, Norton
Dasgupta P., and M. Weal, 1992, On Measuring the Quality of Life, World Development, 20, pp 119-31
De la Torre, A., E. M. Yeyati, , S. Schmukler, 2003, Living and Dying with Hard Pegs : The Rise and Fall of Argentina's Currency Board, WP 2980, World Bank, Washington D.C.
De Haan, A., 1999, Livelihoods and Poverty: The Role of Migration – A Critical Review of the Migration Literature, Journal of Development Studies, 36(2), pp 1-47
De Soto, H., 2000, The Mystery of Capital : Why Capitalism Triumphs in the West and Fails Everywhere Else, London, Bantam Press
Deutsch, K., 1953, Nationalism and Social Communication – an Inquiry into the Foundation of Nationality, New York, Wiley
Devetak, R., 1995, The Project of Modernity and International Relations Theory, Millenium –Journal of International Studies, 24/1, pp 27-51
Diamond, J., 1997, Guns, Germs and Steel: The Fate of Human Societies, New York, Norton
Diamond, L., 2002, Elections without Democracy: Thinking about Hybrid Regimes, Journal of Democracy, 13/2 pp 21-35
Dillard, M., J. Hennard, 2002, The Approaching Age of Virtual Nations, The Futurist, July-August 2002,
Dombrowski, P., 1998, Haute Finance and High Theory: Recent Scholarship on Global Financial Relations, Mershon International Studies Review 1998(42), pp 1-28
Downs, A., 1957, An Economic Theory of Democracy, New York, Harper
Doyle, M., N., Sambanis, 2001, International Peace Building : A Theoretical and Quantitative Analysis, American Political Science Review, 94/4

Drucker, P., 1994, The Age of Social Transformation, Atlantic Monthly, vol. 274/4, pp 53-94
Duffield, J., 2001, Transatlantic Relations after the Cold War: Theory, Evidence, and the Future, International Studies Perspectives, 2001/2, 93-115
Durning, A., H. Brough, 1992, Taking Stock: Animal Farming and the Environment, New York, World Watch Institute
Easterly, W., 2001, The Elusive Quest for Growth: Economists' Adventures and Misadventures in the Tropics, Cambridge Mass, MIT Press
Easterly, W., R. Levine, 2001, What we have learned from a decade of empirical research on growth? It's not the factor accumulation. Stylized facts and growth models, The World Bank Economic Review, 2/2001, pp 177-219
Easterly, W., 2002, Tropics, Germs and Crops: How Endowments Influence Economic Development, Washington DC, NBER Working Paper 9106,
Easterly, W., 2002, Inequality Does Cause Underdevelopment: New Evidence, Center for Global Development, Working Paper 1, Washington DC
Easterly, W., 2002, The Cartel of Good Intentions, Foreign Policy, July/August 2002
Eatwell, J., V. Taylor, 2000, Global Finance at Risk: The Case for International Regulation, New York, New Press
Edelmann, G., 1987, Neural Darwinism: The Theory of Neural Group Selection, New York, Basic Books
Edison, H., C. Reinhart, 2000, Capital Controls During Financial Crises: The Case of Malaysia and Thailand, New York, The Federal Reserve Board, International Finance Study Papers, No 662
Ehrlich, P., 1968, The Population Bomb, New York, Ballantine Books
Eichengreen, B, 1996, Institutions and Economic Growth: Europe after World War II, in N. Crafts and G. Toniolo (eds.), Economic Growth in Europe since 1945, Cambridge, Cambridge University Press, pp 38-72
Eichengreen, B., (ed) 1998, Transatlantic Economic Relations in the Post – Cold – War – Era, New York, Council on Foreign Relations
Eichler, M., 2002, The State of Gender in IR, manuscript, for a ws of ÖIIP, April 2003, Vienna
Elias, N., 1939, Über den Prozess der Zivilisation, Suhrkamp, Frankfurt
Elmeskov, J., 2002, Structural Reforms and Competitiveness: Where Does Europe Stand Today? Paper at the ANB conference, Vienna, November 2002
Engen, E., and J. Skinner, 1996, Taxation and Economic Growth, National Bureau of Economics, Working Paper No 5826
Etzioni, A., 1993, The Spirit of Community: Rights, Responsibilities and the Communitarian Agenda, New York, Crown Publishers

Etzioni, A., 1996, The New Golden Rule – Community and Morality in a Democratic Society, New York, Basic Books

European Commission, 1999, Forward Studies Unit, Scenarios for Europe 2010, EC, Brussels

European Commission, 2000, European Trend Chart on Innovation: the European Innovation Scoreboard, DG Enterprise

Evangelista, M., 1999, Unarmed Forces: The Transnational Movement to End the Cold War. Ithaca, Cornell University Press

Evers, A., H. Nowotny 1987, Über den Umgang mit Unsicherheit – Die Entdeckung der Gestaltbarkeit von Gesellschaft, Frankfurt, Suhrkamp

Falk, R., 1999, Predatory Globalisation: A Critique, Cambridge, Cambridge University Press

Fallows, J., 1993, How the World Works, Atlantic Monthly, Dec 1993

FAO, 2000, The State of Food Insecurity in the World, Rome

Feng, Ai, 2001, Political Freedom, Political Instability, and Political Uncertainty: A Study of Political Institutions and Private Investment in Developing Countries, International Studies Quarterly, 45, pp 271-294

Florini, A., 2000, The Third Force: The Rise of Transnational Civil Society, Washington DC, Carnegie Endowment for International Peace

Ford, J., 2003, A Social Theory of Trade Regime Change: GATT to WTO, International Studies Review, 4/3, fall 2002, pp 115-140

Fox, J., 2001, Religion as an Overlooked Element of International Relations, International Studies Review, 3/3, fall 2001, pp 53-73

Frank, R., P. Cook, 1995, The Winner – Take – All Society: Why the Few at the Top Get So Much More than the Rest of Us, New York, The Free Press

Frantz, D., C. Collins, 2000, Celebration USA: Living in Disney's Brave New Town, New York, Henry Holt

Freeman, R., (ed) 1994, Working Under Different Rules, Boston Bureau of Economic Research, Boston

Frey, E., 2003, Feuding Friends: Transatlantic Trade Relations and US Trade Policy during the Clinton Presidency, Dissertation, University of Vienna, Austria

Friedman, T., 2000, The Lexus and the Olive Tree, New York, Farrar, Strauss Giroux

Friedrichs, J., 2002, The Meaning of New Medievalism, European Journal of International Relations, 7/4, pp 475-502

Fukuyama, F., 1992, The End of History and the Last Man, London, Penguin,

Fukuyama, F., 1999, The Great Disruption, Atlantic Monthly, vol 283/5, pp 55-81

Fukuyama, F., 2000, Second Thoughts – The Last Man in a Bottle, The National Interest, Sommer 1999, pp 16 –33

Fukuyama, F., 2000, Social Capital, in L.E Harrison, S.P. Huntington, Culture Matters: How Values Shape Human Progress, New York, Basic Books

Fukuyama, F., 2002, Our Posthuman Society: Consequences of the Biotechnology Revolution, New York, Farrar Strauss and Giroux

Gabriele, A., 2002, S&T Policies and Technical Progress in China, Review of International Political Economy, 9/2, summer 2002, pp 319-358

Gaddis, J.,1999, Living in Candlestick Park, Atlantic Monthly, vol. 283/4, pp 65-78

Gallarotti, G., 1991, The Limits of International Organisations: Systematic Failure in the Management of International Organisations, International Organisation 45 (2), pp 183-220

Gallup, J., J. Sachs, 1998, Geography and Economic Growth, Paper presented at the World Bank Annual Conference on Economic Development, Washington DC, April 20-21, http://www.worldbank.org/html/rad/abcde/html/sachs.htm

Garrett; G., 1998, Global Markets and National Politics: Collision Course or Virtuous Circle? International Organisation, 52/4, autumn 1998, pp 787-824

Gates, J., 2000, Democracy at Risk: Rescuing Main Street from Wall Street, Cambridge, Mass., Perseus Books

Geithner, T., G. Nankani, 2002, Market Access for Developing Country Exports – Selected Issues, September 26, IMF and IBRD, Washington

Gellner, E., 1983, Nations and Nationalism; Ithaca, Cornell University Press

Gellner, E., 1993, Nationalism and the Development of the European Societies, in: Ivonen, J. (ed.), The Future of the Nation State in Europe, North Hampton, Edward Elgar

Gerschenkron, A., 1962, Economic Backwardness in Historical Perspective, Cambridge Mass, Belknap Press

Giddens, A., 1990, The Consequences of Modernity, Stanford, Stanford University Press

Giddens, A., 1991, Modernity and Self – Identity, Cambridge; Polity Press

Gilpin, R., 1987, The Political Economy of International Relations, Princeton, Princeton University Press

Gilpin, R., 2001, Global Political Economy: Understanding the International Economic Order, Princeton, Princeton University Press

Glaeser, E., A. Schleifer, 2001, The Rise of the Regulatory State, National Bureau of Economic Research, working paper 8650, Cambridge, Mass.

Gordon, R., 1999, US Economic Growth Since 1870: One Big Wave?, American Economic Review, Papers and Proceedings, vol. 89(2) pp 123-28

Gordon. D., 1996, Underpaid Workers – Bloated Corporations, Dissent, spring 1996, pp 23-35

Gordon, R., 2000, Does the new economy measure up to the great inventions of the past, Journal of Economic Perspectives 14 (4), pp 49-74

Gore, A., 1992, Earth in the Balance: Ecology and the Human Spirit, Boston Houghton Mifflin

Grossman, L., 1996, The Electronic Republic: Re-Shaping Democracy in the Information Age, New York, Viking

Guehenno J-M., 1995, The End of the Nation State, Minnesota, University of Minnesota Press

Gurr, T., 1974, Persistence and Change in Political Systems, 1800-1971, American Political Science Review, 68/4, December 1974, pp 1500 ff

Gurr, T., 1994, Ethnopolitical Conflict and the Changing World System; International Studies Quarterly 38, pp 347-377

Haas, E., 1964, Beyond the Nation State, Functionalism and International Organisations, Stanford, Stanford University Press

Habermas, J., 1968, Erkenntnis und Interesse, Frankfurt, Suhrkamp

Habermas, J., 1984, The Theory of Communicative Action, Boston, Beacon Press

Habermas, J., 1996, The European Nation State – Its Achievements and its Limits. On the Past and Future of Sovereignty and Citizenship, in Gopal, B. (ed) Mapping the Nation, London, Verso

Hacker, A., 1992, Two Nations – Black and White, Separate, Hostile and Unequal, New York, Scribner

Haggard, S., B. Simmons, 1987, Theories of International Regimes, International Organisation, 41, pp 491-518

Hall, R. B., 2003, The Discursive Destruction of the Asian Development Model, International Studies Quarterly, 47/ pp 71-99

Hann, C., E., Dunn, (eds.), 1996, Civil Society: Challenging Western Models, New York, Routledge

Hardin, G., J., Baden, 1977, Managing the Commons, San Francisco, W.H. Freeman

Hassner, P., 1992, Nous Entrons dans un Nouveau Moyen Age, le Monde, 27th Oct., p 2

Hayek, F., 1945, The Use of Knowledge in Society, American Economic Review, 35 (4), pp 519-530

Head, S., 1996, The New, Ruthless Economy, New York Review of Books, February 1996

Heilig, G., and others, 2001, Can China Feed Itself?, IIASA, Wien

Held, D., A. McGrew, D. Goldblatt, J. Perraton, 1999, Global Transformation: Politics, Economics and Culture, Policy Press

Held, D., A. Mc Grew (eds.), 2000, The Global Transformation Reader: An Introduction to the Globalisation Debate, Cambridge, Polity Press

Helleiner, E., 2002, Economic Nationalism as a Challenge to Economic Liberalism? Lessons from the 19th Century, International Studies Quarterly, 46, pp 307-329

Herbst, J., 2000, States and Power in Africa: Comparative Lessons in Authority and Control, Princeton, Princeton University Press

Hirsch, F., 1976, Social Limits to Growth, Cambridge, Harvard University Press

Hobsbawm, E., 1968, Industry and Empire, London, Weidenfeld & Nicolson

Hobsbawm, E., 1992, Nations and Nationalism Since 1780, Cambridge, Cambridge University Press

Hobsbawm, E., 1994, The Age of Extremes, New York, Pantheon Books

Hoffman, S., 1977, An American Social Science: International Relations, Daedalus, 106 (3), pp 41-60

Hoffmann, S., 1992, Delusions of World Order, New York Review of Books, 9 April, 1992

Hopkins, T., I. Wallerstein, (eds.), 1980, Processes and the World System, Beverly Hills, Sage

Howard, M., 2000, The Invention of Peace: Reflections on War and the International Order, Newhaven, Yale University Press

Howard, P., 2001, The Collapse of the Common Good – How America's Lawsuit Culture Undermines Our Freedom, New York, Ballantine

Hunter Wade, R., 2002, US hegemony and the World Bank: the fight over people and ideas, Review of International Political Economy, 9/2, pp 201-229

Huntington, S., 1991, The Third Wave: Democratisation in the Late Twentieth Century, Norman, University of Oklahoma Press

Huntington, S., 1993, The Clash of Civilisations, Foreign Affairs, summer 1993, vol. 73, pp 22 –28

IBRD World Development Report 2003

ICRC Forum, 2000, War Money and Survival, ICRC, Geneva

Illich, I., 1971, De-Schooling Society, New York, Harper

Izetbegovich, A., 1984, Islam between East and West, Indianapolis, American Trust Publications

Jervis, R., 1997, System Effects: Complexity in Political and Social Life, Princeton University Press, Princeton

Johnston, A., 2001, Treating International Institutions as Social Environments, International Studies Quarterly, 2001/45, pp 487-515

Jorgenson, D., and K. Stroh, 1999, Information Technology and Growth, American Economic Review, Papers and Proceedings, vol. 89, pp 109-115

Kagan, R., 2002, Warrior Politics – Why Leadership Demands a Pagan Ethos, New York, Random House

Kahn, H., 1970, The Emerging Japanese Super State – Challenge and Response, Englewood Cliffs, Prentice Hall

Kahneman, D., A. Tversky, 2000, Choices, Values and Frames, Cambridge, Cambridge University Press

Kaminsky, G. Reinhart, 1999, The Twin Crises: The Causes of Banking and Balance of Payment Problems, American Economic Review, vol. 89, pp 473-500

Kanbur, R., N. Lustig 1999, Why Inequality is Back on the Agenda, Annual Conference on Development Economics, World Bank, Washington

Kaplan, R., The Coming Anarchy, The Atlantic Monthly, February 1994

Kapstein, E., 1996, Workers and the World Economy, Foreign Affairs, May/June 1996, pp 16-37

Kaufman, G., 1998, Central Banks, Asset Bubbles and Financial Stability, Paper at the Conference on Transitional Economies, Dubrovnik, summer 1998

Kennedy, P., D. Messner, F. Nuschler, 2002, Global Trends and Global Governance, London, Sterling

Kennedy, P., 1989, The Rise and Fall of Great Powers; Economic Change and Military Conflict from 1500 to 2000, New York, Vintage Books

Keohane, R., 1984, After Hegemony: Cooperation and Discord in the World Political Economy, Princeton, Princeton University Press

Keohane, R., L. Martin, 1995, The Promise of Institutionalist Theory, International Security 20, pp 39-51

Keynes, J. M., 1930, Economic Possibilities for our Grandchildren, in Essays in Persuasion, New York, Norton

Kindleberger, C., 1978, Manias, Panics and Crashes. History of Financial Crisis, Basic Books; London

Kindleberger C., 1996, World Economic Primacy, New York, Oxford University Press

Klotz, A., 2002, Transnational Activism and Global Transformations: The Anti-apartheid and Abolitionist Experiences, European Journal of International Relations, 8/1, pp 49-76

Knack, S., P. Keefer, 1997, Does Social Capital Have an Economic Pay – Off? A Cross – Country Investigation, Quarterly Journal of Economics 112 (4), pp 1251-1288

Kondratieff, N., 1984, The Long Wave Cycle, New York, Richardson and Snyder

Krasner, S., 1999, Globalisation and Sovereignty, in Smith, D., Solinger, D., Topik S., (eds.) States and Sovereignty in the Global Economy, London, Routledge

Kristol, I., 2001, Is Technology a Threat to Liberal Society, The Public Interest, 143, Spring 2001, pp 45-52

Krugman, P., 1994, Competitiveness – A Dangerous Obsession, Foreign Affairs, 73(2), 28-44

Krugman, P., Nov 1996, What Economists Can Learn from Evolutionary Theorists, http://web.mit.edu/krugman/www/evolute/html

Krugman, P., For Richer: How the Permissive Capitalism of the Boom Destroyed American Equality, New York Times Magazine, 20. October 2002

Kuhn, T., 1962, The Structure of Scientific Revolution, Chicago, University of Chicago Press

Kupchan, C., 2002, The End of the American Era: US Foreign Policy and the Geo-Politics of the Twenty – First Century, New York, Knopf

Kurth, J., 1998, Inside the Cave: The Banality of I.R. Studies, The National Interest, No 53, fall 1998, pp 29-41

Kuttner, R., 1984, The Economic Illusion – False Choices Between Prosperity and Social Justice, Philadelphia, University of Pennsylvania Press

Kuttner, R., 1999, Everything for Sale, Chicago, Chicago University Press

La Beber, W., 2002, The Post September 11th Debate, Political Science Quarterly, 117/1, Nov 2002, pp 1-17

Lakatos, I., 1970, "Falsification and the Methodology of Scientific Research Programmes". In "Criticism and the Growth of Knowledge", Lakatos, I. and Musgrave, A. (eds.), pp 91 –196, New York, Cambridge University Press

Laqueur, W., 1999, The New Terrorism, Oxford, Oxford University Press

Landes, D., 1997, The Wealth and the Poverty of Nations: Why Some are so Rich and Some are so Poor, New York, Norton

Lasch, C., 1991, The True and Only Heaven: Progress and its Critics, New York, Norton

Latham, A., 2002, Warfare Transformed: A Braudelian Perspective on the "Revolution in Military Affairs", European Journal of International Relations, 8/2, pp 231-266

Leibfritz, W., 2002, Adjusting Welfare Systems to Ageing Populations – Challenges and Experiences in OECD Countries, paper at the ANB East/West Conference, Vienna, November 2002

Lenin, V., 1916, Imperialism, the Highest Stage of Capitalism, http://www.stetson.edu/department/russian/leninimperialism0100.html

Leontief, W., 1982, The Distribution of Work and Income, Scientific American, September 1982, p 188-205

Levin, Y., 2002, Politics after the Internet, The Public Interest, 149, fall 2002, pp 80-96

Levy, J., 1983, War in the Modern Great Power System, Lexington, University of Kentucky Press

Lieber, R., (ed.) 2001, Eagle Rules? Foreign Policy and American Primacy in the Twenty First Century, Upper Saddle River, Prentice Hall

Lieven, A., 1997, Qu'est-ce-qu'une nation? National Interest, No 49, fall 1997, pp 10-23

Linz, J., A. Stepan, 1996, Problems of Democratic Transition and Consolidation: Southern Europe, South America and Post – Communist Europe, Baltimore, Johns Hopkins University Press

Light, D., 1986, Corporate Medicine for Profit, Scientific American, Dec 1986

Lipset, S., 1996, American Exceptionalism, New York, Norton,

List, F., 1904, The National System of Political Economy, London, Longmans, Green

Lomborg, B., 2002, The Sceptical Environmentalist; Measuring the Real State of the World, Cambridge University Press, Cambridge

Luttwak, E., 1992, Is America on the Way Down? Yes!, Commentary, vol 93/3, March 1992

Maddison, A., 1991, Dynamic Forces in Capitalist Development: A Long – Run, Comparative View, New York, Oxford University Press

Maddison, A., 1995, Monitoring the World Economy 1820-1992, Development Centre Studies, OECD, Paris

Maddison, A., 2001, The World Economy: A Millenium Perspective, OECD

Madrick, J., 2002, Why Economies Grow: The Forces that Shape Prosperity and How to Get them Working Again, New York, Century Foundation

Mansfield, E., J. Snyder, 2002, Incomplete Democratisation and the Outbreak of Military Disputes, International Studies Quarterly, 2002/46, pp 529-549

Maoz, Z.V., 1997, The Controversy over Democratic Peace, International Security, 22, pp 162-198

Marty, M., Appleby, S., 1991, Fundamentalism Observed, Chicago, University of Chicago Press

Matzner, E., 2000, Monopolare Weltordnung: zur Sozialökonomie der US Dominanz, Marburg, Metropolis

Meadows, D. et al., 1972, The Limits to Growth: a Report for the Club of Rome's Project on the Predicament of Mankind, New York, Universe Books

Meadows. D., 1992, Beyond the Limits, Chelsea Green Publishing Company

Mearsheimer, J., 1990, Back to the Future: Instability in Europe after the Cold War, International Security, summer 1990, pp 5-56

Mearsheimer, J., 2001, The Tragedy of Great Power Politics, New York, Norton

Melchior, J., 1998, Democratic Foundations of Political Community in the European Union, WP at the Vienna – Austria ISA Congress, September 1998
Mendoza, G., 1995, Do Taxes Matter for Long Term Growth? IMF working paper 1995/79, Washington
Metcalfe, J., 2002, Knowledge of Growth and the Growth of Knowledge, Journal of Evolutionary Economics, 12/1+2, pp 3-15
Michalopoulos, C., 2002, Developing Countries in the WTO, New York, Palgrave
Michels, R., 1914, Les parties politiques : essai sur les tendences oligarchiques des démocracies, Paris, Flammarion
Milanovic, B., 2002, True world income distribution, 1988 and 1993 – first calculations, based on household surveys alone, WPS 2244, World Bank, Washington DC
Minc, A., 1993, Le Nouveau Moyen Age, Paris, Gallimard
Mitchell, R., 1999, British Historical Statistics, UK Ministry of Agriculture
Mitchell, R., 1988, European Historical Statistics, Cambridge, Cambridge University Press
Mittelmann, J., 2002, Globalisation: An Ascendant Paradigm? International Studies Perspectives, 2002/3, pp 1 -14
Modelski, G., W. Thompson, 1996, Leading Sectors and World Powers: The Co – Evolution of Global Economics and Politics, Columbia University of North Carolina Press
Morgan, C., 1997, Fools Suffer Gladly – The Use of Economic Sanctions in International Crises, International Studies Quarterly, 1997/4, pp 27-50
Morgenthau, H., 1978 (5th revised edition), Politics Among Nations – The Struggle for Power and Peace, New York, Alfred Knopf
Moynihan, P., 1993, Pandemonium – Ethnicity in International Politics, New York, Oxford University Press
Mueller, J., 1989, Retreat from Doomsday: The Obsolescence of Major War, New York, Basic Books
Murray C., 1994, Losing Ground. American Social Policy 1950-1980; New York, Basic Books
Murshed, M., 2002, Conflict, Civil War and Underdevelopment, http://www.wider.unu.edu/whoswho/murshedpapers.htm
Nelson R., S. Winter 1982, An Evolutionary Theory of Economic Change Cambridge Mass, Harvard University Press,
Nincic, M., 1997 Democratic Costs: The US Public and the Isolationist Calculus, International Studies Quarterly. 1997 / 4 p 493 ff
Nordhaus W., 1994, Managing the Global Commons: The Economics of Climate Change, Cambridge, MIT Press

North, D., 1981, Structure and Change in Economic History, New York, Norton
North, D., 1990, Institutions, Institutional Change and Economic Performance, New York, Cambridge University Press
Nowotny, T., 1993, Europtimismus – oder warum das Abendland nicht untergeht, Wien, Böhlau,
Nowotny, T., 2001, Europa muss die Hand ans Steuerruder legen, Europäische Rundschau 2001/2, pp. 81 -96
Nowotny, T., 2002, Markets, Democracy and Social Capital, Österreichische Zeitschrift für Politikwissenschaft, 2000/2, pp 217-229
Nowotny, T., 2003, The Trade – Off between Inflation and Unemployment; other Unsubstantiated Claims; and Why Economists Can Get Away with Them, Global Society, January 2003
Nye, J., 1990, The Misleading Metaphor of Decline, Atlantic Monthly, March 1990
Nye J., 2002, The Paradox of American Power: Why the World's Only Superpower Can't Go It Alone, New York, Oxford University Press
Ohmae, K., 1993, The Rise of the Region – State, Foreign Affairs, 72, pp. 78-87
O'Rourke, K., J. Williamson, Globalisation and History: The Evolution of a Nineteenth – Century Atlantic Economy; Cambridge, MIT Press
Ozawa, T., 2000, The Flying Geese Paradigm: Toward a Co – Evolutionary Theory of MNC Assisted Growth, in K. Fatemi (ed.), The New World Order: Internationalism, Regionalism and the Multinational Corporations, Amsterdam and New York, pp 209-223,
Olson, M., 1971, The Logic of Collective Action: Public Goods and the Theory of Groups, Cambridge Mass, Harvard University Press
Orenstein, M., 2001, Out of the Red: Building Capitalism and Democracy in Postcommunist Europe, Ann Arbor, University of Michigan Press
Park D., 1999, Inter – Country Income Inequality – an Expansion and Update, Comparative Economic Studies, 41(4) 103-8
Parker, G., 1988, The Military Innovation and the Rise of the West 1500 –1800, Cambridge, Cambridge University Press
Peng, D., 2002, Invisible Linkages: A Regional Perspective of East Asian Political Economy, International Studies Quarterly, 46, pp 423-447
Perrucci, R., 2003, The New Class Society: Goodbye American Dream, Lanham, Roman & Littlefield
Pfaff, W., 1991, Re-Defining World Power, Foreign Affairs 90/91
Phelps, E., 1985, Political Economy – An Introductory Text, London, Norton
Phillips, K., 2002, Wealth and Democracy – A Political History of the American Rich, New York, Broadway Books

Piketty, T., 1995, Social Mobility and Re-Distributive Politics, Quarterly Journal of Economics, August 1995

Platteau, J-P:, …Behind the Markets Stage – Where Real Societies Exist, Journal of Development Studies, vol. 30/3 pp 533 –577 ; and vol. 30/4, pp 754-817

Polyani, K., 1944, The Great Transformation, New York, Rinehart

Popper, K., 1963, The Open Society and its Enemies, 4th revised edition, Princeton, Princeton University Press

Porter, M., 1990, The Competitive Advantage of Nations, London, Macmillan

Porter, B., 1994, War and the Rise of the State, New York, Free Press

Prasad, E., K. Rogoff, Sh. Wei, A. Kose, 2003, Effects of Financial Globalization on Developing Countries: Some Empirical Evidence, IMF, March 2003, Washington DC

Preston, 1975, The Changing Relation between Mortality and the Level of Economic Development, Population Studies, vol. 29 pp 231-248

Priest, D., 2002, The Mission: Waging War and Keeping Peace with America's Military, Norton, New York

Purcell, M., 2002, The state, regulation, and global re-structuring: reasserting the political in political economy, Review of International Political Economy, 9/2, summer 2002, pp 284-318

Putnam, R., 1993, Making Democracy Work, Princeton, Princeton University Press

Putnam, R., 2000, Bowling Alone: The Collapse and Revival of American Community, New York, Simon and Schuster

Quinlan, J., 2003, Drifting Apart or Growing Together? The Primacy of the Transatlantic Economy, Johns Hopkins University, School of Advanced International Relations, Washington DC

Rae, G., 2002, Chaos Theory: A Brief Introduction, http://www.imho.com/grae/index.html

Rauch, J., 1994, The Hyper – Pluralism Trap, The New Republic, June 6, 1994

Reich, R., 1987, Tales of a New America, New York, Times Books

Reich, R., 1992, The Work of Nations – Preparing Ourselves for the 21st Century Capitalism, New York, Vintage Books

Reus-Smit, C., 1997, The Constitutional Structure of International Society and the Nature of Fundamental Institutions, International Organisations, 51/4, autumn 1997, pp 555-589

Richards D., R. Gelleny, D., Sacko, 2001, Money with a Mean Streak? Foreign Economic Penetration and Government Respect for Human Rights in Developing Countries, International Studies Quarterly 45, pp 219 -239

Rifkin, J., 2000, The Age of Access: The New Culture of Hyper-Capitalism; When All of Life is a Paid For Experience, New York, Putnam

Rigby, A., 2001, Justice and Reconciliation: After Violence, Boulder, Lynne Rienner

Robinson, J., 1978, Marx, Marshall and Keynes, reprinted as pp 61-75 in J. Robinson, Contributions to Modern Economics, Oxford, Basil &Blackwell

Rodrik, D., 1998, Who Needs Capital Market Convertibility, Essays in International Finance, Princeton, No 207, May

Rodrik, D., 1998, The Global Fix, The New Republic, 2 November 1998, pp. 17 -20

Rodrik, D., 2002, Institutions, Integration and Geography: In Search of Deep Determinants of Economic Growth, http://ksghome.harvard.edu/~.drodrik.academic.ksg/papers.html

Rodrik, D., 1997, Has Globalization Gone Too Far? Washington DC, Institute for International Economics

Rosenberg N., and L. Birdzell, 1986, How the West Grew Rich, London, Tauris

Rostow, W., 1960, Stages of Economic Growth. A Non-Communist Manifesto, Cambridge University Press

Roy, D., 1995, Hegemon on the Horizon? China´s Threat to East Asian Security, International Security, 19/1, pp 149-168

Sabel, C., 1994, Flexible specialisation and the re-emergence of regional economies, in A. Min (ed), Post – Fordism: a reader, Malden, Blackwell

Sala, M., 1996, Transfers, Social Safety Nets and Economic Growth, IMF, WP 1996/40

Sarkes, M., F. Wayman, J. Singer, 2003, Inter – State, Intra – State and Extra – State Wars: A Comprehensive Look at Their Distribution over Time , 1816-1997, International Studies Quarterly, 2003/47, pp 49-70

Sassen, S., 2001, The Global City: New York, London, Tokyo, Princeton, Princeton University Press

Sassen, S., 2003, Globalization and Denationalisation? Review of International Political Economy, 10/1, February 2002, pp 1-22

Saul, R., 2001, Rethinking Theory and History in the Cold War: The State, Military Power and Social Revolution, London, Frank Cass,

Scarpetta, S., T. Tressel, 2002, Productivity and Convergence in a Panel of OECD Industries: Do Institutions Matter?, OECD Economics Department, working paper, 342, Paris

Schampel, J., 1994, Parity or Preponderance: One More Look , International Studies Notes, vol. 19/3, pp 1-3

Schirm, S., 2002, Handel und Politik; der Einfluss lokaler Märkte auf National Interessen, International Politik, 57/6, Juni 2002, pp 1-10

Schlesinger, A., 1986, The Cycles of American History, Boston, Houghton Mifflin

Schumpeter, J., 1934, The Theory of Economic Development, Cambridge, Harvard University Press

Schumpeter, J., 1942, Capitalism, Socialism and Democracy, New York, Harper

Schumpeter, J., 1991 (English translation), Imperialism and Social Classes, Philadelphia, Orion Editions

Schwartz, H., 1994, States Versus Markets: History, Geography and the Development of the International Political Economy, New York, St Martins Press

Sen, A., 2000, East and West: The Search for Reason, New York Review of Books, 20 July 2000,

Shaw, M., 2000, Theory of the Global State: Globality as an Unfinished Revolution, Cambridge UK, Cambridge University Press

Shiller, R., 2000, Irrational Exuberance, Princeton University Press, Princeton

Simon, H., 1995, Economics, Bounded Rationality and the Cognitive Revolution, New York, E. Elgar

Simon, J., 1981, The Ultimate Resource, Princeton, Princeton University Press

Singer, D., 1979, The Correlates of War, New York, Free Press

Small, M., D. Singer, 1982, Resort to Arms: International and Civil War, 1816-1980, Beverly Hills, Sage

Smith, T., 2002, The New Law of War: Legitimizing Hi-Tech and Infrastructural Violence, International Studies Quarterly, 46, pp 355-374

Smythe, E., 1998, Who Writes the Rules: Europe and the United States Negotiate Investment Rules at the OECD, paper at the Pan European International Relations Conference, September 1998, Vienna

Solingen, E., 2001, Mapping Internationalisation: Domestic and Regional Impacts, International Studies Quarterly, 45, pp 517-555

Solow, R., 2000, Notes on Social Capital and Economic Performance, in Dasgupty, P. and I. Serageldin (eds.) Social Capital: A Multi-Facetted Perspective, Washington DC, World Bank

Sorel, G., 1969 (Engl Translation), The Illusions of Progress, Berkely, University of California Press

Stalker, P., 2000, Workers without Frontiers: The Impact of Globalisation on International Migration, Boulder, Lynne Rienner

Stein, A., 1983, Coordination and Collaboration: Regimes in an Anarchic World, in S.D. Kramer, (ed), International Regimes, pp 115-140, Ithaca, Cornell University Press

Stiglitz, J., 1985, Credit Markets and the Control of Capital, Journal of Money, Credit and Banking, vol17/2, May 1985

Stiglitz J., 1996, Some Lessons from the East Asian Miracle, World Bank Research Observer, 11(2), 151-177

Stiglitz, J., 2000, What I Learned at the World Economic Crisis, The New Republic, April 17/2000, pp 56-60
Stiglitz, J., 2000, More Instruments and Broader Goals: Moving towards the Post – Washington Consensus, Wider Annual Lectures; http://www.wider.unu.edu/stiglitz.htm
Stiglitz, J., 2002, Globalization and its Discontents, New York, Norton
Stockholm International Peace Research Institute (annual) SIPRI Yearbook: Armament; Disarmament and International Security, Oxford, Oxford University Press
Stoessinger, J., 1974, Why Nations Go to War, New York, St Martins Press
Strange, S., 1986, Casino Capitalism, Oxford, Blackwell
Strange, S., 1988, States and Markets: An Introduction to Political Economy, Cambridge, Cambridge University Press
Strange, S., 1996, The Retreat of the State: The Diffusion of Power in the World Economy, Cambridge, Cambridge University Press
Streek, W., 1991, On the Institutional Conditions of Diversified Production, in: Matzner, E., Streek, W. (eds): Beyond Keynesianism: The Socio-Economics of Production and Employment, London, Edward Elgar, pp. 21-61
Sucharipa, E., 1997, The United Nations – An Impossible Dream: Indispensable Nations versus Indispensable Organisations; The Austrian Experience, manuscript, Wien
Sunstein, C., 2001, Republic.com, Princeton, Princeton University Press
Svejnar, J., 2002, Structural Reforms and Competitiveness: Where Does Europe Stand Today? Paper at ANB conference, Vienna, November 2002
Swaine, M., A. Tellis, 2000, Integrating China's Great Strategy: Past, Present and Future, Santa Monica, Rand Corporation
Szompka, P., 1993, Civilisational Incompetence: The Trap of Post – Communist Societies, Zeitschrift für Soziologie, 1993/22, p 33 and ff
Tanzi, V., 1994, Taxation in an Integrating World, Washington, Brookings Institution
Tarp, F., 2000, Foreign Aid and Development, New York, Routledge
Tate, N., T. Vallinder, 1995, The Global Expansion of Judicial Power, New York, New York University Press
Taylor, T., 2001, Thinking about the "New Economy", The Public Interest, 143, spring 2001, pp 3-19
Teilhard de Chardin, P., 1955, Le Phénomene Humain, Paris, Editions du Seuil
Teschke, B., 2002, Theorising the Westphalian System of States : International Relations from Absolutism to Capitalism, European Journal of International Relations, 8/1, pp 5-48

Thaa, W., 2001, "Lean Citizenship": The Fading Away of the Political in Transnational Democracy, European Journal of International Relations, 7(4), pp 503-523

Tickner, A., 2002, Feminist Perspectives on 9/11, International Studies Perspectives, 2002/3, pp 333-350

Tietenberg,T., 1992, Environmental and Natural Resource Economics (3rd ed) Harper Collins, New York

Toynbee, A., 1946, A Study of History, Oxford, Oxford University Press

UNDP Human Development Report 2002, New York

UN Habitat, 1998, Global Urban Indicators Database

UN, 1998, World Urbanisation Prospects, The 1996 Revision, New York

Utgoff, V., 2000, The Coming Crisis: Nuclear Proliferation, US Interests, and World Order, Cambridge Mass., MIT Press

Van Creveld, M., 1989, Technology and War from 2000 BC to the Present, New York, Macmillan

Van Creveld, M., 1999, The Rise and the Decline of the State, Cambridge, Cambridge University Press,

Van Wolferen, K., 1989, The Enigma of Japanese Power, New York, Alfred Knopf

Vogel, E., 1991, The Four Little Dragons, Cambridge/ Mass, Harvard University Press,

Vonnegut, K., 1985, Galapagos, New York, Seymour & Lawrence

Wallerstein, I., 1974, The Modern World System, New York, Columbia University Press

Wallerstein, I., 1979, The Capitalist World Economy, Cambridge, Cambridge University Press,

Wallerstein, I., 2002, The Eagle has Crash-Landed, Foreign Policy, July/August 2002

Waltz, K., 1959, Man, the State and War – A Theoretical Analysis, New York, Columbia University Press

Waltz, K., 1967, International Structure, National Force and the Balance of World Power, Journal of International Affairs 21, pp 215-231

Waltz, K., 1979, Theory of International Politics, Readings, Addison – Wesley

WCED, 1987, – The World Commission on Environment and Development for the General Assembly of the United Nations – (The Brundtland Report"), New York, Oxford University Press,

Weber, M., 1978, Economy and Society: Volume I, New York

Weidenfeld, W., 1996, America and Europe: Is the Break Inevitable? Gütersloh, Bertelsmann Foundation

Weitzman, M., 1998, Why the Far Distant Future Should Be Discounted at Its Lowest Possible Rate, Journal of Environmental Economics and Management 36 (3), pp 201-208
Welch, D., 1993, Justice and the Genesis of War, New York, Cambridge University Press
Wendt, A., 1987, The Agent – Structure Problem in International Relations Theory, International Organisations, 41, pp 335-370
Wendt, A., 1992, Anarchy is What States Make of It, International Organisation, 46/2, pp 394 ff
Wendt, A., 1999, Social Theory of International Politics, Cambridge, Cambridge University Press
Williamson, J., 1997, Globalisation and Inequality: Past and Present, IBRD Research Observer, vol. 12/2, August 1997, pp 117-136
Williamson, J., 1990, What Washington Means by POLICY Reform; in J. Williamson, (ed) Latin American Adjustment. How much has happened, Washington DC, Institute for International Economics
Wilson, W., 1987, The Truly Disadvantaged, Chicago, University of Chicago Press
Wilson, W., 1994, What to Do about Crime? Commentary, September 1994, pp 25-34
Wittfogel, K., 1957, Oriental Despotism: A Comparative Study of Total Power, New Haven, Yale University Press
Wolf, A., 2002, Does Education Matter? Myths about Education and Economic Growth, London, Penguin Books
Wolfe, T., 1987, Bonfire of Vanities, New York, Farrar, Straus& Giroux
Woo-Cumings, M., (ed), 1999, The Developmental State, Ithaca, Cornell University Press
Woolcock, H., 1998, Social Capital and Economic Development: Towards a Theoretical Synthesis and Policy Framework, Theory and Society 27, pp 151-208
World Bank, 1994, Averting the Old Age Crisis: Policies to Protect the Old and to Promote Growth, New York, Oxford University Press
World Bank, 1998, Assessing Aid: What Works. What Doesn't and Why? New York, Oxford University Press
Zakaria, F., 2002, The Future of Freedom: Illiberal Democracy at Home and Abroad, New York, Norton

Useful References and Web-Sites

Amnesty International: *"Amnesty International report" and country reports*: www.amnesty.org

Attac: *(a quite young global movement critical of (some aspects) of globalisation)*: http://www.attac.org

Bank for International Settlements – *BIS: The BIS Consolidated International Banking Statistics:* www.bis.org

Centre for International Development and Conflict, *at the University of Maryland, annual publication analysing the world's conflicts;* http://www.cidm.umd.edu./insc/peaceconflict.pdf

European Bank for Reconstruction and Development – EBRD*; annual "Transition Report" on the state of the economy in the so – called "transition countries";* www.ebrd.org

Food and Agricultural Organisation – FAO: *"The State of Food and Agriculture"* FAO stat: www.fao.org

"Foreign Policy" (Globalisation Index): http://www.foreignpolicy.com/issuejan feb_2003/

Freedom House: *annual report on civic and political freedom; the much quoted "Freedom House Index" for these two freedoms:* www.freedomhouse.org

Heidelberger Institut Für Konfliktforschung, *annual publication on ongoing conflicts,* http://www.hiik.de

International Bank for Reconstruction and Development/ Worldbank – IBRD: *Flagship publication (basic for whoever is active in the field) "World Development Report" (released in summer of each year, comprehensive source of comparative statistics). Furthermore a host of cutting edge working papers on development economics, on a vast array of topics; and based on widely differing values (or ideologies) :* www.worldbank.org

International Energy Agency – *IEA World Energy Outlook;* http://www.iea.org/

International Food Policy Research Institute: *surveys research on globa,l regional, national supply and demand issue; as well as on sectoral questions; http://*www.ifpri.org

International Fund for Agricultural Development – IFAD: *publishes the "Rural Poverty Report*, http://www.ifad.org

International Institute for Applied Systems Analysis – IIASA: *series of working papers and other publications using the systems analysis approach to a host of complex global issues; for instance "Global Agro-Ecological Assessment for Agriculture in the 21st Century: Methodology and Results", March 2002* www.iiasa.org

International Institute for Strategic Studies- IISS . *"Military Balance" – an inventory of the world's armed forces; "Strategic Survey" – last years salient political and military trends:* www.iiss.org

International Labour Organisation – ILO: " *World Employment Report"; and other statistics on labour markets:* www.ilo.org

International Monetary Fund – IMF: *"World Economic Outlook; "World Economic and Financial Survey", "International Capital Markets"; chapter 4 consultations (reviews of economic/monetary policy of member countries), other statistics on international capital movements and global monetary affairs; interesting and far ranging working papers. On average there is a tendency, though, to view problems and issues from the perspective of financial institutions (and markets):* www.imf.org

Inter University Consortium for Political and Social Research: http://www.icpsr.umich.edu

Library of Congress. *Biggest library in the world; excellent search engine*: http://lcweb.loc.gov

National Intelligence Council 2000, Global Trends 2015: *A Dialogue about the Future with Nongovernment Experts*, http://www.odci.gov/cia/publications

Neue Zürcher Zeitung – NZZ. *idiosyncratic but unique, the best European newspaper, good on-line archives; in German though : www.nzz.ch/*

New York Times*: very comprehensive; good archive www.nytimes.com/*

Organisation for Economic Co-operation and Development – OECD: *"OECD Economic Outlook", DAC statistics on Official Development Assistance* ; *OECD Historical Statistics: The OECD is a treasure trove of many other data and analyses on the world's wealthiest countries. Publications from the OECD Economic Directorate tend to have a narrow ideological focus; but those from other Directorates don't. Unfortunately, few of these publications are accessible via the INTERNET*: www.oecd.org

PAIS – Public Affairs Information System : *expansive international databank on publications relevant to public policy. Accessible via authorised channels only*

RAMSES *Rapport Annuel sur le Systeme Economique et les Strategies*, IFRI (institut francais des relations internationales)

http://www.ifri.org/F/publications/ramses

Smelser, N., P., Baltes (eds.), 2001, International Encyclopedia of the Social & Behavioral Sciences. New York, Elsevier,

Social SciSearch: *database accessible via Dialogue (and for a rather steep fee), excellent for search in recent social science literature, as it includes abstracts*: http://library.dialog.com

Social Science Information Gateway, http://www.sosig.ac.uk

Stockholm International Peace Research Institute – SIPRI: "*SIPRI Yearbook – Armament, Disarmament and International security*" : www.sipri.se
The Economist: www.economist.com
Transparency International: *publishes the "Corruption Perception Index":* www.transparency.org
Union of International Associations, *provides links to several thousands of IGOs and NGIOs, publishes the "Yearbook of International Organisations"; and statistics on international organisations and meetings,* http://www.uia.org
United Nations Conference on Trade and Development – UNCTAD: *"Trade and Development Report", "World Investment Report"; focus on the problems of the poorer countries:* www.unctad.org
United Nations Development Programme – UNDP : "*Human Development Report" including the Human Development Index and the Human Poverty Index:* www.undp.org
United Nations Educational, Scientific and Cultural Organisation – UNESCO: *various series on educational statistics.*www.unesco.org
United Nations Environment Programme – UNEP, "*Global Environmental Outlook"* : www.unep.org
UNEP – World Conservation Monitoring Centre, *data bank and annual publication on conservation bio diversity etc;* http://www.unep-wcmc.org
United Nations – Habitat, *Global Report on Human Settlements,* http://www.unhabitat.org
United Nations Industrial Development Organisation – UNIDO : *"The International Yearbook of Industrial Statistics", "Industrial Development Report",* www.unido.org
United Nations Population Fund – UNFPA: "*The State of the World Population*": www.unfpa.org
UN Statistics Division: "*UN Statistic Yearbook", host of other statistics, unfortunately most not accessible over net:* http://unstats.un.org/unsd/
UN Statistics Division: the implementation of the so called "Millenium Targets" (of poverty reduction, educational improvement; etc.): http://unstats.un.org/unsd/mi/mi_results
US Department of State *: noteworthy the largely unbiased human rights reports that appear at the end of February of each year:* www.state.gov
Vienna Institute of International Economic Studies: *first rate source on statistics on the economic performance of the formerly Communist countries (save Central Asia)*; www.wiiw.ac.at
World Economic Forum: *Organises the well known (perhaps notorious) Davos – Get – Togethers; publishes a "Competitiveness Ranking"*, http://www. weforum.org

World Health Organisation – WHO : *"the World Health Report", "Global Health Situation and Projections", other health statistics:* www.who.org
World Trade Organisation – WTO : " *WTO Annual Report* " : www.wto.org
Worldwatch Institute: *"State of the World", an annual report on environmental problems; and Vital Signs" on trends that "are changing the world" (publications tend to promote"green" positions* : www.worldwatch.org

Peter Lang · Europäischer Verlag der Wissenschaften

Gustav Dieckheuer / Boguslaw Fiedor (eds.)

Competition, Environment and Trade in the Globalized Economy

Frankfurt am Main, Berlin, Bern, Bruxelles, New York, Oxford, Wien, 2002.
VIII, 194 pp., num. fig. and tab.
Internationale Marktwirtschaft. General Editor: Gustav Dieckheuer. Bd. 3
ISBN 3-631-39684-8 / US-ISBN 0-8204-6001-X · pb. € 39.00*

There is an ongoing discussion about causes and consequences of economic globalization. The effects of growing international trade, worldwide integration and international policy co-ordination are widespread and thus call our attention. This book focuses on four major topics of the debate: the conditions for a country's trade on worldwide growing markets for goods and capital; environmental problems caused by international economic growth; effects of increasing international competition; national macro-policies under the influence of increasing international interdependencies.

Contents: Preparing a World Antitrust Framework – An Ordoliberal Approach · Global Information Techniques and their Economic Consequences · Regional Dimensions of National Integration · Some Theoretical and Empirical Aspects of Poland's Integration in the EU